W9-CVA-020

The Rise of Instrumental Music and Concert Series in Paris 1828-1871

Studies in Musicology, No. 65

George Buelow, Series Editor

Professor of Musicology
Indiana University

Other Titles in This Series

No. 36 *The Early French Parody Noël* — Adrienne F. Block

No. 57 *American Women Composers before 1870* — Judith Tick

No. 60 *Louis Pécour's 1700* Recueil de dances — Anne L. Witherell

No. 62 *Dr. Burney as Critic and Historian of Music* — Kerry S. Grant

No. 63 *The Fertilizing Seed: Wagner's Concept of the Poetic Intent* — Frank W. Glass

No. 64 *The Secular Madrigals of Filippo di Monte, 1521-1603* — Brian Mann

No. 66 *The Crumhorn: Its History, Design, Repertory, and Technique* — Kenton Terry Meyer

No. 67 *A History of Key Characteristics in the Eighteenth and Early Nineteenth Centuries* — Rita Steblin

No. 69 *The Concerto and London's Musical Culture in the Late Eighteenth Century* — Thomas B. Milligan

The Rise of Instrumental Music and Concert Series in Paris 1828-1871

by

Jeffrey Cooper

Ann Arbor, Michigan

Produced and distributed by
UMI Research Press
an imprint of
University Microfilms International
Ann Arbor, Michigan 48106

Library of Congress Cataloging in Publication Data

Cooper, Jeffrey.
The rise of instrumental music and concert series in Paris, 1828-1871.

(Studies in musicology ; no. 65)
Thesis (Ph.D.)–Cornell University, 1981.
Bibliography: p.
Includes index.
1. Instrumental music–France–Paris–19th century–History and criticism. 2. Concerts–France–Paris–19th century. I. Title. II. Series.

ML497.8.P4C6 1983 785'.0944'361 83-1062
ISBN 0-8357-1403-9

Contents

List of Tables *vii*

List of Abbreviations *xi*

Preface *xiii*

1 Introduction *1*

2 Musical Life in Paris, I: Customs and Conditions; Concert Series *13*

"The Season"
Concert Halls
Programs, Programming, Performances, and Performers
Concert Series
The Société des Concerts du Conservatoire
The Societe Sainte-Cécile
The Société des Jeunes-Artistes
The Concerts Populaires
The Société Alard-Franchomme (Société de Musique de Chambre)
The Société des Derniers Quatuors de Beethoven
The Société des Quatuors de Mendelssohn (Quatuor Armingaud or Quatuor Armingaud-Jacquard)
The Séances Populaires
The Gouffé *Séances*
The Lebouc *Séances*
Remaining Concert Series

3 Musical Life in Paris, II: Other Musical Events; The Audience *85*

Single Concerts by Individuals
Charity Concerts
Salons
State Concerts

Outdoor Concerts and Café Concerts
Representative Musical Years
Audiences and the Music Business
Audiences and Musical Events

4 Repertory *105*

Repertory: The Broad Picture
Changes in the Repertory: A Chronological Study
Performed Repertory of Individual Composers

5 Perceptions of Musical Life in Nineteenth-Century France *135*

Instrumental Music in France before 1828
Descriptions and Explanations, 1828 to 1871
Postwar Developments
Historical Commentary

6 French Instrumental Works *169*

7 A Half-Century of Change *207*

Appendix A: Parisian Concert Series *217*

Appendix B: Provincial Concerts *279*

Notes *285*

Bibliography *355*

Index *367*

List of Tables

2.1. Instrumentation of the Orchestra of the Société des Concerts du Conservatoire *27*

2.2. Performances of Instrumental Works (Listed by Composer) at the Société des Concerts du Conservatoire, 1828-1870 *31*

2.3. Performances of Major Instrumental Works *32*

2.4. Performances of Symphonies *32*

2.5. Cumulative Percentage of Performances of Works by Beethoven, Haydn, and Mozart *34*

2.6. Performances of Instrumental Works (Listed by Composer) Conducted by Théophile Tilmant, 1860-1863 *35*

2.7. Performances of Instrumental Works (Listed by Composer) Conducted by François Hainl, 1864-1870 *35*

2.8. Percentage of Performances of Instrumental Works (Listed by Composer), 1828-1870 *35*

2.9. Percentage of Performances of Major Instrumental Works (Listed by Composer), 1828-1870 *35*

2.10. Percentage of Performances of Symphonies (Listed by Composer), 1828-1870 *36*

2.11. Other Statistics Comparing Four Conductors of the Société des Concerts du Conservatoire, 1828-1870 *36*

2.12. Performances of Instrumental Works (Listed by Composer) by the Societe Sainte-Cécile, 48 Concerts, 1850-1855 *40*

2.13. Performances of Major Instrumental Works *40*

2.14. Performances of Symphonies *41*

2.15. Performances of Instrumental Works (Listed by Composer) by the Societe Sainte-Cécile, Excluding Special Programs of Contemporary Music, 43 Concerts, 1850-1855 *41*

2.16. Performances of Instrumental Works (Listed by Composer) by the Société des Jeunes-Artistes, 59 Programs, 1853-1861 *44*

2.17. Performances of Major Instrumental Works *45*

2.18. Performances of Symphonies *45*

2.19. Performances of Instrumental Works (Listed by Composer) by the Concerts Populaires, 219 Programs, 1861-70 *49*

2.20. Performances of Major Instrumental Works *50*

2.21. Performances of Symphonies *50*

2.22. Comparison of Number of Performances of Works by the Five Most-Performed German and French Nineteenth-Century Composers, by the Concerts Populaires, 1861-1870 *51*

2.23. Representative Repertory of the Société Alard-Franchomme: Performances (Listed by Composer) in 55 Concerts, 1847-1870 *54*

2.24. Performances of Instrumental Works (Listed by Composer) by the Société des Quatuors de Mendelssohn, 39 Programs, 1856-1867 *58*

2.25. Known Performances of Major Instrumental Works (Listed by Composer) at the Lebouc *Séances,* 1855-1870 *65*

4.1. Known Performances of Instrumental Works in Paris, 1828-1870 *108*

4.2. Known Performances of Major Works (Listed by Composer) in Paris, 1828-1870 *109*

4.3. Known Performances of Major Instrumental Works by French and Non-French Composers, Paris, 1828-1870 *110*

4.4. Known Performances of Instrumental Works (Listed by Composer) in Paris, 1828-1870, in Six Periods *112*

List of Abbreviations

The following abbreviations appear in footnotes to the text and throughout the Appendix and Bibliography.

FétisB	F.-J. Fétis: *Biographie universelle des musiciens*, 2nd rev. ed. Paris: Firmin Didot frères, 1866–70, many subsequent impressions with later dates.
FétisB Supplement	*Supplément et Complément* to the above, ed. Arthur Pougin. Paris: Firmin Didot frères, 1878–80, many subsequent impressions.
GMdP	*Gazette musicale de Paris*, weekly journal, 1834–5.
Grove 5	*Grove's Dictionary of Music and Musicians*, 5th ed., ed. Eric Blom. London: Macmillan and Co., 1954; other numbers (e.g., *Grove 3*) refer to earlier editions.
Grove 6	*The New Grove Dictionary of Music and Musicians*, ed. Stanley Sadie. London: Macmillan Publishers Limited, 1980.
MGG	*Die Musik in Geschichte und Gegenwart*, ed. Friedrich Blume and Ruth Blume. Kassel and Basel: Bärenreiter Verlag, 1949–79.
ReM	*Revue musicale*, weekly journal, 1827–35. Other journals with the same name are spelled out.
RGMdP	*Revue et gazette musicale de Paris*, weekly journal, from 1835; this journal resulted from a merger of *GMdP* and *ReM*.

Preface

The present volume is a revised version of my dissertation, "A Renaissance in the Nineteenth Century: the Rise of French Instrumental Music and Parisian Concert Societies, 1828-1871" (Cornell University, 1981). The revising process has provided a welcome opportunity to correct errors, resolve inconsistencies, and incorporate recent or overlooked research. But most of the revising has involved making the contents more accessible and easier to assimilate. The writing has been polished and several ambiguous passages have been clarified. A much-needed index has been added. Perhaps most important, the structure has been reworked. In the dissertation, the fourth chapter discussed various facets of French musical life. For this volume, a portion of it involving customs and conditions of concert life has been moved to the beginning of chapter 2, to provide context for all that follows. Another part of chapter 4, a brief description of provincial musical activity, has become a second appendix. The remainder of the chapter, a discussion of musical events other than concert series and of the new role of the audience in an increasingly commercial concert scene, has been transposed with the original chapter 3 (on repertory); now chapter 2 (on concert series) and the new chapter 3 provide a continuous survey of Parisian entertainment offering instrumental music. Finally, the general discussion of concert series in chapter 2 is now chronological rather than topical.

After five years of responding to enquiries concerning my research by either reciting the dissertation's unwieldy title or summarizing its contents as "the performance, composition, and appreciation of instrumental music in Paris, 1828-1871," I am becoming accustomed to the questioners' subsequent looks of disbelief, horror, or amusement. It is indeed an enormous topic, and one that a single volume can only survey. But a survey seemed to be needed because previous works concerning music in nineteenth-century France have either relegated instrumental music to a minor part of an even broader discussion or restricted their examination to single musicians, single concert series, or single aspects related to instrumental music. Because this is a survey, its many individual topics can each be investigated further, and in fact a widespread awakening of interest in related subjects is evident in journal articles of the early 1980s. These articles and, in particular, the many fine papers delivered at a conference on "Music in Paris in the Eighteen-Thirties" (Smith College, April 1982) have demonstrated the wealth of information to be found in heretofore little-explored archival documents and other available primary sources. One of the participants in the Smith conference, Joël-Marie Fauquet, has recently completed a dissertation on chamber music societies in nineteenth-century France, which I regret not having seen before preparing the current volume. In the acknowledgments to my dissertation I wrote,

> It pleases me to express my appreciation to the chairperson of my graduate committee, Don M. Randel, particularly for his patience and levelheaded punctiliousness, and to the other members of that committee, Esther Dotson and Robert Palmer; all provided valuable suggestions. Michael Keller, music librarian at Cornell University while this study was done, helped well beyond the call of duty. I also thank the staff of the Cornell music library and the staffs of music libraries at the Paris Bibliothèque Nationale, the Library of Congress, the University of Illinois, and Yale University. I am indebted to Steven Stucky for his graciously given advice on translating German texts. My parents, William and Ruby, were a constant source of encouragement. Finally, my wife, Peggy Daub, assisted in countless ways, among them reading drafts or listening to ideas and always responding with sound advice, aiding in the unrewarding task of proofreading, and through her love constantly preserving my well-being.

While revising I have incurred several additional debts. I appreciate the helpful suggestions and corrections supplied by various persons who read the dissertation after its completion. The library of the University of Michigan provided solutions to most of the new problems that arose, and Barry Kernfeld promptly checked details I had overlooked in sources at Cornell. Working with the editorial staff of UMI Research Press has been a pleasure. Finally (again), I thank Peggy for her continuing support, encouragement, and love, her ready answers, and, more important, her thoughtful questions.

Jeffrey Cooper
Ann Arbor
March 1983

1

Introduction

French music and musical life of the mid-nineteenth century have thus far received little scholarly attention and consequently are not well understood. Writings about nineteenth-century France commonly portray a nation manic over opera and ballet but otherwise familiar only with "salon" music—a term that should mean "music heard in salons" but which has come to connote works of dubious artistic merit. Because Berlioz almost alone is cited in historical sources as a significant French composer of works not intended for stage or *salon,* readers may conclude that in France composition and even performance of orchestral and chamber works were nearly unknown.

A survey of twentieth-century descriptions of nineteenth-century France demonstrates the emphasis that opera there has traditionally received, but also indicates a long-standing awareness among a few authors that other, little-remembered forms of music existed. Arthur Hervey, whose *French Music in the XIXth Century* appeared just after that century ended (1903), wrote that

> French genius seemed more adapted to dramatic music, and Berlioz invested his great tone-creations with a dramatic sentiment. The symphony proper was only cultivated in a modest, unobtrusive fashion.[1]

Edward Burlingame Hill, who had more time in which to gain historical perspective, wrote in 1924 that "Parisian distaste for orchestral concerts constituted the normal state of affairs in the early career of Berlioz." But he observed that in the years following midcentury there was

> a revolution in public taste due to the establishment of orchestras and chamber music societies with a consequent awakening of interest in their respective literatures. Saint-Saëns, Lalo, and César Franck, the pioneers of instrumental music in France, may be regarded as the direct outcome of this movement.[2]

Gerald Abraham, when writing *A Hundred Years of Music* (1938), did not follow Hill's lead, and had apparently not revised his opinion by the time of the fourth edition (1974). His statement that "in France, almost as much as in Italy, a composer had to succeed at opera to succeed at all," may hold true, especially in economic terms, and particularly for the first half of the century; but the evidence weighs heavily against Abraham's declaration that in the period following Beethoven's death chamber music as a genre "was played everywhere except in France and Italy but composed by few non-German musicians."[3] Paul Henry Lang's monumental *Music in Western Civilization* (1941) stressed the dominance of opera in nineteenth-century France, noting "the complete decline of instrumental music, the complete extinction of the fine symphonic school that started so auspiciously with Gossec, Méhul, Cherubini, and others." Referring to the mid-nineteenth century, Lang wrote, "With the exception of Berlioz, who declared himself to be 'three-fourths a German,' music became to the French synonymous with the lyric stage." He repeated this idea (using, in fact, the same words) to describe "the latter part of the nineteenth century":

> The musical despot in France was the opera . . . *Musique* was synonymous with the lyric stage, and no one paid serious attention to anything else.

Lang did, however, finally acknowledge a school of instrumental composers who, in the second half of the century, "attacked the undisputed reign of grand opera"; he added that Jules Pasdeloup, through founding the Concerts Populaires (in 1861, a date Lang did not mention), "created a veritable renaissance of French music, acquainting the public with the works of Berlioz and Wagner."[4]

More recently, historians of nineteenth-century music have noted interest in instrumental music both before and after 1850. Kenneth Klaus, in *The Romantic Period in Music* (1970), admitted,

> In all fairness it must be mentioned that chamber music in France was not dead. Performers played the classics, such as Haydn and Mozart. As early as 1814 Baillot, the great violinist, was giving such concerts. The public found his own music too modern and preferred the quartets of such men as Onslow.[5]

William Weber, who has explored sociological aspects of music in nineteenth-century Europe, has documented "dramatic growth" in the number of public concerts in Paris beginning after 1830.[6] Rey M. Longyear, in *Nineteenth-Century Romanticism in Music* (1973), observed that "quartet societies and symphony orchestras had been founded between 1850 and 1870."[7]

Nevertheless, statements ignoring the composition and performance of French instrumental music remain prevalent, even in scholarly publications. Discussing chamber music in particular (though orchestral music is subject to equal neglect), J.-M. Nectoux has written of Saint-Saëns,

> But in his quintet [Op. 14, composed in 1855], as in his first cello sonata Op. 32 [composed in 1872], Saint-Saëns remained heavily influenced by the Germanic aesthetic; and how could it be otherwise during a time when there was no chamber music but that of Beethoven and Schumann?[8]

Donald Grout's *History of Western Music* (all editions), which of course discusses only the most significant composers of any era, names only Berlioz as a French composer of orchestral or chamber music between 1828 and 1871. While Grout's selectivity is perhaps proper for the purpose of his book, the result reinforces the prevalent impression that instrumental music by French composers other than Berlioz was nonexistent in mid-nineteenth-century France.

If twentieth-century accounts of nineteenth-century France are sketchy (and possibly onesided), the fault lies not so much with historians as with the absence of dependable sources. Only recently has scholarly investigation in this area begun; previously historians relied in large measure on the retrospective writings of renowned nineteenth-century musicians—memoirs, autobiographies, and essays widely available in published form but not necessarily historically accurate. These musicians recalled the mid-nineteenth century as a discouraging time for instrumental activity in France. Berlioz's *Mémoires,* a well-studied account of French musical life, describe the author "deciding to become a composer (which to the French means the theatre)." In the same source Berlioz observed,

> The composer who would produce substantial works in Paris outside the theatre must rely entirely on himself. He must resign himself to sketchy and tentative and thus more or less misleading performances, for want of the rehearsals he cannot afford; to halls which are inconvenient and uncomfortable from the point of view of both performers and audience; to the numerous difficulties raised, quite reasonably, by the opera houses, whose players one is obliged to employ, and who naturally have the needs of their own repertory to think of; to the barefaced appropriations of the poorhouse tax-collectors, who take no account of what a concert costs, and contribute to the deficit by walking off with one eighth of the gross receipts; and to the hasty and inevitably erroneous judgements pronounced on large and complex works which are heard under these conditions and rarely heard more than once or twice. He must, in the last analysis, have a great deal of time and money to spend—not to mention the humiliating expense of will-power and spiritual energy required to overcome such obstacles.[9]

Two slightly younger French composers supported Berlioz's contentions. Saint-Saëns, in *Harmonie et mélodie* (1885), wrote that before 1870

> a French composer who had the audacity to venture into the field of instrumental music had no way of having his works performed other than to give a concert himself and to invite his friends and the critics. As for the public, the real public, one could not think of them; the name of a living French composer, printed on publicity, had the property of putting everyone to flight.[10]

Charles Gounod, in his autobiography (begun in 1877), stated,

> There is only one road for a composer who desires to make a real name—the operatic stage. The stage is the one place where a musician can find constant opportunity and means of communicating with the public.
>
> Religious and symphonic music, no doubt, rank higher, in the strictest sense, than dramatic composition; but opportunities for distinction in that highest sphere are very rare, and can only affect an occasional audience, not a regular and systematic one like the opera-going public.[11]

Berlioz, Saint-Saëns, and Gounod were each generalizing about a large period in the nineteenth century; the latter two were able to compare the decades before 1870 with the years afterward. Reports of contemporary musical activity written within the period 1828 to 1871 seem less onesided. There were many complaints, but these were countered by notices commending native performers and composers and, increasingly as the period progressed, by occasional expressions of optimism: In 1828 F.-J. Fétis deplored the dismal state of Parisian concerts, particularly the abandonment of orchestral concerts in favor of piano-dominated *soirées,* most of which (he said) offered only poor music.[12] The following year, however, he maintained that France was becoming the primary musical center of Eruope.[13] Franz Liszt, in 1835, signed his name to an article declaring that in Paris serious composers could not obtain adequate performances of their works, especially religious and instrumental compositions.[14] The same year François Stoepel, a performer, educator, and writer on music, opined that concert music in France was becoming steadily worse, descending from (mainly eighteenth-century) classics to the *contredanses* of Musard and Tolbecque (leaders of popular dance orchestras). Most public events he considered beneath criticism, though he was careful to except the presentations of Baillot and Berlioz as well as the concerts of the Conservatoire.[15] The composer and writer Georges Kastner, reviewing a new trio by Jupin in 1838, claimed that serious chamber music had become passé, but noted that works of classical composers were still performed.[16] An anonymous commentator remarked in 1854 that ensemble works (including chamber works) were becoming increasingly rare;[17] on several occasions in the 1850s, however, Henri Blanchard (the main critic for the *Revue et gazette musicale*) noted the proliferation of chamber music. Antoine Elwart, in his *Histoire de la Société des Con-*

certs du Conservatoire (1860), expressed extreme discouragement with contemporary programs. He wrote:

> We have only some rare symphonies performed, at great expense, at even rarer concerts. Chamber music is performed scarcely at two or three gatherings of fervent *amateurs*; but arrangements upon *motifs* from opera form the major portion of the musical program of even the slightest family entertainment.[18]

He added that "the majority of our composers must attempt to prove themselves at the *théâtre lyrique,* or risk vegetating without success or glory."[19] Yet he remained optimistic about the abilities of native composers, suggesting that "we now have symphonists worthy of competition with the Germans."[20] Only one year later—and some months *before* the advent of the Concerts Populaires, a series that exceeded all Parisian predecessors in its successful promotion of orchestral music—the critic Scudo noted rapidly increasing interest in instrumental works. He praised the Conservatoire concerts and chamber music societies, and told of the disappearance of "toute musique futile," including *airs variés,* impromptus, and so forth, which (he said) no longer interested publishers.[21]

Reports from Paris in the Leipzig *Allgemeine musikalische Zeitung,* 1863, deplored the conservatism of French programs and described the public's fascination with German music, yet added that there were native composers eager to write symphonies, quartets, and trios, among them Bizet, Adolphe Blanc, Mme. Farrenc, Franck, Gouvy, [Léon] Kreutzer, Reber, and Saint-Saëns.[22] A review of musical life in 1866, in the *Revue et gazette musicale,* described a trend of increasing musical conservatism; the author believed that established composers were writing less, and that times were ever more difficult for young composers, as nobody performed new works.[23] Just two years later, however, Mathieu de Monter remarked that music was becoming more a part of French daily life, and that well-performed renditions of masterpieces were presented in Paris and major provincial towns.[24] Finally, an anonymous reviewer for the *Revue et gazette musicale* wrote in February 1870 that chamber music societies and private concerts were multiplying at an "edifying" rate.[25]

Although the above sample of nineteenth-century statements may seem predominantly negative, and especially so in the period preceding the 1860s, it shows clearly that some concert activity existed throughout the period. Most of the laments mention exceptions. Two sides can also be seen in the lack of "official" support for concerts, a circumstance often decried by contemporary composers. In 1845 the French government curtailed the number of concerts that could be scheduled and limited admission prices for concerts to the sums charged by the *théâtres ly-*

riques.[26] Although these restrictions added to the frustrations of composers, performers, and lovers of instrumental music, their implementation suggests that concerts were viewed as a threat to the state-subsidized operas and theatres.

Concurrent with the prevalent twentieth-century image of the mid-nineteenth-century French instrumental scene as a near wasteland is the idea that following the Franco-Prussian War (1870–71) and the establishment of the Third Republic (1871), a renaissance took place, in which native instrumental music, encouraged by new nationalism (or anti-Germanic sentiment) and particularly by the new Société Nationale de Musique—founded in 1871 under the motto "Ars Gallica"—suddenly blossomed. Donald Grout has expressed this idea succinctly:

> The French musical renaissance is usually dated from 1871, with the foundation at the end of the Franco-Prussian War of the National Society for French Music. . . . One effect was a marked rise, both in quantity and quality, of symphonic and chamber music. The entire movement that was symbolized by the Society was at the outset nationalistic, both in that it was motivated by patriotism and that it consciously sought to recover the characteristic excellences of the national music.[27]

Earlier, Paul Henry Lang had written, "The foundation of the Société Nationale de Musique (1871) finally made it possible for the newer French composers to present their works to the public, and it was thanks to these efforts that music other than theatrical became again acceptable." Lang also stated that "Franck's [postwar] activity not only gave French music new vitality but largely determined its future course, for it was he and his disciples who at a time when young French composers could think of nothing but opera led them to the appreciation of instrumental music."[28] Rey Longyear, who has demonstrated more awareness of instrumental activity before the Franco-Prussian War, has also described a transformation in the musical scene afterwards:

> The principal musical change in France after 1870 was the acceptance of French composers in more than one field of music. . . . Between 1780 and 1870 the proper province for the French composer was a certain kind of opera: the rescue opera, *opéra comique,* or *opéra lyrique.* After 1870, however, critics and audiences accepted the absolute music of French composers, showing them an appreciation which had only hesitantly been granted Berlioz.[29]

Economic and social conditions of postwar France are widely accepted as reasons for this alleged renaissance; Longyear has mentioned the effects of the war and the Paris Commune on musical activity in the early 1870s. Martin Cooper had ventured such an explanation as early as 1951:

> In 1871 the war with Prussia and the Commune had left France shattered. . . . For a short while, at least, the overpowering predominance of the opera was broken, for opera needs money and a stable social system. Here was an opportunity for the more austere musical forms of orchestral and chamber music to gain a footing in Paris, and it was in these forms that the members of the Société Nationale first distinguished themselves.[30]

The concept of a "French musical renaissance" after 1871 is plausible only if one imagines an antecedent "French musical Dark Ages." For many historians the era preceding 1871 has indeed remained "dark," meaning "obscure." But publishers' advertisements, announcements and reviews in nineteenth-century journals, and the holdings of major research libraries suggest a picture of nineteenth-century France that is far from "dark"—a picture in which instrumental music (which henceforth will mean, primarily, orchestral and chamber music) played a substantial role. Two issues relevant to instrumental music are involved here, and these must be considered separately: the first concerns performance of instrumental works in general; the second regards composition of instrumental works by native contemporaries and the subsequent reception of these works. (In that an active concert life did not necessarily ensure performance of contemporary compositions, the nineteenth century more closely resembles the twentieth than the eighteenth.) To explore these two issues, separate sets of questions should be asked. The first set, applying to all instrumental music in the period 1828 through 1870, might include: How much was publicly performed in France? What works were programmed and which of them were most popular? Which musicians and what audiences supported instrumental music? The second set, restricted to contemporary French works, might entail: What instrumental music was written? Was it worthy of performance? What opportunities existed for its performance, and how much was it actually played?

Once the two sets of questions have been examined, they might be reconsidered for the years immediately following the Franco-Prussian War. Then one could compare the pre- and postwar eras and determine when and to what extent a musical renaissance occurred.

Seeking answers to these questions, I have surveyed various aspects of French musical life in the nineteenth century:

First, the nature of Parisian musical entertainment. Instrumental music was presented at more than 100 series of concerts or *séances*; these included programs by orchestras, chamber ensembles, soloists, composers, teachers, amateur societies, and groups associated with educational institutions.[31] Although this survey emphasizes the history of such series, it also examines music at nonseries concerts, *salons,* cafés, outdoor programs, and festivals. Furthermore it describes the setting and conditions for musical events—the musical season, concert locations, programming practices, and the class structure of the audience. The interaction of social, political, and industrial revolutions with musical developments eventually resulted in musical entertainment attracting a greatly expanded audience that was divisible not so much by wealth as by stylistic preference.

Second, the repertory and how it developed through the period. Beethoven, Mozart, Haydn, Weber, and Mendelssohn dominated concert programs, effectively shutting out most French composers; nonetheless, native, contemporary composers such as Berlioz, Adolphe Blanc, Georges Onslow, and Louise Farrenc attained some popularity. As the century progressed, chamber music replaced virtuosic works on many programs.

Third, contemporary and subsequent writings about music and musical activity during the nineteenth century. The divergent interpretations of nineteenth-century musicians and journalists regarding the musical scene and, particularly, the role of instrumental works, contrast vividly with the twentieth-century historians' almost unanimous agreement that instrumental music in France from the Revolution to the Franco-Prussian War is barely worth acknowledgment.

Finally, French music from the period in question. Composers from Cherubini to Castillon wrote impressive amounts of well-crafted instrumental music, yet most of it was soon forgotten and only a few composers—Louise Farrenc, for example—have been revived by any segment of the musical community.

The boundaries of this study are musical and chronological. I have examined the composition, performance, and reception of chamber and orchestral music—thus works for two or more instruments, but subject to one further restriction. In the following chapters, use of the terms "art" music and "popular" music has, with regret, been found too convenient to forgo; these terms are perhaps impossible to define precisely, and seem to have attained their nebulous connotations through common usage rather than through application of clear criteria. The subject of this study is "art" music, which henceforth will refer to genres commonly associated with concert halls. "Art" music will include duos, trios, quartets, quintets, and so forth, symphonies, concertos (some of which are better examples of virtuosic showpieces than of the art of musical composition), *symphonies concertantes,* suites, divertimentos, serenades, concert overtures, symphonic poems and excerpts from the above. Also included will be some works for unaccompanied solo orchestral instruments (when these seem appropriate to concert halls), works in which voices are involved relatively briefly (for example, Beethoven's Ninth

Symphony and Mendelssohn's music to *A Midsummer Night's Dream*), and instrumental excerpts from vocal or stage works (for example, opera overtures, ballet music, and instrumental movements from instrumental-vocal works such as Berlioz's *Roméo et Juliette*). Works for keyboard instruments, harps, or guitars exclusively will not be considered. "Popular" music, which has only secondary importance in this study, will refer to music widely regarded as being ephemeral—that which is often played at occasions where music is not the sole entertainment. It will include works for military band, dances (for example, *quadrilles* and *contredanses,* usually based on themes from other works and performed by dance orchestras), variations and fantasias on themes from operas or celebrated *romances,* and other "salon" works (many of which were intended mainly to display the virtuosic talents of performers).

The chronological boundaries within which this study explores concert life in Paris are the years 1828 and 1871. In 1828 the newly established Société des Concerts du Conservatoire (one of the few musical institutions that remained active through the entire period) initiated a new level of performance for orchestral works, and introduced to Parisian audiences several major compositions—particularly those of Beethoven. These achievements signalled the end of a musical nadir (affecting, especially, instrumental music) that had begun in 1815 with the return of the Bourbon regime;[32] beginning in 1828 instrumental composition and performance experienced a slow but unmistakable revival. French interest in instrumental music after 1871—more precisely, from autumn 1871, when the interruption effected by the Franco-Prussian War and Commune ended—has been recounted and is generally acknowledged; some compositions from the postwar period have remained in the repertory. Hence this period is less in need of examination.

The musical scene from 1828 to 1871 changed slowly. The stages through which it evolved seem to be reflected in six chronological subperiods, upon which some of the following chapters are structured. The subperiods represent, in part, a continual alternation between a relatively adventurous approach to concert life and a desire to maintain the status quo (the first subperiod reflects both attitudes). Briefly, the subperiods are:

1) 1828–33—a period of confusion, in which optimism resulting from the establishment of new concert societies and musical *salons,* after the pre-1828 musical depression, was followed by disappointment because of unrealized expectations. Musical activity after the July Revolution in 1830 seemed rather directionless.

2) 1833–39—a time of new concert series, performing both "art" and "popular" music for new (less aristocratic) audiences.

3) 1839–46—static musical years, an increase in the performance of instrumental works notwithstanding.

4) 1847–53—a period when, despite the interruption of the February Revolution, chamber music achieved unprecedented public success and significant orchestral societies appeared.

5) 1854–60—a less eventful time, although several more musical series were established.

6) 1860–70—a decade when new and highly varied concert series appeared and disappeared with alarming rapidity, but lively years, leading directly, save for the interruption of the Franco-Prussian War and consequent events, to the alleged renaissance of concert activity in 1871.

The main sources of information in this study are the weekly periodicals, *Revue musicale* (1827–35) and *Gazette musicale de Paris* (1834–35), and the result of their merger in 1835, the *Revue et gazette musicale de Paris* (also published weekly, occasionally more often). I have scrutinized each issue from 1827 through 1871 for program announcements, reviews, advertisements of publications, and articles on instrumental music, concert societies, and French musical life. These three interrelated journals were selected as the primary source on weekly musical activity partly because they provide continuous, relatively consistent coverage of the entire period, and partly because, as Dorothy Hagan has maintained, the *Revue et gazette musicale* patronized composers known for operatic and orchestral innovations, and was considered less conservative than many contemporary publications.[33] Although some music critics for the *Revue* were rather backward in their attitudes toward new styles, instrumental programs and works of progressive composers were widely reported in its pages.

Other sources include: additional nineteenth-century periodicals; memoirs, letters, and books by contemporary musical figures (the writings of Berlioz and Saint-Saëns, and those signed by Liszt are especially noteworthy); biographies and autobiographies of French performers and composers (Jacques Barzun's *Berlioz and the Romantic Century*[34] is particularly enlightening and thought-provoking); general music histories, studies of nineteenth-century music history, and books on special aspects of the century (such as Leo Schrade's *Beethoven in France*[35] and William Weber's *Music and the Middle Class: The Social Structure of Concert Life in London, Paris, and Vienna*); dissertations on individual musicians, repertory, criticism, and French musical life; music encyclopedias and biographical dictionaries (F.-J. Fétis's *Biographie universelle*[36] is, despite its many errors, most informative about nineteenth-century French musicians); books and articles on specific concert societies (notably Elwart's

Histoire de la Société des Concerts du Conservatoire and Elisabeth Bernard's article on the Concerts Populaires[37]); books about life in nineteenth-century Paris (those by foreign visitors are most helpful) and descriptions of musical *salons*; chamber and orchestral music of French composers (most of which I examined at the Paris Bibliothèque Nationale and the Library of Congress), writings about this music (*Cobbett's Cyclopedia of Chamber Music*[38] is a uniquely useful reference), and library catalogs; Constant Pierre's *Le Conservatoire National de Musique et de Déclamation*[39] deserves special mention; although it tells little about concert series, musical activity, or music, it provides a wealth of information about the obscure French musicians who performed instrumental music.

Finally, apart from proposing that activities relating to instrumental music in mid-nineteenth-century France have been seriously underrated, this study attempts some explanations. Why had instrumental music fallen out of favor earlier in the century and what, before 1871, led to its recovery? Why did young, native composers encounter such difficulties having their works performed or published? Why were so many projects that promoted new music unsuccessful, and why, given these circumstances, did such projects continue to appear? Why, in a period in which the new, emotionally charged Grand Opera made a successful debut in Paris, did so much French instrumental music remain conservative and staid? To what extent, directly or indirectly, did audiences, performers, institutions, and writers affect instrumental music, and how did they influence its course? Why have historians recognized the historical importance of French operas long absent from the standard repertory, yet continued to neglect instrumental works of the same provenance?

2

Musical Life in Paris, I: Customs and Conditions; Concert Series

If Dr. Burney's travels had taken place six, eight, or ten decades later, what would he have observed about Paris? What were the conventions of musical life? What was the viewpoint of the audience (or potential audience) on a day-to-day basis during this evolutionary period? What sorts of musical entertainment were available to, say, a connoisseur, a wealthy government official, a middle-class tourist, or a local artisan during, for example, the height of the concert season or the summer off-season in 1828, in 1848, in 1868?

The following two chapters describe the wide range of entertainment involving instrumental music, and explore details of concert life. The first defines the concert season, discusses concert locations and programming customs, and then examines the roughly 120 concert series that presented orchestral and chamber "art" music. The second depicts other sorts of musical events—among them enormous festival concerts, intimate *matinées* and *soirées,* benefit and state concerts, and nightly presentations of dance music in stylish cafés—and eventually summarizes available musical entertainment from single years early and later within the period 1828–1871; it also describes the audiences at various sorts of events, and attempts to explain what drew them there.

Information in these chapters comes from announcements and reviews in the weekly periodicals *Revue musicale, Gazette musicale de Paris,* the *Revue et gazette musicale de Paris,* and *Ménestrel,* and from a sampling of memoirs, histories, travel guides, novels, books of socialites, and other scattered sources as well as recent books and articles.

"The Season"

In nineteenth-century Paris, "the season" (meaning the social season) generally encompassed the period from early November to late April or early May.[1] It began when the upper classes returned from yearly visits to the country, where they had gone in August or early September; indoor concerts usually began in November or early December.[2] *Matinées* and *soirées,* held in private *salons,* also began late in the calendar year. In January the wealthy held balls (at which musicians were employed) in their own homes.[3] Later that month or early in February, the concert season began in earnest. Established series, which began at this time, commonly constituted six concerts at bi-weekly intervals, and thus lasted ten weeks, or into mid-April.[4]

During "the season," concerts were held weeknights, nearly always at 8:00, and Sunday afternoons, almost invariably at 2:00. Midweek afternoon concerts, private *matinées* excepted, were rare. Given the length of contemporary programs, evening concerts must have run quite late; there are occasional reports of concerts continuing past midnight.[5]

The number of programs dwindled in late April, and the season effectively ended by mid-May, simply once warm weather arrived, audiences no longer wished to remain indoors.[6] Musical life did not entirely cease in summer; concerts of light music, often suitable for dancing, were held outdoors, at parks, or in cafés.

Naturally, "the season" varied slightly from year to year; it appears that from 1828 to 1870, the concert season gradually became somewhat, though not significantly, longer. But despite the inevitable variation in quantity and quality of events on the calendar, the pattern of the musical season changed little. Exceptions to the usual routine were generally caused by nonmusical occurrences—revolutions, wars, recessions, and so forth—which made certain seasons poor samples of Parisian musical life:

1830–31. The results of the July Revolution disrupted musical life, though the revolution itself, occuring in the "off-season," and before regular outdoor summer concerts were established, had little direct effect. The revolution was followed by a damaging financial crisis, described by Edouard Fétis late in 1830: theatres were not attended and *soirées* were no longer given because of the financial risk involved.[7] Most persons had no money for concerts, and the rich stayed home.[8] Fétis *père* noted in early 1831 that since the revolution there had been much less activity for musicians at court, and that lower pay, loss of pensions, and other changes had hurt the opera houses.[9] Happily, the *Revue musicale* reported soon thereafter that the (spring 1831) concert season had suddenly and unexpectedly blossomed.[10]

Spring 1832. In March a cholera epidemic that eventually killed about 20,000 Parisians[11] caused the cancellation of many concerts. The rich left town, and persons who remained avoided concert halls. The Société de l'Athénée Musical (see p. 67) suspended its series for a few months, but some series endured, and Paganini played a special benefit concert for victims of the *maladie* in April.[12]

Spring 1848. The effects on musical life of the February Revolution were drastic. Erupting as the high plateau of the concert season was beginning, it brought most musical events to a standstill, permanently terminating a series sponsored by the *Revue et gazette musicale* (see p. 70). That journal had little to review, and most musical gazettes halted publication altogether, for concerts vanished "as if by magic."[13] Barzun has written that in the aftermath of the revolution "all cultural activity in Paris immediately ceased."[14] In a letter of 26 July, Berlioz described the scene as follows:

> All the theatres closed, all the artists ruined, all the professors idle, all the students in flight, poor pianists playing sonatas in the public squares, historical painters sweeping streets. . . .[15]

Several commentators remarked that the only music heard was patriotic or mob songs in the streets. Blanchard lamented the general unemployment and ridiculously low wages, and reported that the rich, many of whom were leaving town, were not investing money.[16] It is only fair (and does little to alleviate the gloomy picture of spring and summer 1848) to point out that certain series (notably the Société des Concerts du Conservatoire, the Société Philharmonique, the Enfants d'Apollon, Ettling's "Société des Amateurs", and the Alard-Hallé-Franchomme concerts, see pp. 21–37, 52–54, 65–66, and 71) persevered through the season. There were benefit concerts even in March and April. Ironically, in this impoverished musical season, there were enough events to prompt Blanchard's complaint that, though the February Revolution had disrupted everything else, concert programs *still* comprised mainly *fantaisies, romances, chansonnettes,* and *airs variés.*[17]

Summer 1860. An inclement summer eventually forced closure of the popular outdoor summer concerts.

1867. In a reversal of usual procedures, outside events helped musical life. The year was dominated by the Exposition Universelle, for which several special musical events were presented. A number of foreign musical organizations provided additional concerts.

1870–71. Entertainment during the 1870–71 season, the time of the Franco-Prussian War, the Siege of Paris, the Commune, and the consequent second siege, was, to understate it, greatly curtailed. Musical activity continued after the declaration of war (July 1870), but was halted during the first siege (beginning in late September). There was occasional activity again before the period of the Commune; Pasdeloup conducted a few concerts in February 1871, there were *soirées musicales* at the Opéra,[18] and benefit concerts offered (mainly) military music. The *Revue et gazette musicale* ceased publication from 28 August 1870 to 1 October 1871. Not until June 1871 did music begin to regain a foothold in Paris.

Concert Halls

I count nearly 50 Parisian concert halls active at some time between 1828 and 1871, not including the many private *salons* where music was heard.[19] Yet throughout the 1800s, the complaint was often voiced that Paris had no good concert hall, especially no place suitable for large forces. Although several new halls were built in the course of the century (and even more were announced), few found much favor, as the following contemporary comments demonstrate. In 1827 Fétis lamented the lack of satisfactory concert halls, contrasting this dearth with the plentiful supply of adequate theatres.[20] The establishment of the Gymnase Musical on the boulevard Bonne-Nouvelle in 1835 was greeted with optimism because of an interior regarded as exquisite and well-designed for the public. It was called the first respectable concert hall in Paris (the Grande Salle des Concerts of the Paris Conservatoire, excepted) and contrasted with undesirable contemporary rivals: the *salles* of Musard and Masson were thought to be fit only for social gatherings; the salle Chantereine, noted for uncomfortable, dirty little seats, was too small to seat a full orchestra, as was the salle Taitbout; the Hôtel de Ville was regarded as satisfactory but too remote.[21] The acoustics of the new Gymnase, however, turned out to be disappointing.[22] In 1852 Henri Blanchard wrote that concert halls were neither large enough nor plentiful enough to accommodate all the events of that season.[23] Five years later, while commenting on the thriving Parisian concert life, Blanchard deplored the constant competition for three or four meager concert halls, all with poor acoustics and facilities.[24] In 1861, Léon Kreutzer's review of a *matinée* by the composer and cellist Jacques Franco-Mendès pointed out that Franco-Mendès had composed symphonies, overtures, and other orchestral works, but that on this visit to Paris he presented only solos and chamber works because halls for large performing groups were unavailable.[25] Even in the first years of the twentieth century, Romain Rolland stated that Paris still had no respectable concert hall.[26]

To compound the problem, the few acceptable concert halls that did exist were difficult to obtain. In 1837 Blanchard, noting the tribulations one had to undergo to present an orchestral concert in Paris, especially cited this difficulty, confirming Berlioz's reports that Habeneck refused the Menus-Plaisirs to other persons or organizations because of professional jealousy.[27]

Occasionally, concerts were held in theatres, especially the Opéra and the Théâtre-Italien; Fétis found the Opéra unsatisfactory for orchestral concerts.[28] Smaller concert halls sponsored by instrument makers Bernhardt, Erard, Herz, Pape, Pleyel, Sax, and others, were used constantly. Most of these manufacturers provided a piano for their own halls, thereby gaining publicity for their products at each program. Particularly popular were the salles Erard, Pleyel, and Herz; the first two were used primarily for chamber or solo concerts. Berlioz thought the salle Herz too was suitable only for small performing groups, but orchestras did perform there, and Maurice Bourges found it less satisfactory for chamber music than the smaller salle Sax.[29] The salle Sainte-Cécile on the rue de la Chaussée d'Antin (just east of the present Opéra) was popular in the 1850s; Berlioz praised its acoustics, elegance, and good location.[30]

Carse has observed that in the nineteenth century the change to public concerts in larger concert halls led to the development of larger orchestras.[31] Confirmation for the first part of this statement can be easily established in a sampling of Parisian halls used from 1828 to 1871. The Conservatoire concert hall, opened in 1811, seated 956.[32] The hall (later called the salle Valentino) built on the rue Saint-Honoré in 1835 seated 2000.[33] The salle Barthélemy on the rue Saint-Nicolas, inaugurated in 1851, had about 3000 seats.[34] The Cirque Napoléon, where the Concerts Populaires were founded in 1861, had a capacity of 5000.[35] Subsequent Parisian halls did not all maintain this scale (the Athénée Musical, opened about 1864, seated only 1500 in a long rectangular room with a circular amphitheatre),[36] but an auditorium projected by Maurice Strakosch in 1869 was also to seat 5000.[37] Evidence regarding growth in the size of orchestras after 1828 is considerably less conclusive. At mid-century there were still, as in Germany, several orchestras of no more than 50 players. The most important Parisian orchestra, that of the Conservatoire, had over 80 members (not all of whom necessarily performed at once) upon its establishment in 1828, but had not expanded by 1859.[38] A trend toward larger orchestras may have been exemplified by the Concerts Populaires (see pp. 46–51), which had 101 members in 1861. There were of course much larger orchestras gathered for outdoor festivals.[39]

Programs, Programming, Performances, and Performers

At public concerts, as well as private *matinées* and *soirées*, printed programs were evidently not yet regularly available, for reviewers not infrequently commented on performers "dont le nom m'échappé." Too, critics often mentioned that programs published in advance bore little relationship to what was actually performed (and by whom).

Nineteenth-century programs were notable for their length and variety. Generally, they comprised either a few long works or numerous short, disparate pieces, as the representative sample below indicates. Although the following programs are of slightly above-average duration, they are by no means extreme within the period.

Example 1: Concert by Ferdinand Hiller, salle du Wauxhall, 23 March 1833.[40]

1) Hiller: A new symphony (premiere)
2) A duo, vocal
3) A violin solo, performed by Ernst
4) Beethoven: Piano Concerto No. 5
5) Bach: Allegro from Concerto for three keyboard instruments (performed on three pianos)
6) An air, vocal
7) Hiller: *Etudes* and *caprices,* piano
8) Franchomme: A cello solo
9) A duo, vocal
10) Hiller: Duo, two pianos
11) Hiller: Overture, orchestra (premiere)

Example 2: Concert organized by the violinst Charles Dancla, salons d'Hesselbein, 30 March 1853.[41]

1) Dancla: String Quartet No. 1
2) Dancla: Piano Trio, D Major
3) Dancla: Three *Romances sans paroles,* violin
4) Beethoven: Violin Sonata, Op. 30, No. 2
5) Dancla: *Fantaisie* on a theme from Bellini's *Norma,* violin
6) Haydn: String Quartet, Op. 64, No. 4

Example 3: Concert de l'Opéra, 21 November 1869.[42]

1) Weber: *Freischütz* overture
2) Berlioz: *Fragments* of *La Damnation de Faust,* orchestra
3) Saint-Saëns: Suite, orchestra
4) Air from *La Prise de Jéricho,* vocal[43]
5) Reyer: *Fragments* from *Sélam,* vocal
6) Beethoven: Symphony No. 7
7) Gluck: *Fragments* from *Alceste,* vocal
8) Schumann: *Kinderscenen,* No. 7, arranged for strings and oboe by Litolff

9) Schumann: "Scherzo" from Overture, Scherzo, and Finale, orchestra
10) Handel: "Hallelujah" Chorus from *The Messiah*

Some private *soirées* had programs of similar length.

The above programs demonstrate two common practices of the period: the extent to which excerpts (denoted by the unspecific French term "fragments") were performed, and the presentation of various and dissimilar genres at single events. It was not unusual to hear orchestral, solo instrumental, piano, and vocal works in one evening. Even if the instrumental portion of a concert was executed by an orchestra or chamber musicians exclusively, the distinction between chamber and orchestral music was not rigidly observed. String quartets were often rendered by string orchestras; other well-liked works, notably Weber's *Invitation à la danse,* and Beethoven's Septet, Op. 20, were also orchestrated.[44] Conversely, in concertos or other works for a soloist (or soloists) with orchestra, the orchestra was frequently replaced by a string quartet, other ensembles, or even a piano. The reviewer of a concert given by M. Panseron in 1830 explained that substituting a piano or pianos for an orchestra improved execution, as orchestras tended to be too hastily rehearsed.[45] The order of programs does not appear to have followed consistent patterns, with two exceptions: many orchestral concerts began with an overture, which thus functioned as an *ouverture* to the remainder of the program; often (especially in the late 1860s), concerts given by pianists opened with a piano trio, even if the entire rest of the program comprised piano solos.

Although some of the best music was heard at small *séances,* there were frequent complaints that at *soirées,* as well as concerts, the same *fantaisies, nocturnes, romances,* and *potpourris,* played by the same musicians, were heard over and over; Liszt (or his ghostwriter) wrote that three-quarters of all concerts were "ennuyeux".[46] The objection was also voiced that most young instrumentalists performed only their own (virtuosic) compositions.[47] As late as 1852, a reviewer stated that the programs by Stamaty's pupils *introduced a new path* for piano recitals by including piano concertos of Mozart, Beethoven, Weber, and Mendelssohn, as well as chamber works, rather than the usual *fantaisies, souvenirs,* and so forth.[48]

Many performing groups, especially those that played at private gatherings, comprised amateurs or a mixture of amateurs and professionals. Particularly popular, early in the period, were solo performances by children; examples of this phenomenon include concerts by four Swiss children named Koëlla, ages 6 to 11 in 1831, who sang and performed string quartets; the brothers Eichhorn, ages 8 and 10 in 1832, who played virtuosic violin music in the style of Paganini; and Camille Saint-Saëns, who was 8 years old in July 1844, when he performed piano concertos of Mozart and Field, and works by Beethoven, Handel, and Bach.[49]

Concert Series

Between 1828 and 1871 instrumental "art" music was performed at thousands and thousands of events. These may be divided into single programs—festivals, benefit concerts, presentations by travelling virtuosos, and individual *matinées* and *soirées*—and series. The concept of "series," somewhat problematic, is largely a matter of intent on the part of the organizer or organizers. For the purposes of this study, three or more programs at fairly regular intervals, either in one season or as single annual events for three or more consecutive years, constitute a "series." Furthermore, for the remainder of this chapter, "series" will refer not to the weekly or nightly café or outdoor concerts, the repertories of which included a small portion of "art" music, but only to concerts or *séances* that emphasized "art" music. About 120 such series were established (or remained active) in Paris between 1828 and 1871. Some of the organizers were foreign artists visiting for a few weeks, during which they performed only three or four times. But others were societies of local musicians who had some formal organization and maintained a steady schedule over several years or decades. Whether by design or otherwise only about 60 series lasted more than one season, and slightly fewer than half of these survived more than four years. Unquestionably, many of these transitory series had only limited importance as single entities; yet cumulatively they dramatically changed the musical life of nineteenth-century Paris.

The concert series, or the societies that established them, had various *raisons d'être*. Some series were associated with schools or other institutions. Individuals—composers, soloists or teachers—organized series to display, respectively, their compositions, performing abilities, or the talents of their pupils. Wealthy amateur musicians who wished to perform or nonmusicians who wanted to listen or to entertain their guests arranged concerts or *séances*. Other amateur players, who main purpose was to learn the literature, gathered together and offered occasional public programs. Some chamber groups concentrated on a particular genre or works of a single composer. Other organizations were especially receptive to new or native music. Finally, some series sought sizable audiences from the lower and middle classes; these were known as *concerts populaires,* "populaires" here referring not to the repertory, but the audience—meaning "intended for the people."

Organizers of most concert series followed the programming practice described above in that they offered several genres. Events in which orchestras participated also included instrumental solo, piano, and vocal works. Similarly, chamber works shared programs with other sorts of music, though some organizations, such as string quartets or quintets, played chamber music exclusively. Thus the terms "orchestral series" and "chamber music series" are not always appropriate if interpreted strictly. Nonetheless, most groups that provided instrumental "art" music can be categorized loosely by their emphasis on either orchestral or chamber music. About 50 series presented at least some orchestral music,[50] and in approximately 30 of these the orchestra was prominent. Chamber music was performed in the programs of nearly 85 series, and was primary in the repertory of about 50.

The discussion that follows begins with detailed descriptions of ten most significant series. Some of these, notably the Conservatoire concerts and the Concerts Populaires, have been documented elsewhere with varied success. Questions remain about each. Other series have been virtually ignored by historians; nearly all the information on these comes from nineteenth-century sources. The remaining organizations have received some recent notice—notice that, unfortunately, is blemished by much long-perpetuated misinformation.

The detailed accounts of individual series are followed by a general discussion of the many lesser series in a roughly chronological progression. Further information on these is provided in Appendix A.

The Société des Concerts du Conservatoire (from 1828)

Introduction. The Société des Concerts du Conservatoire, founded in 1828, was the first major orchestral organization in Paris after 1816, the year in which the *exercices* performed by Conservatoire students were discontinued because of political events that had led to reorganization of the Conservatoire. The Société's orchestra, now recognized as one of the finest in the nineteenth century, gained repute for polished renditions that eventually established new European performance standards. Because of the Société's chronological and qualitative precedence, it has been more thoroughly investigated than any other French concert organization of the nineteenth century; the considerable research, archival and otherwise, into the Conservatoire concerts by past scholars has made possible the detailed description in the pages below. Yet the position of these concerts in the French musical scene, and, especially, the role of the concerts' founder and first conductor, François-Antoine Habeneck, have too often been misunderstood. The Société's reactionary programming after 1848 represented neither contemporary Parisian repertory nor Habeneck's original intentions.

Harold Schonberg has called the Société's orchestra "the first of the great modern orchestras," and Carse has stated that in the first half of the nineteenth century it was "the finest orchestra in Europe, and therefore in the world."[51] Contemporaries also appreciated its excellence. Mendelssohn thought it "the best orchestra I have ever heard" and mentioned that the strings "start with exactly the same bowing, the same style, the same deliberation and ardor."[52] Wagner lauded the orchestra's persistent rehearsing, perfect execution, and ability to find and sing the melody in each bar and to discover exactly the correct tempo.[53] John Ella wrote that he had heard the best orchestras of Germany and London, but that none compared with that of the Conservatoire. He cited their *esprit de corps* and unity of style, taste, and expression.[54]

The establishment of the Société des Concerts had far-reaching effects. An anonymous critic wrote in the 17 February 1849 *Illustrated London News* as follows:

> Habeneck . . . brought the execution of symphonies and overtures of the great masters to a pitch of unparalleled perfection. The fire and energy of Habeneck's conducting, his observance of rhythmical time, and the precision and finish which he obtained from his forces, have led to the improvement of the other great orchestras in Europe; and to Habeneck's colouring may be ascribed the perfection afterwards attained by the Leipzig band, and by our own Philharmonic orchestra. The dazzling brilliancy of the stringed instruments in the Conservatoire band, perhaps, has never been equalled—certainly never surpassed.[55]

The same critic wrote that Habeneck brought about a "revolution in orchestral execution" and that "unity and coherence were the distinctive qualities of Habeneck's system."[56]

Other contemporaries also proclaimed the influence of the Conservatoire concerts to have been widespread. Elwart wrote:

> The activity of the Société des Concerts was felt not only in France, but in all Europe; the greatest artists regarded it as an honor to have their talents consecrated there; composers, singers, and instrumentalists all solicited the benefit of [a performance] on the magnificent programs of these concerts which, from the start, have placed their orchestra at the head of all the orchestras in Europe.[57]

And F.-J. Fétis, quoted by Elwart, stated that the establishment of the Conservatoire concerts regenerated French music.[58]

More recently, Emile Haraszti has said:

> The founding of the Société des Concerts du Conservatoire . . . and its performance under Habeneck's leadership . . . signified the beginning of a new epoch, not only in

the history of performance and the cultivation of Beethoven, but also in the musical taste of Europe.[59]

Beginnings of the Société. The person mainly responsible for the creation of the Société des Concerts was François-Antoine Habeneck (1781–1849), a violinist and an experienced conductor with a passion for the music of Beethoven. Habeneck had been attempting to acquaint the French public with Beethoven's string quartets—works that were unknown to even prominent French musical figures before 1828—as early as the first decade of the nineteenth century,[60] and, according to Schrade, had begun to study Beethoven's first symphonies in 1802.[61] He conducted Paris premieres of Beethoven's early symphonies in the Conservatoire's student orchestra programs from 1807 to 1811.[62] His father-in-law, the publisher Georges-Julien Sieber (who, with his father, had considerable commercial interest in German music), may have introduced new German works to Habeneck or encouraged his interest in Beethoven. Habeneck's appointment to the Conservatoire staff as a violin teacher in 1825 provided the necessary link with that institution for the establishment of the Société des Concerts three years later.

The promotion of Beethoven's music in Paris was, apparently, Habeneck's main purpose in founding a concert society, although he was also dismayed at the rarity with which orchestral works were performed there. The Concerts Spirituels, which had few programs per year, had reportedly fallen to a low level of execution,[63] and there was no other orchestral society meeting regularly. According to legend, Habeneck's initial step was a "luncheon" invitation (with a request that instruments be brought) to several prominent members of the Opéra orchestra in November 1826; when the musicians arrived, they found that preparations had been made for a reading of Beethoven's Third Symphony. Although enthusiasm was not unanimous among the group, more readings took place the following year, eventually leading to establishment of a society, on Habeneck's initiative. Cherubini, then director of the Conservatoire, carried out the official transactions, though his personal role in the proceedings remains controversial. Haraszti maintained that Cherubini was among the leading opponents of Habeneck's project,[64] and Berlioz opined that Cherubini viewed the Société with little enthusiasm, because of his jealousy of Beethoven.[65] Other sources supply persuasive arguments against this theory. Elwart stated that "when Cherubini was informed of Habeneck's plan, he agreed to the request that the latter should obtain the authority of the minister [of the *maison du roi*] with a degree of warmth that does honor to his memory."[66] Cherubini's actions in the establishment of the Société and his subsequent role as president of the society are cited. Ludwig Bischoff wrote that "Cherubini knew very well that Habeneck's object was the performance of the works of Beethoven. Had he entertained so mean an opinion of the latter as he is reported to have entertained, he certainly would not have promoted and arranged the whole affair with the zeal that he did."[67]

In any event, Cherubini was asked to obtain authorization for the presentation of concerts in the *grande salle* of the Conservatoire. M. Sosthène de Larochefoucault, a minister of the *maison du roi,* was approached. Habeneck had offered to pay personally for the expenses of lighting, heat, publicity, and programs,[68] but M. de Larochefoucault thought so highly of the idea that he granted permission for six concerts a year and provided an allocation of 2000 francs per annum for expenses. The *arrêté* from the minister, issued on 15 February 1828 (thus the official date of the establishment of the society), included the following instructions:

1) Each year there are to be six public concerts at the Conservatoire, beginning, at the latest, on the first Sunday in March. The director shall arrange that there be an interval of no longer than two weeks between concerts.
2) Participation in the concerts is open to past and present students of the Conservatoire.
3) No artist from outside the Conservatoire can perform in the concerts, regardless of his talent. [This regulation was soon suspended.]
4) Students presently enrolled at the Conservatoire are required to participate (gratuitously) in the concerts on the request of the director. Students who refuse to participate, or miss rehearsals for which they have been summoned, will lose student status at the Conservatoire.
5) Former students will be paid. The fee will be fixed at the end of the series, on the basis of the number of rehearsals and concerts in which they have participated. First desk players will receive double pay.
6) Concerts will take place in the *grande salle* of the Conservatoire. Prices are fixed: Premières loges—5 francs; Galerie, deuxièmes loges, rez-de-chaussée—4 francs; parterre—3 francs; amphithéâtre des troisièmes—2 francs.
7) Members of the Comité d'administration et d'enseignment, titled and honorary professors, inspectors from the department of

Beaux-Arts, directors of the Institution royale de musique religieuse, the Académie royale de musique [the Opéra], the Opéra-Comique, the Théâtre-Italien, and the Odéon shall have free entry to seats at any level.

8) At the end of the series, a financial account shall be realized.

9) The director of the Conservatoire [Cherubini] is granted the execution of this order.

This decree was read by Cherubini at a meeting of enthusiastic faculty and students of the Conservatoire. At this gathering the society was officially named the Société des Concerts du Conservatoire.[69]

The first program was presented on Sunday, 9 March 1828:

Beethoven: Third Symphony
Rossini: Duo from *Semiramis*
Meifred: Horn solo
Rossini: Air
Rode: Concerto "nouveau" for violin
Cherubini: Chorus from *Blanche de Provence*
Cherubini: Overture to *Abencérages*
Cherubini: Kyrie and Gloria from the *Messe du Sacre*

The second concert took place two weeks later; the following day, 24 March, the general assembly of the founder-members held their first meeting. The provisional committee was led by Cherubini (president), Habeneck (vice-president and conductor), and Guillon (secretary); other members were Dauprat, Brod, Halévy, Kuhn (the *chef de chant*), Meifred, Amédée, Albert Bonet, A. Dupont, and Tajan-Rogé. Fifty-two articles that had been proposed by the committee were approved by members of the Société; the most significant are the following:[70]

4) No person who is not a native Frenchman or a naturalized citizen can take part in the Société.
5) The committee shall choose guest artists.
7) The number of Société members is fixed at 100.
10) The committee shall consist of seven members: a conductor, a secretary, a commissioner of personnel, a commissioner of materials, an accountant, an archivist, and a professor from the ensemble class of the Conservatoire.

Many of the remaining articles describe the responsibilities of committee members. A telling statement in the job description for the conductor mentions that he *alone* has the right to beat time.

Among modifications and additions made to these rules in 1841 is a detailed description of the procedure for the admission of new works to the repertory of the Société: the final decision on admission was made by a group of members of the Société, chosen by the governing committee. Thus the conductor (in 1841, Habeneck) did not totally control the programming.

Physical characteristics of the *grande salle* at the Conservatoire have been described and illustrated in several sources.[71] There was general agreement that the hall had excellent acoustics but was otherwise less than glamorous. Chorley called it the "*ne plus ultra* of shabbiness," and reported that it was "small and filthy, airless and uncomfortable."[72]

The musicians. It appears that the size of the orchestra and chorus at the Conservatoire varied slightly from year to year, and that individual concerts did not require the services of all members. Elwart's account of the society's size in 1828 and in 1859 is surely accurate, for he compiled lists of personnel. He named 86 orchestral musicians and 74 choristers the former year, and an orchestra of 85 and chorus of 72 the latter.[73] Schindler reported that in 1841 the orchestra had 85 members plus percussion, but that only about 60 participated in any one concert.[74] Elwart quoted Meifred as stating that in 1844 there were an orchestra of 63, a chorus of 32, and 11 soloists;[75] these figures may represent the personnel at a single or typical concert, thus supporting Schindler's qualification. Three lists indicating the distribution of the orchestra are shown in table 2.1.

As stated in the bylaws of the Société, the instrumentalists were faculty, graduates, and students of the Conservatoire. Many members were famous performers, composers, or teachers.[76]

Programs. Because of benefit concerts, extra concerts for special occasions, and *concerts spirituels* (concerts performed during Holy Week, in which oratorios and other vocal works prevailed), there were each year more than the six scheduled subscription concerts—never fewer than seven concerts and often more. During Habeneck's conductorship (1828–48) there were 191 concerts in 21 years, an average of 9.1 per year; the figure was slowly increasing, and continued to do so in the mid-1860s. Beginning in the season of 1866–67, after the hall was redecorated and made somewhat smaller, many programs were performed twice, sometimes with minor alterations, such as the replacement of one piece. Thus in 1866–67, 18 concerts were presented but only 13 different programs. Between 1864 and 1870 there were 100 concerts and 81 programs, for respective yearly averages of 14.3 and 11.6.[77]

Early programs usually comprised six to nine compositions, divided about equally between instrumental and vocal works. Many of the pieces

Table 2.1 Instrumentation of the Orchestra of the Société des Concerts du Conservatoire

	Elwart 1828	**Schindler 1841**	**Elwart 1859**
First violins	15	15	15
Second violins	16	12	14
Violas	8	10	10
Cellos	12	13	12
Double Basses	8	11	9
Flutes	4	4	4
Oboes	3	3	2
Clarinets	4	2	2
Bassoons	4	4	4
Horns	4	4	4
Trumpets (or Cornets)	2	4	3
Trombones	3*	3	3
Ophicleide	1	—	1
Percussion	1	?**	1
Harp	1	—	1
	86***	85+	85***

*Elwart actually said there were 4 trombones including one ophicleide.

**Schindler noted that there was percussion, but did not number the players.

***Elwart said that the 86 players in 1828 included one extra, and that the 85 players in 1859 included six extras.

were excerpts, overtures, or other short works; still, the concerts were long by twentieth-century standards. Within a few years a new pattern developed: programs generally comprised four to seven works and nearly always opened and closed with instrumental works (often two symphonies, and sometimes two Beethoven symphonies). The following programs are typical:

1 April 1832

Beethoven: Third Symphony
Weber: Chorus from *Euryanthe*; solo by Mme. Damoreau
Anonymous: Cello solo, performed by M. Desmarets
Beethoven: Portions of string quartets, performed by string orchestra
Rode: Variations, sung by Mme. Damoreau [originally for violin]
Weber: Overture to *Oberon*

12 April 1835

Mozart: Symphony in E-flat [probably No. 39]
Anonymous: *Laudi spirituali* from the 16th century, for unaccompanied chorus

Haydn: Andante from a symphony
Brod: *Nouvelle fantaisie* on Swiss airs, for oboe, performed by the composer
Mozart: *Ave Verum*
Beethoven: Second Symphony

The nature of individual concerts changed little over the years. In the late 1860s there appears to have been a trend toward programs with fewer but longer works (sometimes as few as three, and rarely more than five). More often than before, the program finale was a vocal work. An example follows:

14 and 21 February 1869

Beethoven: Second Symphony
Mendelssohn: Chorus from *St. Paul*
Beethoven: *Coriolanus* Overture
Haydn: "Autumn," from *The Seasons,* solos sung (in French) by Mlle. Marimon, M. Achard, and M. Gailhard

As the examples reproduced above demonstrate, the Conservatoire's programming exemplified common nineteenth-century practices already described. Excerpts, such as one movement of a symphony or a scene from an opera or oratorio, appeared frequently. Chamber works were sometimes performed by orchestral forces. The Conservatoire's string section often played string quartets—mainly those of Beethoven and Haydn; *fragments* of Beethoven's Op. 59 No. 3 were performed in this manner ten times between 1837 and 1865, and the slow movement (usually entitled "Hymne") from Haydn's Op. 76 No. 3 was presented 19 times from 1852 to 1869. A favorite work of the Société was Beethoven's Septet Op. 20, originally scored for violin, viola, cello, double bass, clarinet, bassoon, and horn; at the Société concerts it was performed with its original instrumentation in 1831, but in its 46 representations from 1837 to 1869 it was usually rendered by string orchestra with doubled clarinets, bassoons, and horns (and often only *fragments* were played). Less typical was the division of one work into two: the Société's program of 15 April 1832 opened with the first two movements of Beethoven's Ninth Symphony, proceeded with short works by Cherubini, Beethoven, and Weber, and concluded with the final two movements of the Ninth.

Repertory. The Société's professed goal of promulgating the music of Beethoven was carried out to an incredible degree. Of 1276 performances[78] of instrumental works at the Société concerts from 1828 through 1870, 547 (43 percent) were of Beethoven's works; of 647 performances of major instrumental works[79] in the same period, 391 (60 percent) were Beethoven's, as were 360 of the 548 symphonies performed (66 percent). From 1828 to 1832 (not 1831, as is sometimes stated), Habeneck conducted all of Beethoven's symphonies; this was the first time that the nine were performed as a set in Paris.

Haydn and Mozart were also popular. Haydn's instrumental works account for 11 percent of the total performances, 13 percent among major works, and 15 percent among symphonies. The respective percentages for Mozart are 6, 9, and 10. (See Table 2.2 for more details.) Together, performances of Beethoven, Haydn, and Mozart totalled 60 percent of the instrumental-work performances, 83 percent for major works, and 91 percent for symphonies. Weber's name appears on the programs more often than Mozart's, but only three of the performances involved major works, and none involved symphonies. Mendelssohn's representation is approximately as impressive as Weber's; he had fewer total performances but more major works. These five Germanic composers, all but one of whom had died before the Conservatoire concerts were founded, were the most popular by far at this series (and, eventually, throughout Paris). Together their works made up 74 percent of all instrumental works programmed by the Société, and 88 percent of the major works. The most popular French composer at the Société concerts was Méhul, whose 16 performances of instrumental works rank him a distant seventh, behind Rossini. From Méhul's *oeuvre,* the Société performed only overtures, that of *Jeune Henri* 14 times; his symphonies were sadly neglected.

Probably the most significant French composer given a respectable number of hearings was Georges Onslow (1754–1853), actually of Anglo-French descent. His four symphonies were performed a total of eight times between 1831 and 1847. Only a few other French composers figured even relatively prominently on the instrumental portions of the Société's programs: works of Henri Brod (1799–1839) received 13 performances from 1828 to 1845; all of the works were for an oboe soloist (himself), and only one, a concerto, was major. The overture and an "air de danse" from Gluck's *Iphigénie en Aulide* were played, collectively, 12 times from 1838 to 1868. The cellist Auguste Franchomme (1808–84) appeared as a composer 9 times between 1829 and 1842.

Table 2.2 lists all composers whose instrumental works received four or more performances, and tables 2.3 and 2.4 list the most-performed composers of major works and symphonies.

Best known among the 88 composers whose instrumental works received three or fewer performances are Adam, Alkan, Auber, J. S. Bach, de Bériot, Berlioz, Chopin, Félicien David, Ferdinand David, Deldevez, Louise Farrenc, Handel, Herz, Hummel, Rodolphe Kreutzer, Mayseder, Moscheles, Paganini, Ries, Saint-Saëns, Schumann, Spohr, and Vieuxtemps. Among names notable by their absence are Schubert,[80] Liszt, and eighteenth-century symphonists, such as Gossec, Beck, and Devienne.

The Evolution in programming. Although the nature of the Société's concerts changed little from 1828 to 1870, the repertory did evolve. Statistical studies suggest that the four conductors active during the period, Habeneck, Girard, Théophile Tilmant, and Hainl, were influential in selecting the programs.[81]

Habeneck's tenure (1828–48) covered 191 concerts, on which were programmed 617 instrumental works.[82] Carrying out his goal, he conducted much Beethoven: 279 instrumental works (45 percent of the total), 192 major works (62 percent, and just over one per concert), and 178 symphonies (70 percent.)[83]. He also led many works by Haydn and Mozart. Surprisingly, the relatively modern Weber was the second-most-performed composer of instrumental works under Habeneck: his works were performed 45 times, but only one major work (a piano concerto) was played; the other works were all overtures. Brod received 13 performances, while Mendelssohn, who was introduced to the programs in 1842, received 12. Other composers whose works were heard relatively frequently were Franchomme (9 performances), Méhul (8), Onslow (8), Dancla (6), Kalkbrenner (6), Tulou (6), and Vogt (5); all were either French or active in France. Among contemporary French composers with major instrumental works performed on Habeneck's programs were Onslow (8), Dancla (4), Reber (2), Rode (2), Rousselot (2), Félicien David (1), Gallay (1), Tulou (1), and Vogt (1).

During his career, Habeneck led the Paris premieres of several works that have since become part of the standard orchestral repertory. Altogether, works by 97 composers (plus anonymous works) were heard, though 55 composers were given only one trial. It is to Habeneck's credit that he was willing to program the music of so many composers. The statistics demonstrate that the criticism he later received for being too conservative was not entirely warranted, and that later conductors of the Société (such as Deldevez) who defended the conservatism of their repertory as being in Habeneck's tradition were misled. The most notable trait reflected in Habeneck's programs is not conservatism, but his obsession with the music of Beethoven. His promulgation of Beethoven was, early in the century, too advanced for a conservative public but, by the end of Habeneck's career, too persistent for the taste of young native composers, who hoped to hear more performances of their own works.

Table 2.2 Performances of Instrumental Works (Listed by Composer) at the Société des Concerts du Conservatoire, 1828–1870

Composer	Performances (x)	Percentage of total performances (x ÷ 1276)	Major-work performances
Beethoven	547	43%	391
Haydn	138	11	85
Weber	112	9	3
Mendelssohn	76	6	33
Mozart	76	6	60
Rossini	19	1	0
Méhul	16	1	0
Brod	13	1	1
Gluck	12	under 1	0
Franchomme	9	under 1	0
Meyerbeer	8	under 1	0
Onslow	8	under 1	8
Cherubini	6	under 1	0
Dancla, Charles	6	under 1	?4
Kalkbrenner	6	under 1	4
Tulou	6	under 1	2
Altès	5	under 1	0
Reicha	5	under 1	0
Vogt	5	under 1	1
Alard	4	under 1	0
Baillot	4	under 1	1
Chevillard, A.	4	under 1	0
Gallay	4	under 1	1
Habeneck	4	under 1	0
Hérold	4	under 1	0
Masset	4	under 1	1
Mayseder	4	under 1	2
Reber	4	under 1	4
Rode	4	under 1	3
Romberg	4	under 1	2
Viotti	4	under 1	3
Wagner	4	under 1	0
88 others + anon.	151	12	38
120 composers + anon.	1276		647

Table 2.3 Performances of Major Instrumental Works

Composer	Performances	Percentage of all major works performed
Beethoven	391	60%
Haydn	85	13
Mozart	60	9
Mendelssohn	33	5
Onslow	8	1
Dancla, Charles	4	under 1
Kalkbrenner	4	under 1
Reber	4	under 1
David, Félicien	3	under 1
Rode	3	under 1
Viotti	3	under 1
Weber	3	under 1
37 others	46	under 1
49 composers	647	

Table 2.4 Performances of Symphonies

Composer	Performances	Percentage of all symphonies performed
Beethoven	360	66%
Haydn	83	15
Mozart	55	10
Mendelssohn	24	4
Onslow	8	1
Reber	4	under 1
David, Félicien	3	under 1
Rousselot	2	under 1
Schumann	2	under 1
Schwenke	2	under 1
Taeglichsbeck	2	under 1
Farrenc, Louise	1	under 1
Gouvy	1	under 1
Ries	1	
14 composers	548	

Although Habeneck was chastised by those with more modern attitudes (notably Berlioz), a remark made in an anonymous article on him in the *Allgemeine musikalische Zeitung* a few years before his death, is noteworthy: "To understand the significance of Habeneck, . . . one can look to Italy. . . . Who there knows Beethoven, or even the major instrumental works of Mozart?"[84] Because of Habeneck, many Parisians did.

A realistic assessment of Habeneck's conducting is difficult. Although he conducted from a first-violin part (with added cues) and used a violin bow rather than a baton, he was renowned for a thoroughness and strict discipline that evidently produced excellent results. Carse, having previously cited pertinent evidence of Wagner, Ella, Schindler, and other contemporaries, wrote, "Nowhere else were symphonies so thoroughly practiced as for the Paris Conservatoire concerts." He added that works were not performed there until they were familiar to the entire orchestra through repetition.[85] Many contemporaries agreed that no one performed Beethoven symphonies as well as Habeneck. Yet to the disgust of Berlioz and others, Habeneck occasionally rewrote portions of the symphonies that he thought ineffective.

Narcisse Girard (1797–1860), conductor from 1849 to 1859, had a career not unlike Habeneck's.[86] The repertory of the Société had become somewhat established by the time Girard succeeded Habeneck, but Girard's programs reveal less imagination than his predecessor's. He conducted 125 concerts, on which were programmed 313 instrumental works (2.5 per concert, down from 3.2 during Habeneck's regime). The most popular composers on Girard's programs (figures in parentheses represent number of instrumental works performed) were Beethoven (131), Haydn (58), Mozart (30), Weber (22), Mendelssohn (17), Rossini (13), and Gluck (8). The most-performed composers of major works were Beethoven (104), Haydn (24), and Mozart (22); no other composer received more than three such performances. Although there were many performances of symphonies by Beethoven (97), Haydn (24), and Mozart (22), no other composer received more than one hearing. Girard's programs included about the same amount of Beethoven as Habeneck's had, but the cumulative percentage of works by Beethoven, Haydn, and Mozart rose sharply (see table 2.5).

During Girard's 11 years as conductor, only 27 composers appeared on the programs (four anonymous works were played) as authors of instrumental works; only 8 of these names, of which Handel and Paganini are the best known, were new to the Société's programs, while 79 names disappeared. Many of the composers whose works were no longer played at the Conservatoire concerts were nineteenth-century musicians who

Table 2.5 Cumulative Percentage of Performances of Works by Beethoven, Haydn, and Mozart

Conductor	Instrumental Works	Major Works	Symphonies
Habeneck	54%	80%	91%
Girard	70	93	97

had been active in France, among them Cherubini, Kalkbrenner, Onslow, and Viotti.

Programs under the conductorship (1860–63) of Girard's successor, Théophile Tilmant, were no more progressive. Tilmant conducted 43 concerts, on which were played 117 instrumental works. The usual repertory was followed—Beethoven, Haydn, and Mozart, although Weber returned to second place in frequency of performance, and Mendelssohn now equalled Mozart. Otherwise, no composer was heard more than twice. Table 2.6 lists the most-performed composers.

Table 2.6 Performances of Instrumental Works (Listed by Composer) Conducted by Théophile Tilmant, 1860–1863

Composer	Performances	Major Works	Symphonies
Beethoven	48	33	30
Weber	18	1	0
Haydn	16	11	9
Mozart	10	8	6
Mendelssohn	10	6	4
12 others	15	4	2
17 Composers	117	63	51

The programs for all 43 concerts comprised the instrumental works of only 17 composers, only one of whom was new to the Société concerts: Hérold, whose *Zampa* overture was performed in 1861, 30 years after its composition.

Tilmant's successor, François Hainl (1807–73), displayed some more interest in works of contemporary composers, but not enough to alter significantly the conservative repertory of the Société. Between 1864 and 1870, Hainl conducted 100 concerts comprising 81 programs, during which he led 229 instrumental works. Twenty-eight composers were represented, of which 12 were new to the concerts: Adam, Auber, Garcin, Gernsheim, Gouvy, Joncières, Meyerbeer, Anton Rubinstein, Saint-Saëns, Schumann, Vaucorbeil, and Wagner. Table 2.7 shows the most-performed composers during Hainl's regime.

Table 2.7 Performances of Instrumental Works (Listed by Composer) Conducted by François Hainl, 1864–1870

Composer	Performances	Major Works	Symphonies
Beethoven	89	62	55
Mendelssohn	37	18	12
Haydn	27	17	17
Weber	27	1	0
Mozart	11	9	7
Meyerbeer	8	0	0
Wagner	4	0	0
Schumann	3	2	2
20 others	23	10	1
28 Composers	229	119	94

Beethoven was still clearly the favorite composer, and the combination of Beethoven, Haydn, Mozart, Weber, and Mendelssohn continued to dominate the repertory. Mendelssohn become the second most popular composer, while Mozart lost ground.

Tables 2.8–2.11 compare the repertory under each of the Société's conductors, from 1828 to 1870.

Table 2.8 Percentage of Performances of Instrumental Works (Listed by Composer), 1828–1870

Composer	Habeneck	Girard	Tilmant	Hainl
Beethoven	45%	42%	42%	39%
Haydn	6	19	14	12
Mendelssohn	2	5	9	17
Mozart	4	10	9	5
Weber	7	7	15	12
All Others	37	18	12	16

Table 2.9 Percentage of Performances of Major Instrumental Works (Listed by Composer), 1828–1870

Composer	Habeneck	Girard	Tilmant	Hainl
Beethoven	62%	65%	52%	52%
Haydn	11	15	17	14
Mendelssohn	3	1	10	15
Mozart	7	14	13	8
Weber	0	0	2	1
All Others	17	6	6	10

Table 2.10 Percentage of Performances of Symphonies (Listed by Composer), 1828–1870

Composer	Habeneck	Girard	Tilmant	Hainl
Beethoven	70%	66%	59%	59%
Haydn	13	16	18	18
Mendelssohn	3	1	8	13
Mozart	8	15	12	7
All others	7	2	4	3

Table 2.11 Other Statistics Comparing Four Conductors of the Société des Concerts du Conservatoire, 1828-1870

	Habeneck	Girard	Tilmant	Hainl
Years Active	21	11	4	7
Number of composers of instrumental works programmed	98	27	17	28
Composers introduced	98	8	1	12

The figures in the above tables show not only general trends (such as a decrease in the amount of Beethoven performed and a great increase in the popularity of Mendelssohn), but also statistically significant differences in the repertories of the four conductors. A similar statistical study indicates that it is unlikely that the directors of the Conservatoire, Cherubini (from 1822 to 1842) and D.-F.-E. Auber (1842 to 1871), influenced the programs greatly. Another possibility is that the programs were selected by committee, although no such body is mentioned in the bylaws. If this were true, it would be difficult, if not impossible, to trace the relationship between the repertory and the personnel that chose it.

Success of the concerts. Notices in contemporary periodicals often echoed a statement concerning the Société in the *Monde illustré* of 1861: "Concerts can be attended only by those who have the forethought to subscribe thirty years in advance."[87] In other words, the concerts were immensely successful. Nearly all seats were sold via subscriptions, and as subscribers retained the right to renewal, new listeners were all but shut out. Although only the affluent could afford subscriptions (especially at the Société's relatively high admission charges), demand for tickets always exceeded supply. This is in part explained by the small capacity of the hall: originally it seated only 956, and when it was redecorated in 1866 the *parterre,* which seated 150, was removed,[88] necessitating thereafter double presentations of some programs (and concerts two of every three Sundays) in order to accommodate enthusiastic audiences. Conservatoire concerts were, like performances at the Opéra, prestigious social events, attended by wealthy persons (some of whom knew little about music). Yet the numerous accolades of contemporary musicians indicate that the Société's success was not merely commercial.

Conclusions. After Habeneck's retirement, the Société des Concerts du Conservatoire became, at best, extremely conservative; Habeneck had not intended it to be so. His own programs demonstrate a willingness to try music by young or unknown composers, and if he allowed many writers only one hearing, history's verdict on some of these has been that they deserved no more; the notable exception to this verdict is Berlioz, whom Habeneck probably neglected for personal reasons.[89] Although he initiated the practice of playing an excessive amount of Beethoven, he did so at a time when Beethoven's music was little known in France; therefore, for Paris, Beethoven was a "new" composer (despite his having died the year before the Société's establishment). Under Habeneck, the Société served several valuable purposes: it provided an excellent musical alternative to opera and ballet, introduced much fine music to French audiences, and supported the best concert orchestra in Europe.

By the time Girard succeeded Habeneck, however, it was clear that Beethoven was no longer new and unknown; nor were Girard and his successors interested in new music. The institution evolved into a museum that provided little inspiration or hope for contemporary composers.[90]

The Société Sainte-Cécile (1850–1855; 1864–?1866)

History. Notice of the founding of the Société Sainte-Cécile was given in the *Revue et gazette musicale de Paris* on 3 November 1850.[91] Edouard Monnais related that disagreements among members of the Union Musicale (see pp. 73–74 and 274–75) in autumn 1850 had led to the departure of their conductor, F.-J.-B. Seghers, as well as several other members, whereupon Seghers established the Société Sainte-Cecile to perform orchestral and vocal music.[92] One M. de Bez, ex-president of the Union Musicale, presided over the new Société; the orchestral conductor until June 1854 was Seghers, and the choral conductor J.-B. Wekerlin.[93] Including the chorus, there were about 130 performers.[94] Six concerts per season were scheduled in the salle Sainte-Cécile, rue de la Chaussée d'Antin, at two-week intervals, alternating Sunday afternoons with the Société des Concerts du Conservatoire. Subscription prices for the season ranged from 15 to 30 francs;[95] the cost was neither exorbitant nor inexpensive, and was comparable to that of the Conservatoire concerts. After the inaugural concert (not part of the subscription series), presented 24 November 1850, Henri Blanchard, a reviewer for the *Revue et gazette musicale,* wrote that the orchestra was possibly the finest in Paris.[96] The wide-ranging program of that concert follows:

1) Beethoven: Fourth Symphony
2) *Pavane:* Chorus "from the sixteenth century," four voices, unaccompanied
3) Grétry: Air from *Anacréon*
4) Beethoven: *fragments* from the Octet for winds
5) Beethoven: "Chant élégiaque", chorus and strings
6) H.-M. Berton: Air from *Montano et Stéphanie*
7) Wagner: Overture to *Tannhäuser* (Paris premiere)

The first subscription concert was given 19 January 1851; regular subscription concerts continued for five seasons. Each season there were additional concerts, usually two before the subscription series started and sometimes one after. One of these was always devoted to music of contemporary composers; the first, given in late April 1851, included instrumental works by Wagner, Gouvy, and Greive.[97] The following season the "contemporary" concert comprised unpublished works. The same season the Société sponsored a contest for a new cantata on a given subject,[98] thus supporting more new music. In the three seasons from autumn 1852 to spring 1855 the concerts of contemporary music were held in December. French composers whose works were heard on these concerts include Berlioz, Deldevez, Gouvy, Georges Mathias, Prumier *fils,* and Saint-Saëns. Two notes in the *Revue et gazette musicale* described the procedure for selecting works for the contemporary programs.[99] Manuscripts were sent anonymously (with an accompanying envelope stating the name of the composer) to the committee of the Sainte-Cécile, which included the conductor, assistant conductor, and choral conductor, as well as Halévy, Ambroise Thomas, Gounod, and Reber.

By June 1854 Seghers had "regrettably" resigned; at the annual *assemblée générale* of the society, A.-M.-B. Barbereau (1799–1879, previously conductor at the Théâtre-Français) was elected his successor.[100] Dandelot wrote that Seghers's retirement led to the Société's dissolution.[101] Hill, who blamed the cessation (which he thought happened in 1854) on lack of funds, also mentioned the competition from the recently established Société des Jeunes-Artistes (see pp. 42–46).[102] Although the explanations of both Dandelot and Hill may be valid, both authors neglected the fact that a full six-concert season took place without Seghers in 1854–55.

After the final subscription series concert, the society had a strange history. A postseason *concert spirituel* was conducted by a newcomer, Edouard-Charles Muratet (born 1812), of the Théâtre Montmartre.[103] For the first time, summer orchestral concerts, given by the society in the Jardin d'hiver, were reported; at the new location, more light works—particularly overtures—were introduced to the programs. The last reported program comprised only vocal works and ephemeral instrumental compositions.[104] In December 1864 a notice appeared, stating that the Société Sainte-Cécile was resuming under the leadership of Wekerlin, who intended to concentrate on vocal works but also program piano and organ pieces.[105] Only vocal works were mentioned in the review of the inaugural concert (7 January 1865); the program included both the old and the new, offering works of Lassus, Carissimi, J. S. Bach, Lully, Rameau, Wekerlin, Hignard, Saint-Saëns, Wagner, and others.[106] The society was still active in February 1866, when it performed several vocal works and Saint-Saëns's *Sérénade* for piano, organ, violin, and cello at the salons Pleyel-Wolff.[107]

The degree of popular success of the Société Sainte-Cécile has not been established. It never enjoyed the reputation of the Conservatoire concerts, but it provided an attractive alternative for the many *amateurs* who could not obtain seats at the Conservatoire. A large audience was reported to have attended a concert in January 1854,[108] but the review of a preseason program of traditional music in December 1852 had stated that the audience comprised mainly instrumental dilettantes, many of whom were from Belgium and Germany.[109] The switch to programs of ephemeral works in June 1855, shortly before the society's demise, does not necessarily reflect a lack of success during the regular season; at that time no Parisian organization had yet been able to attract listeners to symphonic concerts in the summer months, during which only dance orchestras had sizable audiences. About May 1852, the Société received 1000 francs from the government, as official encouragement.[110]

Repertory. Programs are printed in the *Revue et gazette musicale* for all 48 known concerts given by the Société Sainte-Cécile, 1850 to 1855.[111] At these concerts were heard 135 instrumental works (about 2.8 per concert), of which 54 were major; 50 were complete symphonies (just over one per concert). Programs generally comprised five to seven works, about evenly divided between instrumental and vocal music. Major vocal works were performed less than major instrumental works, but were not entirely neglected.[112] Apart from symphonies, both opera and concert overtures held prominent positions in the repertory. *Fragments* of symphonies and concertos were also heard frequently, solos and marches somewhat less often. Only rarely was chamber music played.[113]

As at the Conservatoire concerts, Beethoven's name dominated the programs, appearing more than twice as often as that of any other composer. A considerable distance behind were Mozart, Haydn, Mendelssohn, and Weber. The works of these five composers appeared 82 times, about 61 percent of the total. Among the other 30 composers represented (plus the anonymous composer of a pavane) were many contemporaries, both foriegn and French: Auber, Berlioz, Deldevez, Fessy, Gade, Gouvy, Mme. de Grandval, Greive, Léonard, Georges Mathias, Meyerbeer, Pilet, Prumier *fils,* Reber, Rossini, Saint-Saëns, Schumann, Stadtfeld, and Wagner. But none of these persons received more than six performances, and 19 composers were played only once. Tables 2.12–2.14 show composers whose works, major works, and symphonies appeared most.

Table 2.12 Performances of Instrumental Works (Listed by Composer) by the Société Sainte-Cécile, 48 Concerts, 1850–1855

Composer	Performances (x)	Percentage of total performances (x ÷ 135)	Major-work performances
Beethoven	34	25%	22
Mozart	14	10	9
Haydn	12	9	7
Mendelssohn	11	8	3
Weber	11	8	0
Gouvy	6	4	4
Mathias, G.	4	3	2
Reber	4	3	2
27 others + 1 anon.	39	29	5
35 composers + 1 anon.	135		54

Table 2.13 Performances of Major Instrumental Works

Composer	Works	Percentage of all major works performed
Beethoven	22	41%
Mozart	9	17
Haydn	7	13
Gouvy	4	7
Mendelssohn	3	6
6 others	9	17
11 composers	54	

Table 2.14 Performances of Symphonies

Composer	**Symphonies**	**Percentage of all symphonies performed**
Beethoven	21*	42%
Haydn	7	14
Mozart	7	14
Gouvy	3	6
Mendelssohn	3	6
6 others	9	18
11 composers	50	

*The Société performed only Symphonies Nos. 3 through 7.

These statistics include the nonsubscription programs of contemporary music, on which five composers, Deldevez, Gade, Mme. de Grandval, Greive, and Prumier received their only hearing. The repertory of the subscription concerts, shown in Table 2.15, was much more conservative: works of mid-nineteenth-century Paris's most popular five (Beethoven, Haydn, Mendelssohn, Mozart, and Weber) constitute 68 percent of all instrumental works performed and 82 percent of all the major works.

Table 2.15 Performances of Instrumental Works (Listed by Composer) by the Société Sainte-Cécile, Excluding Special Programs of Contemporary Music, 43 Concerts, 1850–1855

Composer	**Performances (x)**	**Percentage of total performances (x ÷ 121)**	**Major-work performances**	**Symphony performances**
Beethoven	34	28%	22	21
Mozart	14	12	9	7
Haydn	12	10	7	7
Mendelssohn	11	9	3	3
Weber	11	9	0	0
Gouvy	4	3	3	2
Reber	4	3	2	2
Gluck	3	2	0	0
22 others + 1 anon.	28	21	4	4
30 composers + 1 anon.	121		50	46

In spite of this conservatism, the programming of the Société Sainte-Cécile was more adventurous than that of the Conservatoire, particularly during the same years. The Société Sainte-Cécile was responsible for the first performance of any Schubert symphony in Paris, in November 1851.[114] And the Société did use its concerts of new music as a testing ground for young composers' works; some of these were later performed for the subscription audiences, thus gaining a certain degree of respectability. Nevertheless, the society received criticism for its conservatism. Léon Kreutzer complained that the society duplicated the function of the Conservatoire concerts, and suggested more performances of works by Berlioz, David, Gounod, Gouvy, and Reber.[115]

The Société des Jeunes-Artistes (1853–1861)

History. The Société des Jeunes-Artistes was an organization of Conservatoire students and graduate prize winners led by Jules Pasdeloup in biweekly concerts of traditional and recent orchestral and vocal works. The society was founded in late 1852 or early 1853.[116] According to Elwart, Pasdeloup decided to establish a musical organization after the "chef d'orchestre d'une société alors en pleine exploitation dans la capitale" [presumably Girard of the Société des Concerts du Conservatoire] refused even to read through a scherzo of Pasdeloup's, stating that his orchestra performed only works by established masters.[117] Pasdeloup intended his new organization to perform serious works by young composers as well as those of better-known authors. His project was regarded as having much educational value for Conservatoire students, as it provided instrumentalists and vocalists with experience in group performances, and enabled student composers to hear their own works.[118] Pasdeloup's group comprised 62 instrumentalists and 40 choristers; the choral conductor was Edouard Batista. Profits were to be distributed among the performers.[119]

The inaugural program took place Sunday, 20 February 1853:

1) Beethoven: First Symphony
2) *Pavane,* Chorus "from the sixteenth century," with vocal soloists
3) Louis Lacombe: "New" overture
4) Georges Bousquet: Duo from *Tabarin*
5) Berlioz: *Roman Carnival Overture*

Thereafter at least six biweekly concerts were presented each year, on Sunday afternoons, generally between December and March, and always at the unspacious salle Herz, rue de la Victoire. From 1856 or earlier, supplementary concerts were given after the regular season ended; these comprised benefit concerts and *concerts spirituels*. In addition, the group performed at various state occasions and in churches.[120]

Most members of the Société des Jeunes-Artistes were students. Consequently, their talents, though considerable, were somewhat less than professional, and the personnel changed dramatically from year to year. For these reasons, and because Pasdeloup was an inexperienced conductor, the Jeunes-Artistes could not hope to match the polished performances of the carefully rehearsed professionals in the Société des Concerts du Conservatoire. The Jeunes-Artistes became renowned, however, for willingly performing new works, propagating masterpieces among middle-class audiences, and training young musicians in the art of ensemble playing.[121]

Despite critical acclaim and a faithful audience, and even with financial aid from the Conservatoire, the Société had financial difficulties.[122] Some of their monetary problem can be attributed to the small capacity of the salle Herz. Lasalle and Thoinan suggested that admission prices were too high to draw crowds,[123] but other reports indicate that generally there were eager audiences.[124]

Repertory. From nine musical seasons (1853–61), there are 62 known concerts—54 series concerts and eight postseason concerts. Programs have been examined for 59 of these concerts; all statements below concerning repertory are based on the 59 known programs.[125] Fifty-two composers are represented by instrumental works (roughly twice as many as were represented at the Conservatoire concerts during the same period); in addition, four works were performed for which the author is unknown. The repertory ranged chronologically from Stradella (although he was the only composer earlier than Haydn) to new works. The Jeunes-Artistes presented several Paris premieres, including that of Schumann's "Spring" Symphony. Performed on the known programs were 191 instrumental works (somewhat more than three per concert), among them 86 major works, 66 of them symphonies (more than one per concert). Only 18 composers had major works performed, and only 12 had symphonies on the programs.

Programs averaged five to seven numbers, about evenly divided between instrumental and vocal music. (Individual programs sometimes had a preponderance of one or the other.) By twentieth-century standards, many of the programs seem long, though they tended to include many short works rather than fewer long. The program of a series concert, presented 4 January 1857, is typical:[126]

1) Gouvy: Symphony in F Major
2) Alard: *Fantaisie* (on a theme of Beethoven), violin
3) Rameau: Chorus
4) Haydn: *Fragment* of a string quartet, arranged for string orchestra
5) [? C.-E. Lefebvre]: Air from *Zaïre*
6) Gounod: Symphony in D Major
7) J. S. Bach: Prelude, arranged for chorus and orchestra by Gounod

Symphonies and overtures were most popular, and concertos, orchestrations of chamber works, *fragments* (usually single movements) of symphonies, and solos (particularly for the violin) were also played regularly. Tables 2.16–2.18 show which composers were most performed by the Jeunes-Artistes.

Table 2.16 Performances of Instrumental Works (Listed by Composer) by the Société des Jeunes-Artistes, 59 Programs, 1853–1961

Composer	Performances (x)	Percentage of total performances (x ÷ 191)	Major-work performances
Beethoven	34	18%	27
Haydn	14	7	5
Mozart	13	7	6
Gounod	11	6	10
Mendelssohn	11	6	9
Weber	10	5	0
Alard	9	5	4
Rossini	7	4	0
Lefébure-Wély	6	3	5
Cohen, Jules	5	3	0
Gouvy	5	3	5
Schumann	5	3	4
Meyerbeer	4	2	0
39 others + anon.	57	30	9
52 composers + anon.	191		86

The repertory of the Jeunes-Artistes was broader and more modern than those of the Conservatoire and the Société Sainte-Cécile. Although Beethoven is again the most popular composer by far, his works make up just 18 percent of all instrumental works performed. Paris's favorite five, who so dominated the programs of the two other major orchestras, account for only 43 percent of all instrumental-work performances by the Jeunes-Artistes, and 55 percent among major works. Gounod's works rank second among major works and symphonies performed, and con-

Table 2.17 Performances of Major Instrumental Works

Composer	Performances	Percentage of all major works performed
Beethoven	27	31%
Gounod	10	12
Mendelssohn	9	10
Mozart	6	7
Gouvy	5	6
Haydn	5	6
Lefébure-Wély	5	6
Alard	4	5
Schumann	4	5
9 others	11	13
18 composers	86	

Table 2.18 Performances of Symphonies

Composer	Performances	Percentage of all symphonies performed
Beethoven	23	35%
Gounod	10	15
Haydn	5	8
Lefébure-Wély	5	8
Mendelssohn	5	8
Gouvy	4	6
Mozart	4	6
Schumann	4	6
4 others	6	9
12 composers	66	

temporary compositions by Alard, Lefébure-Wély, Gouvy, and Schumann figure prominently in the repertory. Contrary to expectations, few works by Conservatoire students were programmed, although the orchestra may have read student compositions at rehearsals; works by recent graduates were presented often.

Edouard Monnais suggested that the Jeunes-Artistes had inspired a new era of symphonic writing, citing as examples the symphonies of Gouvy, Rosenhain, and Litolff.[127] Unlike many contemporary organizations, the Société never abandoned its policy of programming recent works; even in the final season (1861), compositions of Gade, Alard, Constantin, Litolff, Schumann, and Wagner were tried. One notable absentee from the Société's programs is Reber, whose works had been played repeatedly by the Société Sainte-Cécile in the early 1850s.

The Concerts Populaires (1861–1884)

History. The Concerts Populaires evolved from the Société des Jeunes-Artistes in 1861. Many of the same personnel remained, including the director and man responsible for the transformation, Jules Pasdeloup. Financial problems, if nothing else, must have forced Pasdeloup to consider changing the Société des Jeunes-Artistes. Some contemporaries believed that he had been disappointed in his search for interesting contemporary music.[128] Elisabeth Bernard, whose article in *Revue de musicologie*[129] is the best recent scholarship on the Concerts Populaires, has suggested that the success both of British music festivals in the 1850s and of similar festivals organized by Pasdeloup prompted him to reconsider the purpose of his organization: instead of promoting new music to an enthusiastic but necessarily small audience, he would present established masterpieces and talented soloists to a larger, less affluent (and presumably less cultured) audience, in an enormous hall, with low admission fees.[130] He would initiate the multitudes to the enjoyment of the best music.[131] As it had been impossible for nonsubscribers to attain seats at the Conservatoire concerts, much of the Parisian public had only periodically had the opportunity to attend orchestral concerts (and even less often at affordable prices).

To execute his plan, Pasdeloup, supported by a rich moneylender, moved his orchestra to the Cirque Napoléon, boulevard des Filles-du-Calvare.[132] The setting, a short distance south-southeast of the Place de la République, was later called the Cirque d'hiver and is now also known as the Place Pasdeloup. Botte said that the hall was somewhat less well located than the Conservatoire, but that the seating was well planned, the temperatures not too extreme, and the acoustics reasonable.[133] Edouard Monnais, who thought the acoustics fine, reported that the orchestra was situated on a platform on one side of the hall.[134] Bernard has stated that the hall seated about 5000 in steeply angled banks.[135]

The orchestra was enlarged to 101 members, comprising 20 first violins, 20 second violins, 12 violas, 12 cellos, 12 double basses, 3 flutes, 2 oboes, clarinets, and bassoons, 4 horns, 2 trumpets, 3 trombones, 1 ophicleide, 1 set of tympani, 1 triangle, and 4 harps.[136] Elwart said the orchestra included 44 past winners of *premiers prix* at the Conservatoire.[137] The list of personnel is impressive, and the guest soloists no less so: among them were the violinists Alard, Vieuxtemps, Garcin, Mme. Norman Neruda, and Besekirsky; the cellists Jacquard and Poëncet; the pianist Marie Pleyel, flutist Brunot, horn player Mohr, and various singers.

Concerts were scheduled weekly on Sunday afternoons through the musical season. With only few exceptions, there were 24 subscription concerts per year, divided (temporally—but with no discernible differences) into three series of eight. Most seasons there were optional *concerts spirituels* or benefit concerts. Admission fees for single concerts were fixed at 75 centimes to six francs,[138] and apparently remained the same for many years. Subscription prices for a series of eight concerts in 1867 cost 24 to 48 francs.[139] These fees contrasted favorably with those of the Conservatoire concerts (at that time two to twelve francs per concert);[140] furthermore, seats were usually available at the Concerts Populaires, whereas the few places at the Conservatoire concerts had been reserved by subscribers years in advance.

The first program, a major success, took place Sunday, 27 October 1861:[141]

1) Weber: Overture to *Oberon*
2) Beethoven: Sixth Symphony
3) Mendelssohn: Violin Concerto Op. 64
4) Haydn: "Hymne" (Poco adagio from String Quartet Op. 76, No. 3), arranged for string orchestra
5) Méhul: Overture to *Jeune Henri*

Nearly 5000 persons attended, and the press was favorable. Berlioz,[142] reviewing the first concert in the *Journal des débats* (12 November 1861), mentioned the sincere enthusiasm of the inexperienced audience, and complimented Pasdeloup on fulfilling a much-needed function. A week after the inauguration Monnais wrote that to understand the Concerts Populaires, one must imagine the Conservatoire concerts suddenly made available to thousands, rather than hundreds, of persons.[143] Shortly thereafter, Botte made a similar analogy, describing the Concerts Populaires as a counterpart to the Conservatoire concerts, but for the less wealthy; Botte also drew parallels between the careers of Pasdeloup and Habeneck.[144] Everyone applauded the low prices. At the second concert, 3 November, the hall was overflowing; more than 500 persons could not find seats.[145]

This impressive success continued through the 1860s. Hervey wrote that "every Sunday afternoon [the concerts] were crowded. It became the correct thing to go either to the Conservatoire or to Pasdeloup's . . . and as admittance to the former temple of art was extremely difficult to obtain, the latter profited thereby."[146] Adolphe Jullien also mentioned the popularity of the concerts and described the competition for tickets.[147] Apart from regular concerts in Paris, the orchestra toured in the provinces (thus inspiring, according to Bernard,[148] the formation of music societies in Toulouse, Nantes, Marseilles, Brest, Versailles, and Lyons; see Appendix B) and in other countries, particularly Belgium and Italy.

After the Franco-Prussian War, the Concerts Populaires continued with slowly diminishing popularity until 1884. The society was hurt by competition from new organizations: the Concert National (or Concerts Colonne, founded in 1873 and modeled on the Concerts Populaires) and the Concerts Lamoureux (founded in 1881). The Concerts Colonne were particularly successful (and, therefore, damaging) after their move from the Odéon to the Châtelet in 1874; they undersold the Concerts Populaires, charging only 50 centimes to three francs per concert.[149] Bernard attributed the organization's eventual downfall, however, to deficiencies in the orchestra's execution and Pasdeloup's interpretations,[150] which drew criticism from Bizet ("quel triste musicien"), Wagner (who referred to Pasdeloup's "grande maladresse"), and Reyer ("Pasdeloup est bien dirigé par son orchestre"),[151] among others.[152] Pasdeloup's shortcomings were probably little noticed by the audience of novices in the early 1860s who welcomed the opportunity to hear good music at affordable prices. But Pasdeloup could not compete with the superior conducting techniques of Colonne and Lamoureux;[153] eventually his audience and even some of his musicians deserted him.[154]

Repertory. Information on the repertory comes from study of 219 programs presented in the nine seasons between autumn 1861 and spring 1870.[155] The Concerts Populaires were almost exclusively instrumental. Rare exceptions to this practice included performances of works in which the vocal portion was relatively brief, such as Beethoven's Ninth Symphony (which was, in any case, sometimes performed without the last movement). The society also programmed some major vocal works (for example, Mendelssohn's *Elijah*) at special, nonseries concerts. Series programs generally comprised four or five works, exceptionally three or six, mixing relatively substantial works with relatively light ones. Most programs included one or more symphonies and at least one overture (in many cases performed first). Concertos, orchestral suites, symphonic poems, arrangements of chamber works for string orchestra (some with winds), individual movements of larger works, excerpts from ballets, and instrumental solos made up most of the remainder of the repertory.

On the 219 known programs were 1037 performances of more than 200 instrumental works. There were 400 performances of major works and 280 performances of symphonies. Tables 2.19–2.21 show the composers whose works were most performed.

As with nearly all nineteenth-century Parisian concert societies, Bee-

Table 2.19 Performances of Instrumental Works (Listed by Composer) by the Concerts Populaires, 219 Programs, 1861-70

Composer	Performances (x)	Percentage of total performances (x ÷ 1037)	Major Works
Beethoven	259	25%	159
Mendelssohn	143	14	59
Haydn	126	12	60
Mozart	114	11	53
Weber	77	7	0
Wagner	37	4	0
Meyerbeer	35	3	1
Schumann	28	3	11
Rossini	25	2	0
Bach	16	2	1
Berlioz	16	2	0
Lachner	14	1	9
Gounod	11	1	1
Schubert	8	under 1	5
Wallace	8	under 1	0
Gade	7	under 1	4
Nicolai	7	under 1	0
Rameau	6	under 1	0
Cherubini	5	under 1	0
Gluck	5	under 1	0
Méhul	5	under 1	0
Paganini	5	under 1	5
Vieuxtemps	5	under 1	1
Viotti	5	under 1	4
42 others	70	7	26
66 composers	1037		399

thoven was by far the most popular composer. Mendelssohn's being second is not unusual among post-1850 repertories. The dominance of these two composers, plus Haydn, Mozart, and Weber, indicates a conservatism almost comparable to that of the Conservatoire concerts. The works of these five composers constituted 69 percent of all performances of instrumental works, 83 percent for major works, and 91 percent for symphonies. (It is only in the list of next-most-performed composers that a change from this traditional programming is noticeable: Wagner, Meyerbeer, Schumann, Berlioz, Lachner, and Gounod rank among the top 13.) This basic conservatism can be explained by Pasdeloup's announced intention to popularize masterpieces rather than to explore new compositions.

Table 2.20 Performances of Major Instrumental Works

Composer	Performances	Percentage of all major works performed
Beethoven	159	40%
Haydn	60	15%
Mendelssohn	59	15%
Mozart	53	13%
Schumann	11	3%
Lachner	9	2%
Paganini	5	1%
Schubert	5	1%
Gade	4	1%
Viotti	4	1%
Massenet	3	under 1
Rubinstein, A.	3	under 1
Spohr	3	under 1
17 others	21	5
30 composers	399	

Table 2.21 Performances of Symphonies

Composer	Performances	Percentage of all symphonies performed
Beethoven	119	43%
Haydn	59	21
Mozart	44	16
Mendelssohn	33	12
Schumann	10	4
Schubert	5	2
Gade	4	1
Rubinstein	3	1
3 others	3	1
11 composers	280	

A number of recent composers were, however, represented once at the Concerts Popularies; Bernard noted that Pasdeloup was often willing to read works of young composers at rehearsals.[156] As early as February 1862 it was announced that Pasdeloup intended to intersperse relatively new works among the masterpieces;[157] but the change in programming thereafter was hardly remarkable, and some contemporary composers—Molique, Mohr, Brunot—had appeared on earlier programs. Regarding Pasdeloup's attitude toward modern symphonies, Hill reported him to have said "Write symphonies like those of Beethoven, and I will play them."[158] Hervey wrote that "Pasdeloup had aroused an interest in the symphonic works of the great German masters. Occasionally some young French composer was able to find favor."[159] Georges Favre maintained that Pasdeloup disliked contemporary French composers and catered to the German school.[160] The programs reveal that although more contemporary French composers than Germans were given a hearing, the works (and particularly major works) of contemporary Germans were performed much more. Figures for the five most performed nineteenth-century composers from both countries demonstrate this dramatically, even if Meyerbeer is allowed to be considered a Frenchman (see table 2.22.)

Table 2.22 Comparison of Number of Performances of Works by the Five Most-Performed German and French Nineteenth-Century Composers, by the Concerts Populaires, 1861–1870

German Composers			**French Composers**		
Composer	*Performances*	*Major Works*	*Composer*	*Performances*	*Major Works*
Mendelssohn	143	59	Meyerbeer	35	1
Wagner	37	0	Berlioz	16	0
Schumann	28	11	Gounod	11	1
Lachner	14	9	Massenet	3	3
Spohr	3	3	Saint-Saëns	3	2
	225	82		68	7

Pasdeloup's selection of programs does not appear to have been strongly influenced by his audience or critics; at times he actively opposed their wishes.[161] This is particularly true in the case of Wagner, whom Pasdeloup championed in spite of vocal opposition by much of the audience. Beginning in autumn 1864, Wagner's works, mainly the overtures and other opera excerpts, were performed with increasing frequency—nine times in both the 1868–69 and 1869–70 season,[162] eventually winning some enthusiasts. After Pasdeloup's performance of the Prelude to *Lohengrin,* 6 December 1868, part of the audience demanded immediate repetition of the work (not an uncommon practice at the time), while the rest of the listeners vehemently opposed this request. Pasdeloup resolved the conflict by agreeing to repeat the Wagner at the end of the concert, so that those who wished to leave could do so.[163]

The Société Alard-Franchomme (Société de Musique de Chambre) (?1847–?1872)

History. The Société Alard-Franchomme, founded by the violinist Delphin Alard (1815–88) and cellist Auguste Franchomme (1808–84), counted among its other members another violinist, two violists, and a pianist. This combination enabled the society to perform a repertory of violin and cello sonatas, and trios, quartets, and quintets, with or without piano. From the late 1840s until after the Franco-Prussian War[164] they gave, with few exceptions, six public concerts a year.

I have not been able to pinpoint an exact date for the founding of the Société Alard-Franchomme. Alard and Franchomme had performed together occasionally in the early 1840s, but evidently not as a *société*. Martin Cooper has stated that the organization was founded in 1848.[165] The beginning of its sixth season was announced in November 1852,[166] which would indicate that its first season was no later than 1847–48. The earliest record I have seen of Alard and Franchomme combining as an official society is an announcement of the *resumption* of concerts by the Société de Musique de Chambre on 20 January 1850.[167] Official society or not, Alard and Franchomme began to meet regularly with others for *séances* of chamber music by 7 February 1847, when the first of a series took place at the Petite salle du Conservatoire; other performers at the *séance* were pianist Charles Hallé (1819–95, of Hallé Orchestra fame), Jules Armingaud (second violin), "Casimir Ney" (whose real name was Louis-Casimir Escoffier[168], viola), and Deledicque (viola). The repertory was to include sonatas, trios, quartets, and quintets by "grands maîtres."[169] Maurice Bourges, reviewing the inaugural concert, mentioned that the series would help to alleviate the notable lack of public chamber music concerts. (He allowed that chamber music was performed in private *salons*.)[170]

In spite of the February Revolution, at least three concerts were announced at the salle Chantereine in early 1848 by the same personnel. I have found no record of concerts by Alard and Franchomme in the 1848–49 season, but thereafter they gave yearly series in various locations and with various performers:

Locations of concerts by the Société Alard-Franchomme. (Concerts took place in spring each year.)

1847	petite salle du Conservatoire
1848	salle Chantereine
1850	petite salle du Conservatoire

1851 salle Sax
1852–70 salle Pleyel

Participants in the Société Alard-Franchomme, with known dates of participation, 1847–70.

First violin—Delphin Alard (1847–70)
Second violin—Jules Arminguad (1847–51); Adolphe Blanc (1852–58); L.-V.-A. Viault (1859); Emile Magnin (1860–67); [?Joseph] White (1864); Joseph Telesinski (1868–70)
Viola—"Casimir Ney" [Escoffier] (1847–66); Trombetta (1867–70)
Viola—L.-B.-E.-C.-H. Deledicque (1847–70, possibly with interruptions)
Cello—Auguste Franchomme (1847–70)
Piano—Charles Hallé (1847–48); Paul Gunsberg (1850–51); Mlle. Mear (1852); Valentin Alkan (1853); Thomas Tellefsen (1854); Ferdinand Hiller (1854); Georges Mathias (1845–55); Francis Planté (1855–60); Louis Diémer (1861–70); Mlle. Marie Colin (1867); Henri Fissot (1870)
Others—René Franchomme (cello); Claude-Paul Taffanel (flute); Achille Gouffé (cello and double bass); and more.

The Société Alard-Franchomme's concerts usually occurred at two-week intervals, alternating Sunday afternoons with the Conservatoire concerts (in which both Alard and Franchomme participated). After the Société des Concerts du Conservatoire expanded their schedule to two concerts every three weeks in 1867, the Société Alard-Franchomme performed only once every third week but still presented six programs a year.

Performances of the Société Alard-Franchomme were highly esteemed. Blanchard wrote in 1850 that its concerts attracted all the serious music lovers in Paris.[171] Scudo, in 1861, called it the best of Parisian chamber music societies (though the reactionary Scudo may have been favorably prejudiced by its conservative repertory), and the previous year described it as a "petite succursale" [little branch] of the Société des Concerts du Conservatoire.[172] Botte too referred to it as a "brillante miniature" of the Société des Concerts, and praised the members' consistent perfection.[173]

Repertory. Of the at least 135 programs known to have been given by the Société Alard-Franchomme from 1847 through 1870, I have examined only the 55 reported in the *Revue et gazette musicale*. Coverage of the concerts was best in the early 1850s, but the 55 examined programs span the period, and here will be considered representative of the Société's repertory.

Alard and Franchomme did, as planned, emphasize works of "grands maîtres," even more than the Société des Concerts du Conservatoire. About 84 percent of all performances, and nearly 88 percent of the performances of major works, involved compositions by Beethoven, Mozart, and Haydn. Adding Mendelssohn to this group increases the respective percentages to 92 and 93. On known programs only 11 composers were heard, and four of these only once. The survey of known performances below (see table 2.23) indicates that most (85 percent) of the performances were of complete works. Three additional characteristics of the Société's programs are noteworthy:

1) Among the 26 performances of Beethoven string quartets in which the quartet is identifiable (5 remain unidentified), none is of a Late quartet.

2) The marked preference for Mozart over Haydn (Mozart was played about twice as often) was unusual among contemporary Parisian programs (though, admittedly, Haydn had been less well known for chamber music in Paris before the late 1840s).

3) Onslow was the only nineteenth-century French composer on the programs; his name disappeared after 1854, the year following his death.

Table 2.23 Representative Repertory of the Société Alard-Franchomme: Performances (Listed by Composer) in 55 Concerts, 1847–1870

Composer	Performances (x)	Percentage of all known performances (x ÷ 230)	Major works (y)	Percentage of known performances of major works (y ÷ 196)
Beethoven	94	41%	87	44%
Mozart	66	29	60	31
Haydn	33	14	25	13
Mendelssohn	19	8	11	6
Weber	7	3	5	3
Onslow	4	2	4	2
Schubert	2	under 1	2	1
J. S. Bach	1	under 1	1	under 1
Hiller	1	under 1	0	under 1
Rameau	1	under 1	0	under 1
Schumann	1	under 1	1	under 1
Anonymous	1	under 1	0	under 1
11 composers + 1 anon.	230		196	

The Société des Derniers Quatuors de Beethoven (from ?1851)

History. As its title indicates, the society organized by violinist Jean-Pierre Maurin (1822–94) and cellist Alexandre Chevillard (1811–77) was established to perform the Late quartets of Beethoven, then little known (but not unknown) in Paris and still controversial. The society's beginnings are difficult to fix. Maurin had organized several *séances* of string quartets before 1850,[174] and Chevillard had arranged private readings of the Late quartets. Martin Cooper has claimed that the Société was founded in 1851, and Hill said 1852.[175] Notices in the *Revue et gazette musicale* in the *late* 1850s support Cooper,[176] but the Société was not mentioned in this journal until 29 February 1852, when at least one concert was discussed in the past tense.[177]

The original group included Maurin (first violin), Sabattier (second violin), J.-L.-M. Mas (viola), and Chevillard (cello). The earliest concerts were given in the Cercle de la Libraire, but by December 1852 the society was installed in the salle Herz.[178]

At first the "Société Maurin-Chevillard" intended to perform Beethoven's Late quartets almost exclusively; the repertory gradually expanded slightly. Blanchard wrote in 1853 that the Société's well-rehearsed renditions made the Late quartets better understood than ever before.[179] Praise for the group's execution and news of their public appeal appeared frequently in contemporary sources during the following years. Blanchard mentioned in 1854 that their concerts were attended by a large, distinguished, and attentive audience.[180] About December 1855 (or January 1856) the group made what was probably the first of several successful winter tours to Germany, where their playing also won acclaim.

Poor coverage of the Société des Derniers Quatuors in the *Revue et gazette musicale* (particularly during the 1860s) impedes thorough study of the group's subsequent history. From 1852 to 1867 they scheduled six concerts a season (usually at two-week intervals on Wednesdays, Thursdays, or Fridays—changing the day from year to year) in Paris; from 1868 they played only four times a season. Their location remained the salle Herz until at least November 1855, but from January 1856 was the salle Pleyel.[181] In autumn 1855 the pianist Théodore Ritter became a "permanent" member of the group; thereafter the Société always included a pianist among its members. An incomplete account of the group's personnel from 1852 to 1870 follows:

First violin—Maurin (1852–70, and later)
Second violin—Sabattier (1852–66); Colblain (1867–70)
Viola—Mas (1852–57); Viguier (1858–65); Mas (1865–70)

Cello—Chevillard (1852–?65); Valentin Müller (1866–67); Ernest Demunck (1868–70)
Piano—Ritter (1855–66); Saint–Saëns (67–70)

Guest pianists included Louise Mattmann, Thomas Tellefsen, and Mme. Tardieu de Malleville. Although Chevillard had left the group by 1866, Maurin was still leading a string quartet in Paris in the 1870s.[182]

Repertory. From 1852 through 1870 the Société des Derniers Quatuors should have played 108 concerts.[183] Unfortunately, I have found relatively few complete programs—too few to gain a full understanding of the repertory. Partial programs and other commentary, however, indicate the nature of the concerts. The 72 known performances of chamber works include 59 presentations of works by Beethoven, and a handful by F.-J. Fétis, Haydn, Mendelssohn, Mozart, Schumann, and Weber. String quartets were, of course, the most popular genre, but instrumental sonatas, trios, quartets, and quintets, most with piano, were also presented. Programs in which pianists participated generally included solo piano music. Almost no ephemera were played; most programs comprised few works, all substantial. Early programs each offered two of Beethoven's Late quartets. Slowly the repertory grew to include the Middle quartets (I have found no record of the Société having performed the Early quartets), other genres, and other composers. To the end, however, Late Beethoven was the group's *raison d'être*; even the pianists played Beethoven. As late as 1868, by which time only one of the original members remained, the group announced plans to continue emphasizing the works that had made them famous.[184]

The Société des Quatuors de Mendelssohn (Quatuor Armingaud or Quatuor Armingaud-Jacquard) (1856–1867)

History. The Société des Quatuors de Mendelssohn was established in 1856.[185] Probably inspired by the success of the Société des Derniers Quatuors de Beethoven in propagating little-known works of Beethoven, the new society hoped to do the same for Mendelssohn's quartets and other chamber works.[186]

The founding members were Jules Armingaud (1820–1900, first violin), Lapret (second violin), Edouard Lalo (1823–92, viola), and Léon Jacquard (1826–96, cello). Only one change occurred among the core personnel during the group's twelve-year existence: in 1861 Lalo took over the second violin part and was succeeded as violist by Mas. The pianists Ernst Lubeck (1829–76) and Mme. Massart (*née* Masson, 1827–87) performed with the group often, and other players were added when necessary (as in performances of Mendelssohn's Octet).

The first program was presented in late January 1856 (probably 30 January)[187] at the salle Erard:

> Mendelssohn: Piano Trio No. 2 in C Minor, Op. 66
> Mozart: String Quartet "No. 9"[188]
> Beethoven: "Andante con variazioni" and *finale* of the "Kreutzer" Violin Sonata
> Mendelssohn: String Quartet in D Major, Op. 44

Three more concerts were presented that year in the same location. Thereafter, six concerts were scheduled each season, biweekly, on Wednesday evenings. In 1858 the group moved permanently to the salons Pleyel et Cie. The last known concert occurred 10 April 1867. There was no announcement of the Société's permanent closure at that time (it was the sixth and final concert of the season), but I have found no records of concerts after this year.[189]

There are, in contemporary journals, several references to the society's success. Botte paid tribute to its members' consistently high level of performance—particularly their remarkable ensemble, excellent style, and delicacy of nuance, and said that "beaucoup de pureté et de sobriété caractérisent ce quatuor."[190] Scudo reported that they were appreciated by a distinguished audience.[191] As late as March 1867, shortly before the group's final concert, their much-deserved success was remarked upon in an anonymous review in the *Revue et gazette musicale*.[192]

Repertory. Of the 70 concerts scheduled by the Société des Quatuors de Mendelssohn, I have seen programs for 39. Most programs comprised four (or, exceptionally, five) substantial works, sometimes including a selection for solo piano. String quartets were, of course, the most-performed genre, but instrumental sonatas, piano trios and quartets, some works for larger ensembles, and even keyboard concertos with the soloist accompanied by string quartet were heard regularly. Few excerpts and almost no light works were played; from the 39 programs and descriptions in other sources, I know of 156 instrumental-work performances by the Société, of which 140 involved complete and "major" works.

In accordance with its goal, the Société played Mendelssohn's works most.[193] Programs from 1856 through 1858 included, as a rule, two major works by Mendelssohn. In 1858 plans were announced to perform all of Mendelssohn's quartets (including posthumous works), plus the octet, in order of the opus numbers;[194] this plan was not, however, strictly carried out. After 1858 the works of Mendelssohn no longer dominated the repertory. Some programs in the 1860s neglected Mendelssohn entirely, and the name "Société des Quatuors de Mendelssohn" was abandoned. (The society had always been popularly called the "Quatuor Armingaud-Jacquard," or just "Quatuor Armingaud," and retained these labels.)

Although the names of only 11 composers appear on the programs I have examined, the Société's repertory was less traditional than that of many other chamber music societies. Apart from their promotion of Mendelssohn, the members played Paris premieres of two Schumann string quartets, performed Chopin's cello sonata and a Marschner piano trio, and programmed much Schubert chamber music (including the piano trios D. 898 and 929 and the string quartets D. 804, 810, and 887) before it became popular in Paris. Table 2.24 provides a complete list of known performances.

Table 2.24 Performances of Instrumental Works (Listed by Composer) by the Société des Quatuors de Mendelssohn, 39 Programs, 1856–1867

Composer	**Performances (x)**	**Percentage of total performances (x ÷ 156)**	**Major works (y)**	**Percentage of all major works performed (y ÷ 140)**
Mendelssohn	51	33%	48	34%
Beethoven	35	22	34	24
Mozart	23	15	22	16
Haydn	17	11	11	8
Schubert	12	8	9	6
Schumann	9	6	7	5
Bach, J. S.	3	2	3	2
Weber	3	2	3	2
Boccherini	1	under 1	1	under 1
Chopin	1	under 1	1	under 1
Marschner	1	under 1	1	under 1
11 composers	156		140	

The Séances Populaires (from 1863) (Lamoureux Séances; from 1860)

History. The Séances Populaires were a series of concerts, mostly of chamber music, organized by the violinist (and later conductor) Charles Lamoureux. The name "Séances Populaires" invites comparison with the Concerts Populaires, discussed above; like the Concerts Populaires, the Séances presented public concerts with low admission fees,[195] and emphasized a traditional repertory.

Lamoureux's *séances* (not yet called the Séances Populaires) began 12 January 1860 in the salons Pleyel; the program follows:[196]

Mozart: String Quartet in B-flat, "Op. 18"[197]
Beethoven: String Quartet, Op. 18 No. 4
Beethoven: Violin Sonata, Op. 30 No. 3
Mendelssohn: Canzonetta from String Quartet, Op. 12
Haydn: String Quartet in D, "No. 67" (Op. 64 No. 5)

Thereafter at least three, and usually six, *séances* were held each season at two-week intervals. In the 1863–64 season, when the name "Séances Populaires de Musique de Chambre" was adopted, the group moved to the salle Herz and presented eight weekly concerts in December and January. In later seasons, however, the biweekly format was restored, and concerts spanned the months of January to early April. From 1862 concerts, regardless of their frequency, were always on Tuesdays. In 1867 the society returned to the salons Pleyel.

The "permanent" personnel of Lamoureux's concerts comprised a string quartet and pianist. Members included the following:

First violin: Charles Lamoureux (1860–postwar)
Second violin: Edouard Colonne (1860–64); Colblain (1865–postwar)
Viola: Adam (1860–postwar)
Cello: Louis-Marie Pilet (1860–61); Emile Rignault (1862–66); H.-M.-J. Poëncet (1867–68); Hippolyte-François Rabaud (1869); Ernest Demunck (1870); Auguste Tolbecque (1872–?)
Piano: Bernard Rie (1860–61); Georges Pfeiffer (1863–?64); Henri Fissot (1862–70); Marie Mongin (1866); Albert Lavignac (1866); Delaborde (1869)

Botte's review of an early Lamoureux *séance*[198] noted the group's success, but suggested that they lacked unity, finesse, and a sustained or authoritative style. Within four years, however, the players were drawing praise for their overall talent and magistral style in the interpretation of string quartets.[199] Thereafter, reports of the group's success and large audiences were frequent.

Repertory. From 1860 through 1870 Lamoureux presented about 56 *séances,* possibly a few more. Of these, I have found programs for roughly half, and seen references to the content of another few. Most programs comprised three to five works, nearly all of them major and complete. Among 119 known performances of chamber works, 107 were of major works, 44 of them string quartets; instrumental sonatas, chamber works with piano, and piano solos (many of them sonatas) were also common.

The repertory was traditional. Among known performances, the favorite composer was Beethoven (late works were avoided), followed at some distance by Haydn, Mozart, Mendelssohn, and Boccherini; the works of these composers constitute 80 percent of the known repertory.[200] On the other hand, the Séances Populaires were among the earliest concerts to program Brahms's chamber works in Paris: a piano quartet (either Op. 25 or Op. 26), the String Sextet Op. 18, and the Piano Quintet Op. 34 were performed in 1869 and 1870.[201] Among other contemporaries, Adolphe Blanc, Félicien David, Rubinstein, and W. H. Veit were given hearings. Schubert's String Quartet D. 804 received a performance, and at least one violin sonata attributed to Porpora[202] was revived, as was a concerto for two violins and cello (soloists), attributed to Handel.[203] Among known programs, however, only 16 composers were played. Vocal works were introduced to the programs for the first time when the *séances* resumed after the Franco-Prussian War, in January 1872.[204]

The Gouffé Séances (ca. 1836–?1874)

History. The musical *séances* sponsored by the double bass player Achille Gouffé (1804–74) were, for over 30 years, among the most important events in Paris for serious musicians, and particularly for young composers. Yet today they remain the most obscure of the significant musical series; an attempt to trace their history yields many unanswered questions, and answers that appear to be contradictory.

Gouffé's *séances* began, according to most reports, in the 1830s, possibly about 1836.[205] Curiously, I have found no mention of these *séances* in the *Revue et gazette musicale* before 16 May 1847; in this issue, the editors refer to a recent *séance,* apparently expecting readers of the journal to be familiar with the series.[206] The editors mention that the audience at this *séance* included well-known musicians—Onslow, Rigel, Dourlen, Dauprat, and Aristide Farrenc.

Information regarding the frequency of these concerts is also problematic. Most sources agree that the *séances* took place every Wednesday, though Blanchard reported in 1849 that they met biweekly;[207] perhaps the 1849 season was an exception to the usual practice. Occasionally Gouffé sponsored *séances* on other days as well (that is, more than one *séance* a week), usually special programs of new music. Several references, mainly from the early 1850s, maintained that the *séances* took place year round;[208] in June 1854 Blanchard stated specifically that the *séances* continued through the summer, regardless of the heat.[209] But in late autumn of several years (even years in which year-round concerts had been mentioned) the series was said to have "resumed."[210] And from 1867, in spring of some years, "final" concerts were noted. Such announcements seem to indicate that the concerts were not presented throughout the year. It is conceivable that the phrases "toute l'année" and "tous les mercredis de l'année" should not be interpreted literally, but actually mean "extending well beyond the regular musical season." Notices of Gouffé's *séances* are, admittedly, sparse and sporadic, but over a period of 24 years none was mentioned in August or September, while several can be found in all other months. After 1856 I have discovered no announcements during the months June through October. It appears likely that Gouffé's *séances* had a ten-month season from the early 1850s (possibly earlier) through 1856 and a shorter season beginning sometime thereafter.

Even the social aspects of Gouffé's *séances* are not clearly understood. The presentation of the *séances* in Gouffé's private residence (its location is unknown before autumn 1856 when Gouffé moved to the rue la Bruyère),[211] the absence of references to an admission charge, and the distinction made in announcing Gouffé's *concerts annuels* (held in larger halls; see below) as public concerts,[212] seem to indicate that the *séances* were for invited guests only. Bannelier remarked that Gouffé received no pay for his work and often presented *séances* at his own expense, and that the events were for a "public choisi."[213] The lack of publicity before 1847 suggests also that the *séances* were not then public. Yet the weekly *séances chez* Gouffé were announced and reviewed among public concerts in the *Revue et gazette musicale,* and in 1855 Blanchard mentioned crowds so large that it was sometimes difficult to gain admittance.[214] The high performance standards of these events must have spread their fame among music lovers; many readers of the *Revue et gazette musicale* were surely also regular attenders.

Private or public, Gouffé's *séances* boasted some of Paris's best performers. A string quartet and pianist presided at most events. Among the performers from 1847 to 1870 were the pianists Mlle. Picard, Georges Bizet, and Mme. Béguin-Salomon, violinists Auguste-Antoine Guerreau, Adolphe Blanc, and Emile Rignault, violists "Casimir Ney" [Escoffier] and Trombetta, the cellist Charles Lebouc, flutist Joseph-Henri Altès, clarinettist J.-V.-A. Blancou, bassoonist L.-M.-E. Jancourt, horn player J.-F. Rousselot, and, of course, Gouffé on double bass.

Repertory. Repertory is another area of ambiguity, for insufficient coverage of Gouffé's programs prevents a thorough understanding thereof. It is clear from the personnel, and from the few known programs, that string quartets, chamber music with or without piano, and some solo piano works made up most of the programs. Instrumental solos and sonatas, and works for large chamber groups (sextets, septets, even octets, some with winds) were not uncommon. Most of the works were substantial, but some light works, especially among the solos, found their way on to programs.

General descriptions of Gouffé's *séances* indicate a traditional repertory with occasional exceptions. Blanchard wrote in 1852 that most programs included works of Haydn, Mozart, and Beethoven,[215] and that good performances of quartets by "grands maîtres" could be heard consistently, while contemporary works were played occasionally.[216] The scarce records of individual programs, however, mention much contemporary music. A possible explanation, of course, is that programs including new music attracted notice in the press because they were unusual. In any case, Gouffé was clearly willing to present recent works by little-known authors, and did not restrict these works to his special concerts of new music. Among contemporaries whose chamber works were performed *chez* Gouffé were Bellon, Blanc, Blanchard, Bousquet, Chopin, Deldevez, Dorus, Franchomme, de Garaudé, Gastinel, Goldner, Gouffé, Habeneck, Kontski, Léon Kreutzer, Lavainne, Malibran, Mendelssohn, Onslow, Mlle. de Reiset, Rosenhain, Salesses, Salvator, Sowinski, Spohr, Verroust, Walckiers, and Zimmermann. Gouffé must have particularly admired the music of Adolphe Blanc (1828–85), whose name appeared on the known programs more often than that of any other composer, beginning by 1852.[217]

From the slender evidence, I picture the Gouffé *séances* as programs for musicians. Talented instrumentalists gave good performances both of established masterpieces and new works[218] before an audience that included composers and other instrumentalists. As the *séances* were apparently not commercial, one cannot attribute to them financial success. But the longevity of the weekly programs, the consistent acclaim of critics, and the appreciation earned from contemporary composers made them one of the most significant musical series in nineteenth-century Paris.

As noted above, Gouffé also offered public concerts of chamber music; these took place once each spring, beginning in the late 1830s[219] and continuing past 1870. The *concerts annuels* were much like the weekly *séances chez* Gouffé and involved the same personnel, though programs of the public events comprised shorter selections and fewer contemporary works.

The Lebouc Séances (from 1855)

History. The *séances* established by the cellist Charles-Joseph Lebouc (1822–93) and the vocalist "Paulin" (actually Louis-Joseph Lespinasse, 1814–67) in 1855 cannot compare with the Gouffé *séances* in sheer number, or in concentration on major chamber works; the Lebouc *séances* happened only a few times each year, and the repertory combined substantial chamber works with piano pieces, vocal music, and ephemeral instrumental solos. Yet Lebouc's *séances* remain significant because of the number of first-rate musicians who presented the best chamber music, and because of Lebouc's willingness to program recent works.

The first program took place 20 January 1855 in the salle Pleyel:[220]

Boccherini: a string quintet
Méhul: Air from *Stratonice*
Gluck: "Air de Thoas," from *Iphigénie en Tauride*
Mozart: "Air de la Zerlina," from *Don Giovanni*
Spontini: Prière, from *La Vestale*
L'Abbé Clari: Vocal Duo "from 1669"
Salieri: Air de Danaüs, from *Les Danaïdes*
Hummel: Septet for piano, flute, oboe, horn, viola, cello, and double bass, Op. 74
Beethoven: Andante and Minuet from a piano sonata[221]
Bach: Gavotte, performed on the piano

The earliest notice in the *Revue et gazette musicale* described the series as *séances* of "bonne musique rétrospective," intended to provide *amateurs* with the opportunity to hear masterpieces of chamber music and vocal excerpts from operas and oratorios by "grands maîtres."[222] Four *séances* were held in 1855; thereafter the format of the concerts varied considerably from year to year. In 1856 and 1857 they were referred to as *soirées* of "musique classique et historique." *Séances* are mentioned in the *Revue et gazette musicale* each year until (and immediately after) the Franco-Prussian War, 1861 excepted.

Concerts were held in the salle Pleyel from 1855 to 1859. In 1860 they took place in the new salons Erard,[223] but by 1862 they had returned to the salle Pleyel.[224] From the beginning of the 1863–64 season, *séances* were held *chez* Lebouc, 12 rue Vivienne,[225] though single concerts for a larger audience were given in the salle Herz in 1864 and 1865.[226] After the war the *séances* were advertised as *matinées* of M. and Mme. Lebouc.[227]

Schedules changed yearly. From 1855 through 1860, three to six *soirées* were presented each season, usually at two-week intervals, with the day of the week changing from one year to the next. Only one concert is known from spring 1862; three were mentioned during the 1862–63 season. After the move to Lebouc's residence in autumn 1863, *matinées* took place twice a month, Mondays, from November to April. Thus there were about 12 *séances* each season.

The earliest concerts were sponsored jointly by Lebouc and Paulin. By 1857 Paulin no longer shared in organizing the concerts, though he returned to sing on occasion. The impressive list of participants in Lebouc's *séances* includes pianists Mlle. Mattmann, Louis Lacombe, Caroline Rémaury, Mme. Béguin-Salomon, Louise Farrenc, Marie Mongin, and Georges Pfeiffer; violinists Maurin, Blanc, Ernst, Charles Dancla, Viault, White, Comtat, Léonard, and I.-L. Diepedaal; violists "Casimir Ney" [Escoffier] and Trombetta; cellist, Lebouc; double bass player, Gouffé; flutists Dorus and Brunot; oboists Roméden, Triébert, and Berthélemy; clarinettists Leroy and Rose; bassoonist, Jancourt; horn players, Rousselot and Duvernoy; vocalists Pauline Viardot, Mme. Gaveaux-Sabattier, Mme. Barthe-Banderali, M. Euzet, and Paulin.

There are several references in the *Revue et gazette musicale* to good attendance at Lebouc's *séances*. Most such references emphasize that the audience comprised music lovers and distinguished society.[228]

Repertory. Before the Franco-Prussian War, Lebouc sponsored about 110 *séances.*[229] Of these I have program information on nearly half.[230] Most programs included vocal works (usually opera excerpts) and light instrumental solos, particularly piano works; thus they comprised many numbers (the inaugural program, shown above, is not atypical), of which only two or three were major chamber works. Among over 50 known programs I count 122 performances of complete, major instrumental works. The mainstays among chamber works presented at the *séances* were instrumental sonatas, and trios, quartets, and quintets for strings with or without piano. But, perhaps because the performing body was not standardized, a variety of genres was tried, among them chamber works with winds (including a Reicha wind quintet), works for larger ensembles (sextets and septets), reductions of piano concertos for piano and solo strings, and works for unusual combinations (for example, Haydn's *Echos,* a double trio for four violins and two cellos).

The most popular of the 27 composers whose major instrumental works appeared on known programs are listed in table 2.25.[231] It is possible that programs on which recent or unusual works were performed received more publicity than others, and that the actual repertory was

Table 2.25 Known Performances of Major Instrumental Works (Listed by Composer) at the Lebouc *Séances*, 1855–1870

Composer	Major Works	Percentage of all known performances of major works
Blanc, Adolphe	26	21%
Beethoven	18	15
Mozart	16	13
Hummel	9	7
Mendelssohn	9	7
Weber	5	4
Boccherini	4	3
Haydn	4	3
Schumann	4	3
Bach, J. S.	3	2
17 others	24	20
27 composers	122	

somewhat more traditional than table 2.25 suggests. But the popularity of Blanc on the known programs reflects a readiness to present new works. Among contemporary composers whose instrumental works were programmed at least once (not including those listed above) were Damcke, Ernst, Louise Farrenc, D.-J.-G.-F. Godefroid, Lebouc, G. Pfeiffer, Raff, Saint-Saëns, Salvator, Vieuxtemps, Vignier, and Walckiers. The *Revue et gazette musicale* reported in 1868 that a new work was attempted at each *séance*.[232] Clearly, a young composer might better attract attention at Gouffé's or Lebouc's, in spite of the small audiences, than at more major concert series.

Remaining Concert Series[233]

Although instrumental music received little attention in the years preceding 1828 (see the beginning of chapter 5, pp. 136–41), it did not altogether disappear from concerts. Thus as the season for 1828 commenced there were already established a few series that presented orchestral or chamber works. The *Société académique des Enfants d'Apollon,* founded in 1741, held musical *séances* yearly until 1848, more often thereafter. The composers, performers, and dilettantes who constituted the Enfants' membership sometimes participated in its *séances,* but nonmembers, among them some of Paris's best musicians, were also engaged to entertain. As the performing personnel changed from year to year, so did the repertory.

Programs included orchestral, chamber, solo instrumental, and vocal works, and though much of the repertory was light, the Société welcomed recent "art" music.

Three orchestral societies involving amateurs were active in the 1820s. The *Société Philharmonique de la Ville de Paris* (?1822–?1854), comprising amateurs and young professionals, was led (at least part of the time) by professional conductors. It performed mainly overtures, orchestral excerpts from operas, and light works, but also accompanied renowned soloists in concertos. The *Concerts d'Emulation,* begun about 1823 and still active in 1829, programmed vocal and instrumental music, including works of Haydn, Mozart, Beethoven, Boccherini, Krommer, and "Onslorre" (presumably Onslow) as well as 80 recent overtures, at weekly *séances* that may or may not have been open to the public. The director, M. Egasse (in whose *salon* these events took place), offered to provide string instruments to amateurs who wished to participate. The *Concert des Amateurs,* led by Tilmant *aîné* and Henri Barbereau at the Tivoli d'Hiver and later at Vauxhall, performed orchestral works by young French composers.[234]

The most important of early chamber music series were those organized by the eminent violinist Pierre *Baillot,* beginning in 1814. With the leading Parisian string players, Baillot presented quartets and quintets of Haydn, Mozart, Boccherini, Beethoven (including Late quartets), Onslow, and, only occasionally, other composers. According to a contemporary report, an attentive audience of 600 to 700 attended Baillot's *soirées* in 1833.[235] As the schedule and location of Baillot's *séances* changed from year to year, his presentations must be considered as several consecutive series (rather than a single, consistent series), but series were presented every year from 1827 through at least 1836, and further concerts were reported in 1838 and 1840.

The brothers *Bohrer,* Anton (violin) and Max (cello), with other string players and pianists, presented concert series in 1830 and 1831, and reputedly gave annual concerts from 1827 through 1829. Their performances of Beethoven's Late string quartets in 1830 and 1831 were among the earliest in Paris (and among the few offered there before the foundation of the Société des Derniers Quatuors de Beethoven two decades later).

Finally, the Conservatoire gave public concerts in conjunction with its annual distribution of prizes, beginning in 1797. Until about 1850 the programs were evenly divided between instrumental and vocal works, sometimes including as many as six of each; thereafter, fewer instrumental works were presented. Most concerts began wth an overture, and concertos (and other works for one or more soloists) figured prominently in the repertory. Occasionally, chamber music was essayed. The participants included student prize winners, and many of the works performed were by students or graduates. Among the 65 composers who were represented by instrumental works at these concerts (1828 through 1870), the most popular were Viotti (10 performances), Tulou (9), Bazin and Vogt (8), Alard (7), Rodolphe Kreutzer (6), and Baillot, Berr, and Charles Dancla (5).

The founding of the Société des Concerts du Conservatoire in 1828, and the magnitude of its achievement, suggested that date as the starting point for this study. The eventual influence of the Conservatoire concerts on repertory and performance standards has already been noted. A direct result of the Société's appearance and immediate success was the establishment of concerts by Conservatoire students. Two concerts, presented within weeks of the Société's premiere, were well attended, and consequently in June the *Concerts d'Emulation* ("de la Société mineure des jeunes élèves de l'Ecole royale de musique," 1828–?1834, not to be confused with the earlier Concerts d'Emulation of Egasse) were founded. An orchestra of about 50, a choir, and soloists performed overtures, solos, and *fragments* by student composers, among them Alard, Chevillard, Elwart, Franchomme, and Ambroise Thomas; the composers sometimes conducted their own works.

In 1829 appeared the *Société de l'Athénée Musical,* a society of professionals and amateurs who performed orchestral, chamber, solo instrumental, and vocal works several times a year until 1844, and whose announced intention was the presentation of new or little-known compositions. The *Société des Amis de l'Enfance* (evidently founded in the late 1820s, but little mentioned in contemporary journals),[236] sponsored concerts, aided by the patronage of several members of the nobility. In 1853 they engaged the Société des Jeunes-Artistes to play for them. An unnamed amateur society, mentioned in 1830,[237] announced plans to perform symphonies of Haydn, Mozart, and Beethoven, as well as works of contemporary composers, but may not have given any actual concerts.

The concerts of Berlioz, the first of which occurred in 1828 and only some of which were arranged in series, were probably the most important organized by and around an individual during the entire period under consideration. Both Berlioz and his biographers have described in detail the concerts and festivals that revealed his talents not only as a composer but also as a conductor and organizer of the enormous forces that his works required. Berlioz gave few such concerts in Paris after 1848, though according to Barzun he held "sessions of chamber music at his own house" from the 1830s until his death.[238] Of similar historical importance—because of their effect on Liszt—but of limited artistic significance were the series presented by Paganini in 1831 and 1832, at which he played mainly his own concertos and solos.

In the mid-1830s outdoor and café concerts became fashionable in Paris (see chapter 3). These offered dance music, overtures, and other light works at low prices, thus attracting large audiences and (not incidentally) the services of commercially oriented virtuosos. As these virtuosos abandoned concert halls, the frivolous solos that they had performed there were replaced by "art" music. In effect, there took place a partial division of public musical events into exclusively "popular" entertainment and concerts of "art" music. The latter quickly imitated the former in pursuing the growing number of people with money to spend on entertainment. The earliest notable series of *concerts populaires* emphasizing "art" music was that of the *Gymnase Musical* (1835),[239] advertised as an open arena (figuratively) for all genres of music, including stage works, sacred works, and "folk" music. Its main goal was to satisfy public taste.[240] New works and old compositions previously unperformed in Paris were to receive emphasis. Before the series opened, the government forbade the performance of vocal works, probably because it feared competition to the state-subsidized musical theatres. Nevertheless, from May 1835, in a hall that seated about 1000, the Gymnase Musical presented four concerts a week of symphonies, concertos, overtures, and instrumental solos on nights when the Théâtre-Italien, with whose orchestra it shared musicians, had no performances. A reviewer of its early concerts wrote that the performances of symphonies by Weber, Beethoven, and Spohr were "played with a verve, dash, and drive that recall the musical entertainment of the Conservatoire"[241] (that is, the Conservatoire concerts). Edouard Fétis praised its willingness to try new works.[242] It appears that the society's repertory gradually became both more conservative and more "popular." Plans were announced in October to perform more works of Beethoven, Haydn, and Mozart, "composers that everyone speaks of, though their music is rarely heard."[243] Apparently the society's demise shortly thereafter was caused by financial hardship. The government ban on vocal music had surely discouraged some potential attenders, and having begun the concert series in May was a major error, as Parisians were reluctant to attend concerts during the summer.

Somewhat more successful were the *Concerts Valentino* (1837–41), nightly concerts in a hall on the rue Saint-Honoré that seated 2000 persons; admission was only one franc.[244] Four nights a week the orchestra of about 85 musicians was led by Valentino in programs of symphonies, overtures, and other instrumental works (vocal works were, again, prohibited by the state). The remaining nights, Fessy conducted *contredanses* and other popular works. Valentino had reputedly intended a concert series in which a diverse public could acquaint themselves with music of the German masters.[245] But he also made a sincere effort to enlarge the repertory;[246] the programs comprised a healthy mixture of Beethoven, Mozart, Haydn, Weber, and contemporary composers both native and foreign. Praise for the "Concerts Valentino" appeared often in the pages of the *Revue et gazette musicale de Paris,* and Elwart later wrote that these were the first concerts other than those of the Conservatoire in which the music of Beethoven and other German masters was performed "in a manner worthy of them."[247] Schindler, on the other hand, thought that the orchestra hurried the tempos, lacked enthusiasm, and wanted variety of style. He also suggested that they performed too many concerts.[248] Large crowds are reported throughout the duration of the concerts, although it was admitted that the dance orchestras of Musard and Tolbecque were more popular.[249] The supplement to Fétis's *Biographie universelle* stated that attendance slowly dwindled, and that when the audience demonstrated their preference for lighter works Valentino retired.[250] The last reported concert took place 30 April 1841; the following year the salle Valentino was used for public dances.[251]

Two other orchestral series that appeared about this time were not dependent on steady mass appeal. The *Institution des Jeunes Aveugles* sponsored concerts by its students and faculty at irregular intervals from no later than 1836 through the end of the period. The members performed orchestral, chamber, and vocal music; their handicap did not prevent them from tackling Beethoven symphonies, and their concerts were well attended. The *Cercle Musical des Amateurs,* founded about 1837 and still active in 1870, was a group of wealthy amateurs (with some professionals) who met for weekly study but presented only one concert a year, priced for the upper classes.[252] Their repertory combined old and new orchestral, instrumental solo, and choral works.

Programs of chamber music series were in many cases more experimental than those of orchestral series, for a chamber ensemble could survive without a large audience. The *Cercle Musical,* founded in late 1834 and soon transformed into the *Société Musicale,* was established as a private club for its founders (among them several composers) plus 100 members; their goal was to perform chamber music and an expanded repertory of salon music with standards similar to those of the Société des Concerts du Conservatoire. (Members of the Cercle Musical felt that lack of rehearsal time limited the repertory of music played in *salons,* as performers tended to repeat pieces they knew well rather than learn new ones.)[253] Amid some intrasociety strife, the goals of the organization fluctuated, but eventually the public was invited to concerts and began attending in increasing numbers.[254] Both salon music (instrumental and vocal) and more substantial works were presented; the composers most performed were some of the society's founding members—Bertini, Brod, Labarre, and Gallay.

Concerts of this Société Musicale lasted only one season, but four seasons later (late 1838) a second *Société Musicale* was formed; its members included many persons who had been in the first Société, and its goal was related though not identical: to reform the music of *salons* by providing good performances of "serious" chamber music, using the Conservatoire concerts as a model.[255] The programs combined works of Beethoven and Mozart, more recent chamber music by Reicha and Bertini, and frivolous fare, both instrumental and vocal. This series ceased after about two months.

The *"Concerts Tilmant,"* so called because the brothers Tilmant played first violin and cello in the concerts, performed all varieties of chamber music—mainly trios, quartets, and quintets, both old and new—in series lasting from 1833 to 1838. They sometimes performed Beethoven's Late string quartets. *Liszt, Urhan, and Batta* gave four concerts of chamber, piano, and vocal music in January and February 1837. Their progressive programs included piano trios and instrumental sonatas of Beethoven, and piano works of Chopin and Liszt.[256] In late 1837, years before the establishment of the renowned Alard-Franchomme and Maurin-Chevillard chamber music societies, Alard and Chevillard joined with Charles Dancla (violin) and Croisilles (viola) to form a "permanent" string quartet, sometimes adding another string player to perform quintets. Their society lasted three seasons, playing mainly works of Beethoven, Mozart, Haydn, and Chevillard.

In 1838 the *Revue et gazette musicale de Paris* initiated for its subscribers a series to promote the performance of string quartets and quintets, which the journal feared were being replaced by piano music and *romances*.[257] The programs, which continued until 1848, comprised various genres of chamber music (as well as vocal works, light instrumental works, and, occasionally, orchestral works), and included music of young composers. The "house" performers were some of the best musicians in Paris, among them Alard, Chevillard, and Franchomme, and pianists César Franck, Louise Farrenc, and Charles Hallé.

Three other noteworthy chamber series appeared in the mid to late 1830s. The *séances* of Gouffé have already been described. *Matinées* of string quartets, sponsored by M. le baron de Trémont [Louis Philippe Joseph Girod de Vienney], were reported in 1838; these may not have been open to the public. And *matinées* (ca. 1838–ca. 1840) of the Belgian violinist Seghers attracted many serious musicians. Liszt sometimes performed in Seghers's *salon,* where quartets and piano trios of the young Henri Reber[258] and "posthumous" quartets[259] of Beethoven were essayed.

In the 1840s several noteworthy series disappeared, among them the Concerts Valentino (in 1841), the Société de l'Athénée Musical (in 1844), the series of the *Revue et gazette musicale* (in 1848), and the chamber music concerts of Alard and Chevillard (probably in 1840). Furthermore, no truly significant new series arrived until 1847, and the few series that were established were short-lived. The Concerts of *Herz and Labarre* (season of 1840–41), intended for the upper classes, offered orchestral, chamber, and vocal music as well as piano, harp, and other instrumental solos. The brothers *Franco-Mendès,* Joseph (violin) and Jacques (cello), presented traditional and contemporary chamber works for two seasons, 1840 and 1841; their admission fee too was rather high. At *matinées* in 1844, the violinist Javault programmed string quartets and quintets of Haydn, Mozart, Beethoven, and Onslow. Last, a *Société d'Harmonie,* publicized as an *orchestre* of 80, began rehearsing in 1845 but had no concerts reported in the *Revue et gazette musicale.*[260]

The *Concerts Viviennes* lasted a bit longer, presenting weekly concerts summer and winter from 1840 to at least 1845. Their programs emphasized light orchestral music but "Concerts Extraordinaires" were devoted to "grandes compositions" and new works.[261] In 1843 the organization announced monetary gifts to encourage young composers. For at least three seasons, beginning in December 1845, the composer *Emile Ettling* led an *amateur orchestra* that mainly programmed light works (including instrumental solos by professionals) but also essayed symphonies and concertos.

Few concerts of the *Association des Artistes-Musiciens* were part of a series, but the society deserves mention. The Association was "a group of Paris musicians [who] had agreed to band together for mutual aid and the furtherance of modern music."[262] Its foundation, by Baron Taylor (Isidore-Justin-Severin Taylor), in 1843, was prompted by the poor economic status of musicians. For a modest annual fee, members qualified for assistance, pensions, and so forth.[263] The Association, in turn, sponsored concerts, thereby attempting to relieve individual composers of financial risks,[264] and organized numerous concerts (some by nonmembers) to benefit members. At irregular intervals and in various locations it presented programs of diverse instrumental and vocal works, sometimes employing enormous forces. For its first concert, scheduled for August 1843 but repeatedly postponed and eventually cancelled, Berlioz and Spontini had planned to conduct 400 musicians in a program of vocal, dramatic, and orchestral works.[265] At a festival presented by the Association in 1846, Tilmant *aîné* led an orchestra of 1800 to 2000 in a program of light works plus the finale of Berlioz's *Symphonie Funèbre.*[266] In 1852 the Association organized separate series of orchestral and chamber music at the salle Bonne-Nouvelle. In addition it sponsored (musical) masses on St. Cecilia's Day, Easter, and, sometimes, other occasions. The repertory ranged chronologically from Corelli and J. S. Bach to Berlioz, Louise Farrenc, Prudent, and many other contemporaries. By 1864 the Association had 4844 members.[267]

Beginning in 1847 public chamber music concerts proliferated in Paris. The series of the Société Alard-Franchomme (from 1847) and the Société des Derniers Quatuors de Beethoven (from 1852), already described, represent only the tip of the iceberg.

The *Société de Musique Classique,* whose founding members included a vocalist, a pianist, five strings, and five winds, was established in November 1847. Alternating Sunday afternoons with the Conservatoire concerts during two seasons, it made a serious effort to present the best chamber music to an upper-class public. Prices were 5 to 10 francs per concert.[268] The repertory, which comprised Beethoven, Haydn, Mozart, and Bach, as well as contemporaries (Bertini, Fesca, Onslow, Spohr, and others), evidently reflected an attempt to allow each member as much participation as possible; it included septets, octets, nonets, and even a work for ten strings and winds.

The composer and violinist *Charles Dancla* had ventured early into chamber music *séances.* In 1841 he had given a *matinée* of his own compositions; single concerts followed, and his first series—performances of string quartets by distinguished composers—was announced in 1847. Thereafter, until the mid-1860s,[269] he organized many chamber music concerts, some of which were arranged in series. The repertory included works (primarily string quartets) of Beethoven, Haydn, and Mozart, as well as by Dancla and other contemporaries. Dancla was assisted by two of his musical brothers and other fine musicians. Another violinist, Lambert Massart, held weekly *soirées* from 1848 through 1851 (possibly over a longer period). Some of Paris's best instrumentalists and pianists (among the latter group Massart's wife, from 1849, Aglaé Masson) assisted him in unadventurous programs of chamber, piano, vocal, and light instrumental works.

Several series were established by pianists. Mlle. *Mattmann,* with the violinist *Maurin,* cellist *Lebouc,* and others, presented four concerts of traditional and recent chamber works in winter 1847–48. Mlle. Mattmann also gave single concerts at which she programmed some chamber music. *Charlotte de Malleville* (later Mme. Tardieu de Malleville) gave, generally, four concerts a year of chamber works (many of them with piano), keyboard works, and, occasionally, concertos with chamber ensemble accompaniment from 1849 to the early 1860s. Although her concerts took place in the salle Sax and salle Pleyel, it appears that, for at least some of them, the audience was invited by the pianist. The repertory was conservative. Mme. *Pierson-Bodin* began presenting concerts in her home by 1849, either performing herself or sponsoring other celebrated musicians, including pianists. Some years weekly *séances* were mentioned; other years gatherings were less regular. Frequent *séances* of her piano students and invited artists were reported in the late 1860s and after the war. Programs included piano, vocal, and light instrumental works, as well as old and new chamber music; especially prevalent were chamber works of Louise Farrenc (who often participated in their performance), evidently a close friend of Mme. Pierson-Bodin.

Little is known of two other midcentury chamber music series, both of which were intended for high society: works of Haydn, Mozart, Beethoven, and Boccherini were played at the *soirées* of the violinist *Eugène Sauzay*;[270] *séances* in the *salon* of M. le duc *Charles de Caraman,* mentioned in 1851, also emphasized a traditional repertory.

In the first half of the nineteenth century virtuosos had generally performed solo or *concertante* works. But as the century progressed a new breed of virtuosos, following in the footsteps of Baillot, Alard, and Liszt, became increasingly involved with chamber music; among the best known of those who played in Paris are Vieuxtemps, Sivori, Saint-Saëns, and Louise Farrenc (whose concerts will be examined below). An early example of this phenomenon is the series of three *soirées* of chamber music presented by the violinist *Joachim* during a visit to Paris in spring 1850. At these *soirées,* compositions of J. S. Bach (keyboard concertos and violin works), Mozart, Beethoven, Mendelssohn, and Farrenc were heard. That same season Joachim participated in a brief series of chamber, piano, and vocal music organized by the German pianist and composer *Jakob Rosenhain.*

Like chamber music series, orchestral series increased about midcentury. But Paris could evidently support only a few orchestras, and most of the new series had only a brief run. The most durable were the Société Sainte-Cécile (1850–55) and the Société des Jeunes-Artistes (1853–61), discussed above.

The *Société de l'Union Musicale* lasted only three seasons, 1849–51. At biweekly concerts (alternating Sundays with the Conservatoire programs) its 160 members performed orchestral and choral works; the programs also included instrumental solos and songs. The first conductor, Manera, died after the spring 1849 season and was replaced by Seghers; Seghers left the following year to found the Société Sainte-Cécile and was succeeded by Félicien David (orchestra) and Louis Dietsch (chorus) for a final season. Publicity issued in November 1850 promised a repertory of Haydn, Mozart, Beethoven, Mendelssohn, Palestrina, Allegri, Marcello, Handel, J. S. Bach, Weber, Gluck, Cimarosa, Paisiello, Cherubini, Grétry, Méhul, "etc.," and newer works.[271] Clearly, many of these composers contributed only to vocal portions of the program; the list of instrumental music performed there includes works of Berlioz, Félicien David, Gouvy, Reber, and other nineteenth-century composers, as well as more traditional repertory. Subscriptions for six yearly concerts cost 12 to 20 francs, which was fairly reasonable.

The *Grande Société Philharmonique de Paris* (1850–51), a grandiose orchestral-choral society run almost single-handedly by Berlioz, played a mixed assortment of instrumental and vocal music. It carried out a plan[272] to program numerous recent works (particularly those of Berlioz), and announced the intention (which it did not survive long enough to execute) to perform each year a work of any genre by a Prix de Rome winner, upon his or her return from the prize winners' stay abroad. Always hampered by limited capital, the series ended after 18 months, having given no more than 12 concerts.

The *Association des Musiciens-Exécutants* (1851) attempted, unsuccessfully, to revive *concerts populaires*. An orchestra of 70 to 80, organized by the violinist, composer, and critic Alexandre Malibran, performed just one concert, in the Casino Paganini; the program included Elwart's vocal symphony *Ruth et Booz* and overtures by Auber and Méhul.[273] Later that season Malibran formed another orchestra under the title *Cercle Musical et Littéraire*. According to Henri Blanchard, Malibran planned to make the orchestra available to instrumental or vocal soloists for a reasonable "rental" fee.[274] The group gave five concerts (but apparently not with soloists) from February to April 1852; its repertory, which included overtures, concertos, other orchestral works, and chamber and vocal compositions, was unadventurous.

Three other contemporary series offering orchestral works were equally short-lived. The *Société de Sainte-Cécile* (1847–48), founded by the composer and writer Elwart and originally called "L'Essai Musical," presented only two concerts. It promoted music by contemporary French composers—orchestral and choral works as well as instrumental and vocal solos. Pupils of the pianist *Stamaty* played concertos of Beethoven, Laffite, Mozart, and Weber at three concerts organized by their teacher in April 1852; they were accompanied by members of the Théâtre-Italien orchestra.[275] Finally, a *Société Symphonique,* founded in autumn 1852 under the direction of Aristide Farrenc, publicized a repertory of established and little-known (but not necessarily new) works. The society was apparently discontinued after two concerts.

The midcentury wave of new orchestral series passed rather quickly, and following the establishment of the Jeunes-Artistes in 1853, no significant orchestral series appeared until the 1860s. Chamber music, meanwhile, continued to thrive in concert halls and *salons*. But many new series from the mid to late 1850s were transitory, the notable exceptions being the Lebouc *séances* and the concerts of the Société des Quatuors de Mendelssohn (both already examined).

A single season (or part of a season) was of course the planned length for series by visiting musicians. The Belgian violinist *Vieuxtemps* presented four concerts of string quartets, quintets, and violin solos in winter 1858–59. The programs emphasized works of Beethoven and Vieuxtemps and the admission fee for the series was high—40 francs. A few weeks after the final concert Vieuxtemps began another four-concert series, in which a lighter, more diverse repertory of concertos, overtures, and piano and vocal works was performed. The following autumn the Italian violinist *Sivori,* pianist *Théodore Ritter,* and others gave four concerts of chamber works, violin and piano solos, and vocal music. Their programs were scheduled to resume in spring 1860 but apparently did not.

The *Nouvelle Société de Musique de Chambre,* however, was originally intended to endure longer. Founded by the amateur composer and cellist le comte Louis de Stainlein, the society performed four benefit concerts in the salle Pleyel in 1857 and was expected to return the next year, but was discontinued when the count went to Nice for the winter. It is not clear whether Stainlein participated in the concerts though his chamber music was programmed with Beethoven's and Mendelssohn's.

Reasons for the apparent brevity of two other chamber music series are not known. The *Société des Quintettes Anciens et Modernes,* established by M. le baron de Ponnat in 1858, comprised a quintet of string players (including two cellists) and a pianist. In its single season of four concerts its members performed chamber works (not exclusively quintets) mainly of Blanc, Boccherini, and Onslow. Professors and students of the *Ecole Beethoven,* a music school founded in autumn 1857, gave programs of chamber music plus piano and vocal works during two seasons. From the second season only the premiere concert was mentioned in the *Revue et gazette musicale,* but there may have been others as only three of 14 concerts from the first season had been reported. *Matinées* organized by the composer *Félicien David* and the vocalist *Paulin* [Lespinasse], at which several chamber works of David were played, were also limited to one season.

Two contemporary series did assume a more stable role in the Parisian musical scene. Mme. *Clara Pfeiffer,* pianist and mother of the composer and pianist Georges Pfeiffer, presented frequent concerts in the late

1850s and 1860s. It is not clear which of these constituted series, but her programs were mentioned in a list of chamber music organizations in 1857[276] and her *matinées* of chamber music were noted in 1862. Beginning in spring 1867 two or three *séances* were announced each season through 1870. Mme. Pfeiffer's programs included much piano and vocal music, as well as chamber works. The Friday *soirées* of M. le comte de *Nieuwerkerke* (Directeur général des musées nationaux from 1849), at the Louvre, were first reported in 1856. Although the best musicians performed (for many years Pasdeloup was musical director for the *soirées*) for a prestigious audience, the programs, which included chamber, solo instrumental, piano, and vocal works, were primarily light. The *soirées* were still scheduled in 1870 and may have continued after the war.

In the 1860s orchestral and chamber music series together were established at a rate roughly double that of the previous three decades. Because most new series were short-lived, the number of closures in the 1860s was also unprecedented; but the percentage of series that did not survive was no higher than before.

Jules Pasdeloup's Concerts Populaires (described above) dominated orchestral series of the 1860s, not only through sheer quantity of concerts (24 per season), but also via their success in attracting large audiences. The series provided a model for the *Concerts Classiques* (1864), an unsuccessful attempt to extend *concerts populaires* into the summer. On successive Sundays in April (beginning three weeks after the final Concert Populaire of the season), the conductor Deloffre led two substantial programs of orchestral works at the Cirque de l'Impératrice; the series was expected to continue, but no further concerts were reported. Three seasons later, Pasdeloup expanded the activities of the Concerts Populaires orchestra, directing it and a large chorus at concerts of the *Société de l'Athénée*. The banker Raphael Bischoffscheim, who had built a commodious and elegant concert hall[277] (complete with organ) near the Opéra, loaned it to the "Athénée" with the stipulation that half of the profits from its activities would be donated to a professional school for girls. Concerts took place thrice weekly from November 1866 through May 1867; each week, one night was scheduled for oratorios, one night for purely orchestral music, and one night for various works for orchestra and voice.[278] Light instrumental solos, masses, and other sorts of works were also performed. Contemporary compositions constituted a large share of the repertory, and it appears that instrumental music received increasing emphasis as the season progressed. Although no announcement has been found of the concerts' permanent termination, the series did not resume in 1867–68. Mathieu de Monter wrote in 1870 that the

Athénée had continued its battle to become a fourth *scène lyrique;*[279] thus it seems to have abandoned concerts.

Almost nothing is known of the *Société Symphonique de Paris* (1861), an apparently short-lived orchestra whose only reported concert followed the premiere of the Concerts Populaires by six weeks. A contemporary orchestra with a similar name, the *Société des Symphonistes,* proved more durable, though it was never (nor was it intended to be) a major part of the Parisian scene. Its members, most of whom were amateurs, met weekly (during the season) from about 1861 through 1870 to read through old and new symphonies, but performed only once a year. Its programs included chamber works and instrumental and vocal solos as well as symphonies, and promoted works of young composers.

Other contemporary orchestral series (or societies) that supported new music included:

—The *Cercle de l'Union Artistique* (1860 through 1870), founded by the Polish tenor and composer Prince Poniatowski as an attempt to aid young artists by performing their works and opening doors to Parisian *salons.* The seldom-reported programs of the Cercle included major works of composers from Bach to contemporaries; a program in 1864 comprised three new symphonies, by Lacherier, Polignac, and Lefebvre. By 1862 the Cercle had 500 members.

—*The Société Nationale des Beaux-Arts* (later known as the *Concerts des Beaux-Arts*), active from 1862 to 1865. Under the leadership of Félicien David in its first season, it drew praise for performances of contemporary orchestral and orchestral-choral works; in many cases these works were conducted by their composers, who included Saint-Saëns, Bizet, and Debillemont. In subsequent seasons chamber music, then light music (both instrumental and vocal), and, finally, theatrical representations were programmed. Although the repertory became more conservative the second season, some modern works were still presented.

—Three concerts of the violinist *Jean Becker* (1863). Although these were described as "historical" concerts, the survey of Italian, German, French, and Belgian violin concertos and solos continued into the contemporary era. Thus programs offered compositions of Alard and Bazzini as well as those of Leclair and Tartini.

—Eight concerts arranged by *Camille Saint-Saëns* in 1864 and 1865. The repertory for the six concerts in 1864 included, particularly, Mozart piano concertos (with an orchestra), but also traditional and modern chamber works, piano pieces, and vocal music. Another six concerts in series and one nonseries concert were planned for 1865. At the nonseries concert Saint-Saëns gave the Paris premiere of Robert Schumann's piano concerto; and he intended to present contemporary or little-known orchestral and chamber works during the ensuing series. But in spite of favorable reviews, the series was cancelled after one concert because of disagreement between Saint-Saëns and the management of the concert hall (the salle Pleyel) regarding the selections performed. Perhaps the management felt the repertory too modern, although the final program was not particularly avant-garde, comprising works of Beethoven (Op. 74), Félicien David, Henry Litolff, Mendelssohn, and Saint-Saëns.

—The *Grands Concerts des Compositeurs Vivants,* a brief series organized by the lawyer and amateur composer Antonín Prévost-Rousseau at the hôtel du Louvre in 1865. The series's title accurately describes the two known programs, which included orchestral and orchestral-choral works of Louis Lacombe, Wagner, and Prévost-Rousseau.

—The *Société Philharmonique de Paris* (spring 1866), an orchestra of 100 and chorus of 150 that presented both established and recent works. Only two of its three scheduled concerts were reviewed.

—The equally short-lived *Concerts de l'Opéra* (1869), which programmed Classical and modern orchestral and choral compositions. Contemporary composers were invited to conduct their own works. The orchestra of 100 musicians (called the "necessary number"[280]) comprised members of various theatre orchestras. Despite public success the series dissolved after two concerts following the resignation of the regular conductor, Henry Litolff.

Most of the new works heard at concerts of *Anton Rubinstein* were his own—mainly piano concertos and solos, but also symphonies and chamber pieces. Rubinstein gave many concerts during visits to Paris in 1857, 1858, 1868, and 1870, but only five (of seven) from spring 1868 can be considered a series.

New "art" music may have been played at the *concerts-promenades* which took place at the *hôtel Laffite,* beginning in 1864. Contemporary reports mentioned an orchestra of 50, with many good soloists, performing both classical and modern music, specifically works of young composers. Held in conjunction with exhibitions of art, science, and industry, these concerts were intended for the upper classes.

The frequent inclusion of contemporary works was not the only new practice in orchestral programming of the 1860s; the juxtaposition of "art" and "popular" music in a single concert became less common, and as symphonic works were played more, "popular" works were, as in the mid-1830s, disappearing from concert halls. Light music remained, however, prominent in the orchestral programs of the *lycée Louis-le-Grand,* reported from 1860 to 1866.[281]

Light music was combined with chamber works (or *fragments* thereof) at the *soirées of Mme. Erard* (ca. 1862–ca. 1865, possibly for a longer period) and at concerts of the *Cercle des Beaux-Arts* (or *Cercle Artistique,* beginning in the season of 1864–65 and continuing past the Franco-Prussian War). But, as in orchestral series, such mixed programming diminished in public chamber music series of the 1860s. Instead, new series not only concentrated on "art" music but, in many cases, also specialized in a single genre or the works of specific composers. In a sense, earlier series had also specialized, in that many had a repertory comprising only five or six celebrated composers. But the intent of the early, conservative chamber groups was different from that of musicians in the 1860s. Probably, as chamber music organizations flourished and commercial competition became more lively, new societies sought a unique "cause" that would distinguish them from other performing bodies.

The *Société des Quatuors Français,* whose members included a string quartet and pianist, was established in 1862 to perform French chamber works written within the previous 30 years. Several living composers agreed to write especially for the series. The society presented only a few programs before its demise in 1865, but these included works of A. Blanc, Boëly, C. Dancla, L. Gastinel, L. Kreutzer, G. Mathias, A. Morel, Onslow, G. Pfeiffer, Reber, and Vaucorbeil.

The *Société de Musique de Chambre Jacobi-Willaume,* named after two participating violinists, gave concerts in 1865 and 1866 that were described as "fort brillante."[282] Its other label, the *Société de Quatuors et Quintetti,* aptly describes its repertory of works for strings with or without piano.

The *Société des Trios Anciens et Modernes* also gave concerts in 1865 and 1866, programming works for piano trio and other compositions involving combinations of those three instruments. The trio of de la Nux (piano), White (violin), and Lasserre (cello) was praised for its fine ensemble and for the promotion of little-known recent works, including piano trios of Schumann, Damcke, Rosenhain, and Gade.

Visiting Paris in spring 1869, the *Quatuor Florentin,* under the leadership of first violinist Jean Becker, performed four concerts. Its repertory was unadventurous but its ensemble was said to be "unequaled" and its balance particularly praised because, unlike most other groups, the first violin was not too prominent.[283]

The following season the *Société des Quintettes Harmoniques,* which comprised young performers, played music for winds and keyboard instruments on the Left Bank. The *Société Schumann,* emulating groups that had promoted quartets of Beethoven and Mendelssohn, imported chamber works of yet another German master. Apart from Schumann, the quartet of string players and the pianist Delahaye [? Lepot] played other works little known in Paris, including those of Brahms, de Castillon, Raff, and Volkmann.

Apparently the name of the *Société de l'Avenir Musical* was misleading; its only known program presented chamber works as early as Beethoven's, as well as more recent compositions. The society gave only a few concerts, during the season of 1869–70.

Several chamber music series were associated with individuals (or small groups of individuals) and lasted only a season or two. Such series include:

—Three *lecture-recitals* by the scholar *Aristide Farrenc* and his wife, the composer, pianist, and scholar *Louise Farrenc,* spring 1862. With the assistance of other pianists and instrumentalists, the Farrencs demonstrated selections from their historical anthology of keyboard music, *Le Trésor des pianistes* (then in progress), as well as Mme. Farrenc's own chamber works.

—Four concerts, in which instrumental and piano solos as well as vocal music were performed, by the pianist *Rosa Escudier-Kastner,* violinist *Vieuxtemps,* and the Belgian cellist *Alexandre Batta,* early 1863.

—Five *matinées* by the violinist *Antoine Bessems,* 1865. Programs comprised chamber, piano, and vocal works. Since the 1840s Bessems had given numerous single concerts in which he offered chamber music and violin solos of established composers.

—Weekly *séances chez Adolphe Sax,* established to display his new wind instruments, season of 1865–66. For the same purpose, Sax had organized several other short-lived series; his programs included arrangements of orchestral "art" works.

—Five concerts of established and recent compositions (among the latter, works of Schumann, Damcke, Hiller, Raff, and Rubinstein) by the pianist Mme. *Szarwady* and the *brothers Müller,* a string quartet from Germany,[284] spring 1866.

—Five *séances* at the lycée Louis-le-Grand, organized by the English violinist and composer *Alfred Holmes* to promote classical masterpieces among *lycée* students, spring 1866.

—Three *lecture-recitals* arranged by the critic *de Gasperini* and the pianist and composer *Georges Pfeiffer,* spring 1867. Lectures on Haydn and Mozart, Beethoven, and Mendelssohn and Schumann were complemented by performances of these composers' chamber, piano, and vocal works.

—*Matinées* of chamber and piano music, established by the violinist *Edouard Colonne,* season of 1867–68.

—*Soirées* of chamber music, organized by the pianist *Alphonse Duvernoy,* spring 1869.
—Four *séances* by *Louise Farrenc,* involving her own chamber and piano works, and pieces from *Le Trésor des pianistes,* spring 1870. Participants included Farrenc's former and current piano students, as well as string and wind players. From the 1840s through the 1860s Mme. Farrenc had organized and played in many single concerts, in which she promoted her own music.

More significant were series that had a certain degree of permanence, even if they were less formally organized. The most notable of these were arranged by pianists; those of Mme. Tardieu de Malleville and Mme. Pfeiffer, which continued into the 1860s, have already been mentioned. The pianist, composer, and teacher *Thérèsa Wartel* (*née* Andrien) gave Saturday *soirées* (probably weekly) at the salle Erard in spring 1862 and weekly *soirées* in her home the following season. She had also presented three *soirées* in 1847 and several individual concerts from the mid-1840s until the mid-1860s. The programs comprised chamber, piano, vocal, and light instrumental works, performed by some of the best musicians in Paris. *Louise Béguin-Salomon* (*née* Cohen), a pianist and teacher, held weekly *soirées* of chamber music with piano in her home from 1866 (and probably earlier) through 1868. In addition, she received high praise for her single concerts, presented 1862–66, 1868, 1870, and possibly other years.[285] Little definite is known about the *séances* of pianist Mlle. *Adrienne Picard.* The contemporary press reported seasonal closings and resumptions of weekly *séances chez* Mlle. Picard, but rarely reviewed these events or listed programs. The concerts evidently attracted crowds[286] and had the reputation of being particularly hospitable to new works. They had begun by spring 1867 and continued after the war.

As has been noted for Mme. Pierson-Bodin, some piano teachers arranged public concerts in which their students performed chamber music with professional musicians. What began as *exercices* for pupils of the pianist and composer *Paul Bernard* developed into real concerts as the students improved and guest artists, both vocalists and instrumentalists, were invited to join them. These *séances,* which occurred from about 1862 until sometime after the war, seem to have emphasized light music. Similarly, the pianist and composer *Jean-Henri Bonewitz* included his students in several concerts of chamber and piano works, many by young composers, from 1867 to 1870.

Not all of the individuals who sponsored series were professional musicians. Sauzay recalled his own participation in weekly musical *séances* of Princess Mathilde Bonaparte, held from 1861 through the end of the Second Empire. The *séances* were virtually private the first year, but subsequently more persons, among them visiting heads of state, were invited to hear both established and new chamber, piano, and vocal works.[287] The amatuer cellist Baron Molitor hosted and played in summer *matinées* in 1866 (possibly other years too). His programs offered a traditional repertory plus chamber works of Adolphe Blanc.

During any given year from 1828 through 1870 a number of concert series were active in Paris. The scene changed from year to year, of course, as individual musicians took the initiative to introduce new series and as different sorts of music became popular. The founding of the Conservatoire concerts in 1828 sparked interest in instrumental works and introduced Parisians to orchestral works of Beethoven. Many early series presented both "art" and "popular" music. Beginning in the mid-1830s, series tended to emphasize one or the other, a practice which became temporarily less prevalent during the 1840s. Until nearly midcentury chamber music was associated with *salons,* but public concerts of chamber works appeared suddenly and attained a popularity that never waned; as more chamber groups were formed, their individual repertories became increasingly specialized. If the several new orchestral series established at midcentury did not experience comparable lasting success, together they proved the existence of interested listeners other than subscribers to the Conservatoire concerts. In the 1860s Pasdeloup took advantage of this discovery, steadily drawing large audiences to programs of orchestral "art" music. As the period progressed, amateur orchestras became less common (or less newsworthy). Their replacement by series such as the Concerts Populaires, and the move of chamber music from *salon* to concert hall, indicate the increasingly pervasive view of musical entertainment as a commercial activity, in which professionals performed for the general public.

Although the concert scene changed continuously, there were always series promoting new or little-known music. Some organizations that supported the unfamiliar failed miserably, but others, such as the quartets that specialized in Late Beethoven and Mendelssohn, had considerable success. Noteworthy efforts on behalf of contemporary music were made by groups or series such as the Société de l'Athénée Musical, the Gymnase Musical, the Sociétés Musicales (I and II), the Concerts Valentino, concerts of the *Revue et gazette musicale,* the Association des Artistes-Musiciens, the Société Sainte-Cécile (II), the Grande Société Philharmonique de Paris, the Société des Jeunes-Artistes, the Société Nationale des Beaux-Arts, the Société des Quatuors Français, the Société des Symphonistes, the Séances Populaires, and the Société Schumann, and by individuals such as Berlioz, Gouffé, Lebouc, Dancla, the Bohrers, the Tilmants, Saint-Saëns, and Mlle. Picard.

The persistent attempts of groups and individuals to promote music of contemporary (and, in many cases, native) composers necessitate a reevaluation of the organization most widely recognized for such activity, the Société Nationale de Musique (founded in 1871). Traditionally, the Société Nationale has been considered the first significant promulgator of new music (other than stage and *salon* works) by French composers. But how does it compare with the prewar societies mentioned above?

The goals of the Société Nationale, as stated by its secretary, Alexis de Castillon, were specific:

> The aim of the society is to aid the production and the popularization of all serious musical works, published or unpublished, by French composers; to encourage and bring to light, so far as is in its power, all musical endeavor, whatever form it may take, provided that there is evidence of high artistic aspiration on the part of the author. . . . Members of the society will contribute, each in his own sphere of activity, to the study and performance of works which they will be called upon to select and interpret.[288]

Henri Duparc recalled that members of the Société (which numbered 150 by early February 1872),[289] met weekly to listen to each other's works.[290] Ursula Eckart-Bäcker, citing Arthur Pougin, has noted that there had been 37 concerts (beginning in November 1871) by late spring 1874;[291] thus there were approximately 12 per season. On early programs there were few major works; short pieces for small groups abounded. Duparc remembered a program that included 14 *mélodies,* and Pougin noted that the first 37 programs comprised over 400 works—more than ten per concert.[292] The repertory included orchestral, chamber, piano, solo vocal, and choral works. At early concerts an orchestra of 40 was available, but composers generally chose their own performers.[293] Composers whose works were performed in the first three concerts included Bizet, Bourgault-Ducoudray, de Castillon, Théodore Dubois, Fissot, Franck, Garcin, Guiraud, Massenet, Pfeiffer, and Saint-Saëns.[294]

Apparently, the initial success of the group was greater among composers than with the public. Midway through the first season, however, a special concert was given of works most successful on earlier occasions, to which musical leaders of Paris were invited. James Harding has written that "on that date the aim of the society was achieved, and from then onwards French names appeared on concert programs to which no-one had hitherto dared admit them."[295]

The Société Nationale was unquestionably a success. Already in February 1872, Mathieu de Monter thought he noticed increased individual initiative among young composers, more self-reliance, and more reliance on each other. He also praised the increased fraternization among young and old composers.[296] Duparc stressed the educational value of the Société's providing composers the opportunity to hear their own works.[297] Rolland wrote:

> All that was great in French music found a home there. Without it, the greater part of the works that are the honor of our music would never have been played; perhaps they would not ever have been written.[298]

Eckart-Bäcker, who had more time for historical perspective, thought the Société opened nontheatrical genres to French composers, and allowed French composers to discover each other and thereby develop a path separate from the Wagner school.[299] The promising composers whose works were performed during the first 40 years of the Société's existence included Alkan, Boëllmann, Bordes, Chabrier, Chausson, Camille Chevillard, Coquard, Debussy, Dukas, Duparc, Fauré, Gouvy, d'Indy, Jacobi, Louis Lacombe, Paul Lacombe, Lalo, Lekeu, Magnard, Marty, Messager, Ravel, and many others.[300]

Clearly the Société Nationale de Musique was more effective in promoting works of living French composers than earlier series had been. Yet without intending to depreciate in any way the Société's importance, I must conclude that its achievement has been exaggerated by historians; for its efforts to explore and promulgate nineteenth-century French music, though more concentrated and successful than those of earlier series, were not unique. The fact that contemporary composers found the prewar series inadequate to their needs does not justify the neglect that these series have suffered in histories of French music.

3

Musical Life in Paris, II: Other Musical Events; The Audience

Apart from series, events that offered instrumental music include single concerts by individuals, charity concerts, *salons,* state concerts, and outdoor and café concerts. "Art" music constituted only a small portion of programs at state, outdoor, and café concerts. The diverse repertory of the other events does not lend itself to generalizations.

Single Concerts by Individuals

Because orchestras and chamber ensembles, once formed, tended to give multiple concerts, most single (nonseries) events were organized by individuals. Composers, such as Berlioz and Charles Dancla, presented concerts to program their works; William Weber has noted 20 such events in the season of 1845–46 alone.[1] Similarly, Adolphe Sax gave concerts to exhibit his "works"—new musical instruments. But most of the individuals who scheduled single events were performers. Their programs, like those of many series discussed in chapter 2, comprised various combinations of chamber, instrumental solo, piano, and vocal works, though solo works outnumbered chamber pieces as individuals tended to demonstrate their own abilities. Orchestras were relatively rare at such concerts, no doubt because it was difficult to organize and pay a large body of musicians.

Both performers and composers organized "benefit concerts", of which they were, individually, the *bénéficiares;* there is no apparent difference between an individual's "benefit concert" and any other presentation by a needy musician. William Weber has suggested that the audience for such events generally comprised persons closely associated with the performer—family, teachers, pupils, sponsors.[2] The concerts might involve only a few performers, though musicians aided each other in these enterprises, thereby increasing the number of performers at individual concerts.[3] Some benefit concerts were organized to enable a performer to buy his way out of military conscription; if the conscript was a member of a permanent orchestra, other members of the orchestra might assist in presenting the concert. Programs of these personal benefit concerts commonly consisted of about 12 numbers, including both vocal and instrumental works.

Although most musicians found organizing a concert to be extremely difficult and prohibitively expensive, Flotow described a method for giving concerts that brought him success in the 1830s:

> One makes several appearances [at private salons] in the course of the winter and then, at the beginning of Lent, one announces a concert and sends a dozen high-price tickets, generally at ten francs, to the hostess of every salon at which one has played. That is the usual practice. It practically never happens that all, or even any, of the tickets are sent back.[4]

Flotow added that the cost of such a concert was negligible if given during the day, because no lighting or heating was needed; and no publicity or box office was necessary as the audience had been supplied with tickets by the various hostesses.

Charity Concerts

There were also benefit concerts organized for a wide variety of charitable causes: assistance to groups of impoverished musicians or other artists; pension funds for retired artists and employees of the Opéra; schools for children of poverty-stricken artists; and relief for the Parisian poor or indigents of a particular *arrondissement* (rarely, for a particular family), the needy of other countries (for example, the Poles during their uprising against Russia in 1831), victims of natural disasters, and men wounded or women widowed in wars. Many of these charity concerts employed enormous forces, thereby creating a spectacular effect, which attracted large crowds. A benefit festival for impoverished musicians and artists in September 1848 at the Elysée National engaged 300 instrumentalists and 900 choristers, plus 300 military musicians.[5] Prices for most, but not all, benefit concerts were high (as much as ten francs), presumably in order to retain some money for the cause after expenses were met.

Salons

One of the few safe generalizations about *salons* (that is, *matinées* and *soirées* in private homes), is that each was unique, according to the taste of the host and hostess, and the nature of the invited guests.[6] Some *salons* offered no music. For others, music was the *raison d'être;* the *séances* of Gouffé and Lebouc, held in private homes, were among the most important musical events in Paris in the mid-nineteenth century. At some *salons,* music was relegated to the background—a forerunner of MUZAK. In others, guests who interrupted the musical proceedings were chastised.

The nineteenth-century British journalist James Grant equated *soirées* with English "at-homes". He noted that *soirées,* rather than dinner parties, were the main evening social events in Paris. Usually they began at 7:30 or 8:00 and lasted until 11:00 or 12:00; wine, coffee, tea, and cake were served. They were well attended (sometimes 150 to 200 persons crowded into relatively small quarters), and the guests were not necessarily acquainted with each other.[7] Frances Trollope agreed that *salons* were extremely crowded, but remarked upon the informality and absence of ceremony, relative to similar social events in London.[8] Among historians, Burnand has described *salons* as poorly lit rooms filled with cushioned chairs, and observed that musical *salons* were restricted to homes of the wealthy because owning a piano was a luxury.[9] And Kracauer has written that *salons* were run by the nobility and the richer members of the bourgeoisie in town houses; in a more scholarly approach to the subject, Weber has found that *salons* were sponsored mainly by the upper-middle class—and primarily by persons in the business and banking worlds.[10]

According to Kracauer, music was offered at nearly every *salon* (but, with few exceptions, was mediocre).[11] An anonymous critic in 1838 described the "multiplication" of concerts in aristocratic *salons,* and a report issued in January 1850 stated that there were four or five *soirées* nightly.[12] A Parisian journalist in 1846 estimated "that during the previous season about 850 *salons* had substantial enough musical interludes that they could be called private concerts."[13] Clearly, the repertory at these "private concerts" varied from one *salon* to another. In 1828 Fétis deplored the abandonment of orchestral concerts for piano-dominated *soirées* at which the music was poor.[14] François Stoepel in 1835 stated that *soirées* and *matinées,* apart from those of Baillot and Berlioz, were beneath musical criticism,[15] and several other reviews of *salons* indicate that much of the music performed there was of little worth. Conversely, before 1848 chamber works of Mozart, Beethoven, and other *grands maîtres* were heard primarily in *salons.*

Weber's contention that persons attended concerts because they really enjoyed music (or, at least, enjoyed virtuosos), but attended *salons* to carry on the social routine[16] is supported by contemporary comments: an anonymous critic wrote in 1835 that because Paris had no good concert hall there were many musical *soirées,* but that music was not really taken seriously at these.[17] Liszt opined that at *salons* music was only a pretext for socializing.[18] Few of the guests at *salons* had any musical expertise, but a pretended knowledge of the arts was considered mandatory. Regarding *matinées* of chamber music at the mansion of the Marquis de Prault, Legouvé wrote "the Marquis' *matinées* had become the fashion, society was delighted to air its real or assumed appreciation of high-class music."[19] Taine even suggested the following approach to conversation at musical *salons:*

> Learn a few technical terms: "skilful *reprise,* change of key, minor passage, these trills are strings of pearls, etc." The high style consists in knowing the names of the chief works of the great masters, and in repeating them in a low voice in a familiar way.[20]

There was, however, an opposing view regarding the musical merits of *salons.* An anonymous critic writing in 1831 praised *soirées* for having eliminated the ceremony attached to concerts, thereby making it possible for listeners to devote all their attention to music.[21] Ten years later the idea was expressed, again anonymously, that sometimes the best music was saved for small, intimate *soirées.*[22] The truth of course is that the musical worth of *salons* varied greatly, depending on the hosts and guests. Apart from the *séances* of Gouffé and Lebouc, *soirées* sponsored by P-.J.-G. Zimmermann, Kalkbrenner, Rossini, Mme. Orfila, Mme. Viardot, and Saint-Saëns were particularly highly regarded. The *salons* of Zimmermann became the main place for Parisian debuts in the 1830s and 1840s. Later, Mme. Orfila's *salon* assumed this function; performing there was like receiving a certificate of talent.[23]

Many *salons* earned a reputation via the musicians who played or sang there. Weber claimed that as *salons* were more fashionable than public concerts, some of the best musicians performed only in *salons.*[24] But at some *salons* the participants were amateurs.[25] In 1838 an anonymous critic commented that the aristocrats were performing (mainly vocal and piano music) so much at their own *soirées* that there would soon be more performers than listeners.[26] Many *salons* engaged music teachers, artists of moderate talent, or young performers who viewed *salons* as steppingstones to wider fame.[27] Like Zimmermann and Mme. Orfila, Marmontel held *soirées* at which young performers were encouraged.[28]

Regardless of the repertory, ability of the performers, or attentiveness of the audience, *salons* played a significant role in the musical life of nineteenth-century Paris. They employed struggling musicians, and some provided a forum for music (particularly chamber music) that was not heard elsewhere. Although at some *salons* the music was incidental, at others the musical presentation rivalled or even surpassed public concerts.

Finally, it should be noted that some of the concert halls run by instrument manufacturers and others were referred to as *salons* (for example, the salons Pleyel), but were generally open to the public.

State Concerts

Concerts sponsored by the state were, with the exception of the subsidized Société des Concerts du Conservatoire, not well publicized in the *Revue et gazette musicale de Paris,* possibly because many of them were private. Even determining which concerts were government-sponsored is in some cases difficult. According to contemporary reports, formation of a body of musicians to play for *fêtes* and *spectacles* at the royal palace was considered in 1832, but King Louis-Philippe offered only 40,000 francs annually for such a venture, too small a figure to interest any organizers.[29] Sauzay, on the other hand, recalled weekly private concerts presented for Louis-Philippe by a small instrumental ensemble (in which Sauzay participated), beginning in 1832, and annual concerts of the Musique du Roi, in which vocal music predominated.[30] In November 1848 the Préfet de la Seine announced that the city of Paris would present a series of concerts led by Tilmant *aîné,* and in 1857 it was reported that the Saturday receptions of the Préfet (by then the famous Baron Haussmann) were devoted to concerts by the best artists, including the Société des Jeunes-Artistes. Musical *soirées* "du Préfet de la Seine," attended by government officials and the wealthy, were held at the Hôtel de Ville from about 1855; opera singers and an orchestra led by Pasdeloup participated.[31] On special occasions the government sometimes supported concerts by military or brass bands, often in the Tuileries.

Concerts that may have been associated with the government were reported increasingly in the 1860s. These include operatic "Concerts des Tuileries" for invited guests,[32] several private or official concerts in 1867 (none with musically interesting programs, in spite of the participation of first-rate artists), and musical activities such as those for the "high-life" [original in English], reviewed in 1868:[33] vocal concerts *chez* the Hôtel de Ville, the Marquise d'Aoust, and the Président du Conseil d'Etat and *soirées* of Count Nieuwerkerke. Most of these events were not associated with any known series, and all took place in government buildings or in the homes of government officials; few offered noteworthy instrumental music.

Outdoor Concerts and Café Concerts

Summer concerts and huge music festivals, both held outdoors, were popular throughout the mid-nineteenth century. Berlioz led some of the largest outdoor events, among them a concert at the first great exhibition of industrial products in Paris, August 1844, for which he recruited 1200 musicians, and a concert at Versailles in October 1848, in which there were 450 performers.[34] Other samples of vast outdoor concerts (few of which offered music comparable to those of Berlioz) include a program by 22 choral societies from Paris and the Département Seine in March 1867, and a concert at the Exposition Universelle of the same year, at which there were a chorus of 500, an orchestra of 700, and an audience of 15,500.[35]

Many of the smaller concerts held during summer months also took place outdoors, generally under a structure that protected performers and some of the audience from the elements. These concerts, which "combined music, dancing, refreshment, shelter, and fresh air,"[36] offered (mainly) frivolous fare: arrangements of opera tunes as popular dances, military band music, and virtuosic fantasias and variations. Regular outdoor summer concerts began in the early 1830s, probably 1833.[37] Their immediate success effected not only the prompt formation of indoor winter concerts presenting the same "popular" repertory for the same audience, but also (as noted in chapter 2) the establishment of *concerts populaires* promoting "art" music a few years later. Seemingly the most significant and enduring of the *concerts d'été* were those held on the Champs-Elysées, founded in (again, probably) 1833. These were performed in an enclosure at the "lower" end of the Champs-Elysées (presumably the southeastern end). Frances Trollope described the setting as a round space enclosed by a rail, within which were circular rows of chairs, sheltered by a light awning; the band played in the center, on a stage covered by a canopy; ubiquitous statues of graceful nymphs had lights built into their heads; the price of admission was one franc.[38] Evidently, concerts were held nightly. The first conductor was Philippe Musard (1793–1859), a violinist and composer of light music who was already a celebrated orchestra leader at Parisian balls. Musard's orchestra, renowned for its precision and execution of nuance, performed overtures by Mozart, Weber, and Rossini, symphonies (rarely), and quadrilles by the conductor; the small repertory was repeated often. Carse, citing Rivière, stated that the orchestra was about 80 strong when Musard moved to the salle Valentino in 1837, but a contemporary description of the first summer concerts, in 1833, mentioned only about 40 musicians.[39] The initial series lasted, with one interruption, until 1839. When Musard moved to the rue Saint-Honoré in 1835 he was succeeded on the Champs-Elysées by the horn player Mohr, but much of the audience followed Musard and the Champs-Elysées series quickly declined, finally closing for financial reasons in August of that year. The concerts reopened the following summer, and by 1839 were directed by MM. Tilmant *aîné* and Dufresne (a cornettist and singer).[40]

An early rival to the summer Champs-Elysées series was that of the Jardin Turc, on the boulevard du Temple, in a lower-middle-class area.[41] Concerts were presented there by 1833 (probably no earlier),[42] in a café decorated in a pseudo-oriental style; the orchestra played in a pagodalike structure.[43] The first conductor, Tolbecque (probably Jean-Baptiste-Joseph), led an orchestra of 40 through (mainly) overtures, quadrilles, and galops. Criticized for poor ensemble playing, they nevertheless received praise for attempting to interest lower classes in orchestral music.[44] A plan to program vocal music, in 1834, was forbidden by the government.[45] An organ, introduced about 1835, was thought to be the first outdoor organ in Paris.[46] In 1836 Jullien followed Tolbecque as conductor, the orchestra was expanded to 60, and fireworks were sometimes presented with the music.[47] I have no record of nightly concerts at the Jardin Turc after 1839.

Indoor concerts of "popular" music took place mainly at *cafés* and *bazars*.[48] Cafés, which had formerly relied upon street musicians, began to engage professionals (including many of the same groups that played at summer concerts), and evolved nearly into informal concert halls.[49] The programs, intended for all levels of society, took place in lavish, capacious surroundings.[50] Again, Trollope provided a description of such events:

> [at 7:30 in the evening] you lounge into a fine, large, well-lighted room, which is rapidly filled with company: a full and good orchestra give you during a couple of hours some of the best and most popular music *of the season* [italics mine]; and then you lounge out again, in time to dress for a party.[51]

She added that the cost was one franc and that the attraction brought the "best company" in Paris.

Among the earliest of the café orchestras was that of Musard, which, immediately following its initial summer on the Champs-Elysées in 1833, moved to an odd sheltered garden (heated, yet containing vegetation) at 359 rue Saint-Honoré.[52] By 1835 the orchestra was installed on the rue Saint-Honoré year round, presenting instrumental solos, overtures, and symphonies, but mainly (by popular demand) Musard's own quadrilles, valses, and galops. The concerts owed their extreme success not only to the repertory, but also to the fine orchestra, which included some of the best players in Paris.[53] In 1837 Musard moved his orchestra to a new concert hall, designed for 90 musicians and eventually capable of seating 2000 persons, on the rue Vivienne.[54] This particular series was abruptly liquidated in December 1839, a few weeks after A.-C. Fessy (who had played organ in the Musard orchestra) became director of the concerts.[55]

An amusing chapter in the history of café concerts involves the short-lived success of the Casino, a café of unrivalled luxury, which opened in December 1837 on the rue Mont-Blanc.[56] The orchestra of Pugni (and later Jullien) played mainly dance music there;[57] according to all reports, it attracted the highest aristocracy. The Casino was closed abruptly after printing the following notice:

> Aujourd'hui, 20 août, la Symphonie en MER, musique DE Rossini, exécutée POUR la première fois au Casino, en attendant que L'AUTORITE permette la deuxième Nuit vénitienne.[58]

Few outdoor or café concerts were reported from the early 1840s until the mid-1850s. In May 1840, only a few months after the cessation of the concerts Fessy had led on the rue Vivienne, the Concerts Viviennes (mentioned in chapter 2) opened under Fessy's direction.[59] Elwart succeeded Fessy as conductor in 1843 and the series lasted until 1845. Meanwhile, "Concerts Musard" were reported in 1841; Weber has claimed that they lasted until 1846.[60] From 1848 concerts of light music, ranging from fanfares and works for military bands to vocal solos, choral music, waltzes, and symphonic movements, were held regularly at the Jardin d'hiver. A group called the Société des Concerts was established there by Fessy in July 1848; its concerts happened thrice weekly (sometimes to the accompaniment of fireworks), and attracted all classes.[61] Subsequently, concerts were led there by Musard (almost certainly Alfred Musard, 1828–1881, son of Philippe).[62]

From the late 1850s through the remainder of the period, series of outdoor and café concerts proliferated. Concerts on the Champs-Elysées were revived in summer 1858 under Musard *fils*.[63] In 1859 these were christened the Concerts du Prince Impérial, and presented in a new establishment behind the Palais d'Industrie. Six thousand persons attended the inaugural concert in May, at which 100 musicians performed works (probably overtures) of Auber, Méhul, Mendelssohn, Meyerbeer, and Rossini.[64] A genteel atmosphere, excellent soloists, and a wide repertory made these nightly concerts a great success; when the weather was favorable the concerts attracted 3000 to 4000 persons. Even high society attended.[65] The series evidently remained active throughout the 1860s. In

1861, autumn Sunday-afternoon concerts were inaugurated, after the nightly summer series had stopped; at about the same time the cornettist Arban succeeded Musard as conductor. Arban, in turn, was succeeded by Eugène Prévost for the 1864 season. The final concerts of the 1863 season were led by an interim conductor, one Gobert.[66] The programs on the Champs-Elysées comprised dance music more than symphonies or concertos. Nevertheless, the orchestra performed opera and concert overtures of the best nineteenth-century composers and showed a willingness (more common to organizations that performed "popular" music than to those that played "art" music) to attempt new works by untried composers.

Sunday concerts by Musard's orchestra, under the direction of Arban, had been announced at the parc d'Asnière as early as 1857.[67] Orchestral concerts led by Marx at the same location were mentioned in 1859, and a reopening, in which Rochefort led quadrilles and other works, was noted and reviewed in 1864.[68]

Somewhat more consistently reported was the series at the Pré Catelan (in the Bois de Boulogne, on the west side of Paris). A variety of concerts by several orchestras and bands (including the *guides* and *garde* of Paris) was held there in 1859. Programs included favorite overtures and symphonic movements, arranged for military band. Often, several orchestras and bands participated (not simultaneously) in festivals there; other sorts of entertainment were provided as well.[69] In 1862 an orchestral series of varied but mainly light music was inaugurated on Sunday afternoons (and sometimes on Thursday afternoons).[70] Although the orchestral concerts continued, references to concerts by military bands and fife, drum, and bugle corps were increasing. From 1868 the band of the *garde*, choral groups, children's dances, dramatic representations, scientific experiments, and games dominated activity there,[71] and serious orchestral music apparently disappeared.

Other summer series mentioned in passing in the *Revue et gazette musicale* are the Concerts de Paris, led by Arban at Ranelagh (just east of the Bois de Boulogne) in 1858,[72] band concerts at the Tuileries, Palais Royal, and place Vendôme in 1865,[73] concerts of light music led by Mey at the Jardin Mabille the same year,[74] and nightly programs for lovers of music and dance at the Château des fleurs on the Champs-Elysées in 1867.[75] In late summer, Parisians attended concerts in the provinces (see Appendix B).

The enterprising Musard *fils* was also busy with indoor series. Early in 1856 his orchestra opened at the hôtel d'Osmond[76] where, according to several contemporary reports, it had great success performing opera overtures, symphonies, instrumental solos, and quadrilles; an anonymous critic (probably Blanchard) stressed that Musard *fils,* in contrast to his father, believed in playing the orchestral repertory as well as dance music, and that in doing so he rendered a real service to composers and publishers.[77] These concerts evidently took place year round until summer 1857.[78] In 1866 Musard *fils* was contracted to present, at the Théâtre du Prince Impérial on Sunday afternoons, winter counterparts to the summer concerts held on the Champs-Elysées. Overtures, symphonies, and concertos (including works by contemporary French composers) were presented with much success, and the concerts were commended for propagating a taste for serious music among the *quartiers industriels.*[79]

Following Musard at the hôtel d'Osmond in 1857, Arban led an orchestra in the "Concerts de Paris." Highly-regarded renditions of overtures and dances led to much popular success, and Blanchard complimented the orchestra's unusual willingness to perform new symphonies.[80] By 1858 the orchestra had moved to the rue du Helder (just east of the present Opéra) and had established a schedule of dances thrice weekly with concerts on the remaining days; in 1859, by which time the conductor was Charles Hubans, the concerts moved to the salle Barthélemy on the rue du Château d'Eau (which runs northwest from the place de la République).[81]

In February 1859 Arban began a series of thrice-weekly concerts (alternating with balls) at the Casino de la rue Cadet.[82] An orchestra of 50 of "incontestable superiority,"[83] played overtures and movements of symphonies; a chorus also participated. The series thrived until 1868, when the entrepreneurs of the Casino Cadet decided to limit the repertory to dance music. Arban then left[84] to establish the Concerts Arban with the same orchestra and repertory at the refurbished salle Valentino.[85] These concerts too were extremely successful, and continued after the war; Arban's conducting won frequent praise.

New and fashionable in the 1860s at the Café Eldorado, the Casino Cadet, and elsewhere were *concerts de famille,* the "wholesome" atmosphere of which contrasted them with the many café concerts intended mainly for beer drinkers.[86] Kracauer has mentioned that café concerts proliferated in that decade, and it was reported in 1869 that there were 63 café concerts (series) that attracted an estimated 3500 persons nightly.[87]

Both summer concerts and café concerts were criticized for the limitations of their programs. Castil-Blaze and Blanchard noted, early in the period, that dance music was much more popular with the general public than overtures, much less symphonies.[88] Even those who preferred light music had reason to complain. Vocal music was prohibited at many such concerts, and the orchestras or bands (particularly the weaker ones) tended to confine themselves to a small, often-repeated collection of overtures and dances by Jullien, Musard, the Tolbecques, and a few others.

Representative Musical Years

Lists of Parisian musical events (at which, unless otherwise noted, instrumental music was presented) during two representative years (not seasons), 1840 and 1869, provide an idea of the musical calendar early and late in the period.

1840

Series Concerts

Société des Concerts du Conservatoire (orchestral), 8 series concerts plus 3 additional concerts.
Société Philharmonique (orchestral), 6 concerts.
Concerts Valentino (orchestral, solos, light music), nightly, with a summer respite.
Société de l'Athénée Musical (orchestral), 8[?] concerts.
Cercle Musical des Amateurs (orchestral), 1 annual concert.
Revue et gazette musicale concerts (chamber), 3[?] concerts.
MM. Franco-Mendès concerts (chamber), 4 concerts.
Baillot concerts (chamber), 3 concerts.
Enfants d'Apollon (mixed), 1 annual concert.
Annual concert for prize distribution at the Paris Conservatoire (mixed).
Herz-Labarre concerts (mixed), first 2[?] concerts in a series of 6[?].
Concerts Viviennes (mixed), unknown—at least weekly from May, with some respites.

Other series believed to have been active in 1840, but for which no concerts were announced, include the Institution des Jeunes Aveugles (orchestral, unknown frequency), and the Gouffé *séances* (mostly chamber, weekly[?]).

That year the *Revue et gazette musicale de Paris* reported few non-series concerts (among them five orchestral-vocal concerts by Berlioz, one orchestral concert by Deldevez, one chamber music concert by Franck, and some benefit concerts), roughly two dozen *matinées* and *soirées* (none from April through early October; the organizers included Alard, Louise Farrenc, P.-J.-G. Zimmermann, and MM. Herz and Géraldy), and over 75 other recitals (none between April and October), counting some at *salons* and some of vocal or piano music. There were of course many unreported concerts, *matinées,* and *soirées,* and numerous musical events at which only light music was performed. Three years earlier, it was reported that the musical season included 983 musical events (including vocal programs), of which 133 were public;[89] the figures for the 1840 season would likely be similar.

1869

Series Concerts

Société des Concerts du Conservatoire (orchestral), 15 concerts.
Concerts Populaires (orchestral), 24 weekly concerts, none from 4 April to 17 October.
Société des Symphonistes, 1 concert.
Gouffé *séances* (chamber), weekly concerts, none from 17 March to December[?].
Alard-Franchomme series (chamber), 6 concerts in spring.
Séances Populaires (chamber), 6[?] concerts.
Lebouc *séances* (chamber), biweekly[?], none between April and November.
Quatuor Florentin (chamber), 4 concerts, spring.
Maurin *soirées* (chamber), 4 concerts, spring.
Louis Lacombe concerts (chamber), 3 concerts, spring.
Mlle. Adrienne Picard *séances* (chamber), weekly concerts ending in May (beginning unknown).
Concerts de l'Opéra (mixed), 2 concerts before series aborted, autumn.
Institution des Jeunes Aveugles (mixed), 1 concert, January.
Société des Enfants d'Apollon (mixed), monthly[?] concerts.
Cercle des Beaux-Arts (mixed), 5 or more concerts.
Paul Bernard *soirées* (mixed), 4[?] *soirées*.
J.-H. Bonewitz *soirées* (mixed), 2[?] *soirées*.
Alphonse Duvernoy *séances* (mixed[?]), 3[?] *séances*.
Mme. Clara Pfeiffer *matinées* (mixed), 2 or more *matinées*.
Mme. Pierson-Bodin *matinées* (mixed), 2 or more *matinées*.
Mme. Tardieu de Malleville *séances* (orchestral[?]), 3 or more *séances*.
Société des Quintettes Harmoniques, 1[?] concert, December.

Other series believed to have been active that year, but for which no events were announced, include those of Nieuwerkerke (weekly *soirées*), Gouffé (annual public concert), the Cercle Musical des Amateurs (annual concert), and the Cercle de l'Union Artistique (whose schedule is unknown). In addition, the Concerts des Italiens were scheduled as a weekly series, beginning 6 December,[90] but no concert was ever reviewed and the series was not mentioned again.

The *Revue et gazette musicale* noted more than 30 nonseries concerts at which noteworthy orchestral or chamber works were performed. A great many other public concerts, not to mention private *séances,* were not reported. Apart from performances of "art" music, lighter music was provided at the Hôtel de Ville (by Pasdeloup and others), the Pré Catelan, the Casino Cadet, the "Concerts Valentino" (led by Arban), Arban's annual concert, and several less well-known events.

Officially, 701 concerts took place in Paris in 1869, not counting café concerts (of which there were 388 in the first four months alone) or most outdoor summer concerts.[91] These statistics, and the above lists, suggest that Parisians had many opportunities to hear instrumental music *before* the Franco-Prussian War.

Audiences and the Music Business

Many historians have noted great economic change in the concert life of the early to mid-nineteenth century—change that particularly affected the relationship between performers and audience. Paul Henry Lang has concisely described a large part of this change:

> By 1830 the cheap and easily accessible musical mass culture that resulted from the spiritual and economic alliance of the bourgeoisie, the virtuoso, and the impressario was rapidly displacing these last representatives [that is, the generation slightly younger than Beethoven; Lang is referring specifically to Spohr, Hummel, and R. Kreutzer] of a proud artistic tradition.[92]

No discussion of nineteenth-century music and its audiences can ignore William Weber's recent study regarding sociological aspects of European musical life in the first half of the century, *Music and the Middle Class: the Social Structure of Concert Life in London, Paris, and Vienna.*[93] Several of Weber's findings pertain to the Parisian scene:

1) The early nineteenth century brought a "professionalization" of musicians. The increasing wealth of the middle class led to more demand for public concerts, thereby enabling musicians to act as independent agents, who quickly developed new methods for management and promotion.[94] As career virtuosos (a phenomenon made possible by both the collective wealth and taste of the new audience) made concert life more commercial than ever before, they "eroded the traditional power of the

aristocracy in musical life and forced it to accept the upper-middle class on a more equal basis."[95]

2) After about 1830 there were concerts in increasing numbers, intended not only for the bourgeoisie but also for lower classes. The establishment of professional concerts for the less wealthy was viewed as a threat by the elite, who regarded this entertainment as an exclusive social event.[96]

3) Audiences could be categorized by taste as much as by wealth. The two major "taste-publics" (Weber's term) were those who preferred "high culture" (basically, the Classical German style) and those who preferred "popular" music (the Rossinian operatic style).[97] There was little direct relationship between affluence and taste (though before 1848 the rich had greater access to "high culture" music). The division into "taste-publics" was least sharply defined among the lower classes.[98] "High-culture" music was supported primarily by men, and mainly by those in liberal professions and the bureaucracy—who placed status value on intellect rather than wealth;[99] persons in the business or banking worlds, on the other hand, sought escape at concerts and, rather than seeking musical "depth," supported virtuosos, to whom they looked "for an exaggerated picture of the success and glamour they saw in themselves."[100]

4) The more prestigious the audience, the better were the performers, regardless of the repertory.[101]

5) Printed music and instruments were more widely available than before. The rising income of the middle class made possible unprecedented musical activity in the home as well as attendance at professional concerts.[102]

6) "Popular" music was characterized by novelty. Virtuosic technique, new instruments (and the "latest" *contredanses*) were more important than other musical considerations.[103]

Audiences and Musical Events

What encouraged (or discouraged) audiences to attend various sorts of events? Surely, cost was a major factor. Known prices of individual concerts (from 1828 to 1871) range from 75 centimes to 12 francs. (There was little fluctuation in price through the period.)[104] Many outdoor events were free; *salons* also were free, but presumably restricted to guests affluent enough to return the hospitality. Contemporary descriptions of a given admission charge are sometimes misleading, for a price of five francs was sometimes described as "low"; this apparently meant "low for the expected (elite) audience," as it was prohibitive for many music lovers. The middle classes might, rarely, spend as much as five francs for a concert, and the lower classes generally paid only one franc, almost never more than two.[105] Subscription concerts, for which the price per concert was a bargain (relative to that of single concerts), were the province of the wealthy, as only they could afford the necessary lump sum.

For the rich, then, the whole range of musical entertainment was available: intimate *salons,* some of which offered the finest chamber music and best virtuosos; prestigious subscription concerts, such as those of the Société des Concerts du Conservatoire; single concerts by famous soloists; concerts or *salons* sponsored by government officials; benefit concerts; café concerts (and their equivalents, in splendid hotels); and so forth, as well as operas and ballets. Although, as Weber has indicated, upper-class events generally engaged the best performers, many offered only frivolous music. Despite the fact that an artistic education was becoming *de rigueur* for the elite,[106] the development of sophisticated musical taste did not automatically result, as F.-J. Fétis noted in 1833:

> A revolution recently brought about in musical taste had injected into people's minds a false and worthless idea, namely, that this art was nothing but a fashionable object whose ephemeral results were destined to have but a short existence and to be reduced to nothingness, after having burned themselves out with a more or less lively flame.[107]

Middle-class audiences had far fewer opportunities to enjoy public musical events, though several respectable concert societies answered the increasing demand for affordable public concerts, among them the Société Philharmonique de la Ville de Paris, the Société de l'Athénée Musical, the Association des Artistes-Musiciens, the Grande Société Philharmonique de Paris, the Société des Jeunes-Artistes, the Concerts Populaires, the Société Nationale des Beaux-Arts, the Athénée, and the Concerts de l'Opéra. Occasional nonseries concerts by virtuosos of the second rank, café concerts, and outdoor concerts were also enjoyed by the middle classes.

As the lower classes had limited buying power, their public musical entertainment primarily comprised, in the first half of the century, café concerts, outdoor concerts, and concerts by amateurs.[108] Early attempts to introduce "art" music to lower-class audiences were short-lived. Most noteworthy of these were the Concerts Valentino where, for one franc, one could hear traditional works and dance music; both sorts of music were offered in hopes of attracting a wider public,[109] but it became clear there and elsewhere that the public preferred dancing to listening.

The relationship between admission fees and attendance was most evident within the lower classes. Cost apparently mattered little to the rich, who could easily afford the top prices, but the reduction of admission charges from 75 centimes to 50 had a substantial effect on attendance, as was proved when the Concerts Colonne began to undersell the Concerts Populaires by that amount in 1874.[110]

Other factors that most attracted audiences were repertory, performers, and environment. Repertory was a significant determinant mainly among the wealthy (and among musicians). As Weber noted, the battle between "taste-publics" was most apparent among those who could afford all options and who had enough experience to know what music they enjoyed. Although before 1850 the lower classes appeared to prefer "popular" music, during many seasons there was little choice of repertory at events they could afford.

The quality (or reputation) of performers carried more weight than repertory for most listeners. Announcements regarding upcoming concerts in the *Revue et gazette musicale* emphasized performers but often neglected the program. Personalities were particularly important to audiences interested in "popular" music, who were eager to hear the most celebrated virtuosos. A less personal emphasis on performance occurred at concerts of "art" music for the elite, as they expected to hear professionals. (Some *salons* were an exception, but the best engaged professionals.) Lower-class concerts were sometimes presented by amateurs, though talented young musicians used these events to launch themselves into the musical scene.

Frequent (sometimes yearly) glowing reports of redecoration in the favorite cafés demonstrate how important environment was for less expensive events. Audiences who could not afford to hear the best performers were evidently eager to listen in the most elegant (or, at least, fashionable) surroundings. As Weber noted, concern with fashion carried over to repertory and performers too. Other forms of entertainment, such as dancing and fireworks, also attracted persons to café concerts.

Good attendance at various concerts, as mentioned regularly in contemporary journals, seems incompatible with the brief life of most concert series. (As Berlioz demonstrated, financial failure did not necessarily indicate poor attendance: after expenses and taxes were paid, entrepreneurs sometimes lost money, even with a full house. Berlioz's concerts were, because of the large forces engaged and the tenuous position of his music with contemporary audiences, more prone to financial failure than many enterprises.) Certainly, sizable audiences attended café concerts, outdoor concerts, *salons,* concerts of major virtuosos, and certain series, notably the Société des Concerts du Conservatoire and Concerts Populaires. Poor attendance did, however, cause the downfall of several series, either through closure, or by forcing series managers to change the nature of the concerts in an attempt to attract a wider public.

Finally, the relationship between programs and the class structure of the audience changed as the century progressed. While upper-class events embraced the entire spectrum of "taste" throughout the period, members of the lower and middle classes would less likely have attended "high-culture" concerts in the first half of the century; most had had little previous exposure to "art" music, and as they had minimal access to *salons* and subscription concerts, opportunities to gain familiarity with it were rare. The few societies that attempted to present "art" music to the general public succumbed to popular taste. After mid-century, however (and particularly in the 1860s), organizations such as the Concerts Populaires, Séances Populaires, Concerts des Beaux-Arts, and the Athénée sold inexpensive tickets in large numbers, attracting neophytes to performances of traditional orchestral and chamber music. At last, all varieties of instrumental music were available to the entire population.

Chapters 2 and 3 have painted a picture of musical life in nineteenth-century Paris, surveyed events offering instrumental music, and examined the relationship between musical entertainment and its audience. The major variables affecting the audience's selection of this entertainment seem to have been time and money: time, in that the musical scene changed between 1828 and 1871, bringing new sorts of musical events and opening public concerts to larger audiences; money, in that the wealthy always had more musical options than did others.

One striking discovery of this survey is the sheer quantity of musical events that took place during most musical seasons. The amount of concert acitivity, which increased steadily as the period progressed, was not lost on contemporary observers (even if the quality was often deplored). An anonymous contributor to the *Gazette musicale de Paris* viewed Parisian musical life in 1834 as being at an all-time high, citing especially the new musical establishments, new artistic associations, new music periodicals, and developments in vocal music.[111] Twenty years later, Paul Duprat described the concert season as "unabating," adding that pianists were in the majority among performers.[112] In 1857 Blanchard wrote that the thriving concert scene provided too much for a critic to attend, and probably too much to be economically viable for the artists.[113]

Although interest in all instrumental music developed and expanded throughout the period, the reawakened appreciation of chamber music, leading after 1846 to regular public concerts thereof, is particularly notable. In 1856 Blanchard reported that chamber music concerts were still gaining popularity; he called it "l'ère du quatuor."[114]

The development of "popular music" events, beginning in the mid-1830s, effected a major revolution in concert life of the nineteenth century—the advent of public musical entertainment for the lower classes. Not too much earlier, concerts or even performances (in the sense of practiced, polished renditions) of secular works had been almost exclusively the domain of the aristocracy; "plebians" might have gathered to perform chamber music with each other or for small groups of acquaintances. In the nineteenth century, public concerts, presented by professionals (or, at least, talented amateurs), were established for all classes, and the earliest concerts to attract those in the lower-income brackets were programs of "popular" music. As the period progressed, "art" music drew wider audiences and eventually there was little if any class distinction between "popular" and "art" music.

Apart from the spreading of "art" music to lower-class audiences, trends involving the relative appreciation of "art" music versus "popular" are not always clear. Berlioz remarked in 1840 that Beethoven had lost his snob appeal and that "the dilettantes in the boxes no longer feel they have to keep up the pose which they had been assuming for ten years past. They are frankly bored."[115] And there were continued laments that *salons* were inundated by *fantaisies, romances,* and so forth. Weber, however, has concluded that by the 1840s audiences were tiring of virtuosity and flashiness, and wanted more substantial music.[116] Regardless of what audiences wanted, what they got was a period in the early 1840s when "art" and "popular" music were mixed on many programs, followed by growing emphasis on "art" music at many series. The outdoor and café concerts that flourished in the late 1850s and 1860s may have been a reaction against the increasing (but still relative) neglect of "popular" works by the better musicians. The division into "art" and "popular" concerts was never clear-cut; many musical events continued with "mixed" programs, and the rich sponsored whatever they liked at *salons,* but there appears to have been a slow, partial separation (eventually among all classes) along the lines of Weber's "taste-publics." Weber, incidentally, has suggested that the continuous battle between followers of "popular" and "art" music led to changes for both groups, for virtuosos (who originally pursued the "popular" market) were gradually attracted to "art" music, thereby exposing their followers to that repertory while simultaneously raising the performance standards of "art" music (and inspiring, if not forcing, those who *had been* playing "art" music to do the same).[117]

Regardless of what music was preferred by French listeners, the new role of the middle and lower classes as buyers of musical entertainment led to a new relationship between performers (now more independent than ever before) and audiences. As Weber has stated, by 1848 a commercial concert world existed, over which the middle class exerted substantial control, and from 1848 to 1870 there was "a consolidation of the concert world in its modern form."[118]

How, though, does one reconcile this expansion of concert activity with the repeated pessimistic statements of keen and sincere contemporaries such as Berlioz? Although Berlioz is not renowned for complete factual accuracy in, for instance, his own memoirs, it would be presumptuous to claim that Berlioz's understanding of nineteenth-century Parisian musical life was erroneous. Berlioz wrote, for example, in 1846:

> Here [in Paris] we have nothing but shabby scores, sprinkled with shabby melodies, accompanied by shabby orchestras, sung by shabby singers, and listened to by a shabby public, which fortunately never listens to them twice and forgets them at once.[119]

This comment concerned the quality of the Parisian musical scene (composition, performance, and appreciation) rather than the quantity of musical activity, and was perhaps just. But Berlioz seems to have distorted the facts when he wrote in 1862 that the public was interested only in *opéras comiques*.[120] The Concerts Populaires, established a few months earlier, had achieved immediate popular success with orchestral programs and several other instrumental series appear (from this chronological distance) to have been thriving.

Berlioz's opinions were not without prejudice (he naturally wanted more Parisian support for his own music and was, after all, attempting to influence readers to change their attitudes), yet most of his complaints were valid. It *was* difficult to obtain good performances of instrumental music, especially contemporary works. It *was* difficult to persuade the Opéra to attempt anything new or different. It *was* difficult to cope with frivolous Parisian taste, and the overwhelming popularity of Herz, the Musards, Offenbach, and others. All of this was understandably discouraging, yet Berlioz may have ignored slow improvements that occurred during his lifetime. This act of neglect may be attributed partly to human nature: constructive persons like Berlioz are likely to express themselves about matters that bother them, circumstances in which they see room for improvement; as letters to editors demonstrate, persons rarely write to express approval of the status quo, except perhaps in response to criticism or threatening change. Too, and perhaps more to the point, one who lives through an era may be more aware of sudden changes than of gradual trends. Thus Berlioz fumed when economic recessions, revolutions, new musical fads, or personal failures made the outlook bleak, but was less likely to have noticed gradual advances made in the course of 40 years. These trends are more obvious to historians.

Finally, apart from Berlioz's thoughts, it would be wrong to suggest that instrumental music enjoyed complete acceptance in French culture before 1871. Critics and the state deserve as much blame as musicians and audiences for this neglect. In weekly reviews and annual summaries, contemporary journals treated opera as primary, relegating all other music to the background.[121] The Opéra, Opéra-Comique, Théâtre-Italien, Comédie Française, and the Société des Concerts were subsidized, and other organizations found it difficult to break even. Through taxes, limitations on the number of concerts that single organizations could present, price regulation, prohibition of vocal music, denial of concert halls, and through a rule that prevented orchestra members of royal theatres (including the Opéra) from participating in public concerts even up to three years after their retirement (a rule that discouraged departure from these orchestras),[122] the government thwarted the success of public concerts.

Despite these obstacles, interest in and performances of instrumental music grew steadily. The increased emphasis on instrumental music after the Franco-Prussian War was not, as is sometimes stated, revolutionary; a new appreciation for instrumental works had been developing for years.

4

Repertory

From 1828 through 1870, I have records of 7646 performances of instrumental works in Paris.[1] The number 7646 has no significance as an exact integer. As stated in chapter 2, for some concert series fewer than half the programs are known. The announcements for many concerts mentioned only that the program would include (for example) "works of Mozart, Beethoven, and Onslow"; similarly, there are series described in which works of (for example) Haydn, Beethoven, and Mendelssohn were reportedly heard "regularly," but for which few specific programs are recorded. Worse yet, no composers were named in several contemporary program announcements,[2] and there were many concerts never announced at all. In establishing the number 7646 only fairly specific references to individual works have been counted.[3] Thus, the actual number of performances of instrumental works in Paris from 1828 through 1870 was certainly much higher.[4]

The 7646 known performances, then, are significant only in that they provide a large sample of the contemporary repertory. An examination of these performances reveals which composers were most popular and which individual works were most performed. For example, among known performances of instrumental works, those of Beethoven's works make up 23 percent of the total, nearly triple the percentage of any other composer's; from this it should not be concluded that exactly 23 percent of all works performed were Beethoven's, but it could safely be assumed that Beethoven was by far the most performed composer of the period. Such statistics not only provide a picture of contemporary taste, but also suggest which works might have been best known and which, therefore, may have served as models for contemporary French composers.

The list of 7646 performances encompasses the works of about 469 composers,[5] plus many compositions for which the author is unknown, grouped under the heading "anonymous." Certainly if all programs were available and if the composers of anonymous works were known, the number of composers who contributed to the repertory of instrumental music would increase greatly; it seems not likely that it would surpass 600. Of the 469 known composers, 191 received only one known performance, and another 131 fewer than five known performances. Only 87 composers are known to have been performed ten or more times. Again, if all performances were known, the number of performances for most composers would increase significantly. But it is clear that the number of composers whose music was performed regularly was relatively small.

A close relationship between repertory and publication (particularly of works by foreign composers) might be supposed. Carse has mentioned that the repertory of symphonies by Mozart and Schubert performed in the nineteenth century was limited by a lack of printed parts; by 1837 only four of Mozart's symphonies were available in Paris (the "Prague" and the last three) and as late as 1870 only two of Schubert's symphonies (numbers Eight and Nine) had been printed.[6] Publication, however, hardly guaranteed performance. Publishers' advertisements abound with works for which no performances are known. There are even a surprising number of composers who had several works published, but whose names appeared on no known programs; perhaps most notable among this unfortunate group is one Grenet (presumably Claude de Grenet, 1771–1851), whose 21 quartets, 24 quintets, and 3 sextets, advertised for sale by Gaveaux *aîné* in 1828, are not known to have been performed in public. Even published works that eventually became favorites suffered temporary obscurity: Mendelssohn's Piano Quartet Op. 1 was advertised in 1828 and his Octet in 1834, yet none of his instrumental works is known to have been programmed in Paris before 1839. Undoubtedly, if all programs were known, the discrepancy between works published and works performed would be reduced; most composers who published works intended for the concert hall must have attained some performances. But the number of printed works for which there is no record of performance, and the number of works programmed before being published, indicate less direct relationship between publication and performance than might be expected.

Identifying works on concert programs is a serious problem in studying the repertory of mid-nineteenth-century Paris. Before the introduction of Köchel numbers (1862), Deutsch numbers (1950), and other numbers from thematic catalogs, labelling of performed works was imprecise. Many times works were identified only by key; this aided knowledgeable musicians of the time more than it does their twentieth-century counterparts, for they knew the limits of contemporary repertory. For example, "Mozart's Symphony in E-flat" could mean any of four works today, but in mid-nineteenth century France it signified only the work now identified as K. 543. Likewise, "Beethoven's Symphony in F" apparently referred only to the Eighth Symphony; the Sixth was always called the "Pastorale." But identification by key was not always so specific; "Beethoven: String Quartet in F" could have signified then, as now, any of three quartets. Compositions were also identified by number, but the numbering systems provided by publishers differed from systems developed more recently. Haydn string quartets were rarely identified by opus numbers, but commonly by the Pleyel and Eulenberg numbers, still used on occasion. His symphonies, however, were identified by Sieber's numbering system (which runs only to 53). Mozart's piano concertos were known by Richault's numbers, and his string quartets by three numbering systems—opus numbers (used by J. André, Boyer, Sieber, and Forster) and two other systems, making positive identification impossible in some instances: contemporary programs included string quartets "no. 4" in C and E-flat, "no. 6" in C and G, "no. 7" in C and D, "no. 9" in A and F, and so forth. Other equally problematic cases abound.

Repertory: The Broad Picture

Table 4.1 lists all composers whose instrumental works received 30 or more known performances in Paris from 1828 through 1870. The amount that five Germanic composers were performed is striking: performances of works by Beethoven, Mozart, Mendelssohn, Haydn, and Weber total 3802—roughly half of all known performances. By mid-century, all of these composers were deceased, and all but Mendelssohn were renowned as established "masters"—that is, for contemporary audiences their names equalled or exceeded in significance the quality of their music. Weber, the least played of these five, received well over three times as many performances as the next-ranked composer, Berlioz, who arranged performances of his own music by organizing concerts and festivals and directing the short-lived Grande Société Philharmonique de Paris. Close behind Berlioz were several French composers whose popularity has not endured: Adolphe Blanc (who became renowned at *séances* of chamber music in the 1860s), Charles Dancla (who, like Berlioz, vigorously promoted his own music), Georges Onslow (who paid for the publication of his own works), and Louise Farrenc (one of the most successful woman composers of the nineteenth century). Somewhat less often heard, but still having a notable number of significant works played, were nineteenth-century Frenchmen Emile Prudent, Camille Saint-Saëns, Félicien David, Henri Brod, Henri Herz, Louis Lacombe, Charles Gounod, Léon Kreutzer, Georges Pfeiffer, Henri Reber, and Théodore Gouvy. Less substantial works of other French composers (or composers active in France) appeared often on programs; these included overtures of Meyerbeer, Méhul,

Table 4.1 Known Performances of Instrumental Works in Paris, 1828–1870

(Figures in column A represent the number of known performances of instrumental works—or excerpts thereof—by the composer listed adjacently. Column B shows what percent the matching number in column A represents of all known performances. For example, Beethoven's 1790 performances represent 23 percent of the total, 7646.)

Composer	A	B
Beethoven	1790	23%
Mozart	586	8
Mendelssohn	549	7
Haydn	482	6
Weber	395	5
Berlioz	121	2
Schumann	115	2
Blanc	113	1
Hummel	112	1
Dancla, Charles	96	1
Onslow	92	1
Bach, J. S.	88	1
Rossini	83	1
Farrenc, Louise	73	under 1
Bériot	61	under 1
Meyerbeer	60	under 1
Wagner	60	under 1
Schubert	57	under 1
Vieuxtemps	56	under 1
Alard	55	under 1
Prudent	51	under 1
Spohr	51	under 1
Mayseder	49	under 1
Méhul	49	under 1
Saint-Saëns	47	under 1
David, Félicien	40	under 1
Rubinstein, Anton	39	under 1
Boccherini	38	under 1
Viotti	38	under 1
Chopin	37	under 1
Rosenhain	32	under 1
Brod	31	under 1
Litolff	30	under 1
436 others	1861	24
Anonymous	209	3
469 composers + anonymous	7646	(100%)

Gluck, and Auber, and solos of little musical interest by instrumental virtuosos Alard, Franchomme, Baillot, Tulou, and Chevillard.

The Bach revival reached Paris by midcentury; his works were seldom played there before 1850, though according to Albert Palm Baillot and friends had performed several works of Bach in concerts played between 1809 and 1813.[7] Bach joined Mozart, Haydn, Boccherini, and Gluck as eighteenth-century composers whose music became a substantial portion of the concert repertory.

Table 4.2 lists all composers whose major instrumental works received 20 or more known performances in Paris from 1828 through 1870.[8] As in table 4.1, these figures are not to be regarded as exact; the real number of performances of major works was considerably higher. The figures should indicate roughly, however, the relative amounts that various composers' major works were performed. Beethoven, Mozart, Mendelssohn, and Haydn again dominate the list, but Weber's position is no longer so prominent, for 248 (over 62 percent) of the performances of his works

Table 4.2 Known Performances of Major Works (Listed by Composer) in Paris, 1828–1870

Composer	Performances
Beethoven	1381
Mozart	409
Mendelssohn	361
Haydn	307
Blanc	105
Weber	98
Hummel	97
Schumann	88
Onslow	76
Farrenc, Louise	68
Dancla, Charles	66
Bach, J. S.	40
Schubert	39
Spohr	36
Mayseder	32
Rubinstein, Anton	32
Saint-Saëns	30
Boccherini	28
Rosenhain	26
Viotti	24
Berlioz	23
David, Félicien	23
Herz	22

involved overtures. Others whose overtures were performed often, Rossini, Wagner, Meyerbeer, and Méhul, had virtually no major instrumental works performed, and Berlioz, whose overtures and instrumental excerpts from large-scale works made up a significant part of the general repertory, had few performances of major instrumental works. Several contemporary French composers retained high positions on the list, among them Blanc, Onslow, Louise Farrenc, Charles Dancla, and Saint-Saëns, although their totals pale beside those of the most performed foreigners (see table 4.3).

Table 4.3 Known Performances of Major Instrumental Works by French and Non-French Composers, Paris, 1828–1870. (Listed are the seven French and seven non-French composers whose major works were performed most.)

French		**Non-French**	
Composer	*Performances*	*Composer*	*Performances*
Blanc	105	Beethoven	1381
Onslow	76	Mozart	409
Farrenc	68	Mendelssohn	361
Dancla	66	Haydn	307
Saint-Saëns	30	Weber	98
Berlioz	23	Hummel	97
David	23	Schumann	88
Total	391	Total	2741

Changes in the Repertory: A Chronological Study

A slow oscillation between experimental and relatively staid musical activity suggests division of the period 1828 to 1870 into six subperiods (first delineated in chapter 1). The experimental activity included not only the establishment of new concert societies and the search for larger audiences, but also the exploration of new music and promotion of genres that had been little performed previously. Thus the evolution of repertory helps to delimit the six subperiods.

Table 4.4 provides data on repertory in each of these subperiods.[9] Most striking in this table is the increase in the total number of known performances from about 70 per year in 1834–39 to about 310 per year in 1861–70. A small percentage of this change might be attributable to changes in reporting habits of contemporary journals (although there is no reason to believe this to be so), but such a dramatic increase can be attributed only to an actual increase in performances of instrumental works. Oddly, nineteenth-century journalists did not universally report the growing popularity of instrumental works; in fact, some commented on the declining state of instrumental music. It is conceivable that growing interest in all varieties of music, which journalists did notice (they were fond of citing statistics regarding the number of concerts that had taken place in a given year[10]), obscured the increased activity in instrumental music.

The lists in table 4.4 also indicate when the music of various individual composers was first performed regularly in Paris and how the popularity of these composers fluctuated as the nineteenth century progressed. Only a few composers maintained a relatively steady degree of popularity throughout the period. Beethoven's instrumental works, almost unknown in France before 1828, were thereafter ardently promoted by the Société des Concerts du Conservatoire and quickly gained astonishing acceptance. From about 1840 they consistently made up about 24 percent of the performed repertory. Only Weber's works enjoyed similarly steady success.

Most important, the lists in table 4.4 reflect changes in Parisian taste as the period progressed. Each subperiod deserves a detailed explanation.

1828–1833

The repertory during these years was characterized by an interest in relatively facile music—short, light works and flashy vehicles for virtuosos. Many of the most-performed composers were "composer-soloists"—that is, virtuosos who wrote music to display their own talents: the 20 performances of works by the Belgian violinist de Bériot comprised primarily violin solos (particularly *airs variés*) and violin concertos; the Austrian violinist Mayseder's 14 presentations included 11 violin solos; at his Paris concerts of 1831 and 1832, Paganini played almost exclusively his own solos and concertos;[11] and among the 11 known performances of the oboist Brod's works were eight oboe solos and an oboe concerto. Known performances of other most-programmed "composer-soloists" follow in abbreviated form: the violinist Habeneck—nine performances including seven violin solos and two excerpts from violin concertos; the oboist Vogt—nine performances, among them eight oboe solos; the cellist Franchomme—eight performances, all cello solos; the German pianist Kalkbrenner—eight performances, mainly works for piano and orchestra (his solo piano music is, by definition, not included in these statistics); the violinist Rode—eight performances, including six violin concertos (or movements thereof) and one violin solo; the flutist Tulou—seven performances, including solos, one flute concerto, and two chamber works

Table 4.4 Known Performances of Instrumental Works (Listed by Composer) in Paris, 1828–1870, in Six Periods (Columns "A" and "B" function as in Table 4.1)

1828–1833			1834–1839			1840–1846		
Composer	*A*	*B*	*Composer*	*A*	*B*	*Composer*	*A*	*B*
Beethoven	99	20%	Beethoven	120	29%	Beethoven	236	24%
Anonymous	66*	13	Weber	27	7	Weber	52	5
Bériot	20	4	Berlioz	18	4	Anonymous	52	5
Weber	20	4	Mozart	16	4	Mozart	47	5
Mayseder	14	3	Haydn	13	3	Berlioz	38	4
Berlioz	13	3	Bertini	11	3	Haydn	30	3
Haydn	13	3	Brod	11	3	Hummel	22	2
Paganini	11	3	Anonymous	10	2	Mendelssohn	22	2
Brod	11	2	Mayseder	8	2	Dancla	20	2
Mozart	11	2	Gallay	7	2	Onslow	17	2
Hiller, F.	10	2	Berr	6	1	Farrenc	16	2
Habeneck	9	2	Chevillard	6	1	Mayseder	16	2
Vogt	9	2	Kalkbrenner	6	1	Alard	14	1
Boccherini	8	2	Méhul	6	1	Osborne	13	1
Franchomme	8	2	Bériot	5	1	Spohr	12	1
Hummel	8	2	Dancla, C.	5	1	Chevillard	11	1
Kalkbrenner	8	2	Franchomme	5	1	Tulou	11	1
Onslow	8	2	79 others	123	30	Bériot	10	1
Rode	8	2				Méhul	10	1
Tulou	7	1				Rossini	10	1
Romberg, B.	6	1				Artôt	9	under 1
72 others	140	28				David, Fél.	9	under 1
						138 others	302	31
92 composers + anonymous	507		95 composers + anonymous	409		159 composers + anonymous	979	

*The actual number of reported performances of "anonymous" works was much higher; my figures include references to "anonymous" works when listed in programs with specific works, but do not consistently include references (particularly prevalent in the first sub-period) to programs of (for example) "solos for violin, flute, and cello".

1847–1853			1854–1860			1861–1870		
Composer	*A*	*B*	*Composer*	*A*	*B*	*Composer*	*A*	*B*
Beethoven	289	25%	Beethoven	346	24%	Beethoven	700	23%
Mozart	111	9	Mozart	136	9	Mendelssohn	339	11
Haydn	73	6	Mendelssohn	128	9	Mozart	265	9
Weber	61	5	Haydn	112	8	Haydn	241	8
Mendelssohn	59	5	Weber	64	4	Weber	171	6
Anonymous	43	4	Hummel	24	2	Schumann	95	3
Farrenc	24	2	Blanc	23	2	Blanc	83	3
Onslow	24	2	Bach, J. S.	21	1	Wagner	54	2
Hummel	22	2	Rossini	19	1	Meyerbeer	52	2
Rossini	20	2	Prudent	18	1	Bach, J. S.	41	1
Berlioz	19	2	Schumann	18	1	Dancla, C.	41	1
Bach, J. S.	18	2	Alard	14	under 1	Saint-Saëns	37	1
Dancla, C.	18	2	David, Fél.	14	under 1	Hummel	33	1
Méhul	13	1	Onslow	14	under 1	Schubert	31	under 1
Vieuxtemps	13	1	Gounod	13	under 1	Rossini	29	under 1
Gouvy	12	1	Mathias	13	under 1	Rubinstein	28	under 1
Prudent	12	1	Schubert	13	under 1	Berlioz	27	under 1
Bériot	11	under 1	Anonymous	13	under 1	Vieuxtemps	26	under 1
Spohr	11	under 1	147 others	467	32	Onslow	25	under 1
140 others	323	27				Anonymous	25	under 1
						Pfeiffer	23	under 1
						Farrenc	22	under 1
						Spohr	21	under 1
						187 others	696	22
158 composers + anonymous	1176		164 composers + anonymous	1470		209 composers + anonymous	3105	

involving flute; the cellist Bernhard Romberg—six performances, all concertos and solos.

The remaining most-performed composers of the first subperiod concentrated on more substantial genres. Beethoven's music soared to prominence because of Habeneck's efforts; about 70 percent of the 99 known performances of Beethoven's works were presented at the Conservatoire concerts. Thus orchestral works, particularly the Third, Fifth, Sixth, and Seventh Symphonies, were played more than chamber pieces. Although the instrumental sonatas and piano trios, which later became highly popular, were rarely heard, the string quartets were rendered both by quartets and by string orchestras. The Early and Middle quartets must have been played at chamber concerts that advertised "works of Beethoven," and particularly at Baillot's *séances,* but *known* performances of the Late quartets, promoted by the brothers Bohrer (and, to a lesser extent, by Baillot), were more numerous.

Surprisingly, in a city noted for conservative taste in instrumental music, two of the most-programmed composers were Weber and Berlioz. Weber, like Beethoven, was promulgated at the Conservatoire concerts. Unlike Beethoven, he became known for short works; all but one of his 20 known performances in the first subperiod involved overtures. Berlioz too became familiar via overtures, though the *Symphonie Fantastique* was heard in its entirety at least thrice.

Haydn and Mozart had not yet attained the acclaim they later enjoyed. The known performances of each are fewer than Weber's, though this statistic may be distorted by contemporary journalism, for orchestral concerts (which presented Weber's overtures) were better reported than chamber music concerts or *salons* (where works of Haydn and Mozart were evidently heard). The early *known* performances of Haydn's works involve symphonies or excerpts thereof (most of them by the Conservatoire orchestra) and string quartets.[12]

The remaining foreigners who experienced notable success were Ferdinand Hiller, Hummel, and Boccherini. Hiller had gained early renown as a pianist; among performances of his works in the early 1830s were three renditions of piano concertos (one only an excerpt), but also symphonies and overtures. Hummel was known for piano concertos and septets, while Boccherini was represented mainly by string quintets, performed at Baillot's *séances.* Other than Berlioz, the only native composer of "art" music to gain much recognition was Onslow. His symphonies were essayed at the Conservatoire concerts and his string quintets at the series of Baillot and the brothers Bohrer.

Because instrumental music had been so neglected in Paris before 1828, the repertory in the years immediately thereafter was somewhat experimental. Musicians tried unfamiliar works (Beethoven's symphonies are the most obvious example) and, sometimes in cooperation with entrepreneurs, attempted to attract listeners from a population that was largely unversed in instrumental "art" music. Despite the experimentation, known programs named only 92 composers, a considerably smaller number than were represented in later subperiods. This figure may be unrealistically low, for a large segment of known performances of the first subperiod involved works for which the composer was not mentioned. Some instances of anonymity can be attributed to inadequate publicity and some to the custom of not providing printed programs (particularly at *salons*). Anonymity also occurred in connection with virtuosic works, for composers of these took a back seat to performers;[13] it is not coincidental that the 66 recorded performances of works by "anonymous" authors include 58 instrumental solos.

1834–1839

In the mid to late 1830s "popular" music—including the works of "composer-soloists"—found a home in the newly established outdoor and café concerts; an apparent consequence of this development was the greater concentration on "art" music in concert halls. This partial separation of concerts that offered "art" music from those that presented "popular" would explain (given that programs of "popular" concerts were rarely announced or reviewed) the smaller number of *known* performances of instrumental works (from about 85 per year in the first subperiod to under 70 in the second),[14] the smaller portion of the known repertory devoted to virtuosic works, and the decrease in "anonymous" works. It would be wrong, however, to stress this separation, as several series still programmed both "art" and "popular" music.

Beginning in the 1830s, a standard repertory of "art" music (which, with additions and modifications, has continued into the twentieth century) was becoming evident. In the second subperiod known performances of works by Beethoven, Weber, Mozart, and Haydn comprised 48 percent of the total performances (up from 28 percent in the previous subperiod) as each of these composer's works was further explored. Beethoven was at the apex of his popularity. His First, Second, Eighth, and Ninth Symphonies joined the standard repertory, and though his chamber works lagged behind his orchestral in acceptance, the Septet Opus 20, "Archduke" Piano Trio, and "Kreutzer" Violin Sonata became better known. Weber's popularity grew as the French discovered his instrumental works (apart from overtures, which continued to receive frequent performances). Mozart also received more attention (especially the late symphonies and various chamber works), while Haydn was represented almost exclusively by symphonies.

Among other composers of "art" music, Berlioz retained a prominent position by presenting performances of *Harold en Italie,* the *Symphonie Fantastique,* and overtures. Henri-Jérôme Bertini (1798–1876) enjoyed brief fame through performances of his chamber music (mainly for large ensembles), particularly his sextets. Previously renowned for violin solos, Mayseder gradually established himself as an author of chamber works. Méhul and young Charles Dancla (1817–1907) attained minor niches in the "art" music repertory with overtures.

The dwindling number of composer-soloists who remained popular in concert halls included the horn player Gallay, the clarinettist Berr, the cellists Chevillard and Franchomme, and the violinist de Bériot.

1840–1846

Most remarkable in the third subperiod was the impressive increase in mentioned performances—from under 70 per year in the previous subperiod to about 140. This occurred despite the cessation of well-established series and the dearth of new societies. The replacement of "permanent" organizations by one-year series and an unusual number of nonseries concerts apparently led to renewed experimentation in repertory. Not only were the best-established composers played somewhat less (proportionately), but the number of composers known to have been programmed increased by roughly two-thirds, from 95 in the previous era to 159. The discontinuation of several "popular" series evidently also caused changes in concert repertory: composer-soloists made a temporary recovery in concert halls and again there were many works played for which the author is not known.

If the position of established masters was slightly diminished, it nonetheless remained strong. Beethoven had gained adulation throughout Paris, and even without the increasing support of the Conservatoire concerts would easily have remained the most-performed composer. His piano trios and the *Leonore* and *Fidelio* overtures were added to the standard repertory. Mozart and Haydn retained their popularity but were still renowned only for a small body of works; Mozart's piano concertos were slowly being discovered. Similarly, Weber's list of performed works expanded little, though his "Invitation à la valse," in an orchestral version by Berlioz, began its climb to substantial popularity.

Berlioz continued to promote his recent works successfully. After *Harold en Italie,* however, his major compositions were vocal: the *Requiem* (first performed in 1837), *Roméo et Juliette* (1839), *Symphonie funèbre et triomphale* (1840), and *La Damnation de Faust* (1846). The overtures, *Harold,* and instrumental excerpts from the above-named vocal works kept his name on instrumental programs. Like Weber and Berlioz, Rossini and Méhul were familiar to concert audiences via overtures.

A significant development of the third subperiod was increased programming of chamber and orchestral works by native composers other than Berlioz. Onslow's chamber music was further explored. Charles Dancla, commonly regarded as a composer-soloist (for he often performed in his own *duo concertantes* and *symphonies concertantes*), also programmed his own string quartets. Louise Farrenc was represented by chamber works for piano and strings, plus a few orchestral pieces. Finally, instrumental works of Félicien David, which never achieved real popularity, were programmed occasionally from about 1840; best known in the 1840s were his symphonies.

Among foreign newcomers to the "most-performed" list, the most important, considering later developments, was Mendelssohn, who had several Parisian premieres in the early 1840s; the First Piano Concerto, Third Symphony, and *Hebrides Overture* were the first of his works to be securely established in the Parisian repertory. Spohr was represented by various orchestral and chamber works, and the Irish pianist-composer Osborne (who gave concerts of his own music in Paris) exclusively by piano trios. The chamber works of Mayseder were popular at this time, as were those of Hummel.

Virtuosic works by composer-soloists remained prevalent, though some of the musicians were new. Joining the already popular Bériot, Chevillard, and Tulou on the list of most-performed composers, were Dancla, the Belgian violinist Artôt, and the French violinist Delphin Alard (1815–88), who gained lasting fame performing classical chamber works but was familiar as a composer through violin solos and concertos.

1847–1853

The fourth subperiod commences with the advent of successful public chamber music series. Suddenly, chamber works of Beethoven, Mozart, Haydn, Farrenc, Onslow, Hummel, and Dancla were heard regularly in concert halls. Simultaneously, four new orchestral societies (the Union Musicale, Grande Société Philharmonique, Société Sainte-Cécile, and the Société des Jeunes-Artistes) allowed orchestral music to hold its own. The increase in performances of chamber and orchestral music can be attributed, then, mainly to the growing number of series, but also, as will be shown below, to declining interest in virtuosic music.

The yearly average of known performances climbed nearly 20 percent, from roughly 140 in subperiod three to 168. This figure would have jumped even more had not the February Revolution halted most musical life in 1848.[15] Except for the Conservatoire concerts and various benefit events, musical activity was restricted to programs of patriotic songs for chorus and/or wind band; many musical events were held outdoors. Regular concert attenders fled the city, and musical *salons* ceased almost completely. If 1848 is counted as only a half-season, then the yearly average of known performances in subperiod four rises to about 180.

While the number of performances was increasing, the repertory was becoming somewhat more narrowly focussed. Performances of works by Beethoven, Haydn, Mozart, Weber, and Mendelssohn, which comprised 40 percent of the performed repertory in the third subperiod, now made up 50 percent. Most of this gain derives from the advancing popularity of Mozart, Haydn, and Mendelssohn. Mozart's renown grew via quintets and trios, to a lesser extent piano quartets and piano concertos, and overtures to *Don Giovanni* and *Marriage of Figaro*. There was sudden interest in Haydn's string quartets (previously seldom played in concerts), due partly to the efforts of the "Société Alard-Franchomme." Mendelssohn's success was still only beginning (relative to his later status), but in this period his Fourth Symphony, *Midsummer Night's Dream* music, and string quartets all became standards.

The first of J. S. Bach's works to experience revival were keyboard concertos and pieces for a violin soloist with or without accompaniment. Other composers who were much performed at this time, all of them only temporarily popular, were the Belgian violinist Henri Vieuxtemps (represented by violin concertos), Frenchman Théodore Gouvy (symphonies and overtures), and French pianist Emile Prudent (best known for his first piano concerto—the Concerto-Symphonie, Opus 34).

Meanwhile, Beethoven, Farrenc, Onslow, and Hummel maintained their status, largely because of the chamber music explosion. Beethoven's Late string quartets, string trios Opus 9, and various violin sonatas were played with increasing frequency. Overtures kept Weber and Rossini on concert programs. Berlioz, who was no longer writing instrumental works, and Dancla experienced a decline, and composer-soloists assumed a lesser role in the concert scene.

1854–1860

In the fifth subperiod the number of known performances of instrumental music again rose significantly—to about 210 per year. Chamber works found eager performers at several new series, among them the *séances* of Lebouc, the programs of the Société des Quatuors de Mendelssohn, and, at the very end of the subperiod, Lamoureux's *séances*. Orchestral series were relatively scarce; after the Société Sainte-Cécile was discontinued in 1855 the only orchestras that met regularly were the Société des Concerts du Conservatoire and the Société des Jeunes-Artistes. Thus chamber music attained a position of unprecedented strength in concert halls, and the ensembles that presented this genre sought out previously unfamiliar (but not necessarily recent) works.

The performed repertory was more conservative and Germanic than ever before. The six most-performed composers had all been active east of the Rhine, and all were deceased. The number of known performances by Paris's "favorite five" (Beethoven, Haydn, Mendelssohn, Mozart, and Weber) increased to 53 percent of the total. And though music by 164 composers was essayed at least once, the number of composers each of whose performances made up one percent or more of the total was only 11 (in previous subperiods it had been as high as 20).

Beethoven, Mozart, Weber, Hummel, Bach, and Prudent each held a fairly stable position in the repertory, though performers, still experimenting, introduced some works of these composers that had been unfamiliar previously. Beethoven became known increasingly for Middle and Late string quartets, piano trios, and cello sonatas; Weber for chamber works; and Prudent for several light pieces involving piano and orchestra. Haydn's works, particularly symphonies, were played more than before and Mendelssohn's popularity absolutely blossomed as Parisians listened to his string quartets, piano trios, cello sonatas, and the Violin Concerto in E minor.

Several contemporary Frenchmen won recognition. Adolphe Blanc achieved public success at an unusually early age with several chamber works.[16] Not quite as popular were the symphonies of Charles Gounod (played by the Société des Jeunes-Artistes) and orchestral works of Georges Mathias. Félicien David, renowned earlier for symphonic odes, presented his chamber works, primarily string quintets, at a series of concerts he organized in 1857. Alard continued to perform his own violin concertos and solos.

Among foreigners, Schumann and Schubert experienced rapidly growing esteem. Schumann was practically unknown in France before 1853, but his chamber music (particularly the Piano Quintet) and the Third Symphony won fame in the late 1850s. Schubert's piano trios and string quartets gained appreciation slowly, but the dispersion of his symphonies was still limited by the lack of printed parts.

Interest in Berlioz, Dancla, Farrenc, Onslow, and Rossini apparently declined. Berlioz had no new instrumental compositions and was no longer promoting his oeuvre in France so ardently, while Onslow's works were already beginning to fade into obscurity. Composer-soloists were less prominent on programs and anonymous works, particularly solos, were no longer as frequently mentioned in announcements and reviews.

1861–1870

The repertory for the final subperiod before the Franco-Prussian War is characterized not only by continued expansion in the number of performances of instrumental works (this expansion can be attributed largely to the establishment of the Concerts Populaires, which programmed over 1000 instrumental works from 1861 through 1870), but also by continued standardization; the works of only 14 composers constituted 70 percent of the performances (in earlier subperiods the top 14 composers had received between 50 and 66 percent of the total performances). This select list of most-performed composers included Paris's "favorite five," whose combined performances now totalled 55 percent of all performances; living composers (Blanc, Wagner, Meyerbeer, Saint-Saëns, and Dancla); deceased composers whose works were belatedly becoming known (Bach, Schubert, and Schumann); and, finally, Hummel, whose music was already well known.

The most notable change among the "favorite five" was the steadily climbing popularity of Mendelssohn, who jumped ahead of Mozart to become the second most-performed composer. Most of Mendelssohn's gain was effected by the many performances of his orchestral works (particularly the overtures, the *Midsummer Night's Dream* music, and the concertos, all often performed at the Concerts Populaires); but the piano trios also accounted for a large share of his performances. Beethoven held his own in the repertory but, as with Mendelssohn, his orchestral works (especially overtures, excerpts from *Prometheus,* orchestrated versions of the Septet, and symphonies) received emphasis. Mozart's and Haydn's symphonies were played nearly twice as often as in the previous period.[17]

Robert Schumann and Adolphe Blanc made astonishing gains in popularity. Schumann, aided only minimally by the establishment of the Société Schumann in 1870, became the most-performed composer after the "favorite five." All genres of his oeuvre won appreciation, but particuarly his orchestral works; several of his compositions received their Paris premieres. The prolific Blanc became the most popular native composer of instrumental works by far; his new chamber works appeared on programs regularly, especially at the *séances* of Gouffé and Lebouc.

Among other living composers on the list, Wagner and Meyerbeer were represented by overtures and opera excerpts; works in several genres by young Saint-Saëns gained quick acceptance; and Dancla's repertory of performed works was little changed.

Bach remained popular, as solo violin works and orchestral pieces (mainly excerpts from the suites) were explored. Schubert's increasing number of devotees were undoubtedly pleased by the publication of his Unfinished Symphony in 1866.

Performed somewhat less, but gaining fame, were works of Anton Rubinstein (chamber works and the "Ocean" Symphony) and Frenchman Georges Pfeiffer (piano trios, piano concertos, and other orchestral and chamber works with piano). Continuing in or returning to the standard repertory were Berlioz, Farrenc, Onslow, Rossini, Spohr (some of whose violin concertos were revived), and Vieuxtemps. Descending in popularity at various rates were Hummel, Prudent, Alard, David, Gouvy (who was now spending most of his time in Germany), Mathias, and Méhul.

Summary

Apart from the rapidly expanding devotion to instrumental music in Paris, various trends are observable concerning the composers, genres, and styles of music preferred. Perhaps most significant was the establishment of certain composers as acknowledged masters, and certain works as "standards." Many of the most-performed composers at the beginning of the period were contemporaries whose works were briefly fashionable but have long been forgotten; the most popular composers at the end of the period included past masters and a handful of contemporaries, several of whom have remained highly esteemed.[18]

The nineteenth century is commonly regarded as a time in which interest in music of earlier periods blossomed. Certainly it was the first period in which instrumental works composed 50 or more years earlier were performed so extensively, and the first in which the idea of a "permanent" standard repertory existed. A well-known manifestation of nineteenth-century historical interest is the "Bach revival"; but the very term "Bach revival" seems to imply a distinction between Bach and other early composers who, having been celebrated during their lifetimes, presumably never lost their popularity. The concepts of a "Haydn revival" or "Mozart revival" in the nineteenth century are not familiar. While this distinction is valid, it is, when applied to instrumental music in Paris, too neat. In a sense, most instrumental music experienced a revival there after 1828, for the composition and performance of chamber and symphonic works had dwindled after the Revolution and was at a particularly low ebb in the period from 1816 (when regular student *exercices* at the

Conservatoire ceased) to 1828 (when the Société des Concerts du Conservatoire was established).[19]

Separately from this general instrumental revival, Haydn and Mozart experienced their own less obvious revivals. It is true that neither had been forgotten as an important historical figure (though Sophie Leo reported in 1817 that Mozart was completely ignored as a composer of operas),[20] that connoisseurs such as Baillot continued to perform their works in *salons,*[21] and that certain of their symphonies were kept alive at the student *exercices* of the Conservatoire prior to 1816; as indicated above, however, in the subperiod from 1828 to 1833 relatively few of their works were played, and their combined known performances made up less than five percent of the repertory.[22] As the period continued, more of their works gained appreciation; by the 1860s their combined known performances made up over 16 percent of the total. Although the "revival" of Haydn and Mozart between 1828 and 1870 in Paris is not comparable to Bach's, their status as "masters" was certainly confirmed and fortified during this period.

Beethoven, on the other hand, was less revived than discovered. His music was hardly known in Paris during his lifetime, but with aid from the Conservatoire concerts its popularity skyrocketed immediately after his death.[23] His name became magic, whether or not the audience knew his music. Likewise, Mendelssohn was discovered but, happily, during his lifetime. Others who, through revival, discovery, or popularity continued from a previous era, became (or started to become) acknowledged as "masters" in Paris before 1870 were Weber, Schumann, Bach, Wagner, Schubert, and Saint-Saëns.

Concurrent with, and inseparable from, the establishment of "master" composers was a change in the genres of instrumental music most appreciated. In 1820 Spohr wrote from Paris that

> all here . . . strive only to shine by mechanical execution . . . in order to create a sensation with it before the public. . . . Hence one seldom or never hears in the musical *réunions* here an earnest well-digested piece of music, such as a quartet or a quintet of our great masters; everyone produces his showpiece; you hear nothing but *airs variés, rondos favoris, nocturnes,* and the like trifles. . . .[24]

This phenomenon was still much in evidence in the 1830s. Although symphonies and a few chamber works were introduced, the most prevalent genres were overtures, concertos, and solos. To Parisian audiences, virtuosos were more celebrated than composers, who, as mentioned, often remained anonymous; shallow works of "composer-soloists" were ubiquitous.[25]

The appeal of virtuosic performances never entirely disappeared, but appreciation for more subtle genres of music developed as the period progressed. Performances of chamber music proliferated in the 1850s, and by the 1860s symphonies, quartets, piano trios, and other forms of orchestral and chamber music were performed often for a wide audience.

Performed Repertory of Individual Composers

Following is a discussion of the "standard" Parisian repertory of the mid-nineteenth century, arranged alphabetically by composer. For each composer there are remarks concerning which genres or specific works were most successful, a description of changes in the composer's performed repertory as the period progressed (if not already discussed in the general section on chronological changes in repertory), and an acknowledgement of significant Parisian premieres. Included are composers (such as Chopin) whose instrumental works received occasional performances throughout the period even though they may not have been particularly popular in any single subperiod.

The violinist *Delphin Alard* was a true "composer-soloist." Of the 52 known performances of his works, 31 involved violin solos, ten involved works for two violins, and ten involved violin concertos (or *fragments*). The earliest known performance was a *Fantaisie* for violin, at a Conservatoire concert in 1836 when Alard was 21. His works were most popular in the 1840s and 1850s.

A movement of one of *J. S. Bach's* concertos for three keyboard instruments was played by Chopin, Liszt, and Ferdinand Hiller at a concert by Hiller in March 1833.[26] The ensuing years brought occasional renditions of keyboard works and violin solos, these works being among the few compositions of Bach published before 1850, but the real Bach revival began after that date, as more printed music became available. Eventually, keyboard concertos, excerpts from orchestral works (probably the suites), and compositions (many times only *fragments*) for unaccompanied violin were widely sampled. Specific identification for most of these works is difficult, if not impossible, but particularly popular were a keyboard concerto in D minor (presumably BWV 1052) and a chaconne for unaccompanied violin (probably from BWV 1004).

Beethoven's symphonies, which won immediate acclaim following their introduction at the Conservatoire concerts in 1828,[27] accounted for 644 of his 1790 performances.[28] Most popular were (in order) the Fifth, Sixth, and Seventh, each of which was played more than twice as often as any of the others. Most of the concertos were sampled early but slow to win fame; the Second Piano Concerto is not known to have been performed in its entirety until 1865. Incidentally, the following year the Concerts Populaires presented his Piano Concerto "No. 6" in D Major (apparently an arrangement of the Violin Concerto). Ironically, Beethoven's best-known chamber work, the Septet (109 known performances), was often rendered by a string orchestra with doubled winds, and seldom in its complete form. The string quartets were introduced early but, Op. 59 No. 3 and Op. 74 excepted, not often programmed until after 1848. The piano trios accounted for over 200 performances; especially popular were Op. 1 No. 3, in C minor, and the "Archduke" Trio, Op. 97. The only two instrumental sonatas to become repertory standards were the "Kreutzer" Violin Sonata, Op. 47, and the Cello Sonata Op. 69. Also well-known were the Serenade for string trio (from the early 1840s) and excerpts from the *Prometheus* music. Most of Beethoven's works did not become standards until after 1840, but the insistent repetition of the symphonies[29] at the Conservatoire concerts from 1828 ensured his reputation and encouraged exploration of his other compositions.

The Belgian violinist *de Bériot* had 61 known performances, most of them in nonseries concerts before 1860. Nearly all of the works performed were for a violin soloist; especially prevalent were *airs variés* and concertos (at least six separate concertos were performed).

Although *Berlioz* wrote few major works without voices, his instrumental music was performed in Paris perhaps more than that of any other French composer.[30] As his large works after *Harold en Italie* include vocal parts (and because he generally promoted his most recent compositions), there were few performances of major instrumental works after 1844, but his overtures, especially *Roman Carnival* and *Francs Juges,* continued to appear on programs.

The first known performance of a work by *Adolphe Blanc* did not occur until 1852, yet during the entire period surveyed in this chapter (beginning in 1828), Blanc had more *major* instrumental works performed than any other native composer, and from the mid-1850s, he was by far the most popular French composer of instrumental music.[31] All but three of the known performances involved chamber works; Blanc was a prolific composer of trios, quartets, and quintets, both with and without piano, and each genre was well-represented on Parisian programs.

In nineteenth-century Paris *Boccherini* held a status as a "master" that has since diminished. Often mentioned in the same breath as Haydn and Mozart early in the period, and evidently programmed at private *soirées,* he fell out of favor in the late 1830s, but by the 1860s again received a respectable number of performances, particularly at the Séances Populaires. His string quintets accounted for about three-quarters of the known performances.

Chopin's instrumental works were of course secondary in importance to his piano music. They never formed a large part of the instrumental repertory, but from at least 1832 (when his Second Piano Concerto was played at his own concert[32]) to 1870, his piano concertos, cello sonata, and Polonaise for cello and piano all received occasional hearings.

Through self-promotion *Charles Dancla* became one of the most-performed French composers of instrumental music; of the 96 known performances of his works, 55 took place at his own concerts. An overture of Dancla's was performed in 1836,[33] but his best known works were string quartets (at least eight were played), piano trios, and violin duos (especially *symphonies concertantes*) and solos.

At midcentury *Louise Farrenc* was one of the most popular native composers in Paris. Unlike her colleagues Blanc and Dancla, she achieved celebrity without either organizing a major concert series of her own or receiving much help from the *salons* of Gouffé and Lebouc; although she presented some concerts herself, and was supported by her friends (particularly women pianists), most of her music was played at "nonseries" concerts. A concert overture was performed as early as 1835[34] at the Gymnase Musical, but her works were not programmed regularly until the mid-1840s. Most often heard were chamber pieces with piano, particularly quintets and trios.

Charles Gounod's symphonies, since nearly forgotten, received at least 11 complete performances from 1855 through 1864; excerpts from these two works were also programmed occasionally.

Haydn was always regarded as a "master," but his music received real prominence in the Parisian repertory only after 1846. A partial explanation for this change is the profusion of chamber music societies in the late 1840s and 1850s, and subsequent "discovery" of Haydn's string quartets by a larger audience: of 212 known performances of the string quartets or excerpts thereof, 204 occurred after 1846.[35] By far the most popular work for string quartet was the second movement "Poco Adagio" of Op. 76 No. 3, usually labelled "Hymne"; this received over 50 performances, nearly all of them after 1848, and was frequently performed (as were Haydn's other quartets) by a string orchestra. Parisians apparently had no other favorite quartets and sampled widely among various sets. The symphonies were played throughout the period; best-known were No. 85 ("La Reine"), No. 88, and the London symphonies (particularly the "Surprise").

Hummel was among the most popular composers of the period; unfortunately for him, performances of his works were notably more frequent after his death, in 1837. Most famous were his two septets, though his quintets and piano concertos were programmed regularly.

The works of the pianist *Henry Litolff* (1818–91) received occasional performances in the 1850s and 1860s, primarily at concerts presented by himself or other pianists. His Parisian debut as a composer may have occurred with the performance of two movements of a piano trio at a concert of Mlle. Graever, 23 November 1851; this work and two other piano trios continued to attract attention, as did various orchestral overtures, but his most renowned works were the *concertos symphoniques* for piano and orchestra (especially No. 4, which was programmed at least nine times in the late 1850s and 1860s).

Mayseder was introduced to Paris as a violin soloist and composer of works for himself, but from the mid-1830s (and coinciding with slowly dwindling popularity), he programmed chamber works, particularly piano trios.

His several[36] symphonies notwithstanding, *Méhul* was known to concert-goers only by opera overtures and excerpts; the overture and "Chasse" from *Jeune Henri* received at least 34 performances, distributed evenly throughout the period.

The earliest known public performance of an instrumental work by *Mendelssohn* in Paris was a rendition of a Duo for clarinet and basset horn at the concerts of the *Revue et gazette musicale* on 27 January 1839.[37] Various other chamber works were attempted in the following years and by the mid-1840s Mendelssohn's music was established in the repertory; the first work to gain popularity was the *Hebrides Overture*. A taste for more substantial orchestral and chamber works developed in the 1850s. Eventually the favorite works were (numbers in parentheses indicate number of known performances) *Midsummer Night's Dream* music (including *fragments,* 55, from 1851), the First Piano Concerto (at least 39, from 1842; several performances of "a piano concerto" are not further identified, but the Second was not performed there until 1856), the E minor Violin Concerto (33, from 1848), the Third and Fourth Symphonies (each 30, from 1844 and 1852, respectively), the *Hebrides Overture* (29, from 1840), the Canzonetta of String Quartet Op. 12 (at least 20, counting complete performances of the quartet; this was sometimes performed by a string orchestra), and the two piano trios (together 86, from 1847; many announcements do not specify which trio was performed).

Overtures and excerpts from *Meyerbeer*'s stage works reached concert programs in the 1860s. The incidental music to *Struensée* (and excerpts thereof) accounted for roughly half of the known performances.

Mozart was best known in mid-nineteenth-century Paris for the same genres that have remained most famous, though only a small body of works was played regularly. His symphonies were performed throughout the period (at first only by the Société des Concerts du Conservatoire).

As mentioned above, only four were available in Paris by 1837; subsequently more were programmed, although the lack of an established numbering system makes identification of some of these impossible. It is clear that only the final three (K. 543, K. 550, and K. 551) were played often. The piano concertos were discovered in the 1840s;[38] K. 466 in D minor became especially popular. Overtures to *Marriage of Figaro, Don Giovanni,* and *Magic Flute* (often referred to as *Mystères d'Isis*) became standards, but other overtures remained unknown. Among Mozart's fine quintets, only the String Quintet K. 516 (in G minor) and the Clarinet Quintet K. 581 achieved wide appreciation; excerpts of the latter were often performed by a string orchestra with a clarinet soloist. From the 1840s, various string quartets were attempted. A curiosity of the Parisian Mozart repertory were occasional performances of single movements, variations, and even a sonata, for cello and piano, for which Mozart is not known to have composed any complete works; these are probably arrangements of works originally written for violin.

Georges Onslow, one of the most-performed native composers, was known mainly for chamber works—string quartets, string quintets, and a few works for larger ensembles. Acclaimed throughout the period, he was a particular favorite at Gouffé's *séances.* His four symphonies received occasional performances at the Conservatoire but rarely elsewhere; they disappeared from the repertory after 1847.

Compositions of the pianist *Emile Prudent* include works for piano (both with and without orchestra),[39] which he often played himself. His best-known instrumental works were the *Concerto-Symphonie* Op. 34 (his first piano concerto) and the *Danse des fées* Op. 41, also for piano and orchestra.

The German pianist and composer *Jakob Rosenhain* (1813–94) was never outstandingly popular, but held a steady place in the repertory from about 1840. Most famous were his piano trios, which received 16 performances; other chamber works and the symphony *Im Frühling* were played occasionally.

Rossini was familiar to concert audiences almost exclusively through his opera overtures. By far the most popular was that to *William Tell,* which (although it was not played regularly before 1840) accounted for 46, or more than half, of Rossini's known performances.

Anton Rubinstein's works were introduced to Parisian audiences at concerts given by the composer in April 1857; the first works performed were the Second Violin Sonata (Op. 19), a piano quartet, the Third Piano Concerto (Op. 45), and a symphony.[40] Thereafter, various sonatas, trios, quartets, and piano concertos were played occasionally, but only the

"Ocean" Symphony, first performed in Paris in 1865, received repeated performances, nearly all at the Concerts Populaires.

In December 1853, shortly after *Saint-Saëns*'s eighteenth birthday, his First Symphony was presented by the Société Sainte-Cécile.[41] This was the first of many instrumental performances for the young composer: nearly every instrumental work that he wrote before 1871 (including the unpublished Symphony in D) was performed within a few years of its completion. Although some of these works later became "war horses" of the repertory (for example, the "Introduction et Rondo Capriccioso" for violin and orchestra and the Second Piano Concerto), there were few favorites with the prewar Parisian audiences; only the First Violin Concerto (Op. 20) is known to have received more than five performances.

Schubert's instrumental works were heard in Paris as early as 1837, when a piano trio[42] was given its Paris premiere at a concert of Franck, Alard, and Chevillard, but did not join the standard repertory until the mid-1850s.[43] Like Saint-Saëns, Schubert had many works of various genres (mostly chamber works) performed a few times but no real "hits." Most popular were the Piano Trio in E-flat (Op. 100, D. 929), and a string quartet in D minor labelled "no. 4" (almost certainly D. 810, the "Death and the Maiden" quartet). As noted above, an absence of printed parts limited Schubert's appearances on orchestral programs.

Most of *Schumann*'s instrumental works date from the 1840s; there was a delay of ten to fifteen years before they found their way to Parisian concert halls. The Piano Quintet and *Manfred* overture were performed in Paris in 1853,[44] but his compositions received regular hearings only from 1857, the year after his death. The Piano Quintet became a favorite, receiving 31 known performances by 1870. The First Symphony (Paris premiere announced in 1860[45]), Third Symphony and Piano Quartet (first known performances of both in 1857[46]), and the *Manfred* and *Genoveva* overtures eventually achieved some popularity, but most of the many works sampled were played only a few times. The Société Schumann, founded in 1870, promoted chamber works.

Some of *Ludwig Spohr*'s instrumental works were known in Paris before 1828,[47] but his oeuvre was rarely heard there before 1840. It appears (although the sample of known performances—51—may be too small to warrant the following conclusion), that Spohr's works experienced two waves of popularity: in the 1840s and early 1850s chamber works (particularly those for large ensembles, often involving winds) and symphonies (especially No. 4, "Die Weihe der Töne") were played occasionally; in the 1860s most of these works were neglected while violin concertos (mainly Nos. 8 and 9) and violin solos received attention.

Vieuxtemps wrote mainly for violinists (presumably himself). Over half the known performances of his works in Paris (all after 1840) were violin solos, and the remaining performances comprised primarily violin concertos or duos for violin and another string instrument. The only known exceptions are two performances of a string quartet (or two quartets; he wrote three) in 1870 at concerts in which the composer participated.

Overcoming the reputation established by the fiasco of the Parisian premiere of *Tannhäuser* in 1861, excerpts from *Wagner*'s operas became quite popular in the 1860s, largely through Pasdeloup's stubborn promotion of them at the Concerts Populaires (though the works had received attention before Pasdeloup's efforts began). Overtures (or Preludes) to several operas were played regularly (those to *Flying Dutchman, Tannhäuser,* and *Lohengrin* were especially well known); the "March" from *Lohengrin* (presumably from the beginning of act 3) also became a favorite. Scudo reported that Wagner led a performance of the *"Prélude et l'introduction"* to *Tristan and Isolde* in 1860.[48]

Best known among *Weber*'s instrumental works were the overtures to *Oberon* (106 known performances), *Freischütz* (often called *Robin des Bois,* after Castil-Blaze's infamous reworking of the original; 68 known performances), and *Euryanthe* (50 known performances); these three pieces, which alone account for more than half the known performances of Weber's works, enjoyed steady popularity throughout the period. By contrast, the works intended for the concert hall were almost unknown before 1840. Nonetheless, the instrumental works eventually received an enviable number of performances: particular favorites in Paris were (apart from Berlioz's orchestration of "Invitation à la valse") the *Concertstück* for piano and orchestra, the two piano concertos, the Piano Quartet, and the Trio for piano, flute, and cello. Other chamber works (particularly duos) were played occasionally, but the two symphonies were almost entirely neglected.[49]

Parisian repertory in the years following 1828 can perhaps best be understood by imagining what music would seem accessible to the potential audience (and to performers). A few listeners would remember Parisian life before the Revolution, when the Concert Spirituel performed regularly, when there was an active school of French symphonists and composers of chamber works, and when works of Haydn, Mozart, and other foreigners were produced there, sometimes under the direction of the composer.[50] A few more listeners would have experienced the Revolution and its immediate aftereffects, which included the performances at large outdoor festivals of hymns and other patriotic works (in a simple, straightforward style) by the leading native composers.[51] A few would recall the student *exercices* at the Conservatoire from 1800 to 1815 at which symphonies of Haydn and Mozart, and concertos, solos, and overtures by foreign and native contemporaries formed the instrumental portion of the program.[52] The youngest generation of listeners would be familiar primarily with salon music and with operas recently produced in Paris: works of Auber, Berton, Boieldieu, Catel, Cherubini, Dalayrac, Hérold, Isouard, Lebrun, Méhul, Rossini, Spontini, and others.[53]

The genres and styles that were performed in the period following 1828 seem, for the most part, to have continued from (or developed directly from) the music prevalent at various times in the preceding 50 years.[54]

1) The enduring popularity of military bands (particularly at outdoor festivals) possibly stemmed from musical activities of the immediate post-Revolutionary period, when bands and choruses presented patriotic music. The informal atmosphere of the outdoor concerts and the facile music played there made few demands on listeners.

2) Virtuoso soloists, who had attracted attention before 1828, remained prominent. Several factors contributed to their success throughout the first half of the nineteenth century. Improvements to musical instruments (for example, the addition of valves to brass instruments, new fingering mechanisms for woodwinds, the advent of the Tourte bow, the development of the one-piece cast-iron frame for pianos) allowed and inspired new technical feats; philosophies that placed more emphasis on the individual (developed in the eighteenth century and reflected politically in, especially, France and America) may have led to idolization of individual artists, including soloists (such as Paganini);[55] the economic change from a system of receiving patronage to a dependence on wide public support (concurrent with the French Revolution) caused many artists to compose or perform spectacular but shallow music that they hoped would have mass appeal.

3) Opera, traditionally a keystone of French musical culture (and undoubtedly aided by the emphasis on vocal music during the post-Revolutionary festivals and after the return of the Bourbon regime), continued to be the most emphasized form of musical entertainment in Paris. It received support from the government and the wealthy, and the combination of music, drama, ballet, theatrical effects, and "star" performers attracted listeners with little musical background. At concerts, the liking for opera resulted in frequent performances of excerpts as well as overtures of Beethoven, Gluck, Méhul, Meyerbeer, Mozart, Rossini, Wagner, and Weber.

4) Finally, chamber and orchestral works that had been well known at one time returned to (or remained in) the repertory; thus the popularity of Haydn and Mozart and success of Boccherini.

Concerning French taste in "art" music during the eighteenth century Schrade has written:

> Haydn provoked less resistance among the French than any other composer of the classic period. The balance of form and idea in his work, the well-designed proportions, the adjustment of dynamics, the avoidance of procedures that might be thought disturbing or abrupt or too much burdened by ideas; the singing qualities of his melodies, all this and more appealed to the spirit of eighteenth-century France. If these attributes seem to reveal little of the essential quality of Haydn's composition, they are nevertheless the terms in which the French expressed their admiration.[56]

Curiously, the qualities of Haydn's music appreciated in eighteenth-century France remained prime criteria for nineteenth-century audiences and musicians evaluating instrumental music of their contemporaries. Consequently, most of the successful composers wrote in a traditional style, taking care to avoid "procedures that might be thought disturbing." Among popular native composers, Blanc wrote works in the "ancient style";[57] Onslow was noted for his conservatism; Saint-Saëns followed eighteenth-century models (especially in his early works); Louise Farrenc's works were traditional, if somewhat more imaginative than those of her contemporaries; Dancla's music was unadventurous; and many less-performed French composers wrote "textbook" sonatas that showed little innovation.[58] Even Félicien David, whose interest in exoticism led to musical experimentation, left surprisingly conservative chamber works. The one notable innovator among the French was Berlioz, whose works were performed frequently not because of popularity but because of Berlioz's ambition and organizational ability.[59] Among foreign composers, many of those who gained extreme or rapid success were traditionally oriented—for example, Mendelssohn, Hummel, and Rubinstein—while more inventive composers, such as Schumann and Wagner, were less quickly welcomed, if at all; the avant-garde instrumental works of Liszt were ignored.[60] This theory does not account, however, for the popularity of Beethoven, whose departures from tradition provided the groundwork for later nineteenth-century innovators, and whose music surely seemed, upon its introduction in France, strikingly different from any instrumental "art" music with which the French were familiar.[61]

The French environment and the heritage of French music must also have affected French musicians' taste for foreign composers. For musicians familiar with eighteenth-century French works or even with the relatively uncomplex French operas and ballets of the early nineteenth century, and for audiences accustomed to classical French architecture, furniture, painting, literature, and so forth, the leap to Mendelssohn's elegant music must have been easier than the leap to Schumann's instrumental works (which probably seemed weighty and possibly, sometimes, muddy and morose) or Bach's (which probably seemed abstruse). Stated in simple, if subjective, terms, most of Mendelssohn's music sounds more French than Schumann's, Bach's, or Brahms's. But the assumption that French cultural bias influenced attitudes toward foreign music, like the theory that the French preferred the traditional to the innovative, apparently fails to explain the popularity of Beethoven in France. Or does it? Peter Bloom has suggested that in several ways Beethoven was influenced by French models: the Eroica Symphony was affected by Napoleon and in its slow movement the influence of Gossec and Cherubini can be detected; *Fidelio* is a rescue opera in the French tradition; the storm scene in the Sixth Symphony borrows naturalistic effects from French operas; the frequent use of rapid four-four meters, dotted figures and upbeat patterns, and pulsating rhythms beneath *cantabile* melodies also seems characteristically French.[62] One might conclude that Beethoven and the French were not so far apart after all were it not that later French composers did not, for the most part, adopt his innovations.

Beethoven's music was timely for a revolutionary age; its spirit was more nearly approached by rescue operas than by contemporary French instrumental works. Schrade wrote:

> The door, then, through which the French admitted the genius of Beethoven . . . was opened by the romantics. . . . Not until romanticism struck the intellectual world like lightning was the way cleared and Beethoven let in. . . . From the first romantic concerts, he proceeds into the center of the French musical repertory, which he is to dominate for forty years to come.[63]

Yet Beethoven's relationship to French romanticism, and any attempted explanation of his popularity in Paris, is complicated by several factors, all of which have been mentioned above. First (and most relevant), because it became socially fashionable to attend performances of Beethoven's music, programs thereof were frequented by audiences who could not distinguish it from that of lesser composers—audiences for whom the name "Beethoven" meant more than the music. Although these listeners were largely responsible for Beethoven's commercial success, it is difficult to guess whether they truly empathized with the spirit of the music. Second, Beethoven's Late works found less public acceptance than his earlier, more traditional compositions. While it can be argued that the reflective mood of the Late works was too far removed from the more explicit emotionalism of some French romantics (whose style was perhaps more nearly approached by some of Beethoven's Middle works) to satisfy the spirit of the age, it is equally significant that the Late works are the farthest removed from the traditional idiom the French apparently preferred. Furthermore, even some innovations of the Middle works were regarded with suspicion in France. Third, the works of Beethoven now considered most romantic were an exception to the rule within the standard Parisian instrumental repertory. Others whose music seems to express romantic ideals or revolutionary spirit were generally less successful than composers who emulated classical models. The "romantic concerts" to which Schrade referred were, Beethoven's works excepted, dominated by nonromantic music.

Philip George Downs has proposed ideas about repertory[64] which, when extended to Beethoven, suggest a possible explanation for his unique role in Parisian musical life. Downs has attributed the establishment in the nineteenth century of a standard "permanent" repertory to 1) the rise of historical consciousness (resulting in the revival of earlier music); 2) a new philosophy of art, in which music is regarded as a noble expression of emotion and human aspirations rather than a mere entertainment resulting from sound craftsmanship; and 3) the development (concurrent with improvements in communication and transportation) of a European repertory, replacing separate local repertories. Furthermore (Downs has stated), once these phenomena had taken effect (that is, as the repertory became standardized), it became increasingly difficult for new works to gain a foothold in the concert hall. Beethoven could have benefited in Paris from all of the occurrences that Downs has cited. As he died in 1827, his music could, in 1828, already have been helped by the sense of historical consciousness. Because of the dearth of instrumental-music performances in Paris before 1828, a standard repertory did not yet exist when Beethoven's music was introduced; yet within a few years the repertory became set, and was thereafter less open to new music. Finally, Beethoven's works fit, perhaps better than anyone's, the new view of music as statement. In other words, for Beethoven's music in Paris, the timing was perfect.

The above is not intended to deny the possibility that the popularity of Beethoven was caused by the sheer excellence of his music. But if quality was the primary criterion for success, why did the music of Haydn and Mozart (much of which was also readily available) lag so far behind?

The mystery of Beethoven's rapid and overwhelming success at a time when most of the remaining instrumental repertory was conservative leads to a greater puzzle: why, during a period of great political excitement and social upheaval, a period in which Grand Opera—through unprecedented flamboyance—attracted new middle-class audiences, did composers, performers, and audiences interested in instrumental music favor eighteenth-century compositions and a conservative approach to new music? Were musicians and listeners who preferred instrumental "art" works generally backward? Did a taste for symphonies and string quartets exclude art that might reflect revolutionary aspects of the age? Or did the new music that attracted middle-class audiences turn some listeners against all new music?

Answers to these questions require a better understanding of contemporary thought on music and French nineteenth-century music itself. These topics are the subjects of the following chapters.

5

Perceptions of Musical Life in Nineteenth-Century France

Perceptions of musical life in nineteenth-century France, including both descriptions and explanations (or, at least, theories), came from the pens of performers, composers, critics, and aestheticians. The best known of these perceptions, which survive as often-repeated quotations, have formed the basis upon which historians have built our present understanding of the period—an understanding that is inaccurate and strikingly incomplete. To fill historical voids, one seeks a broader sample of contemporary accounts, even though, as shown in chapter 3, some of these (especially statements concerning the quantity and quality of instrumental music performed) appear to be at odds with historical data.

Despite the inherent problems, opinions of contemporaries and historians must be considered. Persons who experienced the period first-hand developed attitudes toward the state of music that are in some ways more telling than statistical studies compiled a century later. (It is not so much events that influence human activity as interpretation of those events.) And observations by historians should be confirmed or refuted but not ignored.

Of particular concern are opinions of nineteenth-century writers and twentieth-century historians on the following questions: How did the musical scene during the period 1828 to 1871 differ from that of the preceding era, and what changes took place within the period? How did French musical life compare with that of other European countries? How were chamber and orchestral works viewed, relative to other genres? Did the position of instrumental music improve and, if so, was this trend considered desirable? Among those who appreciated instrumental works, how were modern compositions regarded, especially in contrast with eighteenth-century music or recent works based upon eighteenth-century models? What was the relationship between style and genre, and why? (Why were Parisians intrigued by new Grand Opera but reportedly cool to contemporary instrumental works?) Finally, how did the post-Revolutionary social structure affect French musicians and composers?

Instrumental Music in France before 1828[1]

To understand properly the attitudes of French musical figures after 1828, one must have some idea of earlier musical activities. One might guess that performances of traditional "art" music would have disappeared during the French Revolution and political events that followed. Aristocratic patronage ceased. The most famous eighteenth-century concert series, the state-sponsored Concert Spirituel, halted in 1791. Instrumental music did suffer in the 1790s, but musical life in general recovered quickly from the Revolution, and reached a surprisingly high level by 1800. The worst blow to instrumental music seems to have occurred later, when the Bourbon regime resumed control in 1815; the resulting nadir lasted until the late 1820s.

It can be argued that even pre-Revolutionary France had not offered an environment conducive to the development of instrumental music. William Weber has written that the growth of "art" music in France of the 1700s was weakened by a lack of aristocratic dilettantism and by state restrictions on public concerts.[2] Certainly there were no eighteenth-century French composers of instrumental works comparable to Haydn or Mozart, and a modern synopsis of the period would likely emphasize the operatic activities of Rameau, Gluck, and Grétry, rather than the instrumental school. Yet, as the writings of Brook, La Laurencie, and Pierre have demonstrated well, France boasted prolific symphonists, an active school of violinists (and composers for that instrument), and a lively concert series, the Concert Spirituel.[3] Furthermore, biographies of various contemporary figures describe warm receptions accorded their instrumental works in Paris.

Music (and especially vocal music) enjoyed surprising popularity in the wake of the Revolution, as indicated by Boris Schwarz:

> With the revolutionary events of 1789, the entire social structure collapsed, and with it centuries of musical culture and tradition. . . . [But] the fact is undeniable that throughout the revolutionary decade (1789–99), musical life in Paris continued to pulsate with undiminished intensity. Neither Revolution, nor terror, nor war could suppress the artistic needs of the people.[4]

To support his argument Schwarz quoted an article from the *Allgemeine musikalische Zeitung,* 1800:

> Perhaps never before in Paris has music been so much appreciated and performed as now. Never has there been such a number of excellent composers and virtuosos from all the world.[5]

He admitted that the outlook for instrumental music was not quite as rosy:

> Compared with activity in the realm of opera, the concerts played a subordinate role in the musical life of Paris in 1789–99. Being a subtler form of musical entertainment, they suffered more than the opera from the loss of their aristocratic clientele, and it took a number of years before a new concert audience was built, after the old *amateurs* were dispersed by the impact of the Revolution. The established concert organizations did not survive for long; the Concerts de la Loge Olympique closed in December 1789, the Concert Spirituel in 1791. Short-lived enterprises tried to fill the gap.[6]

The post-Revolutionary emphasis on vocal music can be attributed largely to the music festivals organized by the new government, and the audience for which they were intended—an audience not accustomed to traditional art. Lockspeiser wrote that the music required for the festivals of the Republic—or celebrations of victorious battles—"had to be strikingly suggestive," and had to "portray in a rather obvious and realistic manner" certain events.[7] Lockspeiser continued with a quotation from LeSueur's *Exposé d'une musique, une, imitative et particulière:* "that the aim of composers should be to get 'le plus de poésie, de peintre, et d'expression dans leurs ouvrages.' "[8] Thus, description and imitation were more appropriate to the times than abstract music. Lockspeiser concluded that descriptive music, the appreciation of which was passed from LeSueur to his pupil Berlioz, became one of the main influences on the latter's orchestral-vocal works and on the "program" music that blossomed later in the century. But if LeSueur's understanding of the Republic was correct, then vocal music better satisfied the needs of the time than programmatic instrumental works. In fact, vast numbers of simple *hymnes* and *chansons* were written during the Republic; their authors include even the best French composers.[9]

Schwarz, whose main interest was instrumental music, noted the same sort of musical change that Lockspeiser had described earlier:

> [After the Revolution] music . . . became a civic act, a social function, a moral force in the service of the fatherland and in the cult of glory and liberty. . . . The concept of composer-artist was now replaced with that of the composer-citizen. His task was not to express individualized emotion, but to speak the collective language of the people.
>
> The new era called for a new musical style, built along clear lines, with strong rhythm, easy melody, simple harmony, brilliant orchestral color painted with broad brush strokes; in short, a fundamental simplification of musical forms, means, and expression. Music was needed that [was] music of action, not of reflection.[10]

In spite of an atmosphere unfavorable to traditional concerts, concert societies were not unknown in the 1790s. The Concerts du Théâtre Feydeau were active from 1796 to 1802, and concerts on the rue de Cléry were established in 1798.[11] A short-lived concert society founded by Fridzeri performed at the Palais Royal and later at the Magasin of the Opéra, also about 1798.[12] Schwarz has related that in the 1790s, instrumental works were performed during intermissions at theatres.[13]

After the turn of the century, music continued as a prominent part of French culture, and vocal music remained predominant. Schwarz wrote:

> More than ever, the musical center of gravity was the opera, for it satisfied the general desire for pomp and display, as well as light entertainment.[14]

Two reports from the *Allgemeine musikalische Zeitung,* both cited (and translated) by Schwarz, provide different views of concert life in Paris, though they agree that interest was high:

> Never was our [Paris's] musical sky more brilliant than during this winter season [early 1800]. The works of the most prominent Italian, German, and French composers were performed by exquisite artists and excellent orchestras. The music-loving public listened with enthusiasm to symphonies by Haydn and Mozart, given with such perfection and precision at the Concerts Cléry.[15]

> With all the interest in music, it is surprising that Paris should have so few public concerts. . . . At present there is only one organization, the Concerts Rue Cléry.[16]

The concerts of the rue de Cléry moved to the rue Chantereine in 1805; they programmed, among other works, symphonies of Haydn and Reicha,[17] and contemporary reviews were complimentary. At concerts on the rue Grenelle, begun in 1803, solo and chamber works were heard. In the same year the Théâtre-Italien attempted, without success, to reestablish the Concert Spirituel.[18] The regular "public exercises" of the Conservatoire students, lasting from 1800 to 1815 (with the exception of the 1801–2 season, when the students organized their own *Concerts français,* independent of the institution), "acquired international reputation by the high excellence of performance and freshness of approach."[19] At these concerts some of Beethoven's symphonies received their Paris premieres (beginning in 1807),[20] though the orchestra played mainly works of Haydn and Mozart. The short-lived, semiprivate concerts of the Cercle Musical de la rue Mandar were active in 1808.[21] As noted above, Baillot, with the cellist Lamare and pianist Mme. Marie Bigot, played works of J. S. Bach as early as 1809, and established a "permanent" series of chamber music *séances* in 1814.

His own descriptions of musical activity in the 1790s notwithstanding, Schwarz has written of the early 1800s:

> After a period of comparative inactivity during the revolutionary decade, concert life in Paris began to re-establish itself with the return of more stable conditions.[22]

He also has noted that before 1815 instruction at the Paris Conservatoire was much stronger for instrumentalists than for vocalists, and that this imbalance showed at the student exercises.[23] Apparently both teachers and students at the school had some interest in composing instrumental works: Méhul's four numbered symphonies (for which exact dates of composition are unknown) were performed in 1809 and 1810;[24] Hérold wrote two symphonies in 1813 and 1814 while in Rome (as winner of the Prix de Rome).[25] Fétis wrote in 1831 that chamber music had been cultivated in France about 20 years earlier, but since then had almost disappeared.[26]

After 1815 nearly all instrumental music faded from the picture, not to return until the mid to late 1820s. Other forms of music had difficulty too: Sophie Leo wrote that Mozart was *completely* ignored and that music in 1817 was in a "lethargy."[27] Ludwig Spohr reported of his visit to Paris in 1820 that native artists believed the French not to be musical, and that they "frequently reply, when I speak of Germany in this respect: 'Yes, music is loved and understood there, but not here.' "[28] Writing 150 years later, the historian William Weber agreed with these sweeping judgements:

> During the 1820's Paris . . . had a vacuum of taste and leadership among serious musicians and amateurs.[29]

Clearly, though, instrumental music suffered more than other forms. Sophie Leo wrote:

> However discouraging the condition of the opera may have been during those years, the concerts were in an even more deplorable state. Even the most capable artist dared not offer his unappreciative audience a quartet or quintet, much less an entire concerto . . . and in private circles where music was cultivated, the display of ignorance and lack of taste was still more striking.[30]

She added that as late as 1825 "the Parisians had an almost total absence . . . of any feeling for the serious German symphonic style."[31] Schwarz has stated that when the Bourbon regime resumed control, changing the Conservatoire back to the Ecole Royale, "the emphasis in instruction was shifted to the vocal department, favoring operatic preparation at the expense of instrumental teaching."[32] Regular student concerts were discontinued, and no replacement appeared. Spohr found that writing music for theatre was much more lucrative in France than in Germany. He also reported that French instrumentalists emphasized virtuosity rather than musical depth, and expressed surprise that Cherubini (soon to become head of the Conservatoire) was unfamiliar with the string quartets and quintets of Mozart and Beethoven.[33] Berlioz arrived in Paris shortly after Spohr's visit, and later recalled his early years in the city:

> Instrumental music still meant nothing to me; the only concerts I had heard were those given at the Opéra, where the feebleness of the performances was not calculated to awaken my interest.[34]

When, a few years after his arrival, Berlioz asked to have one of his works performed at the Concert Spirituel (resurrected by the Opéra), the conductor, Rodolphe Kreutzer, is said to have replied, "We cannot perform any new compositions at these concerts; we don't have time to rehearse them."[35] Fétis confirmed that the Concert Spirituel, the only noteworthy series at the time, had only a single rehearsal for their concerts.[36] Schwarz wrote that when Cherubini became director of the Conservatoire in 1822 he intended to revive student concerts, and announced that there would be 12 per year, but that a total of 9 were presented in 1823 and 1824, and none thereafter.[37] Summarizing the relationship between instrumental and stage music during the 1820s, Schwarz has written:

> Untouched by the turmoil of revolutions and wars, the taste of the Parisian public remained unchanged; it still preferred the lyric stage to instrumental music and even to the spoken theatre.[38]

Well-founded pessimism about concert life continued into the late 1820s. William Weber has discovered that in the 1826–27 season there were only 78 public concerts in Paris; 19 seasons later there were 383.[39] Much of the pessimism was expressed by F.-J. Fétis in his new *Revue musicale* (founded in 1827). Fétis's complaints included the lack of suitable places for the performance of religious works and symphonies, the publishers' lack of interest in orchestral and chamber music (which made composition of these works economically unfeasible), the singular importance of opera to the exclusion of all other music, the extremely limited repertory of the Concert Spirituel, and the poor musical education of the Parisian public (which he believed led to their alleged poor taste).[40] Fétis also felt that the increasing popularity of the piano and the (to some extent consequent) development of musical *salons* contributed to the replacement of orchestral and chamber music by piano solos and instrumental or vocal solos with piano accompaniment, noting that with few exceptions French musicians *no longer* gathered together to perform chamber music.[41]

This environment discouraged the composition of instrumental works, as, perhaps, did the "expressionist" aesthetic prevalent among French writers on music in the late 1820s. The belief that music should express feelings or ideas may have derived from the post-Revolutionary goal of satisfying a mass audience that could not appreciate music for musical reasons. In an article on the French violin school, Schwarz has observed that:

> As the social pattern of the audience changed [during and after the Revolution], the concerto—like the opera—acquired a nervous intensity, a militant boldness, a technical brilliance geared to impress an unruly public.

(finally becoming mainly virtuosic with the advent of Paganini in the 1820s).[42]

As early as 1827, however, some musicians found cause (albeit limited) for optimism. Even Fétis saw occasional bright spots. He wrote enthusiastically about the expansion and development of the orchestra[43] and suggested that fine teaching at the Conservatoire was helping to make France the musical equal of Germany and Italy.[44] Three amateur orchestral series had been active since the mid-1820s: Egasse's Concerts d'Emulation, the Société Philharmonique de la Ville de Paris, and the Concert des Amateurs (see chapter 2, p. 66). Looking back from 1831, an anonymous critic for the *Revue musicale* discussed a decline in French music that (he believed) had begun 15 years before, citing as evidence the preference for shorter instrumental works, the abandonment of student exercises at the Conservatoire, and the disappearance of chamber music; he saw signs of recovery by 1827, however, in the establishment of public (vocal) *exercices* at Choron's school, Habeneck's preparations for the Conservatoire concerts, and the chamber concerts of Baillot and the brothers Bohrer.[45]

Even the greatest optimists of 1827 must have been surprised by the events of the following five years. At least six new concert series were established, including the immensely successful Société des Concerts du Conservatoire, whose performances of Beethoven's symphonies surely astonished musically backward Paris. Berlioz provided further reason for shock with his *Symphonie Fantastique,* premiered in 1830. Fétis's novel *concerts historiques* took place in 1832. On the vocal side of the musical coin, Grand Opera began. Parisians greeted premieres of Auber's *La Muette de Portici* (1828), Rossini's *Guillaume Tell* (1829), and Meyerbeer's *Robert le Diable* (1831), as well as new *opéras comiques*—Auber's *Fra Diavolo* (1830) and Hérold's *Zampa* (1831) and *Le Pré aux Clercs* (1832).

Descriptions and Explanations, 1828 to 1871

Printed descriptions and explanations of musical life in France between 1828 and 1871 represent a wide range of interpretations and opinions. Apart from differences among individual authors, some divergence in opinion can be attributed to significant changes that took place during the period—changes that led to reevaluations and new ideas. Because of this evolution, a temporally unrestricted sampling of opinions could be confusing and misleading. Therefore, in the ensuing discussion the period is again divided into six subperiods (1828–33; 1833–39; 1839–46; 1847–53; 1854–60; and 1860–70; this division, suggested by changing patterns of musical activity, was first outlined in chapter 1 and used for statistical purposes in chapter 4). Following this survey of contemporary statements is a summary of pertinent historical thought since 1871.

1828–1833

Consequent to the above-mentioned revival of various musical activities in France in or by 1827, a brief period of optimism was expressed by Parisian musicians. They were particularly excited about the new Conservatoire concerts, which not only introduced Beethoven's works and other unfamiliar music, but performed known works better than they had ever before been heard in Paris. Among other new societies founded at that time, a frequently stated intention was the programming of music by young or little-known (particularly, French) composers: societies that promised this included the Conservatoire's Concerts d'Emulation,[46] the Gymnase Lyrique (which may not have actually performed any concerts),[47] the Athénée Musical, and a society of amateurs. (See chapter 2, p. 67 and Appendix A.) By 1828 Fétis was saying that France was the primary musical center in Europe. He still attributed this alleged condition to the good work of the Conservatoire, but also credited the naturalization of Cherubini, the good fortune to have had native composers such as Méhul, LeSueur, Berton, and Boieldieu, the advent of instrumental virtuosos such as Baillot, Rode, Tulou, and others, the establishment of the Conservatoire concerts, and a greater interest in music among the general public. He blamed the wars with Germanic nations for the French people's ignorance of the German repertory.[48] Using a combination of statistics and educated guessing, he discussed the increasing number of music professors in Paris (he believed that there were 207 in 1788 and about 8000 in 1829); he also mentioned the development of public music schools, philharmonic societies, and musical theatres in the provinces.[49] Edouard Fétis, writing in spring 1830, thought that music in France was progressing well and cited, apart from new philharmonic societies and schools, an expanding concert schedule and a new interest in the arts, as audiences escaped the post-Revolutionary governments' inattention to culture.[50]

Regarding the position of instrumental music in particular, the rarity of positive statements indicates the dominance of vocal music. Chorley (later) described the revolutionary emphasis on instrumental works at the Conservatoire concerts as a case of not just "turning" but "absolutely overthrowing the tables on the choralists."[51] Also looking back to the period, Edouard Fétis regarded the performances of Onslow's symphonies as an important model to native orchestral composers, who, he said, were still discouraged by the lack of success that Méhul and Cherubini had experienced with this genre.[52] Ironically, one of the few bright spots concerning instrumental activity is the obituary of one Lagrave, a Prix de Rome contestant who died from a "nervous fit" after losing the competition (to Ambroise Thomas); the notice reported that Lagrave had already written many promising quartets and symphonies.[53]

Many contemporaries saw little hope for music of any sort. Young or little-known composers found it difficult to gain a foothold, as neither publishers nor theatre directors were interested in the unfamiliar; the most promising young composers, the Prix de Rome winners, were deported for three years, a time that Berlioz and other recipients felt could have been better spent taking advantage of their official recognition to promote themselves in Paris.[54] Explaining the foundation of the Gymnase Lyrique in 1828, Stéphen maintained that all young composers were discouraged by the lack of opportunities to hear their own music. He felt that their only chance was in the theatre, but other sources indicated that there was no hope even there.[55] In 1828 F.-J. Fétis cited one Schneitzhoeffer as an example of a promising young composer who had abandoned his career in disgust with the French musical scene.[56] The same year a *soirée* in the *salons* of Pleyel was described as highly unusual in that it presented good music well performed, and by 1829 there were reported fewer benefit concerts and *soirées,* allegedly because of competition from the Conservatoire concerts.[57]

Comments on instrumental music (excepting the rare examples mentioned above) were particularly pessimistic. An 1828 advertisement for three new string quartets by F. Bonjour may be paraphrased as follows: "It takes real love of the art to devote oneself to string quartets, which are so little in favor at this time."[58] Similarly, in 1830 the composition of symphonies was described by J.-A. Delaire as a most ungrateful pursuit—one for which the composer would receive little admiration until his death. The same author noted a general trend toward smaller forms—overtures, sonatines, caprices, arrangements of popular tunes, and so forth.[59]

It was widely acknowledged that instrumental music in the tradition of Gossec, Devienne, and Méhul suffered from several causes, among them the French public's fondness for vocal music and the entrepreneurs' attempts to interest new audiences with easily approachable music. The preference for vocal music (seemingly a habitual state of affairs in France) is demonstrated by several (anonymous) contemporary comments. The reviewer of a concert by the horn player Schuncke in 1828 stated that the French public had a weakness for singing, always favoring a cavatina or modest *romance* to a sonata or concerto; a review of 1832 maintained that operas and *romances* had driven chamber music from the scene; an unsympathetic reviewer of the Conservatoire concerts in 1832 thought concerts that presented only (or primarily) instrumental music to be boring.[60] But public bias toward vocal music did not deserve or receive all the blame for the poor standing of instrumental music. Another anonymous observer, writing in 1831, noted a scarcity of estimable native instrumental works, stating that the leading French instrumental composers (he cited Baillot, Kalkbrenner, Kreutzer, Onslow, Reicha, and Rode) were weak.[61] Likewise, Fétis in 1833 saw no followers in France (or elsewhere) to the recently deceased Beethoven and Weber.[62]

Fétis also saw (and more recent writers have agreed) that social revolutions caused cultural revolutions that precipitated changes in the musical scene. Nineteenth-century audiences, no longer exclusively aristocratic, had less appreciation for instrumental music in the traditional styles; and composers, no longer supported by individual patrons, felt compelled to accommodate the new audiences. The composers' dependence on commercial success—thought Fétis—was intensified by increasingly materialistic attitudes resulting from the industrial revolution; composers now demanded money, rather than the security of a permanent position, to purchase goods that flooded the market. Fétis concluded (prematurely, and with a somewhat naive view of history) that the era of composer as independent genius was over.[63] Fétis's intentions, as reflected in his *Revue musicale,* have been described by Peter Bloom as an attempt at "rapprochment between serious music and the new, growing, middle-class public, the bourgeoisie whose tastes were to characterize the July Monarchy of Louis-Philippe."[64]

As early as the mid-1820s, the famous publishing house of Sieber, which had once offered many symphonies and chamber works, turned to potpourris, arrangements, and variations (in addition to vocal works).[65] Edouard Fétis remembered the increasing prevalence of virtuosos, especially pianists.[66] After 1830 (the date of the second major revolution) change in the musical scene accelerated. The emphasis on light music led Tiersot to conclude that in nineteenth-century France the symphony was regarded as an academic achievement—something for Prix de Rome winners to write while in Rome.[67] And Kracauer has noted that after 1830 "novelty and innovation became the rage, and license in clothing and speech and fashion."[68]

Following the July Revolution, as William Weber has indicated, the new and insecure Orléanist regime was seeking to

> legitimise its authority after the overthrow of the Bourbon monarchy. By sanctifying classical [that is, "art"] music as official high culture, it established a link with a prestigious national heritage.[69]

Like previous governments, the new regime sponsored a few musical organizations (among them the Société des Concerts du Conservatoire); this relationship not only provided the desired connection with "high culture," but also allowed the state to exert some control over art (at the very least, through the threat of withdrawing financial support).

Thus the July Revolution effected a wide musical separation between the new government (which supported "art" music) and the new middle-class public (which preferred "popular" idioms). But its other effects were sooner apparent: in its wake some musical series were temporarily discontinued, and many musicians suffered during the post-revolutionary recession.

The social and political upheaval of the few years neighboring the July Revolution seems to have caused in music as much diversity and confusion as revolution. The direction of musical trends was not immediately clear, and critics alternated between extremes of optimism and pessimism. The establishment of the Conservatoire concerts was itself a minor revolution, but these concerts were restricted to a small segment of a rapidly expanding audience. The advent of Grand Opera heralded not only a new musical style, but also an attempt to interest the bourgeoisie through spectacle.[70] For the new audience, spectacle was perhaps the most enticing development; in instrumental music, this attitude was reflected by the new emphasis on virtuosic compositions. During the same years a small segment of the minority interested in instrumental "art" music considered a different departure from the prevalent conservative aesthetic. Their thesis, expressed in several articles in the *Revue musicale,* was that music without words can in fact move the soul and express passions or vague emotions (but should not attempt to depict concrete images).[71] Conservative critics did not readily accept musical changes that this philosophy suggests, and were for the most part unappreciative of compositions that departed from "classical" patterns (less flexible in the minds of critics than they had been for classical composers) for the sake of expressiveness. Clarity and melodic charm were still regarded as necessities. The virtuosic works that appeared with increasing frequency after the July Revolution may well have strengthened critical opposition to all works that did not meet the contemporary narrow conception of the

Classical style, and thus diminished acceptance of innovators such as Berlioz.

1833–1839

As noted in chapters 2 and 3, the mid-1830s saw the arrival of outdoor and café concerts, a profusion of *salons,* and, from 1835, *concerts populaires* of "art" music and a few chamber music series (see chapter 2, pp. 68–71 and chapter 3, pp. 86–89 and 90–95). Excitement was expressed at the founding of each new concert series; sometimes "progress" was mentioned. Yet the mood of the period (at least among writers for the *Revue musicale* and *Gazette musicale*) was, though not entirely unhopeful, one of discouragement and frustration. Those who acknowledged the increasing musical activity nearly all spoke disparagingly about the quality of contemporary musical events. Edouard Fétis wrote in 1835 that interest in music was growing at an incalculable rate, but that the music was no better than before. He elaborated that never had there been so many concerts or musical gatherings in a single season, but that few or none had reached a standard of excellence.[72] An anonymous contributor to the *Gazette musicale de Paris* had, a few months earlier, indicated that Parisian musical life was at an all-time high, citing new musical establishments, associations, and journals, as well as the introduction of German opera and the debuts of various singers; yet he also predicted that the new Gymnase Musical (then still being planned) would have difficulty finding competent instrumentalists and conductors, and that a repertory of works by young composers would never attract an audience.[73] Another critic, at the end of the same season, stated that music had become a fad—an entertainment that was expected everywhere.[74] Judging by the numerous notices describing music's proliferation, it was reaching more persons (and more often); but appreciation of music as a fine art was dwindling. Surely the announcement of a new series of *soirées équestres et musicales* in the same year[75] is, from a musician's viewpoint, a discouraging reflection of popular taste.

A single article signed by Liszt covers most of the major complaints voiced by musicians in the 1830s: the difficulty composers had in organizing and presenting concerts in Paris (especially the lack of appropriate locations); the shortage of proficient and available performers; the limited number of persons appreciative of instrumental works; and (conversely), the necessity of composing *romances, chansonnettes, mosaïques, contredanses,* and *galops,* and of arranging favorite *motifs* from selected operas in order to attract an audience or publisher.[76] To be fully representative, this list might be supplemented by two further grievances: the deluge of virtuosos and the poor standard of performance by many other musicians, especially singers.[77] Elwart confirmed the presence of deterrents to musical events, stating in 1838 that Paris was perhaps the most difficult of European cities in which to present a concert, no matter how small.[78]

The lack of musical sophistication among audiences and the popularity of virtuosic pieces and dance music are nearly inseparable, although it is possible to depict an audience's ignorance of "art" music (as in the above-mentioned instance of confusion concerning piano trios by Beethoven and Pixis when their order of performance was reversed from that of the program) without indicating a preference for "popular" works. An anonymous writer in 1835 observed that everyone spoke of Beethoven, Haydn, and Mozart, but that their music was rarely heard.[79]

Most listeners, however, preferred "popular" music. In reviewing the final Conservatoire concert of the 1836 season, Berlioz stated that the *amateurs* in the audience would not bother to seek other music until the following season, and that the *dilettantes* would, having fulfilled their social obligation to appear at the Conservatoire, go straight to the Musard concerts or Jardin Turc to hear music that they truly enjoyed.[80] A year earlier, in a letter to Humbert Ferrand, Berlioz had written:

> At present we sit dumb under the triumph of Musard, who, puffed up by the success of his dancing-den concerts, looks upon himself as a superior Mozart. Mozart never composed anything like the "Pistol-Shot Quadrille," so Mozart died in poverty. Musard is earning 20,000 francs a year.[81]

The pervasiveness of virtuosic works or dance music at both private and public musical events was reported frequently. Liszt wrote in 1835 that he would prefer sonatas by *anyone* to more *romances,* potpourris, and so forth.[82] Elwart noted that *romances* and works for cornet were replacing chamber music in *salons*.[83] The anonymous "N.," discussing the popularity of Musard's orchestra in 1835, remarked that publishers were mainly interested in *contredanses* and *quadrilles,* and would not publish even opera scores unless they included material suitable for conversion to *contredanses*.[84]

Whatever problems composers experienced were compounded for newcomers. The latter met resistance from both performers and publishers. Announcements that new societies would perform works of young composers suggest that some musicians were awakening to the problem, but also indicate that the practice was perceived as unusual. An anonymous writer in 1834 declared that young composers, regardless of their talent or determination, were usually condemned to await unlikely acceptance by the Opéra-Comique—and that opportunity at the Opéra was altogether unthinkable.[85] In 1835 Edouard Fétis called the Gymnase Musical the only hope for unestablished composers.[86] One wonders whether the difficulty of obtaining performances did not inhibit whatever original ideas young composers might have had; some newcomers must have hoped that if they did not rock the boat, they might be able to climb in. In fact, a critic who signed himself "F. B." described composition in the mid-1830s as an act of imitation: composers either continued in traditional styles (Onslow is mentioned as a contemporary who followed this path), or imitated Rossini or Beethoven (but not the Late works, which were thought unworthy).[87]

In instrumental music the piano was attaining a drastically new role, gaining significance in chamber music and replacing the violin as the most prominent solo instrument.[88] Causes for this change (which are interrelated) were thought to include mechanical improvements to the piano, the advent of performers such as Liszt, Chopin, and Thalberg, the richer harmonies of nineteenth-century music, and the social need to utilize the pianos found in increasing numbers of private *salons*. The prevalence of *romances* and instrumental solos (particularly at *salons*) led to further use of the piano in an accompanying role.

A demise in chamber music was noted in some quarters (but not always mourned; in 1838 Blanchard complained that the Société Musicale programmed too many instrumental works, especially multi-movement compositions).[89] The more sympathetic Kastner was saddened that string quintets and quartets were so neglected; he felt that their demise was caused by contemporary composers' increasing effort to attract mass audiences,[90] yet realized that this was necessary in order to survive.[91] Concert music was coming to be considered passé—a genre of "auteurs classiques," played by habit and appealing only to the erudite.[92] An article from April 1834 mentioned that the Athénée Musical was the only performing orchestra in Paris other than those of the Société des Concerts du Conservatoire and the Opéra.[93]

It is tempting to agree with François Stoepel, who in 1835 argued that concert music in France was steadily declining—from the classics, through the variations of Herz and arrangements of melodies from ballets and operas, to the *contredanses* of Musard and Tolbecque.[94] The appearance and immediate success of commercial "popular" orchestras in 1833 and 1834 makes this evaluation seem particularly apt. But one must also recall that there *were* new series established to play orchestral or chamber music.

Persons alert to chronology might conclude that the subperiod of 1833 to 1839 would be viewed more realistically as two subperiods: 1833–35, in which "popular" orchestras arrived and proliferated, causing alarm among traditionalists; and 1835–39, in which supporters of "art" music regrouped. This categorization is certainly defensible. Equally important, however, and characteristic of the entire subperiod, was the musicians' attempt, through new organizations, to attract less affluent audiences. The most significant musical events of the previous subperiod (1828–33)—the establishment of the Conservatoire concerts and developments at the Opéra—had affected mainly the wealthy (both aristocrats and the *nouveaux riches*). In this second subperiod musicians and entrepreneurs sought to tap a larger portion of society, and therefore presented music (often in combination with other forms of entertainment) that could be enjoyed by persons with little musical background. Following the success of concerts offering "popular" music, attempts were made to interest the new audiences in traditional "art" music; these early efforts were largely unsuccessful, yet remain important historically as forerunners of the Concerts Populaires and Concerts Colonne.

1839–1846

Although statistics cited in chapter 4 suggest a substantial increase in "art" music performances in Paris during the early 1840s, the subperiod 1839 to 1846 suffered from artistic stagnation and the public's fascination with "popular" music. The best-established musical organizations persevered, but some series that supported "art" music foundered and were not replaced. The Concerts Valentino were succeeded by public dances and the Société de l'Athénée curtailed its schedule, probably for financial reasons. Even well-known series of "popular" and dance music became scarcer. For all repertories, single concerts and short series were replacing established institutions. Concerning the relationship between "art" music and "popular," Kastner wrote in 1843 that performers were too eager to perform solos, and therefore unwilling to accept the subordinate roles required in chamber music.[95]

Nearly all positive comments from the period were inspired by the (infrequent) founding of new series. Even these examples reflected the cultural indigence of the time, for excitement about new concerts was generally accompanied by declarations that such concerts had been badly wanted to fill some large gap in the Parisian musical scene. An article on the Cercle Musical des Amateurs (founded in 1837) cited the need for amateur orchestras—to revive old works that had disappeared from the repertory, and to provide young composers with the chance to hear their own music.[96] A good performance of Beethoven's Sixth Symphony in 1841 at the Concerts Vivienne (where both "popular" and "art" music were heard) elicited the wish that the management might program more works of such caliber.[97] The establishment of the Association des Artistes-Musiciens in 1843 (see chapter 2, pp. 71–72) is perhaps the best example of a positive step being taken because professional life for musicians had become nearly intolerable.

Berlioz excepted, French critics seem to have been reticent in describing the contemporary scene; indirect remarks, though, indicate the poor state of music. The announcement of a *matinée* of chamber works presented by Alard and Chevillard in 1839 included the comment that such *salons* were too rare.[98] Shortly before Berlioz left to tour Germany in 1842, Liszt wrote him an open letter stating that "Germany is the country of symphonies; it is therefore yours";[99] by implication, France was not. When a benefit concert was planned for the recently widowed Mme. H.-M. Berton in 1844, the organizers were unable to find enough orchestral players to execute a Beethoven symphony, and Liszt's piano reduction of the Sixth Symphony's finale was hurriedly substituted.[100] Finally, a common attitude (and misunderstanding) regarding chamber music is revealed by publishers' catalogs from the mid-1840s, which listed string quartets and quintets under "violin."

Chorley was more direct; his view of composition in France, published in 1841, was hardly encouraging:

> With all their zeal, there have never been any signs among the French of the foundation of a school of national orchestral composition. . . .
>
> [The French lack] the possession of that poetical enthusiasm, balanced by sound and ancient science—that sufficiency of fantasy and sufficiency of judgement united—necessary to combine elements of melody and harmony, for the production of such masterpieces as Haydn, Mozart, and Beethoven have left.[101]

Berlioz regarded the early to mid-1840s as a particularly hard time; in 1840 he observed that Beethoven had lost his snob appeal and that the dilettantes in the boxes were bored.[102] A century later, Berlioz's biographer Barzun made several perceptive remarks on the period, also venturing thoughtful explanations. Concerning France in 1840, Barzun has written:

> The "railroad decade" was underway and the spectacle of its greedy folly was beginning to discourage all sensitive minds.[103]

Of the early 1840s:

> The intellectual eclipse that Renan ascribed to the Second Empire beginning in 1852 had in reality begun a decade before.[104]

Of Berlioz's return to Paris (from Central Europe) in 1846:

> He could see that when compared with Central Europe Paris was stagnant. It was no longer the hub which it had been three decades before. . . . Prague now had a great Conservatory, Vienna the best orchestra, and the separate German states an enormous urge to produce and perform.[105]

Barzun has not ignored the remaining supporters of "art" music, but has suggested that resistance to the Italian composers made upholders of the native tradition conservative and academic, so that even Mendelssohn seemed "modern and venturesome."[106]

Much space in the preceding chapters has been devoted to the idea that musical life in nineteenth-century France was not as drear as is usually believed. The period of 1839 to 1846 may warrant an exception to this thesis. Barzun's comments on this era suggest that much of the fault lay with the audience. On one hand, there was the lack of support for the Concerts Valentino, the boredom with Beethoven, and the ignorance of symphonic form;[107] and in fact both musicians and entrepreneurs appear to have temporarily abandoned efforts to interest the uncultured audience in "art" music. On the other, as indicated by Barzun and by statistics in chapter 4, the minority that supported "art" music became increasingly narrow-minded in the first half of the century, thereby discouraging composition in a modern idiom. H.-M. Berton explained in 1840 that contemporary composers did not attempt string quartets and quintets because they were intimidated by the prototypes of Haydn, Mozart, Boccherini, Beethoven, and Onslow.[108] Caught between Scylla and Charybdis, serious young composers saw little reason to write music that would never be performed or published.

This analysis ignores a few bright spots: performances of new works by Charles Dancla, Félicien David, Louise Farrenc, and Mendelssohn; the lively but largely unpublicized *séances* of Zimmermann and Gouffé; the (unsuccessful) attempts of a few amateur instrumental groups (such as the Société d'Harmonie) to establish series. With these rare exceptions, however, the period of 1839 to 1846 matches the popular conception of musical life in France between the Revolution and the Franco-Prussian War.

1847–1853

The frequency of social revolutions in nineteenth-century France notwithstanding, it seems improbable that a revolution in artistic taste could occur within a short period; yet the Parisian musical scene changed dramatically in the years between 1847 and 1853. To some extent, musicians became more independent, playing music that they liked for whatever audience would listen. Significant new orchestral (or orchestral-choral) societies included the Union Musicale, Berlioz's Grande Société Philharmonique de Paris, the Société Sainte-Cécile, and the Société des Jeunes-Artistes (see chapter 2, pp. 37–46 and 73–74). The cause of chamber music was embraced with new determination by Dancla, the Société Alard-Franchomme, the Société de Musique Classique, and the Société des Derniers Quatuors de Beethoven. Little if any of this change seems directly related to the February Revolution, which was mentioned by musicians only as a terrible disruption to the 1848 season (see chapter 2, p. 15).

The new societies were, rather, the result of crying needs in the Parisian musical scene, and announcements of their establishment typically described them as oases in an expansive desert. Each society brought promise, but critics pointed out that accomplishments of the new organizations were long overdue or distressingly unique. For example, the Société de Musique Classique (which promoted chamber music, especially that for large ensembles with winds) was said to fill a major gap.[109] Léon Kreutzer expected the Grande Société Philharmonique to rival similar societies *already long established* in London, Vienna, and St. Petersburg.[110] The Société des Derniers Quatuors de Beethoven was lauded because its repertory consisted of music previously little known in France.[111]

Other aspects of French musical life also elicited mixed reports. In May 1852 the press noted that the government had given the Société Sainte-Cécile 1000 francs as encouragement[112] (a surprising departure from earlier governments' behavior toward musical institutions); yet two months later Edouard Fétis complained about the lack of government support for music.[113] Regarding the promotion of new music, Léon Kreutzer maintained that, contrary to announced intentions, the Société Sainte-Cécile performed only old, well-established works (see chapter 2, note 115). Gouffé's *séances* were still considered to be conspicuous for their frequent presentations of new compositions,[114] yet the Grande Société Philharmonique, having committed itself to perform each year a work of any genre by a Prix de Rome winner upon his or her return from abroad, found response to this offer to be disappointing.[115]

Perhaps most confusing for both contemporaries and historians were developments relating directly to instrumental music and its audience. Good attendance at concerts of orchestral and chamber music was reported frequently; Berlioz, however, claimed about 1854 that the public was increasingly indifferent to all music other than opera.[116] Despite the enthusiasm for the many new series promoting instrumental music, several of these lasted only briefly. Blanchard remarked in 1847 that Paris offered better performances of string quartets than did any other European city, but that the *amateurs'* interest in this genre was diminishing.[117] In 1851 Edouard Fétis wrote that performers had kept chamber music alive, though composers were not supplying new works.[118] A. de la Fage held the same view, maintaining—not quite accurately—that Mme. Farrenc was practically the only French composer cultivating "la haute musique instrumentale."[119] Yet composers complained that performers had little interest in new music. Efforts to propagate "art" music among broader audiences (that is, lower classes) were renewed,[120] even though Blanchard wrote that concerts of the Société Sainte-Cécile, in the medium price range, attracted mainly instrumental dilettantes, many of them foreigners.[121]

As confusing as the period of 1847 to 1853 may seem, it can perhaps be summarized by the following sequence of events: the sudden development of new interest (among musicians almost exclusively, at first) in chamber music, demonstrated by new series; a brutal interruption to musical life by the February Revolution; resumption, with continued promotion of chamber music (evident in the multiplication of minor series presenting this genre) and the establishment of new orchestras,[122] leading to increasing but hardly unanimous optimism in the early 1850s. The summary above is supported by a sample of contemporary comments. Blanchard had noted late in 1846 that performances of string quartets and quintets seemed to have diminished since the 1830s (though he mentioned the activities of the violinists Alard and Tilmant as exceptions to this trend).[123] Looking back to 1847, Bourges (in 1849) remarked upon a manifestation of interest in chamber music, immediately preceding (and interrupted by) the February Revolution.[124] Of Paris in 1848, Berlioz wrote bitterly:

> A man must have a tri-color flag over his eyes to fail to see that music in France is now dead and that it is the last of the arts to which our rulers will pay attention.[125]

And further:

> Nothing is left of what used to exist in art. . . . No one even thinks of it or talks about it.[126]

As "art" music was revived after 1848 by the new societies mentioned above, confidence returned.[127] Displaying long-range optimism in 1853, Edouard Monnais ventured renewed hope for music in the second half of the century, citing the growing number of new operas being performed, and the progress of concert music at the Conservatoire, the Société Sainte-Cécile, and the Association des Artistes-Musiciens.[128]

1854–1860

By some indications, the period of 1854 to 1860 appears to have been the liveliest era for music yet described. Major new series appeared, among them the *séances* of Lebouc and Lamoureux and the concerts of the Société des Quatuors de Mendelssohn. Several new short series dotted the concert scene, while the only significant organization to cease activity was the Société Sainte-Cécile. There were probably more concerts, and certainly more performances of "art" music, than before. Chamber music enjoyed unprecedented success. Monnais suggested that a new regime of symphonic writing, in which the outstanding artists included Gouvy, Litolff, and Rosenhain, had been inspired by the Société des Jeunes-Artistes.[129]

Yet there was a lull in the excitement with which music was regarded and a respite from the rapid change of the previous few years. Contemporary observers expressed a sensation of stasis, and with good reason; the series that offered the best performances were in a rut. The Conservatoire concerts were directed by the unadventurous Girard (see chapter 2, pp. 33–34). The Maurin-Chevillard Quartet's promotion of Beethoven's Late quartets was no longer novel. Similarly, programs of the Société des Quatuors de Mendelssohn attracted attention at first, but soon became repetitive. And the Société Alard-Franchomme, whose high performance standards were no longer unique in Paris, retained a limited and conservative repertory. Consequently, the best organizations were increasingly ignored by the press, who sought something new. Journalists' neglect of these organizations should not be interpreted solely as a contemporary obsession with novelty; the repertories of the four organizations mentioned above were extremely small, and critics found it ever more difficult to say something fresh about the same few works repeated by the same performers.[130] Complaints about the lack of programming variety and absence of new works from the standard repertory were common. Liszt wrote in 1855 that Paris (like London, Leipzig, Berlin, and many other cities) had stopped at Beethoven.[131] The normally conservative Adolphe Botte, a new music critic for the *Revue et gazette musicale de Paris,* congratulated Sivori for programming recent works, remarking that new music was often banned elsewhere.[132] Even the reactionary critic Scudo commented that in 1859 the programs of the Société des Jeunes-Artistes, which had been established to perform works of young composers, lacked newness.[133] The promotion of young composers was specifically encouraged by Botte (who in 1859 suggested that Paris needed a society devoted to new works),[134] by Blanchard (who commended the Institution Impériale des Jeunes Aveugles for presenting a program of recent compositions),[135] and, most imaginatively, by F.-J. Fétis in a series of articles entitled "Que peut-on faire pour améliorer la condition des jeunes compositeurs?"[136] Fétis stated that the only way to reverse the declining taste of the general public was to make more performances of good music available via government subsidy. He suggested that the government should support 1) a large-scale revival of music in 15 cathedrals (which, theoretically, would in turn benefit church schools and organ teachers), 2) presentation of new operas at five cities other than Paris, and 3) the establishment at conservatories of quartet societies and orchestras that would be obliged to perform new works during the summer, when other musicians had time to listen. Promotion of new efforts was clearly rare. (Paris was hardly more receptive to preclassical music; Fétis's attempt to revive *concerts historiques* in 1855 was a failure.[137])

Opportunities to hear orchestral music decreased in the late 1850s; from 1856 through 1860 there were only two major orchestral series. Chamber music, however (and despite the unchanging nature of the three most renowned chamber music societies), was experiencing unprecedented public success, as critics (mainly Blanchard) repeatedly noted. Early in 1855 Blanchard declared, "La musique classique et de chambre est plus que jamais en honneur."[138] Later that year he chastised soloists for continuing to play light music when the public had developed an interest in "art" music.[139] By 1856 he was writing of "l'ère du quatuor," and reporting that chamber music concerts had their own set of dilettantes and fanatics.[140] He also saw (somewhat belatedly) a termination in German instrumental music with the deaths of Beethoven, Weber, and Mendelssohn, and wished that a French composer might follow their footsteps.[141] In 1857 Blanchard noted that audiences were overflowing at *séances* of chamber music, and remarked upon the growing number of chamber music groups, citing nine.[142] Apparently because of public demand, soloists in the late 1850s often included one chamber work on their programs.

Although the Préfet de la Seine sponsored concerts, and the government aided the Société des Jeunes-Artistes (indirectly, through the Conservatoire), the granting of permission to Félicien David to present concerts of his own music in the Conservatoire concert hall was still considered an exceptional favor.[143] The government remained protective of the few institutions that it subsidized.

Lest readers be misled by the growing enthusiasm for chamber music, they should be aware that opera remained central in the Parisian musical scene. In weekly issues and annual reports of the *Revue et gazette musicale,* opera news received top billing, and the most space. Apart from having become habit, this practice seems to have reflected contemporary taste. But the best-established instrumental groups hindered their own publicity, for the simple reason that newspapers present news.[144]

1860–1870

Among the roughly 50 new series that appeared in the final decade before the Franco-Prussian War, only a few achieved lasting importance, and many foundered after a single season. But, as in the past, nearly all were established with the intention of filling voids in Parisian musical activities, and the announced goals of each institution reflect various sorts of improvement that contemporaries felt were needed. Primary among these goals were two familiar ideas involving expansion: a larger audience that would include the middle and lower classes; and a larger repertory, with more instrumental music and more works of young composers.

The spreading of concerts to the less wealthy is best exemplified by the accomplishments of the Concerts Populaires. To reiterate briefly, the Concerts Populaires, founded in 1861, presented good performances of fairly traditional "art" music in a hall large enough to permit low individual admission charges, thereby consistently attracting large crowds of persons who had not previously heard such music. An anonymous writer for the *Revue et gazette musicale* believed that the Concerts Populaires were established at a propitious time (for both the Concerts and the general public), suggesting that, as every school and organization then had its own band, it was essential to guide the taste of the multitude by providing the opportunity to hear musical masterpieces well executed.[145]

The success of the Concerts led to immediate and continuing optimism concerning the enthusiastic response of the new audience toward "art" music. Monnais, in reviewing musical events in 1861, described the concerts as a great equalizer of classes.[146] Maurice Cristal wrote in 1867 that instrumental music in particular was no longer a pleasure reserved for connoisseurs and dilettantes, having been "popularized" in all major cities.[147] By 1870 the public had reputedly developed a decided taste for "art" music.[148] The Concerts Populaires also inspired many imitators; most notable was Lamoureux's series, which appended the label "Séances Populaires" in 1863, but several less renowned organizations also helped to spread the musical wealth. The announced intentions of the Société Philharmonique de Paris (1866) included popularizing the repertory of the Conservatoire concerts and promulgating new works.[149] The

Société des Quintettes Harmoniques (1869) hoped to alleviate the need for music on the Left Bank.[150] Other new organizations that catered (or intended to cater) to the less affluent include the Athénée Musical (1864), the Société du Grand Concert (1864), and Holmes's concerts for *lycée* students (1866). (See Appendix A.)

Expansion of the repertory was effected by several new series, particularly by those specializing in either single genres or contemporary works (see chapter 2, pp. 77–80). Meanwhile, older organizations enlarged their repertories. The Armingaud-Jacquard Quartet, originally established to propagate Mendelssohn, paid more attention to other composers after 1860.[151] By 1868 Lebouc was attempting a new work at each of his *séances*. Nonetheless, the feeling that older music was better remained widespread. Elwart, historian of the Conservatoire concerts, regarded the late eighteenth century as the highpoint of music history.[152] In lists of favorite composers, Scudo included Bach, Haydn, Mozart, Weber, Beethoven, and Schubert, and Cristal (limiting himself to instrumental music) named Boccherini, Haydn, Mozart, and Beethoven.[153]

Such opinions continued to make life for young composers difficult. A report from Paris in the Leipzig *Allgemeine musikalische Zeitung,* 1863, deplored the conservatism of French programs:

> Works more recent [than Beethoven's] are heard here extremely seldom, and it has been only a few years since even Mendelssohn was first accepted on the programs of the Conservatoire concerts. Schumann and Schubert are but little known as instrumental composers; . . . a few cautious attempts have been made, in concerts established especially for this purpose, to present works of living composers to the public . . . but the attempts met with no real sympathy, and the public, quite content not to compromise itself, would rather be allowed to admire pretty much the same pieces by famous masters every year; the artists, for their part, find this so convenient that they do not feel impelled to challenge this routine.[154]

In the same year, F.-J. Fétis discussed problems living composers had in obtaining performances. The most significant orchestras and chamber music societies, as well as music publishers, were interested only in works of established writers, yet there was no way to become established without being performed or published. Fétis believed that worthy French instrumental music was being written, but not performed, and asked the government to subsidize concerts (by Paris's best organizations, the Conservatoire orchestra and three major chamber music societies) of music by living French composers.[155]

Several commentators blamed the audience for young composers' difficulties. Elwart maintained that the Société des Concerts du Conservatoire had provided good performances of symphonies by newcomers, but that the public liked only Haydn, Mozart, and Beethoven.[156] Charles Bannelier stated in 1868 that the conservative programming of the Conservatoire concerts was difficult to criticize as it was so successful.[157] Writing years later, Duparc (who was in his teens in the 1860s) mentioned the hostility of audiences toward all that was new.[158] Saint-Saëns declared that in the 1860s "one had really to be devoid of all common sense to write music."[159] Today, it is impossible to know the true reaction of those audiences, but it is clear that many societies offered them little opportunity to hear new works, and it is probable that they received the unfamiliar with little enthusiasm. One wonders what the effect might have been had an established organization persistently promoted new works. As late as 1867 Monnais felt that while interest in music was increasing, taste was becoming more conservative.[160]

There were, however, more organizations and individuals awakening and reacting to the problems of contemporary composers. Even the conservative Elwart claimed to encourage more performances of works by faculty and students of the Conservatoire.[161] Other conservatives, such as Botte, praised societies that tried new works.[162] And there were several series deserving such praise (see chapter 2, pp. 77–79). But as late as 1869 the practice of supporting contemporary music was still considered too rare[163]—a sad commentary on the limited success of earlier groups in this endeavor.

A concern related to the hardships of young composers was the minor role of French composers in the repertory (and complementary prominence of Germans). A fascination with Germanic "art" music was noted by the Parisian correspondent of the *Allgemeine musikalische Zeitung* in 1863:

> Increasingly, German music is becoming fashionable here. It is so delightful that good music is no longer heard exclusively at the Conservatoire, the Concerts Populaires, and the quartet societies (which multiply each year), but also at most concerts and private *soirées* where, only a short while ago, virtuoso pieces and operatic fantasias of all kinds were widespread—although so far it is much more fashion that is causing this revolution than greater public understanding. . . . In the *salons* [of high society], spendidly illuminated, grand, replete with gold and silk, is assembled a large circle of the most elegant Parisian ladies in brilliant "ball dress," but not necessarily to dance the quadrille or polka. No, it is a musical *soirée,* and what is being presented to these elegant ladies? Is it a celebrated virtuoso who is showing off? Is it Mlle. Patti, the prima donna of the Théâtre-Italien, who is now turning everyone's head? No, it is Beethoven's Late Quartets.[164]

Duparc later wrote that there was no French symphonic art,[165] but Elwart, referring to symphonies in particular, suggested that France in the 1860s had composers who could potentially compete with German artists.[166] Some support was provided by the Concerts Populaires, though their repertory emphasized German works. More nationalism was exhibited by the Société des Quatuors Français (see chapter 2, p. 79).

Regardless of the handicapped position of young or native composers, there was general agreement that in the 1860s instrumental music excited unprecedented interest. In 1861 Scudo wrote:

> Each day the public, and particularly Parisian high society, further initiates itself to great instrumental music; the works of Beethoven, Haydn, Mozart, Weber, Mendelssohn, Schubert, Fesca, Boccherini, and even Schumann are finding in Paris an enlightened audience which thirty years ago did not exist.[167]

Discussing the Alard-Franchomme chamber music society, Botte reported that in its early years the participants had had to struggle against popular taste, but that by 1862 they were well accepted.[168] Mathieu de Monter, in 1867, remarked upon booming interest in instrumental music all over Europe; in Paris he cited the success of the Concerts Populaires and the Athénée and the expanded schedule of the Société des Concerts du Conservatoire.[169] Reports of enthusiasm for instrumental "art" music appear in many reviews of individual concerts and *salons*. The Chartier prize, a yearly award for composers or editors of chamber music, was established (actually bequeathed) in 1861.

Despite the apparent progress of instrumental music with the public, it still suffered from lack of recognition and disappointing, sometimes old-fashioned performances. Bannelier in 1866 lauded the courage of one Oechsner for writing chamber music when it brought little fame and no money.[170] Astonishingly, in summaries of the musical seasons 1864 and 1865 (banner years for performances of instrumental music), the *Revue et gazette musicale* mentioned no instrumental activity other than the visit of a Russian military band in 1865.[171] When Berlioz travelled to St. Petersburg in 1867 he wrote back to Mme. Massart:

> The orchestra [here] is superb and does exactly what I want. If you could hear them play Beethoven's symphonies, I think you would say things that don't occur to you at the Conservatoire.[172]

Like the Conservatoire orchestra, the primary Parisian chamber music societies were highly regarded by the natives, yet when the Quatuor Florentin visited France in 1869, surprised critics described its ensemble playing and balance (in which the first violin was not overly prominent) as "unequaled."[173]

New styles of orchestral music (particularly symphonies) provoked widely varied reactions. Elwart approved the symphonies of Scipion

Rousselot, Reber, Félicien David, Gouvy, and Louise Farrenc, but felt that the less traditional works of Berlioz and Douay were destroying the genre.[174] Botte argued that music's purpose is to depict the soul, and predicted that contemporary attempts to depict local color would never become musically significant.[175] Ives Kéramzer defended the "modern" symphony, however, urging remembrance that art must be continuously transformed and renewed. He believed it unfair to compare the classical symphony, which had reached its pinnacle, with the more recent "narrative" symphony, which he happily greeted as a new form—still in its formative stage.[176]

New attitudes toward the symphony (by someone other than Berlioz), new interest in instrumental music, new societies, new repertory, new audiences—all indicate that the 1860s were a giant step toward the postwar "renaissance."

Postwar Developments

This study's chronological terminus is the period of the Franco-Prussian War, after which, according to traditional thought, the French musical renaissance arrived. Historians defining this renaissance have generally cited three interrelated developments: 1) a new sense of nationalism (perhaps more accurately, anti-Germanic sentiment) created sudden interest in French art; 2) postwar financial difficulties particularly affected opera production, causing a turn to instrumental music (previously primarily a Germanic genre); and 3) the newly founded Société Nationale de Musique strongly supported French music, especially instrumental works, and thereby led the renaissance movement. Some occurrences during the years immediately following the war do not support this version of history. In the first postwar issue of the *Revue et gazette musicale* (October 1871, a time when anti-Germanic feeling should theoretically have been high), the French publisher Maho advertised works of Haydn, Mozart, Schumann, Brahms, Raff, Rüfer, Eckert, and Hoelzel.[177] The Séances Populaires returned in 1872 with programs of Bach, Handel, Haydn, Mozart, and Beethoven, and *introduced* vocal works to their concerts. Of 51 known performances of instrumental works at the Concerts Populaires in 1871, 8 involved French works, while 37 involved German (or Austrian). Furthermore, both the Opéra and the Opéra-Comique had resumed active schedules by early October 1871, before the concert season began and before the first concert of the Société Nationale de Musique.

It seems correct, nevertheless, to acknowledge a surge of interest in native instrumental music after the war. Mathieu de Monter stated that there had never been as much music in Paris as in the final three months of 1871. He believed that "absolute" music was gaining favor with the public, and saw the possibility of a bright future for the French symphonic school (he mentioned works of Bizet, David, Gouvy, Guiraud, and Reber).[178] The Concerts Danbé, beginning in October 1871, supported instrumental music and programmed (not exclusively instrumental) works of Adam, Baillot, Gounod, Leclair, Meyerbeer, Saint-Saëns, and Thomas.[179] The Concerts Mozart, established a month later, played Adam, Auber, Hérold, and Halévy, and seemed to avoid German works. The Société Nationale, whose concerts also commenced at this time, eventually became the most renowned promoter of French music. Its immediate effect, however, was probably less than that of the successful Concerts Danbé and Concerts Mozart, for its earliest concerts attracted mainly composers.[180] In 1873 the Concerts Colonne came into being; they successfully promoted the music of Berlioz and several living French composers. Even the Conservatoire concerts complied to some extent with changes in taste: according to Deldevez's statistics, the Conservatoire added only 5 French instrumental works to its repertory from 1861 to 1870, but from 1872 to 1880 introduced 19 such works.[181]

Did France experience a musical "renaissance" after the war? Clearly there was considerable interest in native music, especially instrumental works—more than at any time in the nineteenth century, and possibly more than ever before. In this sense, "renaissance" is the appropriate term. But "renaissance" is, in this context, often interpreted as "feast after famine," and construed this way is misleading. The last true musical famine occurred in the 1820s, and though the early to mid-1840s were lean years, the musical fare that preceded the feast became increasingly substantial after 1846.

Historical Commentary

Remaining are comments, descriptions, and explanations that concern (or purport to concern) the entire period of 1828 to 1871. Until recently, French instrumental music of the mid-nineteenth century has suffered relative neglect by historians and musicologists. This lack of attention is attributable partly to the Germanic origins of musicology (German scholars understandably concentrated on German music) and partly to the (not unrelated) assumption that there was little French music worthy of investigation. Writers on the subject, therefore, have had surprisingly few sources, and have relied heavily on published remarks by the era's most famous musicians active in Paris—Berlioz, Liszt, Gounod, Lalo, Saint-Saëns. The comments of these artists, valuable as personal perceptions of musical life (and fascinating reading), are not necessarily the most reliable versions of history. Author-musicians were not overly careful with their chronology; as Martin Cooper noted years ago, Saint-Saëns's often-quoted passage from *Portraits et souvenirs* (1900), which provides a horribly bleak picture of Paris "when Gounod came on the scene," "fifty years ago," is really more applicable to the 1840s.[182] Berlioz and Saint-Saëns in particular practiced the art of hyperbole (the writings on Paris that Liszt signed seem, by contrast, particularly fair and free of exaggeration), yet have sometimes been interpreted too literally. When Berlioz wrote in his *Mémoires* (in the 1850s) of "the public's increasing indifference to all music that was not opera,"[183] he was undoubtedly frustrated by the recent failure of major Paris orchestras (including his own Grande Société Philharmonique), and by his lack of public success in France, but was ignoring the recent advances of chamber music that many of his contemporaries described. One must always bear in mind that when Berlioz et al. complained about the barren musical scene, they were usually ignoring musical activities that did not satisfy their own high expectations, and that acknowledgement of the worst aspects of French musical life need not indicate a total absence of good.

Another major source of information (and misinformation), particularly about concert societies, is the writings of the theorist, composer, and historian Antoine Elwart. Clearly his books on the Société des Concerts du Conservatoire (1860) and the Concerts Populaires (1864) have been relied upon heavily, for incorrect dates and other errors stated therein have been widely dispersed. Similarly, his descriptions of the period (for example, "La musique de chambre [in 1860] s'exécute à peine dans deux ou trois réunions d'amateurs fervents")[184] have too frequently been accepted without question. His books are significant and unique sources, but are colored by his conservative taste, his determination to defend the Conservatoire and its concert society at any cost, and his reluctance to acknowledge rival musical organizations.

Early twentieth-century authors relied on the nineteenth-century sources mentioned above, and could still have obtained first-hand memories from musicians, such as Saint-Saëns (1835–1921), Massenet (1842–1912), and even Dancla (1817–1907), who had been active in France before 1870. These authors, secure that their interpretation of the nineteenth century would not affect its future, wrote with considerably more historical detachment than Berlioz or Elwart. Romain Rolland emphasized, by analogy with "Great Man" histories, Great Events. He wrote that Paris was a musical town until about 1840, suffered complete apathy in the Second Empire except for a slight revival in the 1860s, and finally reawakened in the 1870s. As a basis for this analysis he cited the discovery of Beethoven's symphonies at the Conservatoire concerts, performances of Spontini and Gluck, and the appearance of Berlioz's early works (all before 1840), the Concerts Populaires and Berlioz Festival (1860–70), and the establishment of the Société Nationale and the Colonne concerts (early 1870s).[185] Each of these events is important, but Rolland ignored day-to-day musical life, which suggests a drastically different interpretation: Paris offered much more "art" music in the 1850s than before 1840.

Other early twentieth-century historians began to attempt explanations of nineteenth-century musical life and its transformations, sometimes simplistically. Tiersot wrote that in the mid-1800s a group of composers decided it was time that French music be known by something other than Auber operas, and began writing orchestral suites.[186] (It is difficult to understand how Tiersot, who wrote extensively about music in nineteenth-century France, could maintain than when the Quatuor Armingaud-Jacquard was founded in the mid-1850s, "nowhere could the quartets of Beethoven, Mozart, or Haydn be heard."[187]) Arthur Hervey believed that the Concerts Populaires had inspired among composers an interest in symphonic music.[188] Many of the better-known symphonies, however—Berlioz's, Gounod's, Bizet's, four of Saint-Saëns's—date from before the establishment of the Concerts Populaires. One of the more imaginative histories is E. B. Hill's *Modern French Music*. Hill noted the establishment of orchestral and choral societies in the second half of the century, and blamed the lack of French instrumental music on the Conservatoire's dominant influence. Hill said that the Conservatoire had not encouraged instrumental writing, as it offered no courses in advanced instrumental forms, and invariably required the composition of a cantata for the Prix de Rome contest. He sometimes, however, overstated a case; his remark that Castillon "was drawn particularly toward chamber music at a time when this branch of musical art was not appreciated or even understood" is unjust and seemingly inconsistent with even his own version of history.[189]

Later historians remained slow to acknowledge prewar French instrumental activity. Landormy stated, "From 1830 to 1870, one can say that France was closed to all symphonic music,"[190] and Gerald Abraham maintained that in the period after Beethoven's death, chamber music was not played in France.[191] Lang developed an intriguing theory to explain the advent of Grand Opera and (what he termed) "the complete decline of instrumental music" in France—namely, that "Reduced to inactivity by historical events, the French nation spent the two decades between 1825 and 1845 in imagining what could no longer be achieved."[192] Pierre Meylan must have been thinking along similar lines when he stated that the Romantics viewed music as a *"phénomène extérieur,"* little related to the real world depicted in literature and painting.[193] I believe Meylan was implying that traditional opera, sacred music, and instrumental works must have seemed far removed from everyday life—and, similarly, from the empathy aroused by the portrayal of basic human emotions in Grand Opera and other Romantic art forms—and therefore did not satisfy the French Romantics. Lang also wrote that as late as 1870 "young French composers could think of nothing but opera," though on the same pages he commended the activity of Pasdeloup (whose Concerts Populaires began in 1861) and noted that "in the second half of the century" some composers (he mentioned Franck, Lalo, and Saint-Saëns) wrote instrumental works.[194] Landormy, Abraham, Lang, and others used the best sources available to them (short of doing primary research on this topic), and their generalized depictions reflect widely held beliefs concerning concert life in mid-nineteenth-century France; yet the picture they present is misleading, for it exaggerates the plight of instrumental music. One wonders why historians for so long ignored one major indication of Parisian instrumental activity: the article "Paris" in *Grove's Dictionary,* from the third edition (1927–28)[195] through the fifth, provides a fairly accurate (though by no means complete) list of concert societies in nineteenth-century France.

In the period from the 1920s to the 1950s, scattered new investigations into instrumental music appeared. Georges Servières wrote "La Symphonie en France au XIXe siècle (avant 1870)" in 1923.[196] Pierre Soccanne's research on Pierre Baillot[197] furnished information on Baillot's *soirées,* and Leo Schrade examined the history of attitudes toward Beethoven's music in France.[198] About midcentury, three major works arrived: Jacques Barzun's revolutionary *Berlioz and the Romantic Century;* Boris Schwarz's dissertation on French instrumental music before 1830; and Martin Cooper's *French Music from the Death of Berlioz to the Death of Fauré,* which reappraised some aspects of French music before Berlioz's death.[199] Recent historians of the nineteenth century, such as Longyear and Klaus, have demonstrated greater awareness of both composition and performance of instrumental works in France before 1870 (see chapter 1, page 2). Dorothy Hagan, who investigated French musical criticism, has concluded that "abundant evidence exists of strong support for serious music during the July Monarchy,"[200] and William Weber's archival research has indicated that after 1830 the concert schedule expanded dramatically.[201]

Apart from describing concert activity (or lack thereof), a few writers have discussed the music itself; some have tried to explain why so little of it has been deemed noteworthy, and why so much of it was conservative. Elwart is again a major nineteenth-century source; his conservative thinking, examples of which were provided in the section on the

1860s, was representative of the Parisian musical establishment—and especially the Conservatoire. Redecoration of the Conservatoire's concert hall in the 1860s provided an opportunity to monumentalize esteemed composers, and the selection is revealing: around the hall were busts of "grands maîtres"—Bach, Haydn, Mozart, Gluck, Handel, and Beethoven—and in the balcony were Cherubini, Mendelssohn, Weber, Méhul, Boieldieu, Grétry, Spontini, Donizetti, Hérold, Halévy, Meyerbeer, and Rossini.[202] Elwart's feeling that Berlioz and Douay had destroyed the symphony was echoed almost exactly by Deldevez in his supplement to Elwart's history of the Conservatoire concerts, which covers the period from 1860 to 1885. In defending the backward programming of the Conservatoire concerts, Deldevez portrayed the series as the last bastion of the symphony proper, and argued for a retention of the classical style. He believed that Beethoven's symphonies, the Sixth in particular, carried the genre to its absolute limits, but admitted that composers who had continued in the classical vein had not experienced success. Of Beethoven's position on the Conservatoire's programs he wrote:

> S'il conserve ce premier rang, c'est qu'aucun autre compositeur *classique* n'est venu le détrôner. Et cela ne pourrait se faire jamais que par un auteur symphoniste de l'Ecole classique.

He was particularly critical of descriptive effects, *fantaisie,* and new harmonies that increased dissonance.[203]

Deldevez's proclamation "Pour assurer l'avenir le passé commande"[204] died hard. As late as 1902, Elwart's and Deldevez's conception of French symphonic history was reiterated by Julien Tiersot, who wrote that with Berlioz the French symphony took a step in the wrong direction. Tiersot suggested that Berlioz attempted to follow Beethoven's lead,[205] a view of both Berlioz and the venerated Beethoven that would have struck earlier French critics as peculiar. If I understand Tiersot correctly, he was implying that Beethoven himself sometimes strayed far from approved paths.

Rolland, conveniently forgetting Berlioz, Debussy, and others, suggested that there were (and had been) no masters of French style; he wrote, "all our greatest composers are foreigners," citing as examples Lully, Gluck, Duni, Grétry, Rossini, Meyerbeer, and Franck. Rolland continued, "France in the nineteenth century acquired the habit of speaking German in music."[206] Regarding Germanic influence, Prod'homme believed that exoticism in works of Berlioz, Hérold, and Félicien David was inspired by Weber.[207] Rolland, however, was more likely referring to the many "textbook" sonatas manufactured by minor composers in what they took to be the classical style. William Weber has suggested that these overly academic attempts to imitate Beethoven repulsed listeners, discouraging interest in all instrumental "art" music.[208] Conversely, Barzun has theorized (as mentioned above) that reaction against the new Italian operatic style inspired this academic manner.[209]

Many writers have agreed that composers of instrumental music either continued in an outdated "classical" style, or tried to adapt the dramatic, virtuosic style of Italian opera (or French Grand Opera) to instruments and thus abandoned chamber and symphonic works. Most composers in the first half of the century saw little reason to explore further the alternative paths suggested in Beethoven's late works, as these compositions were little known in France, and were regarded as the efforts of a slightly mad deaf man. Music's recently gained freedom from dance and words[210] had in some ways made original composition more difficult, forcing creators to take the plunge into the unknown, or driving them back to familiar but old-fashioned ground. Probably the most innovative of native composers was Berlioz, but he did not gain a wide following. Critics, then and for a long time afterwards, thought his music overly reliant upon dramatic effect. Hervey, attempting to explain the low profile of the symphony "proper" in France, felt that French genius lay in dramatic music, citing Berlioz specifically.[211] The nineteenth century excepted, however, this has not been true of French music; Martin Cooper has stated that Berlioz influenced French music so little because he was unique.[212] Lockspeiser agreed that Berlioz's music, like Delacroix's paintings, contrasted with the delicacy and refinement characteristic of French art in other periods; he attributed the styles of both Berlioz and Delacroix to the emotional fervor of the period, and criticized Berlioz's music for its lack of depth.[213] Modern critics have discovered more to Berlioz's works than dramatic effect, but in the nineteenth century the very label "program music," whether or not justified, curtailed a work's success with some audiences. The earliest critic mentioned in this section, Stoepel, expressed an opinion that was widespread among French connoisseurs and musicians in the middle of the nineteenth century—namely, that instrumental music was intended to express inner thoughts, sentiments of the soul, and emotions, rather than specific descriptions.[214] Because of this popular aesthetic theory, certain inventive composers were neglected by the only listeners who could have appreciated their musical worth.

Some recent attempts to describe or explain musical activities in nineteenth-century France have concentrated on the audience. This is, of course, not a new topic; Berlioz often mentioned the audience, complaining, for example, in 1836 of wealthy dilettantes who attended even the best concerts for reasons primarily social rather than musical.[215] For a long time, however, the effect of different segments of the population on both concerts and music itself was little appreciated or explored.

Barzun has divided the Parisian public of the first half of the nineteenth century into two main groups:

> a public of exclusive opera-goers . . . [and] a fashionable and academic circle of amateurs, reared on the eighteenth-century classics and contemporary "little pieces," to whom Bach meant C. P. E. or J. C. but never J. S. All but a few felt that the uncouth Beethoven went too far.[216]

Neither group would have appreciated innovative instrumental works. William Weber has brought a sociological viewpoint to the topic, investigating the audiences involved in the conflict between (what he labelled) the German Classical style and the Rossini opera style. He has also convincingly demonstrated the dominating influence of middle-class commercialism on music after 1830.[217]

Finally, nineteenth-century French composers themselves have become the subject of scholarly investigation in recent years. Apart from impressive achievements in Berlioz studies, scholarly works have appeared on Saint-Saëns, Félicien David, Louise Farrenc, F.-J. Fétis, and Alexis de Castillon.[218] As the lives and works of these musicians are examined, new sources and facts come to light.

Future surveys of music (particularly that of the nineteenth century) will benefit from the historical accuracy, depth, and collective scope demonstrated by the writings mentioned above (and, presumably, of works still to come). Whether this greater availability of reliable material will inspire fuller treatment of nineteenth-century French music therein remains to be seen. But whatever space is allotted to this music, the conclusions drawn regarding instrumental music and concert life must be different than those accepted through most of the twentieth century.

6

French Instrumental Works

After chapters that repeatedly deplore the hardships of French composers and the troubles they experienced attempting to obtain performances of their works, it seems essential to ask what sort of instrumental music they wrote during the mid-nineteenth century. Berlioz's works have slowly become part of the standard repertory and gained a large following. Some of Saint-Saëns's prewar music is widely played (especially the Second Piano Concerto and "Introduction et Rondo Capriccioso"), even if it is not universally considered of the first rank. But who knows chamber works of Henri Bertini, Louise Farrenc, or Félicien David; or symphonies of Théodore Gouvy, Henri Reber, or even Gounod? Was nineteenth-century music worthy of performance, or was its neglect justified, and is the oblivion into which it has fallen deserved? Furthermore, are there noteworthy musical differences between works that received some contemporary performances, and those that were almost ignored? What were musicians and critics seeking in instrumental music?

French "art" music of the nineteenth century has not yet received much scholarly investigation, and some of the composers who were popular then have long since disappeared from musical reference sources. (The reader may note, in the following pages, frequent citations of *Cobbett's Cyclopedic Survey of Chamber Music* and F.-J. Fétis's *Biographie universelle des musiciens,* with its supplement, edited by Arthur Pougin;[1] for numerous obscure composers, these were the only sources I located, other than contemporary reviews, that mention their music.) Because of this state of research, I have chosen to sample many composers' instrumental works rather than to examine in detail the works of a few. But the list of composers whose music is surveyed here is in no way intended to be comprehensive; the main criteria for inclusion are 1) that the composer's oeuvre comprises "art" music, and 2) that the composer's works were performed a moderate number of times. Exceptions to the latter condition have been allowed for some little-played composers whose works are of particular musical interest. Further, there is no account of Berlioz's music, which is already familiar through performances, recordings, editions, and extensive coverage in recent publications. In the course of discussing instrumental "art" music, I shall attempt to describe various paths that French composers followed, to recognize musical ideals, to note trends that developed as the period progressed, and to seek a "renaissance" in style comparable to the resurgence found in the performance of "art" music.

A surprising number of French nineteenth-century composers produced instrumental works.[2] Complete "works" lists for many of them may be found in music encyclopedias and dictionaries, but it is perhaps useful to note here some of the major contributors between 1828 and 1871. Berlioz wrote nearly all his works after 1828 (he died in 1869). By 1871 Saint-Saëns had completed four symphonies, three piano concertos, two violin concertos plus the "Introduction et Rondo Capriccioso", an orchestral suite, a piano quintet, a piano quartet, a piano trio, a suite for cello and piano, and some lesser works. In the same period, Adolphe Blanc contributed a symphony, an overture, and approximately 35 chamber works, among them a septet, seven string quintets, two piano quintets, and three to five each of string quartets, piano quartets, piano trios, other trios, violin sonatas, and cello sonatas. Georges Onslow composed 35 string quartets and 34 string quintets, as well as several works for smaller and larger chamber ensembles, and four symphonies;[3] the majority of his oeuvre was completed after 1828. Louise Farrenc's works comprise three symphonies, an incomplete piano concerto, two overtures, and 13 chamber works, among them four trios and two piano quintets. Summary lists of instrumental works by many other prominent artists are included below, with descriptions of their music. A majority of the works by well-known composers were published.

More chamber music was written than orchestral, probably because the opportunity for performance was greater. Among chamber works, piano trios and string quartets were somewhat less predominant than they have since become in the "standard" repertory; many trios, quartets, and quintets required unusual combinations of instruments, including mixtures of strings, winds, and piano. This practice suggests that composers were writing for amateurs or for informal gatherings of professionals in musical *salons,* rather than for "permanent" professional groups, which comprised mainly string quartets and piano trios.

Instrumental "art" music was produced continuously throughout the period of 1828 to 1871; at no time was there a drought. As the era progressed composers increasingly lost interest in virtuosic works and turned to more complex and substantial genres.[4] Concertante pieces and *fan-*

taisies were replaced by sonatas and string quartets, though flashy solos, never entirely abandoned, continued to occupy a major portion of publishers' catalogs.

What was the nature of French "art" music in the period? We must examine, describe, and evaluate it with our own criteria, but we may be aided by a familiarity with contemporary ideals. A few composers wrote of their own music and aesthetics. Berlioz, for example, discussed extensively the relationship of music and drama, among other points; the formalist Saint-Saëns believed the organization of pure sounds to be of primary importance.[5] To find less personal aesthetic goals, one turns to contemporary criticism. An informal survey of reviews in the *Revue musicale, Gazette musicale de Paris,* and *Revue et gazette musicale de Paris* reveals which musical features attracted notice, which traits were praised, and which faulted. There was great concern with attractiveness of melody, little with thematic development; reviewers liked the harmony to be rich (frequent modulation was praised) and original (but not too much so); counterpoint *per se* was rarely mentioned, but equality of voices and interesting material for each instrument were stressed; novel orchestration was lauded; formal structure was discussed primarily in terms of tradition versus innovation; variety within a composition, contrast, surprise, good effects, and handling of details were all praised in early reviews, while unity, proportion, and economy later became more valued ideals. Favorite qualities were verve, liveliness, and brilliance, elegance, grace, and finesse, richness, and strength. Considering the nature of the music, it is surprising that clarity and classicality were only occasionally cited. Above all other criteria was originality. That this trait was emphasized more than correctness, *facture,* taste, or depth now seems odd, as the most innovative works of the period were often faulted for lacking some or all of the four latter qualities. Terms relating to expressiveness or inspiration were used infrequently, but many works were praised for their warmth.

Nineteenth-century writers distinguished between contemporaries who (they believed) continued in the tradition of eighteenth-century Classicism and those who sought something new,[6] and recognized that the two groups existed side by side. When, in 1853, the Académie Royale de Belgique sponsored a competition for the best new symphony, F.-J. Fétis (whose verbal report was recorded in the *Revue et gazette musicale*) noted that the works of the 12 finalists fell distinctly into two categories: 1) imitations of Haydn, Mozart, and Beethoven—works that "appartiennent à l'ancienne forme," and 2) works demonstrating innovation in, especially, form, sentiment, harmony, and rhythm. The winning symphony, by Hughes Ulrich, belonged to the first category.[7]

In placing certain nineteenth-century composers in the classical tradition, one is tempted to compare them with the most familiar composers of the classical period—Haydn, Mozart, and Beethoven. Charles Rosen, contrasting the composers whose works epitomize the Classical style with the " 'anonymous' style or musical vernacular of the late eighteenth century," has written that

> Even if Haydn and Mozart improbably differed in all essentials from their contemporaries, their work and their conception of expression would have to remain the center of the history.[8]

If one accepts the Viennese classicists as paragons against which French works are to be judged, one introduces a Germanic bias; there is, in theory, no reason why French composers' goals should match those of Germans (or Austrians) and an evaluation using Germanic standards is likely to be inappropriate.

This bias, however, is perhaps not as problematic as it first seems, for the nineteenth-century French musicians themselves associated a "traditional" style with the most famous representatives of Viennese classicism. Fétis's equation of Haydn, Mozart, and Beethoven with "l'ancienne forme" is typical among French critics. As statistics on programs clearly show, these three composers were not only familiar but absolutely dominant in the contemporary repertory, while other eighteenth-century composers of instrumental works were practically unknown. (From the late eighteenth century, the only other composer whose works received regular performances was Boccherini; works of French composers were completely neglected.) If critics and performers were acquainted mainly with Haydn, Mozart, and Beethoven among classical composers, and regarded them as the epitome of traditional music, it seems unlikely that contemporary classically oriented composers were working in some other tradition; almost unquestionably, these composers used Germanic models. When, in the pages below, I suggest that the nineteenth-century French version of classical music was less than successful, I am concerned not with a lack of Germanic traits therein, but with the French composers' inability to realize the classical style even when using these traits. Put simply, many French composers did write Germanic music, but less well than the Germans.

Most music does not fall as neatly into Fétis's two classifications as did the competitors' in the Belgian competition. The concept of a continuum, however, from the most traditional compositions to the most innovative, provides a convenient framework for placing nineteenth-century French composers, and therefore has been adopted as a means of organizing the discussion below.

A great number of composers belong at the conservative end of such a continuum. This was acknowledged in 1851 by Edouard Fétis, who stated that chamber works especially were often modeled upon eighteenth-century patterns.[9] "Patterns" is the appropriate word, for some composers seem to have regarded the formal plan as more crucial than the music; the resulting works resemble "textbook sonatas." A hypothetical sonata that combines the least imaginative features of contemporary French works might be described as follows: It has three or four movements, the inner ones being an "Andante" and (if there are four movements) a light, dancelike work (some pieces still had a Minuet and Trio).[10] At least one movement (and possbily as many as three) is in "sonata form," which here becomes a mold into which insipid themes and unmusical figuration are poured. Development sections are undramatic parades through related keys, separated from recapitulations that are not substantially changed from expositions, except for the retention of the tonic. The work is melody-oriented, yet the (usually diatonic) melodies lack lyricism and variety and are sectionalized into even, square phrases. Despite the emphasis on melody, there are many sections of static figuration—repeated cascades of scales and arpeggios, or simply broken-chord patterns. The combination of mechanical tunes and stale passage-work yields a mood commonly associated with études (in the worst sense). The texture comprises mainly an accompanied melody; the accompaniment often consists of unvarying, monorhythmic, chordal figuration. Harmonies are simple and diatonic, and there is little variety among the metrically oriented rhythmic patterns. In a symphonic work, written for an eighteenth-century orchestra, phrases or even entire themes are assigned to single melodic instruments or groups of instruments (that is, themes are not shared horizontally). The piano is unusually prominent in a chamber work, particularly one written by a pianist. Perhaps the most general difference between a "textbook sonata" and the examples of Haydn, Mozart, and Beethoven, is that the former lacks surprises. Whereas the Viennese classical composers established a set of melodic, harmonic, rhythmic, and formal expectations in order to work against them, many nineteenth-century compositions are studies in predictability; they lack the touches that give the best classical works life.

Contemporary criticism suggests that the "textbook sonata" was regarded as the direct descendant of works by the Viennese classicists; composers, and writers too, seemingly ignored the ways in which their famous predecessors had "broken the rules." For the remainder of this chapter, when the word "classical" is used, it refers more to the nineteenth-century image of "classicism" and a concept of "classical ideals" (such as simplicity, clarity, proportion), than to the actual music of Haydn, Mozart, and Beethoven.

Few works were as unimaginative in all aspects as the "model" sonata described above. To varying degrees, composers wrote innovatively within a traditional style, or broke from classical principles. The influence of the classical masters (and the nineteenth-century concept of classicism) was, however, clearly strong. Many nineteenth-century works reveal experimentation in only one or two aspects, remaining otherwise conventional.

Among the least imaginative examples are works by or for virtuosos. Because of exacting technical difficulties, uncontrolled flights of fancy, and perhaps some formal innovations to suit the soloist, these works could never be mistaken for eighteenth-century Classical music; but the melody, phrasing, harmony, key structure, rhythm, texture, and so forth are in many cases unoriginal and old-fashioned.

Most chamber and orchestral "art" works surpass virtuosic pieces in musical interest, though some (particularly, it seems, those by virtuosos) are no more innovative: the works of the violinists Habeneck and Lafont, and the flutist Tulou (among better-known musicians) come immediately to mind. The cellist Franchomme tried some formal experiments and essayed contemporary orchestration, but his music is otherwise unremarkable. Except for occasional colorful harmonies and abrupt modulations, the works of Nicolas Louis seem undistinguished. Eugène Walckiers's generally conservative works include imaginative rhythmic patterns and some interesting interplay among instruments.[11] But the following "Avis," inserted before the finale of his *1re Sonate pour Piano et Clarinette,* Op. 91 (by 1855), is antithetical to the philosophy of those prototypical Romantic artists who composed, as Donald Grout has described it, "for infinity, for posterity, for some imaginable ideal audience which, they hoped, would some day understand and appreciate them":[12]

> At gatherings in which the end of a work never arrives soon enough for the tastes of impatient persons or enemies of thoroughly-developed pieces, one will do well to suppress the Marche [of the finale] and not to begin the FINALE until the 2/4; but in this case, one will play the SCHERZO before the ADAGIO. One can even suppress the entire FINALE. Finally, one can also play only two movements: the PREMIER and the SCHERZO; or the ADAGIO and the SCHERZO; or, finally, the first movement and the FINALE.[13]

It was of course common practice to program only one or two movements of a multi-movement work, but hardly a habit that many composers wished to encourage.

Composers with more facility and imagination than those just mentioned did exist at the traditional end of the continuum. Historians have not considered them to be particularly significant, probably because they were neither truly innovative nor equal to the best classical composers; nonetheless, their works are not without rewards for performers and listeners. Most important among this group are Onslow, Reber, Louise Farrenc, and Adolphe Blanc. Charles Dancla, Elwart, Brod, and, for part of their oeuvres, Félicien David and Emile Douay might also be noted.

Many of the 69 string quartets and quintets of *Georges Onslow* (1784–1853) were produced in the quarter century between 1828 and his death. Onslow was an affluent amateur who resided in the provinces and paid for the publication of his own works; nevertheless, his were among the most-performed chamber works in Paris, and his symphonies were played at the Conservatoire concerts. Criticized by his contemporaries for lacking originality,[14] he has since been described as having been "careful to avoid all semblance of innovation" in his correct but unemotional music.[15] Although his conservatism was widely acknowledged, his taste and ability to write elegantly were never questioned. Berlioz praised his orchestration and rich, distinguished harmonies, and an anonymous critic lauded his counterpoint and thematic development, while comparing his themes favorably to Spohr's.[16] Among the samples of Onslow's works that I have seen (some of the quartets), the early ones are good examples of "textbook" sonatas, but are redeemed by lively rhythms, extreme dynamics (including effective silences), and occasional tonal surprises. For the most part a French tradition of treating the string quartet as a work for accompanied solo violin is followed. Although there is some interplay among instruments, the inner parts are generally dreary.

The later quartets, however, yield pleasant surprises. The formal structures, though still traditional, are less thematically oriented and more varied; the processes of development and recapitulation are no longer separate and some of the quick middle movements are five-part (Scherzo—contrasting section—Scherzo—contrasting section—Scherzo). There are colorful chromatic passages (see examples 1 and 2) in which the individual chords remain simple. More significant than chromatic alterations to individual lines, or the odd chromatic progression, is Onslow's ability to move confidently and easily from one tonal center to another, never abandoning the underlying tonal structures associated with classical forms. Even the late quartets, though, have an unrelieved "notey" quality; some simple, lyrical sections, contrasting with Onslow's predominantly rich, bold, brilliant writing, might have led to more permanent success.

Henri Reber (1807–1880) was probably most celebrated for his four symphonies. Saint-Saëns, who did not bestow praise lightly (and who appreciated Berlioz's music), called Reber the first French composer to

Ex. 1 Georges Onslow: String Quartet No. 35, Op. 66, D Major, introduction to first movement

Ex. 2 Onslow: String Quartet No. 35, theme from the Finale

succeed completely in this difficult genre.[17] An early review (by someone who was aware of Schubert's chamber works) cited bold harmonies, original rhythms and modulations, and expressive (even passionate) melodies in Reber's trios and quartets,[18] but a critique of the second symphony five years later (1839) compared the overall effect to that of Haydn's works,[19] and many subsequent reviews mentioned Reber's fondness for traditional forms. Hervey, much later, agreed that the symphonies were possibly modeled upon Haydn's.[20] Nearly everyone agreed that Reber's works were well-crafted, especially in the handling of details, and that his instrumental writing was praiseworthy. Of Reber's oeuvre I have examined only some chamber works from the middle of his career. They are well-constructed, with obvious concern for melody and form, and have imaginative development sections. The phrasing is less constricted than that of many contemporary works, and the harmonies are spiced with chromatic alterations, but usually in the form of passing tones amid familiar diatonic progressions (see example 3). The idiom, however, is basically traditional. Reber's works, though not likely to be mistaken for authentic Classical pieces, are in many ways no more modern than early Beethoven.

Louise Farrenc (1804–1875) was one of the foremost woman composers of the century, as well as a distinguished pianist and scholar of early keyboard music.[21] Like Reber, she wrote symphonies, but these attracted less attention than her chamber works (in performances of which she often participated): these twice (in 1861 and 1869) won the Prix Chartier. Bea Friedland has lauded Farrenc's mastery of the craft and consistently high standards as a composer, and has noted many beautiful and inspired passages as well as a "motoric energy and élan." Yet Friedland has admitted that Farrenc's works (particularly the symphonies) are little

Ex. 3 Henri Reber: Piano Trio No. 3, Op. 16, opening of second movement

different from earlier models, and suffer in comparison with the best of them.[22] I have studied only a violin sonata (Opus 39) and two trios (Opus 44 and Opus 45) of Farrenc. The simplicity of the works is striking: rarely do the harmonies exceed a diminished-seventh chord in complexity; and there are few surprises in the formal structure. Nevertheless, Farrenc succeeded in building traditional materials into a successful entity. The *facture* is solid, the music lively, and the extended forms well supported. The works have rhythmic vitality and passages of intriguing tonal structure; nonmelodic voices sometimes approach the status of a countermelody. Rather than having imitated classical works, Farrenc seems to have absorbed their principles and worked with them comfortably, while occasionally exhibiting a touch of Romantic drama.

Of less consistent quality are works of the prolific *Adolphe Blanc* (1828–1885). F.-J. Fétis suggested that they reveal the evident haste with which they were produced.[23] They are soundly rooted in tradition; Adolphe Piriou labeled Blanc "one of the last representatives of the purely classical school," a composer in the "ancient style."[24] Nonetheless the works reveal flexibility and imagination, and incorporate some Romantic traits, such as vivid dynamic contrast and occasional expression of melodrama. Most important, Blanc (who mastered compositional techniques early) understood how to use simple elements effectively. His individual chords are ordinary, but employed in unusual ways (the finale of the Trio for piano, clarinet, and cello, Opus 23 in B-flat Major, opens with an E-natural diminished-seventh chord leading to a B-flat minor six-four) and linked in interesting modulations. There is some alternation between major and minor modes. Melodies are rather plain—though in some movements they grow out of each other—and the parts for individual instruments are sometimes stark (surprisingly long sections of the piano parts comprise nothing but parallel octaves); yet Blanc's talent for utilizing all voices yields a satisfying texture, as melodic lines are divided horizontally among instruments, brief countermelodies duck in and out, and motifs become the subject of lively exchanges. Frequent rhythmic variation and occasional syncopation prevent stodginess, as does the elision of phrases. In many of Blanc's sonata movements the processes of development and recapitulation are merged, and there are other departures from "textbook" models. Even though the working-out is sometimes slipshod, and the music lacks subtlety, Blanc's flair for drama elevates his work above the prosaic efforts of many contemporaries. One senses that a composer of his cleverness and imagination could have essayed a more modern idiom. Perhaps he preferred conventional writing or perhaps he found it easier and more profitable to dash off works in the traditional style favored by the majority of the public; it is difficult to argue with his immediate (albeit short-lived) success.

Charles Dancla (1817–1907) was an extremely prolific author of works for one or two violin soloists, some with orchestral accompaniment; these he performed regularly at his own concerts. Persons who know only these compositions are apt to dismiss, as Cobbett did, Dancla's efforts as melodious but "purely violinistic salon music."[25] His *concertante* works do seem to have been designed mainly for virtuosos,[26] but he also wrote overtures and chamber music (at least nine string quartets and four piano trios by 1871), and these reveal a more serious bent. The sixth string quartet, which I examined, is in the classical mode, but somewhat étude-like, and its inner voices are consistently dull. An "Ouverture dramatique," dedicated to Jules Pasdeloup, though also old-fashioned, has more variety and spirit. The orchestration is forceful, but largely because there is so much "tutti" writing; possibly Dancla had grown too accustomed to treating the orchestra as "filler" behind violin soloists.

Like Dancla, *Félicien David* (1810–1876) led a dual role as a composer. Best known are his symphonic ode *Le Désert* and other orchestral-choral works (many on Eastern subjects), which were regarded as modern and exotic. Berlioz acknowledged his distinctive melodies and picturesque orchestration.[27] David's four untitled (nonprogrammatic) symphonies are in a different vein. Despite their rich instrumentation and minor innovations, they struck the critic Bourges as being closely related to the "elegant manner" of Haydn.[28] A string quartet in F minor, published in 1868, has traditional, Germanic form, and sectionalized themes that are anything but distinctive; except for some lively rhythms, the imaginative traits found in David's programmatic works are conspicuously absent.

Yet another dual artistic personality was *Emile Douay* (born 1802).

F.-J. Fétis portrayed him as an "independent spirit" who "sought new paths" and Edouard Fétis opined that his programmatic orchestral works (among them a *Symphonie poétique*) were too vast for his limited resources, and sometimes vulgar.[29] As late as 1887 Deldevez ranked Douay alone with Berlioz as a destroyer of the symphony proper (because of his programmatic approach).[30] Actually, Douay was more fecund as a composer of chamber works, none of which was much performed. His rather tame piano trio in C minor (the only work of Douay's I have seen) is conservative in nearly every way. Only in virtuosic variations of the second movement and in its somewhat unconventional, though hardly adventurous, tonal structure does it stray from classical models.

The music of theorist and writer *Antoine Elwart* (1808–1877), better crafted than Douay's, is consistent with Elwart's written opinion that musical composition reached its apex in the late eighteenth century (see chapter 5, p. 157). Most of Elwart's instrumental works remained unpublished.[31] His first string quartet (released by G. Brandus et S. Dufour in 1867, but apparently composed in 1833) is traditional, yet displays solid technique and expressivity. Dynamics are used effectively, and there are some examples of motivic development and simple imitative counterpoint (generally, a canon between two voices at the unison, with the second entering a measure after the first, and the two proceeding briefly in parallel thirds).

Unremarkable but popular was the music—mainly works in which the oboe was prominent—of composer and oboist *Henri Brod* (1799–1839). By audiences accustomed to virtuosic works, Brod's simplicity was considered refreshing, "plus agréable qu'un déluge de notes."[32] His works displayed the oboe as much through graceful melodies as through technical feats. In Brod's trio in G minor for piano, oboe, and bassoon, Op. 56 (in two movements: a marchlike Maestoso with modulations to closely related keys, and a theme with variations), the instruments have equal roles, and the staid quality resulting from square phrasing and predictable harmonic progressions is lessened by syncopation and some structural surprises.

Next on the traditional-to-innovative continuum belong a number of composers who retained a conventional approach while employing some new traits, either experimenting themselves or borrowing contemporary ideas from more progressive composers. Some of the persons mentioned below were no more modern than Blanc (who was discussed earlier because he was one of the most significant of the highly traditional composers); others were more innovative.

There is, possibly, a curious relationship between the number of composers who sought originality within the confines of secure classical traditions, and the popularity of Weber in French concert halls. Weber was best known to concert audiences for his overtures, which some listeners may have regarded as classical works with modern touches. The overture to *Der Freischütz,* for example, is in sonata form,[33] but the emphasized and (harmonically) nonfunctional diminished-seventh chords and eerily colorful orchestration create an atmosphere decidedly more modern than that associated with works of Haydn or Mozart. In a period when critics and audiences were impressed by *effets,* composers may, consciously or not, have sought to emulate their conception of Weber's music by attaching new devices to otherwise old-fashioned forms.

For many French composers, the influence of Weber was probably more substantial than that of Beethoven, the latter's enormous popularity in Paris notwithstanding. In France Beethoven's Late works were seldom heard before 1850 and even some compositions from the Middle Period (particularly the Sixth Symphony) were regarded with suspicion. Had Beethoven never existed, the writing of the more conservative French nineteenth-century composers might have been little affected. One can imagine a progression leading from Haydn, Mozart, and French eighteenth-century musicians, through Weber, Schubert (the earlier works, though even these were little known in France until about 1850), and lesser composers, to some of the conservative French artists discussed here; in this scheme, Beethoven would be an outsider, a figure who had leapt away from the mainstream. In fact, contemporary critics not infrequently expressed the wish that composers could start afresh from the eighteenth-century style, to avoid being "sidetracked" by nineteenth-century musical developments. Many of these developments had been initiated or explored by Beethoven, but his name seldom appeared in such comments. This conception of music history is not intended to refute Longyear's declaration that "no composer of the nineteenth century could wholly escape Beethoven's influence" any more than does his own statement that several of "Beethoven's contemporaries" (included under this chapter heading in Longyear's book are Dussek, Hummel, Spohr, Weber, Schubert, and "lesser composers, mostly pianists") "had a more immediate influence [than Beethoven] on most of the younger composers who reached musical maturity between 1830 and 1850."[34]

First chronologically among the "progressive classicists" mentioned below is *Luigi Cherubini* (1760–1842), a man who, for diverse reasons, is difficult to classify. Is it fair to label him a French nineteenth-century composer of classical instrumental works? A native Italian, he became a French citizen and wrote roughly half of his operas in French; more significantly, the Paris musical establishment accepted him enough to appoint him director of their chauvinistic Conservatoire. The concert public knew him almost exclusively for opera overtures, but he produced five string quartets after 1828.[35] Unlike most of the classical-sounding composers mentioned in this chapter, he was not an imitator but a true child of the Classical era, being only four years younger than Mozart. On the other hand (and despite Cherubini's intolerance of new ideas, as reported in Berlioz's *Mémoires*), his chamber works are among the most original composed in France before 1850.

His quartets have been discussed elsewhere in more detail than can be afforded them here—notably by Saint-Foix and Mansfield.[36] Each quartet stems from the classical style and each evolves in its own way. The powerful third quartet shows increasing formal freedom (without abandoning traditions); Saint-Foix, who described it as "somewhat symphonic," believed that it showed the influence of Beethoven.[37] Contrapuntal writing, for which Cherubini was renowned, is particularly notable in the fourth and fifth quartets, as are greater chromaticism, a fairly advanced sense of key relationship, and (in the fifth) more abrupt modulations. The sixth is the most modern structurally, being an example of cyclic writing; in the finale, initial phrases from the three preceding movements successively reappear. Saint-Foix felt that the quartets lacked individuality, suggesting that Cherubini was too much the scholar, but Mansfield viewed them as an attractive alternative to the standard repertory.[38] The quartets' energy, drama, and variety of style were unusual for any French chamber works of the 1830s, much less those of a septuagenarian.

Two other composers of instrumental "art" music, both active in the 1830s but quite different from one another, were *Scipion Rousselot* (born 1804) and *Henri-Jérôme Bertini* (1798–1876). By 1831 Rousselot's list of works had reached 26 opus numbers, of which most were chamber music, but thereafter he was known in Paris concert halls through occasional performances of at least one symphony;[39] his symphonic writing was criticized by Edouard Fétis as labored and without inspiration and by Bourges as inconsistent.[40] His String Quartet No. 5, Op. 26 (which I examined at the Bibliothèque Nationale, Paris), is, however, an expressive and musical work, despite lackluster inner parts and overly regular phrasing. Its tonal structure is almost daring: in both the first movement (in E minor) and the finale (in E Major) the tonal center resides briefly in E-flat Major. Most French contemporaries—unlike Schubert—stayed within more closely related keys.

The prolific Bertini wrote mostly for piano, but also left a great many chamber works, of which the sextets (he also wrote septets and nonets, as well as works for fewer instruments) were particularly popular. Contemporary critics were generally complimentary to his music, though

Schumann's comment that many of his movements are too long,[41] and Blanchard's wish for more unified structures[42] are probably valid. Bertini seems to have assimilated the classical style. He relied upon traditional forms, but was not controlled by them; his phrasing is balanced, but rhythmic variety is achieved (sometimes by rearranging rhythmic or melodic motifs relative to the bar lines). All instruments play significant roles in his music, exchanging themes and motifs. Most remarkable is his chromaticism. His melodies abound with accidentals and brief chromatic runs, and modulations to any scale degree are common. Even if his music had no redeeming features (which it does), Bertini would deserve mention here for an astonishing passage in the slow second movement of his Violin Sonata Opus 152, in which rapidly changing tonal centers outline a whole-tone scale (see example 4). This developmental section may be viewed as either an original stroke of genius or a trick involving too much repetition while leading the tonal center only back to its starting point; either way it is an unusual event for a piece dating from the 1840s.

In the mid-1850s, during a respite from operatic activities (caused, according to the composer, by the recent failure of his *La Nonne sanglante*),[43] *Charles Gounod* (1818–1893) penned two symphonies (in D Major and E-flat Major) that quickly joined the French symphonic repertory. Of ample dimensions (perhaps too much so for the material; Gounod favored long preparations for returns of keys or themes), they are attractive works, if not overly original. Both were recorded some years ago;[44] this listener was reminded, at various times, of Beethoven's and Schumann's symphonies. In both of Gounod's, a relatively small orchestra is handled ably (in the slow second movement of the E-flat Major work there is motivic imitation among various instruments), and there are lively rhythms. If the developmental passages sag a bit, other places are, not unexpectedly, unusually lyrical.

Howard Shanet has argued convincingly that *Georges Bizet*'s Symphony in C Major (a work familiar to twentieth-century audiences, though its existence was "not generally known" until 1933) was strongly influenced by Gounod's D Major Symphony.[45] Shanet pointed out remarkable structural similarities between the middle movements of the two works, and noted that Bizet had made a four-hand piano arrangement of Gounod's work in the few months separating its first performance (4 February 1855, middle movements only) and the composition of his own auspicious symphony.

One can only be astonished that *F.-J. Fétis* (1784–1871), amid activities as a scholar, editor, critic, conductor, and educator, found time to compose. His instrumental works include a pair of symphonies, at least two overtures, some string quartets and quintets, and a sextet for string

Ex. 4 Henri-Jérôme Bertini: Violin Sonata No. 1, Op. 152 (ca. 1844), from the second movement ("Andante")

quartet and piano four hands; the quintets and sextet were played in Paris during the 1860s. I have seen Fétis's concert overture dedicated to Liszt, and the first of his three quintets. Not surprisingly, considering Fétis's criticism, his music is conventional. In the overture a relatively large orchestra is required, but the winds (especially the brass) are used percussively rather than melodically, mainly in an accompanying role; exceptions to this practice include effective crescendos created by piling up imitative entries among the woodwinds. Nonfunctional diminished-seventh chords appear briefly and there are some rich harmonic progressions. Otherwise the overture is remarkable only for sometimes superimposing duple (4/4) and triple (12/8) meters.

The string quintet (with two violas), in A minor, is more substantial. Its main points of interest are a tonal scheme that includes modulations upward by half-steps, as well as key changes effected via enharmonic progressions, and a second movement that combines the structures of rondo and theme with variations (the "rondo" theme is varied at each successive reappearance). There are many examples of syncopation and contrametrical writing, but elsewhere the rhythm plods. The inner parts are tedious, and the style conservative for a work that dates from 1859.[46]

There remain some traditional composers whose place in the French concert scene was of little significance, but who perhaps deserve brief mention for their attempts at originality within a classical setting. *Ferdinand Lavainne* (born 1810) wrote at least one symphony and several chamber works. Two piano trios dating from the 1840s, which I examined, reveal formal experimentation, clever handling of instruments, some brief counterpoint, and much developmental writing in which the music moves freely—sometimes abruptly—through diverse keys. *Auguste-François Morel* (1809–1881), known mainly for chamber works, wrote well for instruments, both individually and together. His formal and tonal plans, though based on classical models, are nonetheless somewhat unconventional, and syncopation is used to create dissonance via anticipation and suspension. He was not averse to programmatic titles or effects: the second movement of his string quartet Op. 1, entitled "Echos et danse des montagnes," is an attempt to sound folklike. The horn virtuoso *Jacques Gallay* (1795–1864) appears to have borrowed dramatic effects (particularly harmonic progressions involving diminished-seventh chords) from Grand Opera for his solos and 12 concertos for horn.[47] Regarding one *Salvator,* I know only that he had a handful of chamber works performed and published in Paris in the 1850s. Although in most ways extremely conservative, his music is expressive and his melodies are unpredictable. He experimented with unusual phrase lengths and contrametrical rhythmic patterns (for example, six-beat motives in 4/4 time), and emphasized the development of short motifs. *Adolphe Vogel* (1808–1892), active throughout the period of 1828 to 1871, was known by contemporaries as a violinist and composer of operas; he also wrote orchestral and chamber works. F.-J. Fétis twice suggested that his early works lack clarity, but complimented the orchestration and elegance of an early symphony.[48] I have seen only his first violin sonata (dated 1862), in which extremely conservative writing accentuates the few unorthodox traits: surprising chromatic alterations to the melody; infrequent harsh dissonances, usually created by suspension; the insertion of four syncopated 2/4 measures amid the 3/4 scherzo; and the juxtaposition of outer movements in G Major with inner ones in F Major and B minor.

The composers discussed in the remainder of this chapter should probably be labeled "romantic," though their collective romanticism is wide-ranging. Some continued to rely on classical models, while working on a vaster scale, and generating greater (or less subtle) drama. Their works became longer and more complex; chromatic alterations and rich chords prolonged the life of established harmonic progressions, and an expanded orchestra made possible increased power and colorful effects. Other composers, while falling short of the revolutionary inventiveness of Liszt, Musorgsky, or Berlioz, forsook some of the foundations of classical writing via experiments with tonality and formal structure. In the following pages I have attempted to retain the concept of a traditional-to-innovative continuum. It is of course impossible to establish a "proper" order on this continuum, as there are so many aspects of music to consider. If some composers constructed novel forms from conservatively written fragments, while others coated traditional structures with a veneer of new effects, which are more modern?

Louis Théodore Gouvy (1819–1898) composed much of his instrumental music (which, before 1871, included five symphonies, two concert overtures, serenades for strings and for piano quartet, a piano quintet, two string quartets, and five piano trios) during his residence in Paris; as his career progressed, he spent more and more time in Germany, where his music was better appreciated, and devoted his attention increasingly to major choral-orchestral works.[49] At Parisian concerts, only his orchestral works were performed regularly. He used a conservative repertory of compositional techniques that appears to stem from Beethoven and Weber. Contemporaries compared his music with Mendelssohn's, especially in its elegance, but found it less original. Too many critics have categorized Gouvy as an unimaginative producer of serious but lightweight works, considered at best to be graceful, delicate, transparent, balanced, well-crafted, spirited, and feeling, and at worst uninspired, scholastic, empty, and long-winded. Berlioz, however, apparently admired the beauty and originality of the Third Symphony,[50] and the works that I studied have more weight and expressiveness than contemporary criticism leads one to expect. Although some of Gouvy's themes are undistinguished, many are developed dramatically. He seems to have been best at frolicsome ideas in quick tempos. Chromatic writing with more than a hint of whole-tone patterns is demonstrated in the opening of the Scherzo (in D minor) from the Second Symphony in F Major, Opus 12 (ca. 1848; see example 5). Yet the chromaticism never penetrates beneath the surface: harmonic procedures are traditional (the unusual number of pedal points in all registers excepted), as are the formal structure and rhythms. In Gouvy's chamber and orchestral works there are many examples of imitative interplay among instrument. His orchestration is well varied, and in all his music there is effective dynamic contrast.

Ex. 5 Théodore Gouvy: Symphony No. 2, Op. 12, F Major, opening of the second movement (Scherzo)

Georges Pfeiffer (1835–1908), son of the pianist Clara Pfeiffer, himself first gained recognition as a pianist. By 1871, however, he had composed a symphony, two piano concertos, an Allegro-symphonique for piano and orchestra, an overture, a piano quintet, a piano trio, and a cello sonata, all of which had been performed in Paris. Fétis and Pougin might have classified Pfeiffer's music with Gouvy's; they noted its clarity, sentiment, melodic variety (not associated with Gouvy's works), polished form—and lack of originality; both critics also thought that Pfeiffer overemphasized a search for "effects".[51] Of Pfeiffer's prewar compositions I have seen only the Piano Trio in G minor, Op. 14 (from about 1861). In structure, rhythm, and texture, the Trio is indeed similar to Gouvy's music: the forms are traditional; the rhythm is never startling, but is highly varied and includes instances of syncopation and hemiola; simple imitative counterpoint (most often a two-voice canon at the unison or octave) occurs frequently. Not surprisingly, perhaps, the piano introduces most of the major themes and is otherwise somewhat predominant. Pfeiffer was a more inventive and powerful melodist than Gouvy, but the Piano Trio, composed when Pfeiffer was only in his mid-twenties, exhibits less interest in thematic development. His writing was sometimes chromatic, as example 6, from the first movement of the Piano Trio, demonstrates. Chromaticism is more evident in his much later Piano Quartet, Op. 119, composed after the Wagner craze had swept France, and after the appearance of Debussy's early works; the Quartet even presents a chromatic progression in which the motion is exclusively parallel. In both the early and late works, however, the chromaticism is ornamental—a piquant device that affects the otherwise conventional harmonic progressions only slightly and the large-scale, traditional tonal schemes not at all.

Ex. 6 Georges Pfeiffer: Piano Trio in G minor, Op. 14 (ca. 1861), from the first movement

Between 1863 and the Franco-Prussian War *Jules Massenet* (1842–1912) produced a concert overture, the first of seven numbered orchestral suites, a symphonic suite entitled *Pompéia,* and "Deux pièces" for cello and piano.[52] Only the orchestral suite, promoted by Pasdeloup, was played regularly. It received adverse criticism after the first performance (1867), but Pougin later praised its original formal structure (none of the four movements is in sonata form, and the theme of the first-movement "Pastorale" returns in the finale) and brilliant, varied orchestration.[53] The large orchestra, which includes piccolos, trombones, a saxtuba, and two harps, is indeed handled flashily, though the delicate instrumental writing of Massenet's later operas is not manifest. Perhaps the Suite's biggest surprise is the amount of imitative counterpoint—in both the "Pastorale" and "Fugue" of the first movement and in the finale, "Marche et Stretto."

Housed in the Paris Bibliothèque Nationale are quantities of symphonies, overtures, violin concertos, string quartets (at least ten), piano trios, violin sonatas, and similar works by the otherwise obscure violinist *Célestien Tingry* (1819–96). Only a few Parisian performances of these works are known, all in the 1840s. Tingry, who later left Paris for Cambrai,[54] evidently did not ardently promote his (largely unpublished) music, and it warrants mention here solely for artistic reasons. Blanchard, reviewing three string quartets and a string quintet in 1845, felt that Tingry was overly concerned with details, and that his works were rather constricted and uninspired; he nonetheless remained optimistic about Tingry's future.[55] The single work that I examined (the Second Piano Trio, Op. 57, published about 1856) is unusually expressive and progressive. The long-breathed melodies, characterized by large leaps and overlapping phrases, have a Schumannesque quality. The formal-tonal structure is uncommonly free (in three of the four movements sonata-allegro form was probably in the back of Tingry's mind), and there are brief instances of imitative counterpoint. Also noteworthy are the "exoticism" of the second movement ("Bolero") and occasional humorous touches. Tingry was still composing in 1880,[56] but by then had evidently been long forgotten in Paris.

In the compositional career of *Louis Lacombe* (1818–84), the emphasis changed gradually from piano and chamber music to dramatic symphonies (with solo voices and chorus) to opera. Thus most of the purely instrumental works, which include two overtures, a piano quintet (with parts for oboe and bassoon or bass clarinet, replacing one violin and one of two cellos), two piano trios, possibly a quartet, and several light works for violin and piano, had been completed by 1860; some works were not published until much later, if at all.[57] Because of Lacombe's descriptive symphonies for large forces, F.-J. Fétis grouped him (disapprovingly) with Berlioz, David, and Douay;[58] such a categorization seems unwarranted (or, in the case of David and Douay, warranted for the wrong reasons), for Lacombe's works are in many ways conventional.[59] He was a capable orchestrator, given to much variety, and in both his orchestral and chamber music, the individual voices have melodic interest. His attempts to be expressive (his works include such indications as "avec une expression naïve" and "avec âme") were not without success, but occasionally led to grandiloquence. Some of his melodies are interestingly developed through the addition of new "tails." Most notable, however, are the formal structures. Unexpected modulations spice sonata-process movements. The fantasialike fourth-movement finale of the Piano Trio No. 2 in A minor, Op. 41 (composed by 1851), has 14 major tempo changes and several meter changes; it begins with the theme of the second-movement "Scherzo," and later resurrects, transformed, a prominent theme from the first movement (see example 7), thereby establishing Lacombe as an early French explorer of cyclical structure.

Ex. 7 Louis Lacombe: Piano Trio No. 2 in A minor, Op. 14 (by 1851)

From the first movement.

From the fourth movement.

The violinist *Eugène Chaine* (1819–82) wrote two symphonies and violin concertos, one overture, nonet, woodwind quintet, piano quartet, and piano trio, and several light works for violin; none of these achieved popularity, in spite of the talent Chaine demonstated. In his Second Violin Concerto, Op. 19 (1856[?]), the spirited and original themes abound with ambitious melodic leaps and rhythmic variety, and chromaticism infiltrates the harmonic scheme. In both the first and third (final) movements there is some tonal ambiguity between B minor and D Major (the second movement is in G minor, B-flat minor, and G Major). Tempo changes and dynamics are utilized expressively, and there are contrametrical accent patterns in the finale. Blanchard, who reviewed both violin concertos in 1856, called Chaine one of the best virtuoso-composers, and particularly praised his democratic orchestration.[60]

According to Fétis and Pougin, the composer, pianist, and critic *Léon Kreutzer* (1817–68, nephew of Rodolphe Kreutzer) was ahead of his compatriots in musical thinking, and was a purist who disdained frivolities.[61] The one work of Kreutzer's that I have seen, his monumental Piano Concerto in E-flat Major (ca. 1861), does not seem to exemplify purism, but does deserve Pougin's additional criticism that Kreutzer, in his eagerness to be original, sometimes attained "la bizarrerie." Commencing this work, Kreutzer may have recalled Beethoven's "Emperor" Concerto in the same key: two measures of orchestral chords are followed by 79 measures for piano solo. Later in the movement, influence of Liszt is suggested, as the key signature changes often (and to remote tonal centers), and within the virtuosic piano part, notes are grouped together 11, 17, or 24 to a beat. There is, however, much small-scale repetition, the solo writing is cluttered with extended trills and tremolos, the orchestration is unvaried, and the work seems too long for the material (its four movements comprise over 2300 measures). Perhaps the concerto is a poor representative of Kreutzer's instrumental works, which include two symphonies, lesser orchestral pieces, a sextet for piano and winds, a piano trio, and at least eight string quartets.

Kreutzer as critic would surely not have appreciated the commercially successful works of his contemporary, the pianist *Emile Prudent* (1817–63). More impressed by the playing and writing of Thalberg than by theory courses at the Conservatoire,[62] Prudent eventually composed (for his own performances) numerous graceful, descriptive piano solos, some with (negligible) orchestral accompaniment. He also wrote two piano concertos, notable mainly for their melodic ornamentation (possibly inspired by Chopin) and for their unusual formal plans. The first movement of the Concerto-Symphonique, Op. 34 (composed about 1847, published in 1849) introduces several themes but remains unrelievedly in B-flat Major until a 12-bar piano recitative in G Major, which leads directly into the second movement (also in G). Prudent carried the idea of connecting movements to its extreme in his second concerto, "La Prairie," in D Major, Op. 48 (1856); it is in one continuous movement with many changes of tempo, meter, tonal center, and mode.[63] Like the earlier concerto, it was clearly designed to display the pianist's virtuosity.

The careers of *Edouard Lalo* (1823–92) and *César Franck* (1822–90) could be Exhibits "A" and "B" for those who maintain that a "renaissance" of musical creativity occurred in postwar France. Both composed a few instrumental works early in their careers, abandoned the genre (having experienced little success), then renewed their efforts in the 1870s, eventually gaining more fame as instrumental composers than most of their French contemporaries.

By the late 1850s Lalo had composed a string quartet, two piano trios, a violin sonata, and some smaller works either for violin or cello (and piano).[64] These works were tried in Paris but appreciated by only a handful of connoisseurs;[65] disappointed by this reception, Lalo turned away from instrumental music in the 1860s. I have not seen scores for any early works, but have heard a recording of the First Piano Trio, Op. 7, in C minor.[66] Its outer movements are severe and economical (the handling of the traditional formal structures is almost abrupt), yet forceful and spirited, surely influenced by Beethoven. I also note a hint of pseudo-Gypsy influence, especially in the first movement. The second movement,

"Romance" (the most typically French and the most sentimental), has delicate harmonic shading reminiscent of Chopin. In the "Scherzo," occasional eighth-note duplets in a contrametrical pattern give rhythmic life to an otherwise common theme (see example 8). Lalo's forte is the writing for instruments, both individually and together. The cello part is most expressive, and the piano assumes a remarkable variety of roles; the ensemble combines effectively, sharing themes, developing motifs, imitating, and presenting melodies with countermelodies. In the slightly later String Quartet Op. 19, Florent Schmitt noted a more romantic approach to formal and harmonic schemes.[67]

Ex. 8. Edouard Lalo: Piano Trio No. 1, Op. 7, C minor, opening theme of third movement ("Scherzo")

Lalo was in his late 20s when his first piano trio appeared, and had already developed artistic maturity and a personal style. Franck completed his first opus, three piano trios, by 1841 when he was 19.[68] To Franck's youthfulness, then, one can attribute the curious juxtapositions of naivety and invention, and of inspired experimentation and lack of self-criticism (one can argue that the latter trait remained with him) that characterize these works. Innovative features of the first trio, in F-sharp minor (the best-known of the set), have been well documented:[69] the first movement, which has a formal outline of A-B-A-A-B, retains F-sharp as a tonal center throughout, changing only the mode (to major in the "B" sections); the second-movement "Scherzo" has two (different) "trios" (not so labeled); most important, three themes introduced in the first movement return, sometimes in different guises, in the Scherzo and the finale. This cyclicism is an advance over that essayed by Cherubini in his sixth string quartet, in that Franck not only reiterated themes, but also transformed them, making a few serve as material for the entire work—thus being economical while building in unity. The integration of the cyclic themes into the various movements is not, however, accomplished as subtly here as it is in Franck's later works. Other traits that distinguish Franck's mature works are already observable: chromatic harmonies; the immediate repetition of phrases (often one step) lower or higher; lively syncopation; and worthy, if unusual, parts for all instruments (there is even some nonimitative counterpoint, which, Berlioz's works excepted, was unusual in France at this time). Despite the obvious attention to detail, Franck's inexperience shows. One of his prominent themes seems, even if interpreted as self-conscious *naïveté,* particularly uninspired (see example 9).[70] The piano writing in the lower register is sometimes too thick to "sound." There are awkward modulations and the work is repetitive and long-winded, especially in the finale. If this trio is less than first-rate, it is nonetheless important as an innovative creation, a harbinger of Franck's later, more polished works, and a refreshing, dramatic example of the young romantic spirit.

Ex. 9 César Franck: Piano Trio in F-sharp minor, Op. 1 No. 1, theme introduced in the first movement

In the half of his career that preceded the Franco-Prussian War, the pianist-composer *Georges Mathias* (1826–1910) wrote at least one symphony,[71] the "Hamlet" overture, a piano concerto, two piano quintets, four piano trios, and lesser works; most of these received a few performances. When Blanchard reviewed the piano quintets in 1848 he cited, among other attributes, their purity, clarity of ideas, traditional form, and eighteenth-century aura.[72] Six years later, the Symphony in D Major was described as being in the Classical mold, at times reminiscent of Weber and Mendelssohn, and well-crafted but unoriginal.[73] If these criticisms are fair, Mathias's style must have developed rapidly, for the Fourth Piano Trio in A Major, Op. 36, completed by 1866, does not warrant such comments. The opening measures of the Finale (see example 10) are representative: the piano introduction (motivically similar, incidentally, to the first prelude in the *Well-Tempered Clavier I*) begins suspensively with a tonic chord in first inversion followed by a minor tonic, also in first inversion, continues with a series of diminished chords moving downward by half-steps, then recommences the entire three-bar pattern a half-step higher in B-flat. Eventually, via a strong cadence that culminates with the cello's entrance, A Major seems to regain its footing. The cello melody, however, immediately leaps to a C-natural before sliding chromatically back to A (echoing the movement of bars 1 to 3); a subsequent cadence in A Major is effected through an upward chromatic scale in the melody over a colorful (but functional) chord progression, all vivified by a "crescendo molto fuoco." The trio's fantasialike formal plan is also unusual: within movements abundant with tempo and meter changes, numerous themes are introduced in a bewildering variety of keys; some melodies return, often in a drastically different key; there are passages in which themes are motivically developed as the tonal center changes rapidly, rather than a single development section *per se*; and though movements begin and end in the same key, there is not always a thematic recapitulation. (The formal structure of the later Violin Sonata, Op. 68, reveals that that of the Paiano Trio was not a one-time experiment; in the later work the number of themes is reduced, and greater unity is achieved by finally stating these themes—sometimes simultaneously—in the home key.) Individual instruments have significant parts, frequently providing countermelodies or sharing in the process of thematic development. The trio's melodies, many of which consist of short, even, repetitive, purely diatonic phrases, often seem incongruous amid the exciting dramatic structures and sophisticated handling of harmonies and rhythms.[74]

The small body of instrumental works by *Alexis de Castillon* (1838–73) has become familiar to a few musicians and historians,[75] but remains unknown to concert audiences. Because Castillon's mature works[76] (a piano concerto, a concert overture, symphonic sketches, a piano quintet, piano quartet, and string quartet, two piano trios, a violin sonata, and some incomplete works) were composed between roughly 1870 and 1873, and because he was the active first secretary of the Société Nationale de Musique, his name is often cited among those preeminent in the alleged postwar renaissance of French "art" music. One must recall, however, that Castillon had written instrumental works before the Franco-Prussian War. Rather than inspiring a new activity, the war tragically interrupted and ultimately terminated his brief career, as the hardships of active duty eventually led to his death.

Although Castillon was later described by Duparc as the most talented of all Franck's pupils,[77] his works were at first thought unintelligible. One can imagine the listeners' mystification upon hearing the opening of the Violin Sonata in C Major, Op. 6 (see example 11): a motif built upon C, F-sharp, and G, introduced by the piano, quickly settles into a contrametrical ostinato pattern that emphasizes the tritone C to F-sharp; soon the violin enters (above the ostinato), seeming to be in the Dorian mode[78] on D, and accompanied by D minor chords on the piano (right

Ex. 10 Georges Mathias: Piano Trio No. 4 in A Major, Op. 36, opening of the fourth movement

mi - - nu - - en - - do
p
crescendo molto con fuoco
sf
subito pp
pp
fpp

Ex. 11 Alexis de Castillon: Violin Sonata in C Major, Op. 6, opening of the first movement

cresc.
f
dim.
p
cresc.
f
dim.
f
dim.
p
f
dim.

p
cresc.
f
dim.
dim.
p
p
pp
pp
pp
un peu marqué

hand); from bar 25 the violin and piano (right hand) continue their respective roles in G Major; finally, at bar 37, both resolve to C, while the Lydian-sounding ostinato continues relentlessly. The entire introduction, an elongated ii-V-I cadence, suggests something about the scale in which the movement was conceived.

Classical ancestors can, with difficulty, generally be traced for Castillon's formal structures. But some consecutive movements are connected, and themes (in transformed versions) are shared between them. Individual movements are sectionalized by numerous tempo and meter changes, and the tonal plan includes modulations to remote centers. Oddly, many of these tonal leaps are followed by a return to the original tonic, even at the very end of exposition sections (a practice that stultifies dramatic structure); conversely, the first movement of the above-mentioned violin sonata (in C Major) ends with 36 measures about E, a balance to the 36-bar introduction and a preparation for the second movement in A Major.[79] Most critics agree that Castillon's developments are overly dependent on repetition (in various tonal centers) rather than motivic *Entwicklung,* and are too long (though the processes of development and recapitulation overlap in some instances).

One notes in Castillon's music unusual rhythms and accented contrametrical patterns, varied textures (including fugal passages), and an absence of the figuration so common in works of his compatriots. The influence of Beethoven and Schumann is apparent[80] (Castillon was an ardent student of earlier works), but a characteristically French grace is retained. If the music is inconsistent, it nonetheless deserves recognition for its tonal and formal innovations, fiery expressiveness, and what Davies praised as "felicitous touches of scoring" and "sheer breadth of melodic invention."[81]

Discussion of the eclectic *Camille Saint-Saëns* (1835–1921) has been postponed to the end of this chapter, for he is difficult to classify; even his prewar works span a wide portion of the traditional-to-innovative continuum represented by the compositions discussed above. As his music has received increasing attention from scholars and performers in recent years,[82] an extensive discussion thereon seems unnecessary; instead, I shall try to place Saint-Saëns relative to his contemporaries, and to note innovative features of early works that he later developed further. Perhaps because he understood the music of Haydn, Mozart, and Beethoven so well (he grew up performing this repertory), he was able to produce unusually good music based upon classical principles. His works have clarity and balance, and though he used established formal structures, he did not write "textbook" sonatas. Even the early Symphony in A (composed in 1850, when he was 15) includes an abridgement that more pedantic contemporaries would not have considered: the distance between statements of the two primary themes in the sonata-form first movement is shortened from 46 bars in the exposition to 17 in the recapitulation. This movement employs the germ motif made famous in the finale of Mozart's "Jupiter" Symphony, but the economical handling of themes is Haydnesque, and the opening of the finale is reminiscent of the first movement of Haydn's Symphony No. 102 in B-flat Major (see example 12). The orchestration in the Symphony in A suggests the influence of Beethoven and, possibly, Mendelssohn; occasional daring harmonic progressions, such as a series of diminished-seventh chords moving downward by half-steps in the finale (anticipating, incidentally, the similar series in Mathias's Piano Trio No. 4), may have been inspired by Weber.

Ex. 12 Camille Saint-Saëns: Symphony in A Major (1850), opening of the fourth movement

As much as Saint-Saëns disdained the music of most French contemporaries, he could not entirely escape its influence. His heritage is made evident in his compositions, not only through their French elegance, but also through more specific traits, found commonly in works of his compatriots: hocketlike writing (for example, the opening of the third and fourth movements of the First Piano Trio, Op. 18); use of drone bass (which, in the second-movement "Andante" of the same work, lends an aura of mystery to an otherwise pedestrian melody); humor, especially in themes of mainly rhythmic interest (the opening of the finale to the First Piano Concerto, Op. 17); and reliance upon diatonic scales as melodic units (coda, finale to the Symphony in A; this practice was carried to extremes in the final measures of the much later "Organ" Symphony, Op. 78, in which four C-Major scales in different rhythms occur simultaneously).

Saint-Saëns's early works, then, were based on classical models and influenced by more recent French music. Quickly, his idiom expanded to embrace both older and newer styles. An interest in baroque music[83] was revealed in the composition of his Suite for cello and piano, Op. 16, in 1862 (before Massenet and Bizet wrote suites), in toccatalike writing (suggested in the "Prelude" of the cello suite, but best demonstrated in the opening of the Second Piano Concerto, Op. 28), and in fugal or quasi-fugal sections (finales of the Piano Quintet, Op. 14, and cello suite; first movement of the Symphony No. 2, Op. 55, composed in 1859). Concurrently Saint-Saëns was developing more sophisticated timbral and harmonic palettes and a repertory of Romantic gestures; the style exhibited in the Second Piano Concerto (1868) remained fashionable (if not avant-garde) the rest of the century. As early as the Piano Quintet (1855), some passages sound more Wagnerian than Mozartian (see example 13). Harmonies became richer and, rarely, common practice functionality was briefly abandoned. Traditional forms were treated more freely: the exposition of the sonata-form first movement of the Piano Quintet in A minor modulates not to the expected relative major or dominant, but to the submediant F Major; the second and third movements of the same work are connected, and in the coda of the finale, a theme from the first movement reappears. Thematic recycling is explored further in the Second Symphony. There, material from the first three movements is transformed, to varying degrees, in the finale. This procedure, halfway between the cosmetic cyclicism of Cherubini's Sixth String Quartet and the integral structural cyclicism of Franck's works, is a precursor of more extensive cyclic writing in the "Organ" Symphony, in which a single theme permeates all but the "Poco Adagio" movement.

Ex. 13 Saint-Saëns: Piano Quintet in A minor, Op. 14 (1855), from the third movement

Saint-Saëns's formalist aesthetic may have contributed to the lack of depth for which his art is faulted; it did not, however, lead to overly academic writing. His early works are surprisingly original, and no matter what style he attempted, he took care that the result was musical.

From the foregoing, one sees that all sorts of instrumental "art" music were composed in France between 1828 and 1871—chamber and orchestral works in traditional and modern idioms, pieces ranging from the trivial to the monumental, and productions demonstrating diverse levels of artistic competency. Admittedly, few great composers of instrumental music were active there, and I find no convincing explanation for what might be considered a shortage of native musical genius. I am not certain, however, that an explanation is needed: how many great composers of instrumental music appeared in Italy, Spain, England, the Netherlands, Scandinavia, or Russia at this time? The Austro-Germanic countries' wealth of talent seems to have been the exception rather than the rule.

Although few French composers can be called "great," some achieved moderate contemporary success. How, if at all, did an individual composer's position on the conservative-to-innovative continuum affect his or her acceptance by French audiences, performers, and critics? The answer necessitates amplification of the continuum.

The continuum, as defined, represents degrees of innovation; its one extreme would be represented by works that utilize only well-established compositional principles, and its other by works that employ new principles exclusively. Clearly, most works display some combination of the innovative and the established (and some traits may be interpreted as either innovations or modifications of established principles). But apart from the degree to which innovative principles are evident, works demonstrate varying amounts of imagination in the handling of given principles. While innovative works of course reveal imagination, a traditional work may also be composed imaginatively. For the purposes of the following discussion only, I shall restrict the meaning of "imaginative" composition to "original treatment of established principles," and use "innovative" composition to imply "extensive utilization of new principles."

Favorite "art" music of French musicians and audiences suggests that they sought the "imaginative." To nineteenth-century listeners, Haydn and Mozart had written imaginatively in what had since become a traditional format. Beethoven's works through the Middle Period were on familiar enough ground that his "innovations" could, with few exceptions, be ignored while delighting in his "imaginative" approach and unequalled ability to sustain drama; his more reflective Late works were too "innovative," and therefore slow to gain appreciation. Weber's overtures and Mendelssohn's oeuvre could also be interpreted as "imaginative." The "innovative" works of Liszt, on the other hand, did not win approval.

The attitude regarding French composers was evidently similar. Among the most popular (in spite of their limited cumulative output of orchestral works) were Onslow, Farrenc, Dancla, and Blanc—all traditional and (possibly excepting Dancla) "imaginative."

An "imaginative" ideal is also suggested by the French critics' preferences (described earlier in this chapter): two of their most prevalent criteria were originality and the presence of "effects." But truly "innovative" works had too much originality and were generally reviewed unfavorably. As Peter Bloom has noted, F.-J. Fétis encouraged experimentation but not to excess.[84] Many effects were superficial—"imaginative" additions to otherwise traditional structures (rare exceptions occurred, notably Félicien David's "effective" procedures in his acclaimed symphonic odes). Other traits that critics sought indicate a liking for music novel enough to sound fresh, but not so new that it seemed unfamiliar. Late in the period a few reviewers displayed more openmindedness.[85]

To the detriment of their popular success, many talented composers were naturally "innovative" and could not remain content within the confines of tradition. Berlioz forged his way to fame through incredible perseverance and with (mainly) unintended help from disapproving critics, but never achieved widespread acclaim in France. Saint-Saëns proved that he could produce pleasing, traditional music, but even his relatively minor departures from convention were viewed with some suspicion.[86] Less comprehensible artists, such as Castillon, left critics and audiences far behind.

The significance of this seeming preference for safe, "imaginative" music may not be restricted to criticism and the performed repertory. Composers less idealistic than Berlioz possibly viewed "imaginative" writing as the only path to even limited success; to attract musicians and audiences, they scrupulously avoided potentially alarming "innovations." This theory would explain the abundance of conservative music originating from nineteenth-century France. A more plausible explanation is that the number of persons with the creative power to conceive major innovations was small. But as taste (reflected by concert programs and criticism) became less conservative in the 1860s, more composers—among them Saint-Saëns, more so Mathias and Castillon—ventured into "innovative" territory.

Did mid-nineteenth-century French instrumental music experience a stylistic change comparable to the gradual renaissance evident in its performance and appreciation? Because Berlioz's contribution so dominates French stylistic development (though his immediate influence was small), the answer is both "yes" and "no": "yes" because Berlioz's compositions created their own stylistic revolution; "no" because this revolution coincided with the beginning of the period in question (*Huit scènes de Faust* appeared in 1829 and the *Symphonie Fantastique* in 1830), and other French composers spent the remainder of the period catching up. There were few, if any, works from the 1860s more advanced than Berlioz's early music; thus stylistic change after this initial leap was, apart from Berlioz's own further development, minor. Certainly, instrumental compositions from the 1860s were, as a group, more modern than the body of works produced in the 1830s, and the contributions of Saint-Saëns, Mathias, Castillon, and others demonstrated significant innovation. But while other changes concerning instrumental music happened gradually, becoming evident mainly after 1850 (and especially in the 1860s), the most important stylistic developments were introduced by Berlioz, well before 1850.

No major stylistic revolution appeared immediately after the Franco-Prussian War, either. The most apparent musical changes occurred in the oeuvre of Saint-Saëns, who in the 1870s suddenly produced four symphonic poems. Both Martin Cooper and Rey Longyear have suggested that these were influenced by Liszt;[87] perhaps too, Saint-Saëns was consciously or subconsciously expressing postwar nationalism by abandoning the Germanic forms on which he had previously relied. His Trumpet Septet of 1881 also avoids Germanic forms in that "its movements, entitled 'Préambule,' 'Minuet,' 'Intermède,' and 'Gavotte' hearken back in spirit to the chamber suites of Couperin and Rameau."[88] After the war, Lalo and Franck renewed their interest in instrumental genres (the latter not until the late 1870s), but their styles, while having matured, were not startlingly altered. And the instrumental music by the younger members of the Société Nationale de Musique was not particularly novel.

Longyear admitted that "the principal musical change in France after 1870 was the acceptance of French composers in more than one field."[89] Other claims of a postwar renaissance are also based on increasing instrumental activity (in both composition and performance). When one appreciates, however, that quantities of instrumental music were composed in France before 1870 (and innumerable French composers not mentioned in this chapter attempted at least a few instrumental works), that some of the music was notably original, and that some received support from critics and performers, then the musical environment of the postwar years seems to lack the newness implied by the term "renaissance."

Finally, the oblivion into which most nineteenth-century French instrumental works have fallen is not uniformly deserved. Several reveal noteworthy compositional technique, imagination (in its broadest sense), originality, and expressive power. These need a widespread reevaluation, accomplishable through performance, listening, and analysis.

7

A Half-Century of Change

Any attempt to summarize and analyze the findings of the preceding chapters must seem to be at cross purposes with itself. On one hand, this study seeks to show that there was more performance and composition of (and interest in) instrumental "art" music in mid-nineteenth-century France than has been previously realized. On the other, like any examination of the period, it must account for the dissatisfaction expressed by contemporaries and must recognize the problems of instrumental musicians—and in doing so must try to explain why there was not more and better instrumental activity. Thus the verdict is mixed.

But most writings on French instrumental activity of the mid-nineteenth century dwell upon its shortcomings, whereas this study considers both its positive and negative aspects: an active concert life is demonstrated by the quantity of concert series performing "art" music, though many of these struggled to survive; contemporary French instrumental music *was* performed publicly, though less than older Germanic works; individuals from nearly every socioeconomic level developed an appreciation for instrumental "art" music, though these persons were fewer than those who preferred "popular" fare; some contemporary musicians were optimistic about the musical scene, while others were not; and French composers produced a surprising amount of well-crafted and, in some cases, innovative music, though little of it has ever been thought comparable to the best contemporary Germanic music.

This bilateral depiction of instrumental activity between 1828 and 1871, when considered with Boris Schwarz's conclusions regarding the period before 1830, suggests the need to reevaluate our conception of French instrumental activity through the entire nineteenth century. A (composite) traditional view of the century, as expressed in books through the first half of the twentieth century (and as still found in record-liner and program notes), implies that, apart from efforts of rare concert societies and the achievements of Berlioz, instrumental music in France was practically nonexistent until 1871 when, inspired by the Société Nationale de Musique, it experienced a momentous renaissance. In the last few decades, musicologists (in particular) have presented a less extreme picture; they have acknowledged the existence of concert activity before 1816 and after 1850, and have explored the music of certain nineteenth-century French composers. They have stopped regarding the happenings after the Franco-Prussian War as a complete revolution but still described the 1870s as a time of major improvement.

Still further emendation is needed. Instrumental music began a significant revival (following the slump begun in 1816) in the late 1820s; and most of the changes that occurred between, say, 1845 (another low point) and the mid-1870s had taken place by 1870—that is, before the war. The concept of a renaissance need not be abandoned; certainly musical life was much improved in the 1870s over the doldrums of 1816 to 1825. But the renaissance was accomplished over a period of 50 years, receiving special boosts at four periods: about 1828, when the Société des Concerts du Conservatoire appeared and introduced Beethoven's music to Paris; the late 1840s and early 1850s, when notable new series were established and new repertories were explored; the early 1860s, when the Concerts Populaires and other organizations succeeded in attracting new audiences (thus facilitating continued expansion in the late 1860s and 1870s); and the early 1870s, when the Franco-Prussian War awakened nationalism.

The renaissance took a half-century to evolve partly because it began at a time that was musically primitive. Its slow, unsteady progress was frustrating to artists, for the many obstacles to instrumental activity nearly smothered the revival of instrumental music that had begun in the late 1820s. While some of these hindrances remained throughout the century, others slowly disappeared, allowing an ever-faster resurgence of instrumental music. Improvement from one year to the next was nearly imperceptible, but the difference between musical life in the early 1840s and the late 1860s is striking.

Fundamental to the unfortunate circumstances of instrumental composers, especially during the first half of the century, was the relationship between social structure and the perceptions of new music (particularly that which departed from traditional styles). Among the most flagrant departures from tradition were the first Grand Operas—works characterized by spectacle, grandiosity, special effects, color, melodrama, and extremes of personal emotion. These attributes attracted to the opera house a new audience, the *nouveaux riches*. Grand Opera was ideal for persons with little musical or cultural background; it could be appreciated without knowledge of literary classics, classical music, and operatic conventions. The apparent instrumental counterpart to Grand Opera, from the point of view of the *nouveaux riches,* was not chamber works of

Onslow, Bertini, or Farrenc, or symphonies of Reber, Gounod, or even Berlioz, but virtuosic music. Therein were found qualities similar to those that made Grand Opera popular: grandiosity, spectacle, special effects, and, possibly, musical or personal drama. No advanced musical intelligence was required to appreciate it, for musical characteristics (niceties of formal structure, melody, harmony, texture, and so forth) were secondary to bravura. Furthermore, the solo virtuoso exemplified the romantic ideal of the heroic individual, a concept with which members of the *nouveaux riches* might empathize. Clever artists, like Paganini, used personal charisma to advantage, creating a "supernatural" aura that drew audiences with limited interest in music.

Meanwhile, those who, in the first half of the century, supported "art" music were musicians (in this category are included not only professional performers, but critics, educators, historians, and amateur players), the aristocracy (who, because of their cultured background, had had more exposure to traditional music, and who, even if they had little real appreciation of music, probably felt obliged to attend "artistic" events), and a small number of listeners who, against the odds, had developed subtle musical sensibilities. In 1828, following the prolonged nadir of concert life, the instrumental music familiar to these musicians and listeners included works of Haydn, Mozart, Boccherini, and possibly Méhul and Reicha; older members might recall some minor eighteenth-century figures. This audience quickly grew fond of Beethoven's music (which, the rarely played Late works excepted, was understandable to persons who enjoyed Haydn's or Mozart's) and Weber's. Many of these supporters had refined, conservative tastes (the latter attribute might be expected of the aristocrats: eighteenth-century music reminded them of better times). They must have found little artistic satisfaction in Grand Opera and virtuosic concert or salon music, and the more snobbish persons in this group may not have wished to condone music associated with the *nouveaux riches*. It appears that this prejudice against certain recent developments in music made supporters of "art" music unduly wary of any modern traits, and any music that was truly innovative.[1] When Berlioz's works were performed, the conservatives noted his dramatic and musical extremes—the programmatic elements, novel coloristic effects, occasional (actually, rare) bombast—and other departures from tradition, rather than evaluating the music on its own terms and recognizing its different ideals.[2]

Early in the period, then, innovative instrumental "art" music had no real audience: listeners who sought novelty (the *nouveaux riches* and, as the period progressed, others who could for the first time afford musical entertainment) did not appreciate orchestral or chamber "art" music, and did not attend programs in which these figured prominently; listeners who could, had they been willing, have realized the musical worth of "modern" works were opposed to innovation.[3] For young composers, backing came almost exclusively from fellow musicians. Such a relationship among composers, performers, and audience explains why so many new societies that announced plans to promote contemporary composers quickly abandoned programs of new music for a more conventional repertory. Well-intentioned musicians established such societies, but soon discovered that there was no public support for "modern" works and turned to safer programs in order to avert economic disaster.

Among contemporary composers, only conservatives (those who were merely "imaginative") found much favor with concert audiences. No living composer of instrumental works, however, experienced unqualified success; those who wrote in a traditional style were inevitably compared, to their disadvantage, with Haydn, Mozart, and Beethoven. What France lacked was a composer conservative enough to maintain the support of audiences interested in instrumental "art" music, yet talented enough to compete with Beethoven, Weber, and Mendelssohn.

Among the most pressing of other problems that besieged instrumental composers were the governments' policy of dissuading competitors to state-supported organizations (at a time when regimes in France—and much of the rest of Europe—were highly unstable, governments were likely to discourage art that was beyond their control) and the lack of concert halls. When, late in the period, the public became less indifferent toward instrumental music, more concert halls appeared.

Inertia, which pervaded the attitudes of performers, institutions, the music business, and the public, affected living composers of "art" music, whatever the genre.[4] A young artist who attempted to obtain performances or publication of his or her work found himself or herself in a vicious, self-perpetuating cycle: opera directors, entrepreneurs, publishers, and many performers had no interest in music by an unknown artist, yet becoming known was almost impossible without their cooperation. Thus, most newcomers depended on *salons* to establish a reputation and to find supporters. This explains the quantity of chamber music written in the first half of the century, before it had become popular at public concerts.

The romantic concept of "composing for posterity" hindered more composers than it helped, as did the related realization that music from preceding eras had lasting artistic value. Works composed 50 or more years earlier had become a mainstay of the repertory, and were viewed as compositional models of permanent worth. Suddenly composers were competing for places on concert programs not as much with each other as with artists of previous generations. Performers questioned the lasting appeal of new music (to their conservative audiences) before agreeing to perform it. Whereas eighteenth-century publishers had been eager to obtain the latest compositions, their nineteenth-century counterparts might reject music that did not seem competitive, over a period of time, with Haydn's, Mozart's, and Beethoven's. Judging from advertisements, publishers did much more business with works of classical composers than with works not yet proven in concert halls.

Conservatism also prevailed at the institution that wielded the most influence on French instrumental activity, the Paris Conservatoire. Its influence was detrimental, for perpetuation of the status quo, whether it concerned instruction in composition or the staid programs of the Conservatoire's concert society, worked against the composition and performance of modern instrumental music. During the period in question the Conservatoire had only two directors, Cherubini and Auber. Both were renowned for vocal works (particularly operas), and evinced only minimal interest in instrumental music.[5] During their respective tenures (within the period 1828 to 1871), their average age was just under 75 (both maintaining their positions until the year of their death, and both living to be octogenarians);[6] neither was especially adventurous musically in his later years, and neither supported avant-garde styles. At the same time, the composition teachers at the Conservatoire included H.-M. Berton (tenure, 1818–44), LeSueur (1818–37), Reicha (1818–36), F.-J. Fétis (1821–33), Halévy (1833–62), Leborne (1836–66), Paer (1838–39), Carafa (1840–69), Adam (1848–56), Thomas (1856–71), Reber (1862–80), and Massé (1866–80).[7] One wonders what students at that institution could have learned about writing string quartets or symphonies from these gentlemen (among whom only Reicha, Fétis, and Reber demonstrated interest in instrumental works), or whether they could even have been encouraged to essay works of this genre.

Furthermore, the Conservatoire's curriculum emphasized vocal music. The Prix de Rome contest, always comprising the composition of a cantata, was judged in a performance with piano accompaniment (thus disregarding the orchestration), and the formation of the Conservatoire's instrumental ensemble class followed that of the vocal ensemble class by more than 20 years. For whatever reasons involving instruction there, many graduates, among them both composers and critics, emerged with narrow, conservative opinions about what did or did not constitute a symphony, concerto, and so forth; the critics frequently remarked that certain untraditional works with these labels did not truly deserve their titles.

The exception, early in the period, to the prevailing preference for established works was in "popular" music. Amateurs performed *mélo-*

dies, romances, arrangements, variations, and fantasias based on currently fashionable tunes. In advertisements publishers emphasized new vocal and instrumental solos, often of a "popular" nature. The acquisition of a piano in upper-class homes created demand for works in which it was used soloistically or as accompaniment to vocal or instrumental performers, and in which the writing was not too difficult for amateur musicians. This demand was met mainly by "popular" works (rather than sonatas or other "art" music); and the piano boom did nothing to promote interest in string quartets or quintets, much less symphonies (except in arrangements for piano).

Beginning shortly before midcentury, significant changes occurred in French musical life. As conscientious musicians grew weary of commercially popular music, a number of new concert societies were formed, some of which achieved lasting renown: the best known are the Union Musicale, the Grande Société Philharmonique de Paris, the Société Sainte-Cécile, and the Société des Jeunes-Artistes (leading ultimately to the Concerts Populaires) among orchestral groups, and the societies of Alard and Franchomme, Maurin and Chevillard, and Armingaud et al. The new organizations expanded the standard repertory in two directions. First, chamber music, previously prevalent only in *salons,* became commonplace in concert halls; its initial public reception was mixed, but in the 1850s and 1860s it achieved popular success. Second, new music was explored, most of which was more modern than that which had formerly made up the concert repertory. The Société des Derniers Quatuors de Beethoven, though not the first group to perform the Late quartets in Paris, probably gave the most carefully prepared renditions to that time, and repeated these works until they became familiar to critics and audiences. The Société des Quatuors de Mendelssohn did the same for that composer's chamber works. In the 1860s societies were founded to promote works of Schumann and living French composers. Meanwhile, a number of new ensembles investigated (generally as a small part of their repertories) works of other contemporary composers, such as Blanc, Brahms, Farrenc, Gounod, Gouvy, Mathias, Pfeiffer, Prudent, Rubinstein, Saint-Saëns, and Wagner. The Parisian introduction of new or previously unknown works, from late Beethoven to Wagner, should have demonstrated two points to concert audiences: one, that pleasing music in a familiar style had been written by persons other than Haydn, Mozart, Beethoven, and Weber; and two (more significant), that departures from tradition could lead to something other than virtuosic works, "popular" music, imitations of (or derivations from) Grand Opera, and programmatic symphonies. Although many critics retained conservative tastes, others (and some musicians) realized that imitation of eighteenth-century styles could not remain the lone compositional ideal forever.

Probably the most important development between 1850 and 1870 was the confluence of "art" music and *concerts populaires*. The earlier success of dance halls, outdoor concerts, festivals, and other low-cost events at which "popular" music was presented had proved that many persons of the middle and lower classes would pay to hear music. Nonetheless, previous attempts to interest the new audience that had been created by the industrial revolution and political revolutions (which, together, led to a large number of persons suddenly having money to spend on entertainment) had failed, probably because the leap was so great from the music of patriotic festivals and dance halls (the public music that lower- and middle-income groups were most likely to have encountered) to Mozart or Beethoven. As the century progressed, this audience was exposed to various sorts of music, and eventually it bridged the gap between "art" and "popular" music; when, in 1861, Pasdeloup founded the inexpensive Concerts Populaires, listeners came in thousands.

If the new audience had less sophisticated taste than that of the aristocracy, its members were also less steeped in tradition and possibly more openminded, more willing to listen to music by innovative nineteenth-century composers. It would be handy to conclude that a direct relationship existed between the advent of low-cost concerts and a broadening of the repertory to include modern works. Study of the individual concert series, however, leads one to believe otherwise. Although the programs of the Concerts Populaires were less traditional than those of the Conservatoire concerts (works of Wagner, Meyerbeer, Schumann, Berlioz, and Gounod were played with some frequency), they were less experimental than those of the relatively unsuccessful Société des Jeunes-Artistes. Some new series that began by presenting recent works to low-income audiences quickly retreated to more traditional or more "popular" repertories (examples are the Athénée Musical of 1864 and the Société Nationale des Beaux Arts). Furthermore, some events (particularly *salons*) that promoted new music were clearly not intended for the less wealthy. The *nouveaux riches,* who like those less affluent, lacked a traditional cultural background, may have supported these.

The acceptance of contemporary works in the concert repertory came about, however, not so much through series that presented new music exclusively as through occasional performances of modern works by groups that otherwise programmed traditional compositions. Again the *nouveaux riches* (and middle-income groups) may have been largely responsible. Weber has stated that in the new, commercial concert world, the old aristocracy and the middle classes joined forces to sponsor public entertainment.[8] One probable result of the social interaction that this cooperation necessitated is that some listeners from the "new" audiences developed more cultural discernment. Some aristocrats' tastes may also have been affected by the new social structure. As this change occurred, concert programming experienced a general progression (involving much chronological overlap) from separate presentation of "art" and "popular" music (common in the 1830s), through individual concerts that presented both repertories (prevalent in the 1840s), to increased emphasis on "art" music but with some promotion of contemporary works (in the 1860s). Although it would be inaccurate to imply that a strict, chronological, step-by-step pattern of cause and effect between these social and musical trends existed, the increasing participation of the middle classes and the changes in programming appear to be interrelated. Perhaps, when the "new" audiences tired of an exclusively "popular" repertory (beginning in the 1840s), and started to cultivate more interest in "art" music, they remained free of aristocratic (traditional) prejudices and encouraged the performance of contemporary "art" music.

Regardless of which social class was most responsible for changes in repertory, what had been the main problem for composers of instrumental music was being alleviated: the genre's previously small clientele (whose tastes were primarily old-fashioned) had been replaced by the 1860s by a substantial audience, part of which welcomed new styles. As segments of the audience previously attracted by Grand Opera, virtuosos, and "popular" music developed more subtle tastes, and as some members (including critics) of the audience that had once enjoyed only works of classical composers awakened to new musical ideals, nineteenth-century composers found more listeners. To be sure, audiences remained that liked only conservative "art" music or only "popular" works, and some series catered to them. But the dichotomy between these two extreme groups was being replaced by a continuum linking them. If conditions remained far from perfect, as composers continued to maintain, they were nonetheless improving.

What, then, of the "renaissance" after the Franco-Prussian War? Did further progress occur, or does the concept of a renaissance in the 1870s represent belated recognition of musical activity already in existence?

The two choices are not mutually exclusive, and one must answer both halves of the question affirmatively. As this study has demonstrated, instrumental music had already experienced a renaissance by 1870. Its position continued to improve after that date. Several developments, each possibly as significant as the immediate consequences of the Franco-Prussian War, effected the continuous advance of instrumental music in France during the second half of the century.

The presentation of "art" music to lower-income audiences, already successful in the 1860s, was carried further in the 1870s. The Concerts Colonne (from 1873) eclipsed the Concerts Populaires, offering better performances and even lower admission prices.

Berlioz's death in 1869 did not transform him into an idol immediately (though a festival was held in his memory a year later—a few months before the war), but may, perversely, have inspired the Concerts Colonne to promulgate his music, as well as that of several young composers, with some success in the 1870s.[9] For the first time Berlioz's name appeared regularly on programs not organized by himself, and his works were seen in a new light.

Early in 1870 (again, a few months before the war) Gabriel Fauré returned to Paris from Rennes. He had studied not at the Conservatoire but at the Ecole Niedermeyer with the comparatively independent-thinking Saint-Saëns, and was developing a style at once personal and French (or, at least, clearly distinct from Germanic traditions). Although he was not a major composer of instrumental music, and several of his most important works—the piano quintets Opus 89 and Opus 115, the piano trio Opus 120, and the string quartet Opus 121—are late, he contributed the violin sonata Opus 13 and the piano quartet Opus 15 in the late 1870s. His eventual influence as an educator was widespread. His several notable composition pupils included Ravel, and during his directorship of the Paris Conservatoire (1905–20) he instituted progressive reforms.[10]

Franck's appointment as organ professor at the Conservatoire (succeeding Benoist) in 1872 suddenly increased his influence. During the remainder of the decade he and his disciples—who adopted and exalted his untraditional ideas about, particularly, form and harmony—started to gain recognition.

Wagnermania spread through France in the 1870s and 1880s; serious musicians made pilgrimages to Bayreuth, and Wagner's ideas were discussed in the *Revue wagnérienne* (1885–88). If in France Wagner's thoughts on drama received more attention than his music, his practices in structure, harmony, and orchestration, and the emotional level of his music were imitated by French composers (though among purely instrumental works his influence was not great, being most notable in works of d'Indy and, perhaps, Chausson and the Belgian-born Lekeu).[11] More significant ultimately was the reaction against Wagnerism, leading to experimentation with new styles.

Finally, Debussy appeared. His inventive ideas opened paths to an era in which French instrumental works not only achieved at least parity with German instrumental music for the first time in more than a century, but did so without mimicking it. As William Austin has written, the influence of Debussy's styles "freed his compatriots in France from their obsession with Beethoven and Wagner."[12] Debussy himself had described Wagner as "a beautiful sunset mistaken for a dawn";[13] with Debussy's help the enduring pervasiveness of Germanic influence on French composition experienced a sunset and consequent darkness.

Before Debussy, such influence had seemed almost inescapable. Romain Rolland wrote of French music in the nineteenth century:

> in consequence of Germany's monopoly of music since the end of the eighteenth century, musical traditions . . . now became almost entirely German. We think in German forms: the plan of phrases, their development, their balance and all the rhetoric of music and the grammar of composition comes to us from foreign thought, slowly elaborated by German masters.[14]

This lack of national independence and personal originality afflicted much mid-nineteenth-century French music. Too many instrumental works were anachronistic imitations rather than vital creations. Again, though, the verdict is mixed. History should not ignore, as many nineteenth-century Parisians did, the innovative compositions that did appear.

More important, however, composers—whether Germanic or Gallic, conventional or inventive, celebrated or neglected—created instrumental music steadily throughout the era. Performers doggedly promoted instrumental works, first playing mainly classics but later expanding their repertory. Eventually the persistence of both groups effected an important change: a renaissance of appreciation. By 1870, composers and performers alike were benefiting from the new and substantial audience for instrumental music—an audience still learning the old, but open to the new, and awaiting the promising future.

Appendix A

Parisian Concert Series

Appendix A provides brief descriptions of series that were active in Paris at any time between 1828 and 1870 and whose repertories included significant portions of instrumental "art" music. Also depicted are a few series that were announced but that, for various reasons, never got underway. The decision regarding the inclusion of a particular series (or even what constitutes a series) was necessarily somewhat arbitrary; some brief, seemingly minor series are described because the repertory was unusual, and a few societies that presented little instrumental music are discussed because the performers or the concerts themselves were particularly renowned. But most of the series mentioned below were clearly involved in the renaissance of instrumental music in France.

Series of outdoor and café concerts are not included in the appendix, even though some of these programs offered symphonies, concertos, and other "art" music. The most famous of these "popular" series are described in chapter 3, pages 90–95.

Entries are arranged alphabetically. Concerts or *séances* associated with an individual are listed under that person's surname. A system of cross-references indicates the location of series associated with more than one individual and organizations with more than one name.

Information within most entries is in tabular format, with short, separate sections headed *Schedule, Location, Personnel, Repertory,* and *Commentary.* Exceptionally, for the benefit of both the reader and writer, this structure has been replaced by full paragraphs; this has occurred when a series could be summarized in a few sentences, when so little was known that the tabular scheme would have led to a series of blank spaces, or when the state of the research needed describing. Although I have tried to be consistent in the spelling of musicians' names, I have made no attempt to standardize nomenclature for concert halls; several halls were known by many titles and I have adopted the name used in the original descriptions of given series.

Following the final entry is another list, naming musicians whose concerts were not series of instrumental music, but who programmed a significant number of instrumental "art" works.

Abbreviations in Appendix A

In addition to abbreviations utilized in footnotes of the preceding chapters (for example, *FétisB, RGMdP*), the following are used throughout the appendix.

Elwart: *HSCC*	Antoine Elwart, *Histoire de la Société des Concerts du Conservatoire Impérial de Musique* (Paris: S. Castel, 1860)
Weber: *MMC*	William Weber, *Music and the Middle Class: the Social Structure of Concert Life in London, Paris, and Vienna* (London: Croom Helm, 1975)

Instruments are abbreviated as indicated below:

bn	bassoon	ob	oboe
cl	clarinet	pf	piano
db	double bass	va	viola
fl	flute	vc	cello
hn	horn	vn	violin

Alard, Delphin and Alexandre Chevillard: Séances (1837–?1840)

Schedule: (? Biweekly) *séances,* on Sunday afternoons in 1838, beginning 7 January. The last known *séance* is that of Saturday, 5 January 1840, but as most of these events were not announced or reviewed in *RGMdP,* the series may have continued through that spring. See also *Commentary.*

Location: salons of M. Petzold.

Personnel: Delphin Alard (1st vn); Charles Dancla (2nd vn), Armingaud (2nd vn); Croisilles (va), Aumont (va); Alexandre Chevillard (vc); and others.

Repertory: String quintets and quartets, piano trios, sonatas, and solos. Main composers: Beethoven, Mozart, Haydn, Chevillard.

Commentary: Alard and Chevillard had performed together, with César Franck, in June 1837. That November they announced the establishment of a series that would offer polished performances of quartets and quintets by Beethoven, Mozart, and Haydn.[1] The rare reviews of their concerts are favorable.

Amateur Society (1830)

An unnamed amateur orchestral society announced early in 1830 was to meet in a salle de concert, rue St. Martin; the amateurs planned to perform symphonies of Haydn, Mozart, and Beethoven, as well as works by members of the society.[2]

Association des Artistes-Musiciens (from 1843)

Schedule: Sporadic. The Association held yearly meetings, but many years presented no more than two concerts. Some years no concerts were reported, while other years several were mentioned. The Association's committee first met 26 January 1843.[3] The first concert was scheduled to take place 24 August 1843 but was repeatedly postponed and eventually cancelled. See *Commentary.*

Location: Various places, including the Théâtre-Italien, the salle du Conservatoire, the Opéra, the Hippodrome, the salle Bonne-Nouvelle, and the Pré Catelan.

Personnel: Many Parisian musicians, both instrumentalists and vocalists, were members; by 1864 there were 4844.[4] Berlioz was one of the 46 founding members. Conductors included Berlioz, Spontini, Habeneck, Tilmant *aîné,* Georges Bousquet, and Forestier (probably Joseph Forestier). See also *Commentary.*

Repertory: Orchestral, chamber, solo instrumental, and vocal music, including "art," "popular," and even sacred works, ranging chronologically from Corelli's to contemporaries' compositions.

Commentary: The Association was a group of Parisian musicians who, promoted by Isidore-Justin-Severin, baron Taylor (Inspecteur général des beaux-arts from 1838) had "agreed to band together for mutual aid and the furtherance of modern music."[5] For a small annual fee, members qualified for assistance, pensions, and so forth.[6] The Association sponsored concerts (many by its own members), thereby attempting to relieve individual composers of financial risks, and organized benefit concerts (generally for the members as a whole).[7] Some of the concerts employed enormous forces: at the Hippodrome in 1846, Tilmant led an orchestra of 1800 to 2000; at an outdoor festival concert in 1865, 1000 players from Parisian military bands performed, attracting an audience of over 15,000.[8] On appropriate holidays the Association sponsored masses, and during the musically bleak season of 1848 it organized festivals. In 1852 the Association supported four orchestral concerts and two chamber music concerts; despite a favorable reception, the Association evidently lost use of the concert hall before the next season, and the series had to be cancelled.[9]

Association des Musiciens-Exécutants de Paris (1851)

Schedule: The only reported concert took place Sunday, 9 November 1851. Formation of the Association had been announced in September.[10]

Location: Casino Paganini.

Personnel: The violinist, composer, and critic Alexandre Malibran led an orchestra of 70 to 80 and a chorus.

Repertory: At the known concert the program included Elwart's vocal symphony *Ruth et Booz* and overtures by Auber and Méhul.

Commentary: Members of the Association intended to propagate music among the general public.[11] The last reference to the society in *RGMdP* is Blanchard's review of the only known concert.[12] The article on Malibran in *FétisB* states that his attempt to establish *concerts populaires* was unsuccessful.[13] The following spring Malibran led the orchestra of the new and somewhat similar Cercle Musical et Littéraire (see this entry).

L'Athénée (1866–67). See Société de L'Athénée.

L'Athénée Musical (1829–44). See Société de L'Athénée Musical.

L'Athénée Musical (1864)

Schedule: The inaugural concert took place Sunday, 17 January 1864; thereafter concerts were scheduled nightly. On 29 May plans were announced to transform the Athénée Musical into the Athénée Dramatique (thereby ending the concert series) by August.[14]

Location: The Athénée Musical, a new concert hall on the boulevard Saint-Germain, near the Musée de Cluny. The auditorium, reportedly decorated in a style associated with Louis XV, seated about 1500.[15]

Personnel: The founder and first director of the society was M. le comte de Raousset-Boulbon. In April he was succeeded as director by one Gérault.[16] The first conductor was Antoine-Victor Paquis, a horn player in the Théâtre-Italien orchestra. An orchestra of 40 to 50, at least one chorus, and instrumental and vocal soloists participated.[17]

Repertory: Few specific programs are known. The original administration intended to propagate vocal and instrumental "art" music, and reputedly welcomed works of young composers.[18] The inaugural program included an overture of Auber and a march of Mendelssohn, as well as choral music, and vocal and instrumental solos. Vocal compositions seem to have been emphasized at subsequent concerts, and in April *romances* and *chansonnettes* were added to this repertory.

Commentary: Saint-Yves wrote that the Athénée intended to provide "art" music in a location unaccustomed to it (that is, the Left Bank).[19] One wonders why, if (as was twice noted)[20] the programs were well attended, the repertory became lighter and the concert series was abandoned in favor of the Athénée Dramatique (which was to present *vaudevilles* and *revues* under the direction of one Oscar) after only one season.

Baillot, Pierre: Séances (?1820–1836 and later)[21]

Schedule: Two to seven *séances* a year, 1827 (probably earlier, see *Commentary*) through 1836, usually at weekly intervals on Tuesday evenings, in spring; some Sunday *matinées* in December 1832; *soirées* on Saturdays, 1834–35. Baillot had presented chamber music concerts in 1814.[22] Elwart mentioned occasional concerts in 1838; three concerts were reported in 1840.[23]

Location: 1827–32, usually in the hôtel Fesch, rue Saint-Lazare, no. 59; 1831, salle Saint-Jean, Hôtel de Ville; December 1832 to spring 1834, *salons* of Duport, the piano manufacturer, rue Taitbout, no. 15, and *chez* Alerme; 1836, *chez* M. Leroux, the banker, rue Bergère; 1840, rue Bergère.

Personnel: Organized by the violinist Pierre Baillot; other participants included Vidal (vn), Urhan (va), Vaslin (vc), Baudiot (vc), Chevillard (vc), Norblin (vc/db), Mialle (pf), Hiller (pf), and sometimes Sauzay (vn) and others.

Repertory: Chamber works, mainly string quartets and quintets. Main composers: Boccherini, Haydn, Mozart, Beethoven (including the Late quartets), Onslow, Baillot.

Commentary: The renowned Baillot had performed works of J. S. Bach in Paris as early as 1809.[24] Pierre Soccanne believed that Baillot's presentations were the first public concerts of chamber music in Paris, and maintained that Baillot's series experienced success from 1820 on.[25] F.-J. Fétis remarked frequently on Baillot's high standards of performance. According to a contemporary source, an audience of 600 to 700 attended Baillot's *soirées* in 1833,[26] but Sauzay recalled that the audience was faithful rather than large, and that only 150 attended in 1832.[27]

Batta, Escudier-Kastner, and Vieuxtemps: Concerts (1863). See Escudier-Kastner, Vieuxtemps, and Batta: Concerts.

Beaumetz, Mlle. Marie: Séances (1864)

According to announcements in *Ménestrel* and *RGMdP,* the pianist Mlle. Marie Beaumetz scheduled three *séances* of "art" music for strings and piano at biweekly intervals on Fridays, 19 February to 18 March 1864.[28] She, Alard (vn), Franchomme (vc), and, possibly, others planned to play works of Beethoven, Haydn, Mozart, and Weber. I have found no other references to these events.

Becker, Jean: Historical Concerts (1863)

Schedule: Three concerts, 16 and 26 March, and 6 April.
Location: salle Herz.
Personnel: The violinist Jean Becker organized the programs and was soloist in many of the intrumental works presented. At the third concert (and probably at the others) the orchestra was led by one Placet. Mme. Ernest Becker and M. Ferranti supervised the vocal works.
Repertory: Violin solos and concertos ranging chronologically from those of Tartini and Leclair to those of Bazzini and Alard. The first program offered Italian works, the second German, and the third French and Belgian. Vocal works were also performed.

Béguin-Salomon, Mme. Louise: Séances and Concerts (?1862–?1868)

Schedule: Unknown. Single presentations were mentioned each year from 1862 through 1865. Series of *séances* were reported in spring 1866 and 1867; weekly *soirées* "resumed" on Thursday, 19 December 1867. The last event publicized in *RGMdP* was a concert on Thursday, 31 March 1870.
Location: Séances, chez Mme. Béguin-Salomon; Concerts, salons Erard.
Personnel: Organized by the pianist and piano teacher Mme. Béguin-Salomon (*née* Louise-Frédérique Cohen); other main performers were Edouard Colonne (vn) and Henri Poëncet (vc); other participants included Langhans (vn), White (vn), Trombetta (va), Lebouc (vc), Rose (cl), and Brunot (?fl).

Repertory: Chamber works, mainly for strings and piano. Main composer: Beethoven; others included A. Blanc, Chopin, Haydn, Mendelssohn, Mozart, Onslow, Spohr, and Weber.

Commentary: The first four presentations mentioned in *RGMdP* were labelled "séances" (1862 and 1863), "annual audition" (1864), and "concert" (1865). Even after regular *séances* commenced,[29] separate concerts—in which the repertory was similar—were reported (1866 and 1868). Bannelier considered Mme. Béguin-Salomon's concert of 1866 to be one of the most interesting of the season; the *séances* of 1867 received a comparable compliment.[30] The *séances* were well attended.[31]

Berlioz, Hector: Concerts (from 1828)

The many concerts organized by Hector Berlioz, described fully in his *Mémoires*[32] and by Barzun,[33] were among the most significant Parisian concerts of the century—partly because they presented premieres of Berlioz's works and partly because from 1836 they reflected Berlioz's remarkable ability to organize and conduct large forces. The first program, comprising his own works, took place 26 May 1828, while Berlioz was a student at the Paris Conservatoire.[34] After he returned from the Prix de Rome trip in 1832, concerts occurred frequently: Macdonald has listed five in 1833, four in 1834, five in 1835 and 1840, and four in 1842.[35] These were not all series, but some might be so considered. In four concerts at the Conservatoire from 9 November to 28 December 1834, a variety of works by Berlioz (including the *Symphonie Fantastique* and *Harold en Italie*) and others were presented. Two similar concerts took place the following year, on 22 November and 6 December, again at the Conservatoire and again with a large orchestra led by Girard.[36] Berlioz conducted four concerts during the 1843–44 season at various locations; his own works were emphasized. In 1845, from 19 January to 6 April, Berlioz directed four *grands fêtes musicales* at the Cirque des Champs-Elysées; 500 musicians participated in the third concert.[37] The programs included orchestral, choral, and dramatic works of Berlioz (*Roméo et Juliette* and overtures), Beethoven (the Fifth Piano Concerto), Félicien David (*Le Désert*), Glinka (opera excerpts), and others. After 1848 Berlioz organized few concerts in Paris apart from those of his Grande Société Philharmonique de Paris (1850–51; see this entry).

According to Barzun, Berlioz "had frequent sessions of chamber music at his own house" from the 1830s until his death.[38] These were not discussed in *RGMdP.*

Bernard, Paul: Soirées (?1862–70 or later)

The *soirées* sponsored by the pianist, composer, and teacher Paul Bernard in his own home began, no later than 1862, as *exercices* for his piano pupils. As the pupils improved the *soirées* became estimable concerts,[39] outside artists (among them the violinists Mlle. Thérèse Liebe, Magnin, Sarasate, and Léonard, the flutist Taffanel, and renowned vocalists) were invited to participate, and the series received more attention in contemporary journals. In the seasons of 1869 and 1870 *soirées* occurred biweekly. The programs were reviewed favorably, but were predominantly light.

Bessems, Antoine: Matinées (1865) and Concerts (ca. 1843–?1866)

From Saturday 20 May to Saturday ?22 July 1865 the violinist and composer Antoine Bessems organized five *matinées* at Saint-Germain-en-Laye.[40] Other participants were Allard (fl), Colonne (?va), Rabaud (vc), Pasquet (db), the pianists Bériot *fils,* Kowalsky, and Mme. Mackenzie, and a vocalist. The single known program included a Hummel Piano Quintet and vocal and piano works.

Single concerts by Bessems were reported in 1843, 1846, and most years from 1851 through 1866.[41] These varied in nature, and were presented in several locations with a wide array of prominent musicians, among them Saint-Saëns (pf), Lee (vc), and Gouffé (db). Most programs included chamber works and violin solos; Bessems sometimes played his own compositions but emphasized works of established composers, particularly Mozart and Beethoven.

Bohrer Frères: Concerts and Séances (?1827–1831 and later)

Schedule: Annual concerts, ?1827, 1828, ?1829;[42] six *soirées,* mainly at biweekly intervals, the first four on Wednesdays, the remaining two on Sundays, spring 1830; four *séances,* spring 1831. Anton Bohrer and his daughter Sophie, then nine, gave two concerts in Paris in June 1838.[43]

Location: salons of M. Pape for known programs, 1828-31.

Personnel: Anton Bohrer (vn) and Max Bohrer (vc), brothers from Germany; other participants included Tilmant *aîné* (vn), Urhan (va), probably Claudel (vn), other string players, and pianists.

Repertory: Mainly string quartets, but also duos, trios, and quintets. Main composers: Beethoven and the Bohrer brothers.

Commentary: The *séances* attracted large audiences[44] in spite of high admission fees, 3 to 10 francs in 1831.[45] Berlioz spoke favorably of the brothers in his *Mémoires*.[46] Their performances of Beethoven's Late quartets in 1830 and 1831 were among the first in Paris.

Bonewitz: Séances (1867–70)

Schedule: Varied. During the season of 1867–68 there were two series of five *matinées* each at biweekly intervals on Sundays, 3 November to 29 December 1867 and 19 January to 15 March 1868. The resumption of *séances,* now as *soirées,* was announced the following autumn, and another resumption was publicized in January 1870,[47] but during these two seasons only four events were reported; and these, not all of which were *soirées,* took place at irregular intervals and varied in nature.

Location: salons Kriegelstein, rue Drouot, no. 11, for both series in 1867–68, one event in 1869 and one in 1870; the series announced in November 1868 was scheduled for the salle Herz.

Personnel: Organized by the composer, pianist, and piano teacher Jean-Henri Bonewitz. Other participants included Telesinski (vn), Ch. Dancla (vn), A. de Czeké (vn), Norblin (vc), Bernard (? va), and piano pupils of Bonewitz.

Repertory: Chamber, vocal, and piano music; many works of contemporaries.

Commentary: The *séances,* apparently for an invited audience,[48] were reviewed favorably in *RGMdP* on several occasions.

Caraman, Charles de: Séances (1850–51)

Schedule: Unknown. A series of *séances* took place the winter of 1850–51.

Location and personnel: salons of M. le duc Charles de Caraman, who organized the *séances*. The performers are not known.

Repertory: Chamber music of Bach, Beethoven, Handel, Kufferath, Lee, Mayseder, Mozart, Onslow, Vanden Abeeln, and Weber.[49]

Commentary: The Caraman *séances* are mentioned only once in *RGMdP* after the end of the season. Evidently they were expected to continue, for plans were announced to program more recent works,[50] but there is no indication in *RGMdP* that another season took place.

Cercle Artistique (?1864–after 1870). See Cercle des Beaux Arts.

Cercle de l'Union Artistique (1860–70 or later)

Schedule: The Cercle was established in spring 1860, but the inaugural concert did not occur until Tuesday, 14 May 1861.[51] Only a few concerts were reported, at irregular intervals from then through 1870, but the publicity (descriptions such as "first of the season") suggests that there were more.

Location: The address of the Cercle was the rue de Choiseul. The inaugural concert took place at the Théâtre-Italien.

Personnel: The society was established and presided over by Prince J. M. K. F. J. Poniatowski (a Polish tenor and composer who had settled in Paris after 1848). Originally there were 200 members; Scudo wrote of 500 in 1862.[52] At the concert of 5 December 1864 an orchestra was led by Jules Pasdeloup.

Repertory: Symphonies, other orchestral works, chamber music, instrumental solos, and vocal works of established masters and contemporaries.

Commentary: The Cercle was mentioned only rarely in the contemporary press. Scudo wrote that its goal was to open the doors of *salons* to talented but little-known artists, and that Prince Poniatowski hoped to encourage performances of works by young composers.[53] At the two publicized concerts of 1864, several unpublished or new works were programmed. It is not clear whether the Cercle sponsored regular concerts or served mainly as a union that promoted young composers and performers. Surely all 500 members did not participate at the Cercle's concerts, but the organization may have supported events by some of its members.

Cercle des Beaux-Arts (?1864–after 1870)

Schedule: Uncertain. Concerts were reported irregularly, but every season, from 1864–65 until after the Franco-Prussian War. A review of the second concert, 13 May 1865, stated that the society had already existed for six months.[54] Biweekly *soirées* were noted in April 1866.[55] At least five *séances* were presented in the season of 1868–69, and seven were mentioned in spring 1870.

Location: The concert of May 1865 took place at the Cercle des Beaux Arts, rue Saint-Honoré, no. 352. By December 1865 the society played in an elegant hall on the rue de la Chaussée d'Antin (near the present Opéra, then under construction).[56] In January 1867 the inauguration of a new hall on the rue de la Chaussée d'Antin, no. 33, was announced.[57]

Personnel: The violinist Georg Jacobi organized concerts from the inauguration through at least December 1867 and again from no later than January 1870 through at least December 1871.[58] The pianist and composer Ernest Stoeger organized the series in spring 1869. Participants included instrumentalists and vocalists; not all members of the Cercle were musicians.

Repertory: Much light music, including instrumental, vocal, and piano solos. Although chamber "art" works appeared on the programs, in many cases only single movements thereof were performed. Main composers of chamber works: Beethoven and Mozart. Contemporary works were presented. Under Jacobi's regime programs included many violin solos.

Commentary: Young artists and *amateurs* founded the Cercle; by December 1865 there were 200 members.[59] Concerts were attended mainly by members.[60] The events were recommended to persons of taste[61] (the light programming notwithstanding); the hall also offered exhibits of painting and sculpture.

Cercle Musical (1834–35) and Société Musicale (I, 1835)

Schedule: Three Sunday afternoon concerts at weekly intervals, 4 to 18 January 1835, followed by five Sunday afternoon concerts at biweekly intervals, 8 February to 5 April 1835.

Location: salle Chantereine.

Personnel: The founding members included Alard, Henri Bertini, Bordogni, Brod, Cuvillon, Franchomme, Gallay, Geraldi, Herz, Théodore Labarre, Tulou, and probably Liszt and Chopin.[62]

Repertory: Chamber works of the founding members, particularly Bertini, Brod, and Labarre; some chamber works of more established composers; instrumental solos; some vocal music.

Commentary: The Cercle Musical intended to expand the repertory of chamber and *salon* music (including vocal works) and to improve performance standards for these genres; programs of Mozart, Beethoven, Hummel, and French composers who followed in this tradition were planned.[63] Although the Cercle was founded as a private club (limited to the founders plus 100 members), the first concert was open to the public at three and five francs.[64] By the third concert (18 January 1835), the group had been reorganized, the membership had changed, and the organization was renamed "Société Musicale."[65] In spite of the announced intentions, programs comprised mainly contemporary works. A review of the seventh concert mentioned increasing and deserved public favor.[66] Although the society was not mentioned the following season, there was an attempt to revive it in autumn 1838; see Société Musicale (II).

Cercle Musical des Amateurs (1837–70 or later)

Schedule: Annual concerts at the end of each season (usually in April), ?1838 to ?1846. A resumption took place in the 1850's. See *Commentary.*

Location: salle Herz.

Personnel: An orchestra of 60, including some professionals but mainly comprising amateurs, and a chorus. The conductor was Tilmant *aîné*; the director of the society's committee was Charles de Bez. See also *Commentary.*

Repertory: Symphonies and overtures, some instrumental solos and vocal works. Known programs through 1844 included only one major work each. Main composer: Beethoven. Some contemporary works were programmed.

Commentary: Members of the Cercle Musical met weekly (sometimes twice a week) during the season to study music but, except for performing accompanying roles, presented only one public concert a year, for which the admission fee was five francs. The earliest notice in *RGMdP* concerning their activity appeared in April 1839.[67] An article from 1870 stated that the society had been founded in 1837.[68] Reviews of the concerts were mixed. Notices of the Cercle's activities disappeared after 1846 until 1854, when a resumption of weekly *séances* under the direction of Georges Bousquet was mentioned.[69] Thereafter I find only one more announcement of the Cercle's activities in *RGMdP,* the notice of a concert led by Tilmant in 1858.[70] But in 1870 *Ménestrel* printed a letter from members of the Cercle, who expressed regret concerning Tilmant's retirement.[71]

Cercle Musical et Littéraire (1852)

Schedule: Five concerts, of which three were on Sundays, at approximately biweekly intervals, 8 February to 18 April 1852.

Location: salle Sainte-Cécile.

Personnel: An orchestra led by the violinist, composer, and critic Alexandre Malibran. Vocalists also participated.

Repertory: Overtures, concertos, other orchestral works, chamber and vocal works, and instrumental solos by various French and foreign eighteenth- and nineteenth-century composers.

Commentary: The Cercle was primarily intended to be an accompanying orchestra, available to instrumental and vocal soloists for a reasonable "rental" fee.[72] It is not clear that it ever served this function, but it did provide its own series of programs. The organization was established subsequent (and possibly consequent) to the failure in autumn 1851 of Malibran's Association des Musiciens-Exécutants (see this entry). I find no reports of the Cercle after spring 1852.

Chevillard, Alexandre and Delphin Alard: Séances (1837–?1840). See Alard, Delphin and Alexandre Chevillard: Séances.

Colonne, Edouard: Matinées (1867–68)

Schedule: Unknown. A series of *matinées* began in December 1867[73] and continued at least until February 1868.

Location: salle Lebouc.

Personnel: Organized by the violinist Edouard Colonne; other participants included Turban (vn), Heiss (? vn/va), Lévy (va), Poëncet (vc), and pianists Mme. Béguin-Salomon, Mlle. Adrienne Picard, and Henri Fissot.

Repertory: The one known program comprised a Mozart piano quartet, a Haydn string quartet, Beethoven's Serenade for violin, viola, and cello, and piano works.

Commentary: An anonymous reviewer for *Ménestrel* wrote that the *séances* were among those most followed.[74]

Concerts Classiques (1864)

Schedule: The only two concerts mentioned in *RGMdP* occurred on successive Sunday afternoons, 10 and 17 April 1864.

Location: Cirque de l'Impératrice.

Personnel: The series was organized by one Dejean (possibly the entrepreneur Louis Dejean). An orchestra was led by L.-M.-A. Deloffre, then *chef d'orchestre* at the Théâtre-Lyrique.

Repertory: According to the advance publicity, programs would include orchestral works of established masters.[75] The two known concerts offered symphonies, concertos, and overtures by Beethoven, Haydn, Mendelssohn, Molique, Mozart, and Weber.

Commentary: Dejean reportedly hoped to provide a summer version of the Concerts Populaires.[76] Only the first of the two known concerts was reviewed,[77] though the second was announced the same day it was to take place. Probably the series did not continue after the second concert; I have found no more references to it in the contemporary press.

Concerts de la Rue Saint-Honoré (1837–41). See Concerts Valentino.

Concerts de l'Opéra (1869)

Schedule: 14 concerts at biweekly intervals on Sunday nights were planned, but only the first two (7 and 21 November 1869) took place. See also *Commentary.*

Location: salle de l'Opéra.

Personnel: The general director was Emile Perrin, director of the Opéra. Henry Litolff, best known as a composer and pianist, organized and conducted the concerts. An orchestra of 100 was recruited from various theatre orchestras,[78] and there were 90 in the chorus.[79]

Repertory: The two programs included Beethoven's Seventh and Ninth Symphonies, symphonic excerpts and short orchestral works by various nineteenth-century composers, and choral music.

Commentary: According to a prospectus in *RGMdP,* the society was to present old and new orchestral and choral music, with emphasis on selected works of young composers from all schools. When feasible, composers were to conduct their own works.[80] Admission fees, the same as those charged for an opera, ranged from one franc 50 centimes to seven francs; a sizable discount was offered on subscriptions.[81] The first concert attracted a capacity audience. Bannelier wrote that the series, through its contemporary repertory, filled a gap in the Parisian musical scene; and by stating that Paris should be able to support a third orchestral society, he granted the series a status comparable to that of the Conservatoire concerts and Concerts Populaires.[82] But the orchestra was criticized for lack of ensemble playing after both concerts.[83] Soon after the second, the society dissolved, reportedly because of dissension within the administration resulting in Litolff's resignation.[84] Dandelot later blamed the society's demise on lack of governmental support.[85]

Between November 1870 and March 1871 (before the Commune), *soirées musicales* resumed at the Opéra (which was otherwise inactive). Overtures, operatic excerpts, and patriotic airs were presented in a Spartan setting.[86]

Concerts d'Emulation (1828–?1834)

(Concerts d'émulation de la Société mineure des jeunes élèves de l'Ecole royale de musique)

Schedule: The first concert took place in June 1828.[87] A fourth concert was reported late in that calendar year.[88] Thereafter, concerts were recorded rarely and irregularly, seldom with exact dates, but at all times of the year. Concerts were discontinued after the July Revolution (1830), but Cherubini authorized their resurrection about October 1832.[89] I find no mention of them after that date, but Elwart and Pierre maintained that the organization continued until 1834.[90]

Location: Petite salle of the Paris Conservatoire.

Personnel: An orchestra comprising about 50 students of the Paris Conservatoire,[91] and a student chorus. According to one reviewer, students conducted their own works.[92] The director from 1828 to 1830 was Antoine Elwart; in 1832 Millault (probably Edouard Millault) was appointed conductor.[93]

Repertory: Works by students of the Conservatoire, among them Alard, Chevillard, Elwart, Franchomme, A. Thomas, and A. Vogel. The compositions included overtures, orchestral and vocal *fragments,* instrumental solos, and piano works.

Commentary: The success of the Société des Concerts du Conservatoire (begun in March 1828) inspired students of that institution to establish a series at which student composers and performers could gain public exposure. Calling themselves the "Jeunes élèves de l'Ecole Royale," they presented two well-attended concerts in ?May 1828.[94] The Concerts d'Emulation followed in June. Reviews of the society's performances were generally favorable, though some of the student compositions were faulted.

Concerts d'Emulation, Egasse (?1823–?1829). See Egasse: Concerts d'Emulation.

Concerts des Beaux-Arts (1865)

Schedule: The concert series was scheduled to begin Wednesday, 15 February 1865; its inauguration was apparently postponed to Sunday the 19th, after which nightly concerts took place. The society was still active in May 1865. A concert to inaugurate the refurbished hall had been planned for Sunday, 11 December 1864, but was not reviewed.[95]

Location: boulevard des Italiens, no. 26. The hall was described as large, comfortable, and elegant, replete with beautiful paintings and sculpture.[96]

Personnel: One Martinet supervised (possibly owned) the hall. An orchestra of about 35 to 40 was conducted by Jean-Jacques Debillemont, and vocalists were led by one Roger[97] (probably the singer and teacher Gustave-Hippolyte Roger).

Repertory: Plans were announced to perform symphonies, overtures, light instrumental pieces, and vocal music, including compositions (particularly, little-known works) of Lully, Rameau, Gluck, Monsigny, Grétry, Haydn, Mozart, Beethoven, and more recent composers.[98] A repertory of 60 works was mentioned, though no specific pieces were cited.[99] At the only known program, chamber and orchestral works of Gluck, Mozart, Beethoven, and Debillemont, as well as piano and vocal music, were presented.

Commentary: The hall was intended to unite "all elements of elegant distraction," yet the concert that inaugurated it cost only one franc.[100] The refined atmosphere, suitable for families,[101] was repeatedly emphasized, and the first concert was attended by a large and glamorous audience.[102] An anonymous reviewer thought the orchestra sounded weak, possibly because of poor acoustics,[103] but the concerts became popular. (Few concerts were mentioned in *RGMdP,* but that journal did not regularly review nightly concerts.) In April Martinet announced a plan to provide both a short concert and a short theatrical presentation each evening.[104]

Concerts des Italiens (1869)

Schedule: Concerts were planned for each Monday evening, beginning 6 December 1869. The first was not reviewed (possibly it did not take place; see *Commentary*), and I find no further references to the concerts.

Location: Théâtre-Italien.

Personnel: Soloists, chorus, and orchestra of the Théâtre-Italien, with some outsiders.

Commentary: According to the single reference in *RGMdP,* the Concerts des Italiens were to provide *représentations-concerts* for subscribers of the Théâtre-Italien.[105] Possibly the series was established to compete with the Concerts de l'Opéra (see this entry), which had begun a month earlier. Ironically, the dissolution of the Concerts de l'Opéra and foundation of the Concerts des Italiens were announced the same day.[106] Perhaps when the competition disappeared the management of the Théâtre-Italien no longer felt it necessary to execute its plan (though the cessation of concerts at the Opéra was then thought to be temporary).

Admission fees were six and seven francs (rather high, but lower than a regular performance at the Théâtre-Italien). The repertory was to include both acknowledged masterpieces and contemporary works; the first program comprised Schumann's *Das Paradies und die Peri* for solo voices, chorus, and orchestra. It is not clear that this concert took place or that the Concerts des Italiens ever intended to perform instrumental "art" music (as the Concerts de l'Opéra did).

Concerts Neuve-Viviennes (1840–?1845). See Concerts Viviennes.

Concerts Populaires (1861–84)

Programs of (almost exclusively) orchestral "art" music, which succeeded via low admission fees in attracting large audiences. A detailed account of the society is provided in chapter 2, pages 46–51.

Concerts Spirituels

In the early decades of the nineteenth century unsuccessful attempts were made by various theatres (notably the Théâtre-Italien and Opéra) to revive a series of *concerts spirituels* (after the Concert Spirituel, a uniquely important concert series in Paris, active from 1725 to 1790).[107] The *concerts spirituels* sponsored by the Opéra in the 1820s were attacked by F.-J. Fétis for their limited (conservative) repertory and poor execution.[108] At three concerts in spring 1828, instrumentalists and singers from the Conservatoire, the Théâtre-Italien, and Choron's Institution Royale de Musique Classique at Religieuse were led by one Lubbert. Instrumental portions of the programs included Beethoven's Third Symphony and concertos, overtures, symphonic excerpts, and solos by, among others, the Bohrer brothers, Cherubini, Hummel, Mayseder, Rode, Schneitzhoeffer, and Winter (all but one of whom were living composers).[109] Reviewing these concerts, Fétis complained of lifeless renditions and poor acoustics, and remarked that the concerts were poorly attended.[110]

During Holy Week each year the Société des Concerts du Conservatoire presented *concerts spirituels*; unlike the Société's regular programs, these were dominated by oratorios and other vocal works. Later, the Concerts Populaires and other societies also provided *concerts spirituels*.

Concerts Valentino (1837–41)

Schedule: Nightly concerts during the season (and some summers), mid-October 1837 to 30 April 1841.

Location: A hall on the rue Saint-Honoré. The auditorium, which seated 2000,[111] became known as the salle Valentino.

Personnel: An orchestra of about 85, including many young musicians.

"Art" music was conducted by H.-J.-A.-J. Valentino; "popular" music was led first by A.-C. Fessy and, from summer 1840, by one Louis (probably Nicolas Louis).

Repertory: Vocal music was forbidden.[112] Programs comprised symphonies, overtures, instrumental and piano solos, and dance music. Main composers of "art" music: Beethoven, Haydn, Mozart, and Weber; contemporary works were played frequently.

Commentary: As the admission fee was only one franc, the Concerts Valentino provided the opportunity for all social classes to hear works of the German masters.[113] The performances were frequently praised but reports regarding their commercial success were mixed. Berlioz wrote that the programs juxtaposed "art" and "popular" music in order to attract the largest possible audience.[114] The salle Valentino eventually became the home of *bals publiques*.[115] See also chapter 2, pages 68–69.

Concerts Viviennes (1840–?1845)

Schedule: At least one concert a week, and usually more, winter and summer seasons from mid-May 1840. The concerts were last mentioned in *RGMdP* in January 1845.

Location: salle Vivienne on the rue Neuve-Vivienne.

Personnel: The concerts were established under the auspices of a society of artists. The orchestra comprised members of theatre orchestras and the Concerts Valentino; in 1843 its members included 15 former winners of *premiers prix* at the Paris Conservatoire.[116] The first conductor, A.-C. Fessy, was succeeded by Antoine Elwart in September 1843.

Repertory: Mainly light, but including some orchestral "art" music of both established masters and contemporaries. Some years there were special weekly series devoted to "art" music (in addition to the regular concerts).

Commentary: The concerts experienced commercial success and the orchestra's execution won critical acclaim. Although plans to promote "art" music were frequently announced, actual performances of it appear to have been relatively rare. On occasion the society provided monetary encouragement for young composers.[117]

Conservatoire: Distribution des Prix: Concerts (from 1797)

Annual concerts were presented in conjunction with the distribution of prizes at the Paris Conservatoire (in November or December from 1828 through 1857, thereafter in August). The performers included student prize winners. Until about 1850 the repertory was evenly divided between vocal and instrumental works (mainly overtures, concertos, and solos, some chamber music); some programs included as many as six of each. After 1850 fewer instrumental works were heard. The instrumental repertory from 1828 through 1870 comprised works of 65 composers, among them students and recent graduates of the Conservatoire as well as renowned masters.[118]

Conservatoire: Exercices des Elèves (1839–62)

Through the beginning of the nineteenth century there were various series in which students of the Paris Conservatoire performed, among them the Concerts d'Emulation (1828–?34; see this entry).[119] Two or more *exercices,* intended to demonstrate progress of the students, were sponsored by the Conservatoire nearly every year (usually in spring) from 1839 through 1862.[120] Little instrumental music was played: there was none at concerts before 1846 and at 35 concerts from then through 1862 there were only 16 performances of 14 works (mainly overtures) representing 12 composers. The orchestra was directed by, successively, Guérin, Alard, Habeneck, Girard, Massart, and Pasdeloup.

Cossmann, Joachim, and Wartel: Soirées (1850). See Joachim, Cossmann, and Wartel: Soirées.

Dancla, Charles (and siblings): Concerts and Séances (?1847–65)

Schedule: Varied. Short series (two or, more often, three concerts or *séances*) many seasons from spring 1847 through 1865. No events were reported in *RGMdP* during the season of 1848–49 or from autumn 1857 through spring 1861, and only single concerts were publicized in the seasons of 1849–50, 1851–52, and 1852–53. Weekly *séances* on Saturdays occurred in 1854; other years concerts took place at wider intervals. Many of the concerts were on Sundays.[121]

Location: salons of Hesselbein, rue Vivienne, most events through 1855; salle Pleyel, most events after 1855.

Personnel: The most renowned of the Danclas was the violinist and composer, Charles Dancla, who presented several concerts on his own. Other participants in the series included Léopold Dancla (vn), Lenepvu (vn), Altès *jeune* (va), Arnaud Dancla (vc), Sebastien Lee (vc), Gouffé (vc/db), and the pianists Laure Dancla, Adolphe Blanc,

Louis Lacombe, Anatole Bernadel, Auguste Wolff, Mlle. Sophie Danvin, Mlle. Sabatier-Blot, and Mme. Escudier-Kastner.

Repertory: Chamber music, primarily string quartets. Main composers: Charles Dancla, Beethoven, Haydn, and Mozart; contemporary works (other than those of Dancla) were performed occasionally.

Commentary: Although the series organized by Charles Dancla and his siblings were irregular, they were part of the Parisian musical scene for many years. It is unclear whether all the concerts were open to the general public, but many were announced or reviewed in *RGMdP.* Charles Dancla presented single (nonseries) concerts in 1841, 1843, 1844, and 1846, and annually in the late 1860's. At these he presented many of his own compositions, among them violin solos, *symphonies concertantes,* and some orchestral works.

David, Félicien and Paulin: Matinées (1857)

Schedule: Five biweekly Sunday *matinées,* 1 February to 29 March 1857, were scheduled; only the first four were separately announced and reviewed in *RGMdP.*

Location: salle Erard.

Personnel: Organized by the composer Félicien David and the vocalist Paulin [Louis-Joseph Lespinasse]. Other participants included two of the Dancla brothers (?vns), Atlès (va), Lee (vc), Bailly (?vc), the vocalist Mme. Gaveaux-Sabattier, and, evidently, a chorus.

Repertory: The announced repertory included vocal and instrumental music by Palestrina, Lassus, Lully, Rameau, Scarlatti, J. S. Bach, Handel, Marcello, Gluck, Jommelli, Haydn, Mozart, Beethoven, Weber, Spontini, Hérold, Schubert, Mendelssohn, Chopin, Schumann, S. Heller, and Schuloff.[122] The actual programs comprised several chamber works by Félicien David as well as vocal and piano music.

Delcroix, Ménétrier, and Vander-Gucht: Séances (1864)

The single reference to this series in *RGMdP,* in late January 1864, described the founding of a chamber music society to perform music "de nos grandes symphonistes" (no specific works were mentioned).[123] The reference noted that the three members of the society, Pierre-Désiré Delcroix (pf), Ménétrier (vn), and Vander-Gucht (vc), would sometimes be joined by additional performers. At the one known concert, in the *salons* of Lebouc (evidently a few days before the reference appeared), other participants included Cohen (?vn),[124] Delamour (db), and Dragone.

Duvernoy, Alphonse: Soirées (1869)

In February 1869 *Ménestrel* reported that the young pianist Alphonse Duvernoy had organized *séances* of chamber music at the salle Erard, in which Léonard (vn), Marsick (vn), Trombetta (va), Jacquard (vc), and Leroy (cl) would participate.[125] Only three *séances* (20 February, 2 and 16 March) were recorded in that journal and the series was not mentioned in *RGMdP.* No programs were provided, but in concerts that Duvernoy presented with some of the same musicians in 1865 and 1870 he played works of Haydn, Mozart, Beethoven, Weber, and Mendelssohn. There was a passing reference to *réunions* of Duvernoy in 1863.[126]

Ecole Beethoven: Concerts (1857–58)

Schedule: The Ecole announced a plan to present two concerts (or *soirées*) a month,[127] beginning on Tuesday, 27 October 1857. Only three events were reported in *RGMdP* the first season, the third of which, on Friday, 16 April 1858, was actually the 14th and last of the season.[128] The first and only concert mentioned the following year took place on Thursday, 4 November 1858.

Location: Ecole Beethoven, salle du passage de l'Opéra. The hall was called both the Galerie du Baromètre and the salle Beethoven.

Personnel: Faculty and students of the Ecole Beethoven. The director of the school was the singer Paulin [Louis-Joseph Lespinasse].

Repertory: Vocal and piano music, some chamber works and instrumental solos of various eighteenth- and nineteenth-century composers.

Commentary: RGMdP provided only limited information on this series. A crowd of about 300 attended the concert in November 1858.[129]

Egasse: Concerts d'Emulation (?1823–?1829)

Schedule: Weekly gatherings, Friday evenings for three months, probably during the spring. Spring 1829 was the seventh season,[130] thus the first would have been 1823. I find no mention of the concerts after 1829.

Location: chez M. Egasse, rue de la Harpe, no. 45.

Personnel: Amateur musicians directed by one Egasse.

Repertory: Orchestral music (including 80 recent overtures), other instrumental works, and vocal compositions. Main composers: Haydn, Mozart, Beethoven, Boccherini, and Krommer.[131]

Commentary: William Weber has listed the series among professionally managed amateur organizations.[132] Egasse evidently owned the music that was performed, and rented instruments to amateurs who wished to participate. Subscribers (that is, the amateurs who performed) paid 15 francs for three months in the organization.[133] Although announcements of the society's activities appeared in *ReM,* there were no reviews; it is not clear whether the public was invited (which the term "Concerts" suggests), or whether the evenings were solely for the enjoyment of the performers.

Enfants d'Apollon (?1741–twentieth century). See Société Académique des Enfants d'Apollon.

Erard, Mme.: Soirées (1862 or earlier–1865 or later)

Series of Sunday *soirées chez* Mme. Erard, widow of Pierre Erard (director of the Paris firm that made pianos and harps), were cited in spring 1862, 1863, and 1865, and may well have taken place other seasons. These were reportedly well attended, especially by professionals and artists.[134] Participants included Maurin (vn), Sabattier (vn), the Holmes brothers (vns), Chevillard (vc), Diémer (pf), and vocalists. Although the programs evidently comprised much light music, performances of a Mendelssohn piano trio and Beethoven's "Kreutzer" Sonata were presented *chez* Mme. Erard in 1863.

Escudier-Kastner, Vieuxtemps, and Batta: Concerts (1863)

Schedule: Four weekly concerts, Wednesdays, 21 January to 11 February 1863.
Location: salle Herz.
Personnel: Rosa Escudier-Kastner (pf), Henri Vieuxtemps (vn), Alexandre Batta (vc), other string players, and the singer Delle-Sedie.
Repertory: Chamber "art" music, instrumental solos, light piano works, and vocal music. Main composers: Beethoven, Mendelssohn, and Vieuxtemps.

L'Essai Musical (1847). See Société de Sainte-Cécile.

Ettling, Emile: Amateur Society (1845–?1848)

For at least three seasons, beginning in December 1845, a society of amateur instrumentalists led by the composer Emile Ettling met (? weekly) at the *salons* of Hesselbein, rue Vivienne, to perform orchestral music.[135] In the third season a chorus participated.[136] The few reported programs included much light "art" music—late-eighteenth- and nineteenth-century overtures and instrumental solos; but at least once Beethoven's Fifth Piano Concerto was essayed, and Beethoven's symphonies were also tried. (Professionals played solos and solo parts in concertos, and may have assisted in the orchestra.)[137] The concerts were public, though according to Blanchard the amateurs played mainly for their own enjoyment.[138] In May 1848 (following the February Revolution), they played a benefit concert for workers and those out of work.

Farrenc, Aristide and Louise: Séances Historiques (1862)

Schedule: Three *séances* (actually, lecture-recitals), biweekly on Sunday evenings beginning 25 January 1862, were mentioned in *RGMdP.* Bea Friedland has described the *séances* as a series;[139] she did not say whether it continued after the third *séance.*

Location: salle Erard.

Personnel: Organized by the scholar Aristide Farrenc and his wife, the composer, pianist, and scholar Louise Farrenc. The keyboard works were performed by Marie Mongin and Caroline Lévy. Other participants included Marie Colin (pf), Magnin (vn), Müller (vc), and Taffanel (fl).

Repertory: Selections from the Farrencs' historical anthology of keyboard music, *Le Trésor des pianistes* (then in progress), and chamber works of Louise Farrenc.

Commentary: The Farrencs had presented a *séance de musique rétrospective* as early as 1857, and a concert comprising mainly works from *Le Trésor* on 8 April 1861.[140] The lecture-recitals of 1862, given to promote music in *Le Trésor,* were well attended, though critics seemed more enthusiastic about Louise Farrenc's own music.[141] She continued to organize concerts in which music from *Le Trésor* was performed through the 1860s.

Farrenc, Louise: Séances (1870)

Schedule: Four *séances,* biweekly on Thursdays, 17 February to 31 March 1870.

Locations: salons Lebouc.

Personnel: Organized by the pianist, composer, scholar, and teacher Louise Farrenc. Other participants included Mme. Louise Béguin-Salomon (pf), Mlle. Barrande (pf), Mlle. Marie Mongin (pf), Mlle. Marie Colin (pf), White (vn), Lebouc (vc), Taffanel (fl), and Leroy (cl). The pianists were present or former pupils of Louise Farrenc.[142]

Repertory: Trios, instrumental sonatas, and piano works of Louise Farrenc; pieces from *Le Trésor des pianistes* (an historical anthology of keyboard music edited by Aristide and Louise Farrenc).

Commentary: Mme. Farrenc had organized and performed in numerous single concerts from the 1840s through the 1860s; often she promoted her own music.

Ferrand, A.: Concerts (1862–65). See Société des Quatuors Français.

Fétis, François-Joseph: Concerts Historiques (1832–33, and later)

Schedule and *Location:* A series of four *concerts historiques* (actually, lecture-recitals), 8 April and 16 December 1832 (at the Conservatoire), 24 March 1833 (salle Ventadour), and 2 April 1833 (salle de l'Opéra-Comique). Fétis presented single *concerts historiques* in Paris on 12 April 1835 (Théâtre Italien) and 14 April 1855 (salle Herz), and possibly on 18 April 1840 (salle Herz).[143]

Personnel: Organized by the musicologist, critic, and composer François-Joseph Fétis. Several of the most renowned singers of the day participated in the series, and Habeneck (conductor of the Société des Concerts du Conservatoire) conducted. Performers in the concert of 1835 included Baillot (vn), Franchomme and Batta ("basse de viole"), and Hiller ("clavecin").

Commentary: Fétis's *concerts historiques* were not properly a series of instrumental music. Of the programs in 1832–33, the first and fourth presented operatic selections; the second, diverse works of the sixteenth century; and the third, seventeenth-century works.[144] Fétis lectured at each event. The concert in 1835 traced the history of melody and harmony in the sixteenth and seventeenth centuries. The programs of 1840 and 1855 repeated material from earlier presentations. None of the concerts experienced much success, according to later sources.[145] Peter Bloom has written that Fétis had promised to provide early instruments but in fact used only modern ones.[146]

France Musicale: Séances

Bea Friedland has noted that the journal *La France musicale* (founded in 1837) sponsored recitals of solo and ensemble music for their subscribers.[147] She mentioned in particular three programs in 1856, one of which included a sextet for piano and winds by Louise Farrenc.[148]

Franco-Mendès, Joseph and Jacques: Séances (1840–41)

Schedule: Four *séances* a season in 1840 and 1841. Those in 1840 occurred weekly on Wednesdays, 11 March to 1 April. Those in 1841 occurred biweekly on Sundays, 31 January to 14 March; an extra concert was presented Monday, 12 April 1841.

Location: salle Bernard in 1840; a hall on the rue Monsigny in 1841.

Personnel: Organized by Joseph Franco-Mendès (vn) and Jacques Franco-Mendès (vc), brothers from Holland. Other participants included Guerreau (vn), Eaucheux (?va), Lebone (?vc), and a pianist.

Repertory: Mostly string quartets, some string quintets and piano trios. Main composers: Beethoven and Jacques Franco-Mendès.

Commentary: The concerts were reportedly well attended[149] despite an admission fee of five francs. On 12 April 1841 the brothers played the Paris premiere of Schubert's Piano Trio in E-flat Major.[150] Jacques Franco-Mendès presented single concerts in Paris in 1842 and in the late 1850s and early 1860s, at which he performed many of his own works.

Gasperini, A. de and Georges Pfeiffer: Lecture-Recitals (1867)

Schedule: Three lecture-recitals ("conférences musicales"), biweekly on Wednesdays, 20 February to 20 March 1867.

Location: salle Pleyel.

Personnel: Organized by the writer on music, A. de Gasperini, who delivered the lectures, and the pianist and composer Georges Pfeiffer. Other participants included Sarasate (vn), White (vn), Comtat (vn), Trombetta (va), Wolff (va), Lebouc (vc), and the vocalists Mlle. Nilsson and Mlle. Marie Battu.

Commentary and *Repertory:* The first lecture-recital was on Haydn and Mozart, the second on Beethoven, and the third on Mendelssohn and Schumann. Several chamber works were presented as well as a few piano and vocal compositions.

Gouffé, Achille: Concerts (?1838–after 1870)

Schedule: Annual public concerts, usually in March or April. The first was evidently about 1838,[151] though I find no pertinent announcements or reviews before 1851. Known concerts took place on Wednesdays.

Locations: salons of Pleyel, 1851 and, apparently, 1854–70; salle (bazar) Bonne-Nouvelle, 1852 and 1853; unknown for other years.

Personnel: Organized by the double bass player and composer Achille Gouffé. Other participants included Guerreau (vn), Rignault (?vn), Casimir Ney [Escoffier] (va), Heiss (va), Lebouc (vc), Dorus (fl), Triébert (ob), Leroy (cl), Rousselot (hn), Jancourt (bn), Mme. Tardieu de Malleville (pf), Mme. Béguin-Salomon (pf), and vocalists.

Repertory: Chamber works (particularly string quartets and quintets), instrumental solos, and vocal works. Most programs comprised many short works (including excerpts), rather than a few major, complete works (as were heard at Gouffé's weekly *séances*). Main composers: Onslow, Mozart, Gouffé, Beethoven, Blanc, Walckiers, and Haydn. Gouffé's compositions excepted, contemporary works were heard somewhat less at the concerts than at the *séances*.

Gouffé, Achille: Séances (ca. 1836–after 1870)

The double bass player and composer Achille Gouffé organized regular *séances* at which traditional and recent chamber works were performed. A detailed account of this series is presented in chapter 2, pages 60–62. See also Gouffé, Achille: Concerts.

Grande Société d'Harmonie (1845–?). See Société d'Harmonie.

Grande Société Philharmonique de Paris (1850–51)

Schedule: Monthly on Tuesdays (with one exception). The first season there were four concerts, one of them a *concert spirituel* (from 19 February to 23 April 1850), and the second seven (including a *concert extraordinaire*) from 22 October 1850 to 29 April 1851. Barzun has stated that a dozen concerts were presented;[152] I am aware of only 11.

Location: salle Sainte-Cécile.

Personnel: The society was organized by Berlioz, who, according to Barzun, ran it almost single-handedly—arranging, rehearsing, conducting, soliciting funds, and managing publicity and finances.[153] Contemporary sources mention an orchestra of 100 (Barzun has stated 90),[154] a chorus of 110 or 120 (comprising members of various theatres and chapels, and led by Louis Dietsch, *chef de chant* at the Opéra), and soloists.

Repertory: Orchestral and orchestral-choral works, instrumental and vocal solos. Main composer: Berlioz. Advance publicity promised performances of Beethoven, Palestrina, Bach, and Handel, as well as more recent composers (other than Berlioz).[155] The society did support contemporary composers and planned to perform each year a work by a Prix de Rome winner upon his or her return from abroad.[156]

Commentary: Individual concerts cost three to six francs the first season, two to six the second; subscriptions were available. Profits were divided among the musicians (Berlioz received four shares and Dietsch three), but were apparently not high enough to ensure faithful attendance.[157] Sponsors of the society included Adam, Armand Bertin, Félicien David, Halévy, Liszt, Meyerbeer, Niedermeyer, Prince Joseph Poniatowski, Spontini, Baron Taylor, Thomas, and several titled members of the aristocracy.[158] According to Barzun and Searle, the society ceased because of financial difficulties.[159]

Grands Concerts des Compositeurs Vivants (1865)

Schedule: Although a series was mentioned, only two concerts were reported; these took place on successive Fridays, 3 and 10 March 1865.

Location: grand salon, hôtel du Louvre.

Personnel: Organized by Antonín Prévost-Rousseau, a lawyer and amateur composer. An orchestra was directed by L.-M.-A. Deloffre, *chef d'orchestre* at the Théâtre Lyrique, and a chorus was led by Amand Chevé.

Repertory: Works of living composers, among them A.-L.-V. Boieldieu, Deloffre (a piano trio), Hignard, Bovy-Lysberg, Louis Lacombe (*Manfred, symphonie dramatique* with chorus), Wagner (March from *Tannhäuser*), and Prévost-Rousseau (*La Ferme, symphonie rustique*).

Commentary: Through organizing programs of music by living composers, Prévost-Rousseau reputedly hoped to complement the Conservatoire concerts and Concerts Populaires. The series was mentioned only twice in *RGMdP*,[160] but no cancellation was announced.

Gymnase Musical (1835)

Schedule: Four concerts a week, beginning Saturday 23 May 1835.[161] At first, concerts were held Sundays, Tuesdays, Thursdays, and Saturdays (days on which the Opéra had no presentations); in October the schedule was changed to Sundays, Mondays, Wednesdays, and Fridays (days on which the Théâtre-Italien had no performances). I find no mention of the society in *RGMdP* after 13 December 1835.

Location: The Gymnase Musical, boulevard Bonne-Nouvelle, near the Porte St. Denis. The Gymnase seated about 1000 persons.[162]

Personnel: The founder was one Sali-Snerbe, the conductor Tilmant *aîné*.

The orchestra had from 60 to about 100 members,[163] most of whom belonged to the Opéra or Théâtre-Italien orchestras.

Repertory: Orchestral works (particularly symphonies and overtures), chamber and solo music. Main composers: Beethoven, Weber, and Spohr; contemporary works were widely sampled.

Commentary: Originally the Gymnase Musical was to engage a large orchestra and chorus, and several talented soloists, to perform all sorts of music (even sacred and theatrical works) from all nations. Programs (which were to be screened by a committee that included Adam, H.-M. Berton, Castil-Blaze, Halévy, Meyerbeer, Paer, and others) were to emphasize both new and old works that were little known in Paris. The founder hoped to attract a relatively large, diverse audience.[164] (The Gymnase Musical was an early form of *concert populaire*.) Even before the programs began (well behind schedule), the government forbade performances of vocal music thereon.[165] The delayed opening probably damaged the series's public success, for Parisians were not interested in attending indoor concerts during the summer. Early reviews were mixed, but after July the concerts, which increasingly emphasized "popular" entertainment, were rarely mentioned in *ReM* and *GMdP.* In October plans were announced to play more Beethoven, Haydn, and Mozart.[166] It is doubtful that a harp concert held in the Gymnase Musical in spring 1836 was part of the same series.

Herz, Henri and Théodore Labarre: Concerts (1840–41)

Schedule: Six biweekly concerts were planned,[167] but only five presentations, at less frequent intervals, are reported. The first occurred on Sunday, 29 November 1840; the remainder took place on Thursdays, the fifth on 25 March 1841.

Location: ? salle Herz.

Personnel: The pianist and composer Henri Herz, the harpist and composer Théodore Labarre, and others. At the third through fifth concerts an orchestra was led by Valentino.

Repertory: Chamber, orchestral, and vocal works, as well as instrumental, piano, and harp solos. Main composers: Beethoven, Herz, Labarre.

Commentary: The concerts were intended for an upper-class audience (tickets were sold by subscription at 25 francs for six concerts or at six frances for a single concert), and Blanchard reported that they became fashionable among high society.[168] At the fifth concert a work for six pianos was performed.

Historical concerts. See Becker, Jean; Farrenc, Aristide and Louise; Fétis, François-Joseph

Holmes, Alfred: Séances (1866)

Schedule: Five séances, mainly biweekly on Sunday afternoons, 21 January to 22 March 1866; possibly there were more after the latter date.

Location: lycée Louis-le-Grand.

Personnel: Organized by the English violinist and composer Alfred Holmes. Other participants included Mme. Viard-Louis (pf), de la Nux (pf), Georges Pfeiffer (pf), Léhon (vn), Bessems (?va), Lasserre (vc), Müller (?vc), Brunkmann (probably a string player), and V. de Merizki (unknown).

Repertory: Chamber music for strings with or without piano; some instrumental solos. Composers included Bach, Beethoven, Haydn, Mozart, and Spohr.

Commentary: Holmes established the *séances* to promote "musique classique de chambre" among students of the *lycée.*[169] The concerts were authorized by the minister of *l'instruction publique.*

Hôtel de Ville: Concerts (?1848–70 or later)
(M. le préfet de la Seine: *Réceptions*)

In November 1848 M. le préfet de la Seine announced that the city of Paris would sponsor concerts, which Tilmant *aîné* would direct.[170] Little, if anything, concerning these concerts was reported in the musical press. From 1855, however, musical *réceptions* of the Prefect (by then the renowned Baron Haussmann), held at the Hôtel de Ville, were reported regularly. Attended by government officials and other members of Parisian high society, these took place weekly on Saturdays, usually from about the beginning of Lent until later in the musical season.[171] Jules Pasdeloup was musical director. He conducted an orchestra (first that of the Société des Jeunes-Artistes, later that of the Concerts Populaires, both of which organizations he led; see these entries) and chorus, and many leading opera singers performed solos. The repertory was light, the orchestral portion usually comprising overtures and excerpts.

Hôtel Laffite: Concerts Promenades (1864–?)

Schedule: Nightly concerts beginning Saturday, 10 December 1864, and continuing for an unknown period of time.

Location: salons de l'Exposition Internationale, hôtel Laffite.

Personnel: At the inaugural concert an orchestra of 50 was led by one Varney (probably P.-J.-A. Varney, then director of the Bouffes-Parisiens).

Repertory: No specific works known. A repertory of "musique classique," as well as works of young composers, was promised,[172] but the programs were probably fairly light.

Commentary: "Concerts promenades" were scheduled to commence 1 November under the leadership of Forestier, director of summer concerts at the Pré Catelan; the music, and the exhibitions of art, science, and industry, presented in the same location, were expected to attract an upper-class audience.[173] The series did not, however, begin until 10 December and was then led by Varney. The inaugural concert was considered a major success; the soloists were particularly praised.[174] Although only this concert was reviewed, there was no indication that the plan to present nightly concerts had been changed; and nightly concerts, more significant socially than musically, would not have been reviewed regularly anyway. The series was scheduled to move eventually to the still unfinished Jardin d'hiver.[175]

A concert comprising various instrumental solos inaugurated the salons de l'Exposition Internationale on 16 October 1864;[176] this was apparently not related to the later series. Concerts of light music at the hôtel Laffite had been mentioned as early as the 1830s.[177]

Institution des Jeunes Aveugles (?1836–1870 or later)

Schedule: Irregular. No concerts were mentioned some years, several in other years. The first known performance took place 27 April 1836. Annual concerts were announced from 1865.

Location: Institution des Jeunes Aveugles, boulevard des Invalides, no. 56; occasionally elsewhere.

Personnel: Students, graduates, and faculty of the Institution des Jeunes Aveugles. The orchestra had 30 members in 1836, 40 in 1843;[178] there was also a chorus. For many years the conductor was Claude-Joseph Roussel (?1824–?1869),[179] *maître de chapelle* and professor at the Institution, and himself blind. Frequently there were renowned guest soloists.

Repertory: Mainly vocal and light instrumental works of contemporaries (including blind composers), but many programs included one major orchestral work. Main composers: Beethoven (symphonies) and Haydn.

Commentary: Concerts of the Jeunes Aveugles were well attended and consistently praised, particularly for precise execution. The organization participated in several benefit events; in 1853 they performed a concert in honor of Louis Braille.

Jacobi, Georg: Concerts (?1864–?1866). See Société de Musique de Chambre Jacobi-Willaume.

Javault, Louis-Marie-Charles: Matinées (1844)

In the musical season of 1844 the violinist Louis-Marie-Charles Javault presented four Sunday *matinées*[180] in the *salons* of Duport. Assisted by Boucher (vn), Casimir Ney [Escoffier] (va), Lebouc (vc), and Gouffé (vc), he programmed string quartets and quintets of Haydn, Mozart, Beethoven, and Onslow.

Jeunes-Artistes: Concerts (1853–61). See Société des Jeunes-Artistes.

Jeunes Aveugles: Concerts (?1836–70 or later). See Institution des Jeunes Aveugles.

Joachim, Cossmann, and Wartel: Soirées (1850)

Schedule: Three *soirées,* 28 February, 11 and 21 March 1850.[181]
Location: salle Erard.
Personnel: The violinist Joseph Joachim, the cellist Bernhard Cossmann, and the pianist Mme. Thérèsa Wartel received top billing. Other participants included Rivals (?vn), Casimir Ney [Escoffier] (va), and Gouffé (db).
Repertory: Chamber works for various combinations of strings and piano, solo violin works, and a J. S. Bach keyboard concerto. Other composers included Haydn, Mozart, Beethoven, Mendelssohn, and Louise Farrenc.
Commentary: In January 1850 an earlier series of *soirées* by Joachim (at which he performed concertos of Beethoven and Mendelssohn, fugues of Bach, and chamber works) was mentioned in *RGMdP.*[182]

Labarre, Théodore and Henri Herz: Concerts (1840–41). See Herz, Henri and Théodore Labarre: Concerts.

Lacombe, Louis: Séances (1869)

Schedule: Three *séances,* 21 February, 21 March, and 20 April 1869.
Location: salons Erard.

Personnel: Organized by the pianist and composer Louis Lacombe. Other participants included Armingaud (vn), Samary (?vn), Jacquard (vc), and the vocalists Mmes. Barthe-Banderali and Andrée Favel.[183]

Repertory: Chamber, piano, and vocal works, mainly by Lacombe; a piano trio by Beethoven was played at the first *séance.*

Commentary: Lacombe established the series to promote his own compositions. He had been presenting concerts in Paris for four decades, but apparently not as part of a series.

Lamoureux, Charles: Séances (1860–after 1870). See Séances Populaires de Musique de Chambre, and chapter 2, pages 58–60.

Lebouc, Charles-Joseph: Séances (1855–after 1870)

At the *séances* organized by the cellist Charles-Joseph Lebouc, contemporary works were often included on programs of chamber, solo instrumental, piano, and vocal compositions. A detailed account of the *séances* is provided in chapter 2, pages 63–65.

Liszt, Franz: Concerts (1837)

Schedule: Four weekly *soirées* on Saturdays, 28 January to 18 February 1837.

Location: salle Erard.

Personnel: Organized by Franz Liszt (pf); other participants were Urhan (vn), Batta (vc), and the vocalists MM. Geraldi and Nourrit.

Repertory: Sonatas, duos, piano trios, solo piano works, and vocal music. Composers: Beethoven, Weber, Pixis, Liszt, Chopin, and Batta.

Commentary: Reviews of the *soirées* indicate that they were well attended. Berlioz wrote, in his review of the first *soirée,* that Beethoven's piano trios had been performed in Paris previously only by the Bohrer brothers,[184] but Baillot had presented at least one of them in 1835.[185]

Litolff, Henry: Concerts (1869). See Concerts de l'Opéra.

Malleville, Mlle. Charlotte de: Séances (1849–?1863)

Schedule: The first *séance* took place Thursday, 1 March 1849. Thereafter, through at least 1863, there were generally four each season, usually biweekly on Saturdays. See also *Commentary.*

Location: salle Sax, 1849–51; salle Pleyel, from 1852 (with some exceptions).

Personnel: Organized by the pianist Mlle. Charlotte de Malleville, who in 1853 became Mme. Tardieu de Malleville. Other participants included Maurin (vn), Colblain (vn), Mas (vn), Casimir Ney [Escoffier] (va), Givre (va), Lebouc (vc), Vaslin (vc), Chevillard (vc), Gouffé (vc, db), Dorus (fl), Verroust *aîné* (ob), Leroy (cl), Verroust *jeune* (bn), and Méreaux and Saint-Saëns (additional pianists).

Repertory: Chamber "art" works (including sonatas), keyboard music, and, occasionally, piano concertos with chamber ensemble accompaniment. Main composers: Mozart and Beethoven. The programs were conservative.

Commentary: The *séances* were announced and reviewed as public events with an admission fee of five francs, but Blanchard indicated that they were for invited guests, and Scudo wrote that the audience comprised members of the Institute and the scholarly world.[186] Two keyboard concertos (one for three instruments) by J. S. Bach were programmed from 1856 to 1858, and the solo keyboard music included works of Couperin (presumably François Couperin *le grand*) and Rameau. Mme. Tardieu de Malleville gave three *séances* with Sivori (vn) and Piatti (vc) in 1864; *Ménestrel* reported three *séances,* at least one with orchestra, in 1869.[187] The pianist also presented single (nonseries) concerts, some with orchestra.

Massart, Lambert: Soirées (?1848–?1851)

From 1848 (possibly earlier) the violinist and teacher Lambert Massart held weekly *soirées* in his home on Thursdays during the musical season; in 1849 he married the pianist Aglaé Masson (who had participated in the *soirées* earlier), and thereafter they hosted the *séances* together. According to an article in *RGMdP* in November 1848, works of Beethoven, Mozart, Haydn, Weber, and more recent composers were played there by distinguished artists, among them the pianists Mme. Wartel, Joseph Wieniawski, and Edouard Wolff, Reynier (vn), Casimir Ney [Escoffier] (va), and Lebouc (vc).[188] Other participants included Chéri (va), Jacquard (vc), Altès (fl), Triébert (ob), Rousselot (hn), Verrimst (db), and vocalists. The few known programs offered considerable conservative chamber music (as well as vocal, piano, and light instrumental works). The known repertory from 1851 was rather light and the series was not reported after that year, though *soirées* of Mme. Massart were mentioned in 1855 and 1858.

Mattmann, Mlle. Louise: Séances (1847–48)

Schedule: Four *séances*; the second took place Tuesday, 4 January 1848, the last four weeks later on 1 February.[189]
Location: salle Bernhardt.
Personnel: Mlle. Louise Mattmann (pf), Maurin (vn), Lebouc (vc), and other string players.
Repertory: Chamber works for strings, with or without piano, by Beethoven, Mozart, Haydn, various early nineteenth-century composers, and contemporaries Onslow and Franchomme.
Commentary: Mlle. Mattmann also gave several single (nonseries) concerts in the 1840s and 1850s, at which she programmed some chamber music.

Ménétrier, Delcroix, and Vander-Gucht: Séances (1864). See Delcroix, Ménétrier, and Vander-Gucht: Séances.

Molitor, Baron: Matinées d'été (1866)

The single known reference to this series describes the ninth and last *matinée d'été* (on Saturday, 6 October 1866) *chez* the amateur cellist Baron Molitor.[190] At this series, chamber music of Haydn, Mozart, Boccherini, Onslow, Spohr, Mendelssohn, Schumann, and especially Adolphe Blanc was performed for a small, elite audience by Boulart (?vn), de Bailly (?vn), Adam (?va), Gouffé (vc/db), and Molitor.

Müller Brothers and Mme. Szarwady: Concerts (1866). See Szarwady, Mme. and Müller Brothers: Concerts.

Nieuwerkerke, M. le comte Alfred Emilieu de: Soirées (?1856–1870 or later)

M. le comte de Nieuwerkerke, General Director of National Museums, sponsored elegant musical *soirées* at the Louvre,[191] weekly on Fridays during the season, from 1856 or earlier through 1870. There Parisian high society heard a variety of renowned artists; apparently there were no regular performers apart from Jules Pasdeloup, the musical director. The repertory included some chamber "art" music, but mainly comprised vocal solos and duets, light instrumental solos, and piano pieces. Nieuwerkerke's *soirées* were seldom mentioned in the musical press.

Nouvelle Société de Musique de Chambre (1857). See Stainlein, M. le comte Louis de: Concerts.

Paganini, Nicolò: Concerts (1831–32)

The Parisian concerts of Nicolò Paganini are renowned because his playing there so inspired the young Liszt; their significance as a series presenting instrumental "art" music is small. Paganini played almost exclusively his own works, among them concertos. According to Boris Schwarz, he was scheduled to play 12 concerts in six weeks at the Opéra (begining 9 March) and twice at court in 1831.[192] The Italian violinist returned to Paris in spring 1832 and presented additional concerts in spite of the detrimental effect that the cholera epidemic had on attendance.

Pfeiffer, Mme. Clara: Séances (?1855–1870 or later)

Schedule and *Repertory:* Mme. Pfeiffer began presenting regular *séances* of piano music no later than 1855. Her programs were mentioned in a list of chamber music organizations in 1857,[193] and at her *matinées* in March 1858 and December 1860, chamber works were performed. In January 1862, *Ménestrel* reported that her *matinées* had resumed, and listed chamber, piano, and vocal works in the repertory.[194] From 1867 through 1870 Mme. Pfeiffer gave at least two *séances* a year, perhaps many more, though no more than three were cited any one season in *RGMdP*; most took place Sunday afternoons, roughly one month apart. At these the repertory included traditional and recent chamber "art" works as well as piano, vocal, and light instrumental music. See also *Commentary.*

Location: chez Mme. Pfeiffer.

Personnel: Organized by the pianist and teacher Mme. Clara Pfeiffer. Other participants included her son, the pianist and composer Georges Pfeiffer, Mlle. Louise Paloc (pf), Léonard (vn), White (vn), Sighicelli (vn), Lebouc (vc), Albert (vc), Donjon (fl), and vocalists.

Commentary: Most programs in the series appear to have been predominately light. One, however, included four examples of "art" music (among them a Beethoven piano trio and a Mozart violin sonata) as well as lighter works.[195] In the 1860s Mme. Pfeiffer also offered instruction in music requiring more than one piano (mainly arrangements of orchestral works); at the end of each season her pupils presented a concert of such works.

Pfeiffer, Georges and A. de Gasperini: Lecture-Recitals (1867). See Gasperini, A. de and Georges Pfeiffer: Lecture-Recitals.

Pfeiffer, Georges and Pablo Sarasate: Séances (1870)

In February 1870 *Ménestrel* announced that the pianist and composer Georges Pfeiffer and the Spanish violinist and composer Pablo Sarasate would present four *séances* of chamber music biweekly on Thursdays, 17 February to 31 March, at the salle Pleyel.[196] The *séances* were not subsequently discussed in *Ménestrel,* and only the first, at which chamber works of Haydn, Beethoven, Mendelssohn, and Raff were played by Pfeiffer, Sarasate, Trombetta (va), and Lasserre (vc), was mentioned in *RGMdP.*[197]

Picard, Mlle. Adrienne: Séances (?1867–after 1870)

Schedule: Weekly *soirées* were reported in February 1867 and May 1869 (the latter at the close of the season).[198] A resumption of *séances* was announced in December 1871.[199]

Location: chez Mlle. Picard.

Personnel: Organized by the pianist Mlle. Adrienne Picard. Other participants included Lelong (vn), Gary (?vc), Heiss (va), Poëncet (vc), Taffanel (fl), and Turban (cl).

Repertory: Chamber and piano music, including established, little-known, and recent works.

Commentary: According to *RGMdP,* Mlle. Picard's attractive *séances* were among those most hospitable to contemporary music.[200] An unpublished violin concerto of Max Bruch was performed there (presumably with piano accompaniment) in 1867. Mlle. Picard had also given single concerts in the 1850s.

Pierson-Bodin, Mme. Sophie: Séances (1849–after 1870)

Schedule: Irregular. The first known *séance* was a Sunday *matinée* on 23 December 1849. Thereafter, until 1865, *séances* were reported sporadically: many years no events were publicized, but series were mentioned in 1854 and 1858.[201] From autumn 1865 until (and after) the Franco-Prussian War, *matinées* were described somewhat more frequently. All known *séances* occurred on Sunday afternoons, during the season.

Location: chez Mme. Pierson-Bodin, rue de Louvois, no. 10.

Personnel: Organized by the pianist, harpist, and teacher Mme. Sophie

Pierson-Bodin. Other participants included, at various times, her close friend Louise Farrenc (pf), Sighicelli (vn), A. Lebrun (?vn), Casimir Ney [Escoffier] (va), A. Marx (?vc), Gouffé (vc/db), Taffanel (fl), Dorus (fl), Berthélemy (ob), Lalliet (ob), Leroy (cl), Turban (cl), Verroust (bn), Rousselot (hn), Schlottmann (?hn), Mme. Gaveaux-Sabatier (pf), Hermann-Léon (voice), Pagans (voice), and Mme. Emile Louis (unknown). In the late 1860s many of the *séances* were publicized as performances by Mme. Pierson-Bodin's students, but professional musicians continued to appear on the programs.

Repertory: Chamber "art" works, instrumental solos, piano and vocal music. The chamber music was mainly traditional, though several of Louise Farrenc's works were presented.

Commentary: Only a few *séances* of Mme. Pierson-Bodin were mentioned in *RGMdP.* Some of the descriptions, however, suggest that the *séances* were a regular part of Parisian musical life; the editors clearly expected them to be familiar to readers. The performances of Mme. Pierson-Bodin's students were lauded.

Préfet de la Seine: Réceptions (1848–70 or later). See Hôtel de Ville: Concerts.

Prévost-Rousseau, Antonín: Concerts: (1865). See Grands Concerts des Compositeurs Vivants.

Quatuor Armingaud or Quatuor Armingaud-Jacquard (1856–67). See Société des Quatuors de Mendelssohn.

Quatuor Florentin: Séances (1869)

Schedule: Four *séances,* spring 1869: 1, ca. 10, and 18 March; 12 April.

Locations: salons Erard.

Personnel: The Quatuor Florentin was led by the violinist Jean Becker; other members were Enrico Masi (2nd vn), Luigi Chiostri (va), and Frédéric Hilpert (vc).

Repertory: String quartets of Beethoven, Cherubini, E. de Hartog, Haydn, Mendelssohn, Mozart, Rosenhain, Schubert, and Schumann.

Commentary: The quartet had established its reputation first in Florence, later elsewhere in Italy and in Germany.[202] The critic for *RGMdP* praised the group's "unequalled" ensemble—especially its balance, in which the first violin was not overly prominent.[203] On 17 March the quartet made an additional appearance at the *salon* of the *Revue et gazette musicale*.

Quatuor Maurin-Chevillard (?1851–?1865). See Société des Derniers Quatuors de Beethoven.

Revue et Gazette Musicale de Paris: Concerts (1838–48)

Schedule: Irregular. Three to eight concerts a year (the season of 1842–43 possibly excepted) on various days of the week. The first occurred Sunday, 23 December 1838, and the last known concert took place Friday, 11 February 1848, shortly before the February Revolution; these concerts did not resume after the revolution, but see *Commentary.*

Locations: Various, including the salons de Pape, salle Erard, salle du Wauxhall, salle Vivienne, salons Pleyel, salle du Casino des Familles, and salle Herz.

Personnel: Various professional musicians, including Alard (vn), Armingaud (vn), Chaine (vn/va), Croisilles (va), L. Dancla (va), Casimir Ney [Escoffier] (va), Franchomme (vc), Chevillard (vc), Rignault (vc), Gouffé (vc/db), the pianists Louise Farrenc, César Franck, Charles Hallé, and Georges Mathias, and vocalists. A few concerts offered an orchestra, directed on some occasions by A.-C. Fessy.

Repertory: Primarily chamber works (for various combinations of instruments) and vocal music; some instrumental solos, piano works, and orchestral pieces. Individual programs differed greatly from one another. Main composers of instrumental music: Beethoven, Mozart, and Onslow; contemporary works were performed regularly.

Commentary: Concerts were for subscribers to the *Revue et gazette musicale*. The society was originally founded to promote the performance of string quartets and quintets,[204] but the repertory quickly expanded to include other genres. Some years concerts were presented on a regular schedule, in one location, by the same personnel, and thus resembled a true series; but other years concerts had little in common with each other.

One finds references after 1848 to concerts in the *salon* of the *Revue et gazette musicale,* but these programs emphasized, with few exceptions, vocal and light instrumental works.

Ritter, Théodore and Camillo Sivori: Soirées (1859)

Schedule: Four *soirées,* weekly on Wednesdays, 30 November to 21 December 1859. See also *Commentary.*

Location: salle Beethoven, passage de l'Opéra.

Personnel: Organized by the pianist Théodore Ritter and the Italian violinist Camillo Sivori. Other participants included Accursi (vn), Casimir Ney [Escoffier] (va), Rignault (vc), and Mme. Laborde (voice).

Repertory: Chamber music for strings with and without piano, violin solos, piano solos, and vocal works. Music of various composers, ranging chronologically from Gluck to Sivori.

Commentary: The series was suspended after four *séances* while Ritter travelled to Marseilles and Sivori to London. The *soirées* were scheduled to resume in February 1860,[205] but none was reported in *RGMdP* or *Ménestrel* at that time.

Rosenhain, Jakob: Soirées (1850)

In spring 1850 the German pianist and composer Jakob Rosenhain presented three *soirées* (15 and 23 March, 6 April) at the salle Erard with Massart (vn), Joachim (vn), Cossmann (va/vc), Demunck (va/vc), Verroust *aîné* (ob), Leroy (cl), Rousselot (hn), and Verroust *jeune* (bn). Programs included chamber works for piano and strings or winds, as well as piano and vocal music. The admission fee for each *soirée* was six francs.[206]

Rubinstein, Anton: Concerts (1857–70)

The Russian pianist and composer Anton Rubinstein presented concerts in Paris during at least four seasons before the Franco-Prussian War: three in 1857, three in 1858, seven in 1868, and six in 1870. Most of the concerts were not arranged as series; they took place in various locations with various musicians, and offered different sorts of music—orchestral, chamber, and solo piano works. The only concerts that might be called a series were five in 1868 that, apparently, took place at the salle Herz with Saint-Saëns leading the orchestra at least some of the time. Most of the programs presented by Rubinstein included only one or two instrumental "art" works, and most of the compositions were Rubinstein's—particularly piano concertos and solos, but also symphonies and chamber works.

Saint-Saëns, Camille: Concerts (1864–65)

Schedule: In 1864, six concerts at irregular intervals on Fridays, 12 February to 29 April. In 1865, one nonseries concert on Friday, 20 January, and the first of a planned series of six on Tuesday, 7 February; the remaining five were cancelled. See also *Commentary.*

Location: salons Pleyel-Wolff et Cie.

Personnel: Organized by the pianist and composer Camille Saint-Saëns.

In 1864 he was the primary soloist, and an orchestra including many musicians from the Théâtre-Italien was led by Portehaut.[207] In 1865 the Spanish violinist Pablo Sarasate was to play a prominent role, and Jules Pasdeloup conducted an orchestra; other participants included Brossa (?vn), Mas (va), and Lasserre (vc).

Repertory: In 1864: mainly Mozart piano concertos; some chamber, piano, and vocal works. For the series in 1865 the repertory was to include chamber works by various composers, among them Saint-Saëns. See also *Commentary*.

Commentary: Saint-Saëns established the series largely in order to present Mozart piano concertos, and performed at least seven the first year. On 20 January 1865 he played two more, and gave the Paris premiere of Robert Schumann's piano concerto.[208] In the series that year he planned to present chamber and orchestral music, particularly contemporary or little-known compositions, among them Italian works.[209] The first and only program of that series offered piano trios of Félicien David and Henry Litolff. After that concert the series was cancelled. The critic Maurice Cristal attributed the cessation to disagreements between Saint-Saëns and the "maître du logis" (presumably the Pleyel-Wolff firm) concerning the repertory, and lamented that some of the best concerts of the season had been lost.[210] Saint-Saëns presented many nonseries concerts in the 1860s.

Sarasate, Pablo and Georges Pfeiffer: Séances (1870). See Pfeiffer, Georges and Pablo Sarasate: Séances.

Sax, Adolphe: Concerts and Séances

The instrument maker and inventor Adolphe Sax organized many events to demonstrate his new instruments, beginning with a series of public *auditions* in 1844. In May 1853 he founded the Société d'harmonie des premiers prix du Conservatoire, a band that included several of his instruments. In the first concert, at the Jardin d'hiver, one Mohr led the group in renditions of the overture to *Zampa* (Hérold) and Berlioz's *Roman Carnival Overture*; vocalists also performed.[211] An "orchestre féminin" organized by one Sax[212] gave a "first" concert (again, with vocalists) at the salle Herz in August 1865. The "orchestre" of ten played *saxomnitoniques à cinq pistons*; its ensemble was praised.[213] I find no further mention of this group, but weekly *séances chez* Adolphe Sax, at which he presented new instruments, were reported as resuming in November 1865 and continuing in April 1866.[214] At the *séance* of 3 April, *instruments à six pistons et à tubes indépendants* were played by Hollebeke, Schlottmann, Massart, Robyus, Verlève, and Monsen.

Séances Populaires de Musique de Chambre (1863–after 1870)

Séances of chamber music, with some solo piano music, were organized by the violinist Charles Lamoureux in 1860. In autumn 1863 the name "Séances Populaires de Musique de Chambre" was adopted, in evident imitation of the successful (orchestral) Concerts Populaires (founded in 1861; see this entry); as the name suggests, the admission fee was low, but the repertory was decidedly not "popular." A detailed account of the *séances* is provided in chapter 2, pages 58–60.

Seghers, François: Matinées (ca. 1838–ca. 1840)

Private *matinées* of the Belgian violinist François Seghers (who later conducted the Société Sainte-Cécile II) were mentioned in 1838 as one of three series that presented string quartets.[215] A few years later Chorley praised the *matinées* at rue Lafitte, no. 42, in which Seghers led a group that included the cellist Alexandre Batta in renditions of Beethoven's "posthumous" quartets.[216] Liszt sometimes performed at Seghers's *séances*.[217]

Sivori, Camillo and Théodore Ritter: Soirées (1859). See Ritter, Théodore and Camillo Sivori: Soirées.

Société Académique des Enfants d'Apollon (?1741–twentieth century)

Schedule: La Laurencie stated that the society was founded in 1741, and various statements in the nineteenth-century press indicate a similar date of origin.[218] Through 1848 I find mention only of annual *séances,* generally occurring on or about Ascension Day (in May or early June); thereafter, more than one concert was cited many years, and there are several references to monthly *séances*.

Location: ? salle Herz. The location of *séances* was not often mentioned, but notices and reviews in 1842, 1867, and 1869 all place them at the salle Herz.[219]

Personnel: See *Commentary.*

Repertory: Varied. Includes symphonies, concertos, overtures, chamber works, solos, light instrumental pieces, and vocal works. The extremely limited sample of programs suggests that favorite composers in the mid-nineteenth century were Beethoven and Blanc.

Commentary: The Enfants d'Apollon was a society of composers, professional and amateur musicians, and dilettantes.[220] Often its programs included works of members. It appears that the society sponsored *séances* rather than actually presenting them (though members sometimes participated); guest performers included some of Paris's best-known professional musicians, among them Maurin (vn), Lebouc (vc), Gouffé (db), Blanc (pf/vn), Charles Dancla (vn and conductor), and Dietsch (conductor). There was, however, no permanent group of performers; thus an orchestra played at some concerts,[221] while others offered only chamber music and solo works.

Société Alard-Franchomme (?1847–?1872)

The series organized by the violinist Delphin Alard and the cellist Auguste Franchomme presented unusually good performances of traditional chamber "art" music. A detailed account of this series is provided in chapter 2, pages 52–54.

Société Calco-Philharmonique (mid-1850s)

In the mid-1850s the Société Calco-Philharmonique, a wind ensemble that included instruments manufactured by Adolphe Sax, played several concerts. Its repertory included symphonies for winds, particularly those of one Bellon.[222]

Société de la Grande Harmonie (1853). See Sax, Adolphe: Concerts and Séances.

Société de l'Athénée (1866–67)

Schedule: Concerts thrice weekly, Mondays, Wednesdays, and Fridays, from Wednesday, 21 November 1866, to Friday, 31 May 1867. Occasionally a fourth concert took place, generally on Sunday.

Location: salle de l'Athénée, an elegant new hall on the rue Scribe, near the present Opéra (then under construction).

Personnel: The banker Raphael Bischoffsheim supervised programming in the Athénée. Jules Pasdeloup, the music director, led the orchestra of the Concerts Populaires and a large chorus. Among the soloists were Joachim (vn) and Saint-Saëns (organ).[223]

Repertory: Oratorios, orchestral works, music for chorus and orchestra, some chamber and solo vocal works. Much of the orchestral repertory was relatively light, comprising overtures, incidental music, and marches; but some symphonies and several concertos were played. Main composers of instrumental works: Beethoven, Mendelssohn, Mozart, Wagner, Weber, J. S. Bach, Massenet, and Spohr. Many contemporary works were programmed.

Commentary: Bischoffsheim, who endowed the salle de l'Athénée, let the Société use the hall free of charge with the stipulation that half the profit be donated to a professional school for young women.[224] Jules Pasdeloup planned from the beginning to present a mixture of orchestral, vocal, and organ music, with a fair share of contemporary works.[225] Eventually the Société decided to devote one night weekly to oratorios, one night to symphonic works, and one to various works for orchestra or voices;[226] as concerts at the Athénée were usually summarized weekly in *RGMdP,* one cannot determine whether this schedule was followed, but there is no reason to believe that, with occasional exceptions, it was not.

In December 1866 admission fees were *lowered* to two and four francs,[227] prices affordable by the middle classes. A series of even less expensive chamber music concerts, to be led by Georg Jacobi, was announced in January 1867, but never took place.[228] An evening of chamber music was presented by Alard and Magnin (vns), Trombetta (va), and Franchomme (vc) on 15 March.[229] By May the Société's programs mainly comprised instrumental music.[230] There is no mention of the concert society after that month. Elisabeth Bernard has stated that the series was replaced by operetta and *vaudeville*.[231] Reviewing musical activity of 1869, Em. Mathieu de Monter wrote that the Athénée continued its battle to become a fourth *scène lyrique*.[232]

Société de l'Athénée Musical (1829–44)

Schedule: Originally, 12 concerts a year at monthly intervals on Thursdays; the first took place 26 November 1829.[233] The concerts were suspended for several months in spring 1832, presumably because of the cholera epidemic. In summer 1834, concerts were cancelled because of the heat; thereafter concerts took place from late November to late May or early June. The series stopped in 1844.[234]

Location: salle Saint-Jean, Hôtel de Ville.

Personnel: The society was founded by H.-A.-B. Chelard, a composer and conductor. The orchestra had about 80 members, among them Girard (vn), Urhan (va), Vaslin (vc), other professionals, and some amateurs.[235] Conductors included Chelard, Barbereau, Jean J. Vidal, Girard, and Grasset. Soloists by 1832 had included Kalkbrenner,

Field, Liszt, Herz, Labarre, Hiller, Habeneck, Brod, and Rousselot.[236] In 1834, Onslow was president of the society.[237]

Repertory: Orchestral, chamber, solo, and vocal works, but mainly overtures and light orchestral works. Beethoven's music was played often.

Commentary: The society was founded to propagate new compositions (particularly those by little-known composers), or unfamiliar works by established composers; Chelard originally wished to perform sacred music (then in decline in France) at half the concerts, but this plan was abandoned.[238] The society was established under the auspices of the Préfet de la Seine; the Hôtel de Ville was allowed it free of charge.[239] The Athénée drew praise for its performance standards and willingness to program works of young artists. William Weber has suggested that its closure in 1844 was caused by the rising cost of engaging professional musicians.[240] The organization was reunited for a benefit concert in 1848.[241]

Société de l'Avenir Musical (?1869–70)

Schedule: I have records of only the fifth *séance,* on Tuesday, 8 March 1870. According to a review of this *séance* the society had been established a few months earlier.[242]

Location: salle Sax.

Personnel: R. Pugno (pf), J. Salvaire (vc), and other string players.

Repertory: The society was founded to perform works of established masters and young composers. The one known program included Beethoven's Serenade for string trio, Mendelssohn's Variations Op. 17 for cello and piano, G. Salvaire's Sextet for piano and strings, and part of Schumann's Piano Sonata Op. 22.

Commentary: Execution at the single reported concert was praised.

Société de l'Union Musicale (1849–51). See Union Musicale.

Société de Musique Classique (1847–49)

Schedule: The first concert took place Sunday, 28 November 1847, the last on Thursday, 3 May 1849 (postponed from the previous Sunday). Sunday concerts at biweekly intervals (alternating with the Conservatoire concerts) were planned,[243] but in neither season was the biweekly pattern strictly followed (though in both seasons six concerts were presented).

Location: 1847–48, salle Herz; 1849, salle Sax.

Personnel: Mme. Wartel (pf), Delsarte (voice), Tilmant *aîné* (vn), Guerreau (vn), Casimir Ney [Escoffier] (va), Tilmant *jeune* (vc), Gouffé (vc, db), Dorus (fl), Verroust *aîné* (ob), Klosé (cl), Rousselot (hn), and Verroust *jeune* (bn). Delsarte may not have participated in the second season.

Repertory: Chamber "art" works, including some for large ensembles (septets, octets, nonets). Main composers: Beethoven and Mozart; works by early nineteenth-century composers were performed, as were two keyboard concertos and a violin sonata by J. S. Bach.

Commentary: Admission fees for individual concerts, five and ten francs, indicate that attenders were wealthy. More concerts may have been planned for the first season; the February Revolution occurred shortly after the sixth.

Société de Musique de Chambre (?1847–?1872). See Société Alard-Franchomme.

Société de Musique de Chambre Jacobi-Willaume (?1864–?1866)

Schedule: Unknown in 1864; six biweekly concerts on Saturdays in 1865, 14 January to 25 March. The only known concert in 1866 occurred on Thursday, 15 March.

Locations: Société Nationale des Beaux-Arts, boulevard des Italiens, no. 26, in 1864; salons Pleyel for the first five concerts in 1865; salle Herz for the final concert of 1865 and the known concert in 1866.

Personnel: The president was the German violinist Georg Jacobi. In 1864 he may have led a small orchestra. Participants in 1865 were Jules-Louis Willaume (vn), Dumas (? vn/va), Aubery (? vn/va), Waque (?vc), and the pianists Mlle. Rémaury[244] and Georges Pfeiffer. Additional performers in 1866 included Taffanel (fl), Barthélemy (?ob), and vocalists from the Opéra.

Repertory: Known programs date from 1865. These emphasized quartets and quintets for strings, with or without piano. Composers included Beethoven, de Bériot, Boccherini, Haydn, Onslow, Spohr, and Weber.

Commentary: The nature of Jacobi's concerts in 1864 is not clear. An article from January 1865 states that the previous season Jacobi's organization had performed chamber music at the Société Nationale des Beaux-Arts.[245] And Martin Cooper has written that the Société de Musique de Chambre Jacoby-Villaume [sic] was founded in 1864.[246] But the entry on Jacobi in *Grove 6* states that he led an orchestra of 16 at the Société Nationale des Beaux-Arts.[247] In 1865 and 1866 the group played mainly chamber music (though a Spohr violin concerto and Weber's Concertstück for piano and orchestra were listed on programs in 1865);[248] its renditions of quartets and quintets were described as "fort brillante."[249] The final *séance* of 1865 was replaced by a concert in which a violin concerto by de Bériot and a violin solo as well as piano and vocal works were performed. Although no schedule was announced in 1866, a chamber group led by Jacobi evidently remained active.[250] Jacobi gave many single concerts in Paris in the 1860s.

Société de Quatuors et Quintetti (?1864–?1866). See Société de Musique de Chambre Jacobi-Willaume.

Société de Sainte-Cécile (1847–?1848)

In June 1847 *RGMdP* announced that Antoine Elwart had established a new organization, "L'Essai Musical."[251] By July the name had been changed to "Société de Sainte-Cécile,"[252] and by late August subscription tickets were available.[253] At the first public presentation, a *concert-spécimen* on Sunday, 26 September, at the salle Sax, Edouard Millault led the Société in a program comprising an overture, a symphony movement, a horn solo, and choral and solo vocal works of various contemporary French composers. The Société planned a mass composed by eight of its members for St. Cecilia's Day (25 November).[254] A second *concert-spécimen* was scheduled for 16 January 1848, after which I find no more references to this Société; perhaps the disastrous effects of the February Revolution on concert life that spring discouraged further activity. Blanchard wrote that the Société hoped its performances of works by Conservatoire laureates and other contemporaries would help these composers escape obscurity.[255]

Société des Concerts du Conservatoire (1828–twentieth century)

An orchestra and chorus comprising faculty, graduates, and students of the Paris Conservatoire. The first major Parisian orchestra after 1816, it set a new standard for precision and provided a model for orchestral or orchestral-choral societies throughout Europe. For a detailed account of the Société, see chapter 2, pages 21–37.

Société des Derniers Quatuors de Beethoven (?1851–after 1870)

A chamber music society established by the violinist Jean-Pierre Maurin and the cellist Alexandre Chevillard, it promoted Beethoven's Late quartets. A detailed account of the society is provided in chapter 2, pages 55–56.

Société des Jeunes-Artistes (1853–61)

A society of Conservatoire students and graduates led by Jules Pasdeloup, it presented programs of traditional and recent orchestral and vocal music. A detailed account of the society is provided in chapter 2, pages 42–46.

Société des Musiciens-Exécutants de Paris (1851). See Association des Musiciens-Exécutants de Paris.

Société des Quatuors de Mendelssohn (1856–67)

A string quartet that (usually with other musicians) at first promoted chamber works of Mendelssohn. Later it adopted a more varied repertory and dropped the reference to Mendelssohn's name, becoming known as the Quatuor Armingaud or Quatuor Armingaud-Jacquard (after the group's first violinist and cellist). A detailed account of the society is provided in chapter 2, pages 56–58.

Société des Quatuors et Quintetti (?1864–?1866). See Société de Musique de Chambre Jacobi-Willaume.

Société des Quatuors Français (1862–65)

Schedule: Irregular. A "specimen" *matinée* was presented Tuesday 25 November 1862, and two concerts were reported the following April. Three biweekly concerts on Thursdays were scheduled in 1864, from 28 January to 25 February; the second was evidently postponed a week. In 1865 there were again three events, on Mondays, 13 and 27 March and 24 April.

Location: salons Erard in 1862; salle Pleyel in 1864 and 1865.

Personnel: Organized by Albert Ferrand (1st vn); other participants included Colblain (2nd vn), Rinck (2nd vn), A. Viguier (va), E. Bernhard (va), S. Lee (vc), Lasserre (vc), Mme. Viguier (pf), and Fissot (pf).

Repertory: "Art" music for strings with and without piano by the nineteenth-century French composers A. Blanc, Boëly, C. Dancla, L. Gastinel, L. Kreutzer, G. Mathias, A. Morel, Onslow, G. Pfeiffer, Reber, and Vaucorbeil.

Commentary: The society was established to perform French chamber works composed within the previous 30 years (nearly 20 composers were cited whose music fell within this category).[256] At the *séance-spécimen* only excerpts were played.

Société des Quintettes (Anciens et Modernes) (1858)

Schedule: Four biweekly concerts, Tuesdays, 26 January to 9 March 1858.

Location: salons of MM. Pleyel, Wolff et Cie.

Personnel: The society was founded by M. le baron de Ponnat. Performers included White (1st vn), Otto Bernard (2nd vn), Adam (va), Louis Pilet (1st vc), Alfred Bernard (2nd vc), and de la Nux (pf).

Repertory: String quintets and other works for strings (some with piano) by Adolphe Blanc, Boccherini, and Onslow. Although the intention to perform quintets by Fesca was announced,[257] none of his works appeared on the first three programs (the fourth program is not listed in *RGMdP*).

Société des Quintettes Harmoniques (1869–?1870)

Schedule: The inaugural *séance* was scheduled for 2 December 1869, the third and fourth *séances* for 3 February and 3 March 1870. The dates of these *séances* (the only ones of which I have any record) suggest that the Société performed the first Thursday of each month.

Location: salle Gay-Lussac, on the Left Bank.

Personnel: Organized by the organist and pianist Adolphe Populus; other participants were Donjon (fl), Triébert (ob), Turban (cl), Garigue (hn), and Lalande (bn). All of the performers were relatively young.

Repertory: The single known program (the third) comprised two wind quintets by Reicha, a duo for flute and horn by Hasselmans (probably Alphonse Hasselmans), an oboe solo by Solar, and a polonaise for harmonium by Populus. Pougin later wrote that the group played works of "Reicha, Rossini, Adolphe Blanc, Adrien Barthe, etc."[258]

Commentary: The admission fee was one to three francs. An anonymous commentator for *RGMdP* hoped that the society would help meet the need for "art" music on the Left Bank.[259]

Société des Symphonistes (ca. 1861–1870 or later)

Schedule: The Société, evidently founded in 1860 or 1861, gave annual concerts, at the end of the season (usually in late April or early May), from then through at least 1870. See also *Commentary.*

Location: salle Pleyel, Wolff et Cie.

Personnel: An orchestra of amateurs and some professionals, led by L.-B.-E.-C.-H. Deledicque (a violinist at the Théâtre-Italien).

Repertory: Symphonies, other orchestral music, some chamber works, and instrumental and vocal solos. Composers ranged chronologically from Haydn and Mozart to Alard, Vaucorbeil, and Adolphe Blanc.

Commentary: In May 1865 Maurice Cristal described an orchestral concert led by Deledicque "destiné principalement à inaugurer la fondation d'une société des symphonistes";[260] much later the usually reliable Constant Pierre agreed that the organization had been founded in 1865.[261] But in February 1864 an article in *Ménestrel* stated that the Société had existed under Deledicque's leadership for four years.[262] And reports in 1869 and 1870 indicate that the Société had begun no later than 1861.[263] I find no explanation for Cristal's description.

According to the article in *Ménestrel,* members of the Société met every Sunday morning from January until the end of the season to familiarize themselves with the symphonic repertory, then presented a concert; most of the participants were amateurs, but professionals assisted.[264] Cristal, thinking he was describing the group's inauguration, wrote that it intended to propagate works of young composers.[265] *Ménestrel* noted in 1870 the Société's considerable progress.[266]

Société des Trios Anciens et Modernes (1865–66)

Schedule: In 1865, four concerts at biweekly intervals on Fridays, 17 February[267] to 31 March. Further *séances* were mentioned, but without details, in 1866.[268]

Location: salle Pleyel.

Personnel: de la Nux (pf), White (vn), and Lasserre (vc).

Repertory: Mainly piano trios by various nineteenth-century composers; some solo piano music and other works.

Commentary: An anonymous reporter for *RGMdP* wrote that the trio evoked admiration from connoisseurs for its ensemble and its propagation of little-known works.[269] Among the relatively recent compositions the group essayed were piano trios of Damcke, Gade, Rosenhain, and Schumann.

Société d'Harmonie (1845–?)

Late in 1845 *RGMdP* announced the establishment of a "grande Société d'harmonie," an orchestra of 80 musicians under the direction of Mohr;[270] the first rehearsal had taken place on 26 November. The announcement provides no more details, and I find no further references to the Société's activities.

Société du Grand Concert (1864–65)

Schedule: No concerts are known to have taken place. The series was originally scheduled to begin in November 1864, but several postponements were announced after that date. See also *Commentary.*
Location: The Colonnes d'Hercule, rue Richer, no. 32, northeast of the boulevard Montmartre. The hall seated approximately 3000.[271]
Personnel: Félicien David was the director-general; the pianist and composer "Magnus" (probably Magnus Deutz) was the director. The artistic committee comprised Berlioz, David, Gevaert (probably F.-A. Gevaert), Victor Massé, Prince de Polignac, Prince Poniatowski, and Edouard Rodrigues. An orchestra of 85 and a chorus of 200 were planned.[272]
Commentary: In July 1864 *RGMdP* reported that, according to the *Phare de la Loire,* a new society was forming in Paris to perform, with exceptional execution, works old and new, French, German, and Italian, instrumental and vocal (but mainly for large forces).[273] A later note explained that though the planned repertory was extremely broad, only music of incontestable merit and "d'un effet certain" would be accepted; composers could, if they wished, conduct their own works.[274] Capital for the society was underwritten by early December, but the hall was still being prepared and the inauguration was postponed until January or February; the price of admission was to be one to five francs. By Christmas further delay was expected because of Félicien David's rheumatism.[275] No actual concerts are reported in *RGMdP.* In establishing the Société du Grand Concert, David was perhaps trying to recreate the programming the Société Nationale des Beuax-Arts had offered, under his direction, in its first season (1862–63; see this entry).

Société du Gymnase Lyrique (1829)

Schedule: Four biweekly concerts, beginning Friday, 16 January 1829, were planned. I find no mention of any of these actually having taken place.
Location: Unknown.
Personnel: 65 instrumentalists and 55 choristers.
Repertory: See Commentary.
Commentary: The organization was to have been funded through sub-

scription; for 100 francs a subscriber would receive five tickets for each of the four concerts. Subscribers could include composers, performers, and *amateurs*. The society planned to perform works of subscribers, and thereby benefit students or recent graduates of the Paris Conservatoire. Works of foreign or deceased composers could be presented only if the performance constituted a French premiere.[276]

Société Libre des Beaux-Arts (from ca. 1835)

Several years *RGMdP* mentioned annual *séances* of the Société Libre des Beaux-Arts (an *institution philanthropique et artistique* established about 1835),[277] at which members made speeches, awarded prizes, and listened to music. Professional musicians were engaged for the occasion; evidently the repertory mainly comprised vocal and keyboard works, but some chamber "art" music was played.

Société Musicale (I, 1835). See Cercle Musical

Société Musicale (II, 1838–39)

Schedule: Biweekly concerts, Wednesdays, from 2 December 1838 to January or February 1839. See also *Commentary.*

Location: salle Erard.

Personnel: Members included Alard, Henri Bertini, Brod, Alexandre Chevillard, Croisilles, Cuvillon, Charles Dancla, Doehler, Dorus, Franchomme, Gallay, and Urhan.

Repertory: Chamber works, light instrumental solos, and some vocal music. Main composer: Beethoven. Contemporary works (especially those by members) were performed.

Commentary: The Société's formation was announced in November 1838.[278] Several members of the short-lived Société Musicale (I, see under Cercle Musical) had reassembled, hoping to reform the music of *salons* by performing chamber "art" music therein. The last review of the Société's activity in *RGMdP* appeared 24 January 1839. On 21 February *RGMdP* reported that the Société no longer existed.[279]

Société Nationale des Beaux-Arts (1862–65)

Schedule: The first concert occurred on Sunday, 14 December 1862; four or five more were presented that season, all on Sundays, at intervals of two weeks or more. Ten or more concerts took place the following season, some or all on Fridays, beginning in late October. A single concert was mentioned in spring 1865.

Location: A new hall, boulevard des Italiens, no. 26.

Personnel: Félicien David was director of the concerts. An orchestra and chorus, frequently conducted by composers whose works were being performed (among them Saint-Saëns and Bizet), participated the first season, but apparently only a small group of (mainly) string players performed the second. See also *Commentary.*

Repertory: 1862–63: Orchestral, orchestral-choral, and vocal works, many of them major, most by contemporary French composers (notably Berlioz, Bizet, and Félicien David). 1863–64: Chamber works (mainly string quartets and quintets) by various eighteenth- and nineteenth-century composers, among them Haydn, Mozart, Onslow, and David; concertos were also programmed, probably without a full orchestral accompaniment. See also *Commentary.*

Commentary: Reviewing the inaugural concert, Botte described the orchestra as "élite", but thought the new hall less than successful.[280] Later that season he praised the society for its willingness to program works of young composers but harshly criticized the orchestra and its composer-conductors.[281] The nature of the society changed dramatically the second season as chamber music replaced works for large forces and the repertory became conservative. At the beginning of the third season another major transformation occurred: MM. Debillemont, Roger, and Martinet succeeded David and scheduled nightly concerts of both "art" and dance music in a redecorated hall.[282] This series became known as the Concerts des Beaux-Arts (see this entry). In early April 1865, however, Cristal wrote, "Les concerts de la Société des Beaux-Arts ont exceptionnellement renouvelé leur programme";[283] at the single "renewed" concert the Société presented excerpts from Louis Lacombe's opera *L'Amour,* orchestral movements, and solos.

Société Philharmonique de la Ville de Paris (?1822–?1854)

Schedule: Six concerts a year at monthly intervals (usually December to May), Sunday afternoons. The series began perhaps as early as 1822, no later than 1825.[284] I find no mention of the society after May 1854.[285]

Location: 1840 to at least December 1850, salle Montesquieu; by February 1852 the concerts had moved to the salle Sainte-Cécile, by November 1853 to the salle Barthelémy.

Personnel: The orchestra comprised mainly middle-class amateurs and some young professionals; there were professional soloists. By 1840 and through spring 1850 the conductor was Loiseau. From autumn 1850 the conductor was Aimé Roussette.

Repertory: Mainly light works: overtures and excerpts from operas; instrumental solos; concertos; some vocal works.

Commentary: I find no mention of this society before 1840; possibly it drew little attention because of its amateur status. An amateur orchestral society led by Loiseau at the salle de l'Athénée central in 1834 may be the same organization.[286] A review of a concert in December 1850 stated that 2000 had attended.[287] Blanchard wrote that talented artists performed there in an effort to gain a new audience. He also reported that the orchestra comprised mainly amateurs, who paid little attention to nuance.[288]

Société Philharmonique de Paris (1850–51). See Grande Société Philharmonique de Paris.

Société Philharmonique de Paris (I, 1862)

Schedule: The lone announced concert (called the "first"), scheduled for Wednesday, 17 December 1862, never took place;[289] no further concerts were mentioned.

Location: salle du Grand Hôtel, boulevard des Capucines.

Personnel: An orchestra led by the Dutch composer and violinist "Guillaume-Frédéric" Greive; the painist Mme. Aglaé Massart; and the singer Mme. Rosina Penco.

Repertory: The one known program was to have included Mozart's "Jupiter" Symphony, less major orchestral works of Beethoven, G. Mathias, and L. Kreutzer, a chamber "Polonaise" of Moniushko, and two operatic excerpts.

Commentary: There seems to be no relationship between this organization and other Parisian philharmonic societies.

Société Philharmonique de Paris (II, 1866)

Schedule: Three concerts were scheduled for spring 1866, begining Sunday, 18 March.[290] The first two were reviewed in *Ménestrel* two weeks later;[291] I find no reference to the third.

Location: Cirque de l'Impératrice.[292]

Personnel: An orchestra of 100, led by Placet (previously conductor of the orchestra at the Théâtre Lyrique), and a chorus of 150, led by Amand Chevé. The society was directed by a committee.

Repertory: Orchestral and orchestral-choral works. Composers included Beethoven, Weber, Wagner, Bizet, Hignard, and Prévost-Rousseau.

Commentary: When concerts led by Malibran at the Théâtre de la Gaîté were suspended, late in 1865, the orchestra formed a new organization[293]—eventually called the Société Philharmonique de Paris. Its goals were 1) to improve the position of musicians, 2) to popularize the repertory of the Conservatoire concerts, and 3) to propagate new works.[294] The first two concerts were considered highly successful;[295] the critic de Gasperini thought the ensemble was less than satisfactory, but remained optimistic about the Société's future.[296] The organization kept its promise to perform new works—particularly those of French composers.

Société Sainte-Cécile (I, 1839)

The Société Sainte-Cécile was founded under the patronage of Meyerbeer, de Bériot, and other (unidentified) musical celebrities. Only an inaugural concert, on Saturday, 18 May 1839, was reported in *RGMdP.* Chamber and solo works of de Bériot, Osborne, Romberg, and Clara Wieck were presented by the composers.[297]

Société Sainte-Cécile (1847–?1848). See Société de Sainte-Cécile.

Société Sainte-Cécile (II, 1850–55, 1864–?1866)

The most successful of the societies labelled "Sainte-Cécile" presented concerts of (mainly traditional) orchestral and choral "art" music. A detailed account of this series is provided in chapter 2, pages 37–42.

Société Schumann (1869–70)

Schedule: Six *séances,* biweekly on Thursdays, from 27 January 1870; the final session was postponed from 7 to 21 April.

Location: salle Erard.

Personnel: Organized by the pianist Delahaye [? Lepot]; other participants included White (vn), Madier-Montjau (vn), van Waefelghem (va), and Lasserre (vc).

Repertory: The group's goal was the performance of chamber music by Schumann and other composers little known in France.[298] Compositions of Brahms, de Castillon, Raff, Rubinstein, and Volkmann were essayed, but Schumann's works dominated the programs.

Commentary: A subscription for all six *séances* cost 25 francs.[299] An elite, appreciative audience attended the first session, which was favorably reviewed, and by March the society had attracted quite a following.[300] The promotion of composers such as de Castillon was unusual and courageous.

Société Symphonique (1852–53)

Schedule: Six concerts, mainly at biweekly intervals on Fridays, were planned.[301] Apparently, only two concerts, on Monday, 20 December 1852, and Friday, 14 January 1853, actually took place.[302]
Location: salle Herz.
Personnel: The society's director was the publisher and scholar Aristide Farrenc. An orchestra of about 50 was conducted by J.-L.-M. Mas; soloists included the pianists Mlle. Clauss and Mlle. Salomon, the violinist Pazetti, and the singer Mlle. Dietsch.
Repertory: Symphonies, concertos, overtures, and vocal solos of composers ranging chronologically from Stradella to Louise Farrenc.
Commentary: Admission fees for individual concerts were three to six francs. The society announced intentions to present works previously unknown (or not performed for some time) in Paris.[303]

Société Symphonique de Paris (1861–?)

The single known concert (called the "first") took place Saturday, 7 December 1861, at the salons des Arts-Unis, rue de Provence. Evidently the concerts were expected to continue, but there is only one reference to the society in *RGMdP.*[304] It stated that the group's (rather unoriginal) goal was "la perfection de l'exécution instrumentale."

Stainlein, M. le comte Louis de: Concerts (1857)

Schedule: Four biweekly concerts, Fridays, 20 February to 3 April 1857.
Location: salle Pleyel.
Personnel: Organized by the amateur cellist and composer M. le comte Louis de Stainlein. Performers included Sivori (vn), Viault (vn), Casimir Ney [Escoffier] (va), Van Gelder (vc), L. Lacombe (pf), and Lubeck (pf).
Repertory: Chamber works for strings with and without piano. Main composers: Stainlein, Beethoven, and Mendelssohn.
Commentary: Stainlein reportedly intended to give profits from the concerts to the indigent of the *2me arrondissement.*[305] A second season of concerts was planned, but was cancelled in January 1858 as Stain-

lein was spending the winter in Nice.[306] Stainlein's group was also known as the "Nouvelle Société de Musique de Chambre."[307]

Stamaty, Camille: Concerts (1852)

Schedule: Three weekly concerts, Wednesdays, 14 to 28 April 1852.
Location: salle de l'Association des Artistes-Musiciens (probably the salle Bonne-Nouvelle).
Personnel: Piano students of the pianist, composer, and teacher Camille-Marie Stamaty, and members of the Théâtre-Italien orchestra.
Repertory: Programs of piano concertos by Mozart and Beethoven were advertised;[308] the known programs (the first and third) also included other piano concertos and violin solos.
Commentary: Blanchard stated that the programs introduced a new path for piano recitals by presenting piano concertos and chamber works rather than the usual *fantaisies* and *souvenirs*.[309]

Szarwady, Mme. and Müller Brothers: Concerts (1866)

Schedule: Four concerts on Tuesdays, 6, 20, and 27 February and 6 March 1866; a fifth and final concert on Thursday, 15 March 1866.
Location: salons Pleyel-Wolff.
Personnel: The pianist Mme. Wilhelmine Szarwady (née Clauss) and the brothers Müller (Bernhard, Karl, Hugo, and Wilhelm), a string quartet from Germany.
Repertory: Chamber works for strings with and without piano. Main composers: Beethoven, Haydn, Mendelssohn, Schubert, and Schumann. Works of contemporaries such as Damcke, Hiller, Raff, and Rubinstein were also essayed.
Commentary: Charles Bannelier criticized the excessive tempo fluctuation in the group's renditions.[310]

Tardieu de Malleville, Mme. Charlotte: Séances (1853–?1863). See Malleville, Mlle. Charlotte de: Séances.

Tilmant: Concerts (1833–?1838)

Schedule: Short series of Sunday *matinées,* usually at biweekly intervals, announced in autumn 1833 and spring of the years 1835–38. No cancellation was announced, but I find no mention of the series after 1838. A single concert was scheduled on 10 March 1840.

Location: 1833, galerie Colbert, hôtel Fesch; 1835–37, *salons* of M. Pape; 1838, *salons*, of Erard.

Personnel: Théophile Tilmant (*l'aîné,* 1st vn); his brother, Alexandre Tilmant (vc); Claudel (2nd vn, 1835–7), Croisilles (2nd vn, 1838), Urhan (va), Duriez (db), and others.

Repertory: Sonatas, trios, string quartets, and chamber works for larger ensembles. Main composers: Beethoven (including the Late quartets), Mozart, Haydn, and Onslow. More recent compositions included the works of the Tilmants (who wrote works jointly), Bertini, Mayseder, Rousselot, and an unidentified work of Schubert in 1833[311] (one of the earliest Parisian performances of Schubert's music).

Commentary: An announcement in *ReM,* concerning the series beginning in 1835, promised renditions of string quartets and quintets of established masters as well as newer works.[312] A notice the same day in *GMdP* stated the group's intention to perform the Late quartets of Beethoven.[313] Only a few of the actual programs were published in *ReM, GMdP,* or *RGMdP.*

La Trompette (from 1860)

The chamber music society established by Emile Lemoine has been credited, in many twentieth-century sources, with a major role in the propagation of chamber music in France. Most of these sources seem to be based directly or indirectly on Lemoine's own article "La Trompette" (1903).[314] Therein Lemoine, an amateur string player, described how as a student at the Ecole Polytechnique in 1860 he had organized a quartet to read through chamber works.[315] Soon colleagues were invited to listen, and over the years (Lemoine did not provide many dates) the audience expanded, eventually reaching 500 or 600, and the performances moved from private lodgings, to *ateliers,* to halls such as the salle Erard and salle Pleyel. Meanwhile, the name "La Trompette" was adopted and the personnel of the group (never fixed in number or instrumentation) slowly became more professional; among the participants were Alphonse Duvernoy, Louis Diémer, Charles de Bériot, Martin Marsick, and Saint-Saëns (who in 1880 wrote his Trumpet Septet, Op. 65, for the society). Lemoine maintained that the weekly *séances* of La Trompette filled a gap by presenting "art" music when light music predominated in Paris, that they brought new or unknown works into the repertory through persistent repetition, and that they quickly acquired a reputation in the musical world.

Romain Rolland's *Musiciens d'aujourd'hui* (1908) paraphrased (giving due credit) most of what Lemoine had written;[316] since then Lemoine's group has been singled out for praise in sources such as *Cobbett's Cyclopedic Survey of Chamber Music*[317] and *Grove 6*.[318] Whatever La Trompette may have accomplished eventually, its significance before the Franco-Prussian War was limited. The musical press did not discuss it (or Lemoine) in the 1860s. And Augé de Lassus's *La Trompette,* a rambling discussion of the society's activities from 1860 to 1910 (see note 315), devoted only 21 of its 232 pages to the first decade. The earliest known programs (not printed) date from the season of 1867–68. It is not clear when the group first played in public halls or when professionals started to participate regularly, but it was evidently not before the late 1860s. (Saint-Saëns joined the group in 1875.) Existing programs from the late 1860s show that La Trompette tried contemporary works (particularly those of Rabuteau, the Prix de Rome winner in 1868), but played mainly compositions of Beethoven, Mozart, Haydn, and Mendelssohn.

L'Union Artistique (1860–1870 or later). See Cercle de l'Union Artistique.

L'Union Musicale (1849–51)

Schedule: The first concert took place 21 January 1849. Seven biweekly Sunday concerts (alternating with the Conservatoire concerts) were presented in 1849 and again in 1850. Another seven (alternating Sundays with the Société Sainte-Cécile II) were planned for the season of 1850–51;[319] *RGMdP* mentioned none after the fifth, in early March.

Location: salle Sainte-Cécile, rue de la Chaussée d'Antin. The last reviewed concert took place at the Jardin d'hiver.

Personnel: An orchestra was conducted in 1849 by Manera, in spring 1850 (following Manera's death) by F.-J.-B. Seghers, and in the season of 1850–51 by Félicien David. A chorus evidently joined the orchestra, for Reber was announced as the *chef de choeur* in December 1849,[320] and Louis Dietsch was choral director the final season. In November 1850 the society had a membership of 160.[321]

Repertory: Symphonies and overtures; some concertos, orchestral-choral works, instrumental solos, and songs. Main composers: Beethoven, Mozart, and Mendelssohn. Contemporary works were programmed, as were early vocal works (Palestrina, Allegri, Marcello, Handel, and others).

Commentary: Reviewing the inaugural concert, Berlioz wrote that the society intended to avoid major vocal works (partly because of the tax laws),[322] but choral works were presented later that season and by 1850 there was evidently a permanent chorus. Subscription fees for six concerts (the seventh was extra) were 12 to 20 francs,[323] and the concerts were reportedly well attended. According to Monnais, internal strife in the society prompted Seghers to leave (and establish the Société Sainte-Cécile II; see pp. 37–42) after spring 1850.[324] A Union Musicale that sponsored a competition for composers in 1864 does not appear to be related.

Valentino, H.-J.-A.-J.: Concerts (1837–41). See Concerts Valentino.

Vander-Gucht, Delcroix, and Ménétrier: Séances (1864). See Delcroix, Ménétrier, and Vander-Gucht: Séances.

Vieuxtemps, Henri: Concerts (1858–59)

Schedule: Two four-concert series. The first, presenting chamber works, comprised concerts at biweekly intervals, the first three on Thursdays, beginning 25 November 1858, the last on Saturday, 8 January 1859; concerts of the second series, in which there was an orchestra, occurred biweekly on Wednesdays, 2 February to 16 March 1859. See also *Commentary.*

Location: First series, salle Beethoven, passage de l'Opéra; second series, salle Herz.

Personnel: Organized by the Belgian violinist Henri Vieuxtemps. Other participants in the first series included Colblain (vn), Adam (va), Van Gelder (vc), and Mme. Vieuxtemps (pf). In the second series an orchestra was led by Elbel; other participants included E. Forgues (pf) and vocalists.

Repertory: Each of the chamber music programs comprised three string quartets or quintets and one violin solo (for Vieuxtemps); the main composers were Beethoven and Vieuxtemps, but programs included a Chaconne by Bach and one of the rare presentations of a string quartet by Cherubini. The second series offered more varied and generally lighter music—violin concertos, overtures, piano pieces, and vocal works; the main composer was Vieuxtemps.

Commentary: Vieuxtemps had earlier organized similar series in London, St. Petersburg, and Vienna. The admission fee for the chamber music series was high—40 francs for four concerts.[325]

Vieuxtemps presented many concerts in Paris from 1835 to 1870. He appeared there at least three times in spring 1851, gave seven concerts in the season of 1852–53, and played at least four times in spring 1870. But in none of these seasons did his concerts resemble a series; they occurred at various locations, and presented different sorts of music. Most of these individual concerts offered light music (especially violin solos and concertos), though on some occasions Vieuxtemps participated in chamber music *séances*.

Vieuxtemps, Escudier-Kastner, and Batta: Concerts (1863). See Escudier-Kastner, Vieuxtemps, and Batta: Concerts.

Wartel, Mme. Thérèsa: Séances (?1847–?1863)

Series of *séances* by the pianist, composer, and teacher Thérèsa Wartel (née Andrien) were mentioned sporadically from 1847 until 1863. Three separate *soirées* were reported in spring 1847. There were Saturday *soirées* (probably weekly) in 1862, beginning in February and continuing through May,[326] and weekly private *soirées* were noted again in February 1863.[327] Prominent musicians such as Alard (vn), Casimir Ney [Escoffier] (va), Franchomme (vc), Gouffé (vc/db), Dorus (fl), Verroust *aîné* (ob), and Rousselot (hn), joined Mme. Wartel in performances of works by Beethoven, Hummel, Schubert, and Onslow; the few known programs also included piano, vocal, and light instrumental compositions. Mme. Wartel presented individual concerts several years from the mid-1840s until the mid-1860s.

Wartel, Mme. Thérèsa, Joachim and Cossmann: Soirées (1850). See Joachim, Cossmann, and Wartel: Soirées.

Zimmermann, Pierre-Joseph-Guillaume: Soirées (1830s and 1840s)

The private *soirées* of one Zimmermann were frequently described as events in which one always heard something new and in which young artists from all over Europe made their Parisian debuts. Although only his last name appeared in contemporary notices, Zimmermann (sometimes Zimmerman) was often identified as a professor of piano; Pierre-Joseph-Guillaume Zimmermann taught piano at the Paris Conservatoire from 1816 to 1848, and was the most famous Zimmermann in Paris at the time. Furthermore, the obituary notice for P.-J.-G. Zimmermann in *RGMdP* (1853)[328] mentioned his *soirées* using phrases similar to those employed ten years earlier in reviewing *soirées* of the unidentified Zimmermann.[329] The *soirées* were noted as an established series in January 1836, and Blanchard wrote in 1840 that they had become important six or seven years earlier.[330] Monnais stated in 1839 that the *séances* occurred twice a month on Thursdays;[331] later they took place other days. I find no reports of them after 1844.[332] Critics described the *séances* in glowing terms, often mentioning the celebrated artists who attended, and suggesting that success at Zimmermann's *salon* (on the rue Saint-Lazare) practically assured acceptance in the concert world.[333] The critics' enthusiasm notwithstanding, the instrumental, vocal, and piano works on Zimmermann's programs were predominately light. Zimmermann himself seems not to have performed at these events.

Additional Concerts

Many musicians who do not have entries above presented a substantial number of events in which instrumental "art" music was performed. The concerts of these individuals have not been considered series for various reasons: they may have been scheduled infrequently or irregularly; the programs may have been too diverse; or instrumental works may have constituted only a small portion of the repertory (pianists, for example, often included one chamber work on a program otherwise comprising solo music). Nevertheless, such musicians helped to introduce and promote instrumental works in Paris, and their contribution should not be neglected. Below are listed, alphabetically, those whose activities seem most significant; a brief sketch of the relevant repertory and approximate dates of activity are provided for each.

Batta, Alexandre (vc): chamber works of Beethoven and more recent composers, 1840s and 1850s.

Billet, Alexandre (pf): chamber works of eighteenth- and nineteenth-century German composers, mainly in the late 1850s and 1860s.

Chevillard, Alexandre (vc): chamber works and his own concertos, 1840s through 1860s.

Cuvillon, Philippe de (vn): sonatas and other chamber works by established composers and, particularly, Mme. de Grandval, late 1840s and 1850s.

Ernst, Heinrich Wilhelm (vn): concertos of Spohr, Mendelssohn, and Ernst, 1840s and early 1850s.

Franck, César (pf): chamber works of Franck, other contemporaries (the repertory was unusually innovative), and Beethoven, late 1830s to mid-1840s.

Graever, Mlle. Madeleine (pf): piano trios (early 1850s) and concertos (early 1860s) by Beethoven and contemporaries, particularly Litolff.

Greive, Guillaume Frédéric (Dutch composer): single programs most years, 1855–65, which included chamber works (sometimes excerpts thereof) by Greive, Hummel, Onslow, and others.

Hallé, Charles [Carl] (pf): chamber works of Beethoven (particularly piano trios), Mozart, and Hallé, mid-1840s.

Hiller, Ferdinand (pf): symphonies, concertos, overtures, and chamber works by Hiller, concertos and instrumental solos by others, mainly in the early 1830s.

Kreutzer, Léon (pf): his orchestral works (some with piano) and chamber pieces, late 1850s and 1860s.

Krüger, Wilhelm (pf): chamber works, some concertos, by Beethoven, Schubert, Mendelssohn, Schumann, Raff, and Krüger; annual concerts in the 1850s and 1860s.

Langhans, Wilhelm (vn) and Mme. Louise (née Japha, pf): symphonies, concertos, chamber works (including violin sonatas) of Beethoven, Raff, Brahms, and W. Langhans, mid to late 1860s.

Liebe, Mlle. Thérèse (vn, child prodigy): chamber works and concertos of various nineteenth-century composers, late 1860s.

Mayer, Max (vn): chamber works of Beethoven and others, late 1840s and early 1850s.

Osborne, George (pf): chamber works, particularly piano trios, by Osborne and contemporaries, 1830s and early 1840s.

Pleyel, Mme. Marie (pf): works for piano and orchestra by Weber, Mendelssohn, Herz, and Litolff, and some chamber works, 1840s and 1850s.

Prudent, Emile (pf): his works for piano and orchestra, 1840s until his death in 1863.

Sivori, Camillo (vn): his concertos, nineteenth-century German chamber works, 1840s to 1860s.

Szarwady, Mme. Wilhelmine (*née* Clauss, pf): piano trios and other chamber works of Beethoven, Schubert, Mendelssohn, Schumann, and Rust, late 1850s and 1860s.

Telesinski, Joseph (vn): chamber works and concertos of Beethoven and Mendelssohn, late 1850s and 1860s.

Wieniawski, Joseph (pf): concertos and chamber works, early 1860s.

Zompi, Diomède (pf): piano trios of Beethoven and other chamber works, 1850s.

Appendix B

Provincial Concerts

A thorough investigation of musical life in the provinces could well be the subject of several studies such as this one. To treat it properly, one should examine journals and archival material from each of the more than 50 French towns that gained mention in reviews in the *Revue et gazette musicale*. My modest goal in the pages below is to survey the performance of instrumental music in the French provinces in the mid-nineteenth century.

For music, Paris was truly the capital of France; significant developments, for the most part, occurred there and were imitated in provincial towns. Thus orchestral societies, *concerts populaires,* and professional chamber music concerts were first established in Paris, and later adopted in smaller towns. Many of the provincial imitations were less than first-rate: generally, the *sociétés philharmoniques* were small, the musicians and instruments poor, and the repertories limited to "popular" music. Danjou reported, in 1838, that nothing was accomplished at a rehearsal he attended of the *société philharmonique* of Gray because of constant altercations among its 20 members;[1] apparently, such conditions were common. As late as 1862, Mathieu de Monter lamented the position of classical music in the Midi, reporting that most town orchestras attempted only frivolous works (quadrilles, waltzes, gavottes, and overtures); that even the larger *sociétés philharmoniques* clung to an old repertory; that the musicians were generally indifferent, lazy, and jealous; that rehearsals were poorly organized; and that the relationship between conductors and players was unproductive.[2] Because Paris was so clearly the cultural center of the country (if not the world), talented performers and composers abandoned even major provincial towns for Paris, thus perpetuating the sharp qualitative contrast between Paris and the rest of France. As a result, one finds little originality in provincial musical life.

Humphrey Burton has written that eighteenth-century French provincial academies had waned in the closing years of the *ancien régime* because of high taxes, the cost of wars, and competition from provincial theatres, leaving music in the hands of amateurs and part-time professionals. With the Revolution, the concert halls, associated with the aristocracy, were taken over for political purposes.[3] Public concerts of classical music, therefore, had to make a fresh start in the nineteenth century, much as they did in Paris. A new interest in serious nontheatrical music was noticed in 1829 by "Un abonné" to the *Revue musicale,* who cited examples of local philharmonic societies in towns "où naguères on pouvait difficilement réunir quatre musiciens."[4]

Many of the best provincial concerts were presented by guest artists. Soloists and, later, chamber music societies toured France often, especially during Paris's off-season. In the 1860s even the orchestra of the Paris Concerts Populaires travelled to various provincial towns. Throughout the period, accounts of provincial musical events were dominated by news of visiting artists.

There were, however, numerous local musical organizations.

Sociétés Philharmoniques

Foremost among provincial musical groups were the *sociétés philharmoniques* that sprung up in more than 30 towns. Examples are known to have existed at Caen (the Société Philharmonique du Calvados) and La Rochelle as early as 1826, and probably earlier.[5] In 1827 the *Revue musicale* reported that *sociétés* were forming everywhere.[6] A Société des Concerts and Cercle des Arts, performing overtures of Cherubini and symphonies of Beethoven, were said to have already existed in Marseilles for 15 years in 1834.[7] (If they had been performing Beethoven's symphonies since 1819, they were well in advance of Paris.) Other early *sociétés philharmoniques* are known to have existed at Boulogne, Toulouse, and Lyons, and in the mid-1830s, reports of the founding or resurrection of *sociétés* were frequent.[8] By 1838, they were in nearly every sizable town.[9]

The orchestras of the *sociétés* included numerous amateurs.[10] Liszt wrote in 1835 that most provincial orchestras were understaffed and unable to perform the "serious" repertory; he admitted, nonetheless, that they contributed to the development of French interest in music.[11] Programs by provincial *sociétés* included little symphonic music. Often, programs were designed around a visiting soloist, for whom the orchestra provided accompaniment, playing only an overture or two alone. Overtures seem to have formed a large part of the provincial repertory, as did other light works—fantasias, caprices, variations, and so forth. The philharmonic societies also presented religious works on appropriate holidays and included much vocal music on their programs.[12] In 1838, one critic, who had examined programs of several provincial societies, concluded that the general level of programming was improving (especially by the inclusion of more symphonies);[13] yet frivolous music maintained a prominent position on provincial programs. Chamber music was introduced by some *sociétés philharmoniques* late in the period.[14]

Although many nineteenth-century symphonies were beyond the capabilities of individual *sociétés philharmoniques,* they received better treatment at festivals in which several *sociétés* from the same region joined forces. The most significant of these were the festivals of the Association Musicale de l'Ouest, founded in 1835 at the instigation of Désiré Beaulieu (1791–1863), who also sometimes conducted. Musical organizations from Angoulêmes, Châtellerault, Fontenay, Limoges, Niort, Poitiers, Rochefort, La Rochelle, Saint-Jean d'Angely, and Saintes combined to present two or three concerts at each yearly festival, held in one of these cities. The first year they gathered an orchestra of 96, a chorus of 80, and 800 subscribers.[15] By 1859 there were 200 singers and 150 instrumentalists.[16] On the first day (that is, the first concert of each festival), oratorios were performed. The second day brought a program of orchestral music, generally a complete symphony (most often one of Beethoven's, though nineteenth-century French works were occasionally chosen), plus some overtures and other light orchestral works. Often the programs were quite long.[17] Similar regional festivals involving the cooperation (or sometimes competition) of several local orchestras, choruses, or military bands took place throughout the period at Lille, Aix-la-Chapelle, Toulouse, Anger, Meaux, and elsewhere.[18]

Concerts Populaires

Following the success of Pasdeloup's concerts in Paris, series of *concerts populaires* (sometimes performed by local *sociétés philharmoniques*) were established in various French cities in the 1860s. The earliest appear to have been those of Toulouse and Bordeaux, founded in 1862 and 1863 respectively.[19] Series at Nantes, Rennes, and La Rochelle followed. The repertory of these series was similar to that of the Parisian Concerts Populaires.

Chamber Music Societies

Public chamber music concerts were relatively rare in the provinces, though one reporter observed in 1831 that chamber music had not yet, as in Paris, fallen victim to operas and *romances,* and that provincial musicians still gathered to perform this genre.[20] Infrequent performances were reported in subsequent decades, and in 1851 chamber music was considered to be little-known in towns like Tours.[21] Not until the 1860s did the genre make significant inroads in provincial concerts. By far the best-reported provincial chamber music society was the string quartet organized by one Schwaederlé (once a pupil of Baillot) in Strasbourg in 1855;[22] surviving several personnel changes, it was still active in 1867. The quartet played a standard repertory (Haydn, Mozart, Beethoven), and attempted some chamber works of nineteenth-century composers, among them Onslow, Spohr, Hummel, Field, Mendelssohn, Schumann, Hiller, Fétis, and Ernst. Their playing won much praise, and by 1860 the concerts were attracting larger crowds than the Strasbourg Hôtel de Ville could accommodate.[23] A chamber music society at Lille was also active in the 1850s and 1860s.

Summer Concerts

Castil-Blaze wrote in 1839 that the "popular-music" orchestras of Jullien, Musard, Tolbecque, and others were new only to Paris, for similar organizations had existed in the provinces for 60 years.[24] Such orchestras would have drawn little comment from Parisian journals. What did attract notice were musical organizations that performed at summer resorts in the 1860s. Not only did wealthy Parisians visit the resorts—mainly seaside towns or villages with baths—but many musicians were imported from Paris. At Dieppe there were festivals, balls, opera, and operetta throughout the summer holidays (mainly in August), and one M. Placet led an orchestra in "symphonies et ouvertures des grands maîtres" twice daily;[25] soloists also performed. Orchestras provided entertainment at Deauville and Trouville too, mixing traditional "art" music with instrumental *fantaisies* and the like.[26] Summer *séances* of chamber music were reported in the provinces in the early 1860s.[27]

Other Provincial Concerts

The numerous other musical festivals and concerts are not easily categorized. Examples mentioned in the *Revue et gazette musicale de Paris* include benefit concerts and programs by the Garde National, by a Société d'émulation (an orchestra of amateurs and professionals, gathered to perform music by amateur or beginning composers, Douai, 1832),[28] by the Academy of Music at Lille (1841), by a student orchestra at the Strasbourg Conservatory (1866–69), and by the Société Sainte-Cécile of Bordeaux (1869). At the many local festivals, orchestras, bands, choruses, and instrumental and vocal soloists performed.

Provincial Repertory

As is evident from the above descriptions, much of the music played at provincial concerts was "popular"—overtures, instrumental solos, dances, and so forth. A new interest in all forms of instrumental music was attributed to the closing of the *maîtrises* (during the French Revolution) and the diminished emphasis on music in churches,[29] but the instrumental works that attracted "men of the world" were the virtuosic solos of the Herz school.[30] Too, provincial dependence upon guest artists, and a shortage of qualified musicians, discouraged local orchestras from performing symphonies or other substantial works.

Among provincial organizations that did attempt "art" music, the repertory was much like that found in Paris, and possibly even more conservative. Brief announcements of local concerts indicate that Beethoven, Haydn, Mendelssohn, Mozart, and Weber were, as in Paris, clear favorites. Composers known mainly for chamber works (for example, Onslow and Blanc) were heard less often, simply because that genre suffered relative neglect outside Paris.

A sample of 392 known performances at provincial concerts, though too small to have much statistical significance, confirms the popularity of Beethoven (87 performances), Weber (36), Haydn (26), Mendelssohn (23), Mozart (21), and Rossini (19); no other composer received more than nine known performances. Among the 174 known performances of major works, the leaders were Beethoven (60), Haydn (18), Mozart (14), and Mendelssohn (12), with no other composer having more than seven.

Notes

Chapter 1

1. Arthur Hervey, *French Music in the XIXth Century* (London: Grant Richards, 1903), p. 184.
2. Edward Burlingame Hill, *Modern French Music* (Boston and New York: Houghton Mifflin Company, 1924), pp. 20 and 4–5.
3. Gerald Abraham, *A Hundred Years of Music,* 4th ed. (Frome and London: Duckworth, 1974), pp. 17 and 19.
4. Paul Henry Lang, *Music in Western Civilization* (New York: W. W. Norton & Company, 1941), pp. 827, 923, and 925.
5. Kenneth B. Klaus, *The Romantic Period in Music* (Boston: Allyn and Bacon, 1970), p. 336.
6. William Weber, *Music and the Middle Class: The Social Structure of Concert Life in London, Paris, and Vienna* (London: Croom Helm, 1975), p. 7.
7. Rey M. Longyear, *Nineteenth-Century Romanticism in Music,* 2nd ed. rev. (Englewood Cliffs, N. J.: Prentice-Hall, 1973), p. 208.
8. "Mais dans son quintette comme dans la 1re sonate pour violoncelle et piano op. 32, Saint-Saëns reste très influencé par l'esthétique germanique; et comment ne le serait-il pas à une époque où il n'est de musique de chambre que de Beethoven ou Schumann?" J.-M. Nectoux: "Correspondance Saint-Saëns–Fauré", *Revue de musicologie,* 59/1 (1973): 81–82. Schumann's music, incidentally, was little known in France in 1855, but had become part of the standard repertory by 1872.
9. Hector Berlioz, *Mémoires,* trans. and ed. David Cairns as *The Memoirs of Hector Berlioz: Member of the French Institute* (London: Victor Gollancz Ltd., 1969), pp. 64 and 469–70.
10. "Un compositeur français qui avait l'audace de s'aventurer sur le terrain de la musique instrumentale n'avait d'autre moyen de faire exécuter ses oeuvres que de donner lui-même un concert et d'y convier ses amis et les critiques. Quant au public, au vrai public, il n'y fallait pas songer; le nom d'un compositeur, à la fois français et vivant imprimé sur un affiche avait le propriété de mettre tout le monde en fuite." Camille Saint-Saëns, *Harmonie et mélodie,* 3rd ed. (Paris: C. Lévy, 1885), p. 207.

11. Charles Gounod, *Autobiographical Reminiscences,* trans. W. Hely Hutchinson (London: W. Heinemann, 1896), p. 136.

12. F.-J. Fétis, "Nouvelles de Paris: Ecole Royale de Musique: Société des Concerts," *ReM* 4 (1828–29): 516.

13. Fétis, "Revue succinct de la musique pendant l'année 1828," *ReM* 5 (1829): 1.

14. Franz Liszt, "De la situation des artistes, et de leur condition dans la société," *GMdP* 2/30 (26 July 1835): 245–49, particularly p. 247. This article was probably written by Mme. d'Agoult.

15. François Stoepel, "La Musique en France (1835)", *GMdP* 2/39 (27 September 1835): 313–17.

16. Georges Kastner, "Revue critique: Grand trio," *RGMdP* 5/28 (15 July 1838): 290.

17. "Nouvelles," *RGMdP* 21/7 (12 February 1854): 54.

18. "Nous n'avons que quelques rares symphonies exécutées à grands frais dans plus rares concerts. La musique de chambre . . . s'exécute à peine dans deux ou trois réunions d'amateurs fervents; mais des arrangements sur des motifs d'opéra forment la majeure partie du programme musical de la moindre fête de famille." Antoine Elwart, *Histoire de la Société des Concerts du Conservatoire Impériale de Musique* (Paris: S. Castel, 1860), pp. 31–32.

19. "La plupart des nos compositeurs . . . doivent tenter l'épreuve de théâtre lyrique, sous peine de végeter sans fortune et sans gloire." Ibid., p. 32.

20. Ibid., p. 31.

21. P. Scudo: *L'Année musicale* 2 (1861): 181–82. The statement about publishers is odd, for in the same source (p. 294) Scudo reported that the largest portion of published music comprised piano and solo vocal works of an ephemeral nature.

22. R. J. [probably Jakob Rosenhain], "Berichte: Paris," *Allgemeine musikalische Zeitung,* n.s. 1/13 (25 March 1863): cols. 237–38.

23. Paul Smith [Edouard Monnais], "Revue musicale de l'année 1866," *RGMdP* 34/1 (6 January 1867): 1–4.

24. Em. Mathieu de Monter, "Revue musicale de l'année 1868," *RGMdP* 36/1 (3 January 1869): 1.

25. "Concerts et auditions musicales de la semaine," *RGMdP* 37/9 (27 February 1870): 69.

26. "Nouvelles," *RGMdP* 12/8 (23 February 1845): 64.

27. Donald J. Grout, *A History of Western Music,* 3rd ed. rev. (New York: W. W. Norton & Company, 1980), p. 668.

28. Lang, *Music in Western Civilization,* pp. 925–26.

29. Longyear, *Nineteenth-Century Romanticism,* p. 208.

30. Martin Cooper, *French Music from the Death of Berlioz to the Death of Fauré* (London: Oxford University Press, 1951), p. 18.

31. In chapter 2, 10 of the most significant series are described in detail while others are

mentioned in a more general discussion. Appendix A presents brief information—dates of existence, location, personnel, repertory, general commentary—on 122 series.

32. Instrumental music in France before, during, and for a brief while after this nadir has been well documented by Boris Schwarz in his doctoral dissertation, "French Instrumental Music between the Revolutions (1789–1830)" (Columbia University, 1950). Although the Société des Concerts du Conservatoire was not the only organization performing instrumental "art" music in 1828, the impetus it provided for the revival of such music was beyond comparison.

33. Dorothy Hagan, "French Musical Criticism between the Revolutions" (Ph.D. dissertation, University of Illinois, 1965), p. 4.

34. Jacques Barzun, *Berlioz and the Romantic Century,* 3rd ed. rev., 2 vols. (New York: Columbia University Press, 1969).

35. Leo Schrade, *Beethoven in France* (New Haven: Yale University Press, 1942).

36. F.-J. Fétis, *Biographie universelle des musiciens,* 2nd ed. (Paris: Firmin Didot frères, 1866–70); *Supplément et Complément,* ed. Arthur Pougin (Paris: Firmin Didot frères, 1878–80).

37. Elisabeth Bernard, "Jules Pasdeloup et les Concerts Populaires," *Revue de musicologie,* 57/2 (1971): 150–78.

38. W. W. Cobbett, *Cobbett's Cyclopedic Survey of Chamber Music,* 2nd ed., 3 vols. (London: Oxford University Press, 1963).

39. Constant Pierre, *Le Conservatoire National de Musique et de Déclamation: Documents historiques et administratifs* (Paris: Imprimerie nationale, 1900).

Chapter 2

1. James Grant, *Paris and Its People,* 2 vols. (London: Saunders & Otley, 1844), 1:38. Weekly journals from the period confirm Grant's statement.

2. Again, this is evident from the weekly journals. According to "Nouvelles," *RGMdP* 4/42 (15 October 1837): 449, the concert season was considered to begin on 1 November, but Henri Blanchard in "Préface des concerts de la saison," *RGMdP* 13/44 (1 November 1846): 348–49, evidently thought it newsworthy that the concert season was *already* beginning by that date.

3. Robert Burnand, *La Vie quotidienne en France en 1830* (Paris: Hachette, 1943), p. 105. Burnand remarked that balls were social events for persons of all ages, whether or not they enjoyed dancing.

4. Concerts which, following this schedule, would have fallen in Holy Week were usually postponed, thus adding a week to the ten-week season. Many series sold tickets, for some or all concerts, by subscription. Tickets for nonseries concerts were often available at the door but, at least early in the period, were distributed largely by music publishers.

5. This was evidently not, however, the usual practice. Berlioz noted in his *Mémoires* that the Théâtre-Italien "apparently . . . [did] not require the musicians to play after midnight." See *The Memoirs of Hector Berlioz,* trans. and ed. David Cairns (London: Victor Gollancz Ltd., 1969), p. 223.

6. This is mentioned on several occasions. See, for example, A. Botte, "Auditions musicales," *RGMdP* 26/19 (8 May 1859): 153. Low attendance at a concert of M. Langlois in (probably) early May 1829 was attributed to the lateness of the season; see S., "Concert de M. Langlois," *ReM* 5 (1829): 351–52. Edouard Fétis mentioned that the Gymnase Musical (see below, p. 68) fared less well in the summer because audiences preferred to be outdoors: "Nouvelles de Paris: Concerts d'été," *ReM* 15 (26 July 1835): 236. Six years earlier, Fétis had stated outright that June was too late in the year to give a concert: "Concert donné par mademoiselle Elise Vogl," *ReM* 5 (1829): 446.

7. E. F[étis], "Lettre à un étranger sur la musique à Paris," *ReM* 10 (1830–31): 266.

8. "Nouvelles de Paris," ibid., pp. 330–32.

9. F.-J. Fétis: "Variétés: de la nécessité des associations pour préserver la musique de sa décadence en France," *ReM* 11 (1831–32): 73.

10. "Nouvelles de Paris: Concerts," ibid., p. 96. The seemingly simplistic explanation for this blossoming was that artists had to make a living, so they began to perform again.

11. Siegfried Kracauer, *Orpheus in Paris: Offenbach and the Paris of His Time*. (New York: Alfred A. Knopf, 1938), pp. 8–9.

12. "Nouvelles de Paris: Concerts," *ReM* 12 (1832–33): 87.

13. Maurice Bourges, "Première semestre musical de la République," *RGMdP* 15/36 (3 September 1848): 271–72.

14. Barzun, *Berlioz,* 1:524.

15. Hector Berlioz, *Letters,* ed. Humphrey Searle (New York: Vienna House, 1973), p. 108. The letter is to J. W. Davison, music critic of *The Times*.

16. Henri Blanchard: "De la question artistique et musicale," *RGMdP* 15/22 (28 May 1848): 167–68.

17. Henri Blanchard, "Concert donné par M. Ekelheimer," *RGMdP* 15/24 (11 June 1848): 182–83.

18. Em. Mathieu de Monter, "Revue rétrospective: Janvier 1870–Octobre 1871," *RGMdP* 38/36 (1 October 1871): 270.

19. In 1842 alone, 30 concert locations were reported active.

20. F.-J. Fétis, "Sur le Concert Spirituel," *ReM* 1/8 (1827): 206.

21. The above descriptions are summarized from comments in "Gymnase Musical: Ouverture," *GMdP* 2/22 (31 May 1835): 183–85, and "Nouvelles de Paris: Concert du Gymnase Musical," *ReM* 15 (28 June 1835): 205. The anonymous author of the latter notice thought the interior decoration of the Gymnase only mediocre.

22. Barzun, *Berlioz,* 1:266. Barzun has stated that some contemporaries found the acoustics a "disgrace"; other contemporaries were less harsh.

23. Henri Blanchard: "Auditions musicales," *RGMdP* 19/7 (15 February 1852): 50.

24. Henri Blanchard: "Matinées et soirées musicales," *RGMdP* 26/18 (3 May 1857): 146.

25. Léon Kreutzer, "Matinée musicale de Jacques Franco-Mendès," *RGMdP* 28/19 (12 May 1861): 147.

26. Romain Rolland, *Musicians of Today,* trans. Mary Blaiklock, 4th ed. (New York: Henry Holt and Company, 1919), pp. 281–82.

27. Henri Blanchard, "Concerts de M. Panofka," *RGMdP* 4/47 (19 November 1837): 501–2.

28. F.-J. Fétis, "Nouvelles de Paris: Académie Royale de Musique," *ReM* 3 (1828): 248–55. This refers to the building on the rue Le Peletier, used by the Opéra from 1822 to 1873, thus during the entire period under study.

29. Hector Berlioz, "Société de l'Union Musicale," *RGMdP* 16/4 (28 January 1849): 26–28, and Maurice Bourges, "Société de Musique Classique," *RGMdP* 16/6 (11 February 1849), pp. 44–45.

30. Berlioz, "Société de l'Union Musicale," pp. 26–28.

31. Adam Carse, *The Orchestra from Beethoven to Berlioz* (Cambridge: W. Heffer & Sons, 1948), p. 21.

32. Antoine Elwart, *Histoire de la Société des Concerts du Conservatoire Impérial de Musique* (Paris: S. Castel, 1860), pp. 114–15.

33. Carse, *The Orchestra,* p. 100.

34. E. F[étis], "Inauguration de la salle Barthélemy," *RGMdP* 18/26 (29 June 1851): 212–13.

35. Elisabeth Bernard, "Jules Pasdeloup et les Concerts Populaires," *Revue de musicologie,* 57/2 (1971): 157.

36. D.-A.-D. Saint-Yves: "Concerts et auditions," *RGMdP* 31/4 (24 January 1864): 25.

37. "Nouvelles diverses," *RGMdP* 36/8 (21 February 1869): 65.

38. Elwart, *Conservatoire Imperial,* pp. 99–108.

39. A festival given at the Hippodrome in 1846 had an orchestra of 1800 to 2000. See P[aul]. S[mith]. [Edouard Monnais], "Hippodrome: Grand Festival donné par L'Association des Artistes-Musiciens," *RGMdP* 13/30 (26 July 1846): 233–34.

40. "Nouvelles de Paris," *ReM* 13 (1833): 54. The pianists who performed the Bach were Chopin, Liszt, and Hiller.

41. "Nouvelles," *RGMdP* 20/13 (27 March 1853): 111.

42. "Nouvelles diverses," *RGMdP* 36/47 (21 November 1869): 382.

43. In the program announcement the composer is listed as Mozart. According to Clément and Larousse, in *Dictionnaire des opéras,* revised by Arthur Pougin (Paris, 1905); repr. (New York: Da Capo Press, 1969), p. 905, *La Prise de Jéricho* is an operatic pastiche on Biblical themes with music primarily by Mozart, arranged by Lachnith and Kalkbrenner. This particular air may well have been by Mozart.

44. A program presented in 1870 included orchestrations of Mozart's Piano Quartet in G minor and Sonata for two pianos, the "Largo" of Beethoven's Piano Trio Op. 70,

No. 1, and one of Beethoven's three marches Op. 45 for piano four hands. See "Concerts et auditions musicales de la semaine," *RGMdP* 37/19 (8 May 1870): 148.

45. "Nouvelles de Paris," *ReM* 7 (1830): 266–68.

46. Franz Liszt, "De la situation des artistes," *GMdP* 2 (1835): 291. See also "Nouvelles de Paris," *ReM* 11 (1831–32): 13–14 and 387.

47. "Concert de M. Osborne," *ReM* 14 (1834): 94–95.

48. Henri Blanchard, "Auditions musicales," *RGMdP* 19/19 (9 May 1852): 148.

49. See "Nouvelles de Paris," *ReM* 11 (1831–32): 55–56; *ReM* 12 (1832–33): 335; and Henri Blanchard, "Matinées musicales," *RGMdP* 11/27 (7 July 1844): 229–30.

50. It is difficult to know the exact number of series that presented orchestral music because of the limited amount of information available on some organizations, particularly those which were announced but for which no actual concerts were reported. At least 45 societies definitely performed orchestral music; another 5 announced such plans but may never have performed; for a further 3 the repertory is not clear, although it seems likely that they played some orchestral works.

51. Harold Schonberg, *The Great Conductors* (New York: Simon and Schuster, 1967), p. 99, and Carse, *The Orchestra,* p. 17.

52. Cited in Schonberg, *The Great Conductors,* p. 99.

53. Richard Wagner, *On Conducting,* trans. Edward Dannreuther, 2nd ed. (London: W. Reeves, 1897), p. 15, cited by Carse, *The Orchestra,* pp. 94–95.

54. John Ella, *Musical Sketches* (London, 1878), cited by Carse, *The Orchestra,* pp. 97–98.

55. Quoted by Carse, *The Orchestra,* p. 372.

56. Ibid.

57. "L'action de la Société des Concerts s'est fait sentir non seulement en France, mais dans l'Europe entière; les plus grands artistes ont tenu à honneur d'y recevoir la consécration de leur talents: compositeurs, chanteurs, exécutants, tous ont sollicité l'avantage d'apporter leur contingent aux magnifiques programmes de ces concerts, qui, dès le premier, ont placé leur orchestre à la tête de tous les orchestres de l'Europe." Elwart, *Conservatoire Impérial,* p. 1.

58. F.-J. Fétis, loosely quoted by Elwart, *Conservatoire Impérial,* p. 1. Elwart did not give the original source.

59. "Die Gründung der Société des Concerts du Cons. (1828) und deren Auff. unter Habenecks Leitung bedeuten . . . den Beginn einer neuen Epoche, nicht nur in der Geschichte der ausübenden Kunst und der Beethovenpflege, sondern auch in der des mus. Geschmacks in Europa." Emile Haraszti, "Habeneck, François Antoine," *MGG* 5 (1956), col. 1191.

60. "Anton Franz Habenek [*sic*]," *Allgemeine musikalische Zeitung,* 47/28 (9 July 1845), col. 465.

61. Leo Schrade, *Beethoven in France* (New Haven: Yale University Press, 1942), p. 3. Schrade did not state his source, but it may have been Anton Schindler's *Beethoven in Paris* (Münster: Aschendorff'sche Buchhandlung, 1842). Schindler, after visiting

Paris in 1841, reported that Habeneck had told him: "Es sind eben 38 Jahre . . . als ich die ersten Quartette von Beethoven kennen lernte. . . . Bald darauf erhielten wir die 1ste und 2te Simphonie, die wir mit einem kleinen Orchester probirten."

A provable explanation has not been found for the source of Habeneck's early interest in Beethoven. Haraszti theorized that Antonín Reicha was the connecting link; this view seems reasonable. Reicha was in Bonn from 1788 to 1794, played in the same orchestra as Beethoven, and apparently knew him well. From 1799 to 1802, Reicha was in Paris, where he probably met Habeneck.

62. Constant Pierre listed programs for all student *exercices* from 1800 to 1824, in his *Le Conservatoire National de Musique et de Déclamation* (Paris: Imprimerie nationale, 1900), pp. 476–500. According to Pierre, the students had performed the following Beethoven symphonies by 1811:
C Major [No. 1]—22 February 1807
Unspecified—10 May 1807
C minor[!]—10 April 1808
Unspecified [probably No. 1 or 2]—25 March 1810
Unspecified (excerpt)—10 March 1811
E-flat Major [No. 3]—5 May 1811
Although Pierre undoubtedly believed that the performance on 10 April 1808 involved the Fifth Symphony, for he mentioned (p. 466) that the work was played "l'année qui suivit sa composition," Alexander Ringer has pointed out that contemporary announcements in the *Moniteur Universel* and the *Journal de Paris* read simply "Symphony en ut." See "A French Symphonist at the Time of Beethoven: Etienne Nicolas Méhul," *Musical Quarterly,* 37/4 (October 1951): 552. The premiere of the Fifth did not take place until the following December, in Vienna, and parts were not printed until 1809. Thus the work performed in April 1808 must have been the First Symphony. The unspecified symphony listed for 25 March 1810 was composed about 1801, according to a contemporary review in *Courrier de l'Europe et des spectacles* cited by Pierre (p. 466), and thus must have been either the First or Second.

Norman Demuth, in "Habeneck and 'La Société des Concerts'," *Music Survey,* 1/5 (1949): 134, claimed that Habeneck conducted the First in 1807, 1808, and 1810, and the Second and Third in 1811; he gave no source. Carse, *The Orchestra,* (p. 90), citing without author a work entitled *Le Conservatoire National de Musique et de Déclamation* (Paris, 1928), agreed that the First was performed in 1807 and the Second and Third in 1811. The anonymous author of "Nouvelles de Paris; sixième concert du Conservatoire," *ReM* 11 (1831–32), 84–86, wrote that Beethoven's first two symphonies were heard in Paris about 1808.

63. Elwart, *Conservatoire Impérial,* p. 61. Carse,*The Orchestra* (pp. 90-91), stated that the repertory of the Concerts Spirituels was too small and too often repeated, and that the stage (at the Opéra) was not large enough for this sort of concert.

64. Haraszti, "Habeneck" col. 1190–91. See also J.-G. Prod'homme, *Les Symphonies de Beethoven* (Paris: C. Delagrave, 1906), p. 123.

65. Hector Berlioz, *Mémoires,* trans. and ed. David Cairns as *The Memoirs of Hector Berlioz: Member of the French Institute* (London: Victor Gollancz, 1969), p. 105.

66. Elwart, quoted in Edward Bellasis, *Cherubini: Memorials Illustrative of His Life* (London: Burns and Oates, 1874), p. 279.

67. Ludwig Bischoff, "Cherubini," *Niederrheinische Musik Zeitung* 10/5 (1 February

1862): 35, trans. J. V. Bridgeman in *Musical World* 40/37 (13 September 1862): 588. F.-J. Fétis, in "Régénération de l'Ecole Royale de Musique: Société des Concerts," *ReM* 3(1828): 145–49, indicated (p. 145) that Cherubini supported the Société.

68. This statement, and the following information regarding rules, committees, etc. of the Conservatoire is based upon Elwart, *Conservatoire Impérial,* (pp. 62–67), who had access to archival material. When possible, the data have been checked against other sources.

69. Elwart, *Conservatoire Impérial,* pp. 66–67.

70. Ibid., pp. 67–82.

71. See, for example, Carse, *The Orchestra,* p. 474; J.-G. Prod'homme and E. de Crauzat, *Les Menus Plaisirs du roi* (Paris: Delagrave, 1929), pp. 119–41; Albert Vernaelde, "La Société des Concerts et les Grandes associations symphoniques," *Encyclopédie de la musique et Dictionnaire du Conservatoire,* ed. Albert Lavignac and Lionel de la Laurencie (Paris: Delagrave, 1920–31), Part 2, vol. 6 (1931), pp. 3707–8; Victor Blavette, "Théâtres et salles de concert," ibid., p. 3868; and *Musikgeschichte in Bildern,* vol. 4/2, "Konzert," ed. Heinrich W. Schwab (Leipzig: VEB Deutscher Verlag, 1971), p. 81. Illustrations of the hall after its redecoration in the mid-1860s appear in Arthur Dandelot, *La Société des Concerts du Conservatoire (1828–1923),* 3rd ed. (Paris: Delagrave, 1923), pp. 69 and 71.

72. H. F. Chorley: *Music and Manners in France and Germany,* 3 vols. (London: Longman, Orme, Brown, Green, and Longmans, 1841), 3:158.

73. Elwart, *Conservatoire Impérial,* pp. 99–108.

74. Schindler, *Beethoven in Paris,* p. 18.

75. Elwart, *Conservatoire Impérial,* p. 95.

76. Carse discussed the individual personnel of the Société in some detail in his chapter "Orchestras in France," *The Orchestra,* pp. 67–106.

77. All programs for the years 1860 to 1885 are listed in Edouard Deldevez, *La Société des Concerts: 1860 à 1885* (Paris: Firmin-Didot et Cie., 1887), pp. 73–195. Programs for the years 1828 to 1859 are listed in Elwart, *Conservatoire Impérial,* pp. 130–307.

78. These figures, compiled from the programs listed by Elwart and Deldevez, include all *concerts spirituels,* benefit concerts, and other extra concerts. The double programs performed from 1867 on are listed only once: on rare occasions when one work was changed on what would otherwise be a double program, both the new work and the replaced work are counted, but all repeated works are counted only once. This method of counting, although not perfect, seems to cause less distortion than counting all repeated works twice. The statistics are compiled from 440 programs.

79. For the purposes of these statistics, a major work is considered to be a work of substantial length, usually in more than one movement. Complete performances of symphonies, concertos, string quartets, etc. are included as major works, while overtures, fantasias, and single movements from larger works are not.

80. The only Schubert symphonies published before 1884 were the Ninth (in 1840) and the Unfinished (in 1866); see O. E. Deutsch, *Schubert: Thematic Catalogue of All His Works,* with Donald R. Wakeling (New York: W. W. Norton, 1951).

81. Nowhere do the original articles of the Société mention who selected the programs, though members voted on the admission of new works to the repertory. Berlioz (*Memoirs,* p. 469) implied that Habeneck and a committee arranged the programs. Much later, Albert Vernaelde wrote that the composition of programs was fixed by the Société's committee. See "La Société des Concerts et les Grandes associations symphoniques," *Encyclopédie de la musique et Dictionnaire du Conservatoire,* p. 3708.

82. These figures, compiled from the programs listed by Elwart, include benefit concerts, *concerts spirituels,* etc., and a few concerts conducted by Théophile Tilmant (the assistant conductor) during Habeneck's illnesses.

83. Most popular was the Fifth Symphony (40 performances); next came the Sixth (34), Seventh (33), Third (20), Second and Fourth (16), Ninth (12), Eighth (11), and First (4). Two symphonies led by Habeneck were not identified by number.

84. "Von welcher Wichtigkeit Habenek für deren Verbreitung überhaupt ist, wird uns deutlich genug werden, wenn wir auf Italien, die einstige Weige der Musik, sehen. Wer kennt dort Beethoven? Wer selbst die Mozart'schen grösseren Instrumentalstücke?" "Anton Franz Habenek [*sic*]," *AMZ* 47, col. 466.

85. Carse, *The Orchestra,* pp. 94–99 and 468.

86. The highlights of Girard's activities are mentioned in Pierre, *Conservatoire National,* p. 445 and p. 764.

87. The article in *Monde illustré,* 1861 (which I have not seen), is cited by Demuth, "Habeneck," p. 136. The thought, however, is substantiated many times in *RGMdP.*

88. Elwart, *Conservatoire Impérial,* pp. 114–15.

89. Habeneck and Berlioz battled frequently. (Berlioz related many amusing tales about Habeneck in his *Mémoires* and elsewhere.) Habeneck's positions as conductor of both the most important opera company and best orchestra in France made him a powerful figure in the musical world, yet he probably felt threatened by the younger Berlioz's new ideas, musical talent, and organizational abilities. (Berlioz succeeded in presenting a festival of his own works, conducted by himself, at the Opéra in 1840, in spite of Habeneck's attempt to thwart him.)

90. Hainl's successor, Edouard Deldevez, provided lengthy and ridiculous arguments in defense of the society's conservatism in *La Société des Concerts, 1860 à 1885.* Among his more interesting aruments are that 1) the society's first priority should be a high standard of performance, which is impossible to maintain when new works are performed; 2) that it is necessary to maintain the traditions established by Habeneck [though Habeneck was more open-minded than any of his successors]; 3) that "symphony" should be defined as "classical symphony," as written by Haydn and Mozart, and carried to the furthest possible limits by Beethoven. Any works more modern than Beethoven's, and particularly symphonies by Berlioz, are by definition not symphonies, and hence do not belong on the programs of a society created to perform symphonies. (These arguments are a summary of ideas presented on pp. 21–35, 39–40, 51–54, 273, 276, 279, 284–86).

91. "Nouvelles," *RGMdP* 17/44 (3 November 1850): 367. I have found no evidence to support contentions that this society was founded before November 1850. Edward Burlingame Hill, in his *Modern French Music* (Boston and New York: Houghton Mifflin Company, 1924), p. 21, suggested 1848 as the society's beginning, and the

articles "Paris" in both *Grove 5* (by Marie Louise Pereyra, J.-G. Prod'homme, Gustave Chouquet, and Fred Goldbeck) and *MGG* (by Guy Ferchault: "Paris: 19. Jahrhundert: Konzert," 10 (1962), col. 780), state 1849.

This society does not appear to have been related to a Parisian organization of the same name that presented a concert in 1839, or to a Société de Sainte-Cécile, active in 1847–48.

92. P. Smith [Monnais], "Revue de l'année 1850," *RGMdP* 18/1 (5 January 1851): 1–2.

93. "Nouvelles," *RGMdP* 18/8 (23 February 1851): 63.

94. *RGMdP* 17/44 (3 November 1850): 367.

95. Ibid.

96. Henri Blanchard, "Concert de la Société de Sainte-Cécile," *RGMdP* 17/48 (1 December 1850): 397–98.

97. Henri Blanchard, "Concerts," *RGMdP* 18/18 (3 [*sic*, = 4] May 1851): 139.

98. "Nouvelles," *RGMdP* 19/21 (23 May 1852): 174. The contest was won by Saint-Saëns, then 17, the following autumn.

99. "Nouvelles," *RGMdP* 21/36 (3 September 1854): 290; *RGMdP* 21/48 (26 November 1854): 387.

100. *RGMdP* 21/26 (25 June 1854): 210.

101. Dandelot, *La Société dés Concerts,* p. 216.

102. Hill, *Modern French Music,* p. 21. Saint-Saëns had written that Jules Pasdeloup "had plenty of money" and used it to draw the poorly paid musicians of the Société Sainte-Cécile into his Société des Jeunes-Artistes, thereby causing the demise of the former. (See Saint-Saëns, *Musical Memories,* trans. Edwin Gile Rich, (Boston: Small, Maynard & Company, 1919), p. 199.) But this explanation is not entirely satisfactory, not only because the Société Sainte-Cécile continued for three seasons after the foundation of the Jeunes-Artistes, but also because most members of the Jeunes-Artistes were students.

103. Henri Blanchard, "Concerts," *RGMdP* 22/15 (15 April 1855): 114–15.

104. "Nouvelles," *RGMdP* 22/24 (17 June 1855): 190.

105. *RGMdP* 31/51 (18 December 1864): 406.

106. *RGMdP* 32/3 (15 January 1865): 22.

107. "Concerts annoncés," *RGMdP* 33/6 (11 February 1866): 48.

108. Henri Blanchard, "Auditions musicales," *RGMdP* 21/6 (5 February 1854): 42.

109. Henri Blanchard, "Société Sainte-Cécile," *RGMdP* 19/51 (19 December 1852): 467.

110. "Nouvelles," *RGMdP* 19/21 (23 May 1852): 174.

111. This figure includes preseason and postseason concerts, and the final few concerts in the Jardin d'hiver, May and June 1855.

112. At the concert of 12 February 1854, Weber's *Preciosa* was performed in its entirety. Henri Blanchard, "Auditions musicales," *RGMdP* 21/8 (19 February 1854): 61.

113. Excerpts of Beethoven's Octet for winds were heard twice, and a "Minuet-Allegro" from a Mendelssohn String Quartet, arranged for string orchestra, was performed once.

114. Carse (*The Orchestra,* p. 101) pointed this out. The performance took place 23 November 1851; the work is listed as the Symphony in C ("Nouvelles," *RGMdP* 18/47, 23 November 1851, p. 383). This is presumably Schubert's Ninth, as the Sixth had not yet been published.

115. Léon Kreutzer: "Société des Concerts et Société Sainte-Cécile", *RGMdP* 20/13 (27 March 1853): 106-7.

116. Elwart, in his *Histoire des Concerts Populaires de musique classique* (Paris: Librairie Castel, 1864), p. 17, Dandelot (*La Société des Concerts,* p. 217), and many later references maintained that the society was founded in 1851, and that it presented its first concert on 20 February that year. The founding was announced, however, on 13 February 1853 ("Nouvelles," *RGMdP* 20/7, p. 54), and the inaugural concert was mentioned one week later. Elisabeth Bernard, in her "Jules Pasdeloup et les Concerts Populaires," *Revue de musicologie,* 57/2 (1971): 154, said that the statutes date from December 1852; she gave no source, but has done archival work on the subject.

117. Elwart (*Histoire des Concerts Populaires,* p. 15) claimed that Pasdeloup's score was rejected in 1850, and that Pasdeloup founded the Jeunes-Artistes a few months later; the history may be true, despite the chronological inaccuracy.

118. "Nouvelles," *RGMdP* 20/7 (13 February 1853): 54.

119. Bernard, "Jules Pasdeloup," p. 155.

120. Ibid.

121. P. Scudo, ed. *L'Année musicale* (Paris, 1860–62), 3 (1862): 164.

122. Bernard, "Jules Pasdeloup" pp. 155–56. Financial aid began in 1856 when Auber, director of the Conservatoire, having decided that the Jeunes-Artistes provided valuable experiences for Conservatoire students, approved association with the society, which then became the Société des Jeunes-Artistes du Conservatoire Impérial de Musique. A newly established governing committee included several senior faculty members of the Conservatoire.

123. Albert de Lasalle and E. Thoinan [A. E. Roquet], *La Musique à Paris* (Paris: Morizot, 1863), p. 184.

124. Dandelot, *La Société des Concerts,* p. 217, and various reviews in *RGMdP.*

125. I have not been able to examine single programs in the 1852–53, 1858–59, and 1860–61 seasons. I see no reason to believe that the addition of the three missing programs would alter knowledge of the Société's repertory dramatically.

126. "Nouvelles," *RGMdP* 24/1 (4 January 1857): 7.

127. P. Smith [Monnais], "Société des Jeunes-Artistes," *RGMdP* 25/10 (17 March 1858): 73. Oddly, Monnais did not mention the symphonies of Gounod (often performed by the Jeunes-Artistes).

128. "Concerts populaires de musique classique," *RGMdP* 28/41 (13 October 1861): 326.

129. Bernard, "Jules Pasdeloup" pp. 150–78.

130. Ibid., pp. 157–69.

131. "Concerts populaires de musique classique," p. 326.

132. Bernard, "Jules Pasdeloup," p. 150.

133. Adolphe Botte, "Concerts populaires de musique classique," *RGMdP* 28/46 (17 November 1861): 361–62.

134. P. Smith [Monnais], "Concerts populaires de musique classique," *RGMdP* 28/44 (3 November 1861): 346.

135. Bernard, "Jules Pasdeloup," p. 157.

136. "Concerts populaires de musique classique," *RGMdP* 28/41 (13 October 1861): 326; Elwart, *Histoire des Concerts Populaires,* pp. 23–26. Bernard (p. 158) stated that there were 110 members, but listed the same complement of strings (76) and 25 others, giving a total of 101; too, she apparently used Elwart as her source. Probably "110" is a typographical error, as it is an easy transposition from "101."

137. Elwart, *Histoire des Concerts Populaires,* p. 27.

138. Ibid.

139. "Nouvelles diverses," *RGMdP* 34/40 (6 October 1867): 322.

140. Bernard, "Jules Pasdeloup," p. 158.

141. "Nouvelles," *RGMdP* 28/42 (20 October 1861): 333; Elwart, *Histoire des Concerts Populaires*, pp. 29–30.

142. Cited in Bernard, "Jules Pasdeloup," p. 151.

143. P. Smith [Monnais]: "Concerts populaires de musique classique," p. 346.

144. Botte, "Concerts populaires de musique classique," pp. 361–62

145. "Nouvelles," *RGMdP* 28/45 (10 November 1861): 358.

146. Arthur Hervey, *French Music in the XIXth Century* (London: Grant Richards, 1903), p. 177.

147. Adolphe Jullien, *Musique* (Paris: Libraire de l'Art, 1896), cited in Bernard, "Jules Pasdeloup," p. 165.

148. Bernard, "Jules Pasdeloup," p. 159.

149. Ibid., pp. 161–62.

150. Ibid., p. 166.

151. Ibid., pp. 166–67, citing Mina Curtiss, *Bizet* (Paris: La Palatine, 1961), p. 199 for quotations of Bizet and Reyer, and "Wagner à Schuré: Correspondance," *Revue de musicologie,* 54/2 (1968): 206.

152. C[harles]. B[annelier]., "Concerts populaires de musique classique," *RGMdP* 36/43 (24 October 1869): 349, noted that in the Scherzo of Beethoven's Fifth Symphony, Pasdeloup doubled the basses by the cellos, thus abusing the original orchestration in the same way that Habeneck had.

153. Bernard, "Jules Pasdeloup," p. 167.

154. Dandelot, *La Société des Concerts,* p. 219.

155. Nearly all programs are printed singly in *RGMdP.* I am aware of only one missing program, in 1865; possibly there are a very few others missing other years. Programs from the first concert to those of December 1863 appear in Elwart, *Histoire des Concerts Populaires,* pp. 29–78.

156. Bernard, "Jules Pasdeloup," p. 172.

157. "Nouvelles," *RGMdP* 29/8 (23 February 1862): 65.

158. Hill, *Modern French Music,* p. 21.

159. Hervey, *French Music,* p. 165.

160. Georges Favre, *Paul Dukas: Sa Vie—son oeuvre* (Paris: La Colombe, 1948), p. 8.

161. Dandelot, *La Société des Concerts,* p. 219.

162. Immediately after the Franco-Prussian War, Wagner was, for understandable reasons, dropped from the repertory.

163. "Nouvelles diverses," *RGMdP* 35/50 (13 December 1868): 397.

164. It is stated in the article "Alard (Delphin)," in *FétisB* Supplement, that 1872 was the last season of the Société.

165. Martin Cooper, *French Music from the Death of Berlioz to the Death of Fauré* (London: Oxford University Press, 1951), p. 10.

166. "Nouvelles," *RGMdP* 19/47 (21 November 1852): 399. Many announcements in later issues of *RGMdP* suggest that the series began in 1847.

167. "Nouvelles," *RGMdP* 16/51 (23 December 1849): 404.

168. An obituary for Escoffier, "dit Casimir Ney," appearing under "Nouvelles diverses," *RGMdP* 44/6 (11 February 1877): 47, is the only record I have discovered of Casimir Ney's true identity.

169. "Nouvelles," *RGMdP* 14/4 (24 January 1847), p. 35; no. 6 (7 February), p. 51.

170. Maurice Bourges, "Première matinée de musique instrumentale de chambre," *RGMdP* 14/7 (14 February): 57–58.

171. Henri Blanchard, "Auditions musicales," *RGMdP* 17/8 (24 February 1850): 66–67.

172. P. Scudo, ed., *L'Année musicale* (Paris, 1860–62), 2 (1861): 161, and 1 (1860): 185.

173. Botte, "Auditions musicales," *RGMdP* 29/4 (26 January 1862): 29.

174. Blanchard "Appendice aux concerts de la saison," *RGMdP* 14/21 (23 May 1847): 170–72.

175. M. Cooper, *French Music,* p. 10; Hill, *Modern French Music,* p. 7.

176. "Nouvelles," *RGMdP* 25/2 (10 January 1858): 14, noted that the society was beginning its eighth season; 26/2 (9 January 1859): 13, announced the ninth season.

177. Blanchard, "Auditions musicales," *RGMdP* 19/9; p. 67. I have found no record of public concerts by Maurin and Chevillard in 1851, though Maurin gave a solo concert that spring; see Blanchard, "Concerts," *RGMdP* 18/11 (16 March 1851): 85. There

seems to be no reason to consider the suggestion of Gustave Ferrari, in "Chevillard, (Paul Alexandre) Camille," *Grove 2–5* (a suggestion accepted, incidentally, in the article on Chevillard in *Grove 6*), that the society was established in 1835, when Maurin would have been only 13.

178. Blanchard, "Auditions musicales," *RGMdP* 19/48 (28 November 1852): 405, and ibid., 20/1 (2 January 1853): 4–5.

179. Blanchard, "Auditions musicales," *RGMdP* 20/1 (2 January 1853); 4–5.

180. Blanchard, "Auditions musicales," *RGMdP* 21/6 (5 February 1854): 41.

181. "Nouvelles," *RGMdP* 22/43 (28 October 1855): 339, and 23/2 (13 January 1856): 14.

182. "Nouvelles diverses," *RGMdP* 38/49 (31 December 1871): 378.

183. It scheduled six per season from 1852 through 1867 (thus 96) and four per season, 1868 to 1870 (thus 12), for a total of 108. Possibly it played a few extra concerts.

184. "Concerts et auditions musicales de la semaine," *RGMdP* 35/6 (9 February 1868): 46.

185. Blanchard, "Concerts–Auditions musicales," *RGMdP* 23/2 (13 January 1856): 11.

186. Mendelssohn's chamber works had received only a few performances by the Alard-Franchomme and Maurin-Chevillard quartets before 1856.

187. The concert was scheduled for late January ("Nouvelles," *RGMdP* 23/2 (13 January 1856): 14), and had not taken place by the publication of *RGMdP* no. 4, of 27 January. The only date supplied for a concert by the Société des Quatuors de Mendelssohn in 1856 was that of the fourth concert, Wednesday, 12 March; see Blanchard, "Concerts," *RGMdP* 23/11 (16 March): 85. Counting backwards three two-week intervals (the regular schedule later adopted by the group) yields Wednesday, 30 January.

188. Unfortunately, I do not know which edition (and therefore which numbering system) the group used. This may be the String Quartet K. 590 in F Major, which was No. 9 in the edition of Breitkopf & Härtel.

189. The last announcement was "Concerts et auditions musicales annoncés", *RGMdP* 34/10 (10 March 1867): 79. The article "Armingaud (Jules)" in *FétisB* Supplement and G. Ferrari's article "Armingaud, Jules" in *Grove 2–5* reported that the society was transformed, with the addition of wind instruments, into the Société Classique. I have no record of such a transformation, or of a society by that name before the Franco-Prussian War.

190. Botte, "Auditions musicals," *RGMdP* 28/14 (7 April 1861): 106.

191. P. Scudo, ed. *L'Année musicale,* 3 (1862): 167.

192. "Concerts et auditions musicales," *RGMdP* 34/9 (3 March 1867): 70.

193. This is one of the few Parisian concert societies of which Beethoven was not the most popular composer.

194. "Nouvelles," *RGMdP* 25/1 (3 January 1858): 6.

195. "Nouvelles," *RGMdP* 30/45 (8 November 1863): 358.

196. *RGMdP* 27/1 (1 January 1860): 6.

197. This work is probably K. 589, published by J. André (Offenbach) and Boyer, Imbault, and Sieber (all Parisian publishers) as Op. 18 No. 2.

198. Botte, "Auditions musicales," *RGMdP* 27/9 (26 February 1860): 70.

199. "Nouvelles," *RGMdP* 30/45 (8 November 1863): 358.

200. As just over half of the performances are known, I cannot give a complete survey of the repertory. For known performances, the statistics are as follows: Beethoven (34 performances), Mozart (19), Haydn (18), Mendelssohn (16), and Boccherini (8). No other composer was heard more than five times.

201. "Concerts et auditions musicales de la semaine," *RGMdP* 36/10 (7 March 1869): 82; "Concerts et auditions musicales annoncés," *RGMdP* 36/15 (11 April 1869): 127; "Concerts et auditions musicales de la semaine," *RGMdP* 37/7 (13 February 1870): 53.

202. "Nouvelles," *RGMdP* 29/2 (12 January 1862): 14; no. 8 (23 February): 66. The latter announcement refers to a violin sonata dating from 1754. There were three later performances of Porpora violin sonatas. Twelve violin sonatas by Porpora, published in Vienna in 1754, are listed in *RISM,* A/I/7, p. 11.

203. "Concerts et auditions musicales de la semaine," *RGMdP* 37/17 (24 April 1870): 133. This work is perhaps one of Handel's *Concerti Grossi,* Op. 6.

204. "Nouvelles diverses," *RGMdP* 38/48 (24 December 1871): 370.

205. Blanchard, in "Matinées musicales de M. Gouffé," *RGMdP* 18/22 (1 June 1851): 171–72, reported that the *matinées* had taken place for 15 years; thus they would have started in 1836 or 1837. In 1858, however, Blanchard stated that the *séances* were commencing their 21st season, thereby indicating a beginning in spring 1838; see "Concerts et auditions musicales," *RGMdP* 25/14 (4 April 1858): 111. An announcement in December 1871 ("Nouvelles diverses," *RGMdP* 38/47 (17 December 1871): 363) related that the *séances* had begun for the 34th season one month earlier—thus a beginning about 1838 (possibly earlier if no *séances* were held some years) is indicated. The article "Gouffé (Achille)" in *FétisB* Supplement, stated that Gouffé sponsored *séances* for 40 years, which would mean beginning no later than 1835, as Gouffé died in 1874. Charles Bannelier, in "Musique de chambre: M. Gouffé," *RGMdP* 33/4 (28 January 1866): 27, wrote that the concerts had taken place for 30 years, hence, since 1836.

206. "Nouvelles," *RGMdP* 14/20 (16 May 1847): 167.

207. Blanchard: "Les Trois derniers," *RGMdP* 16/41 (14 October 1849): 325.

208. Blanchard, "Matinées musicales de M. Gouffé," *RGMdP* 18/22 (1 June 1851): 171; Blanchard: "Société Libre des Beaux Arts," *RGMdP* 19/24 (13 June 1852): 196; "Nouvelles," *RGMdP* 20/50 (11 December 1853): 432.

209. Blanchard, "Auditions musicales," *RGMdP* 21/25 (18 June 1854): 200.

210. Blanchard, "Les Trois derniers," p. 325; Blanchard, "Auditions musicales," *RGMdP* 21/50 (10 December 1854): 398; "Nouvelles," *RGMdP* 25/48 (28 November 1858): 398; 31/50 (11 December 1864): 397.

211. Blanchard, "Auditions musicales," *RGMdP* 23/43 (26 October 1856): 344.

212. Botte, in "Auditions musicales," *RGMdP* 27/17 (22 April 1860): 149, said, "Cette semaine l'audition était publique"; "Concerts et auditions musicales de la semaine,"

RGMdP 35/12 (22 March 1868): 93, referred to Gouffé's concert as the "séance annuelle publique."

213. C[harles]. B[annelier]., "Musique de chambre: M. Gouffé," *RGMdP* 33/4 (28 January 1866): 27–28.

214. Blanchard, "Des concerts, des matinées et soirées musicales," *RGMdP* 22/50 (16 December 1855): 392.

215. Blanchard, "Société Libre des Beaux Arts," *RGMdP* 19/24 (13 June 1852): 196: "Haydn, Mozart et Beethoven sont toujours là sur le pupitre."

216. Blanchard, "Du quatuor instrumental et du quatuor vocal," *RGMdP* 19/45 (7 November 1852): 379.

217. This does not necessarily mean that Blanc was performed more than any other composer at the Gouffé *séances*; far too few programs are known to make such a claim. Others whose works appeared several times on known programs include Onslow, Beethoven, Mozart, and Walckiers.

218. Bannelier, "Musique de chambre," pp. 27–28, praised Gouffé for his efforts on behalf of both old and new chamber music.

219. Maurice Cristal, in "Auditions et concerts," *RGMdP* 32/12 (19 March 1865): 89, wrote that the annual concerts had taken place for 28 years. I have found no pertinent announcements or reviews before 1851.

220. Blanchard: "Quatre soirées de musique classique instrumentale," *RGMdP,* 22/4 (28 January 1855): 26–27.

221. In the review (ibid.), this is labelled No. 3, from Op. 10. It may be Op. 10 No. 3, but the slow movement of this sonata is usually marked "Largo."

222. Ibid.

223. "Nouvelles," *RGMdP* 27/5 (29 January 1860): 38; P. Scudo, ed., *L'Année musicale* 2 (1861): 165.

224. "Nouvelles," *RGMdP* 29/13 (30 March 1862): 110.

225. "Nouvelles," *RGMdP* 30/48 (29 November 1863): 381; "Nouvelles diverses," *RGMdP* 33/44 (4 November 1866): 350.

226. Y., "Auditions et concerts," *RGMdP* 31/16 (17 April 1864): 124.

227. "Nouvelles," *RGMdP* 38/41 (5 November 1871): 315.

228. See, for example, "Nouvelles diverses," *RGMdP* 34/47 (24 November 1867): 378; 36/1 (3 January 1869): 7; 36/46 (14 November): 374.

229. I have records of 25 *séances* before they took place in Lebouc's home (autumn 1863). Thereafter there were as many as 12 a season for seven seasons (autumn 1863 to spring 1870), thus 84 *matinées* for a total of 109. It is likely that there were some concerts before 1863 of which I am unaware, but also possible that in some years after 1863 fewer than 12 *matinées* were presented.

230. The first 25 known concerts were well reported in *RGMdP,* but programs of the *matinées chez* Lebouc tended to be summarized, when mentioned at all.

231. Because so many of the instrumental works performed at these *séances* were light, it seems impractical to list all known performances; thus only major works appear here.

232. "Concerts et auditions musicales de la semaine," *RGMdP* 35/4 (26 January 1868): 29.

233. Additional details and documentation may be found in Appendix A, in which the series are arranged alphabetically.

234. Elwart, *Conservatoire Impérial,* p. 55, and Georges Servières, "La Symphonie en France au XIXe siècle (avant 1870)," *Ménestrel* 85/39 (28 September 1923): 397–400.

235. "Soirées de M. Baillot," *ReM* 13 (1833): 7.

236. Blanchard, in "Auditions musicales," *RGMdP* 20/10 (6 March 1853): 81, stated that the society had been active for a quarter century. It is not known when the society began to sponsor concerts.

237. "Nouvelles de Paris," *ReM* 7 (1830): 53.

238. Barzun, *Berlioz and the Romantic Century* 1:263 n. 18.

239. This organization is not to be confused with the Gymnase Musical that performed one concert at the Hôtel de Ville in 1831.

240. "Prospectus: Gymnase Musical," *ReM* 14 (14 December 1834): 391–92.

241. The original of this quotation, "dites avec une verve, un éclat, un entraînement, qui rapellent les fêtes musicales du Conservatoire," appeared in *Ménestrel* in 1835. It is cited, without further bibliographic details, in J.-G. Prod'homme, "Le Gymnase musical," *Revue de musicologie* 11/23 (August 1927): 152. Barzun, *Berlioz and the Romantic Century* 1:266, however, has mentioned a concert in which the playing was reportedly "a disgrace."

242. Edouard Fétis, "Gymnase Musical: Concert de la famille Grassll," *ReM* 15 (12 July 1835): 221–23.

243. "Nouvelles," *GMdP* 2/41 (11 October 1835): 335. The more elaborate original is "noms . . . à chaque instant dans toutes les bouches, tandis que . . . leurs oeuvres admirables ne venaient presque jamais charmer nos oreilles."

244. William Weber, *Music and the Middle Class: the Social Structure of Concert Life in London, Paris, and Vienna* (London: Croom Helm, 1975), p. 100, and Carse, *The Orchestra,* p. 100. The article "Valentino (Henri-Justin-Joseph)" in *FétisB* Supplement, however, states that the cost was two francs.

245. Dandelot, *La Société des Concerts,* p. 216.

246. This is evident from an examination of the programs, but is mentioned specifically in "Nouvelles," *RGMdP* 6/58 (10 November 1839): 463.

247. Elwart, *Conservatoire Impérial p. 57: "d'une façon digne d'eux."*

248. Carse, *The Orchestra,* p. 100, cited Schindler without providing bibliographic details; the source is almost certainly Schindler's *Beethoven in Paris.*

249. It is unclear whether the reports of large crowds at this series were representative, or appeared only because sizable crowds were unusual, but as late as December

1839, *RGMdP* reported good attendance nightly ("Nouvelles," 6/68 (15 December): 543). The greater popularity of the dance orchestras is mentioned in "Nouvelles," *RGMdP* 5/22 (3 June 1838): 232.

250. "Valentino (Henri-Justin-Joseph)", *FétisB* Supplement.

251. "Nouvelles," *RGMdP* 8/30 (25 April 1841): 241, and Dandelot, *La Société des Concerts*, p. 216.

252. See especially A. Morel, "De l'utilité des sociétés d'amateurs: Cercle Musical," *RGMdP* 7/43 (5 July 1840): 363–65. An announcement in 1846, "Nouvelles," *RGMdP* 13/12 (22 March): 94, noted that the concerts cost five francs.

253. "Cercle Musical," *ReM* 14 (30 November 1834): 379–80.

254. E. Fétis, "Nouvelles de Paris: Société musicale: Troisième concert," *ReM* 15 (1 February 1835): 37–38, and "Concerts de la salle Chantereine," *GMdP* 2/13 (29 March 1835): 107.

255. "Nouvelles," *RGMdP* 5/45 bis (15 November 1838): 463.

256. At the third of these concerts, the order of the program was changed, reversing piano trios by Beethoven and Pixis, though no announcement was made; the uninformed audience later praised the Pixis (thinking it was Beethoven) and criticized the real Beethoven. See H. Berlioz, "Concerts: Troisième soirée de MM. Liszt, Urhan et Batta," *RGMdP* 4/8 (19 February 1837): 63–64.

257. "Musique de chambre: Soirées de quatuors et quintetti," *RGMdP* 5/31 (5 August 1838): 310.

258. Brigitte François-Sappey, "La Vie musicale à Paris à travers les Mémoires d'Eugène Sauzay (1809–1901)" *Revue de musicologie* 60/1-2 (1974): 176–77.

259. Chorley, *Music and Manners* 1:71n.

260. It is not clear whether this was an orchestra in the strict sense of the word or, as the society's name suggests, a symphonic band.

261. "Nouvelles," *RGMdP* 7/39 (27 June 1841): 322.

262. Barzun, *Berlioz and the Romantic Century* 1:438.

263. Joël-Marie Fauquet, "Notes et documents: Hector Berlioz et l'Association des Artistes Musiciens," *Revue de musicologie* 67/2 (1981): 211. Fauquet notes that the Association still exists.

264. Barzun, *Berlioz and the Romantic Century* 1:440.

265. "Nouvelles," *RGMdP* 10/36 (3 September 1843): 307, and Fauquet, "Berlioz et l'Association," pp. 214–15.

266. P. S[mith]. [Monnais], "Hippodrome: Grand festival donné par L'Association des Artistes-Musiciens," *RGMdP* 13/30 (26 July 1846): 233–34.

267. [Emile Réty], "Association des Artistes Musiciens: Assemblée générale," *RGMdP* 22/19 (7 May 1865): 148.

268. "Nouvelles," *RGMdP* 14/47 (21 November 1847): 383.

269. I have found no records of concerts from 1858 through 1860. In the late 1860s Dancla gave annual concerts.

270. François-Sappey, "La Vie musicale," p. 180.

271. "Nouvelles," *RGMdP* 17/45 (10 November 1850): 375.

272. Léon Kreutzer, "Grande Société Philharmonique de Paris," *RGMdP* 17/4 (27 January 1850): 28.

273. "Nouvelles," *RGMdP* 18/37 (14 September 1851): 304; 18/44 (2 November 1851): 359; Blanchard, "Société des Musiciens Exécutants", *RGMdP* 18/46 (16 November 1851): 371–72.

274. Blanchard, "Auditions musicales," *RGMdP* 19/7 (7 February 1852): 50.

275. "Nouvelles," *RGMdP* 19/14 (4 April 1852): 112; Blanchard, "Auditions musicales," *RGMdP* 19/16 (18 April 1852): 123; "Nouvelles," *RGMdP* 19/17 (25 April 1852):135.

276. Blanchard, "Concerts et auditions musicales," *RGMdP* 24/9 (1 March 1857): 66.

277. P. Smith [Monnais], "Athénée: Séance d'ouverture, mercredi 21 novembre," *RGMdP* 33/47 (25 November 1866): 373.

278. "Nouvelles," *RGMdP* 33/37 (16 September 1866): 294. As musical activities of the Athénée were reviewed by the week (rather than by individual concert), it is impossible to tell whether this announced schedule was followed; there is no reason to believe it was not.

279. Em. Mathieu de Monter, "Revue de l'année 1869," *RGMdP* 37/1 (2 January 1870): 1–2.

280. "Nouvelles diverses," *RGMdP* 36/43 (24 October 1869): 350.

281. See especially "Nouvelles," *RGMdP* 32 (1865), no. 15 (9 April): 117, no. 31 (30 July): 250, and no. 52 (24 December): 422.

282. "Nouvelles," *RGMdP* 32/10 (5 March 1865): 78.

283. "Concerts et auditions de la semaine," *RGMdP* 36/11 and 12 (14 and 21 March 1869): 92–93 and 101.

284. The brothers Müller, Bernhard, Karl, Hugo, and Wilhelm, were the second quartet of Müller brothers. Their father, Karl Friedrich Müller, had, with *his* brothers, Theodor Heinrich Gustav, August Theodor, and Franz Ferdinand Georg, also formed a string quartet. This information comes from the articles "Muller (Les Frères)" in *FétisB,* and "Müller, Gebrüder I, II", in Hermann Mendel, *Musikalisches Conversations-Lexikon* (Berlin: L. Heimann, 1870–83), 7 (1877): 193f.

285. A "first" *séance* was mentioned in 1862, but it is not clear whether this was the first of a series of *séances* presented that year or the first annual concert. See A. Botte, "Auditions musicales," *RGMdP* 29/10 (9 March 1862): 79–80.

286. "Concerts et auditions musicales de la semaine," *RGMdP* 36/22 (30 May 1869): 182.

287. François-Sappey, "La Vie musicale," pp. 206–7.

288. "Le but que se propose la Société, disaient-ils, est de favoriser la production et la vulgarisation de toutes les oeuvres musicales sérieuses, éditées ou non, des compos-

iteurs français, d'encourager et de mettre en lumière, autant que cela sera en son pouvoir, toutes les tentatives musicales, de quelque forme qu'elles soient, à la condition qu'elles laissent voir, de la part de l'auteur, des aspirations élevées et artistiques. . . . C'est fraternellement, avec l'oubli absolu de soi-même, avec l'intention bien arrêtée de s'entr'aider de tout leur pouvoir, que les sociétaires concourront, chacun dans la sphère de son action, aux études et auditions des oeuvres qu'ils seront appelés à choisir et à interpréter." Romain Rolland, *Musiciens d'aujourd'hui,* 19th ed. (Paris: Libraire Hachette, 1949), p. 231.

289. Em. Mathieu de Monter, "L'Esprit d'initiative et le principe d'association dans le mouvement musical français actuel: Société Nationale de Musique," *RGMdP* 39/5 (4 February 1872): 36.

290. Henri Duparc, "Souvenirs de la Société Nationale," *Revue musicale, Société Internationale de Musique,* 8/12 (December 1912): 4.

291. Ursula Eckart-Bäcker, *Frankreichs Musik zwischen Romantik und Moderne: Die Zeit im Spiegel der Kritik* (Regensburg: Gustav Bosse Verlag, 1965), p. 182, citing Arthur Pougin, "La Société Nationale de Musique et le mouvement actuel," *Ménestrel,* 40/25 (1873–74): 197–98.

292. Duparc, "Sociéte Nationale," p. 4, and Eckart-Bäcker, *Frankreichs Musik,* citing Pougin, "Société Nationale" p. 182.

293. Duparc, "Société Nationale," p. 4.

294. "Nouvelles diverses," *RGMdP* 38/49 (31 December 1871): 378.

295. James Harding, *Saint-Saëns and His Circle* (London: Chapman & Hall, 1965), p. 120.

296. Mathieu de Monter, "Société Nationale," pp. 35–36.

297. Duparc, "Société Nationale," p. 5.

298. Rolland, *Musiciens d'aujourd'hui* (Paris: Hachette et Cie, 1908), trans. by Mary Blaiklock as *Musicians of Today,* 4th ed. (New York: Henry Holt and Company, 1919), p. 267.

299. Eckart-Bäcker, *Frankreichs Musik,* p. 183.

300. Duparc, "Société Nationale," p. 6; Rolland, *Musicians of Today,* p. 269; Paul Landormy, *La Musique française de Franck à Debussy,* 5th ed. (Paris: Gallimard, 1943), p. 8.

Chapter 3

1. William Weber, *Music and the Middle Class: the Social Structure of Concert Life in London, Paris, and Vienna* (London: Croom Helm, 1975), p. 73.

2. Ibid., p. 31.

3. Ibid., p. 18.

4. S. Kracauer, *Orpheus in Paris: Offenbach and the Paris of His Time* (New York: Alfred A. Knopf, 1938), p. 47. Kracauer attributed this quotation to Flotow's "memoirs," by which he may have meant *Friedrich von Flotows Leben; von seiner Witwe* (Leipzig, 1892)—the only book on Flotow in his bibliography—or Flotow's "Erin-

nerungen aus meinem Leben," in *Vor den Coulissen,* ed. by Josef Lewinsky, 2 vols. (Berlin: A. Hoffman, 1881–82), vol. 2.

5. "Elysée National," *RGMdP* 15/39 (24 September 1848): 298.

6. This became clear from reading descriptions of *salons,* and is supported by Robert Burnand, who wrote that *salons* were highly variable because they were for invited guests only; See *La Vie quotidienne en France en 1830* (Paris: Hachette, 1943), p. 101.

7. James Grant, *Paris and Its People,* 2 vols. (London: Saunders & Otley, 1844), 2:41–42.

8. Frances Trollope, *Paris and the Parisians in 1835,* 2 vols. (London: Richard Bentley, 1836), 1:35.

9. Burnand, *Vie quotidienne,* pp. 103–4.

10. Kracauer, *Orpheus in Paris,* p. 45, and Weber, *Music and the Middle Class,* p. 33.

11. Kracauer, *Orpheus in Paris,* p. 47.

12. "Nouvelles," *RGMdP* 5/8 (25 February 1838): 94, and 17/4 (27 January 1850): 32.

13. Weber, *Music and the Middle Class,* p. 31; Weber cited an article in *Theaterzeitung* (probably the *Allgemeine Theaterzeitung* of Vienna), 16 April 1846, p. 364.

14. F.-J. Fétis, "Nouvelles de Paris: Ecole Royale de Musique: Société des Concerts," *ReM* 4 (1828–29): 516.

15. François Stoepel, "La Musique en France, (1835)," *GMdP,* 2/39 (27 September 1835): 313–17.

16. Weber, *Music and the Middle Class,* p. 32. Kracauer has also implied that little attention was paid to music at most *salons;* see his chapter on *salons* in *Orpheus in Paris,* pp. 44–59.

17. "Nouvelles de Paris: Concert du Gymnase Musical," *ReM* 15 (28 June 1835): 205.

18. Franz Liszt, "De la situation des artistes," *GMdP,* 2 (1835), p. 291.

19. Ernest Legouvé, *Sixty Years of Recollections* trans. with notes by Albert D. Vandam, 2 vols. (London: Eden, Remington & Co., 1893), 2:220–21.

20. Hippolyte Taine, *Notes on Paris,* trans. with notes by John Austin Stevens (New York: Henry Holt and Company, 1875), p. 57.

21. "Nouvelles de Paris: Soirée musicale," *ReM* 11 (1831–32): 329. Ironically, the particular program being reviewed comprised only light music.

22. "Nouvelles," *RGMdP* 8/10 (4 February 1841): 79.

23. Weber, *Music and the Middle Class,* p. 49; Mme. la comtesse de Bassanville, *Les Salons d'autrefois: Souvenirs intimes,* 4 vols. (Paris: P. Brunet, 1862–66), 4:155.

24. Weber, *Music and the Middle Class,* p. 49.

25. "Nouvelles de Paris," *ReM* 5 (1829): 352–53.

26. "Nouvelles," *RGMdP* 5/8 (25 February 1838): 94.

27. P. Scudo, ed., *L'Année musicale,* 2 (1861): 153.

28. Blanchard, "Concerts," *RGMdP* 18/5 (2 February 1851): 37.

29. "Nouvelles de Paris," *ReM* 12 (1832–33): 255, 279.

30. Brigitte François-Sappey, "La Vie musicale à Paris à travers les Mémoires d'Eugène Sauzay (1809–1901)," *Revue de musicologie,* 60/1–2 (1974): 183 and 196–98.

31. "Nouvelles," *RGMdP* 15/45 (5 November 1848): 348, 24/10 (8 March 1857): 77, 29/11 (16 March 1862): 90, and 32/11 (12 March 1865): 86.

32. "Nouvelles," *RGMdP* 27/11 (11 March 1860): 92.

33. "Concerts et auditions musicales de la semaine," *RGMdP* 35 (1868), no. 12 (22 March): 92 and no. 13 (29 March): 100.

34. "Nouvelles," *RGMdP* 15/43 (22 October 1848): 331. In 1870 the anonymous reviewer of a festival organized in memory of Berlioz noted the appropriateness of the event, as Berlioz had practically invented the music festival in France. See "Festival: Dédié à la mémoire d'Hector Berlioz," *RGMdP* 37/13 (27 March 1870): 97–98.

35. "Nouvelles diverses," *RGMdP* 34/10 (10 March 1867): 78; Em. Mathieu de Monter, "Exposition universelle de 1867," *RGMdP* 34/28 (14 July 1867): pp. 221–24.

36. Kracauer, *Orpheus in Paris,* p. 38.

37. Antoine Elwart, in his *Histoire de la Société des Concerts du Conservatoire Impérial de Musique* (Paris: S. Castel, 1860), Arthur Dandelot, in *La Société des Concerts du Conservatoire (1828–1923),* 3rd ed. (Paris: Delagrave, 1923), p. 215, and Adam Carse, in *The Orchestra from Beethoven to Berlioz* (Cambridge: W. Heffer & Sons, 1948), pp. 101–2, the latter two possibly using Elwart as their source, stated that summer concerts led by Musard began in 1832. I have found, however, no mention of these concerts before 1833. A short notice in *ReM*—"Nouvelles de Paris," 13 (30 November 1833): 350—suggests, albeit inconclusively, that 1833 was the first year of summer concerts in announcing the establishment of similar entertainment indoors during the winter of 1833–34. (It seems unlikely that promoters of such entertainment would have waited until a second summer season had proven successful.) Furthermore, in July 1835 Edouard Fétis reported that outdoor concerts had been important meeting places for two years; see "Nouvelles de Paris: Concerts d'été," *ReM* 15 (26 July 1835): 235.

38. Trollope, *Paris,* 2:348–49. The concerts are also described briefly in "Nouvelles de Paris," *ReM* 13 (1833): 180–82.

39. Carse, *The Orchestra,* p. 57, citing Jules Rivière, *My Musical Life and Recollections* (London: S. Low, Marston & Company, 1893), and pp. 101–2; "Nouvelles de Paris," *ReM* 13 (1833): 180–82.

40. "Nouvelles," *RGMdP* 6/24 (13 June 1839): 196.

41. Weber, *Music and the Middle Class,* p. 110. Weber stated that the concerts of the Jardin Turc were "more mundane" than those of Musard, and attracted a less wealthy audience. The boulevard du Temple is a short street running south-southeast from the place de la République.

42. "Nouvelles de Paris," *ReM* 13 (1833), 260.

43. *Ibid.;* Burnand, *Vie quotidienne,* p. 152; and Kracauer, *Orpheus in Paris,* p. 38.

44. "Nouvelles de Paris," *ReM* 13 (1833): 260; and E. Fétis, "Nouvelles de Paris: Concerts d'été," *ReM* 15 (26 July 1835): 236.

45. "Nouvelles de Paris," *ReM* 14 (24 August 1834): 271.

46. E. Fétis, "Nouvelles de Paris: Concerts d'été," *ReM* 15 (26 July 1835): 236.

47. Kracauer, *Orpheus in Paris,* p. 39, and Carse, *The Orchestra,* p. 102.

48. "Nouvelles de Paris," *ReM* 13 (30 November 1833): 350.

49. Weber, *Music and the Middle Class,* p. 109. Serge Gut and Danièle Pistone have claimed, in their *La Musique de chambre en France de 1870 à 1918* (Paris: Honoré Champion, 1978), p. 21, that Parisian café concerts began in 1770 (though they provide no source for this information). Music may well have been heard in cafés before the 1830s, but it was not mentioned in *ReM* (or other sources which I have examined) during the period immediately preceding, and was treated as a novel development in 1833. Possibly the "professionalization" of café concerts prompted increased reporting thereof in contemporary journals.

50. Weber, *Music and the Middle Class,* p. 109.

51. Trollope, *Paris,* 1:81.

52. "Nouvelles de Paris," *ReM* 13 (1833): 351.

53. E. Fétis, "Nouvelles de Paris: Concerts d'été," *ReM* 15 (26 July 1835): 236; Carse, *The Orchestra,* pp. 101–2.

54. "Nouvelles," *RGMdP* 3/49 (4 December 1836): 431; 4/29 (16 July 1837): 346.

55. E. Fétis, "Nouvelles de Paris: Concerts d'été," p. 236; "Nouvelles," *RGMdP* 6 (1839), no. 57 (7 November): 455, and no. 72 (30 December): 587.

56. "Nouvelles," *RGMdP* 4 (1837), no. 41 (8 October): 442 and no. 49 (3 December): 529.

57. "Nouvelles," *RGMdP* 6/34 (28 July 1839): 271.

58. "Nouvelles," *RGMdP* 6/42 (25 August 1839): 336. The capitalized words form, of course, "MERDE POUR L'AUTORITE."

59. "Nouvelles," *RGMdP* 7 (1840), no. 35 (10 May): 302, and no. 36 (17 May): 309.

60. "Nouvelles," *RGMdP* 8/42 (18 July 1841): 347; Weber, *Music and the Middle Class,* p. 110.

61. Blanchard, "La Société des concerts au Jardin d'hiver," *RGMdP* 15/30 (23 July 1848): 226, and "Concert au Jardin d'hiver," *RGMdP* 15/37 (10 September 1848): 279–80.

62. "Nouvelles," *RGMdP* 22/48 (2 December 1855): 378. Carse (*The Orchestra,* p. 102) wrote that Jules Rivière also led an orchestra of about 80 there at some point.

63. "Nouvelles," *RGMdP* 25/37 (12 September 1858): 306.

64. S. D., "Concert Impérial dirigé par Musard," *RGMdP* 26/23 (5 June 1859): 188.

65. See "Nouvelles," *RGMdP* 26/25 (19 June 1859): 209, 27/26 (24 June 1860): 230, and 28/27 (7 July 1861): 214. An anonymous reporter noted in 1865 that the aristocratic public was noisy and indifferent, but that the provincials and foreigners who attended

in the late summer (when the wealthy Parisians left town) were more appreciative. See "Nouvelles," *RGMdP* 32/34 (20 August 1865): 275. There is an excellent picture of the Musard concerts on the Champs-Elysées in *Musikgeschichte in Bildern,* vol. 4/2, "Konzert," ed. Heinrich W. Schwab (Leipzig: VEB Deutscher Verlag, 1971), p. 133.

66. "Nouvelles," *RGMdP* 30/48 (29 November 1863): 381.

67. "Nouvelles," *RGMdP* 24/22 (31 May 1857): 183.

68. "Nouvelles," *RGMdP* 26/21 (22 May 1859): 174, and 31 (1864), no. 19 (8 May): 152, and no. 21 (22 May): 167.

69. "Nouvelles," *RGMdP* 26 (1859), no. 16 (17 April): 130; no. 19 (8 May): 159; no. 22 (29 May): 182; no. 38 (18 September): 315; no. 41 (9 October): p. 338; A. Lambert, "La Musique au Pré Catelan," *RGMdP* 26/26 (26 June): 217.

70. The first conductor was Alfred Musard; in 1864 he was succeeded by Forestier. See Y., "Auditions et concerts," *RGMdP* 31/14 (3 April 1864): 107.

71. "Nouvelles diverses," *RGMdP* 35/14 (5 April 1868): 111, and subsequent issues.

72. "Nouvelles," *RGMdP* 25 (1858), no. 17 (25 April): 140, and no. 37 (12 September): 306.

73. "Nouvelles," *RGMdP* 32/43 (22 October 1865): 347.

74. "Nouvelles," *RGMdP* 32 (1865), no. 23 (4 June): 186, no. 29 (16 July): 235, no. 32 (6 August): 260.

75. "Nouvelles diverses," *RGMdP* 34/19 (12 May 1867): 155.

76. "Nouvelles," *RGMdP* 23/3 (20 January 1856): 22. The hôtel d'Osmond was probably on the site of the present Opéra (begun in 1861), for it was demolished to make room for a new opera house. See *RGMdP* 25/9 (28 February 1858), p. 70.

77. "Les Deux Musard," *RGMdP* 24/19 (10 May 1857): 154.

78. Blanchard, "Grand concert instrumental et vocal," *RGMdP* 24/35 (30 August 1857): 281.

79. "Nouvelles diverses," *RGMdP* 33/44 (4 November 1866): 350. P. Smith [Edouard Monnais] agreed that audiences at these concerts were unsophisticated, stating that there was no competition between this series and the Concerts Populaires. This series is evidently separate from the summer Concerts du Prince Impérial that Musard began in 1859. See P. Smith, "Revue de l'année 1866," *RGMdP* 34/1 (6 January 1867): 1–4.

80. Blanchard, "Concert de M. Demerssmann," *RGMdP* 25/44 (31 October 1858): 360.

81. "Nouvelles," *RGMdP* 25/49 (5 December 1858): 406, and 26/47 (20 November 1859): 391.

82. "Nouvelles," *RGMdP* 26/6 (6 February 1859): 48; "Concerts du Casino," *RGMdP* 26/7 (13 February 1859): 51. By 1865 the concerts happened four times weekly; see "Nouvelles," *RGMdP* 32/44 (29 October 1865): 359.

83. "Nouvelles," *RGMdP* 26/44 (30 October 1859): 362; 31/42 (16 October 1864): 335. In 1865 the orchestra was described as one of the best in Paris; see "Nouvelles," *RGMdP* 32/43 (22 October 1865), p. 346.

84. Successful musical events continued at the Casino under the conductorships of Auguste Mey (1868–69), Lamothe (1869–70), and Constantin (after the war); see "Nouvelles diverses," *RGMdP* 35/39 (27 September 1868): 310; 36/40 (3 October 1869): 327; 38/38 (15 October 1871): 290.

85. "Nouvelles diverses," *RGMdP* 35/19 (10 May 1868): 151.

86. "Nouvelles," *RGMdP* 31/45 (6 November 1864): 358.

87. Kracauer, *Orpheus in Paris,* p. 258; "Nouvelles diverses," *RGMdP* 36/16 (18 April 1869): 135.

88. Castil-Blaze [F.-H.-J. Blaze], "Un Musicien de province," *RGMdP* 6/50 (6 October 1839): 393–96; Blanchard, "Concerts," *RGMdP* 8/1 (3 January 1841): 5–7.

89. "Nouvelles," *RGMdP* 4/18 (30 April 1837): 155.

90. "Concerts et auditions musicales de la semaine," *RGMdP* 36/49 (5 December 1869): 397.

91. "Concerts et auditions musicales de la semaine," *RGMdP* 37/6 (6 February 1870): 45. These figures are, of course, not limited to concerts of instrumental music.

92. Paul Henry Lang, Editorial, *Musical Quarterly* 39/2 (1953): 239.

93. (London: Croom Helm, 1975), 172 pp.

94. Weber, *Music and the Middle Class,* p. 11.

95. Ibid., pp. 36–37. Not only did virtuosos demand high fees, but also the aristocracy were now less well-off than they had been in previous generations.

96. Ibid., p. 97.

97. Ibid., p. 19. I prefer to think of a range (if not a continuum) from those who supported chamber and orchestral works, through those who enjoyed overtures and virtuosic works, to those who attended musical events to dance or socialize.

98. Ibid., p. 125.

99. Ibid., pp. 55–56. Blanchard wrote in 1840 that *matinées* of the cellist Alexandre Batta were limited to men on the theory that women talked too much and would not, in any case, appreciate the exclusively "serious" repertory. See "Concerts," *RGMdP* 7/75 (24 December 1840): 635.

100. Weber, *Music and the Middle Class,* pp. 33–34.

101. Ibid., p. 119.

102. Ibid., pp. 6 and 85.

103. Ibid., p. 20.

104. That prices changed little is apparent from contemporary announcements. The cost of living evidently varied little too, if the unchanging salaries of the Conservatoire staff, as presented by Constant Pierre in *Le Conservatoire National de Musique et de Déclamation* (Paris: Imprimerie nationale, 1900), pp. 422–30, are any indication. For example, the director was paid 8000 francs each year from 1825 through 1865, and composition instructors received 2500 francs from 1840 through 1875.

105. Weber (*Music and the Middle Class*, p. 24) has stated that the average Parisian artisan in the period of 1830 to 1848 made about 3000 francs annually; he reckoned that such a person might spend one percent or 30 francs a year for entertainment, and thus not much on a single event. Arnold B. Perris cited Bulwer's computation that the Parisian worker in the same period, with an average annual salary of 1000 francs, might spend more on an evening's entertainment than on his daily food—about one-and-a-half francs. See Perris, "Music in France during the Reign of Louis-Philippe: Art as a Substitute for Heroic Experience" (Ph.D. dissertation, Northwestern University, 1967), p. 26.

106. E. F[étis]., "Concerts: Soirée de M. Massimino," *ReM* 7 (1830): 55–57.

107. F.-J. Fétis in *ReM* 13 (27 April 1833): 97, quoted and translated by Peter Bloom, "François-Joseph Fétis and the *Revue Musicale* (1827–1835)" (Ph.D. Dissertation, University of Pennsylvania, 1972), pp. 61–62.

108. In the former two instances entrepreneurs were, as Weber (*Music and the Middle Class*, p. 85) has pointed out, taking advantage of locations in which there was a preexistent audience.

109. Berlioz, "Concerts de la rue Saint-Honoré dirigés par M. Valentino," *RGMdP* 4/44 (29 October 1837): 470–71.

110. Elisabeth Bernard, "Jules Pasdeloup et les Concerts Populaires," *Revue de musicologie*, 57/2 (1971): 161–62.

111. "Du mouvement musical à Paris," *GMdP*, 1/51 (21 December 1834): 409.

112. Paul Duprat, "L'Année 1854: Mouvement musical," *Almanach musical*, 2 (1855): 26. He wrote, "Les concerts ne sont pas ralentis un seul jour; matin et soir les salles MM. Henri Herz, Pleyel, et Erard étaient ouvertes à la foule."

113. Blanchard, "Matinées et soirées musicales," *RGMdP* 24/18 (3 May 1857): 146.

114. Blanchard, "Matinées musicales," *RGMdP* 23/4 (27 January 1856): 26–27.

115. Berlioz, quoted and translated by Jacques Barzun in *Berlioz and the Romantic Century*, 3rd ed. rev. 2 vols. (New York: Columbia University Press, 1969), 1:343.

116. Weber, *Music and the Middle Class*, p. 51.

117. Ibid., p. 60.

118. Ibid., pp. 3 and 7.

119. Berlioz in *Le Musicien errant, 1842–1852; Correspondance publiée par Julien Tiersot* (Paris: Calmann-Lévy, ca. 1919), p. 145, translated in Barzun, *Berlioz*, 1:479.

120. Berlioz in the *Journal des débats politiques et littéraires*, 16 February 1862, cited in Barzun, *Berlioz*, 2:211.

121. The Opéra too had its problems. Financial difficulties headed the list, but many journalists worried that the composition of opera in France was at a nadir.

122. Letter to the editor by "Un artiste de l'Académie Royale de Musique," *RGMdP* 4/53 (31 December 1837): 573. Each of the laws cited was in effect at some time during the period.

Chapter 4

1. These records do not include works exclusively for keyboard instruments, guitars, or harps; nor do they include certain "novelty" works for the many new and short-lived instruments (for example, the *aerophone*) that were invented during the period. The records do include light works for other solo instruments. The main sources for these records are announcements and reviews in *ReM, GMdP,* and *RGMdP.* Programs referred to in books, letters, diaries, and other periodicals were also taken into account if it was provable that the programs mentioned therein had not already been noted in *ReM, GMdP,* and *RGMdP.* Performances at both series concerts (or *séances*) and nonseries events have been counted.

2. Even when a concert announcement does not mention composers, the list of performers may indicate that the program likely included chamber "art" music.

3. This qualification does not mean that only precisely named works were tallied. References to (for example) a quartet, an overture, or even an "Andante" (when the performing body is known) have been included, if it was clear that a single work was intended. References to (for example) "chamber works by Mozart" or even "string quartets by Haydn" have not been counted, though allowance for this omission is mentioned in the text.

4. It is impossible to form even a rough estimate of the total number of performances that occurred. In "Nouvelles," *RGMdP* 30/22 (31 May 1863): 174, it was stated that Adolphe Blanc's chamber works had received 11 performances in concerts and 42 in *réunions* during the previous winter season. My survey uncovered only six presentations of Blanc's chamber works in the calendar year 1863 (and only five in 1862).

5. For various reasons, it is difficult to provide an exact figure. 1) Spelling variants: Clearly "Litz" and "Listz" refer to Franz Liszt, but do "Daniele" and "Danieli" or "Gauthier" and "Gautier" refer to one person or two? (Composers by all four names existed.) Is "Lacherier" (unknown to lexicographers) a misspelling for Eugène Lacheurié? 2) Persons sharing a surname: Among composers there were (at least) four Kreutzers, three Kontskis, and two Blancs, Danclas, Davids, Webers, and Wieniawskis; but nineteenth-century sources sometimes identified these persons only by surnames. 3) Multiple names: Contemporary sources referred to Marie Félicie Clémence de Reiset, Vicomtesse de Grandval, as both Mlle. de Reiset and Mme. de Grandval; she also wrote dramatic works under the names Caroline Blangy and Clémence Valgrand. Are there similar cases yet undetected? 4) "Co-composers": Stephen Heller and Mme. Langhans each shared in the composition of certain instrumental works, but neither has his or her own instrumental works among the list of known performances. The brothers Tilmant composed works together. How should these cases be counted?

6. Adam Carse, *The Orchestra from Beethoven to Berlioz* (Cambridge: W. Heffer & Sons, 1948), pp. 93, 424–25.

7. Albert Palm, "La Connaissance de l'oeuvre de J. S. Bach en France à l'époque préromantique," *Revue de musicologie,* 52/1 (1966): 88–114.

8. As in chapter 2, a major work is here defined as a work of substantial length, usually in more than one movement; excerpts from such works are not counted in table 4.2.

9. The subperiods in table 4.4 differ slightly from those outlined in chapter 1. Because

I originally organized data on repertory by calendar years, the subperiods in the present chapter encompass entire calendar years. In real life, change in the musical scene was usually more notable between musical seasons than between calendar years; the subperiods introduced in chapter 1 and further described in chapter 5 reflect change from one season to the next.

10. "Nouvelles diverses," *RGMdP* 35/38 (20 September 1868): 302, announced that 518 concerts had taken place in Paris from 1 January to 31 July 1868. Em. Mathieu de Monter, "Revue de l'année 1868," *RGMdP* 36/1 (3 January 1869): 1–3, wrote that music was becoming a part of daily life in France and, contradicting the previously cited source, suggested that nearly 700 concerts took place in Paris during the first seven months of 1868. "Concerts et auditions musicales de la semaine," *RGMdP* 37/6 (6 February 1870): 45, reported that 701 concerts happened in Paris in 1869, not counting café concerts. "Nouvelles diverses," *RGMdP* 37/30 (24 July 1870): 238 counted 300 concerts from November 1869 to May 1870 in the salles Erard, Herz, and Pleyel alone (thus eliminating the Conservatoire concerts and Concerts Populaires). It is not clear what sorts of musical events are counted in these statistics; not so many concerts are reported in weekly issues of *RGMdP.*

11. The actual number of performances was higher than the 11 indicated in table 4.4. Unfortunately, only a few specific works were mentioned in accounts of these concerts in *ReM.*

12. Popular, though not included in these statistics, was an arrangement of Mozart's *Magic Flute* overture for three pianos, twelve hands.

13. For many performances of virtuosic works, the composer was the soloist.

14. The infrequent reporting of the nightly Concerts Valentino also makes the figure for the second subperiod unrealistically low.

15. Jacques Barzun has written that after the Revolution "all cultural activity in Paris immediately ceased, and men of all shades of opinion who lived by their art had to seek their living abroad". See *Berlioz and the Romantic Century,* 1:524. The September after the Revolution, Maurice Bourges wrote that concerts had vanished as if by magic. See "Premier semestre musical de la République," *RGMdP* 15/36 (3 September 1848): 271–72. Henri Blanchard mentioned general unemployment, and that the rich who had not fled Paris were not investing their money: "De la question artistique et musicale," *RGMdP* 15/22 (28 May 1848): 167–68. See also P. Seligmann, "Les Béotiens de la musique," *RGMdP* 15/23 (4 June 1848): 173–75; Paul Smith [Edouard Monnais], "Revue de l'année 1848," *RGMdP* 16/1 (6 [*sic,* should read 7] January 1849): 1–3; and Berlioz's letter to Louis Duc of 26 May 1848, cited in Barzun, *Berlioz,* p. 521.

16. A piano trio of Blanc's was performed at Gouffé's *séances* early in 1852, when Blanc was 23. Thereafter his works held a consistent position in the Parisian concert repertory.

17. There are 68 known performances of Mozart's symphonies (or *fragments* thereof) from 1861 through 1870 (6.8 per year), only 25 from 1854 through 1860 (3.6 per year). There are 118 known performances of Haydn's symphonies (or *fragments*) in the sixth subperiod (11.8 per year), 42 in the fifth (6.0 per year). The Concerts Populaires gave 44 complete performances of Mozart's symphonies in the 1860s and 56 of Haydn's.

18. Among the 17 composers most performed from 1861 to 1870, only 2 (contemporary

Frenchmen Blanc and Dancla) are not mentioned in Donald Grout's *History of Western Music,* 3rd ed. rev. (New York: W. W. Norton & Company, 1980). Among the top 18 from 1828 to 1833, 9 are not mentioned by Grout.

19. In "French Instrumental Music between the Revolutions (1789–1830)," (Ph.D. dissertation, Columbia University, 1950, pp. 75–76), Boris Schwarz wrote that the founding of the Société des Concerts du Conservatoire (1828) was "a step of vital necessity and far-reaching consequence, for Paris had been without a regular symphony orchestra since 1816 when the famous orchestral *'exercices'* of the Conservatoire were curtailed by the Bourbon regime. Thus, a whole young generation of musicians and listeners was growing up without adequate knowledge of the symphonic repertoire: the occasional student concerts of the *Ecole royale de musique* . . . or the few *Concerts Spirituels* . . . were wholly inadequate to fill the need."

20. Sophie Leo, "Musical Life in Paris (1817–48)," trans. by Oliver Strunk, *Musical Quarterly,* 17/2 (1931): 261.

21. Pierre Soccanne, "Virtuoses: un maître de quatuor: Pierre Baillot (1771–1842)," *Le Guide du concert,* 24 (1937–38), pp. 743–44.

22. As explained above, the percentage of actual performances of works by Haydn and Mozart must be somewhat higher, for their works were performed at concerts for which specific programs are not known to exist.

23. Sophie Leo wrote that "all at once one was ashamed not to have heard Beethoven's symphonies at the Conservatoire, though until then the very name of Beethoven had been unfamiliar." See "Musical Life in Paris (1817–48)," p. 390.

24. *Louis Spohr's Autobiography,* 2 vols. (London: Longman, Green, Longman, Roberts, & Green, 1865), 2:114; parts of this quotation are cited by Schwarz ("French Instrumental Music," p. 53). Sophie Leo ("Musical Life in Paris," p. 269) added: "However discouraging the condition of the opera may have been during those years [about 1820], the concerts were in an even more deplorable state. The demand was for a long succession of short and varied compositions; often more than twenty pieces were played on a single program. Even the most capable artist dared not offer his unappreciative audience a quartet or quintet, much less an entire concerto with orchestral accompaniment, and in private circles where music was cultivated the display of ignorance and lack of taste was still more striking."

25. Performances of virtuosic showpieces were even more prevalent than table 4.4 would indicate, for throughout the period virtuosos often performed at dance concerts or café concerts, the programs of which (rarely known) are not included in the statistics on repertory.

26. As noted above, Bach's instrumental works had been played in Paris as early as 1809. The performance in 1833 is the first public presentation of an instrumental work that I have found after 1828.

27. Habeneck's earlier attempts to interest Parisians in Beethoven's symphonies had been unsuccessful.

28. This figure includes performances of excerpts, but there were few: Beethoven's symphonies were almost always rendered in their complete form.

29. Of the 219 known performances of Beethoven's works from 1828 to 1839, 123 were of symphonies, 105 of them at the Conservatoire concerts.

30. The 121 known performances of Berlioz's instrumental works, 1828–70, are more than are known for any other French composer. This comparison is perhaps unfair, however, for concerts of Berlioz's works are better reported in secondary sources than are those of, for example, Blanc or Dancla.

31. Blanc was a favorite in the *salons* of Gouffé and Lebouc; 65 of his 113 known performances took place at concerts sponsored by these two string players.

32. On this occasion, 26 February 1832, the concerto was reputedly performed as a piano solo; see Arthur Hervey, *Chopin,* rev. Maurice J. E. Brown, in the *Master Musicians* series (London: J. M. Dent & Sons, 1963), p. 47. An anonymous contemporary reviewer in "Nouvelles de Paris: Concert de M. Chopin", *ReM* 12 (1832–33): 38–39, complimented Chopin's freshness of melodic ideas and overall form, but suggested that the piece sounded too improvisatory and modulated too often.

33. An "ouverture nouvelle" was performed at the prize-awarding ceremonies of the Conservatoire on 20 November. On 22 December a concert overture, possibly the same work, was played by the Société de l'Athénée; see J. A. D., "Athénée musical," *RGMdP* 4/3 (15 January 1837): 25–26.

34. Bea Friedland, *Louise Farrenc, 1804–1875: Composer, Performer, Scholar* (Ann Arbor: UMI Research Press, 1980), p. 17.

35. The actual number of string quartet performances before 1847 must be considerably higher than eight; as mentioned above, reporting of chamber music concerts in this period left much to be desired. Nevertheless, it seems clear that there were many more performances of Haydn's quartets after the February Revolution than before.

36. Méhul may have written as many as six symphonies. See Alexander Ringer, "A French Symphonist at the Time of Beethoven: Etienne Nicolas Méhul," *Musical Quarterly,* 37 (1951): 547, and Barry S. Brook, *La Symphonie française,* 3 vols. (Paris: Institut de Musicologie de l'Université de Paris, 1962), 2:470.

37. This concert was reviewed by Henri Blanchard: "Seconde matinée de chambre," *ReM* 6/6 (7 February 1839): 50–51. The lag between date of composition and Paris premiere can in some, but not all, cases be explained by delays in publication. Some of Mendelssohn's chamber works were not published until after 1840, but others, such as the string quartets Opp. 12 and 13, were published in parts in 1830 but not performed in Paris until at least 1840, when an unidentified Mendelssohn string quartet was performed by the brothers Franco-Mendès.

38. The violin concertos, less readily available, were almost never played.

39. In most of the works for piano and orchestra (the two concertos excepted), the orchestral part is so insignificant that the works were published as piano solos; it is possible that some of the performances listed in tables 4.1 and 4.4 were in fact solo piano renditions, and that the totals for Prudent should thus be lower.

40. Henri Blanchard's review of the second concert ("Rubinstein," *RGMdP* 24/17 (26 April 1857): 140) stated that the symphony was in B-flat. This is probably the unpublished work first called the Symphony No. 3; see Edward Garden: "Rubinstein, Anton," *Grove 6,* 16:299.

41. Blanchard, "Société Sainte-Cécile", *RGMdP* 20/52 (25 December 1853): 446–47.

42. This was evidently the Trio in B-flat (Op. 99, D. 898), for the Paris premiere of Schubert's only other complete piano trio (Op. 100, D. 929), was announced in 1841. See "Séance musicale," *RGMdP* 4/23 (4 June 1837): 193–94, and "Nouvelles", *RGMdP* 8/27 (4 April 1841): 215 for notices of the respective premieres.

43. Schubert's lieder had gained some popularity well before 1848.

44. The Piano Quintet was played at a concert of pianist Wilhelmine Clauss on 10 April ("Nouvelles," *RGMdP* 20/15 (10 April 1853): 135); the *Manfred* received its Parisian premiere at a concert of the Société Sainte-Cécile on 27 November ("Nouvelles," *RGMdP* 20/46 (13 November 1853): 401).

45. The Paris premiere was by the Société des Jeunes-Artistes, 26 February 1860 ("Nouvelles," *RGMdP* 27/8 (19 February 1860): 61).

46. The Third Symphony also was evidently first performed by the Jeunes-Artistes, on 18 January 1857; it was described as a "work still unknown in Paris" ("Nouvelles," *RGMdP* 24/2, (11 January 1857): 14). The Piano Quartet was played at a concert of Louis Lacombe and others, 19 February ("Nouvelles," *RGMdP* 24/7 (16 February): 53–54).

47. Schwarz ("French Instrumental Music," p. 53) mentioned that his Nonet was performed there during a visit in about 1820, and Spohr himself (*Autobiography* 2:133–34) discussed private performances of two of his string quartets on the same visit.

48. P. Scudo, ed., *L'Année musicale,* 3 vols. (Paris: L. Hachette et Cie, 1860–62), 2:140.

49. See also J.-G. Prod'homme: "The Works of Weber in France," trans. Theodore Baker, *Musical Quarterly,* 14/3 (July 1928): 366–68.

50. Constant Pierre, in his *Histoire du Concert Spirituel, 1725–1790* (Paris: Société Française de Musicologie, 1975), lists the programs of that institution (pp. 227–344); concerning French symphonists, see Brook, *La Symphonie française dans la seconde moitié du XVIIIe siècle,* 3 vols. (Paris: Institut de Musicologie de l'Université de Paris, 1962).

51. Descriptions and programs of these concerts are presented in Constant Pierre's *Les Hymnes et chansons de la Révolution: Aperçu général et catalogue avec notices historiques, analytiques et bibliographiques* (Paris: Imprimerie nationale, 1904).

52. Programs for these *exercices* are listed in Constant Pierre's *Le Conservatoire National de Musique et de Déclamation: Documents historiques et administratifs* (Paris: Imprimerie nationale, 1900), pp. 460–510. Schwarz ("French Instrumental Music," p. 16) has remarked that the *exercices* contributed decisively to the development of French musical taste.

53. See chapter 5, pp. 136–41, for a description of French musical life before 1828.

54. This explanation fits the facts only through hindsight; one might equally well have expected that the prolonged absence of regular instrumental concerts would have created an ideal environment for the development of a new style of instrumental music, and a rejection of works that had been popular before 1816 (when instrumental music all but disappeared from concerts).

55. Virtuosic violin schools had, of course, been developing in France and Italy since the early eighteenth century. Regarding the French school, see Lionel de La Laurencie's *L'Ecole française de violon de Lully à Viotti,* 3 vols. (Paris: Delagrave, 1922–24).

56. Leo Schrade, *Beethoven in France* (New Haven: Yale University Press, 1942), p. 15.

57. Adolphe Piriou, "Blanc, Adolphe" in W. W. Cobbett, *Cobbett's Cyclopedic Survey of Chamber Music* (London: Oxford University Press, 1929), 1:126.

58. It seems ironic that the classical style, viewed by many as a reaction against contrivances of the baroque period and a movement towards "natural" writing (See, for example, Grout, *History of Western Music,* pp. 452–53), was imitated in such a restrictive and academic manner by nineteenth-century French composers, who appear to have forced their music into predetermined classical molds.

59. Of course, the large forces required for most of Berlioz's major works discouraged frequent performance. But Berlioz had even less success obtaining performances of his operas in Paris.

60. Georges Servières, "Les Premiers admirateurs français des compositions de Liszt," *Revue musicale,* 19/9 (July 1928): 275, wrote that "dans la période qui s'étend de 1850 à 1870, on pouvait compter sur ses doigts les appréciateurs français de la musique de Liszt."

61. The position of Weber in this "traditional-progressive" duality is ambiguous. His instrumental works were, on the whole, less progressive than his operas; many are in traditional molds. Even the opera overtures, though romantic in atmosphere, follow well-established formal structures. With Schubert, the issue of the duality can be avoided, because the slowness with which his works were published delayed widespread knowledge of his music until late in the period, when tastes were beginning to change.

62. Peter Bloom, "François-Joseph Fétis and the *Revue Musicale* (1827–1835)" (Ph.D. dissertation, University of Pennsylvania, 1972), pp. 95–97.

63. Schrade, *Beethoven in France,* pp. 36–37.

64. Philip George Downs, "The Development of the Great Repertoire in the Nineteenth Century" (Ph.D. dissertation, University of Toronto, 1964). Downs's study, which includes data on Parisian repertory, is at once broader and narrower than my own. He used a computer to formulate and analyze year-by-year statistics on all genres of music performed by representative concert societies in London, Vienna, and Paris. Dividing the repertory into groups ("cores") of composers, he provided extensive statistics on the interrelationships of various groups, comparing those composers who had achieved popularity before 1813 with those who joined the standard repertory later in the century, and so forth. For his Parisian statistics, which cover the same period as my own, Downs used the programs of the Société des Concerts du Conservatoire. He therefore analyzed a sample of works that is relatively small, that deemphasizes chamber music (and thus composers known primarily for chamber works), and that, even for Paris, is unusually conservative and standardized, as a comparison of my tables on the Conservatoire concerts (in chapter 2) and tables for Paris in general (in this chapter) indicates. Examining programs of the Conservatoire alone, one would gain little idea of the significance in Parisian concerts of Berlioz, Blanc, Schumann, Hummel, and Farrenc, but might overestimate the significance of Gluck, Handel, and Cherubini (even allowing for their greater importance as composers of vocal music). Downs's dissertation also provides little information on the relative popularity of various genres or the success of individual works.

Chapter 5

1. For information on instrumental music in France before 1828 I am heavily indebted to Boris Schwarz's doctoral dissertation, "French Instrumental Music between the Revolutions (1789–1830)" (Columbia University, 1950). The section "1789–1870, Concert Life," by David Charlton and John Trevitt, within the article "Paris," *The New Grove Dictionary of Music and Musicians* (London: Macmillan Publishers Ltd., 1980), volume 14, pp. 208–19, has been useful in supplying dates I had not found elsewhere.

2. William Weber, *Music and the Middle Class: The Social Structure of Concert Life in London, Paris, and Vienna* (London: Croom Helm, 1975), p. 70.

3. Barry S. Brook, *La Symphonie française dans le second moitié du XVIIIe siècle,* 3 vols. (Paris: Institut de Musicologie de l'Université de Paris, 1962); Lionel de La Laurencie: *L'Ecole française de violon de Lully à Viotti,* 3 vols. (Paris: Delagrave, 1922–24); Constant Pierre, *Le Concert Spirituel, 1725–1790* (Paris: Société Française de Musicologie, 1975). Pierre's book was completed by 1900 but not published until 1975.

4. Schwarz, "French Instrumental Music," p. 5.

5. Ibid., p. 21, quoting and translating an article in *AMZ,* 2 (May 1800), col. 588.

6. Schwarz, "French Instrumental Music," p. 9.

7. Edward Lockspeiser, "Berlioz and the French Romantics," *Music and Letters,* 15/1 (January 1934): 29.

8. Ibid., p. 30.

9. See Constant Pierre, *Les Hymnes et chansons de la Révolution* (Paris: Imprimerie nationale, 1904).

10. Schwarz, "French Instrumental Music," p. 17.

11. Georges Servières, "La Symphonie en France au XIXe siècle (avant 1870)," *Ménestrel,* 85/39 (28 September 1923): 397–400.

12. J.-G. Prod'homme, under "Nouvelles musicologiques—Documents: la chambre philharmonique," *Revue de musicologie,* 9/15 (August 1925): 127; and "Fridzeri (Alexandre-Marie-Antoine Frixer, dit," *FétisB,* 3:340.

13. Schwarz, "French Instrumental Music," p. 10.

14. Ibid., p. 28.

15. Ibid., p. 30, quoting a report from Paris in the *Allgemeine musikalische Zeitung,* 2 (July 1800), col. 712.

16. Schwarz, "French Instrumental Music," p. 30, quoting a report from Paris in the *Allgemeine musikalische Zeiting,* 3 (Jaunuary 1801), col. 270.

17. Servières, "Symphonie en France," p. 397.

18. F.-J. Fétis, "Sur le Concert Spirituel," *ReM* 1/8 (April 1827): 204.

19. Schwarz, "French Instrumental Music," p. 16. F.-J. Fétis confirmed this opinion of the students' accomplishments. See "Examen de l'état actuel de la musique en France," *ReM* 1/20 (June 1827): 491, and "Sur le Concert Spirituel," pp. 202–3, in which he

wrote that the *exercices* quickly replaced all other concerts, and gained great importance as a meeting place for amateurs and professionals, both native and foreign.

20. See chapter 2, note 62, for details and documentation.

21. A. L. Ringer, "A French Symphonist at the Time of Beethoven: Etienne Nicolas Méhul," *Musical Quarterly,* 37/4 (1951): 548.

22. Schwarz, "French Instrumental Music," p. 29.

23. Ibid., p. 48.

24. Ringer, "Méhul," pp. 543–65.

25. Julien Tiersot, "La Symphonie en France," *Zeitschrift der Internationalen Musikgesellschaft,* 3/10 (1902): 393.

26. F.-J. Fétis, "Nouvelles de Paris: Soirées de quatuors et quintettes de M. Baillot," *ReM* 11 (1831–32): 409.

27. Sophie Leo, "Musical Life in Paris (1817–48)," trans. Oliver Strunk, *Musical Quarterly,* 17 (1931): 261 and 269.

28. Ludwig Spohr, *Louis Spohr's Autobiography,* 2 vols. (London: Longman, Green, Longman, Roberts, and Green, 1865), 2:115.

29. Weber, *Music and the Middle Class,* p. 70.

30. Leo, "Musical Life," p. 269.

31. Ibid., p. 400.

32. Schwarz, "French Instrumental Music," p. 78.

33. Spohr, *Autobiography* 2:114–16 and 133.

34. Hector Berlioz: *Mémoires,* trans. and ed. David Cairns as *The Memoirs of Hector Berlioz: Member of the French Institute* (London: Victor Gollancz, 1969), p. 77. Barzun, in *Berlioz and the Romantic Century,* 3rd ed. rev. 2 vols. (New York: Columbia University Press, 1969), 1:49, wrote that when Berlioz arrived in Paris in 1821 instrumental music "was in the transition between the private patron's orchestra and the establishment of regular public institutions." Although this statement is true, and explains the dearth of concerts, it does not take into account the respectable concert life of the early years of the century. The period in which Berlioz arrived in Paris was really the second musical depression since the decline of private patrons' orchestras, the first having occurred immediately after the Revolution.

35. Berlioz, *Mémoires,* cited by Schwarz, "French Instrumental Music," p. 67.

36. F.-J. Fétis, quoted by Peter Bloom, "François-Joseph Fétis and the *Revue Musicale* (1827–1835)" (Ph.D. dissertation, University of Pennsylvania, 1972), p. 129.

37. Schwarz, "French Instrumental Music," p. 79.

38. Ibid., p. 65.

39. Weber, *Music and the Middle Class,* pp. 16 and 160.

40. See F.-J. Fétis, "Examen de l'état actuel de la musique . . . en France," *ReM* 1

(1827), no. 22, p. 540, and no. 23, p. 558, and "Sur le Concert Spirituel," *ReM* 1/8 (1827): 205–8.

41. See F.-J. Fétis, "Soirées musicales de quatuors et de quintetti, données par M. Baillot," *ReM* 1/1 (February 1827): 37–39, and "Concerts," *ReM* 2 (1827–28): 523–24.

42. Schwarz, "Beethoven and the French Violin School," *Musical Quarterly,* 44/4 (October 1958): 435.

43. F.-J. Fétis, "Des révolutions de l'orchestre," *ReM*, 1/11 (April 1827): 269.

44. F.-J. Fétis, "Examen de l'état actuel de la musique . . . en France," *ReM* 1/20 (June 1827): 492.

45. "Nouvelles de Paris," *ReM* 11 (1831–32): 45. The commentator believed that Baillot's concerts began in 1827, though it is known that Baillot had been presenting concerts more than a decade earlier, and Soccanne wrote that his chamber music series enjoyed great success from 1820. See Pierre Soccanne, "Quelques documents inédits sur Pierre Baillot," *Revue de musicologie,* 23 (1939): 72.

46. F.-J. Fétis, "Quatrième concert d'émulation," *ReM*, 4 (1828–29): 377.

47. Stéphen, "Projet d'Association Musicale: Société du Gymnase Lyrique," ibid., p. 294. Four concerts were scheduled, beginning in January 1829, but none was reviewed.

48. See two articles by F.-J. Fétis, "Nouvelles de Paris: Ecole Royale de Musique: Distribution des Prix," *ReM* 4 (1828–29): 394, and "Revue succinct de la musique pendant l'année 1828," *ReM* 5 (1829): 1, 8–9.

49. F.-J. Fétis, "Statistique musicale de la France," *ReM* 6 (1829–30), pp. 121–29. His source for the statistics of 1788 was Framery's *Calendrier musical universel.* The emphasis on improved teaching seems odd, for only two years earlier he had complained of the French public's poor musical education (see above, p. 140).

50. Edouard Fétis, "Revue de la saison musicale de Paris (1829–30)," *ReM* 8 (1830): 86–91.

51. H. F. Chorley, *Music and Manners in France and Germany,* 3 vols. (London: Longman, Orme, Brown, Green, and Longmans, 1841), 3:63.

52. E. Fétis: "Revue d'un demi-siècle: Musique instrumentale," *RGMdP* 18/27 (6 July 1851): 217.

53. "Nouvelles de Paris," *ReM* 12 (1832–33): 191.

54. See particularly Berlioz's letter to Rouget de Lisle, dated 29 December 1830 (written as Berlioz was about to leave for Italy on his Prix de Rome trip). An English translation of this letter appears in *Hector Berlioz: A Selection from His Letters,* ed. Humphrey Searle (New York: Vienna House, 1973), p. 34. These ideas were also expressed by Berlioz in his *Mémoires;* and most of them had been stated in a letter to the editor of *ReM* by "Un pauvre musicien" (not Berlioz) in 1827; see 1/1 (February 1827): 44–47.

55. Stéphen, "Projet d'Association," pp. 289–90, and "Nouvelles des départemens," *ReM* 4 (1828–29): 134.

56. F.-J. Fétis, "Nouvelles de Paris: Académie Royale de Musique," *ReM* 3 (1828): 253.

57. "Nouvelles de Paris," ibid., p. 116, and "Nouvelles de Paris: Soirée musicale de M. Dietz," *ReM* 5 (1829): 160–61.

58. "Annonces," *ReM* 3 (1828): 48.

59. J.-A. Delaire, "Des differens genres de musique et de la protection qu'ils réclament," *ReM*, 9 (1830): 169 and 170.

60. S., "Nouvelles de Paris: Soirée musicale," *ReM* 3 (1828): 233; "Nouvelles de Paris," *ReM* 11 (1831–32): 409–10; and "Nouvelles de Paris: Concerts du Conservatoire," *ReM* 12 (1832–33): 45.

61. "Revue musicale: Musique instrumentale," *ReM* 11 (1831–32): 223.

62. F.-J. Fétis, "La Civilization et la musique," *ReM* 13 (1833): 345.

63. Ibid., pp. 345–46.

64. Bloom, "Fétis," p. 31.

65. Anik Devriès, "Les Editions musicales Sieber," *Revue de musicologie,* 55/1 (1969): 43–44.

66. E. Fétis, "Revue d'un demi-siècle: Musique instrumentale," *RGMdP* 18/30 (27 July 1851): 241.

67. Tiersot, "La Symphonie en France," p. 393.

68. S. Kracauer, *Orpheus in Paris: Offenbach and the Paris of His Time* (New York: Alfred A. Knopf, 1938), p. 8.

69. Weber, *Music and the Middle Class,* p. 73.

70. Music-lovers' pessimism was not restricted to the instrumental scene; although operas from the period are considered historically important, contemporary critics worried over them. See F.-J. Fétis's review of J.-F. Gail's *Reflexions sur le goût musical en France* (Paris, 1832) in *ReM* 11 (1831–32): 405–7. The book is mainly on operatic taste, and reveals uneasiness about the fate of French opera.

71. See, for example, F.-J. Fétis, "Sur la philosophie et sur la poètique de la musique," *ReM* 3 (1828): 409–16, 509 ff.; Fétis, "Variétés: De l'influence de la musique instrumentale sur les révolutions de la musique dramatique," *ReM* 10 (1830–31): 129–34; J.-A. Delaire, "Variétés," *ReM* 5 (1829): 433–40.

72. E. Fétis, "Nouvelles de Paris: Coup d'oeil sur la saison musicale qui expire," *ReM* 15 (26 April 1835): 131 and 133.

73. "Du mouvement musical à Paris," *GMdP* 1/51 (21 December 1834): 409–12.

74. D. T., "Variétés: Paris Dilettante," *ReM* 15 (24 May 1835): 166–67.

75. "Nouvelles de Paris," *ReM* 15 (5 July 1835): 216.

76. Franz Liszt, "De la situation des artistes, et de leur condition dans la société," *GMdP* 2 (1835), no. 30 (26 July): 245–49 and no. 35 (30 August): 291. This article, like many others signed by Liszt, is thought to have been written by the Countess Marie d'Agoult; see Dorothy Hagan, "French Musical Criticism between the Revolutions," (Ph.D. dissertation, University of Illinois, 1965), p. 69.

77. "Nouvelles," *GMdP* 2/16 (19 April 1835): 139. The remark concerning singers seems somewhat surprising, considering what music from the period has survived.

78. Elwart, "Musique de chambre: Première matinée musicale de MM. Alard, Dancla, Croisilles et Chevillard," *RGMdP* 5/2 (14 January 1838): 12.

79. "Nouvelles," *GMdP* 2/41 (11 October 1835): 335.

80. Berlioz, "Septième et dernier concert du Conservatoire," *RGMdP* 3/19 (8 March 1836): 151.

81. Berlioz to Humbert Ferrand, August or September 1835, in *Hector Berlioz: Selection from His Letters,* p. 60.

82. Liszt, "De la situation des artistes," *GMdP* 2/35 (1835): 290.

83. Elwart, "Musique de chambre," *RGMdP* 5/2 (14 January 1838): 12.

84. N. "Revue de la semaine," *GMdP* 2/30 (26 July 1835): 252.

85. "Nouvelles de Paris: Conservatoire de Musique: Société des Concerts," *ReM* 14 (1834): 53.

86. E. Fétis, "Gymnase musical: Concert de la famille Grassll," *ReM* 15 (12 July 1835): 221–23.

87. "Nouvelles de Paris: Conservatoire de Musique: Société des Concerts," *ReM* 14 (1834): 118–19.

88. See "Nouvelles de Paris: Soirée de M. Baillot," *ReM* 14 (8 February 1834): 45–46, and Henri Blanchard: "Revue critique," *RGMdP* 3/36 (4 September 1836): 312.

89. Henri Blanchard, "Concerts—Société musicale—Soirée de M. Zimmermann," *RGMdP* 5/49 (9 December 1838): 502.

90. G. Kastner, "22e quintette pour instruments à cordes par M. G. Onslow," *RGMdP* 4/21 (21 May 1837): 176–77.

91. See G. Kastner, "Revue critique: Grand trio," *RGMdP* 5/28 (15 July 1838): 290, and (anonymous), "Musique de chambre: Soirées de quatuors et quintetti," *RGMdP* 5/31 (5 August 1838): 310. Oddly, both of these articles cite exceptions to the rules, Kastner mentioning the chamber works being written by Jupin, and the other article describing *séances* at which chamber music was still performed.

92. G. Kastner, "Revue critique: Grand trio."

93. "Athénée musical," *GMdP* 1/17 (27 April 1834): 138. The crucial word in this statement is "performing." There were other orchestral societies, but only the Société Philharmonique (comprising mainly amateurs) met regularly; at that time it was ignored by *ReM* and *GMdP.* There were also some "popular" orchestras. Clearly the Athénée Musical served an unusual function in the Paris musical scene, especially because of its members' willingness to try new works.

94. François Stoepel, "La Musique en France (1835)," *GMdP* 2/39 (27 September 1835): 313–17.

95. Kastner, "Trois quatuors . . . par G. Onslow," *RGMdP* 10/35 (27 August 1843): 297–98.

96. A. Morel, "De l'utilité des sociétés d'amateurs: Cercle Musical," *RGMdP* 7/43 (5 July 1840): 363.

97. "Nouvelles," *RGMdP* 8/61 (28 November 1841): 535.

98. "Nouvelles," *RGMdP* 6/52 (30 December 1839): 587.

99. Cited in Barzun, *Berlioz,* 1:420. Barzun's source was Liszt's *Pages romantiques,* ed. by J. Chantavoine (Paris: F. Alkan, 1912), p. 264.

100. P[aul]. S[mith]. [Edouard Monnais], "Concert au bénéfice de Mme. Ve Berton," *RGMdP* 11/26 (30 June 1844): 223.

101. Chorley, *Music and Manners,* 3:63 and 64.

102. Cited in Barzun, *Berlioz,* 1:343. The original appears in *RGMdP* 7 (1840): 215.

103. Barzun, *Berlioz,* 1:343.

104. Ibid., p. 404.

105. Ibid., p. 479.

106. Ibid., p. 420.

107. See A. Sallès, *Les Premières exécutions à Lyon des oeuvres de Beethoven* (Paris: Jobert, 1927), who wrote that when a Beethoven symphony was performed in Lyons in 1844, the audience complained that they did not wish to hear four consecutive overtures. This story is mentioned in a review by J. T. [Julien Tiersot] in *Revue de musicologie,* 8/23 (August 1927): 168.

108. H.-M. Berton, "Quintetto de M. Turcas," *RGMdP* 7/43 (5 July 1840): 365. Berton added that quartets and quintets did not appear to be lucrative genres.

109. M. Bourges, "Société de Musique Classique," *RGMdP* 16/6 (11 February 1849): 44–45.

110. Léon Kreutzer, "Grande Société Philharmonique de Paris," *RGMdP* 17/4 (27 January 1850): 27.

111. Blanchard, "Auditions musicales," *RGMdP* 19/9 (29 February 1852): 67.

112. "Nouvelles," *RGMdP* 19/21 (23 May 1852): 174.

113. E. Fétis, "De la musique plus que jamais," *RGMdP* 19/30 (25 July 1852): 245–46. I do not wish to imply that Fétis's criticism was unjustified, as the gift to the Société Sainte-Cécile was of relatively minor significance. Fétis suggested that the government should protect theatres, support institutions that performed musical masterpieces, create a national *chapelle* to employ musicians, and provide a place for music in national *fêtes*.

114. "Se distinguent de toutes les autres par de fréquents essais de musique nouvelle." Blanchard, "Auditions musicales," *RGMdP* 16/50 (16 December 1849), 394.

115. "Nouvelles," *RGMdP* 17/7 (17 February 1850): 59, and Barzun, *Berlioz* 1:555.

116. Berlioz, *Memoirs,* pp. 468–69.

117. Blanchard, "Coup d'oeil musical," *RGMdP* 14/11 (14 March 1847): 88.

118. E. Fétis, "Revue d'un demi-siècle: Musique instrumentale," *RGMdP* 18/30 (27 July

1851): 242. Among the contemporary performers cited by Fétis were the brothers Tilmant, Girard, Alard, and Dancla.

119. A. de la Fage, "Concert de Mme L. Farrenc," *RGMdP* 18/14 (6 April 1851): 109.

120. "Nouvelles," *RGMdP* 18/37 (14 September 1851): 304. This article refers particularly to the establishment of the (unsuccessful) Association des Musiciens-Exécutants de Paris.

121. Blanchard, "Société Sainte-Cécile," *RGMdP* 19/51 (19 December 1852): 467.

122. Further evidence of new interest in instrumental genres is suggested by the establishment of a class in instrumental ensemble music at the Conservatoire in 1848, 26 years after the inauguration of its vocal counterpart. See Constant Pierre, *Le Conservatoire National de Musique et de Déclamation: Documents historiques et administratifs* (Paris: Imprimerie nationale, 1900), p. 683.

123. Blanchard, "Préface des concerts de la saison," *RGMdP* 13/44 (1 November 1846): 348–49.

124. Bourges, "Société de Musique Classique," *RGMdP* 16/6 (11 February 1849): pp. 44–45.

125. Berlioz to Pierre Duc, 26 May 1848, in Barzun, *Berlioz* 1:521. Berlioz was in London when he wrote this letter.

126. Cited in Barzun, *Berlioz*, 1:542. Barzun's source is Tiersot's *Le Musicien errant* (Paris: Calmann-Lévy, ca. 1919), p. 240.

127. Barzun (*Berlioz* 1:555) has suggested that consequent to the deaths of Mendelssohn (1847), Chopin (1849), and Spontini (1851), the early 1850s were viewed as the end of an era, from which only Berlioz remained. I believe, however, that this analysis is clouded by historical perspective—that average Parisian musicians, not having esteemed these particular composers as highly as historians have, did not sense such a twilight, and were more interested in day-to-day events. (The French in the early 1850s do not appear to have yet felt a vacuum such as that described by F.-J. Fétis in the early 1830s, following the deaths of Weber, Beethoven, and Hérold.) By 1853 Blanchard was predicting that the coming season would be more serious (that is, better for "art" music) than previous ones; see "Auditions musicales," *RGMdP* 20/1 (2 January 1853): 4.

128. P. Smith [Monnais], "Revue de l'année 1852," *RGMdP* 20/1 (2 January 1853): 1–2.

129. Paul Smith [Monnais], "Société des Jeunes Artistes," *RGMdP* 25/10 (7 March 1858): 73. Monnais might also have mentioned new symphonies by Gounod and Saint-Saëns. Bizet's now famous symphony dates from this period, but remained a carefully guarded secret.

130. This exact problem had been described earlier with regard to the Conservatoire concerts. See "Nouvelles," *RGMdP* 12/4 (26 January 1845): 30 and 18/6 (9 February 1851): 46.

131. Liszt to Freiherr Beaulieu-Marconnay, 21 May 1855, in *Letters of Franz Liszt,* collected by La Mara [Marie Lipsius], 2 vols. (London: H. Grevel & Co., 1894), 1:241–42.

132. Adolphe Botte, "Troisième soirée de musique de chambre," *RGMdP* 26/51 (18 December 1859): 419.

133. P. Scudo *L'Année musicale,* 1 (1860): 184.

134. Botte, "Auditions musicales," *RGMdP* 26/17 (24 April 1859): 136–37.

135. Blanchard, "Concerts à l'Institution Impériale des Jeunes Aveugles," *RGMdP* 25/33 (15 August 1858): 272. The program included works of Grisar, Berthelemy, Boulanger, and Donizetti.

136. See F.-J. Fétis, "Que peut-on faire pour améliorer la condition des jeunes compositeurs?" *RGMdP* 25 (1858): no. 4 (24 January): 25–27; no. 6 (7 February): 41–43; no. 8 (21 February): 57–59; no. 11 (14 March): 81–83; no. 13 (28 March): 101–3.

137. Arthur Dandelot, *La Société des Concerts du Conservatoire,* 3rd ed. rev. (Paris: Delagrave, 1923), p. 214.

138. Blanchard, "Matinées musicales," *RGMdP* 22/9 (4 March 1855): 68. By "classique" Blanchard evidently meant established or "classic," but not "classical" in the stylistic sense, for his examples of *musique classique* included works of J. S. Bach, Scarlatti, and Beethoven.

139. Blanchard, "Des concerts, des matinées et soirées musicales," *RGMdP* 22/50 (16 December 1855): 391–92.

140. Blanchard, "Matinées musicales," *RGMdP* 23/4 (27 January 1856): 26–27.

141. Ibid. Had Blanchard been more worldly, he might have appended to his list the name of Schumann, whose works were not heard regularly in Paris until the following year. F.-J. Fétis expressed, in 1858, a similar sense of loss but for all music, lamenting the disappearance (or inactivity) of Donizetti, Bellini, Rossini, Schubert, Mendelssohn, and Schumann. See "Que peut-on faire pour améliorer la condition des jeunes compositeurs?" *RGMdP* 25/4 (24 January 1858): 26. These sentiments resemble what Barzun has suggested was felt in the early 1850s; see note 127.

142. Blanchard, "Concerts et auditions musicales," *RGMdP* 24/7 (15 February 1857): 49, and no. 9 (1 March): 66.

143. "Nouvelles," *RGMdP* 22/36 (9 September 1855): 279.

144. To be fair, one must acknowledge that the repertory of the Opéra was not always newsworthy. Martin Cooper, in *French Music from the Death of Berlioz to the Death of Fauré* (London: Oxford University Press, 1951), p. 10, has pointed out that only five new French works were introduced there from 1852 to 1870. But its steady repertory, comprising Rossini, Meyerbeer, Donizetti, Auber, and Halévy, was at least postclassical, and it did present new foreign works, such as Verdi's *Luisa Miller* (in 1853), *Les Vêpres siciliennes* (1855), and *Il Trovatore* (1857), and Wagner's *Tannhäuser* (1861). The real point is that, regardless of activities at the Opéra, instrumentalists did little to alleviate their own neglect in the press.

145. "Concerts populaires de musique classique," *RGMdP* 28/41 (13 October 1861): 326.

146. P. Smith [Monnais], "Revue de l'année 1861," *RGMdP* 29/1 (5 January 1862): 1–3.

147. Maurice Cristal, "Histoire de la musique instrumentale," *RGMdP* 34/38 (22 September 1867): 301.

148. "Concerts et auditions musicales de la semaine," *RGMdP* 37/9 (27 February 1870): 69.

149. "Nouvelles," *RGMdP* 33/11 (18 March 1866): 85.

150. "Nouvelles diverses," *RGMdP* 36/48 (28 November 1869): 390.

151. P. Scudo, *L'Année musicale,* 2 (1861): 163.

152. Elwart, *Histoire de la Société des Concerts du Conservatoire Impérial de Musique,* (Paris: S. Castel, 1860), p. 30. Oddly, among his favorite music he cited Handel's oratorios.

153. Scudo: *L'Année musicale,* 2 (1861): 149, and Cristal, "Histoire de la musique instrumentale," *RGMdP* 35/17 (26 April 1868): pp. 129–30.

154. "Von neueren Werken hört man hier äusserst selten etwas, und seit wenig Jahren ist selbst Mendelssohn ersten in den Concerten des Conservatoires aufgenommen. Schumann und Schubert als Instrumental-Componisten kennt man nur wenig; . . . Man hat auch einige schüchterne Versuche gemacht in besonders dafür gegründeten Concerten dem Publikum Werke lebender Componisten vorzuführen . . . aber sie fanden keine rechte Theilnahme, und das Publikum zieht vor, jedes Jahr so ziemlich dieselben Stücke berühmter Meister bewundern zu können, mit aller Sicherheit, sich nicht zu compromittiren; die Künstler ihrerseits finden dies so bequem, dass sie sich nicht gedrungen fühlen, gegen diesen Schlendrian anzukämpfen." R. J. [possibly Jakob Rosenhain]: "Berichte: Paris," *Allgemeine musikalische Zeitung,* n.s. 1/13 (25 (March 1863): cols. 237–38.

155. F.-J. Fétis: "Effets des circonstances sur la situation actuelle de la musique, au point de vue de la composition," *RGMdP* 30/41 (11 October 1863): 323.

156. Elwart, *Histoire de la Société des Concerts,* p. 42. Elwart's claim is exaggerated; although new works were occasionally performed at the Conservatoire (especially before 1848), they were not arduously promoted.

157. Charles Bannelier, "Société des Concerts du Conservatoire impérial de musique," *RGMdP* 35/51 (20 December 1868): 403. The previous year the Conservatoire had begun to play many programs twice, in order to satisfy audience demand.

158. Henri Duparc, "Souvenirs de la Société Nationale," *Revue musicale, Société Internationale de Musique* 8/12 (December 1912): 2.

159. Camille Saint-Saëns in Romain Rolland, *Musiciens d' aujourd'hui,* trans. as *Musicians of Today* by Mary Blaiklock, 4th ed. (New York: Henry Holt and Company, 1919), p. 267.

160. P. Smith [Monnais], "Revue musicale de l'année 1866," *RGMdP* 34/1 (6 January 1867): 1–4.

161. Elwart, *Histoire de la Société des Concerts,* p. 390.

162. See, for example, Botte, "Auditions musicales," *RGMdP* 30/4 (25 January 1863): 27, in reference to the Société Nationale des Beaux Arts.

163. Bannelier, "Société des Concerts de l'Opéra," *RGMdP* 36/46 (14 November 1869): 370–71.

164. "Immer mehr kommt die deutsch Musik hier in die Mode. So erfreulich es auch ist, nicht mehr ausschliesslich nur im Conservatoire, den Concerts populaires und in den mit jeden Jahr sich mehrenden Quartett-Vereinen gute Musik zu hören, sondern auch in den meisten Concerten und Privat-Soiréen, wo noch vor Kurzem die Virtuosen-

kunststücke und die Opernphantasien aller Arten sich breit machten, so ist es bis jetzt eben doch weit mehr die Mode, die diesen Umschwung bewirkt, als ein grösseres Verständnis des Publikums. . . . In den festlich erleuchteten, grossen, von Gold und Seide strotzenden Salons der vornehmen Welt ist ein zahlreicher Kreis der elegantesten Pariser Damen in brillanter Balltoilette versammelt, nicht etwa um Quadrille und Polka zu tanzen; nein, es ist ein musikalische Soirée, und was wird diesen eleganten Damen vorgeführt? Ist es ein berühmter Virtuose, der sich da producirt? Ist es Mademoiselle Patti, die prima donna vom italienischen Theater, die jetzt aller Welt die Köpfe verdreht? Nein, es sind die letzten Quartette von Beethoven." R. J., "Berichte: Paris," *Allgemeine musikalische Zeitung,* n.s. 1/13 (25 March 1863), col. 237.

165. Duparc, "Souvenirs," p. 2.

166. Elwart, *Histoire de la Société des Concerts,* p. 31.

167. "Le public, et particulièrement la haute société parisienne s'initient chaque jour davantage à la grande musique instrumentale et . . . les oeuvres de Beethoven, Haydn, Mozart, Weber, Mendelssohn, Schubert, Fesca, Boccherini, y compris Robert Schumann trouvent en France des auditeurs éclaires qui n'existaient pas il y a trente ans." P. Scudo, *L'Année musicale,* 2 (1861): 181–82. This was written *before* the establishment of the Concert Populaires, which extended the availability of instrumental "art" music to the less wealthy.

168. Botte, "Auditions musicales," *RGMdP* 29/4 (26 January 1862): 29.

169. Em. Mathieu de Monter, "Revue musicale de l'année 1867," *RGMdP* 35/2 (12 January 1868): 9–12. He believed that the new interest was primarily in established works.

170. Bannelier, "Concerts et auditions musicales," *RGMdP* 33/12 (25 March 1866): 90. Oechsner did obtain some performances of his music in Paris.

171. P. Smith [Monnais], "Revue de l'année 1864," *RGMdP* 32/1 (1 January 1865): 1–3, and "Revue de l'année 1865," *RGMdP* 33/2 (14 January 1866): 9–11.

172. Searle, *Berlioz: Letters,* p. 211, letter of 22 December 1867.

173. See "Concerts et auditions musicales de la semaine," *RGMdP* 36 (1869), nos. 11 (14 March): 92–93 and 12 (21 March): 101.

174. Elwart, *Histoire de la Société des Concerts,* p. 40. On Berlioz and Douay's works, Elwart wrote "en dramatisant toutes leurs productions de ce genre, ils ont presque détruit la véritable symphonie, noble, pure et pleine d'unité, pour substituer à sa place les brillantes fantaisies de leur esprit musical et plus ami du merveilleux, que respectueux envers la forme consacrée à la symphonie par tant de chefs-d'oeuvre dus aux patriarches de ce genre admirable."

175. Botte, "Matinée musicale de la Société Nationale des Beaux-Arts," *RGMdP* 29/51 (21 December 1862): 410. Botte's pronouncement was instigated by a performance of David's symphonic ode *Christophe Colomb.*

176. Ives Kéramzer, "De la symphonie moderne et de son avenir," *RGMdP* 37/24 (12 June 1870): 185–86. In his eagerness to defend dramatic or programmatic works, Kéramzer probably gave too little credit to the purely musical organization of compositions such as Berlioz's, yet it is refreshing to read, in a French journal, advocacy of departure from traditional thinking.

177. Advertisement for J. Maho in *RGMdP* 38/38 (15 October 1871): 292. One can legitimately argue that French composers had not yet had time to react with new music, but it is curious that Maho publicized German works rather than prewar French works, if anti-German sentiment was strong.

178. Mathieu de Monter, "Revue de l'année 1871," *RGMdP* 39/1 (7 January 1872): 2–3.

179. See "Nouvelles diverses," *RGMdP* 38 (1871), no. 39 (22 October): 297; no. 40 (29 October): 307; no. 46 (10 December): 354; no. 48 (24 December): 370.

180. James Harding, *Saint-Saëns and His Circle* (London: Chapman & Hall, 1965), p. 120. Regarding the success of the Concerts Danbé and Mozart, see "Nouvelles diverses," *RGMdP* 38 (1871), no. 43 (19 November): 331 and no. 45 (3 December): 346.

181. E.-M.-E Deldevez, *La Société des Concerts: 1860 à 1885* (Paris: Firmin-Didot et Cie, 1887), pp. 220–25. The Conservatoire still did not perform many complete, major works of French composers.

182. M. Cooper, *French Music,* pp. 9–10.

183. Berlioz, *Memoirs,* pp. 468–69.

184. Elwart, *Histoire de la Société des Concerts,* p. 32.

185. Rolland, *Musicians of Today,* pp. 249–52.

186. Tiersot, "La Symphonie en France," p. 395.

187. Tiersot, "Edouard Lalo," *Musical Quarterly,* 11/1 (January 1925): 13.

188. Arthur Hervey, *French Music in the XIXth Century* (London: Grant Richards, 1903), p. 107.

189. Edward Burlingame Hill, *Modern French Music* (Boston and New York: Houghton Mifflin Company, 1924), pp. 4–5, 12, and 154.

190. Paul Landormy, *La Musique française de Franck à Debussy,* 5th ed. (Paris: Gallimard, [1943]), p. 19.

191. Gerald Abraham, *A Hundred Years of Music,* 4th ed. (Frome and London: Duckworth, 1974), p. 19.

192. Paul Henry Lang, *Music in Western Civilization* (New York: W. W. Norton & Company, 1941), p. 827. Lang's suggestion is explored in Arnold B. Perris's doctoral dissertation, "Music in France during the Reign of Louis-Philippe: Art as a Substitute for Heroic Experience" (Northwestern University, 1967).

193. Pierre Meylan, "Delacroix et les musiciens romantiques," *Revue musicale,* 25/209 (March 1949): 9.

194. Lang, *Music in Western Civilization,* pp. 925–26.

195. Marie Louise Pereyra, J.-G. Prod'homme, and Gustave Chouquet, "Paris," *Grove's Dictionary of Music and Musicians,* 3rd ed. (London: Macmillan, 1927–28), 4: 46–51.

196. Georges Servières, "La Symphonie en France au XIXe siècle (avant 1870)," *Ménestrel* 76/39 (28 September 1923): 397–400.

197. Pierre Soccanne, "Virtuoses: un maître de quatuor: Pierre Baillot (1771–1842)," *Le Guide du concert* 24 (1937–38), nos. 24 (11 March 1938) to 30 (22 April), and "Quel-

ques documents inédites sur Pierre Baillot," *Revue de musicologie,* 23/71–72 (1939): 71–78, and série spéciale, no. 2 (July 1943): 15–18.

198. Leo Schrade, *Beethoven in France* (New Haven: Yale University Press, 1942).

199. Barzun, *Berlioz and the Romantic Century,* (Boston: Little Brown, 1950); Schwarz, "French Instrumental Music between the Revolutions (1789–1830)" (Ph.D. dissertation, Columbia University, 1950); Cooper, *French Music from the Death of Berlioz to the Death of Fauré,* (London: Oxford University Press, 1951).

200. Dorothy Hagan, "French Musical Criticism between the Revolutions" (Ph.D. dissertation, University of Illinois, 1965), p. 315.

201. Weber, *Music and the Middle Class: the Social Structure of Concert Life in London, Paris, and Vienna* (London: Croom Helm, 1975).

202. Dandelot, *La Société des Concerts,* p. 61.

203. Deldevez, *La Société des Concerts,* pp. 23–24, 48–49, and 53–54; quotation concerning Beethoven on p. 273.

204. Ibid., p. 288.

205. Tiersot, "La Symphonie en France," p. 394.

206. Rolland, *Musicians of Today,* pp. 44 and 45.

207. J.-G. Prod'homme, "The Works of Weber in France," *Musical Quarterly* 14/3 (July 1928): 385. In chapter 6 I argue that Weber's overtures, his most popular works in France, had nearly the opposite influence.

208. Weber, *Music and the Middle Class,* p. 54.

209. Barzun, *Berlioz,* 1:420.

210. Barzun (*Berlioz* 1:416) pointed out that this development had occurred during Beethoven's lifetime.

211. Hervey, *French Music,* p. 184.

212. Cooper, "The Nineteenth Century Musical Renaissance in France (1870–1895)," *Proceedings of the Royal Music Association,* 74 (1947–48), p. 11.

213. Lockspeiser, "Berlioz and the French Romantics," pp. 26–28.

214. F. Stoepel, "Essai sur la poétique de la musique instrumentale," *GMdP* 2 (15 February 1835): 55–57.

215. Berlioz, "Septième et dernier concert du Conservatoire," *RGMdP* 3/19 (8 May 1836): 151.

216. Barzun, *Berlioz,* 1:420. Saint-Saëns once wrote that the musical public of the mid-nineteenth century "was divided into two hostile camps. There were the lovers of melody, who were in the large majority and included the musical critics; and, on the other side, the subscribers to the Conservatoire and the Maurin, Alard, and Armingaud quartets. They were devotees of learned music; "poseurs," others said, who pretended to admire works they did not understand at all." See *Musical Memories,* trans. Edwin Gale Rich (Boston: Small, Maynard & Company, 1919), p. 202.

217. Among other recent discussions of the relationship between music and audiences in

nineteenth-century France are passages in the doctoral dissertations of Peter Bloom, Dorothy Hagan, and Arnold B. Perris (all cited above) and in Henry Raynor, *Music and Society since 1815* (London: Barrie & Jenkins, 1976).

218. Recent dissertations on French nineteenth-century composers of instrumental music include the following: Sabina Teller Ratner, "The Piano Works of Camille Saint-Saëns" (University of Michigan, 1972); Daniel Fallon, "The Symphonies and Symphonic Poems of Camille Saint-Saëns" (Yale University, 1973); Elizabeth Remsberg, "The Chamber Music of Saint-Saëns" (New York University, 1976); Bea Friedland, "Louise Farrenc (1804–1875): Composer, Performer, Scholar" (City University of New York, 1975), since published under the same title (Ann Arbor: UMI Research Press, 1980); Peter Bloom, "François-Joseph Fétis and the *Revue Musicale* (1827–1835)" (University of Pennsylvania, 1972); Ralph Locke, "Music in the Saint-Simonian Movement; the Political Involvement and Artistic Contribution of Félicien David and Other French Utopian Socialist Musicians" (University of Chicago, 1980); and Joël-Marie Fauquet, "Alexis de Castillon, sa vie, son oeuvre" (doctorat, Ecole pratique des Hautes Etudes, 1977). Three dissertations on Onslow were registered as being in progress in 1977.

Chapter 6

1. W. W. Cobbett, *Cobbett's Cyclopedic Survey of Chamber Music,* 2nd ed., 3 vols. (London: Oxford University Press, 1963), and F.-J. Fétis, *Biographie universelle des musiciens* (hereafter *FétisB*), 2nd ed. (Paris: Firmin Didot frères, 1866–70); *Supplément et complément,* ed. Arthur Pougin (Paris: Firmin Didot frères, 1878–80).

2. This study was inspired partly by my editorial activity for the *New Grove Dictionary of Music and Musicians* (London: Macmillan Publishers Ltd., 1980). In the process of compiling and editing "works" lists therein, I was struck by the large number of nineteenth-century French composers who wrote instrumental works, most of which are unknown to twentieth-century performers and audiences.

3. Some sources credit Onslow with 36 string quartets. For my figures on the quartets and quintets I have relied on the article "Onslow, (André) Georges (Louis)" by Benedict Sarnaker, in the *New Grove Dictionary of Music and Musicians,* 13:543–44. In the "works" list of this article Sarnaker states that the Third Symphony, Op. 69, is a version of the String Quintet Op. 32.

4. Maurice Bourges noted such a change as early as 1843. See "Revue critique: Quatuor en fa . . . par Ch. Dancla," *RGMdP* 10/28 (9 July 1843):243–44.

5. Saint-Saëns wrote in *Les Idées de M. Vincent d'Indy* (Paris, 1919), "Art is form above all else. . . . He who does not feel wholly satisfied with elegant lines, harmonious colors, and a fine series of chords does not understand art." This translation is provided by James Harding in his *Saint-Saëns and His Circle* (London: Chapman & Hall, 1965), p. 219.

6. Of course, even the more Romantic nineteenth-century composers carried forward traits exhibited in late eighteenth-century works.

7. "Concours de symphonies," *RGMdP* 20/36 (4 September 1853):309–10.

8. Charles Rosen, *The Classical Style: Haydn, Mozart, Beethoven,* Norton Library ed. (New York: W. W. Norton & Company, 1972), pp. 21 and 22.

9. Edouard Fétis, "Revue d'un demi-siècle: Musique instrumentale," *RGMdP* 18/30 (27 July 1851):241.

10. See, for example, A.-P.-F. Boëly's sonata for piano and violin, Opus 32 No. 2. The date of the composition is unknown; it was published in either 1858 or 1859, shortly after Boëly's death.

11. I am grateful to Philip Howard, who has done considerable research on Walckiers, for exchanging views with me on Walckiers's music.

12. Donald J. Grout, *A History of Western Music,* 3rd ed. rev. (New York: W. W. Norton & Company, 1980), p. 554.

13. "Dans les réunions ou la fin d'un ouvrage n'arrive jamais assez tôt au gré des impatients ou des ennemis des morceaux développés, on sera bien de supprimer la Marche, et de ne commencer le FINALE qu'au 2/4; mais, dans ce cas, on jouera le SCHERZO avant l'ADAGIO. On pourra, même, supprimer entierement le FINALE. Enfin, on pourra aussi ne jouer que deux morceaux: le PREMIER et le SCHERZO; ou l'ADAGIO et le SCHERZO; ou, enfin, le 1er MORCEAU et le FINALE." Eugène Walckiers: 1er Sonate pour Piano et Clarinette en Si♭, Op. 91 (Paris: S. Richault, ca. 1855). Walckiers also suggested that the Coda to the first movement could be deleted "si l'on trouvait le morceau trop long."

14. See, for example, E. Fétis, "Revue d'un demi-siècle: Musique instrumentale," *RGMdP* 18/27 (6 July 1851):217.

15. H. Woolett, "Onslow," in *Cobbett's Cyclopedic Survey of Chamber Music,* 2:195–200.

16. H. Berlioz, "5e concert du Conservatoire," *RGMdP* 3/13 (27 March 1836):97–98, and P. [possibly Heinrich Panofka], "Revue critique," *RGMdP* 4/9 (26 February 1837):73. The reviews of Berlioz and P. cited here are representative of a much larger number of favorable comments in the contemporary press.

17. Edward Burlingame Hill, *Modern French Music* (Boston and New York: Houghton Mifflin Company, 1924), p. 26.

18. "Revue critique," *GMdP* 1/36 (7 September 1834):290–91.

19. Ad. Guerroult, "Concert de M. Henri Reber," *RGMdP* 6/52 (30 December 1839):579.

20. Arthur Hervey, *French Music in the XIXth Century* (London: Grant Richards, 1903), p. 107.

21. See Bea Friedland, *Louise Farrenc (1804–1875): Composer, Performer, Scholar* (Ann Arbor: UMI Research Press, 1980). A much briefer discussion of Farrenc's activities is Friedland's article of the same title in *Musical Quarterly,* 60/2 (April 1974):257–74.

22. Friedland: "Louise Farrenc (1804–1875): Composer, Performer, Scholar," *Musical Quarterly,* 60/2 (April 1974):266–73.

23. "Blanc, Adolphe," *FétisB,* 1:434.

24. Adolphe Piriou, "Blanc," in *Cobbett's Cyclopedic Survey of Chamber Music,* 1:126.

25. W. W. Cobbett, "Dancla," in *Cobbett's Cyclopedic Survey of Chamber Music,* 1:313.

26. Berlioz, though, in reviewing a *symphonie concertante* of Dancla performed in 1840

mentioned its originality, elegant vivacity, and effective handling of solo parts. See "Deuxième concert du Conservatoire," *RGMdP* 7/10 (3 February 1840):80–81.

27. Francis Hueffer, "David, Félicien (César)," revised by Marie Louise Pereyra, in *Grove's Dictionary of Music and Musicians,* 5th ed. (London: Macmillan and Co., 1954), 2:604–5.

28. Bourges, "Septième concert du Conservatoire," *RGMdP* 13/15 (12 April 1846):113.

29. F.-J. Fétis, "Douay, Emile", *FétisB,* 3:50, and E. Fétis, "Revue d'un demi-siècle: Musique instrumentale," *RGMdP* 18/27 (6 July 1851):219.

30. E.-M.-E. Deldevez, *La Société des Concerts: 1860 à 1885* (Paris: Firmin-Didot et Cie, 1887), pp. 48–49.

31. The Paris Bibliothèque Nationale has only three string quartets and a piano quartet among printed works, but possesses MSS of a fifth symphony, dated 1856, and a 27th string quartet, dated 1855.

32. E. Fétis, "Dernier concert de la société," *Rem* 5 (1829):347–49.

33. The Weber specialist John Warrack has noted that "It is in the three major operatic overtures, to *Der Freischütz, Euryanthe,* and *Oberon,* that a sonata structure is most successfully handled [among Weber's works]." See his *Carl Maria von Weber,* 2nd ed. (Cambridge: Cambridge University Press, 1976), p. 374.

34. Rey M. Longyear: *Nineteenth-Century Romanticism in Music,* 2nd ed. (Englewood Cliffs, New Jersey: Prentice Hall, 1973), pp. 82 and 85.

35. These were his second through sixth quartets; the first dates from 1814. The second, completed in 1829, was actually a reworking of a symphony first performed in 1815. The latter four date from the mid-1830s. Only quartets nos. 1–3 were published during Cherubini's lifetime.

36. See Georges de Saint-Foix: "Cherubini," in *Cobbett's Cyclopedic Survey of Chamber Music,* 1:270–73, and Orlando A. Mansfield, "Cherubini's String Quartets," *Musical Quarterly,* 15/4 (October 1929):590–605; see also Basil Deane: "Cherubini, Luigi . . . ," in the *New Grove Dictionary of Music and Musicians,* 4:209. The quartets are among the few works discussed in this chapter that have been recorded; see phonorecord DG 2710018, on which the Melos Quartet performs worthily.

37. Mansfield, "Cherubini's String Quartets," p. 598, and Saint-Foix, "Cherubini," pp. 271 and 272.

38. Saint-Foix, "Cherubini," p. 273 and Mansfield, "Cherubini's String Quartets," p. 590.

39. The article "Rousselot" in the supplement to *FétisB* (2:456) mentions only one symphony. I note performances of unspecified symphonies by Rousselot in 1834, 1835, 1842, and 1843. This grouping of performances suggests two works, but could, of course, represent any number from one to four. There may also have been performances of which I am unaware, or symphonies that were never performed. Although I have found no published chamber works of Rousselot after 1831, the Bibliothèque Nationale (Paris) possesses, in the Conservatoire collection, the MS of a string quintet dated 1846.

40. E. F[étis]., "Gymnase musical: Concert de la famille Grassll," *ReM* 15 (12 July

1835):221–23; M. Bourges: "Concert du Cercle Musical des Amateurs", *RGMdP* 9/16 (17 April 1842):169–70.

41. From Schumann's *Gesammelte Schriften,* cited in Cobbett, "Bertini," *Cobbett's Cyclopedic Survey of Chamber Music,* 1:124.

42. H. Blanchard, "Concerts—Société musicale—Soirée de M. Zimmermann," *RGMdP* 5/49 (9 December 1838):502. Blanchard's comment was made in connection with the first movement of a septet.

43. Gounod, *Autobiographical Reminiscences,* trans. W. Hely Hutchinson (London: Heinemann, 1896), p. 151.

44. Gounod's Symphony No. 1 is on phonorecord Kapp 9039; Symphony No. 2 is on Decca, DL 9982.

45. Howard Shanet, "Bizet's Suppressed Symphony," *Musical Quarterly,* 44/4 (October 1958):461–76.

46. The quintet in A minor has been recorded by the Brussels String Quartet with Louis Logie, viola; see phonorecord MHS 3266 (Musical Heritage Society, "Music in Wallonia," vol. 2).

47. Other composers of works for virtuosos also utilized a dramatic idiom. Some of Gallay's works, however, are clearly rooted in traditions of "art" music, and seem to be of above average merit.

48. F.-J. Fétis, "Quatrième concert d'émulation, donné par les élèves de l'Ecole royale de musique," *ReM* 4 (1828):377, and "Deuxième concert d'émulation des élèves de l'Ecole royale de musique," *ReM* 5 (1829):495.

49. Otto Klauwell wrote a lengthy biography of Gouvy, which includes a discussion of the works: *Theodor Gouvy: Sein Leben und seine Werke* (Berlin: Harmonie, 1902).

50. See the passage on Gouvy in Jules Combarieu: *Histoire de la musique,* new ed., 3rd vol. (Paris: Libraire Armand Colin, 1928), 3:520–21.

51. See the articles "Pfeiffer" in *FétisB,* 7:22, and Pougin's supplement to *FétisB,* 2:331–32.

52. These works are all mentioned in an appendix of James Harding's *Massenet* (New York: St. Martin's Press, 1970), pp. 215–17. The music for *Pompéia* was later used as incidental music for *Les Erinnyes.* Possibly the list of prewar instrumental works should be longer. The Paris Bibliothèque Nationale possesses a published score entitled "Devant le madone: souvenir de la campagne de Rome," tentatively dated 1864 (published in 1897), and a MS score, "Le Retour d'une Caravane," dated June 1866; both are orchestral. The Bibliothèque Nationale also has a MS entitled "Adagio religioso" for violin and organ, dated September 1867. Pougin mentioned, in the article "Massenet" in the supplement to *FétisB,* 2:180–84, the performance of two orchestral *fantaisies* (not further identified) in July 1866. Furthermore, the second orchestral suite, "Scènes hongroises," was performed in November 1871 and an "Introduction et variations" for string and wind quintets was played in March 1872; either or both may have been completed before the war.

53. Pougin, "Massenet," supplement to *FétisB,* 2:181.

54. "Tingry," *FétisB,* 8:230.

55. Blanchard, "Coup d'oeil musical," *RGMdP* 12/47 (23 November 1845):383–85.

56. The MSS of an "Ouverture solennelle" and a symphony in F, both in the Paris Bibliothèque Nationale, are dated 1880.

57. Lacombe's posthumously published *Philosophie et musique* (Paris: Fischbacher, 1896), edited by his second wife, "Andrée" Lacombe (actually Claudine Duclairfait Lacombe), includes a long list of his unpublished instrumental works. To my knowledge, most of these remain unpublished.

58. "Lacombe," *FétisB* 5:57–58. Fétis evidently had in mind David's and Douay's programmatic works, rather than their more traditional music, discussed earlier in this paper.

59. My observations are based upon an examination of several of Lacombe's works, representing many genres. The prewar instrumental works that I studied include the Piano Trio No. 2 in A minor, the Piano Quintet, and the Overture in B minor.

60. Blanchard, "Revue critique," *RGMdP* 23/12 (23 March 1856):92.

61. See the articles on Léon Kreutzer in *FétisB,* 5:109–10, and Pougin's supplement, 2:50–51.

62. F.-J. Fétis remembered Prudent the student as a born pianist, incompetent in traditional theory and counterpoint. See "Prudent," *FétisB,* 7:131.

63. Edouard Monnais pointed out that the one-movement structure provided a "programmatic" similarity to a vast prairie; he deemed it not a true concerto. See P. S., "Concert d'Emile Prudent", *RGMdP* 23/11 (16 March 1856):83–84.

64. Pougin, in the article "Lalo," supplement to *FétisB,* 2:66–68, also mentioned among Lalo's early works two symphonies and two quintets that had not been published.

65. Although Lalo was also a respected violinist and violist, he was not even mentioned in the second edition of Fétis's *Biographie universelle des musiciens* (1866–70).

66. Phonorecord, Vox-Turnabout, TVC 37002, copyright 1979, by the Caecilian Trio.

67. Florent Schmitt, "Lalo," *Cobbett's Cyclopedic Survey of Chamber Music,* 2:88.

68. The history of Franck's early works is confusing. According to his biographer Laurence Davies, Franck had completed and assigned (nonconsecutive) opus numbers to several juvenile works before 1840. With the composition of the three trios, Franck recommenced with Op. 1, signifying that these were his first professional efforts. See Laurence Davies, *César Franck and His Circle* (Boston: Houghton Mifflin Company, 1970), pp. 46–47. At Liszt's suggestion, the original finale of the third trio (in B minor) was transformed into a fourth trio, Op. 2, in B Major (dedicated to Liszt); a new finale was provided for the third trio. Tiersot claimed that the first three trios were completed by 1840, but most other sources state 1841. See J. Tiersot: "César Franck," *Musical Quarterly,* 9/1 (January 1923):39. All three trios had been performed in Paris by 1841. Franck wrote no other significant instrumental works before the 1870s.

69. See, for example, J. Tiersot, "César Franck," *Musical Quarterly* 9/1 (January 1923):39ff., and Vincent d'Indy, "Franck," in *Cobbett's Cyclopedic Survey of Chamber Music,* 1:419–20.

70. The Peters (Leipzig) edition gives the tempo of the first movement as "Andante con

moto, ♩ = 69''. Because, as in this example, the smallest note value for much of the first movement is a quarter note, the suggested tempo could not possibly be ''con moto.'' I suspect that the correct tempo is 𝅗𝅥. = 69, as it is recorded by the Copinsky Ensemble (phonorecord, Sheffield, Set 3, 145STA). The grace note G-sharp (in parentheses) to the high F-sharp is to be played only in the repeat.

71. The performance of a ''Ballade et Intermezzo'' from a second symphony was announced for a concert of Mathias's music in 1859. See ''Nouvelles,'' *RGMdP* 26/16 (17 April 1859):130. Botte's review of this concert (''Auditions musicales'', *RGMdP* 26/17 (24 April):134–35), however, does not indicate clearly that these were part of a second symphony, and later sources mention only one.

72. Blanchard, ''Deux quintettes inédits par Georges Mathias,'' *RGMdP* 15/9 (27 April 1848):67–68.

73. Blanchard, ''Société Sainte-Cécile'', *RGMdP* 21/52 (24 December 1854):414–15. A committee comprising Halévy, Ambroise Thomas, Reber, and Gounod had unanimously selected Mathias's symphony for performance at the Société Sainte-Cécile's concert of contemporary works; see ''Nouvelles'', *RGMdP* 21/36 (3 September):290, and no. 48 (26 November):387.

74. Blanchard, however, had described the melodies of Mathias's first piano trio as ''sumptuous.'' See ''Revue critique,'' *RGMdP* 16/38 (23 September 1849):300.

75. See especially Vincent d'Indy, ''Castillon,'' in *Cobbett's Cyclopedic Survey of Chamber Music,* 1:232–35; Paul Landormy, *La Musique française de Franck à Debussy,* 5th ed. (Paris: Gallimard, [1943]), pp. 60–64; Hugues Imbert, *Profils d'artistes contemporaines* (Paris: Société anonyme, 1897), pp. 1–29; and Laurence Davies, *César Franck and His Circle,* pp. 114–16 and 124–36.

76. After meeting Franck in 1868, Castillon destroyed works (including a symphony, the first Op. 1) written earlier under the guidance of Victor Massé.

77. André Gauthier, ''Castillon,'' *Die Musik in Geschichte und Gegenwart,* vol. 2 (Kassel-Basel: Bärenreiter-Verlag, 1953), col. 903.

78. Castillon did write modally elsewhere; parts of the third movement of the same sonata are in the Phrygian mode.

79. d'Indy in *Cobbett's Cyclopedic Survey,* p. 234.

80. Gustave Ferrari (and others) suggested that Castillon was also influenced by Bach, Berlioz, and, needless to say, Franck. See ''Castillon,'' *Grove's Dictionary of Music and Musicians,* 5th ed. 2:115.

81. Davies, *César Franck and His Circle,* p. 128.

82. Dissertations on Saint-Saëns's piano, chamber, and orchestral works are cited in the final note of chapter 5. Within the past few years, the following early works have been recorded: Tarantella for flute, clarinet, and piano, Op. 6 (Crystal 642); First Piano Concerto, Op. 17 (Seraphim SIC-6081); Suite for cello, Opus 16 (Philipps 6500459); First Piano Trio, Op. 18 (Turnabout-Vox, TVC 37002); four early symphonies—Op. 2 and Op. 55 (Angel S-36995) and the Symphony in A with the Symphony in F, ''Urbs Roma'' (Angel S-37089). The latter two had not been published and, according to Daniel Fallon's informative liner notes, were performed from parts copied from the MSS at the Paris Bibliothèque Nationale. A score to the Symphony in

A was published in 1974 (Paris: Editions Françaises de Musique). Recordings to many other prewar works have been available for some time.

83. Saint-Saëns later edited the Durand edition of Rameau's works, as well as music of various *clavecinistes*.

84. Peter A. Bloom, "François-Joseph Fétis and the *Revue Musicale* (1827–1835)" (Ph.D. dissertation, University of Pennsylvania, 1972), pp. 381–85.

85. See, for example, Ives Kéramzer, "De la symphonie moderne et de son avenir," *RGMdP* 37/24 (12 June 1870):185–86.

86. Saint-Saëns's concert series in the salle Pleyel was cancelled by the management when in 1865 he replaced the repertory of Mozart piano concertos with his own and other nineteenth-century works.

87. Martin Cooper, *French Music from the Death of Berlioz to the Death of Fauré* (London: Oxford University Press, 1951), p. 19; Longyear, *Nineteenth-Century Romanticism,* p. 211.

88. Longyear, *Nineteenth-Century Romanticism,* p. 211. Later, after the Germans invaded France in World War I, Saint-Saëns openly expressed hostile feelings regarding German art, particularly in his book *Germanophilie* (Paris: Dorbon-aîné, [1916]).

89. Longyear, *Nineteenth-Century Romanticism,* p. 208.

Chapter 7

1. Paul Dukas, writing of Lalo, maintained that symphonic and chamber music were relegated to specialists, amateurs, and attenders of the Conservatoire concerts, and that most in these groups were interested only in the music of dead composers (See "Edouard Lalo," *Revue musicale,* 4/5 (March 1923):97). Dukas's statement accurately summarizes conditions through the late 1840s, the time of Lalo's earliest instrumental works.

2. Reviewing a performance of the *Symphonie Fantastique* and *Lélio* in December 1832, F.-J. Fétis wrote, "Before one can be an innovator in music, one has to be a musician. This is something that M. Berlioz does not appear to have realized." (*ReM* 12, 15 December 1832; the translation is by David Cairns, in his edition of Berlioz's *Mémoires: The Memoirs of Hector Berlioz: Member of the French Institute* (London: Victor Gollancz Ltd., 1969), p. 219, note 9). Although Fétis's criticism was evidently in response to events that he interpreted as a personal attack by Berlioz—for his initial review of the *Symphonie Fantastique* had been much more favorable (see Barzun, *Berlioz and the Romantic Century,* 3rd ed. 2 vols. (New York: Columbia University Press, 1969), 1:151 and 232–33)—this view may have reflected the opinion of conservative listeners.

3. A review of the premiere of the *Symphonie Fantàstique* noted that it was especially well attended by the young. See "Nouvelles de Paris," *ReM* 10 (1830–31):151. This categorization of listeners into two prominent groups, neither of which appreciated modern instrumental music, is similar to but somewhat broader than a categorization proposed by Jacques Barzun (quoted in chapter 5). Barzun maintained that in the first half of the century (the period that my categorization is intended to reflect), the listening public could be divided into "exclusive opera-goers" and a "fashionable and

academic circle of amateurs, reared on the eighteenth-century classics and contemporary 'little pieces.' " See Barzun, *Berlioz and the Romantic Century,* 1:420.

4. For the views of a contemporary on this phenomenon, see F.-J. Fétis: "Effets des circonstances sur la situation actuelle de la musique, au point de vue de la composition," *RGMdP* 30/38 (20 September 1863):297–99.

5. Cherubini's late string quartets are the notable exception to the directors' almost exclusive interest in vocal music; he had also attempted at least one symphony for string orchestra, some light orchestral works, and a string quintet, earlier in his career. Auber's instrumental contributions after 1828 consist of minor orchestral works—a Marche militaire, a Fête venitienne, some dances, and an overture—and pieces for string quartet. Earlier he had composed concertos, *pièces symphoniques,* two string quartets, a piano quartet, and a piano trio. See the list compiled by Rey Longyear in his article on Auber in *Grove 6,* 1:682.

6. Remarkably, this pattern was continued by Auber's successor, Ambroise Thomas. Another opera composer, he assumed the post in 1871, a few months before his 60th birthday, and retained it until his death at the age of 84.

7. Constant Pierre, *Le Conservatoire National de Musique et de Déclamation: Documents historiques et administratifs* (Paris: Imprimerie nationale, 1900), p. 533. Meanwhile, Berlioz was rejected (by Cherubini) as a teacher of harmony classes there, allegedly because of his incompetence at the piano. See Berlioz, *Memoirs,* p. 236.

8. William Weber, *Music and the Middle Class: The Social Structure of Concert Life in London, Paris, and Vienna* (London: Croom Helm, 1975), pp. 36–37.

9. Arthur Hervey, *French Music in the XIXth Century* (London: Grant Richards, 1903), p. 177.

10. Jean-Michel Nectoux, "Fauré, Gabriel (Urbain)," *Grove 6,* 6:419.

11. Martin Cooper, *French Music from the Death of Berlioz to the Death of Fauré* (London: Oxford University Press, 1951), p. 55.

12. William W. Austin, *Music in the Twentieth Century* (New York: W. W. Norton & Co., 1966), p. 1.

13. Rey M. Longyear, *Nineteenth-Century Romanticism in Music,* 2nd ed. (Englewood Cliffs, New Jersey: Prentice-Hall, 1973), p. 183.

14. Romain Rolland, *Musiciens d'aujourd'hui,* trans. Mary Blaiklock as *Musicians of Today,* 4th ed. (New York: Henry Holt and Company, 1919), p. 43.

Appendix A

1. "Nouvelles," *RGMdP* 4/48 (26 November 1837): 513.

2. "Nouvelles de Paris," *ReM* 7 (1830): 153.

3. Joël-Marie Fauquet, "Notes et documents: Hector Berlioz et l'Association des Artistes-Musiciens," *Revue de musicologie,* 67/2 (1981): 211.

4. [Emile Réty], "Association des Artistes Musiciens: Assemblée générale," *RGMdP* 32/19 (7 May 1865): 148.

5. Jacques Barzun, in *Berlioz and the Romantic Century,* 3rd ed. rev. 2 vols. (New York: Columbia University Press, 1969), 1:438.

6. Fauquet, "Notes et documents," p. 211.

7. Barzun, *Berlioz,* p. 440. The Association also sponsored festivals of religious music in the provinces; see Fauquet, "Notes et documents," p. 225.

8. P[aul]. S[mith]. [Edouard Monnais], "Hippodrome: Grand Festival donné par L'association des Artistes-Musiciens," *RGMdP* 13/30 (26 July 1846): 233–34; and "Nouvelles," *RGMdP* 32(1865), no. 20 (14 May): 158, and no. 23 (4 June): 186.

9. Smith [Monnais], "Revue de l'année 1852," *RGMdP* 20/1 (2 January 1853): 1–2.

10. "Nouvelles," *RGMdP* 18/37 (14 September 1851): 304.

11. Ibid.

12. H. Blanchard, "Société des Musiciens Exécutants," *RGMdP* 18/46 (16 November 1851): 371–72.

13. *FétisB,* 5:421.

14. "Nouvelles," *RGMdP* 31/22 (29 May 1864): 174.

15. D.-A.-D. Saint-Yves, "Concerts et auditions," *RGMdP* 31/4 (24 January 1864):25.

16. "Nouvelles," *RGMdP* 31/16 (17 April 1864): 126.

17. "Nouvelles," *RGMdP* 31/3 (17 January 1864): 22, and Saint-Yves, "Concerts et auditions," p. 25.

18. "Nouvelles," *RGMdP* 30/41 (11 October 1863): 326.

19. Saint-Yves, "Concerts et auditions," p. 25.

20. "Nouvelles," *RGMdP* 31/5 (31 January 1864): 38, and no. 16, p. 126.

21. Much information on Baillot's *soirées* can be obtained from reviews in *ReM* and *GMdP.* The best single sources on Baillot and his *soirées* are Pierre Soccanne's "Virtuoses: un maître du quatuor: Pierre Baillot (1771–1842)," *Le Guide du concert* 24 (1937–38), nos. 24 (11 March 1938) to 30 (22 April); the same author's "Quelques documents inédites sur Pierre Baillot," *Revue de musicologie* 23/71–72 (1939): 71–78, and série spéciale, no. 2 (July 1943): 15–18; and Brigitte François-Sappey, "La Vie musicale à Paris à travers les Mémoires d'Eugène Sauzay (1809–1901)," *Revue de musicologie* 60/1–2 (1974): 159–210.

22. Boris Schwarz, "Beethoven and the French Violin School," *Musical Quarterly* 44 (1958): 442; Pierre Soccanne, "Virtuoses" nos. 26–27 (25 March and 1 April): 711–12.

23. Antoine Elwart, "Musique de chambre," *RGMdP* 5/2 (14 January 1838): 12–13, and "Nouvelles," *RGMdP* 7 (1840), no. 21 (12 March): 172, and no. 29 (9 April): 254.

24. Albert Palm, "Le Connaissance de l'oeuvre de J. S. Bach en France à l'époque préromantique," *Revue de musicologie,* 52/1 (1966): 89–90.

25. Soccanne, "Virtuoses" p. 712.

26. "Soirées de M. Baillot," *ReM* 13 (1833): 7.

27. François-Sappey, "Vie Musicale" pp. 193 and 194.

28. "Concerts annoncés," *Ménestrel* 31/12 (21 February 1864): 96; "Nouvelles", *RGMdP* 31/9 (28 February 1864): 70. The latter source mentions only the last two *séances*.

29. Regular *séances,* though first mentioned in *RGMdP* in February 1866, were then described as an already established series; see "Nouvelles", *RGMdP* 33/7 (18 February 1866): 54.

30. C. Bannelier, "Concerts et auditions musicales," *RGMdP* 33/12 (25 March 1866): 91; (anonymous), "Concerts et auditions musicales de la semaine," *RGMdP* 34/15 (14 April 1867): 117–18.

31. "Nouvelles," *RGMdP* 33/7 (18 February 1866): 54.

32. The best English translation is that of David Cairns, *The Memoirs of Hector Berlioz; Member of the French Institute* (London: Victor Gollancz Ltd, 1969).

33. Barzun, *Berlioz and the Romantic Century.*

34. S., "Grand concert donné par M. Berlioz, élève de l'Ecole royale de musique, le lundi 26 mai," *ReM* 3(1828): 422–24.

35. Hugh Macdonald, "Berlioz, (Louis-)Hector," *Grove 6,* 2: 585.

36. "Nouvelles," *GMdP* 2/46 (15 November 1835): 376.

37. "Nouvelles," *RGMdP* 12/9 (2 March 1845): 71.

38. Barzun, *Berlioz,* 1:263, note 18.

39. "Concerts et auditions musicales de la semaine", *RGMdP* 35/14 (5 April 1868): 109.

40. Possibly further concerts were presented but not reported in *RGMdP.*

41. Annual *séances* were mentioned by Blanchard in 1852; see "Auditions musicales", *RGMdP* 19/12 (21 March 1852): 92.

42. According to "Nouvelles de Paris", *ReM* 11 (1831–32): 45, the brothers began giving annual concerts in 1827; I have references only to a *soirée* of 1828.

43. "Nouvelles," *RGMdP* 5 (1838), no. 24 (10 [*sic,* should read 17] June): 251, and no. 25 (24 June): 267.

44. "Nouvelles de Paris," *ReM* 7 (1830): 122.

45. "Nouvelles de Paris," *ReM* 11 (1831–32): 71.

46. Berlioz, *Memoirs,* p. 345.

47. "Nouvelles diverses," *RGMdP* 35/48 (29 November 1868): 384; "Concerts et auditions musicales de la semaine," *RGMdP* 37/3 (16 January 1870): 22.

48. "Nouvelles diverses," *RGMdP* 34/45 (10 November 1867): 362–63.

49. The reference in *RGMdP* does not specify which Kufferath or which Lee had music performed at these *séances*.

50. "Nouvelles," *RGMdP* 18/22 (1 June 1851): 183.

51. "Nouvelles," *RGMdP* 27/17 (22 April 1860), pp. 153–54, and P. Scudo, *L'Année musicale,* 3 (1862): 180.

52. "Nouvelles," *RGMdP* 27, pp. 153–54, and Scudo, *L'année musicale* 3:179.

53. Scudo, *L'année musicale* 3:179.

54. M. Cristal, "Auditions musicales," *RGMdP* 32/21 (21 May 1865): 164. I find no announcement or review of the first concert.

55. "Nouvelles," *RGMdP* 33/15 (15 April 1866): 118.

56. "Nouvelles," *RGMdP* 32/51 (17 December 1865): 413.

57. "Concerts de la semaine," *RGMdP* 34/2 (13 January 1867): 14.

58. The article "Jacobi, Georg" in *Grove 6* (9:445, written by H. V. Hamilton, revised for this edition by John Warrack), states that Jacobi moved to London at the outbreak of the Franco-Prussian War and conducted at the Alhambra Theatre there during the season of 1871–72. But Jacobi was mentioned as organizer and director of the Paris concerts in November 1871, and a viola solo of his was performed at these concerts on 2 December; see "Nouvelles diverses," *RGMdP* 38 (1871), no. 41 (5 November): 314, and no. 46 (10 December): 354.

59. "Nouvelles," *RGMdP* 32:413.

60. "Nouvelles," *RGMdP* 33:118.

61. "Nouvelles diverses," *RGMdP* 34/51 (22 December 1867): 410.

62. Liszt and Chopin are listed among the founders in "Du mouvement musical à Paris", *GMdP* 1/51 (21 December 1834): 410, and are reported to have quit the society in "Nouvelles," *GMdP* 2/4 (25 January 1835): 31. In two lists of founding members in *ReM*—"Cercle Musical", 14 (30 November 1834): 379–80, and "Nouvelles de Paris", 15 (4 January 1835): 7—the two are not mentioned.

63. "Cercle Musical," *ReM* 14:379–80.

64. Ibid. and "Nouvelles de Paris," *ReM* 15:7.

65. "Nouvelles de Paris," *ReM* 15 (25 January 1835), pp. 30–31, and E. Fétis: "Nouvelles de Paris: Société musicale: Troisième concert," *ReM* 15 (1 February 1835): 37–38.

66. "Concerts de la salle Chantereine," *GMdP* 2/13 (29 March 1835): 107.

67. "Nouvelles," *RGMdP* 6/17 (28 April 1839): 136.

68. "Nouvelles diverses: Paris et départements," Ménestrel 37/14 (6 March 1870): 110.

69. "Nouvelles," *RGMdP* 21/4 (22 January 1854): 32.

70. "Nouvelles," *RGMdP* 25/12 (21 March 1858): 97.

71. "Nouvelles diverses: Paris et départements," *Ménestrel* 37:110.

72. Blanchard, "Auditions musicales," *RGMdP* 19/7 (15 February 1852): 50.

73. "Nouvelles diverses," *RGMdP* 34/51 (22 December 1867): 411. The inaugural *matinée* occurred on a Friday, either 13 or 20 December.

74. "Nouvelles diverses," *Ménestrel,* 35/11 (9 February 1868): 87.

75. "Nouvelles," *RGMdP* 31/14 (3 April 1864): 110.

76. Ibid.

77. P. Smith [Edouard Monnais], "Concerts: Du Cirque Napoléon et du Cirque de l'Impératrice," *RGMdP* 31/16 (17 April 1864): 123–24.

78. "Nouvelles diverses," *RGMdP* 36/43 (24 October 1869): 350.

79. Bannelier wrote that there were 190 performers in the orchestra and chorus; see "Société des Concerts de l'Opéra," *RGMdP* 36/46 (14 November 1869): 370–71.

80. "Nouvelles diverses," *RGMdP* 36/37 (12 September 1869): 303; Saint-Saëns did conduct his then unpublished orchestral suite (eventually to become Op. 49) on 21 November.

81. "Nouvelles diverses," *RGMdP* 36/43:350.

82. Bannelier, "Concerts de l'Opéra," pp. 370–71.

83. Ibid., and "Concerts et auditions musicales de la semaine," *RGMdP* 36/48 (28 November 1869): 389.

84. "Nouvelles diverses," *RGMdP* 36/49 (5 December 1869): 397.

85. Arthur Dandelot, *La Société des Concerts du Conservatoire (1828–1923),* 3rd ed. (Paris: Delagrave, 1923), p. 233.

86. Dandelot, *La Société des Concerts,* p. 233, and Em. Mathieu de Monter, "Revue rétrospective: Janvier 1870–Octobre 1871," *RGMdP* 38/36 (1 October 1871): 269–73.

87. André Martinet, in *Histoire anecdotique du Conservatoire de Musique et de Déclamation* (Paris: Ernest Kolb, [?1891]), p. 115, said Thursday, 19 June. Antoine Elwart, in *HSCC,* p. 126, said Thursday, 26 June.

88. F.-J. Fétis, "Quatrième concert d'émulation: Donné par les élèves de l'Ecole royale de musique," *ReM* 4 (1828): 376–78.

89. "Conservatoire de Musique: Concert d'Emulation," *ReM* 12 (27 October 1832): 308.

90. Elwart, *HSCC,* p. 126; C. Pierre, *Le Conservatoire National de Musique et de Déclamation* (Paris: Imprimerie nationale, 1900), p. 475.

91. Elwart, *HSCC,* p. 126.

92. F.-J. Fétis, "Deuxième concert d'émulation des élèves de l'Ecole royale de musique," *ReM* 5 (1829): 495–97.

93. "Conservatoire de Musique," *ReM* 12:308.

94. "Nouvelles de Paris," *ReM* 3 (1828): 472–73 and 521–22.

95. "Nouvelles," *RGMdP* 31/50 (11 December 1864): 397–98.

96. D., "Concerts des Beaux Arts," *RGMdP* 32/7 (12 February 1865): 50–51.

97. "Nouvelles," *RGMdP* 31/47 (20 November 1864): 374; *RGMdP* 32/3 (15 January 1865): 22; no. 9 (26 February): 69; D., "Concerts des Beaux Arts", p. 51.

98. "Nouvelles," *RGMdP* 31:374; D., "Concerts des Beaux Arts," p. 50.

99. D., "Concerts des Beaux Arts," p. 51.

100. "Nouvelles," *RGMdP* 31:374.

101. D., "Concerts des Beaux Arts," p. 50.

102. "Nouvelles," *RGMdP* 32:69.

103. Ibid.

104. "Nouvelles," *RGMdP* 32:16 (16 April 1865): 126.

105. "Concerts et auditions musicales de la semaine", *RGMdP* 36/49 (5 December 1869): 397.

106. "Nouvelles diverses," *RGMdP* 36/49:397.

107. See Constant Pierre, *Le Concert Spirituel, 1725–1790* (Paris: Société Française de Musicologie, 1975). The book was written by 1900.

108. See Fétis's articles "Régénération de l'Ecole Royale de Musique: Société des Concerts," *ReM* 3 (1828): 147, and "Nouvelles de Paris: Académie Royale de Musique," ibid., pp. 248–55.

109. Fétis still suggested that more new music should be played; see "Nouvelles de Paris," p. 250.

110. Fétis, "Nouvelles de Paris," pp. 250–51.

111. Adam Carse, *The Orchestra from Beethoven to Berlioz* (Cambridge: W. Heffer & Sons, 1948), p. 100.

112. F. Danjou, "Concerts Valentino," *RGMdP* 5/52 (30 December 1838): 530.

113. Weber: *MMC,* p. 100.

114. H. Berlioz, "Concerts de la rue Saint-Honoré, dirigés par M. Valentino," *RGMdP* 4/44 (29 October 1837): 470.

115. Dandelot, *La Société des Concerts,* p. 216.

116. "Nouvelles," *RGMdP* 10/38 (17 September 1843): 325.

117. "Nouvelles," *RGMdP* 10/39 (24 September 1843): 333.

118. A complete list of programs from 1797 through 1900 is provided in Pierre, *Le Conservatoire National,* pp. 967–83.

119. For a brief description of earlier student concerts, see chapter 5, p. 138. Programs for student concerts from 1800 through 1900 are listed in Pierre: *Le Conservatoire National,* pp. 476–510; see also the text on pp. 460–76.

120. There was no concert in 1848 and only one a year in 1859, 1861, and 1862. I gather that most concerts were open to the public but not advertised or promoted much.

121. Albert Mell, in his article "Dancla" in *Grove 6* (5:220–21), has written, "About 1839 the Danclas formed their own chamber music group, and from the 1840s their concerts at Hesselbein's home were a regular feature of the Paris season." Although I find reports of concerts by either Charles Dancla or the Dancla family from February 1841, these were presented at various locations and do not appear to have been organized as a series before 1847. But as such concerts and *séances* were not consistently reported in *RGMdP,* Mell's statement may be correct.

122. "Nouvelles," *RGMdP* 24/3 (18 January 1857): 22–23. See also "Nouvelles diverses," *Ménestrel,* 24/7 (18 January 1857): 4.

123. D.-A.-D. Saint-Yves, "Auditions et concerts," *RGMdP* 31/5 (31 January 1864): 35.

124. The most famous musical Cohen in Paris at the time was the pianist and composer Jules Cohen, but as the society already had a pianist, this was more likely the violinist Léonce Cohen.

125. "Soirées et concerts," *Ménestrel,* 36/12 (21 February 1869): 95.

126. "Nouvelles," *RGMdP* 30/22 (31 May 1863): 174 (entry on chamber works of Adolphe Blanc).

127. D., "Ecole Beethoven: Soirée d'inauguration", *RGMdP* 24/44 (1 November 1857): 356.

128. S. D., "Concerts et auditions musicales," *RGMdP* 25/16 (18 April 1858): 129.

129. D. G., "Ecole Beethoven", *RGMdP* 25/46 (14 November 1858): 379.

130. "Exercices et concerts," *ReM* 5 (1829): 114; "Annonces," ibid., p. 615.

131. Ibid.

132. Weber: *MMC,* p. 92.

133. "Exercices et concerts," *ReM* 5:114; "Annonces," pp. 615–16.

134. "Concerts et soirées," *Ménestrel* 30/9 (1 February 1863): 71, and "Nouvelles," *RGMdP* 32/9 (26 February 1865): 69.

135. *RGMdP* announced in October 1845 that the *réunions* would *resume,* but two articles by Blanchard in December described the society as new; see "Nouvelles," *RGMdP* 12/43 (26 October 1845): 355, and Blanchard, "Coup d'oeil musical," *RGMdP* 12/49 (7 December 1845): 400–1, and no. 51 (21 December): 416–17.

136. Blanchard, "Concerts," *RGMdP* 14/49 (5 December 1847): 394–95.

137. See the ambiguous remarks by Blanchard in "Coup d'oeil musical," *RGMdP* 12:416.

138. H. B., "Concert philanthropique," *RGMdP* 15/21 (21 May 1848): 160.

139. Bea Friedland, *Louise Farrenc (1804–1875): Composer, Performer, Scholar* (Ann Arbor: UMI Research Press, 1980), p. 63.

140. Ibid., pp. 60 and 61.

141. Ibid., p. 64.

142. Ibid., p. 77.

143. The concert of 1840 was announced in "Nouvelles," *RGMdP* 7/30 (12 April 1840): 261, and included on a list of upcoming concerts printed in that journal on 16 April (no. 31, p. 270), but not reviewed. Other sources on Fétis's *concerts historiques* that I have seen do not mention this concert.

144. Complete programs for the concerts of 1832–33 and 1835 are printed in Robert Wangermée, *François-Joseph Fétis: Musicologue et Compositeur* (Brussels: Palais des Académies, 1951), pp. 303–8; see also Peter Bloom, "François-Joseph Fétis and the *Revue Musicale* (1827–1835)" (Ph.D. Dissertation, University of Pennsylvania, 1972), pp. 398–413.

145. Dandelot, *La Société des Concerts,* p. 214. Originally there were to be two concerts

in April 1835, but the first was such a failure that the second was cancelled; see Wangermée, *Fétis,* p. 270.

146. Bloom, "Fétis," pp. 413–15.

147. Friedland, *Louise Farrenc,* p. 25.

148. Ibid., p. 45.

149. Blanchard, "Concerts," *RGMdP* 8/22 (18 March 1841): 172.

150. "Nouvelles," *RGMdP* 8/27 (14 April 1841): 215. Franck, Alard, and Chevillard had played the premiere of an unidentified Schubert piano trio in 1837; see "Séance musicale," *RGMdP* 4/23 (4 June 1837): 193–94.

151. Bannelier, in "Concerts et auditions musicales," *RGMdP* 33/13 (1 April 1866): 100, described Gouffé's 29th annual concert. It is possible that no concerts were scheduled some years (for example, 1848, following the February Revolution), which would place the first concert earlier. But in 1865 Cristal wrote that concerts had taken place for 28 years; see "Auditions et concerts," *RGMdP* 32/12 (19 March 1865): 89.

152. Barzun, *Berlioz,* 1:554.

153. Ibid., pp. 554–55.

154. Ibid., p. 555.

155. L. Kreutzer: "Grande Société Philharmonique de Paris," *RGMdP* 17/4 (27 January 1850): 27–28.

156. "Nouvelles," *RGMdP* 17/7 (17 February 1850): 59, and Barzun, *Berlioz,* 1:555.

157. Barzun, *Berlioz,* 1:555.

158. "Grande Société Philharmonique de Paris" [a letter from various of its members, among them Massart, Seligmann, and L. Kreutzer], *RGMdP* 17/5 (3 February 1850): 39.

159. Barzun, *Berlioz,* 1:554, and Humphrey Searle, ed., *Hector Berlioz: a Selection from His Letters* (New York: Vienna House, 1973), p. 113. Searle wrote that the society stopped in March 1851, but the concert of 29 April was reviewed in *RGMdP* 18:140.

160. "Nouvelles," *RGMdP* 32 (1865), no. 9 (26 February): 70, and no. 11 (12 March): 88.

161. J.-G. Prod'homme, "Le Gymnase musical," *Revue de musicologie,* 11/23 (August 1927): 151.

162. "Nouvelles de Paris: Concert du Gymnase Musical," *ReM* 15 (28 June 1835): 205.

163. Sixty, according to "Nouvelles de Paris," *ReM* 15:205; Prod'homme, "Le Gymnase musical" p. 152, stated about 100.

164. "Prospectus: Gymnase Musical," *ReM* 14 (14 December 1834): 391–92.

165. "Nouvelles de Paris," *ReM* 15 (29 March 1835): 103.

166. "Nouvelles," *GMdP* 2/41 (11 October 1835): 335.

167. "Nouvelles," *RGMdP* 7/65 (19 November 1840): 556–57, and Blanchard, "Séance d'inauguration des matinées de MM. Herz et Labarre," *RGMdP* 7/69 (3 December 1840): 588–89.

168. Blanchard, "Concerts," *RGMdP* 8/15 (21 February 1841): 117.

169. "Nouvelles," *RGMdP* 33/3 (21 January 1866): 21.

170. "Nouvelles," *RGMdP* 15/45 (5 November 1848): 348.

171. Most years only the first or second concerts were reported; I have not determined how many weeks the series continued.

172. "Nouvelles," *RGMdP* 31/49 (4 December 1864): 390.

173. "Nouvelles," *RGMdP* 31/42 (16 October 1864): 335.

174. "Nouvelles," *RGMdP* 31/51 (18 December 1864): 407.

175. *Ibid.* I presume that this means the Jardin d'hiver of the hôtel Laffite, rather than a separate institution.

176. "Nouvelles," *RGMdP* 31/43 (23 October 1864): 342.

177. See "Nouvelles," *GMdP* 2/41 (11 October 1835): 335, in which it was reported that M. Masson de Puitneuf was beginning a series of musical *soirées* at the hôtel Laffite.

178. Joseph Mainzer, "Education musicale: Institution des jeunes aveugles," *RGMdP*, 3/26 (26 June 1836): 220–22; F., "Concert donné par des aveugles," *RGMdP* 10/22 (28 May 1843): 187.

179. Roussel's obituary, printed 2 January 1870, stated that he was 45 at his death; see "Nouvelles diverses," *RGMdP* 37/1 (2 January 1870): 7.

180. Blanchard, in "Coup d'oeil musical," *RGMdP* 11/6 (11 February 1844): 44, announced a biweekly schedule lasting from 21 January to 3 March, but this schedule does not seem to have been strictly followed.

181. The second *soirée* had been postponed from 7 March; see "Nouvelles," *RGMdP* 17/6 (10 February 1850): 47 and no. 10 (10 March): 83.

182. "Nouvelles," *RGMdP* 17/4 (27 January 1850): 32.

183. "Mme." Andrée Favel, whose real name was Claudine Duclairfait, became Lacombe's second wife the following October.

184. Berlioz, "Première soirée musicale," *RGMdP* 4/6 (5 February 1837): 50–51. See also Berlioz, "Concerts: Troisième soirée de MM. Liszt, Urhan et Batta," *RGMdP* 4/8 (19 February 1837), pp. 63–64; L. Legouvé, "Les Concerts de MM. Liszt, Batta et Urhan", *RGMdP* 4/10 (5 March 1837): 81–82.

185. "Nouvelles de Paris," *ReM* 15 (15 February 1835): 54.

186. Blanchard, "Concerts," *RGMdP* 22/7 (18 February 1855): 50, and P. Scudo, *L'Année musicale* 3 (1862): 168.

187. "Concerts annoncés," *Ménestrel* 36 (1869), no. 11 (14 February): 88, and no. 15 (14 March): 120.

188. Z., "Une Oasis musicale," *RGMdP* 15/45 (5 November 1848): 343–44.

189. I have no record of the first *séance,* which surely took place in December 1847.

190. "Nouvelles diverses," *RGMdP* 33/41 (14 October 1866): 326.

191. The location was described in 1856 as "au Louvre chez M. le comte de Nieuwerkerke" and in 1865 as the "appartements du Louvre"; see "Nouvelles," *RGMdP* 23/4 (27 January 1856): 30, and *RGMdP* 32/12 (11 March 1865): 86.

192. Boris Schwarz, "Paganini, Nicolò," *Grove 6,* 14:88.

193. Blanchard, "Concerts et auditions musicales," *RGMdP* 24/9 (1 March 1857): 66.

194. "Nouvelles diverses," *Ménestrel,* 29/9 (26 January 1862): 71.

195. Its excessive length was criticized; see "Nouvelles diverses," *RGMdP* 34/52 (22 December 1867): 419.

196. "Nouvelles diverses: Paris et départements," *Ménestrel* 37/10 (6 February 1870): 80.

197. "Concerts et auditions musicales de la semaine," *RGMdP* 37/9 (27 February 1870): 70.

198. "Concerts et auditions musicales de la semaine," *RGMdP* 34/5 (3 February 1867): 37; *RGMdP* 36/22 (30 May 1869): 182.

199. "Nouvelles diverses," *RGMdP* 38/47 (17 December 1871): 363.

200. Ibid., and "Concerts et auditions musicales de la semaine," *RGMdP* 36: 182.

201. Blanchard, "Auditions musicales," *RGMdP* 21/19 (7 May 1854): 152, and *RGMdP* 25/1 (3 January 1858): 5.

202. "Concerts et auditions musicales de la semaine," *RGMdP* 36/11 (14 March 1869): 92–93.

203. Ibid., and ibid., no. 12 (21 March 1869): 101, and no. 16 (18 April): 133.

204. "Musique de chambre: Soirées de quatuors et quintetti," *RGMdP* 5/31 (5 August 1838): 310. Barzun, in *Berlioz and the Romantic Century,* 1:342, has suggested that the concerts may have been Berlioz's idea.

205. "Nouvelles," *RGMdP* 27/1 (1 January 1860): 6.

206. "Nouvelles," *RGMdP* 17 (1850), no. 7 (17 February): 59, and no. 8 (24 February): 68.

207. This was probably Etienne-Marie Portehaut, then *sous-chef* of the Théâtre-Italien orchestra.

208. "Nouvelles," *RGMdP* 32/2 (8 January 1865): 15.

209. Maurice Cristal, "Auditions et concerts," *RGMdP* 32/5 (29 January 1865): 35.

210. Cristal, "Auditions musicales," *RGMdP* 32/7 (12 February 1865): 50.

211. "Nouvelles," *RGMdP* 20/20 (15 May 1853): 183, and L. Kreutzer, "Société de la grande harmonie," *RGMdP* 20/23 (6 June 1853): 210–11.

212. The article in *RGMdP*—"Nouvelles," 32/36 (3 September 1865): 291—names Alphonse Sax (Adolphe's brother) as the founder of the *orchestre*. But in the index to that volume the reference is listed beside Adolphe's name and not beside Alphonse's. As Adolphe was the inventor of the *saxomnitoniques* (and the article states that the organizer's instruments were played) and was much the more ardent promoter of the

two, I believe that the anonymous author of the entry erred and that the indexer was correct.

213. "Nouvelles," *RGMdP* 32:291.

214. "Nouvelles," *RGMdP* 32/45 (5 November 1865): 367, and 33/14 (8 April 1866): 110.

215. "Musique de chambre: Soirées de quatuors et quintetti," *RGMdP* 5/31 (5 August 1838): 310.

216. Henry F. Chorley, *Music and Manners in France and Germany,* 3 vols. (London: Longman, Orme, Brown, Green, and Longmans, 1841), 1:71n.

217. Brigitte François-Sappey, "La Vie musicale à Paris à travers les Mémoires d'Eugène Sauzay (1809–1901)," *Revue de musicologie,* 60/1–2 (1974): 177.

218. Lionel de La Laurencie, "Les Débuts de la musique de chambre en France," *Revue de musicologie* 18/52 (November 1934): 231. Blanchard mentioned the 110th *séance annuelle* in 1851; see "Matinées musicales de M. Gouffé et 110e séance annuelle de la Société académique des enfants d'Apollon," *RGMdP* 18/22 (1 June 1851): 172. In 1867 the society was said to be 127 years old; see "Nouvelles diverses," *RGMdP* 34/42 (20 October 1867): 388–89. According to David Charlton and John Trevitt, the society was inactive from 1789 to 1807; see the article "Paris," *Grove 6,* 14:216.

219. Blanchard, "Concerts: Enfants d'Apollon," *RGMdP* 9/19 (8 May 1842): 205; "Concerts et auditions musicales de la semaine," *RGMdP* 34/23 (9 June 1867): 185; and *RGMdP* 36/21 (23 May 1869): 173–74.

220. La Laurencie and "Nouvelles diverses," *RGMdP* 34/42 (20 October 1867): 338–39.

221. In "Nouvelles," *RGMdP* 28/19 (12 May 1861): 150, a *large* orchestra was mentioned.

222. Blanchard, "Concerts," *RGMdP* 23 (1856); no. 12 (23 March): 90 and no. 20 (18 May): 158.

223. Members of the musical committee included Jules Beer, Chabrier (not Emmanuel), Emile Durier (? the lawyer), E. Duvergier de Hauranne, Galoppe d'Onquaire (the writer), (? Félix) Godefroid, de Guerle, Ferdinand Hérold (the son of the opera composer), Antoine Lascoux (a magistrate), and Roubaud de Gournande.

224. "Nouvelles," *RGMdP* 33/23 (10 June 1866): 181–82.

225. "Nouvelles," *RGMdP* 33/33 (19 August 1866): 263.

226. "Nouvelles," *RGMdP* 33/37 (16 September 1866): 294.

227. "Nouvelles diverses," *RGMdP* 33/52 (30 December 1866): 414.

228. "Nouvelles diverses," *RGMdP* 34/1 (6 January 1867): 6; no. 2 (13 January): 15.

229. "Concerts et auditions musicales de la semaine," *RGMdP* 34/11 (17 March 1867): 85; another concert of chamber music, exclusively by Ernst, was played in May.

230. "Concerts et auditions musicales de la semaine," *RGMdP* 34/19 (12 May 1867): 153.

231. Elisabeth Bernard, "Jules Pasdeloup et les Concerts Populaires," *Revue de musicologie* 57/2 (1971): 159.

232. Em. Mathieu de Monter, "Revue de l'année 1869," *RGMdP* 37/1 (2 January 1870): 1–2.

233. F.-J. Fétis, "Athénée musical: Nouvelle institution: Concert du 26 Novembre 1829," *ReM* 6(1829–30): 451–53.

234. Weber: *MMC,* pp. 91–92.

235. "Concerts: Athénée musical," *RGMdP* 4/23 (4 June 1837): 193.

236. Un amateur, "Variétés: des concerts d'amateurs," *ReM* 12 (1832): 124.

237. "Nouvelles de Paris," *ReM* 14 (16 November 1834): 365.

238. F.-J. Fétis, "Athénée musical: Nouvelle institution: Concert du 26 novembre 1829," pp. 451–53, and "Athénée musical de la Ville de Paris," *ReM* 11 (1831–32), pp. 233–34, and Un amateur, "Variétés: des concerts d'amateurs," p. 124.

239. Un amateur, "Variétés: des concerts d'amateurs" p. 124, and Weber, *MMC,* pp. 91–92.

240. Weber, *MMC,* pp. 91–92.

241. "Nouvelles," *RGMdP* 15/28 (9 July 1848): 210; no. 29 (16 July): 218; Blanchard, "Concerts au bénéfice des blessés de juin," *RGMdP* 15/30 (23 July 1848): 225–26.

242. "Concerts et auditions musicales de la semaine," *RGMdP* 37/11 (13 March 1870): 84.

243. "Nouvelles," *RGMdP* 14/47 (21 November 1847): 383.

244. This was almost certainly Caroline Rémaury.

245. "Nouvelles," *RGMdP* 32/2 (8 January 1865): 15.

246. Martin Cooper, *French Music from the Death of Berlioz to the Death of Fauré* (London: Oxford University Press, 1951), p. 10.

247. H. V. Hamilton, "Jacobi, Georg," rev. John Warrack, *Grove 6*: 445.

248. Possibly a small ensemble played the orchestral parts in the concerto and Concertstück; such a practice was still fairly common.

249. "Nouvelles," *RGMdP* 32/10 (5 March 1865): 78.

250. "Concerts annoncés," *RGMdP* 33/10 (11 March 1866): 79.

251. "Nouvelles," *RGMdP* 14/24 (13 June 1847): 199.

252. "Nouvelles," *RGMdP* 14/29 (18 July 1847): 239, and Blanchard, "Société de Sainte-Cécile et quelques autres choses musicales," *RGMdP* 14/40 (3 October 1847): pp. 325–26.

253. "Nouvelles," *RGMdP* 14/35 (29 August 1847): 288.

254. "Nouvelles," *RGMdP* 14/45 (7 November 1847): 367.

255. Blanchard, "Société de Sainte-Cécile," pp. 325–26.

256. "Nouvelles," *RGMdP* 29/50 (14 December 1862): 406.

257. "Nouvelles," *RGMdP* 24/52 (22 December 1857): 422.

258. Arthur Pougin, "Populus (Nicolas-Adolphe-Alphonse)," *FétisB* Supplement, 2:362.

259. "Nouvelles diverses," *RGMdP* 36/48 (28 November 1869): 390.

260. Cristal, "Auditions musicales," *RGMdP* 32/19 (7 May 1865): 147.

261. Pierre, *Le Conservatoire National de Musique et de Déclamation,* p. 735 (the entry on Deledicque).

262. "Nouvelles diverses: Paris et départements," *Ménestrel* 31/12 (21 February 1864): 95.

263. "Nouvelles diverses," *RGMdP* 36/4 (24 January 1869): 31, announced the beginning of the Société's ninth year; "Nouvelles diverses: Paris et départements," *Ménestrel* 37/23 (8 May 1870): 188, mentioned that the group had existed for ten years.

264. "Nouvelles diverses: Paris et départements," *Ménestrel* 31:95.

265. Cristal, *RGMdP* 32:147.

266. "Nouvelles diverses: Paris et départements," *Ménestrel* 37:188.

267. The date of the first concert, not publicized in *RGMdP,* is calculated from the dates of the second, third, and fourth—3, 17, and 31 March.

268. A. de Gasperini, "Revue des concerts," *Ménestrel* 33/15 (11 March 1866): 117.

269. "Nouvelles," *RGMdP* 32/13 (26 March 1865): 103.

270. "Nouvelles," *RGMdP* 12/48 (30 November 1845): 395. Mohr was identified here as a clarinettist at the Opéra. Pierre later stated that the horn player J.-B.-V. Mohr led the group; see *Le Conservatoire National de Musique et de Déclamation,* p. 815. That Pierre mentioned the society at all suggests that it did get underway.

271. "Nouvelles," *RGMdP* 31 (1864), no. 28 (10 July): 221–22, and no. 32 (7 August): 253–54.

272. Ibid., pp. 253–54.

273. Ibid., pp. 221–22.

274. "Nouvelles," *RGMdP* 31/45 (6 November 1864): 358.

275. "Nouvelles," *RGMdP* 31 (1864), no. 49 (4 December): 390; no. 50 (11 December): 397; and no. 52 (25 December): 413.

276. All information on the Gymnase Lyrique comes from Stéphen, "Projet d'Association Musicale: Société du Gymnase Lyrique," *ReM* 4 (1828–29): 289–96.

277. Blanchard wrote in 1852 that the Société was in its 18th year; see "Société libre des beaux-arts," *RGMdP* 19/24 (13 June 1852): 196. The 31st *séance annuelle* was reported in 1866; see "Nouvelles," *RGMdP* 33/25 (24 June 1866): 198.

278. "Nouvelles," *RGMdP* 5/45bis (15 November 1838): 463.

279. "Nouvelles," *RGMdP* 6/8 (21 February 1839): 66.

280. A. Botte, "Matinée musicale de la Société nationale des Beaux-Arts," *RGMdP* 29/51 (21 December 1862): 410.

281. Botte, "Auditions musicales," *RGMdP* 30/4 (25 January 1863): 27.

282. "Nouvelles," *RGMdP* 31/41 (9 October 1864): 326.

283. Cristal, "Auditions et concerts," *RGMdP* 32/14 (2 April 1865): 106.

284. Several statements from the 1850s in *RGMdP* suggest that the Société began in the

season of 1825–26: "Nouvelles," 17/49 (8 December 1850): 407, announced that it was entering its 26th year; Blanchard, "Auditions musicales," *RGMdP* 19/49 (5 December 1852): 451, stated that it was 27 years old; Blanchard again, "Auditions musicales," *RGMdP* 21/19 (7 May 1854): 152, wrote that the society had just given its 174th concert (which, following the regular schedule of six concerts per season, works out to 29 seasons). In "Nouvelles," *RGMdP* 12/51 (21 December 1845): 419, however, the beginning of the 22nd season was announced, which would indicate a foundation in the season of 1824–25. (There was no interruption in the society's presentations between 1845 and 1850.) William Weber, who has done archival work in Paris, has maintained that the society began in 1822; see *MMC,* p. 92. This date is plausible if one assumes that the society did not meet certain years (say, during the recession of 1831 or the cholera epidemic of 1832).

285. Blanchard, "Auditions musicales," *RGMdP* 21/19 (7 May 1854): 152.

286. "Nouvelles de Paris," *ReM* 14 (19 October 1834): 335.

287. "Nouvelles," *RGMdP* 17/49 (8 December 1850): 407.

288. Blanchard, "Auditions musicales," *RGMdP* 19/49 (5 December 1852): 451, and "Société philharmonique de Paris," *RGMdP* 20/49 (4 December 1853): 421–22.

289. The anonymous author of "Nouvelles," *RGMdP* 29/51 (21 December 1862): 415, stated explicitly that the concert was not performed.

290. "Nouvelles," *RGMdP* 33/11 (18 March 1866): 85.

291. "Concerts et soirées," *Ménestrel* 33/18 (1 April 1866): 143.

292. "Concerts et soirées," p. 143, named the location the Cirque des Champs-Elysées, but all other sources call it the Cirque de l'Impératrice.

293. "Nouvelles," *RGMdP* 32/52 (24 December 1865): 422.

294. "Nouvelles," *RGMdP* 33/11:85.

295. "Concerts et soirées," p. 143.

296. A. de Gasperini, "Revue des concerts," *Ménestrel* 33/20 (15 April 1866): 155.

297. I have discovered only one reference to this organization: "Nouvelles," *Revue musicale* (a subsidiary of *RGMdP* published weekly on Thursdays), 6/21 (23 May 1839): 172.

298. "Concerts et auditions musicales de la semaine," *RGMdP* 36/49 (5 December 1869): 397.

299. Ibid.

300. "Concerts et auditions musicales de la semaine," *RGMdP* 37/5 (30 January 1870): 37, and no. 11 (13 March), p. 83.

301. "Nouvelles," *RGMdP* 19/38 (19 September 1852): 315–16.

302. I have found no more references to concerts, and according to Bea Friedland, *Louise Farrenc,* pp. 45–46, only these two took place.

303. "Nouvelles," *RGMdP* 19/45 (7 November 1845): 381.

304. "Nouvelles," *RGMdP* 28/49 (8 December 1861): 389.

305. "Nouvelle société de musique de chambre," *RGMdP* 24/6 (8 February 1857): 45–46.

306. "Nouvelles," *RGMdP* 25/1 (3 January 1858): 6.

307. "Nouvelles," *RGMdP* 24/13 (29 March 1857): 102.

308. "Nouvelles," *RGMdP* 19/14 (4 April 1852): 112.

309. Blanchard, "Auditions musicales," *RGMdP* 19/19 (9 May 1852): 148.

310. Bannelier, "Concerts et auditions musicales," *RGMdP* 33/10 (11 March 1866): 74.

311. "Nouvelles de Paris," *ReM* 13 (1833): 383.

312. "Nouvelles de Paris," *ReM* 15 (25 January 1835): 32.

313. "Nouvelles," *GMdP* 2 (25 January 1835): 31–32.

314. E. Lemoine, "La Trompette: Histoire d'une société de musique de chambre," *Revue musicale* 3/14 (15 October 1903): 575–79.

315. An early quartet (perhaps the first) comprised the amateurs Peyrot (vn), Lemoine (va), Frédéric Rossel (vc), and Ch. Bazaine (pf); see the photograph following page 12 and text on page 13 in L. Augé de Lassus, *La Trompette: un demi-siècle de musique de chambre* (Paris: Ch. Delagrave, 1911).

316. Romain Rolland, *Musiciens d'aujourd'hui,* trans. as *Musicians of Today* by Mary Blaiklock, 4th ed. (New York: Henry Holt and Company, 1919), pp. 299–300.

317. Marc Pincherle, "French Performing Organizations," *Cobbett's Cyclopedic Survey of Chamber Music,* ed. W. W. Cobbett, 2nd ed., 3 vols. (London: Oxford University Press, 1963), 1:435.

318. The passage on chamber music between 1789 and 1870 by David Charlton and John Trevitt (see "Paris: 1789–1870, Concert Life," *Grove 6* 14:218) overestimates the importance of La Trompette at this time. They write, "Lemoine's success and promotion of the late Beethoven quartets prompted the formation of many other groups, such as the Lamoureux Quartet (1862)." But in the early 1860s the group comprised amateurs who presented private *séances* to a small group of friends. Furthermore, Lamoureux's quartet began giving regular public *séances* in January 1860, before Lemoine had organized his first quartet; see "Nouvelles," *RGMdP* 27/1 (1 January 1860): 6, and chapter 2 of this study, pp. 58–60.

319. "Nouvelles," *RGMdP* 17/45 (10 November 1850): 375.

320. "Nouvelles," *RGMdP* 16/50 (16 December 1849): 397.

321. "Nouvelles," *RGMdP* 17:375.

322. Berlioz, "Société de l'Union Musicale," *RGMdP* 16/4 (28 January 1849): 26–28.

323. "Nouvelles," *RGMdP* 17:375.

324. P. Smith [Monnais], "Revue de l'année 1850," *RGMdP* 18/1 (5 January 1851): 1–2. The histories of Elwart and Dandelot differ from contemporary sources regarding this organization. The historians claim that the Union was founded in 1847, first conducted by Manera, and later by Félicien David and Berlioz, and transformed into the Société Sainte-Cécile in 1849. The Union is not mentioned in *RGMdP,* however, until January 1849; after the first concert, Berlioz referred to it as a new society. See

"Société de l'Union Musicale," *RGMdP* 16/4 (28 January 1849): 26–28. Furthermore, the Société Sainte-Cécile (II) was not formed until November 1850, and was a separate society rather than a replacement. Berlioz does not seem to have been associated with the Union Musicale at all. Georges Servières's suggestion, in "La Symphonie en France," *Ménestrel* 85 (1923): 398, that the Union was founded in 1841, is implausible.

325. "Nouvelles," *RGMdP* 25/46 (14 November 1858): 382.

326. See "Nouvelles," *RGMdP* 29/6 (9 February 1862): 46, and A. Botte, "Auditions musicales," *RGMdP* 29/21 (25 May 1862): 170–71.

327. Botte, "Auditions musicales," *RGMdP* 30/6 (8 February 1863): 42.

328. P. S. [Monnais], "Nécrologie: Zimmerman," *RGMdP* 20/45 (6 November 1853): 391–92.

329. As additional evidence that the Zimmermann in question is P.-J.-G., Blanchard, in "Dernière soirée de Zimmermann," *RGMdP* 6/20 (19 May 1839): 156, described Louis Lacombe as "un de ses adeptes"; Lacombe had studied with P.-J.-G. Zimmermann at the Conservatoire. I should probably not dwell so on the question had not William Weber (*MMC,* p. 49) identified the host of the *salon* as Emile Zimmermann, allegedly a violin teacher at the Conservatoire (though I find no such person on the list of faculty at that institution).

330. "Nouvelles," *RGMdP* 3/2 (10 January 1836): 16, and Blanchard, "Soirée de Zimmermann," *RGMdP* 7/2 (5 January 1840): 16.

331. Monnais, "Une Soirée chez Zimmermann," *Revue Musicale* 6/7 (14 February 1839): 56.

332. The *salon* had surely closed by 1851 when Blanchard wrote that the pianist Marmontel was attempting to recreate the *soirées* of Zimmermann; see "Concerts," *RGMdP* 18/5 (2 February 1851): 37.

333. See, for example, Monnais, "Une Soirée chez Zimmermann," p. 56.

Appendix B

1. F. Danjou: "Deuxième lettre sur l'état de la musique en France," *RGMdP* 5/42 (21 October 1838): 414.

2. Em. Mathieu de Monter, "De la musique et du chant populaire dans le Midi de la France," *RGMdP* 29/34 (7 September 1862): 290–91.

3. Humphrey Burton: "French Provincial Academies," *Music and Letters* 37/3 (July 1956): 274. The original (longer) version of this article is "Les Académies de musique en France au XVIIIe siècle," *Revue de musicologie* 37/2 (December 1955): 122–47.

4. Un Abonné, [under] "Correspondance," *ReM* 5 (1829): 57–59.

5. "Nouvelles des départemens," *ReM* 3 (1828): 42–45; "Nouvelles: Chronique départementale," *RGMdP* 25/19 (9 May 1858): 158. According to a much later source, the Société at La Rochelle was established in 1815; see "Nouvelles," *RGMdP* 32/20 (14 May 1865): 158.

6. "Nouvelles des départemens," *ReM* 1/12 (April 1827): 312.

7. J. d'Ortigue, "Des sociétés philharmoniques dans le Midi de la France," *GMdP* 1/48 (30 November 1834): 384.

8. See, for example, "Nouvelles des départemens," *ReM* 13 (1833): 400; *ReM* 14 (21 September 1834): 302; *ReM* 15 (12 April 1835): 118–19.

9. "Nouvelles," *RGMdP* 4/11 (18 March 1838): 123.

10. That of Rouen, founded in 1834, comprised amateurs exclusively, at least in the beginning. See "Nouvelles des départemens," *ReM* 14 (1834): 143.

11. Liszt: "De la situation des artistes," *GMdP* 2 (1835): 285–92.

12. An anonymous critic in 1832 found it unthinkable that no chorus was to participate in a series of concerts arranged by a local *société symphonique*. See "Nouvelles des départemens," *ReM* 12 (1832–33): 342–43.

13. "Nouvelles," *RGMdP* 5/47 (25 November 1838): 479.

14. See, for example, "Nouvelles: Chronique départementale," *RGMdP* 26/11 (13 March 1859): 91 and 31/6 (7 February 1864): 46.

15. "Nouvelles," *GMdP* 2/26 (28 June 1835): 220.

16. "Grande association musicale de l'Ouest," *RGMdP* 26/17 (29 July 1859): 239. In 1864, however, an orchestra of only 90 and a chorus of 100 were reported by L. Behrnardt, "Festival de Niort," *RGMdP* 31/26 (26 June 1864): 204–5.

17. The second program in 1864 comprised Beethoven's Fifth Symphony and 16 shorter works. See Behrnardt, "Festival de Niort," pp. 204–5.

18. See, for example, "Nouvelles des départemens," *ReM* 5(1829): 353–56 and 569–71; E. Fétis: "Fête musicale du Rhin-Inférieur," *ReM* 14 (1834): 169–71; "Nouvelles," *GMdP* 2/29 (19 July 1835): 243; "Fêtes musicales du congrès méridional," *ReM* 15 (19 July 1835): 227–31 (At this *congrès méridional* at Toulouse, enormous forces were employed, but the acoustics were so poor that the 20,000 spectators heard little); "Nouvelles: Chronique départementale," *RGMdP* 17/15 (14 April 1850): 131–32; "Nouvelles," *RGMdP* 31/19 (8 May 1864): 151; "Concerts et auditions musicales de la semaine," *RGMdP* 37/22 (28 [*sic*, should read 29] May 1870): 174.

19. "Nouvelles," *RGMdP* 29/9 (2 March 1862): 74; "Nouvelles: Chronique départementale," *RGMdP* 30/50 (13 December 1863): 393.

20. "Nouvelles de Paris," *ReM* 11 (1831–32): 409–10.

21. "Nouvelles: Chronique départementale," *RGMdP* 18/12 (23 March 1851): 94.

22. A notice of a concert given in December 1855 mentioned the *resumption* of the chamber concerts, but a notice of March 1858 said that the third season was ending, and subsequent notices also dated the beginning of the series in 1855. I have found no earlier mention of Schwaederlé's series, though *séances* of quartet music were reported in Strasbourg as early as 1842. See "Nouvelles," *RGMdP* 9/17 (24 April 1842): 183; "Nouvelles: Chronique départementale," *RGMdP* 22/48 (2 December 1855): 399 and *RGMdP* 25/13 (28 March 1858): 108.

23. "Nouvelles: Chronique départementale," *RGMdP* 27/4 (22 January 1860): 32, and 28/14 (7 April 1861): 110.

24. Castil-Blaze [F.-H.-J. Blaze], "Un Musicien de province," *RGMdP* 6/50 (6 October 1839): 393–96.

25. "Nouvelles," *RGMdP* 32/28 (9 July 1865): 226; *RGMdP* 33/32 (12 August 1866): 254; "Nouvelles diverses: Départements," *RGMdP* 34/34 (25 August 1867): 275; "Nouvelles des théâtres lyriques," *RGMdP* 35/33 (16 August 1868): 262.

26. "Correspondance", *RGMdP* 34/34 (25 August 1867), pp. 273–74; "Nouvelles diverses", *RGMdP* 34/35 (1 September 1867), p. 282; *RGMdP* 34/38 (22 September 1867), p. 307.

27. See, for example, "Nouvelles: Chronique départementale," *RGMdP* 29/35 (31 August 1862): 287.

28. "Nouvelles des départemens," *ReM* 12 (1832–33): 294–95.

29. "Société philharmonique du Calvados," *ReM* 13 (1833): 208.

30. F. Danjou, "Première lettre sur l'état de la musique dans les provinces," *RGMdP* 5/40 (7 October 1838): 394.

Bibliography

"The real heroes cannot be mentioned individually" is perhaps a cliché. Yet nowhere is it more applicable than in this bibliography, for the main sources of information on concert life are the thousands of columns entitled "Nouvelles," "Nouvelles diverses," "Nouvelles de Paris," and so forth, and the hundreds of reviews of concerts and compositions in the weekly journals *Revue musicale, Gazette musicale de Paris,* and *Revue et gazette musicale de Paris*. The "news" columns appear in every issue. I have also examined similar sections in selected issues of the weekly journal *Le Ménestrel* from 1858 through 1871. Only a few of these articles—items that are particularly helpful in summarizing a concert society or depicting the musical scene—are included in the following list.

Un Abonné. "Correspondance—4 fevrier 1829" [Letter to the editor]. *ReM* 5 (1829): 57–59. (Discusses the development of interest in nontheatrical music.)

Abraham, Gerald. *A Hundred Years of Music*. 4th ed. Frome and London: Duckworth, 1974.

Almanach musical. ed. Pierre Escudier and others. Published yearly. Paris: Alexandre Houssiaux, 1854–67.

Un Amateur. "Variétés: des concerts d'amateurs," *ReM* 12 (1832–33): 121–25.

"Anton Franz Habenek" [*sic*]. *Allgemeine musikalische Zeitung* 47/28 (9 July 1845), cols. 465–68.

L'Art musical. Weekly journal. 1 (1860–61).

"Un Artiste de l'Académie royale de musique." [Letter to the editor] *RGMdP* 4/53 (31 December 1837): 573.

Augé de Lassus, Lucien. *La Trompette: un demi-siècle de musique de chambre*. Paris: Ch. Delagrave, 1911.

Austin, William Weaver. *Music in the Twentieth Century*. New York: W. W. Norton & Co., 1966.

B. "Conservatoire de Musique: Société des Concerts." *ReM* 14 (1834): 53–55. (Discusses difficulties of young composers and reviews a symphony of Scipion Rousselot.)

B., F. "Nouvelles de Paris: Conservatoire de Musique: Société des Concerts." *ReM* 14 (1834): 118–19. (Discusses contemporary trends in music.)

Bannelier, Charles. "Musique de chambre: M. Gouffé." *RGMdP* 33/4 (28 January 1866): pp. 27–28.

———. "Société des Concerts de l'Opéra." *RGMdP* 36/46 (14 November 1869): 370–71.

Barzun, Jacques. *Berlioz and the Romantic Century*. 3rd ed. rev. 2 vols. New York: Columbia University Press, 1969.

Bassanville, Mme. la comtesse de. *Les Salons d'autrefois: Souvenirs intimes*. 4 vols. Paris: P. Brunet, 1862–66.

Bellasis, Edward. *Cherubini: Memorials Illustrative of his Life*. London: Burns and Oates, 1874.

Berlioz, Hector. "Concerts de la rue Saint-Honoré, dirigés par M. Valentino." *RGMdP* 4/44 (29 October 1837): 470–71.

————. *The Memoirs of Hector Berlioz, Member of the French Institute*. Trans. and ed. David Cairns. London: Victor Gollancz, 1969.

————. "Septième et dernier concert du Conservatoire." *RGMdP* 3/19 (8 May 1836): 151–53. (Discusses the musical taste of contemporary audiences.)

————. "Société de l'Union Musicale." *RGMdP* 16/4 (28 January 1849): 26–28.

————. *Les Soirées de l'orchestre*. 2nd ed. rev. Paris: Michel Lévy frères, 1854. Trans. and ed. Jacques Barzun as *Evenings with the Orchestra*. New York: Alfred A. Knopf, 1956.

Bernard, Elisabeth. "Jules Pasdeloup et les Concerts Populaires." *Revue de musicologie* 57/2 (1971): 150–78.

Berton, Henri. "Quintetto de M. Turcas." *RGMdP* 7/43 (5 July 1840): 365. (Discusses the manner in which the continued popularity of older works affected contemporary composers.)

Bischoff, Ludwig. "Cherubini." *Niederrheinische Musik Zeitung* 10/5 (1 February 1862): 35. trans. J. V. Bridgeman in *Musical World*, 40/37 (13 September 1862): 588.

Blanchard, Henri. "Concerts de M. Panofka." *RGMdP* 4/47 (19 November 1837): 501–2. (Discusses the problems of presenting a concert in Paris.)

————. "De la question artistique et musicale." *RGMdP* 15/22 (28 May 1848): 167–68.

————. "Préface des concerts de la saison." *RGMdP* 13/44 (1 November 1846): 348–49. (Discusses performance of chamber music in France.)

————. "Quatres soirées de musique classique instrumentale." *RGMdP* 22/4 (28 January 1855): 26–27. (Discusses the establishment of Lebouc's series.)

————. "Société de Sainte-Cécile et quelques autres choses musicales." *RGMdP* 14/40 (3 October 1847): 325–26.

————. "Soirée de Zimmerman." *RGMdP* 7/2 (5 January 1840): 16–17.

Blaze, François-Henri-Joseph [Castil-Blaze]. "Les Concerts." *GMdP* 2/26 (28 June 1835): 213–17.

————. "Un Musicien de province." *RGMdP* 6/50 (6 October 1839): 393–96.

Bloom, Peter Anthony. "François-Joseph Fétis and the *Revue Musicale* (1827–1835)." Ph.D. dissertation, University of Pennsylvania, 1972.

Botte, Adolphe. "Concerts populaires de musique classique." *RGMdP* 28/46 (17 November 1861): 361–62.

Bourges, Maurice. "Premier semestre musical de la République." *RGMdP* 15/36 (3 September 1848): 271–72.

————. "Première matinée de musique instrumentale de chambre." *RGMdP* 14/7 (14 February 1847): 57–58. (Discusses the beginning of the Alard-Franchomme chamber music society.)

————. "Société de Musique Classique." *RGMdP* 16/6 (11 February 1849): 44–45.

Boyer, Jean. "Sur les relations de Beethoven avec Cherubini." *Revue de musicologie* 36/2 (December 1954): 134–42.

Brook, Barry S. *La Symphonie française dans le second moitié du XVIIIe siècle*. 3 vols. Paris: Institut de Musicologie de l'Université de Paris, 1962.

"Bulletin d'analyse." *ReM* 11 (1831–32): 39–40. (Discusses the lack of rewards for composers of chamber music.)

Burnand, Robert. *La Vie quotidienne en France en 1830*. Paris: Hachette, 1943.

Burton, Humphrey. "Les Académies de musique en France au XVIIIe siècle." *Revue de musicologie* 37/2 (December 1955): 122–47. An abridged version of this article, "French Provincial Academies," appears in *Music and Letters* 37/3 (July 1956): 260–74.

Caradec, François and Weill, Alain. *Le Café-concert.* Paris: Atelier Hachette/Massin, 1980.
Carse, Adam. *The Orchestra from Beethoven to Berlioz: a History of the Orchestra in the First Half of the 19th Century.* Cambridge: W. Heffer & Sons, 1948.
Castil-Blaze [pseud.]. See Blaze, François-Henri-Joseph.
"Cercle Musical." *ReM* 14 (30 November 1834): 379–80.
Charlton, David and Trevitt, John. "Paris: 1789–1870." *Grove 6* 14:208–19.
Chorley, Henry F. *Music and Manners in France and Germany: a Series of Travelling Sketches of Art and Society.* 3 vols. London: Longman, Orme, Brown, Green, and Longmans, 1841.
———. *Thirty Years' Musical Recollections.* London: Hurst and Blackett, 1862.
Clément, Félix. *Histoire de la musique depuis les temps anciens jusqu'à nos jours.* Paris: Hachette et Cie, 1885.
———. *Les Musiciens célèbres depuis le seizième siècle jusqu'à nos jours.* Paris: Hachette et Cie, 1868.
Cobbett, Walter Willson, ed. *Cobbett's Cyclopedic Survey of Chamber Music.* 2nd ed. rev. 3 vols. London: Oxford University Press, 1963.
Combarieu, Jules. *Histoire de la musique.* Vol. 3, new ed. Paris: Armand Colin, 1928.
"Concerts populaires de musique classique." *RGMdP* 28/41 (13 October 1861): 326.
Cooper, Martin. "Charles Gounod and his Influence on French Music." *Music and Letters* 21/1 (January 1940): 50–59.
———. *French Music from the Death of Berlioz to the Death of Fauré.* London: Oxford University Press, 1951.
———. "The Nineteenth Century Musical Renaissance in France (1870–95)." *Proceedings of the Royal Music Association,* 74 (1947–48): 11–24.
Cristal, Maurice. "Histoire de la musique instrumentale." *RGMdP* 34/38 (22 September 1867): 301–3, continued in nos. 40, 42, 44, and 46, and 35 (1868), nos. 3, 9, 10, 15, and 17.
Curtiss, Mina. *Bizet.* Paris: La Palatine, 1961.
D. "Concerts des Beaux Arts." *RGMdP* 32/7 (12 February 1865): 50–51.
D., S. "Concert Impérial dirigé par Musard." *RGMdP* 26/23 (5 June 1859): 188.
Dandelot, Arthur. *La Société des Concerts du Conservatoire (1828–1923), avec une étude historique sur les grands concerts symphoniques avant et depuis 1828.* 3rd ed. rev. Paris: Delagrave, 1923.
Danjou, Félix. "Deuxième lettre sur l'état de la musique en France." *RGMdP* 5/42 (21 October 1838): 413–15.
———. "Première lettre sur l'état de la musique dans les provinces." *RGMdP* 5/40 (7 October 1838): 393–96.
Davies, Laurence. *César Franck and His Circle.* Boston: Houghton Mifflin Co., 1970.
Deane, Basil. "Cherubini, Luigi." *Grove 6* 4: 203–13.
Debay, Victor and Locard, Paul. "Ecole romantique française de 1815 à 1837." *Encyclopédie de la musique et Dictionnaire du Conservatoire.* Ed. Albert Lavignac and Lionel de La Laurencie. Paris: Delagrave, 1920–31. Part I, vol. 3 (1925): 1661–97.
Delaire, Jacques Auguste. "Des differens genres de musique et de la protection qu'ils réclament." *ReM* 9 (1830): 161–73.
———. "Variétés." *ReM* 5 (1829): 433–40. (Discusses aesthetics and orchestration.)
Deldevez, Edouard-Marie-Ernest. *La Société des Concerts: 1860 à 1885 (Conservatoire National de Musique).* Paris: Firmin-Didot et Cie, 1887. (A continuation of A. Elwart's *Histoire de la Société des Concerts du Conservatoire Impérial de Musique.*)
Delvau, Alfred. *Histoire anecdotique des cafés et cabarets de Paris.* Paris: E. Dentu, 1862.
Demuth, Norman. "Antonin Reicha." *Music and Letters,* 29/2 (April 1948): 165–72.

________. "Habeneck and 'La Société des Concerts.' " *Music Survey* 1/5 (1949): 133–36.
"Les Deux Musard." *RGMdP* 24/19 (10 May 1857): 154.
Devriès, Anik. "Les Editions musicales Sieber." *Revue de musicologie* 55/1 (1969): 20–46.
Downs, Philip George. "The Development of the Great Repertoire in the Nineteenth Century." 2 vols. Ph.D. dissertation, University of Toronto, 1964.
"Du mouvement musical à Paris." *GMdP* 1/51 (21 December 1834): 409–12.
Duckles, Vincent. "Patterns in the Historiography of 19th-century Music." *Acta Musicologica* 42 (1970): 75–82.
Dukas, Paul. "Edouard Lalo." *Revue musicale* 4/5 (March 1923): 97–107.
Duparc, Henri. "Souvenirs de la Société Nationale." *Revue musicale Société Internationale de Musique* 8/12 (December 1912): 1–7.
Duprat, Paul. "L'Année 1854: Mouvement musical." *Almanach musical,* 2 (1855): 23–28.
Eckart-Bäcker, Ursula. *Frankreichs Musik zwischen Romantik und Moderne: Die Zeit im Spiegel der Kritik.* Regensburg: Gustav Bosse Verlag, 1965.
Elwart, Antoine. "De la position des jeunes compositeurs français." *RGMdP* 13 (1846): no. 18 (3 May): 141–42, and no. 20 (17 May): 154–55.
________. *Histoire de la Société des Concerts du Conservatoire Impérial de Musique; avec dessins, musique, plans, portraits, notices biographiques, etc.* Paris: S. Castel, 1860.
________. *Histoire des Concerts Populaires de Musique Classique contenant les programmes annotés de tous les concerts donnés au Cirque Napoléon depuis leur fondation jusqu'à ce jour.* Paris: Castel, 1864.
________. "Musique de chambre: Première matinée musicale de MM. Alard, Dancla, Croisilles, et Chevillard." *RGMdP* 5/2 (14 January 1838): 12–13.
Evans, Raymond L. *Les Romantiques français et la musique.* Paris: H. Champion, 1934.
Fallon, Daniel. Liner notes for Phonorecord Angel S-37089 (Saint-Saëns: Symphony in A and Symphony in F "Urbs Roma"), copyright 1975.
Fauquet, Joël-Marie. "Notes et documents: Hector Berlioz et l'Association des Artistes Musiciens." *Revue de musicologie* 67/2 (1981): 211–36.
Favre, Georges. *Paul Dukas: sa vie—son oeuvre.* Paris: La Colombe, 1948.
Ferchault, Guy. "Paris: 19 Jahrhundert: Konzerte." *MGG* 10 (1962), cols. 778–81.
Ferrari, Gustave. "Castillon (de Saint-Victor), Alexis (Vicomte) de," *Grove 5* 2:115.
"Festival: Dedié à la mémoire d'Hector Berlioz." *RGMdP* 37/13 (27 March 1870): 97–98.
Fétis, Edouard. "De la musique plus que jamais." *RGMdP* 19/30 (25 July 1852): 245–46.
________. "Lettre à un étranger sur la musique à Paris." *ReM*, 10 (1830–31): 262–67.
________. "Nouvelles de Paris: Concerts d'été." *ReM* 15 (26 July 1835): 235–37.
________. "Nouvelles de Paris: Coup d'oeil sur la saison musicale qui expire." *ReM* 15 (26 April 1835): 131–34 and 142.
________. "Revue de la saison musicale de Paris (1829–30)." *ReM* 8 (1830): 86–91.
________. "Revue d'un demi-siècle: Musique instrumentale." *RGMdP* 18 (1851), no. 27 (6 July): 217–20, no. 30 (27 July): 241–43, and no. 31 (3 August): 249–51.
Fétis, François-Joseph. "Athénée Musical: Nouvelle institution: Concert du 26 novembre 1829." *ReM* 6 (1829–30): 451–53.
________. *Biographie universelle des musiciens.* 2nd ed. rev. 8 vols. Paris: Firmin Didot frères, 1866–70, many subsequent impressions with later dates. *(FétisB) Supplément et Complément.* ed. Arthur Pougin. 2 vols. Paris: Firmin Didot frères, 1878–80, many subsequent impressions. (*FétisB* Supplement)
________. "La Civilization et la musique." *ReM* 13 (1833): 345–47.
________. "Concours de symphonies." *RGMdP* 20/36 (4 September 1853): 309–10.
________. "De l'exécution musicale." *ReM* 2 (1827–28): 577–83.
________. "Des révolutions de l'orchestre." *ReM* 1 (1827): 269–80.

———. "Effets des circonstances sur la situation actuelle de la musique, au point de vue de la composition." *RGMdP* 30/32 (9 August 1863): 251–52, continued in nos. 35, 38, 41, and 44.

———. "Examen de l'état actuel de la musique: en Italie, en Allemagne, en Angleterre et en France." *ReM* 1 (1827): 11–18 and many subsequent issues; the section on France begins in no. 18, pp. 437–47, and continues on pp. 485–98, 533–42, and 557–69.

———. "Nouvelles de Paris: Ecole Royale de Musique: Distribution des Prix." *ReM* 4 (1828–29): 394–97. (Discusses contributions of the Paris Conservatoire to France's musical stature.)

———. "Nouvelles de Paris: Ecole Royale de Musique: Société des Concerts." *ReM* 4 (1828–29): 515–20.

———. "Que peut-on faire pour améliorer la condition des jeunes compositeurs et pour porter remède à la décadence de la musique?" *RGMdP* 25/4 (24 January 1858): 25–27, continued in nos. 6, 8, 11, and 13.

———. "Régénération de l'Ecole Royale de Musique: Société des Concerts." *ReM* 3 (1828): 145–49.

———. "Revue succinct de la musique pendant l'année 1828." *ReM* 5 (1829): 1–14.

———"Soirées musicales de quatuors et de quintetti données par M. Baillot." *ReM* 1 (1827): 37–39.

———. "Statistique musicale de la France." *ReM* 6 (1829–30): 121–29.

———. "Sur la philosophie et sur la poétique de la musique." *ReM* 3 (1828): 409–16 and 509–14.

———. "Sur le Concert Spirituel." *ReM* 1 (1827): 197–208. (Discusses Parisian concert societies of the late eighteenth and early nineteenth centuries.)

———. "Variétés: de la necessité des associations pour préserver la musique de sa décadence en France." *ReM* 11 (1831–32): 73–75.

———. "Variétés: De l'influence de la musique instrumentale sur les révolutions de la musique dramatique." *ReM* 10 (1830–31): 129–34.

Flagny, Lucien de. "Notes sur Antoine Reicha." *Revue musicale* 7/1 (November 1925): 37–42.

François-Sappey, Brigitte. "La Vie musicale à Paris à travers les Mémoires d'Eugène Sauzay (1809–1901)." *Revue de musicologie* 60/1–2 (1974): 159–210.

"Franz Anton Habeneck." *Allgemeine musikalische Zeitung,* 41/23 (5 June 1839), cols. 440–41.

Friedland, Bea. *Louise Farrenc, 1804–75: Composer, Performer, Scholar.* Ann Arbor: UMI Research Press, 1980. This is the published version of Bea Friedland's doctoral dissertation (City University of New York, 1975). Contents of the dissertation are summarized in an article of the same title in *Musical Quarterly* 60/2 (April 1974): 257–74.

G. "Correspondance" [Letter to the editor]. *ReM* 8 (1830): 115–16.

Gauthier, André. "Castillon de Saint-Victor, Marie Alexis Vicomte de." *MGG* 2 (1953), cols. 901–4.

Gazette musicale de Paris. Weekly journal. 1-2 (1834–35). (*GMdP*)

Gounod, Charles. *Autobiographical Reminiscences with Family Letters and Notes on Music.* trans. W. Hely Hutchinson. London: W. Heinemann, 1896.

Grant, James. *Paris and its People.* 2 vols. London: Saunders & Otley, 1844.

Grout, Donald J. *A History of Western Music.* 3rd ed. rev. New York: W. W. Norton & Co., 1980.

Grove's Dictionary of Music and Musicians. 5th ed. rev. Ed. Eric Blom. 9 vols. London: Macmillan and Co., 1954. (*Grove 5*)

Gut, Serge and Pistone, Danièle. *La Musique de chambre en France de 1870 à 1918*. Paris: Honoré Champion, 1978.

"Gymnase Musical: Ouverture." *GMdP* 2/22 (31 May 1835): 183–85.

Hagan, Dorothy. "French Musical Criticism between the Revolutions (1830–1848)." Ph. D. dissertation, University of Illinois, 1965.

Hamilton, H. V. "Jacobi, Georg." Rev. John Warrack. *Grove 6* 9:445.

Haraszti, Emile. "Habeneck, François Antoine." *MGG* 5 (1956), cols. 1189–93.

Harding, James. *Massenet*. New York: St. Martin's Press, 1970.

———. *Saint-Saëns and His Circle*. London: Chapman & Hall, 1965.

Hervey, Arthur. *Chopin*. Rev. Maurice J. E. Brown. Master Musicians series. London: J. M. Dent & Sons, 1963.

———. *French Music in the XIXth Century*. London: Grant Richards, 1903.

———. *Saint-Saëns*. New York: Dodd, Mead & Co., 1922. Reprinted, Freeport, N. Y.: Books for Libraries Press, 1969.

Hill, Edward Burlingame. *Modern French Music*. Boston and New York: Houghton Mifflin Co., 1924.

Honegger, Marc, ed. *Dictionnaire de la Musique*, vols. 1 and 2, *Les Hommes et leurs oeuvres*. Paris: Bordas, 1970.

Hueffer, Francis. "David, Félicien (César)." Rev. Marie Louise Pereyra. *Grove 5* 2:604–5.

Imbert, Hugues. *Profils d'artistes contemporaines*. Paris: Société anonyme, 1897.

Indy, Vincent d'. "Castillon, Alexis de." *Cobbett's Cyclopedic Survey of Chamber Music* 1:232–35.

———. "Franck, César Auguste." *Cobbett's Cyclopedic Survey of Chamber Music* 1:418–29.

———. "La Première manière de César Franck." *Revue de musicologie*, 4 (1923): 2–7.

J., R. [probably Jakob Rosenhain]. "Berichte: Paris." *Allgemeine musikalische Zeitung* n.s. 1/13 (25 March 1863), cols. 237–38.

Jullien, Adolphe. *Musique*. Paris: Libraire de l'Art, 1896.

Kastner, Georges. "Revue critique: Grand trio." *RGMdP* 5/28 (15 July 1838): 290. (Apart from reviewing a piano trio of Jupin, discusses role of chamber music in France.)

———. "Trois quatuors pour deux violons, alto et basse, par G. Onslow." *RGMdP* 10/35 (27 August 1843): 297–98. (Apart from reviewing the quartets, discusses contemporary performers' reluctance to play chamber music.)

———. "22e quintette pour instruments à cordes par M. G. Onslow." *RGMdP* 4/21 (21 May 1837): 176–77. (Discusses composers' abandonment of chamber works in favor of music with broader appeal.)

Kéramzer, Ives. "De la symphonie moderne et de son avenir." *RGMdP* 37/24 (12 June 1870): 185–86.

Klaus, Kenneth B. *The Romantic Period in Music*. Boston: Allyn and Bacon, 1970.

Klauwell, Otto. *Theodor Gouvy: sein Leben und seine Werke*. Berlin: Harmonie, 1902.

Klein, John W. "Bizet's 'Roma' Symphony." *Musical Times* 76/1114 (December 1935): 1078–79.

Kracauer, Siegfried. *Orpheus in Paris: Offenbach and the Paris of His Time*. New York: Alfred A. Knopf, 1938.

Kreutzer, Léon. "Grande Société Philharmonique de Paris." *RGMdP* 17/4 (27 January 1850): 27–28.

———. "Société des Concerts et Société Sainte-Cécile." *RGMdP* 20/13 (27 March 1853): 106–7.

Lacombe, Louis. *Philosophie et musique*. Ed. Andrée Lacombe [Claudine Duclairfait Lacombe]. Paris: Fischbacher, 1896.

La Laurencie, Lionel de. "Les Débuts de la musique de chambre en France." *Revue de musicologie,* 18/49 (February 1934): 25–34, continued in nos. 50–52.

————. *L'Ecole française de violon de Lully à Viotti.* 3 vols. Paris: Delagrave, 1922–24.

Lalo, Pierre. "La Vie d'Edouard Lalo." *Revue musicale* 4/5 (February 1923): 118–24.

Landormy, Paul. *La Musique française de Franck à Debussy.* 5th ed. Paris: Gallimard, 1943.

Lang, Paul Henry. Editorial. *Musical Quarterly* 39/2 (April 1953): 232–40.

————. *Music in Western Civilization.* New York: W. W. Norton & Co., 1941.

Lasalle, Albert de and Thoinan, E. [pseud., actually A. E. Roquet]. *La Musique à Paris.* Paris: Morizot, 1863.

Lavoix, Henri-Marie-François, *fils. Histoire de la musique.* New ed. Paris: A. Quantin, ?1884.

Legouvé, Ernest. *Soixante ans de souvenirs.* 2 vols. Paris: J. Hetzel et Cie, 1886–87. Translated, with notes, by Albert D. Vandam as *Sixty Years of Recollections.* 2 vols. London: Eden, Remington & Co., 1893.

Lemoine, Emile. "La Trompette: Histoire d'une société de musique de chambre." *Revue musicale* 3/14 (15 October 1903): 575–79.

Leo, Sophie Augustine. "Musical Life in Paris (1817–48)." Trans. and ed. Oliver Strunk. *Musical Quarterly* 17 (1931), no. 2 (April): 259–71, and no. 3 (July): 389–403.

Le Senne, Camille. "Période contemporaine." *Encyclopédie de la musique et Dictionnaire du Conservatoire.* Ed. Albert Lavignac and Lionel de La Laurencie. Paris: Delagrave, 1920–31, Part I, vol. 3 (1925): 1697–1814 (within the section on France).

Liszt, Franz. "De la situation des artistes, et de leur condition dans la société." *GMdP* 2/18 (3 May 1835): 154–55, continued in nos. 19, 20, 30, 35, and 41. The article was probably written by Countess Marie d'Agoult, but was signed by Liszt.

————. *Letters of Franz Liszt.* Ed. La Mara [Marie Lipsius]. 2 vols. London: H. Grevel & Co., 1894.

————: *Pages romantiques.* Ed. J. Chantavoine. Paris: F. Alkan, 1912.

Locke, Arthur Ware. *Music and the Romantic Movement in France.* London: Kegan Paul, Trench, Trubner & Co. and New York: E. P. Dutton & Co., 1920. Reprinted New York: Benjamin Blom, 1972.

Lockspeiser, Edward. "Berlioz and the French Romantics." *Music and Letters* 15/1 (January 1934): 26–31.

Longyear, Rey M. *Nineteenth-Century Romanticism in Music.* 2nd ed. rev. Englewood Cliffs, N. J.: Prentice-Hall, 1973.

Macdonald, Hugh. "Berlioz, (Louis-)Hector." *Grove 6* 2:579–610.

————. "French Music since 1500." *France: a Companion to French Studies.* Ed. D. G. Charlton. 2nd ed. London and New York: Methuen & Co., 1979, pp. 541–78.

Mansfield, Orlando A. "Cherubini's String Quartets." *Musical Quarterly* 15/4 (October 1929): 590–605.

Marix-Spire, Thérèse. *Les Romantiques et la musique: le cas George Sand, 1804–1838.* Paris: Nouvelles éditions latines, 1955.

Martinet, André. *Histoire anecdotique du Conservatoire de Musique et de Déclamation.* Paris: Ernest Kolb, [?1891].

Massart, Lambert et al. "Grande Société Philharmonique de Paris." *RGMdP* 17/5 (3 February 1850): 39. (A letter from members of the Grande Société.)

Mathieu de Monter, Emile. "De la musique et du chant populaire dans le Midi de la France." 29/34 (24 August 1862): 273–74, continued in nos. 36, 38, and 39.

————. "L'Esprit d'initiative et le principe d'association dans le mouvement musical français actuel: Société Nationale de Musique." *RGMdP* 39/5 (4 February 1872): 35–36.

————. "Revue de l'année 1871." *RGMdP* 39/1 (7 January 1872): 1–3.

———. "Revue rétrospective: Janvier 1870—octobre 1871." *RGMdP* 38/36 (1 October 1871): 269–73.

Matter, Jean. "De quelques sources beethovéniennes de César Franck." *Schweizerische Musikzeitung* 89/6 (1959): 231–34.

Mell, Albert. "Dancla." *Grove 6* 5:220–21.

Mendel, Hermann and Reissmann, August. *Musikalisches Conversations-Lexikon: eine Encyklopädie der gesammten musikalischen Wissenschaften.* 11 vols. and supplement. Berlin: L. Heimann, 1870–83.

Le Ménestrel. Weekly journal founded in 1833. I have examined only vols. 26 to 38 (December 1858 to 1872).

Mercier, Alain. "Douze lettres inédites de Richard Wagner à Edouard Schuré." *Revue de musicologie* 54/2 (1968): 206–21.

Meylan, Pierre. "Delacroix et les musiciens romantiques." *Revue musicale* 25/209 (March 1949): 9–16.

Monnais, Edouard [Paul Smith]. "Athénée: Séance d'ouverture, mercredi 21 novembre." *RGMdP* 33/47 (25 November 1866): 373.

———[P. S.]. "Nécrologie: Zimmerman." *RGMdP* 20/45 (6 November 1853): 391–92.

———[P. Smith]. "Revue de l'année 1850." *RGMdP* 18/1 (5 January 1851): 1–2.

———. "Revue de l'année 1861." *RGMdP* 29/1 (5 January 1862): 1–3.

———. "Revue de l'année 1866." *RGMdP* 34/1 (6 January 1867): 1–4.

———. "Revue de l'année 1868." *RGMdP* 36/1 (3 January 1869): 1–3.

———. "Une Soirée chez Zimmermann." *Revue musicale* (a subsidiary of *RGMdP* published on Thursdays) 6/7 (14 February 1839): 56.

Morel, Auguste. "De l'utilité des sociétés d'amateurs: Cercle Musical." *RGMdP* 7/43 (5 July 1840): 363–65.

Die Musik in Geschichte und Gegenwart. Ed. Friedrich Blume and Ruth Blume, 14 vols. and supplements. Kassel and Basel: Bärenreiter Verlag, 1949–79. (*MGG*)

"Musique de chambre: Soirées de quatuors et quintetti." *RGMdP* 5/31 (5 August 1838): 310.

Nectoux, Jean-Michel. "Correspondance Saint-Saëns–Fauré." *Revue de musicologie* 58/1 (1972): 65–89, 58/2: 190–252, and 59/1 (1973): 60–97.

———. "Fauré, Gabriel (Urbain)." *Grove 6* 6: 417–28.

The New Grove Dictionary of Music and Musicians. 20 vols. Ed. Stanley Sadie. London: Macmillan Publishers Ltd., 1980.(*Grove 6*)

"Nouvelle société de musique de chambre." *RGMdP* 24/6 (8 February 1857): 45–46. (Discusses the chamber music society founded by M. le comte Louis de Stainlein.)

"Nouvelles de Paris: Sixième concert du Conservatoire." *ReM* 11 (1831–32): 84–86. (Discusses the French reception of symphonies by Haydn, Mozart, and Beethoven since 1805.)

Ortigue, Joseph d'. "Des sociétés philharmoniques dans le Midi de la France." *GMdP* 1/48 (30 November 1834): 382–87.

Palm, Albert. "La Connaissance de l'oeuvre de J. S. Bach en France à l'époque préromantique." *Revue de musicologie* 52/1 (1966): 88–114.

Pereyra, Marie Louise; Prod'homme, J.-G.; and Chouquet, Gustave. "Paris." *Grove's Dictionary of Music and Musicians.* 3rd rev. ed. Ed. H. C. Colles. 5 vols. New York: The Macmillan Company, 1928, 4:46–51. Rev. with Fred Goldbeck in *Grove 5* 6:547–53.

Perris, Arnold B. "Music in France during the Reign of Louis-Philippe: Art as a Substitute for Heroic Experience." Ph.D. dissertation, Northwestern University, 1967.

Le Pianiste. Journal published twice monthly. 1833–35.

Pierre, Constant. *Le Conservatoire National de Musique et de Déclamation: Documents historiques et administratifs*. Paris: Imprimerie nationale, 1900.

————. *Histoire du Concert Spirituel, 1725–1790*. Paris: Société Française de Musicologie, 1975. (The book was written by 1900.)

————. *Les Hymnes et chansons de la Révolution: Aperçu général et catalogue avec notices historiques, analytiques et bibliographiques*. Paris: Imprimerie nationale, 1904.

Pincherle, Marc. "French Performing Organizations." *Cobbett's Cyclopedic Survey of Chamber Music* 1:434–36.

Piriou, Adolphe and Cobbett, W. W. "Blanc, Adolphe." *Cobbett's Cyclopedic Survey of Chamber Music* 1:126.

Prod'homme, Jacques Gabriel. "Le Gymnase Musical." *Revue de musicologie* 11/23 (August 1927): 150–54.

————. "Nouvelles musicologiques—Documents: la Chambre philharmonique." *Revue de musicologie* 9/15 (August 1925): 127.

————. *L'Opéra (1669 à 1925)*. Paris: Delagrave, 1925.

————. *Les Symphonies de Beethoven*. Paris: Ch. Delagrave, 1906.

————. "The Works of Weber in France." *Musical Quarterly* 14/3 (July 1928): 366–86.

Prod'homme, J.-G. and Crauzat, E. de. *Les Menus Plaisirs du Roi: l'Ecole Royale et le Conservatoire de Musique*. Paris: Delagrave, 1929.

"Prospectus: Gymnase Musical." *ReM* 14 (14 December 1834): 391–92.

Radigeur, Henri. "La Musique française de 1789 à 1815." *Encyclopédie de la Musique et Dictionnaire du Conservatoire*. Ed. Albert Lavignac and Lionel de La Laurencie. Paris: Delagrave, 1920–31, Part 1, vol. 3 (1925): 1562–1660.

Raynor, Henry. *Music and Society since 1815*. London: Barrie & Jenkins, 1976.

Revue et gazette musicale de musique. Journal published weekly (with occasional exceptions), the result of a merger between the *Revue musicale* and the *Gazette musicale de Paris* in 1835; it adopted the volume numbering of the latter. Vols. 2–39 (1835–72). (*RGMdP*)

Revue musicale. Weekly journal. 15 vols. 1827–35. (*ReM*)

"Revue musicale: Musique instrumentale." *ReM* 11 (1831–32): 223–24.

Ringer, Alexander, L. "A French Symphonist at the Time of Beethoven: Etienne Nicolas Méhul." *Musical Quarterly* 37/4 (October 1951): 543–65.

————. "On the Question of Exoticism in 19th Century Music." *Studia Musicologica* 7 (1965): 115–23.

Rolland, Romain. *Musiciens d'aujourd'hui*. Paris: Hachette et Cie, 1908. Trans. Mary Blaiklock as *Musicians of Today*. 4th ed. New York: Henry Holt and Co., 1919.

Rosen, Charles. *The Classical Style: Haydn, Mozart, and Beethoven*. Norton Library Edition. New York: W. W. Norton & Co., 1972.

S., P. [pseud.]. See Monnais, Edouard.

St. Foix, Georges de and Cobbett, W. W. "Cherubini, Maria Luigi." *Cobbett's Cyclopedic Survey of Chamber Music* 1:270–73.

Saint-Saëns, Camille. *Ecole buissonnière: ; Notes et souvenirs*. Paris: Pierre Lafitte, 1913. Trans. and abridged by Edwin Gile Rich as *Musical Memories*. Boston: Small, Maynard & Company, 1919. Reprinted New York: Da Capo Press, 1965.

————. *Harmonie et mélodie*. 3rd ed. Paris: C. Lévy, 1885.

Sallès, Antoine. *Les Premières exécutions à Lyon des oeuvres de Beethoven*. Paris: Jobert, 1927.

Schaal, Richard. "Gesellschaften und Vereine." *MGG* 5 (1956), cols. 6–27.

Schindler, Anton. *Beethoven in Paris*. Münster: Aschendorff'sche Buchhandlung, 1842.

Schmitt, Florent and Cobbett, W. W. "Lalo, Edouard Victor Antoine." *Cobbett's Cyclopedic Survey of Chamber Music* 2: 88–89.

Schonberg, Harold C. *The Great Conductors*. New York: Simon and Schuster, 1967.

Schrade, Leo. *Beethoven in France*. New Haven: Yale University Press, 1942.

Schwarz, Boris. "Beethoven and the French Violin School." *Musical Quarterly*, 44/4 (October 1958): 431–47.

———. "French Instrumental Music between the Revolutions (1789–1830)." Ph.D. dissertation, Columbia University, 1950.

———. "Paganini, Nicolò." *Grove 6* 14: 86–91.

Scudo, P. [Pierre or Paul], ed. *L'Année musicale*. 3 yearly vols. Paris: L. Hachette et Cie, 1860–62.

———. *Critique et littérature musicales*. 2nd series. Paris: Hachette, 1859.

Searle, Humphrey, ed. *Hector Berlioz: a Selection from his Letters*. New York: Vienna House, 1973.

Seligmann, Prosper. "Les Béotiens de la musique." *RGMdP* 15/23 (4 June 1848): 173–75.

Servières, Georges. "Les Premiers admirateurs français des compositions de Liszt." *Revue musicale* 19/9 (July 1928): 272–81.

———. "La Symphonie en France au XIXe siècle (avant 1870)." *Ménestrel* 85/39 (28 September 1923): 397–400.

Shanet, Howard. "Bizet's Suppressed Symphony." *Musical Quarterly* 44/4 (October 1958): 461–76.

Slonimsky, Nicolas. *Music since 1900*. 4th ed. New York: Charles Scribner's Sons, 1971.

Smith, Paul (or P.) [pseud.]. See Monnais, Edouard.

Soccanne, Pierre. "Quelques documents inédites sur Pierre Baillot." *Revue de musicologie* 23/71–72 (1939): 71–78, and série spéciale, no. 2 (July 1943): 15–18.

———. "Virtuoses: un maître de quatuor: Pierre Baillot." *Le Guide de concert* 24 (1937–38): no. 24 (11 March 1938): 647–48, continued in nos. 25–30.

"Société Philharmonique du Calvados." *ReM* 13 (1833): 207–8. (Discusses the role of instrumental music in France.)

"Soirées de M. Baillot." *ReM* 13 (1833): 7.

Spohr, Ludwig. *Louis Spohr's Autobiography*. 2 vols. London: Longman, Green, Longman, Roberts, & Green, 1865.

Stoepel, François. "Essai sur la poétique de la musique instrumentale." *GMdP* 1/41 (12 October 1834): 327–30 and 2/7 (15 February 1835): 55–57.

———. "La Musique en France (1835)." *GMdP* 2/39 (27 September 1835): 313–17.

T., D. "Variétés: Paris dilettante." *ReM* 15 (24 May 1835): 166–67. (Discusses role of music in Parisian daily life.)

Taine, Hippolyte. *Notes on Paris*. Translated, with notes, by John Austin Stevens. New York: Henry Holt and Co., 1875.

Tiersot, Julien. "César Franck." Trans. Frederick H. Martens. *Musical Quarterly* 9/1 (January 1923): 26–55.

———. "Edouard Lalo." Trans. Frederick H. Martens. *Musical Quarterly* 11/1 (January 1925): 8–35.

———. *Le Musicien errant, 1842–1852: Correspondance publiée par Julien Tiersot.* Paris: Calmann-Lévy, [ca. 1919].

———. "La Symphonie en France." *Zeitschrift der Internationalen Musikgesellschaft* 3/10 (July 1902): 391–402.

Trollope, Frances. *Paris and the Parisians in 1835*. 2 vols. London: Richard Bentley, 1836.

Vaines, Maurice de. "Du goût musical en France." *RGMdP* 13/37 (13 September 1846): 289–93, continued in nos. 38–42.

Vernaelde, Albert. "La Société des Concerts et les Grandes associations symphoniques."

Encyclopédie de la musique et Dictionnaire du Conservatoire. Ed. Albert Lavignac and Lionel de La Laurencie. Paris: Delagrave, 1920–31. Part 2, vol. 6 (1931): 3684–3714.

Wangermée, Robert. *François-Joseph Fétis: Musicologue et Compositeur.* Brussels: Palais des Académies, 1951.

Warrack, John. *Carl Maria von Weber.* 2nd ed. rev. Cambridge: Cambridge University Press, 1976.

Weber, William. *Music and the Middle Class: The Social Structure of Concert Life in London, Paris, and Vienna*. London: Croom Helm, 1975.

Woolett, Henri, and Cobbett, W. W. "Onslow, George." *Cobbett's Cyclopedic Survey of Chamber Music* 2: 194–200.

Z. "Une Oasis musicale." *RGMdP* 15/45 (5 November 1848): 343–44. (Discusses the *séances* of Lambert Massart.)

Index

Note: a reference in the following form: Bernard, [? Philippe], 00, indicates that the Bernard in question may or may not have been Philippe. A reference in this form: Bernard, Philippe, 76, 97, 124(?), indicates that only the reference questioned is doubtful, while all others are certain.

Abraham, Gerald, 1-2, 163-64
Académie Royale de Belgique, 171
Académie royale de musique. *See* Opéra (Paris, institution)
Accursi, Roméo-Virgile, 255
Achard, Léon, 28
Adam (violist), 59, 250, 264, 275
Adam, Adolphe, 211, 243, 244; performance of his music, 29, 34, 161
Admission fees. *See* Concerts, admission fees.
Agoult, Marie d', Countess, 4 (and n. 4, p. 286), 320 n. 76
Aix-la-Chapelle, 281
Alard, Delphin, 52, 73, 212, 227, 235, 258; performance of his music (general), 108-09, 112-13, 117, 119, 121, 123; performance of his music (specific), 31, 44-45, 67, 77, 222, 231, 265; as performer, 15, 46, 52-53, 70, 95, 119, 128, 153, 222, 254, 259, 267, 276, 343 n. 150; *séances* with Alexandre Chevillard, 70, 71, 150, 218-19. *See also* Société Alard-Franchomme
Albert (cellist), 251
Alerme (host of *séances*), 221
Alhambra Theatre, London, 339 n. 58
Alkan, Charles-Valentin [Valentin Morhange], 29, 53, 84
Allard, [? Charles-Oscar], 224
Allegri, Gregorio, 74, 224
Allgemeine musikalische Zeitung (Leipzig), 5, 33, 136, 138, 157, 158
Allgemeine Theaterzeitung (Vienna), 305 n. 13(?)
Altès, Ernest *(jeune),* 235, 236
Altès, Joseph-Henri, 31, 61, 249
Amateur performers, 19, 20, 75, 82, 88, 99, 100, 151, 170, 211-12, 250, 271, 273 (and n. 318, p. 350), 280. *See also* Orchestras, amateur
Amédée [François-Amédée Laneau], 25
Ancien regime, music during, 129, 136, 279-80
André, Johann (music publisher), 107, 299 n. 197
Anger, 281
Angoulêmes, 281
Aoust, Marquise d', 89
Appreciation of instrumental music, 2, 10, 209-210; increase in, 1-2, 5, 99, 101-02, 104, 153 (and n. 122, p. 323), 155, 156, 159-61, 207-08, 210, 213-14, 216, 280; lack of, 1-2, 4-5, 69, 94, 99, 103-04, 142-44, 146-47, 151 (and n. 107, p. 322), 152-53, 156, 159, 163), lack of before 1828, 139-141. *See also* Taste, musical
Arban, Jean-Baptiste, 93, 94, 97
Armingaud, Jules, 52-53, 56, 212, 218, 248, 263. *See also* Société des Derniers Quatuors de Beethoven
Artôt, Alexandre [Joseph Montagney], 112, 117
Association des Artistes-Musiciens, 71-72, 82, 99, 150, 154, 219-20; salle de, 272
Association des Musiciens-Exécutants de Paris, 74, 220, 229, 323 n. 120
Association Musicale de l'Ouest, 281 (and n. 16 and 17, p. 352)
Athénée (building), 258-59
Athénée (series). *See* Société de l'Athénée
Athénée Dramatique, 220-21
Athénée Musical (building), 17, 220
Athénée Musical (series, 1829-44). *See* Société de l'Athénée Musical
Athénée Musical (series, 1864), 157, 213, 220-21
Auber, D.-F.-E.: as director of the Conservatoire, 36, 211, 295 n. 122; music of, 163, 211 (and n. 5, p. 336); performance

of his music (general), 109, 130, 324 n. 144; performance of his music (specific), 29, 34, 40, 74, 92, 141, 161, 220, 221
Aubery, [? Jean-Pierre], 261
Audience, 8, 61, 97-103, 129-30, 132, 144, 145, 149, 151-53, 157-58, 166-67 (and n. 216, p. 338), 208-11 (and n. 3, pp. 335-36); at benefit concerts, 85; at café concerts, 91 (and n. 41, p. 306); before 1830, 137, 139-41; expansion of, 8, 46, 82, 94, 101-02, 123, 133, 144-46, 149, 156-57, 160, 207-09, 213-14, 216; at outdoor concerts, 307-08 n. 65; at *salons,* 87-88
Augé de Lassus, Lucien, 274, 350 n. 315
Aumont, [? Henri-Raymond], 218
Austin, William W., 215-16

Bach, C.P.E., 167
Bach, Johann Christian, 167
Bach, Johann Sebastien, 165, 167; music of, 123, 132, 157, 194, 334 n. 80; performance of his music (general), 108-09, 113, 118-23; performance of his music (specific), 18, 20, 29, 39, 44, 49, 54, 58, 63, 65, 72-74, 77, 138, 160, 221, 225, 236, 242, 245, 247, 249, 259, 261, 275
Bach revival, 109, 118, 121, 123
Baillot, Pierre, 66, 73, 142, 144, 164, 221, 240, 248, 282; concerts and *séances* before 1828, 2, 66, 109, 138, 141 (and n. 45, p. 319), 164, 221 (and n. 21, p. 337); later concerts and *séances,* 4, 87, 95, 114, 122, 221-22 (and n. 21, p. 337); performance of his music, 31, 67, 109, 161, 221
Bailly (? cellist), 236
Bailly, de (? violinist), 250
Balls, 14, 90, 94, 234, 282
Bannelier, Charles, 61, 158, 159, 223, 230, 272, 299 n. 205, 300 n. 218, 340 n. 79, 343 n. 151
Barbereau, A.-Mathurin-B., 38
Barbereau, Henri, 66, 259
Barrande, Marie, 239
Barthe, Adrien, 264
Barthe-Banderali, Mme. Adrien, 64, 248
Barthélemy [possibly Berthélemy, Félix-Charles], 261
Barzun, Jacques: own statements on audiences, 151, 166, 167, 335-36 n. 3; own statements on Berlioz, 67, 223, 242, 318 n. 34, 323 n. 127, 345 n. 204; own statements on individual concerts series, 242-43, 301 n. 241; 345 n. 204; own statements on music, 151, 166, 328 n. 210; own statements on the musical scene, 151, 318 n. 34, 323 n. 127, 324 n. 141; own statements on Paris in the 1840s, 15, 150-51, 312 n. 15; writings of, 10, 150-51, 164, 223
Batista, Edouard, 42
Batta, Alexandre, 240, 248, 257, 277; concerts with Rosa Escudier-Kastner and Henri Vieuxtemps, 80, 238; concerts with Franz Liszt, 70, 248; *matinées* of, 309, n. 99
Battu, Marie, 241
Baudiot, Nicolas, 221
Bayreuth, 215
Bazaine, Charles, 350 n. 315
Bazar Bonne-Nouvelle, 241
Bazin, François, 67
Bazzini, Antonio, 77, 222
Beaulieu, Désiré, 281
Beaumetz, Marie, 222
Beck, Franz Ignaz, 30
Becker, Jean, 79, 253; *concerts historiques* of, 77, 222
Becker, Mme. Ernest, 222
Beer, Jules, 346 n. 223
Beethoven, Ludwig van, 3, 23, 102, 132-33, 144, 147, 150, 155, 165, 167, 172, 181; influence of, 131, 148, 165, 166, 171, 181, 182, 192, 201, 202, 216; music of, 51, 106-07, 131-33, 139, 141, 150, 151, 157-59, 165-67, 171-74, 177, 183, 187, 191, 201,204, 209-13, 216; music of, descriptions of, 131-33, 165, 204; performance of his music (general), 8, 9, 19, 23, 55, 87, 105, 107-20, 122-24, 130-33, 158, 172, 283; performance of his music (specific), 18, 20, 23-25, 27-38, 40-42, 44-45, 47-50, 54-60, 62, 63, 65-75, 78-80, 82, 138, 141, 142, 147, 149, 154, 157-60, 162, 163, 165, 208, 212, 218, 219, 221-25, 227-30, 232-34, 236-39, 241, 242, 244-54, 257, 259-62, 267, 269-78, 280-83, 295 n. 113, 302 n. 256, 322 n. 107, 324 n. 138, 350 n. 318, 352 n. 17
Béguin-Salomon, Louise (*née* Cohen): concerts and *séances* of, 81, 222-23; as performer, 61, 64, 229, 239, 242. *See also* Cohen, Louise-Frédérique
Behrnhardt, L., 352 n. 16
Bellini, Vincenzo, 18, 324 n. 141
Bellon, J., 62, 258
Benefit concerts, 85-86, 99, 143; for charities, 86, 150, 239; by individuals, 85-86; instances of, 15, 16, 43, 47, 71, 75, 118, 219, 260, 282
Benoist, François, 215
Béroit, Charles-Auguste de, 270; performance of his music (general), 108, 111-13, 116-17, 124; performance of his music (specific), 30, 261, 262, 270
Bériot, Charles-Wilfrid (son of Charles-Auguste), 224, 273
Berlioz, Hector, 1-3, 16, 33, 37 (and n. 89, p. 293), 83, 103, 137, 139-41, 150-52, 159, 162, 165, 167, 170, 171, 205, 207, 215, 219, 223,

242-43, 266, 323 n. 127, 335 n. 2, 336 n. 7, 345 n. 204, 350-51 n. 24; concerts of, 4, 67, 74, 85, 95, 100, 223 (*see also* Grande Société Philharmonique de Paris); as conductor, 67, 71, 74, 90, 219, 242; music of, 1, 67, 100, 116, 129, 137, 163, 165, 166, 169-71, 187, 205-06, 209, 334 n. 80; music of, appreciation of, 6, 42, 146, 160 (and n. 174 and 175, p. 326), 165, 166, 175, 180, 190, 205, 215, 293 n. 90, 335 n. 2; music of, description of, 131, 166, 194; as organizer of musical events, 67, 90, 100, 131, 223, 242-43; own statements on audiences, 102, 147, 152, 162, 166; own statements on Cherubini, 23, 182; own statements on concert series, 23, 47, 159, 225, 234, 248, 274, 350-51 n. 324; own statements on the musical scene, 3-4, 17, 103, 140, 143 (and n. 54, p. 319), 147, 150, 159, 162, 287 n. 5, 293 n. 81; own statements on individual works of others, 175, 179, 187; own statements on the year 1848, 15, 153; performance of his music (general), 8, 107-10, 112-14, 116-19, 121, 124 (and n. 30, p. 314), 131, 215, 316 n. 64; performance of his music (specific), 18, 30, 38, 40, 42, 49, 51, 67, 72, 85, 141, 161, 213, 223, 242, 256, 268, 335 n. 3; *soirées* of, 67, 87, 223; writings of, 3, 10, 67, 103, 161-62, 223, 293 n. 89
Berlioz festival, 163, 215, 306 n. 34
Bernadel, Anatole, 236
Bernard, Alfred, 264
Bernard Elisabeth, 11, 46, 48, 50, 259, 295 n. 116, 296 n. 136
Bernard, Otto, 225(?), 264
Bernard, Paul, 81, 96, 224, 225(?)
Bernhard, Ernest, 263
Bernhardt, [?P.] (instrument maker), 17
Berr, Friedrich, 67, 112, 116
Berthelemy (composer), 324 n. 135
Berthélemy, Félix-Charles, 64, 253, 261(?)
Bertin, Armand, 243
Bertini, Henri-Jérôme, 182-83, 227, 267; music of, 169, 182-83 (and ex. 4, 184-85), 209; performance of his music, 70, 72, 112, 116, 227, 273
Berton, Henri-Montan, 38, 130, 142, 151 (and n. 108, p. 332), 211, 244
Berton, Mme. (wife of Henri-Montan), 150
Besekirsky, Vasil Vasilevic, 46
Bessems, Antoine, 224, 245; concerts and *matinées* of, 80, 224
Bez, Charles de, 37, 228
Bibliothèque Nationale (Paris), 11, 182, 189 (and n. 56, n. 333), 331 n. 27, 332 n. 52, 334 n. 82
Bigot, Marie, 138
Billet, Alexandre, 277
Bischoff, Ludwig, 24
Bischoffsheim, Raphael, 76, 258-59
Bizet, Georges, 5, 48, 61, 183, 202; music of, 161, 163, 183, 323 n. 129; performance of his music, 77, 83, 268, 270
Blanc, Adolphe, 5, 125, 170, 175, 178-79; music of, 131, 178-80, 205; performance of his music (general), 8, 107-10, 113, 119-20, 124, 212, 283, 312-13 n. 18, 314 n. 30 and 31, 316 n. 64; performance of his music (specific), 60, 62, 65, 75, 79, 80, 212, 223, 242, 250, 257, 263-65, 311 n. 4; as performer, 53, 61, 64, 235, 258
Blanchard, Henri: own statements on concert series, 38, 53, 55, 60-62, 74, 94, 148, 155, 220, 239, 244, 249, 262, 269, 272, 299 n. 205, 301 n. 236, 309 n. 99, 314 n. 37, 338 n. 41, 342 n. 135 and 137, 344 n. 180, 346 n. 218, 348 n. 277, 348-49 n. 284, 351 n. 329 and 332; own statements on the musical scene, 4, 15, 16, 94, 148, 153, 155, 287 n. 2, 309 n. 99, 312 n. 15, 323 n. 127, 324 n. 138; own statements on proliferation of instrumental music, 4, 16, 101, 155; own statements on specific works of others, 183 (and n. 42, p. 332), 190, 191, 194, 334 n. 74; performance of his music, 62
Blancou, J.-V.-A., 61
Blangy, Caroline. *See* Grandval, Marie Félice Clémence de Reiset, Vicomtesse de
Blaze, F.-H.-J. [pseud. Catil-Blaze], 94, 129, 244, 282
Bloom, Peter, 132, 144, 205, 240, 328-29 n. 217 and 218, 342 n. 144
Boccherini, Luigi: music of, 151, 157, 159, 209; performance of his music (general), 108-09, 112, 114, 124, 130, 172; performance of his music (specific), 58, 60, 63, 65, 66, 73, 75, 221, 237 250, 261, 264
Boëllmann, Léon, 84
Boëly, A.-P.-F., 79, 263, 330 n. 10
Bohrer, Anton, 66, 83, 224, 233. *See also* Bohrer brothers, concerts and *séances*
Bohrer, Max 66, 83, 224, 233. *See also* Bohrer brothers, concerts and *séances*
Bohrer, Sophie, 224
Bohrer brothers, concerts and *séances,* 66, 114, 141, 224-25, 248
Boieldieu, Adrien, 130, 142, 165
Boieldieu, Louis, 243
Bonaparte, Mathilde (Princess), 81-82
Bonaparte, Napoléon, 132
Bonet, Albert, 25
Bonewitz, Jean-Henri, 81, 96, 225
Bonjour, F[rançois ?]., 143
Bordeaux, 281; Société Sainte-Cécile, 282

Bordes, Charles, 84
Bordogni, Giulio, 227
Botte, Adolphe, 160 (and n. 175, p. 326), 334 n. 71; own statements on concert series, 46, 47, 53, 57, 59, 159, 268, 299 n. 212; own statements on the musical scene, 154, 155, 158-59
Boucher, Alexandre-Jean, 247
Bouffes- Parisiens, 246
Boulanger, E.-H.-A., 324 n. 135
Boulart, [? V.-J.-B.-C.], 250
Boulogne, *société philharmonique,* 280
Bourbon Restoration, 9, 130, 136, 139, 145, 313 n. 19; music during, 9 (and n. 32, p. 287), 65-67, 114, 121-22 (and n. 19 and 24, p. 313), 133, 136, 139-45
Bourgault-Ducoudray, Louis, 83
Bourges, Maurice, 17, 52, 153, 179, 182, 312 n. 15, 329 n. 4
Bousquet, Georges, 42, 62, 219, 228
Bovy-Lysberg, Charles Samuel, 243
Boyer, Charles-Georges (music publisher), 107, 229 n. 197
Brahms, Johannes, 132, 160; performance of his music, 60, 80, 212, 270, 278
Braille, Louis, 247
Brandus, G. & S. Dufour (music publishers), 180
Breitkopf & Härtel (music publishers), 299 n. 188
Brest, 48
Brod, Henri, 25, 175, 180, 227; music of, 180; performance of his music, 28-31, 70, 107-08, 111-12, 227; as performer, 260, 267
Brook, Barry S., 136
Brossa, Firmin-Jean, 256
Bruch, Max, 252
Brunkmann (? string player), 245
Brunot, Louis-Antoine, 46, 51, 64, 222
Brussels String Quartet, 332 n. 46
Bulwer, Sir Henry, 310 n. 105
Burnand, Robert, 87, 305 n. 6
Burton, Humphrey, 279-80 (and n. 3, p. 351)

Caecilian Trio, 333 n. 66
Caen, 280
Café concerts, 14, 20, 68, 85, 90-95 (and n. 49, n. 307), 97, 99, 100, 102, 115, 146, 147
Café Eldorado, 94
Carafa (de Colobrano), Michele, 211
Caraman, Charles de (le duc): *séances* of, 73, 225
Carissimi, Giacomo, 39
Carse, Adam, 17, 22, 33, 90, 106, 291 n. 62 and 63, 306 n. 37, 307 n. 62
Casimir Ney. *See* Escoffier, Louis-Casimir
Casino, 92
Casino (de la rue) Cadet, 94, 97
Casino des Familles, salle, 254
Casino Paganini, 74, 250
Castil-Blaze. *See* Blaze, F.-H.-J.
Castillon, Alexis de, 8, 83, 163, 167, 195 (and n. 76, p. 334), 201, 205; music of, 195, 201 (and ex. 11, pp. 198-200 and n. 76, 78, and 80, p. 334), 205, 206; performance of his music, 80, 83, 270-71
Catel, Charles-Simon, 130
Cercle Artistique. *See* Cercle des Beaux-Arts
Cercle de la Libraire, 55
Cercle de l'Union Artistique, 77, 97, 225-26
Cercle des Beaux-Arts, 79, 96, 226-27
Cercle Musical (1834-35, later the Société Musicale I), 69-70, 82, 227, 267
Cercle Musical de la rue Mandar, 138
Cercle Musical des Amateurs, 69, 95, 96, 149, 228
Cercle Musical et Littéraire, 74, 220, 228-29
Chabrier, 346 n. 223
Chabrier, Emmanuel, 84
Chaine, Eugène, 191, 254
Chamber works, orchestral performance of, 19 (and n. 44, pp. 289-90), 124-27
Champs-Elysées, 90-94, 307-08 n. 65
Charity concerts. *See* Benefit concerts
Charlton, David, 317 n. 1, 346 n. 218, 350 n. 318
Chartier Prize, 159, 177
Château des fleurs, 93
Châtelet, 48
Châtellerault, 281
Chausson, Ernest, 84, 215
Chelard, H.-A.-B., 259-60
Chéri (probably Victor Cizos), 249
Cherubini, Luigi, 2, 8, 139, 142, 165, 181-82, 211; as director of the Conservatoire, 23-25, 36, 140, 181, 211, 231, 336 n. 7; music of, 132, 143, 181-82 (and n. 35 and 36, p. 331), 193, 203, 211 (and n. 5, p. 336); performance of his music (general), 130, 143, 280, 316 n. 64; performance of his music (specific), 25, 28, 31, 34, 49, 74, 233, 253, 275
Chevé, Amand, 243, 269
Chevillard, Alexandre, 212; performance of his music (general), 109, 112, 116-17; performance of his music (specific), 31, 67, 70, 218, 231; as performer, 55-56, 70, 128, 221, 238, 249, 254, 262, 267, 277, 343 n. 10; *séances* with Delphin Alard, 70, 71, 150, 218-19. *See also* Société des Derniers Quatuors de Beethoven
Chevillard, Camille, 84
Child performers, 19-20, 278
Chiostri, Luigi, 253
Cholera epidemic of 1832, 14-15, 251, 259

Chopin, Fryderyk, 148, 227 (and n. 62, p. 339), 323 n. 127; music of, 192, 193, 314 n. 32; performance of his music (general), 108, 123, 125; performance of his music (specific), 30, 58, 62, 70, 223, 236, 248; as performer, 123, 289 n. 140
Chorley, Henry F., 26, 143, 150, 257
Choron, Alexandre, 141, 233. *See also* Institution Royale de Musique Classique et Religieuse
Chouquet, Gustave, 294 n. 91
Cimarosa, Domenico, 74
Cinti-Damoreau, Laure, 27
Cirque de l'Impératrice, 76, 229, 269 (and n. 292, p. 349)
Cirque des Champs-Elysées, 223, 349 n. 292
Cirque d'hiver, 46
Cirque Napoléon, 17, 46
Cizos, Victor [pseud. Chéri], 249(?)
Clari, L'Abbé, 63
Classical-era music, influence of, 121, 131 (and n. 58 and 61, p. 316), 145-46, 151, 157, 165-67, 171-74, 210, 213, 214; influence of, on individual composers, 174-75, 178, 180-83, 187, 194, 201-02
Claudel (violinist), 224, 273
Clauss, Wilhelmine (later Wilhelmine Szarwady), 271, 315 n. 44. *See also* Szarwady, Wilhelmine
Cobbett, Walter Willson, 11, 169, 179
Cohen, Jules, 44, 342 n. 124
Cohen, Léonce, 236 (and n. 124, p. 342)
Cohen, Louise-Frédérique [pseud. Salomon] (later Mme. Béguin-Salomon), 271. *See also* Béguin-Salomon, Louise
Colblain, A., 55, 59, 249, 263, 275
Colin, Marie, 53, 239
Colonnes, Edouard, 48, 59, 222, 224; *matinées* of, 80, 229; *See also* Concerts Colonne
Colonnes d'Hercule, 266
Comédie Française, 104
Commercialization of music, 82, 91, 97-98, 102-03, 130, 144, 148-49, 167, 213-14, 318 n. 34
Commune, effect on musical life, 6-7, 15-16
Compagnon, Jean-Emile [pseud. Desmarets], 27
Composer-citizen, 137
Composers active 1828-1871: concerts of (see Concerts, composers'); problems for, 3-4, 37 (and n. 90, p. 293), 42, 103, 140-41, 143, 146-48, 151, 154-55, 157-59, 208-11; support for (general), 82-83, 107, 109, 119-21, 149, 151-57, 164, 212-14, 216; support for at outdoor and café concerts, 93, 94; support for by individual series, 20, 37, 38, 42, 45, 50-51, 58, 60, 62-65, 68, 70, 72, 77-78, 80, 143, 226, 242-43, 252, 256, 260, 262-65, 268, 270-71
Comtat (or Contat, violinist), 64, 241
Concert des Amateurs, 66, 141
Concert halls, 16-17, 26, 46, 92, 217; inadequacies of, 3, 16-17, 26, 140, 146; shortage of, 16-17, 88, 146, 210; size of, 16-17
Concert National, 48
Concerts: admission fees of, 98-101 (and n. 105, p. 310); admission fees of selected series, 24, 37-38, 47-48, 75, 215, 230, 232-34, 259, 261, 275; benefit (*see* Benefit concerts); café (*see* Café concerts); composers', 78, 85, 107, 124, 125, 179, 223, 236, 248, 255, 278; financing of, 3, 86, 100; nonseries, 20, 85, 95, 97, 99, 100, 125; outdoor, 14, 15, 20, 68, 85, 90-95 (and n. 37, p. 306), 98-100, 102, 115, 130, 146, 213; programs of (*see* Programs); proliferation of, 95-99, 101, 102, 110-111, 117, 118, 120, 123, 142, 146, 153-55, 164, 212; provincial (*see* Provinces (musical activity in)); pupils', 19, 73, 74, 81, 224, 225, 253, 272; schedule of, 14 (and n. 4, p. 287; *see also* Season, musical); state, 85, 89, 97, 99, 245; summer (*see* Concerts, outdoor); tickets for (*see* Tickets)
Concerts Arban, 94
Concerts Classiques, 76, 229
Concerts Cléry, 138
Concerts Colonne, 48, 100, 149, 161, 163, 215
Concerts Danbé, 161
Concerts de famille, 94
Concerts de la Loge Olympique, 137
Concerts de la rue Saint-Honoré. *See* Concerts Valentino (I)
Concerts de l'Opéra, 18, 78, 96, 99, 230, 232-33
Concerts d'emulation (de la Société mineure des jeunes élèves de l'Ecole royale de musique). *See* Conservatoire, Concerts d'Emulation
Concerts d'Emulation (of Egasse). *See* Egasse, Concerts d'Emulation
"Concerts de Paris," 93, 94
Concerts des Beaux-Arts, 77, 101, 231-32, 268
Concerts des Italiens, 97, 232-33
Concerts des Tuileries, 89
Concerts du Prince Impérial, 92-93, 308 n. 79
Concerts du Théâtre Feydeau, 137-38
Concerts français, 138
Concerts historiques, 77, 80, 141, 155, 222, 239, 240. *See also* Becker, Jean; Farrenc, Aristide; and Fétis, François-Joseph
Concerts Lamoureux, 48
Concerts Mozart, 161
Concerts Musard *See* Musard, Philippe
Concerts Neuve-Viviennes. *See* Concerts Viviennes
Concerts Spirituel (1725-1790), 129, 136-38, 233

Concerts Populaires, 17, 21, 46-51, 82, 99-101, 120, 156, 163, 215, 233; influence of, 2, 46, 58, 76, 156, 163, 208, 229, 257, 281; orchestra of, 46, 245, 258, 280; repertory of, 5, 48-51, 124, 128, 129, 158-60, 213, 243; success of, 5, 47, 76, 100-01, 103, 156, 208, 213, 281; other references to, 77, 96, 149, 164, 212, 230, 308 n. 79, 326 n. 167
Concerts populaires, 20, 90, 99-103, 146, 149, 213, 215, 279, 281; examples of, 68-69, 74, 76, 156-57, 220, 229, 234, 244; in the provinces, 279, 281
concerts promenades, 78, 245-46
Concerts rue (de) Cléry, 138
Concerts rue Grenelle, 138
Concerts Spirituels (in the 19th century), 23 (and n. 63, p. 291), 138, 140, 233
Concerts spirituels, 26, 39, 43, 47, 233, 242
Concerts Tilmant, 70, 272-73
Concerts Valentino (I, 1837-41), 68-69, 71, 82, 95, 99, 149, 151, 233-34, 312 n. 14
Concerts Valentino (II, from 1868), 94, 97
Concerts Viviennes, 71, 92, 95, 149, 234
Congrès méridional, 352 n. 18
Conservatoire (Paris), 21, 23-26, 43, 139, 142, 162, 165, 181, 192, 215, 235, 240, 262, 276, 295 n. 122, 309 n. 104, 351 n. 329; concerts at the distribution of prizes, 66-67, 95, 234-35, 314 n. 33; Concerts d'Emulation, 67, 142, 230-31, 235; concert society (*see* Société des Concerts du Conservatoire); *exercices des élèves,* 21, 23, 121-22, 129-30, 138 (and n. 19, pp. 317-18), 139-41, 235 (and n. 120, p. 341), 315 n. 52; Grande salle, 16, 17, 24, 26, 36-37, 155, 165, 219; influence of, 163, 211; instruction at, 139, 141, 163, 211, 323 n. 122; other student concerts, 67; Petite salle, 52, 231; students and graduates of, 24, 26, 42, 45, 46, 139, 223, 231, 233, 262, 263, 267, 295 n. 122, 351 n. 329
Constantin, Titus-Charles, 45, 309 n. 84
Contat (or Comtat, violinist), 64, 241
Cooper, Martin, 6-7, 52, 55, 162, 164, 166, 206, 261, 324 n. 144
Copinsky Ensemble, 334 n. 70
Coquard, Arthur, 84
Corelli, Arcangelo, 72, 219
Cossmann, Bernhard, 255; *soirées* with Joseph Joachim and Thérèsa Wartel, 73, 247
Couperin, François, 206, 249
Courrier de l'Europe et des spectacles (Paris), 291 n. 62
Court, music at, 14, 89, 251. *See also* Governments' (French) role in musical activity
Cristal, Maurice, 156, 157, 256, 265, 268, 300 n. 219, 343 n. 151
Croiselles, Louis-Jules, 70, 218, 254, 267, 273
Cuvillon, Philippe de, 227, 267, 277
Cyclicism, 182, 189, 191, 193, 201, 203
Czeké, A. de, 225
Dalayrac, Nicolas-Marie, 130
Damcke, Berthold, 65, 79, 80, 265, 272
Damoreau, Mme. [Laure Cinti-Damoreau], 27
Dance orchestras, 9, 39, 69, 90, 148
Dancla, Arnaud, 72, 235-36
Dancla, Charles, 72, 83, 125, 152, 162, 175, 179, 235-36, 322-23 n. 188; concerts of, 18, 72, 85, 125, 179, 235-36 (and n. 121, p. 341); music of, 131, 179, 205; performance of his music (general), 107-10, 112-13, 116-21, 125, 151, 312-13 n. 18, 314 n. 30; performance of his music (specific), 18, 30-32, 67, 72, 79, 85, 236, 263; as performer, 64, 70, 117, 152, 218, 225, 258, 267
Dancla, Laure, 235-36
Dancla, Léopold, 72, 235-36, 254
Dandelot, Arthur, 38-39, 230, 295 n. 116, 306 n. 37, 350-51 n. 324
Danjou, Félix
Danvin, Sophie, 236
Dauprat, Louis-François, 25, 60
David, Félicien, 42, 77, 167, 175, 179, 236, 243, 266, 268; as conductor, 73, 274 (and n. 324, pp. 350-51); *matinées* with Louis-Joseph Lespinasse, 75, 119, 236; music of, 160, 161, 165, 179, 190 (and n. 58, p. 333), 205; music of, description of 131, 165, 179; performance of his music (general), 107-10, 112-13, 117, 119, 121, 151; performance of his music (specific), 30, 32, 60, 74, 75, 78, 155, 223, 236, 256, 268, 326 n. 175
David, Ferdinand, 30
Davies, Laurence, 201, 333 n. 68, 334 n. 75
Davison, J.W., 228 n. 15
Deane, Basil, 331 n. 36
Deauville, 282
Debillemont, Jean-Jacques, 77, 231, 268
Debussy, Claude, 84, 165, 189, 215-16
Dejean, [? Louis], 229
Delaborde, [? Eraïm-Miriam], 59
Delacroix, Eugène, 166
de la Fage, Adrien, 153
Delahaye. *See* Lepot, L.-J.-J.-A.
Delaire, Jacques-Auguste, 143
Delamour, Charles-Joseph or Léon-Charles, 236
de la Nux. *See,* La Nux, de
Delcroix, Pierre-Désiré, 236; *séances* with Ménétrier and Vander-Gucht, 236
Deldevez, Edouard, 95, 161, 165, 180, 292 n. 77, 293 n. 90; as conductor, 30; performance of his music, 30, 38, 40-41, 62
Deledicque, L.-B.-E.-C.-H., 52-53, 265
Delle-Sedie, Enrico, 238

Deloffre, L.-M.-A., 76, 229, 243
Delsarte, François, 261
Demunck, Ernest, 56, 59, 255
Demuth, Norman, 291 n. 62
Départment Seine, 90
Descriptive music, 137, 160, 165, 166, 186, 190, 192
Desmarets [Jean-Emile Compagnon], 27
Deutz, Magnus, 266
Devienne, François, 30, 143
Diémer, Louis, 53, 238, 273
Diepedaal, Ismael-Léon, 64
Dieppe, 282
Dietsch, Caroline-Marie-Victorine, 271
Dietsch, Louis, 73, 242-43, 258, 274
Doehler, Théodore, 267
Donizetti, Gaetano, 165, 324 n. 135, 141, and 144
Donjon, J.-B.-M., 251, 264
Dorus, Louis [originally Vincent Joseph Vansteenkiste], 62; as performer, 64, 242, 249, 253, 261, 267, 276
Douai, Société d'émulation, 282
Douay, Emile, 175, 179-80; music of, 160 (and n. 174, p. 326), 165, 180, 190 (and n. 58, p. 333); performance of his music, 180
Dourlen, V.-C.-P., 60
Downs, Philip George, 133 (and n. 64, p. 316)
Dragone, 236
Dubois, Théodore, 83
Duc, Joseph-Louis, 312 n. 15
Duclairfait, Claudine [pseud, Andrée Favel] (later Claudine Duclairfait Lacombe), 248 (and n. 183, p. 344)
Dufresne (cornet player and singer), 91
Dukas, Paul, 84, 335 n. 1
Dumas, Edouard-Victor, 261
Duni, Egidio, 165
Duparc, Henri, 83-84, 158, 195
Dupont, A. [possibly Pierre-Auguste, *dit* Alexis], 25
Duport (piano manufacturer) *salons* of, 221, 247
Duprat, Paul, 101
Durand (music publishers), 335 n. 83
Durier, Emile (? lawyer), 346 n. 223
Duriez (double bass player), 273
Dussek, Jan Ladislav, 181
Duvergier de Hauranne, E[rnest ?]., 346 n. 223
Duvernoy, Alphonse, 273; *soirées* of, 81, 96, 237
Duvernoy, Frédéric-Nicolas, 64

Early music, interest in, 60, 74, 80, 81, 121, 133, 202-03 (and n. 83, p. 335), 210, 274. *See also Concerts historiques*
Eaucheux (violinist), 241
Eckart-Bäcker, Ursala, 83-84
Eckert, Charles, 160
Ecole Beethoven, concerts of, 75, 237
Ecole Niedermayer, 215
Ecole Polytechnique, 273
Ecole Royale de Musique. *See* Conservatoire (Paris)
Egasse, 66, 237; Concerts d'Emulation, 66, 67, 141, 237-38
Eichhorn brothers, Ernst and Eduard, 19-20
Elbel, [? Victor], 275
Ella, John, 22, 23
Elwart, Antoine, 74, 231, 262; as conductor, 92, 234; music of, 175, 180; own statements on music, 157, 159-60 (and n. 174, p. 326); own statements on the musical scene, 4-5, 147, 158; own statements on the Société des Concerts du Conservatoire, 22, 23, 26-27 (and n. 68 and 77, p. 292), 157-58 (and n. 156, p. 325); own statements on other concert series, 42, 46, 69, 221, 295 n. 116, 306 n. 37, 340 n. 87, 350-51 n. 324; performance of his music, 67, 74, 220, 231; writings of, 10-11, 162, 164, 165
Elysée National, 86
Empire (First, 1804-1815), music during, 129-30, 138-39
Enfants d'Apollon. *See* Sociéte Académique des Enfants d'Apollon
Erard (piano and harp manufactuer), 17, 238
Erard, Pieree, 238
Erard, Mme. Pierre, *soirées,* 79, 238
Ernst, Heinrich Wilhelm: performance of his music, 65, 277, 282; as performer, 64, 277, 346 n. 229
Escoffier, Louis-Casimir [pseud. Casimir Ney], 52-53, 61, 64, 242, 247, 249, 253-55, 261, 271, 276, 297 n. 168
Escudier-Kastner, Rosa, 236; concerts with Alexandre Batta and Henri Vieuxtemps, 80, 238
Essai Musical, 74, 262
Ettling, Emile, 71, 238; amateur society of, 15, 71, 238-39
Eulenberg, Ernst (music publisher), 107
Euzet, L.-G.-E., 64
Exoticism in music, 131, 160, 165, 179, 190, 192
Exposition Universelle of 1867, 15, 90
Expression, music as, 133, 140-41, 145, 160, 166

F.B. (critic), 148
Fallon, Daniel, 329 n. 218, 334 n. 82
Farrenc, Aristide, 60, 74, 239, 240, 271; *séances historiques* with Louise Farrenc, 80, 239
Farrenc, Louise, 5, 8, 73, 153, 167, 175, 177, 239-40; concerts and *séances,* 81, 95, 239-40, music of, 153, 160, 169, 170, 177, 205, 209, 239; music of, description of, 131, 177-78; performance of her music (general), 8, 107-10, 112-13, 117-19, 121, 125, 151, 212, 316 n. 64; performance of her music (specific),

30, 32, 65, 72, 73, 80, 81, 239-40, 247, 253, 271; as performer, 64, 70, 73, 253, 254; pupils of, 81, 239; *séances historiques* with Aristide Farrenc, 80, 239
Fauquet, Joël-Marie, 302 n. 263, 329 n. 218
Fauré, Gabriel, 84, 215
Favel, Andrée [Claudine Duclairfait], 248 (and n. 183, p. 344)
Favre, Georges, 51
February Revolution, 10, 15, 52, 118 (and n. 15, p. 312), 152, 153, 239, 254, 261, 262
Ferchault, Guy, 294 n. 91
Ferrand, Albert, 263
Ferrand Humbert, 147
Ferranti (singer or conductor), 222
Ferrari, Gustave, 297-98 n. 177 and 189, 334 n. 80
Fesca, Alexander, 72, 159, 264
Fessy, Alexandre-Charles, 40, 68, 92, 234, 254
Festivals, 71-72, 86, 213, 220, 223; British, 46; outdoor, 17, 90, 130, 219; post-Revolutionary, 129, 130, 137, 213; provincial, 281, 282, 337 n. 7. *See also* Berlioz festival Fétis, Edouard: own statements on individual series, 68, 148, 288 n. 6; own statements on music, 173, 180, 182; own statements on the musical scene, 142-44, 146, 148, 152 (and n. 113, p. 322), 153; own statements on outdoor concerts, 306 n. 37
Fétis, François-Joseph, 167, 183, 186, 188, 211, 240, 335 n. 2; *Biographie universelle* and other writings, 10, 169, 186, 220, 333 n. 58 and 65; *concerts historiques,* 141, 155, 240; music of, 183, 186, 211; own statements on individual series, 22, 69, 140, 233 (and n. 109, p. 341), 292 n. 67, 317-18 n. 19; own statements on music, 171, 172, 205; own statements on music of individuals, 143, 178, 180, 187, 188, 190 (and n. 58, p. 333), 191, 335 n. 2; own statements on the musical scene, 4, 14, 16, 17, 22, 87, 99, 140-44, 323 n. 127, 324 n. 141, 336 n. 4; own statements on performers, 221; own suggestions for improving the musical scene, 155, 157; performance of his music, 56, 282
Field, John, 20, 260, 282
First Empire (1804-1815), music during, 129-30, 138-39
First Republic (1792-1804), music during, 129, 136-38
Fissot, Henri, 53, 59, 83, 229, 263
Flotow, Friedrich, 86
Fontenay, 281
Forestier, [? Joseph], 219, 246, 308 n. 70
Forgues, Emile-Esprit, 275
Forster (music publisher), 107
Framery, Nicolas-Etienne, 319 n. 49
France, musical position in Europe, 4, 139, 141, 142, 150-54, 158-59, 165, 204
France musicale (Paris), *séances,* 240
Franchomme, Auguste, 52, 212, 227, 258, music of, 174; performance of his music (general), 109, 111-12, 116; performance of his music (specific), 18, 29-31, 62, 67, 231; as performer, 15, 52-53, 70, 222, 240, 250, 254, 259, 267, 276. *See also* Société Alard-Franchomme
Franchomme, René, 53
Franck, César, 1, 5, 164, 192-94 (and n. 68, p. 333), 206, 215; influence of, 6, 215, 334 n. 80; music of, 192-94 (and ex. 9, and n. 68 and 70, pp. 333-34); performance of his music, 83, 277; as performer, 70, 95, 128, 218, 254, 277, 343 n. 150; as teacher, 6, 195, 215
François-Sappey, Brigitte, 337 n. 21
Franco-Mendès, Jacques, 16, 241; presentations with Joseph Franco-Mendès, 71, 95, 241, 314 n. 37
Franco-Mendès, Joseph, 241; presentations with Jacques Franco-Mendès, 71, 95, 241, 314 n. 37
Franco-Prussian War, 195, 208; effect on music, 6-7, 9, 160-61, 214, 339 n. 58; music during, 15-16, 230; renaissance after, 6-7, 9, 83-84, 104, 160-63, 192, 195, 206, 208, 214-16
French culture, 166; effect of, 131-32, 202
French Revolution (1789), 121, 129, 130, 136-37, 141, 280, 283, 318 n. 34
Fridzeri, A.M.A., 138
Friedland, Bea, 177 (and n. 21, p. 330), 239, 240, 329 n. 218, 349 n. 302
Gade, Niels, 40-41, 45, 49-50, 79, 265
Gail, N.-F., 320 n. 70
Gailhard, Pierre, 280
Galerie du Baromètre, 237
Gallay, Jacques, 186 (and n. 47, p. 332), 227, 267; performance of his music, 30-31, 70, 112, 116
Galoppe d'Onquaire (winter), 346 n. 223
Garaudé, Alexis, 62
Garcin, Jules-Auguste, 34, 46, 83
Garde National, 282
Garde of Paris, 93
Garigue, Jean, 264
Gary, Jean-Pierre, 252
Gasperini, Auguste de, 241, 270; lecture-recitals with Georges Pfeiffer, 80, 241
Gastinel, Léon, 62, 79, 263
Gaveaux *aîné,* (probably Simon, music publisher], 106
Gaveaux-Sabattier, Mme., 64, 236, 253
Gazette musicale de Paris, 10, 13, 101, 146, 171, 244, 273, 311 n. 1, 321 n. 93, 377 n. 21, 355

Geraldi [Géraldi, Géraldy], J.-A.-J., 95, 227, 248
Gérault (director), 220
Germanic music: dominance of, 3, 5, 51, 79, 84, 107, 119, 139, 158, 172-73, 207; influence of, 3, 84, 98, 139, 155, 160-61, 165-67, 172, 206, 215-16
Gernsheim, Friedrich, 34
Gevaert, François-Auguste, 266
Girard, Narcisse, 223, 235, 259, 322-23 n. 118; as conductor of the Société des Concerts du Conservatoire, 30, 33-37, 42, 154
Girod de Vienney, Louis-Philippe-Joseph, M. le baron de Trémont, *matinées* of, 70
Givre (violist), 249
Glinka, Mikhail, 223
Gluck, Christoph Willibald, 136, 165; performance of his music (general), 109, 130, 163, 316 n. 64; performance of his music (specific), 18, 29, 31, 33, 41, 49, 63, 74, 232, 236, 255
Gobert (conductor), 93
Godefroid, Félix, 65, 346 n. 223
Goldbeck, Fred, 294 n. 91
Goldner, [? Wilhelm], 62
Gossec, Françis-Joseph, 2, 30, 132, 143
Gouffé, Achille, 60-62, 83, 242; concerts of, 61, 62, 96, 241-42; performance of his music, 62, 242; as performer, 53, 61, 64, 224, 235, 247, 249, 250, 253, 258, 261, 276; *séances* of, 60-63, 65, 87, 88, 95, 96, 120, 125, 127, 151, 152, 242, 254, 312 n. 16, 314 n. 31
Gounod, Charles, 4, 38, 42, 161, 162, 183, 334 n. 73; music of, 163, 169, 183, 209; performance of his music (general), 107, 113, 119, 125, 212; performance of his music (specific), 44-45, 49, 51, 161, 213
Gouvy, Théodore, 5, 42, 45, 154, 187; music of, 160, 161, 169, 187-88 (and ex. 5); performance of his music (general), 107, 113, 118, 121, 187, 212; performance of his music (specific), 32, 34, 38, 40-41, 44-45, 74, 84
Governments' (French) role in musical activity, 89, 130, 137, 145, 153; hindering concert series, 5-6, 68, 91, 92, 94, 104, 210, 244; promoting concert series, 24, 39, 89, 145, 152 (and n. 113, p. 322), 245, 260
Graever, Madeleine, concerts of, 126, 277
Grande association musicale de l'Ouest, 281 (and n. 16 and 17, p. 352)
Grande Société d'Harmone, 71, 151, 265-66
Grande Société Philharmonique de Paris, 74, 82, 99, 107, 117, 152, 162, 212, 223, 242-43
Grand Hôtel, 269
Grand Opera, 2, 133, 135, 141, 145, 163-64, 166, 186, 208-09, 212, 214
Grands Concerts des Compositeurs Vivants, 78, 243
Grandval, Marie-Félice-Clémence de Reiset, Vicomtesse de [pseuds. Caroline Blangy and Clémence Valgrand], 311 n. 5; performance of her music, 40-41, 62, 277
Grant, James, 87
Grasset, Jean-Jacques, 259
Gray, *société philharmonique* of, 279
Greive, Guillaume-Frédéric, 269, 277; performance of his music, 38, 40-41, 277
Grenet, Claude de, 106
Grétry, A.-E.-M., 38, 74, 136, 165, 232
Grisar, Albert, 324 n. 135
Grout, Donald J., 3, 6, 174
Guérin, [? Paul], 235
Guerle, de, 346 n. 223
Guerreau, Auguste-Antoine, 61, 241, 242, 261
Guides of Paris, 93
Guillon, 25
Guiraud, Ernest, 83, 161
Gunsberg, Paul, 53
Gut, Serge, 307 n. 49
Gymnase Lyrique, 142, 143
Gymnase Musical (building), 16, 243-44
Gymnase Musical (society, 1831), 301 n. 239
Gymnase Musical (society, 1835), 68, 85, 125, 146, 148, 243-44, 288 n. 6
Habeneck, François-Antoine, 16, 33, 47, 141, 219, 235, 240, 260, 313 n. 27; as conductor of the Société des Concerts du Conservatoire, 21-26, 29-30, 33-37, 114, 293 n. 90; music of, 174; performance of his music, 31, 62, 111-12; talent as conductor, 33
Hagan, Dorothy, 10, 164, 328-39 n. 217
Hainl, François, 30, 34-36, 293 n. 90
Halévy, Fromental, 25, 38, 161, 165, 211, 243, 324 n. 144, 334 n. 73
Hallé, Charles, 15, 52-53, 70, 254, 278
Hamilton, H.V., 339 n. 58
Handel, George Frideric, 165, 325 n. 152; performance of his music, 19, 20, 30, 33, 60 (and n. 203, p. 299), 74, 160, 225, 236, 242, 274, 316 n. 64
Haraszti, Emile, 22-23
Harding, James, 83
Hartog, Eduard de, 253
Hasselmanns, Alphonse, 264
Haussman, Georges-Eugène, Baron, 89, 245
Haydn, Franz Joseph, 2, 124, 147, 165, 172; music of, 107, 131, 133, 136, 150, 151, 157-60, 171-74, 177, 179, 181, 201, 202, 204, 209-12; performance of his music (general), 8, 107-10, 112-20, 122, 125, 129-30, 133, 147, 163, 172, 283; performance of his music (specific), 18, 28-36, 40-41, 43-45, 47, 49-50, 54, 56, 58-60, 62, 64-74, 80, 138, 160, 218, 219, 221-23, 229, 232, 234, 236, 237, 241, 244-47, 249-50, 252, 253, 261, 265, 272-74, 282

Haydn revival, 121-22, 125
Heiss (violinist or violist), 229, 242, 252
Heller, Stephen, 236, 311 n. 5
Hermann-Léon (singer, evidently not Léonard Hérmann), 253
Hérold, Ferdinand (son of L.-J.-Ferdinand), 346 n. 223
Hérold, J.-J.-Ferdinand, 139, 165, 323 n. 127; performance of his music, 31, 34, 130, 139, 141, 161, 236, 256
Hervey, Arthur, 1, 47, 51, 163, 166, 177
Herz, Henri, 17, 103, 227, 260; concerts with Théodore Labarre, 71, 95, 244; music of, 148, 283; performance of his music, 30, 95, 107, 109, 244, 278
Hesselbein, *salons* of, 18, 235 (and n. 121, p. 341), 238
Hignard, J.-L.-A., 39, 243, 270
Hill, Edward Burlingame, 1, 38-39, 51, 55, 163, 293 n. 91
Hiller, Ferdinand: performance of his music, 18, 54, 112, 114, 272, 278, 282; as performer, 18, 53, 123, 221, 240, 260, 278
Hilpert, Frédéric, 253
Hippodrome, 219, 289 n. 39
Histories of music, 1, 3, 8, 135, 161-67, 207-08
Hoelzel, Gustav, 160
Hollebeke (brass player), 257
Holmes, Alfred, 238; *séances* of, 80, 157, 245
Holmes, Henry (brother of Alfred), 238
Hôtel de Ville (Paris), 16, 89, 221, 245, 260 (*see also* salle Saint-Jean, Hôtel de Ville); concerts and *soirées* at, 89, 97, 155, 245 (and n. 171, p. 344)
Hôtel d'Osmond, 93 (and n. 76, p. 308), 94
Hôtel du Louvre, 78, 243
Hôtel Fesch, 221; galerie Colbert, 273
Hôtel Laffite, 246 (and n. 175 and 177, p. 344); *concerts promenades* at, 78, 245-46; salons de l'Exposition Internationale, 246
Howard, Philip, 330 n. 11
Hubans, Charles-Joseph, 94
Hummel, Johann Nepomuk, 97, 131, 181; performance of his music (general), 108-110, 112-14, 117-21, 125, 131, 282, 316 n. 64; performance of music (specific), 30, 63, 65, 224, 227, 233, 276, 277
Illustrated London News, 22
Imbault, Jean-Jérôme (music publisher), 229 n. 197
Imbert, Hugues, 334 n. 75
Individual, emphasis on, 130, 209
Industrial revolution, 8, 213
Indy, Vincent d', 84, 215, 334 n. 75
Institute, 249
Institution des Jeunes Aveugles, concerts, 69, 95, 96, 155, 246-47
Institution Royale de Musique Classique et Religieuse, 25, 141, 233
Instrument makers, 17, 80, 85, 89, 256
Instruments, improvements in, 130
Isouard, Nicolas, 130
Italian music, influence of, 98, 151, 166, 167

Jacobi, Georg, 84, 226-27 (and n. 58, p. 339), 261-62; as performer, 79, 259, 262
Jacquard, Léon, 46, 56, 237, 248, 249, 263. *See also* Société des Derniers Quatuors de Beethoven
Jancourt, L.-M.-E., 61, 64, 242
Jardin d'hiver, 39, 92, 256, 274
Jardin Mabille, 93
Jardin Turc, 91, 147
Javault, L.-M.-C., *matinées* of, 71, 247 (and n. 180, p. 344)
Jeunes-Artistes. *See* Société des Jeunes-Artistes
Jeunes Aveugles. *See* Institution des Jeunes Aveugles
Jeunes élèves de l'Ecole Royale, 231
Joachim, Joseph, 73, 247, 255, 258; *soirées* with Bernhard Cossmann and Thérèsa Wartel, 73, 247
Jommelli, Nicolò, 236
Joncières, Victorin de, 34
Journal de Paris, 291 n. 62
Journal des débats (Paris), 47
Jullien, Adolphe, 47
Jullien, Louis, 91, 92, 95, 282
July Monarchy, 164. *See also* Orléans Regime (1830-1848), music during
July Revolution, 9, 14, 144-45, 231
Jupin, [? Charles-François], 4, 321 n. 91
Kalkbrenner, Frédéric, 30-32, 34, 88, 111-12, 144, 259, 289 n. 43
Kastner, Georges, 4, 148 (and n. 91, p. 321), 149
Katski, Karol [Charles de Kontski], 62
Kéramzer, Ives, 160 (and n. 176, p. 326), 355 n. 85
Klaus, Kenneth, 2, 164
Klauwell, Otto, 332 n. 49
Klosé, Hyacinthe, 261
Koëlla family, 19
Konski, Charles de [Karol Katski], 62
Kowalsky, Henri, 224
Kracauer, Siegfried, 87, 94, 144, 304 n. 4, 305 n. 16
Kreutzer, Léon, 5, 16, 42, 152, 191-92, 343 n. 158; music of, 191-92; performance of his music, 62, 79, 107, 263, 269, 278; as performer, 278
Kreutzer, Rodolphe, 30, 67, 97, 140, 144, 191
Krommer, Franz, 66, 237
Krüger, Wilhelm, 278

Kufferath (composer), 255 (and n. 49, p. 338)
Kuhn, Georges-Mathieu, 25

Labarre, Théodore, 70, 227, 244, 260; concerts with Henri Herz, 71, 95, 244
Laborde, Mme. [? Rosina], 225
Lacherier (composer; possibly refers to Eugène Lacheurié), 77, 311 n. 5
Lacheurié, Eugène, 311 n. 5
Lachner, Franz Paul, 49-51
Lachnith, Ludwig Wenzel, 289 n. 43
Lacombe, Claudine Duclairfait (wife of Louis), 333 n. 57. *See also* Duclairfait, Claudine
Lacombe, Louis, 190-91, 247-48 (and n. 183, p. 344), 351 n. 329; music of, 190-91 (and ex. 7); performance of his music, 42, 78, 84, 107, 243, 248, 268; as performer, 64, 236, 271, 315 n. 46; *séances* of, 96, 247-48
Lacombe, Paul, 84
La Fage, Adrien de, 153
Laffite, [? J.-B.-P.], 74
Lafont, Charles-Philippe, 174
Lagrave, Pierre, 143
Lalande, D.-A.-J., 264
La Laurencie, Lionel de, 136, 257
Lalliet, Casimir-Théophile, 253
Lalo, Edouard, 1, 161, 164, 192-93 (and n. 65, p. 333), 206, 335 n. 1; music of, 192-93 (and ex. 8, and n. 64, p. 333); performance of his music, 84, 192; as performer, 56
La Madelaine, Stéphen de. *See* Stéphen
Lamare, Jacques-Michel Hurel de, 138
Lamothe [possibly Lamotte, Nicolas-Antony], 309 n. 84
Lamoureux, Charles, 48, 58-59; *séances* of, 58-60, 119, 154, 156, 257, 350 n. 318 (*see also* Séances Populaires). *See also* Concerts Lamoureux
Landormy, Paul, 163, 164, 334 n. 75
Laneau, François-Amédée [pseud. Amédée], 25
Lang, Paul Henry, 2, 6, 97, 163-64 (and n. 192, p. 327)
Langhans, Louise (*née* Japha, wife of Wilhelm), 278, 311 n. 5
Langhans, Wilhelm, 222, 278
Langlois, 288 n. 6
La Nux, de [possibly Véronge de la Nux, G.-M.-F.-Rocheblanche], 79, 245, 264, 265
Lapret (violinist), 56
Larochefoucault, Sosthène de, 24
La Rochelle, 281; *société philharmonique*, 280 (and n. 5, p. 351)
Lasalle, Albert de, 43
Lascoux, Antoine, 346 n. 223
Lasserre, Jules-Bernard, 79, 245, 252, 256, 263, 265, 270
Lassus, Orlande de, 39, 236
Lavainne, Ferdinand, 62, 186
Lavignac, Albert, 59
Lebone (? cellist), 241
Leborne, Aimé, 211
Lebouc, Charles-Joseph, 63-65, 83, 236; concerts with Louise Mattmann, 72, 250 (and n. 189, p. 344); as performer, 61, 64, 222, 239, 241, 242, 247, 249-51, 258; *séances* of, 63-65, 75, 87, 88, 96, 118, 120, 125, 154, 157, 248, 314 n. 31
Lebouc, Mme. (wife of Charles-Joseph), 63
Lebrun, Eugène-Adolphe, 253
Lebrun, Louis-Sébastien, 130
Leclair, Jean-Marie, 77, 161, 222
Lecture-recitals, 80, 239-41
Lee, Sebastien, 224, 225 (and n. 49, p. 338) (?), 235, 236, 263
Lefébure-Wèly, L.-J.-A., 44-45
Lefebvre, Charles-Edouard, 44, 47
Legouvé, Ernest, 88
Léhon (violinist), 245
Leipzig, Gewandhaus Orchestra, 22
Lekeu, Guillaume, 84, 215
Lelong, Z.-E.-C., 252
Lemoine, Emile, 273-74 (and n. 318, p. 350)
Lenepvu, Charles-Frédéric, 235
Leo, Sophie, 122, 139, 313 n. 23 and 24
Léonard, Hubert, 40, 64, 224, 237, 251
Lepot, L.-J.-J.-A. [pseud. Lepot-Delahaye], 80(?), 270(?)
Leroux (banker), 221
Leroy, Adolphe-Marthe, 64, 237, 239, 242, 249, 253, 255
Lespinasse, Louis-Joseph [pseud. Paulin], 63-64, 237; *matinées* with Félicien David, 75, 236
LeSueur, Jean-François, 137, 142, 211
Lévy, Caroline, 239
Lévy, Max, 229
Library of Congress (USA), 11
Liebe, Thérèse, 224, 278
Lille, 281, 282; Académie de Musique, 282
Limoges, 281
Liszt, Franz, 67, 186, 227 (and n. 62, p. 339), 243, 251, 311 n. 5, 333 n. 68; concerts with Alexandre Batta and Chrétien Urhan, 70, 248; music of, 187, 191, 204, 206; own statements on the musical scene, 4, 19, 146, 147, 150, 154; own statements on provincial orchestras, 280; own statements on *salons*, 88; performance of his music, and lack thereof, 30, 70, 131 (and n. 60, p. 316), 248; as performer, 67, 70-71, 73, 123, 148, 254, 260, 289 n. 40; writings of, 10, 161-62, 320 n. 76

Litolff, Henry, 45, 154, 230; as conductor, 78, 230; performance of his music, 78, 108, 126, 256, 277, 278
Locke, Ralph, 329 n. 218
Lockspeiser, Edward, 137, 166
Logie, Louis, 332 n. 46
Loiseau (conductor), 269
London, 275, 323 n. 125, 339 n. 58; Philharmonic, 22, 152
Longyear, Rey M., 2, 6, 164, 181, 206
Louis, Mme. Emile, 253
Louis, Nicolas, 174, 234(?)
Louis-Philippe (king of France), 89, 144
Louvre, 76, 250 (and n. 191, p. 345)
Lubbert (conductor), 233
Lubeck, Ernst, 56, 271
Lully, Jean-Baptiste, 39, 165, 232, 236
Lycée Louis-le-Grand, 80, 245; concerts of, 78
Lyons, 48, 322 n. 107; *société philharmonique,* 280
Macdonald, Hugh, 223
Mackenzie, Mme. (pianist), 224
Madelaine, Etienne. *See* Stéphen
Madier-Montjau (violinist), 270
Magnard, Albéric, 84
Magnin, Emile, 53, 224, 239, 259
Magnus (pianist and composer, probably Magnus Deutz), 266
Maho, J. (music publisher), 160 (and n. 177, p. 327)
Malibran, Alexandre, 62, 74, 220, 228-29, 270
Malleville, Charlotte de. *See* Tardieu de Malleville, Charlotte
Manera (conductor), 73, 274 (and n. 324, pp. 350-51)
Mansfield, Orlando A., 182
Marcello, Benedetto, 74, 236, 274
Marimon, Mlle. [? Marie] (singer), 28
Marmontel, Antoine-François, 88, 351 n. 332
Marschner, Heinrich August, 58
Marseilles, 48, 280; Cercle des Arts, 280; Société des Concerts, 280
Marsick, Martin, 237, 273
Martinet, André, 231(?), 268(?), 340 n. 87
Marty, Eugène-Georges, 84
Marx (conductor), 93
Marx, A., 253
Mas, J.-L.-M., 55, 56, 249, 256, 271
Masi, Enrico, 253
Massart, Aglaé (*née* Masson; wife of Lambert), 159, 249; as performer, 56, 72, 249, 269
Massart, [? Hubert] (brass player), 257
Massart, Lambert, 235, 249, 255, 343 n. 158; *soirées* of, 72, 249
Massé, Victor, 211, 266, 334 n. 76
Massenet, Jules, 162, 189, 202; music of, 189; performance of his music, 50-51, 83, 189, 259
Masset, [? N.-J.-J.] (composer), 31
Masson, Aglaé. *See* Massart, Aglaé
Masson de Puitneuf [or Puyneuf], *soirées* of, 344 n. 177
Materialism, 144
Mathias, Georges, 194, 205; music of, 194-95 (and ex. 10, pp. 196-97, and n. 71, 72, and 74, p. 334), 202, 205, 206; performance of his music (general), 113, 119, 212; performance of his music (specific), 38, 40, 79, 263, 269, 334 n. 71 and 73; as performer, 53, 254
Mathieu de Monter, Emile, 5, 76, 83-84, 159 (and n. 169, n. 326), 160-61, 259, 279, 312 n. 10
Matinées. See *Salons,* musical
Mattmann, Louise, 56, 64; *séances* and concerts of, 72, 250 (and n. 189, p. 344)
Maurin, Jean-Pierre: concerts with Louise Mattmann, 72, 250 (and n. 189, p. 344); as performer, 55-56, 64, 96, 212, 238, 249, 250, 258, 262. *See also* Société des Derniers Quatuors de Beethoven
Mayer, Max, 278
Mayseder, Joseph: performance of his music (general), 108-09, 111-12, 116-17, 126; performance of his music (specific), 30-31, 225, 233, 273
Mear, Mlle. (pianist), 53
Meaux, 281
Méhul, Etienne-Nicolas, 2, 165; music of, 139, 142, 143, 209, 314 n. 36; performance of his music (general), 107-08, 110, 112-13, 116-17, 121, 126, 130; performance of his music (specific), 29-31, 47, 49, 63, 74, 92, 139, 143, 220
Meifred, P.-J.-E., 25, 26
Mell, Albert, 341 n. 121
Melos Quartet, 331 n. 36
Mendelssohn, Felix, 22, 155, 165, 323 n. 127, 324 n. 141; music of, 106, 159, 187, 194, 202, 204, 210, 314 n. 37; music of, description of, 131-32, 151; Parisian premieres of his music, 126, performance of his music (general), 8, 106-10, 112-13, 117-20, 122, 126, 131, 151, 283; performance of his music (specific), 19, 28-36, 40-41, 44-45, 47-51, 54, 56-60, 62, 65, 73-75, 78-80, 92, 157, 212, 221, 223, 229, 236-38, 241, 247, 250, 252-53, 259-60, 263, 271, 272, 274, 277, 278, 282, 295 n. 113
Ménestrel (Paris), 13, 222, 228, 229, 237, 249, 251, 252, 265, 269, 355
Ménétrier (violinist): *séances* with Pierre-Désiré Delcroix and Vander-Gucht, 236
Menus-Plaisirs, 17
Méreaux, Jean-Amédée Le Froid de, 249

Merizki, V. de, 245
Messager, André, 84
Mey, Auguste, 93, 309 n. 84
Meyerbeer, Giacomo, 165, 243, 244; performance of his music (general), 107-08, 110, 113, 120, 126, 130, 324 n. 144; performance of his music (specific), 31, 34-35, 40, 44, 49, 51, 92, 141, 161, 213, 270
Meylan, Pierre, 163
Mialle (pianist), 221
Midi, 279
Military bands, 93, 130, 159, 219
Millault, Edouard, 231, 262
Mohr, [? J.], 265(?) (and n. 270, p. 348)
Mohr, J.-B.-V., 46, 51; as conductor, 91, 256(?), 265(?) (and n. 270, p. 348)
Molique, Bernhard, 51, 229
Molitor, Baron, *matinées d'été,* 82, 250
Monde illustré (Paris), 36
Mongin, Marie, 59, 64, 239
Moniteur Universel (Paris), 291 n. 62
Moniushko [or Moniuszko], Stanislaw, 269
Monnais, Edouard [pseud. Paul Smith or P.S.]: own statements on concert series, 37, 45-47, 156, 275, 276, 308 n. 79; own statements on the musical scene, 5 (and n. 23, p. 286), 45, 153-54, 158; own statements on specific works, 333 n. 63
Monsen, Mons-Johan, 257
Monsigny, Pierre-Alexandre, 232
Montagney, Joseph [Alexandre Artôt], 112, 117
Morel, Auguste-François, 79, 186, 263
Morhange, Charles-Valentin [pseud. Charles-Valentin Alkan], 29, 53, 84
Moscheles, Ignaz, 30
Mozart, Wolfgang Amadeus, 2, 124, 147, 165, 172, 182, 289 n. 43; music of, 136, 139, 150, 151, 157-59, 171-74, 181, 201, 202, 204, 209-13; music of, availability and publication of, 106, 107, 127, 133, 160; music of, influence of, 151, 171-72; performance of his music (general), 8, 87, 106-110, 112-20, 122, 126-27, 129-30, 133, 139, 147, 163, 172, 283; performance of his music (specific), 19, 20, 27-36, 40-41, 44-45, 49-50, 54, 56-60, 62, 63, 65-74, 77, 80, 90, 138, 160, 218, 219, 221-25, 227, 229, 232, 234, 236, 237, 241, 242, 244, 245, 247, 249-51, 253-54, 256, 259, 261, 265, 268, 269, 272-74, 278, 282, 289 n. 44, 312 n. 12, 335 n. 86
Mozart revival, 121-22
Müller, Valentin, 56, 239, 245
Müller brothers (I), August Theodor, Franz Ferdinand Georg, Karl Friedrich, and Theodor Heinrich Gustav, 303 n. 284
Müller brothers (II), Bernhard, Hugo, Karl, and Wilhelm (all sons of Karl Friedrich), 303 n. 284; concerts with Wilhelmine Szarwady, 80, 272
Muratet, Edouard Charles, 39
Musard, Alfred (son of Philippe), 92-94, 103, 308 n. 70
Musard, Philippe, 69, 90-92, 94, 95, 103, 147, 282; concerts of, 90-92, 147, 306 n. 37 and 41; music of, 4, 91, 147, 148
Musical scene in specific historical periods. *See* Ancien regime; Republic (First, 1792-1804); Empire (First, 1804-1815); Bourbon Restoration (1815-1830); Orléans Regime (1830-1848); Second Republic (1848-1852); Second Empire (1852-1870); Franco-Prussian War, renaissance after
Music as civic act, 137
Music histories. *See* Histories of music
Musicology, 161, 208
Musique du Roi, 89
N. (critic), 147
Nantes, 48, 281
Napoleon I (emperor of France), 132
"Narrative" symphony, 160
Nationalism, 6, 79, 159-61, 208, 216, 263-64
Nectoux, Jean-Michel, 3
Neruda, Wilma [Mme. Norman Neruda], 46
Ney, Casimir. *See* Escoffier, Louis-Casimir
Nicolai, Otto, 49
Niedermeyer, Louis, 243
Nieuwerkerke, Alfred Emilieu de, M. le comte, *soirées* of, 76, 89, 96, 250
Nilsson, Christine, 241
Niort, 281
Nonseries concerts. *See* Concerts, nonseries
Norblin, L.-P.-M., 221, 225
Nourrit, Adolphe, 248
Nouvelle Société de Musique de Chambre. *See* Stainlein, Louis de, M. le comte, concerts of
Nux, de la. *See* La Nux, de
Odéon, 25, 48
Oechsner, André, 159 (and n. 170, p. 326)
Offenbach, Jacques, 103
Onslow, Georges, 60, 144, 148, 170, 175, 260, 329 n. 218; music of, 2, 143, 144, 151, 170, 175, 205, 209; music of, description of, 131, 148, 175 (and exx. 1 and 2, pp. 176-77); performance of his music (general), 8, 107-110, 112-14, 117-21, 127, 283; performance of his music (specific), 29-32, 34, 54, 62, 66, 71, 72, 75, 79, 143, 221, 223, 225, 242, 247, 250, 254, 261, 263, 264, 268, 273, 276, 277, 282
Opéra (Paris, building), 16, 17, 219, 230, 232, 251, 291 n. 63, 293 n. 89; *Magasin* of, 138
Opéra (Paris, institution), 37, 104, 160, 230, 232, 243, 293 n. 89, 310 n. 121; concerts of (*see* Concerts de l'Opera); Concert Spirituel

of, 140, 233; orchestra of, 23, 148, 244, 348 no. 270; personnel of, 25, 86, 230, 242, 261, 293 n. 89; repertory of, 103, 147-49, 324 n. 144
Opera, 37, 99, 122, 131-32, 146, 147, 154-55, 160, 162-63, 166, 167, 210; at Dieppe, 282; dominance of, 1-2, 4-6, 37, 104, 130, 137-40, 144, 152, 156, 164; quality of, 139, 310 n. 121, 313 n. 24, 320 n. 70. *See also* Grand Opera; *Opéras comiques*
Opéra-Comique (Paris), 25, 104, 147, 160, 240
Opéras comiques, 6, 103, 141
Operetta, 282
Orchestral works, reduction of, 19
Orchestras: amateur (general), 82; amateur (specific), 66, 67, 69, 71, 77, 141, 142, 149, 219, 228, 237-39, 259-60, 264-65, 268-69, 282; female, 265 (and n. 212, pp. 345-46); provincial, 279-83; size of, 17, 26 (and table 2.1, p. 27), 46, 78, 141
Orchestration of chamber works. *See* Chamber works, orchestral performance of
Orfilia, Mme., *soirées* of, 88
Organ, first outdoor, in Paris, 91
Orléans Regime (1830-1848), 145; music during, 65-72, 90-92, 111-17, 144-53
Osborne, George, 112, 117, 270, 278
Oscar (conductor), 221
Outdoor concerts. *See* Concerts, outdoor
P.S. *See* Monnais, Edouard
Paer, Ferdinando, 211, 244
Paganini, Nicolò, 20, 130, 141, 209; concerts of, 15, 68, 111, 251; performance of his music, 30, 33, 49-50, 68, 111-12, 251
Pagans (singer), 253
Paisiello, Giovanni, 74
Palais Royal, 93, 138
Palestrina, Giovanni Pierluigi da, 74, 236, 242, 274
Palm, Albert, 109
Paloc, Louise, 251
Panofka, Heinrich, 330 n. 16
Panseron, [? Auguste], 19
Pape, Jean-Henri, *salons* of, 17, 224, 254, 273
Paquis, Antoine-Victor, 220
Parc d'Asnière, 93
Pasdeloup, Jules, 42-43, 46-51, 179; as conductor, 16, 42-43, 46-51, 76, 89, 97, 226, 235, 245, 250, 256, 258-59; as director of the Concerts Populaires, 2, 46-51, 76, 82, 129, 164, 189, 213, 281; as director of the Société des Jeunes-Artistes, 42-43, 263, 294 n. 102; talent of, as conductor, 43, 48
Pasquet, Alexis-Ernest, 224
Patronage, 136, 318 n. 34
Patti, Adelina, 158
Paulin. *See* Lespinasse, Louis-Joseph
Pazetti, Pierre-Antoine, 271
Pelletier, Victor-Alfred [pseud. Rabuteau], 274
Penco, Rosina, 269
Pereyra, Marie-Louise, 294 n. 91
Performance, quality of: in Paris, 3, 22, 55, 79, 102, 103, 146-47, 154, 159, 262; in the provinces, 279, 280
Performance practice, 19, 25, 28, 33, 51, 174, 347 n. 248. *See also* Chamber works, orchestral performance of; Programs, structure of
Perrin, Emile, 230
Perris, Arnold B., 310 n. 105, 327 n. 192, 328-29 n. 217
Peters (music publishers in Leipzig), 333-34 n. 70
Petzold, [? Guillaume-Lebrecht], *salons* of, 218
Peyrot (violinist), 350 n. 315
Pfeiffer, Clara, 188, 251; musical presentations of, 75-76, 81, 96, 251 (and n. 195, n. 345); pupils of, 251
Pfeiffer, Georges (son of Clara), 75, 188; lecture-recitals with Augusta de Gasperini, 80, 241; music of, 188-89 (and ex. 6); performance of his music (general), 107, 113, 121, 212; performance of his music (specific), 65, 79, 83, 263; as performer, 59, 64, 245, 261; *séances* with Pablo Sarasate, 252
Phare de la Loire (Nantes), 266
Piano: effect on musical entertainment, 4, 70, 140, 148, 212; improvements in, 130, 148; popularity of, 140, 148; role in chamber music, 148, 173
Piatti, Alfredo, 249
Picard, Adrienne, 61, 83, 229, 252; *séances* of, 81, 96, 252
Pierre, Constant, 231, 265, 291 n. 62, 348 n. 270; writings of, 11, 136, 315 n. 50, 341 n. 107, 118, and 119
Pierson-Bodin, Sophie, 73, 252-53; *séances* of, 73, 96, 252-53
Pilet, Louis-Marie, 40, 59, 264
Piriou, Adolphe, 178
Pistone, Danièle, 307 n. 49
Pixis, Johann Peter, 147, 248, 302 n. 256
Place Pasdeloup, 46
Placet, Auguste-Francisque, 222, 269, 282
Place Vendôme, 93
Planté, Francis, 53
Pleyel (firm): as instrument makers (later Pleyel, Wolff, & Cie), 17, 256; as music publishers, 107; *salons* of (see Salle Pleyel)
Pleyel, Marie (*née* Moke), 46, 278
Poëncet, Henri, 49, 59, 222, 229, 252
Poitiers, 281
Polignac, E.-J.-M.-M., Prince de, 77, 266
Poniatowski, Joseph (prince of Monte Rotondo), 77, 226, 243, 266

Ponnat, M. le baron de, 75, 264
Populus, Adolphe, 264
Porpora, Nicola, 60 (and n. 202, p. 299)
Portehaut, Etienne-Marie, 256 (and n. 207, p. 345)
Pougin, Arthur, 83, 169, 188, 189 (and n. 52, p. 332), 191, 264
Prague Conservatory, 151
Prault, Marquis de, 88
Pré Catelan, 93, 97, 219, 246
Préfet de la Seine, 89, 155, 245, 260; concerts of (*see* Hôtel de Ville (Paris), concerts and *soirées* at)
Président du Conseil d'Etat, concerts of, 89
Prévost, Eugène, 93
Prévost-Rousseau, Antonìn, 78, 243, 270
Prix Chartier, 159, 177
Prod'homme, J.-G., 165, 294 n. 91, 343 n. 163
Program music, 137, 166, 180, 209, 212, 326 n. 176, 333 n. 63
Programs, 17-19, 154, 214; length of, 14, 18-19, 43; provincial, 280-81; structure of, 18-20, 78, 82, 102; structure of, for concerts by individuals, 85, 86, 155; structure of, for piano recitals, 272; structure of, in ca. 1820, 313 n. 24
Provinces: chamber music in, 279, 281-83; *concerts populaires* in, 279, 281; festivals in, 281, 282, 337 n. 7; musical activity in, 142, 279-83; musical activity in, at resorts, 282; program structure in, 280-81; quality of performance in 279, 280; repertory in, 279-83; *sociétés philharmoniques* of, 142, 279-81; summer concerts in, 93, 282
Prudent, Emile, 127, 192 (and n. 62, p. 333), 278; music of, 192 (and n. 63, p. 333); performance of his music (general), 107-08, 113, 118-19, 121, 127 (and n. 39, 314), 212; performance of his music (specific), 72, 192, 278
Prumier *(fils)*, Ange-Conrad, 38, 40-41
Publication of music, 5 (and n. 21, p. 286), 98, 106-07, 140, 143, 144, 147, 150, 157, 210-12; relationship of, to performance, 106, 314 n. 37
Pugni, [? Cesare], 92
Pugno, Raoul, 260
Pupils' concerts. *See* Concerts, pupils'
Quatuor Armingaud (or Quatuor Armingaud-Jacquard). *See* Société des Quatuors de Mendelssohn
Quatuor Florentin, 79, 96, 159, 253
Quatuor Maurin-Chevillard. *See* Société des Derniers Quatuors de Beethoven
Rabaud, Hippolyte-François, 59, 224
Rabuteau [Victor-Alfred Pelletier], 274
Raff, Joachim: music of, 160; performance of his music, 65, 80, 252, 270, 272, 278
Rameau, Jean-Philippe: music of, 136, 206, 355 n. 83; performance of his music, 39, 44, 49, 54, 232, 236, 249
Ranelagh, 93
Raousset-Boulbon, M. le comte de, 220
Ratner, Sabina Teller, 329 n. 218
Ravel, Maurice, 84, 215
Raynor, Henry, 328-29 n. 217
Reber, Napoléon-Henri, 5, 38, 42, 175, 177, 211, 274, 334 n. 73; music of, 160, 161, 169, 175, 209, 211; music of, description of, 175, 177 (and ex. 3, p. 178); performance of his music, 30-32, 40-41, 46, 71, 74, 79, 107, 263
Reduction of orchestral works, 19
Reicha, Antonín, 144, 209, 211, 291 n. 61; performance of his music, 31, 64, 70, 138, 264
Reiset, Marie-Félice-Clémence de. *See* Grandval, Marie-Félice-Clémence de Reiset, Vicomtesse de
Rémaury, Caroline, 64, 261
Remsberg, Elizabeth, 329 n. 218
Renaissance, musical, after 1871. *See* Franco-Prussian War, renaissance after
Renaissance of instrumental music in France, 1828-1871, 2, 9, 104, 205-06, 208, 214, 216
Renan, Ernest, 150
Rennes, 215, 281
Repertory, 15, 100, 105-34, 154, 155, 279; changes in, 78-79, 82, 110-23, 156-58, 160, 208, 212-14; Development of standard, 115, 118, 120-22 (and n. 18, pp. 312-13), 133, 210; provincial, 279-83
Republic (First, 1792-1804), 137; music during, 129, 136-38
Rescue opera, 6, 132
Resorts, music at, 282
Revolution. *See* French Revolution
Revue de musicologie (Paris), 46
Revue et gazette musicale de Paris, 10, 13, 16, 70, 100, 159, 311 n. 1, 355; concerts of, 15, 70, 71, 82, 95, 126, 254; references to reporting in, 4, 38, 39, 53, 55, 57, 60, 61, 63-65, 69, 75, 89, 95, 97, 154, 156, 160, 171, 222, 223, 225, 228-30, 232, 236, 237, 239, 243, 247, 249, 251-54, 259, 262, 264-67, 270-71, 273, 274, 276, 279, 282, 300 n. 230, 342 n. 135 and 139, 348-49 n. 284, 350-51 n. 324; *salon* of, 253, 254
Revue musicale (Paris, 1827-1835), 10, 13, 140, 144-46, 311 n. 1, 355; references to reporting in, 141, 171, 238, 244, 273, 280, 307 n. 49, 312 n. 11, 321 n. 93, 337 n. 21
Revue wagnérienne (Paris), 215
Reyer, Ernest, 18, 48
Reynier, Léon, 249
Richault (music publisher), 107
Rie, Bernard, 59

Ries, Ferdinand, 30, 32
Rigel, Henri-Jean, 60
Rignault, Emile, 59, 61, 242, 254, 255
Rinck, Emmanuel-Guillaume, 263
Ringer, Alexander, 291 n. 62
Ritter, Théodore, 55-56, 254-55; *soirées* with Camillo Sivori, 75, 254-55
Rivals (? violinist), 247
Rivière, Jules, 90, 307 n. 62
Robyus (brass player), 257
Rochefort (conductor), 93
Rochefort (city), 281
Rode, Pierre, 142, 144; performance of his music, 25, 27, 30-32, 111-12, 233
Rodrigues, Edouard, 266
Roger, Gustave-Hippolyte, 231, 268
Rolland, Romain, 16, 84, 162-63, 165, 216, 273
Romanticism, 132-33, 163-64, 174, 187, 210
Romberg, Bernhard, 31, 112, 114, 270
Romédon (oboist), 64
Roquet, A.E. [pseud. E. Thoinan], 43
Rose, Chrysogone-Cyrille, 64, 222
Rosen, Charles, 172
Rosenhain, Jakob [or Jacques], 45, 154, 157 (and n. 154, p. 325), 158, 255; performance of his music, 62, 79, 108-09, 127, 253, 265; *soirées* of, 73, 255
Rossel, Frédéric, 350 n. 315
Rossini, Gioachino, 165, 324 n. 141; music of, 98, 148, 167; performance of his music (general), 108, 110, 112-13, 117-19, 121, 127, 130, 283, 324 n. 144; performance of his music (specific), 25, 29, 31, 33, 40, 44, 49, 90, 92, 141, 264; *soirées* of, 88
Roubaud de Gournande, 346 n. 223
Rouen, *société philharmonique,* 280
Rouget de Lisle, Claude-Joseph, 319 n. 54
Roussel, Claude-Joseph, 246 (and n. 179, p. 344)
Rousselot, Joseph-François, 61, 64, 242, 249, 253, 255, 260, 261, 276
Rousselot, Scipion, 30, 32, 159-60, 182 (and n. 39, p. 331), 273
Roussette, Aimé, 269
Rubinstein, Anton: concerts of, 78, 127, 255; music of, 131; performance of his music (general), 108-09, 113, 121, 127-28, 131, 212; performance of his music (specific), 34, 50, 60, 78, 80, 225, 270, 272
Rüfer, Philippe-Barthélemi, 160
Rust, [? Friedrich Wilhelm], 278

Sabatier-Blot, Sophie-Maria, 236
Sabattier (violinist), 55, 238
Saintes, 281
Saint-Foix, Georges de, 182
Saint-Germain-en-Laye, 224
Saint-Jean d'Angely, 281
St. Petersburg, 152, 159, 275
Saint-Saëns, Camille, 1, 5, 83, 164, 167, 170, 171 (and n. 5, p. 329), 201-03, 205 (and n. 86, p. 335), 206 (and n. 88, p. 335), 215, 294 n. 98; concerts of, 20, 77-78, 255-56, 335 n. 86; as conductor, 77, 255; music of, 163, 169, 170, 201-03 (and n. 82, pp. 334-35), 205, 206, 273; music of, description of, 3, 131, 201-03 (and exx. 12 and 13); own statements on the musical scene, 3-4, 158, 328 n. 216; own statement on Reber and the French symphony, 175; own statement on the Société Sainte-Cécile and Pasdeloup, 294 n. 102; performance of his music (general), 107-10, 113, 120-22, 128, 212; performance of his music (specific), 18, 30, 34, 38-40, 51, 65, 77, 78, 83, 161, 256, 268, 294 n. 98; as pianist and organist, 56, 77, 224, 249, 258, 273-74; *soirées* of, 88; as virtuoso, 73; writings of, 10, 161-62, 335 n. 88
Saint-Yves, D.-A.-D., 221
Salesses, [? L.], 62
Salieri, Antonio, 63
Sali-Snerbe, 243
Salle Barthélemy, 17, 94, 268
Salle Beethoven, 237, 254, 275
Salle Bernard, 241
Salle Bernhardt, 17, 250
Salle Bonne-Nouvelle, 72, 219, 241, 272
Salle Chantereine, 16, 52, 227
Salle de l'Athenée, 258-59
Salle de l'Athénée central, 269
Salle du Wauxhall, 18, 254
Salle Erard (or salons Erard), 17, 310 n. 112, 312 n. 10; as location for individual concerts or series, 57, 63, 81, 222, 236, 237, 247, 248, 253-55, 263, 267, 270, 273
Salle Guy-Lussac, 264
Salle Herz, 17, 42-43, 310 n. 112, 312 n. 10; as location for individual concerts or series, 42, 55, 59, 63, 222, 228, 238, 240, 244, 254-57, 260, 261, 271, 275
Salle Lebouc (or salons Lebouc), 229, 239
Salle Masson, 16
Salle Montesquieu, 268
Salle Musard, 16
Salle Pape. *See* Pape, Jean-Henri, *salons* of
Salle Pleyel (or salons Pleyel or salons Pleyel, Wolff & Cie), 17, 78, 310 n. 112, 312 n. 10; as location for individual concerts or series, 39, 53, 55, 57, 59, 63, 73, 75, 78, 143, 235, 241, 249, 252, 254, 255, 261, 263-65, 271-73
Sallès, Antoine, 322 n. 107
Salle Sainte-Cécile, 17, 37, 228, 268, 274
Salle Saint-Jean, Hôtel de Ville, 221, 259
Salle Sax, 17, 53, 73, 249, 260, 262
Salle Taitbout, 16
Salle Valentino, 17, 69, 90, 94, 233-34

Salle Ventadour, 240
Salle Vivienne, 234, 254
Salomon, Mlle. [Louise-Frédérique Cohen, *dite* Salomon; later Mme. Béguin-Salomon], 271. *See also* Béguin-Salomon, Louise
Salons, musical, 14, 86-89, 96, 114, 158, 226; importance of, for musicians, 86, 87, 89, 210; as main location for chamber music programs, 52, 82, 122, 124, 212; performers at, 88, 100; profusion of, 4, 9, 87, 140, 146; repertory of, 4, 69, 70, 87, 102, 114, 140, 147, 148, 150, 158, 159, 170, 213, 267; social aspects of, 87-88, 98-101, 115; temporary cessation of or decrease in, 14, 118, 143
Salons des Arts-Unis, 271
Salons Erard. *See* Salle Erard
Salons Kriegelstein, 225
Salons Pleyel. *See* Salle Pleyel
Salvaire, G. [probably Gervais-Bernard Salvayre], 260
Salvaire, J., 260
Salvator, [? L.] (composer), 62, 65, 186-87
Salvayre, Gervais-Bernard, 260(?)
Samary, Georges, 248
Sarasate, Pablo, 224, 241, 256; *séances* with George Pfeiffer, 252
Sarnaker, Benedict, 329 n. 3
Sauzay, Eugène, 81, 89, 221; *soirées* of, 73
Sax, Adolphe: as instrument maker, 17, 85, 256, 258; series of, 80, 85, 256-57 (and n. 212 pp. 345-46)
Sax, Alphonse, 345 n. 212
Saxomnitoniques à cinq pistons, 256 (and n. 212, p. 345)
Scarlatti, Domenico, 236, 324 n. 138
Schindler, Anton, 26-27, 33, 69, 290-91 n. 61;
Schlottmann, [probably Frédéric-Antoine, possibly Jacques-Charles], 253, 257
Schmitt, Florent, 193
Schneitzhoeffer, Jean, 143, 233
Schonberg, Harold, 22
Schrade, Leo, 10, 23, 131-33, 164
Schubert, Franz, 30 (and n. 80, p. 292), 181, 324 n. 141; music of, 106, 121, 157, 159, 181, 182, 316, n. 61; Parisian premieres of his music, 42 (and n. 114, p. 295), 128 (and n. 42, p. 315), 241 (and n. 150, p. 343); performance of his music (general): 106, 108-09, 113, 119-22, 128, 157; performance of his music (specific), 42, 49-50, 54, 58, 60, 236, 241, 253, 272, 273, 276, 278
Schuloff [or Schulhoff], Jules [or Julius], 236
Schumann, Clara (*née* Wieck). *See* Wieck, Clara
Schumann, Robert, 183, 324 n. 141; music of, 3, 131-32, 159, 160, 183, 201; Parisian premieres of his music, 43, 58, 77-78, 128, 256, 315 n. 44-46; performance of his music (general), 3 (and n. 8, p. 285), 108-10, 113, 119-20, 122, 128, 131, 157, 316 n. 64; performance of his music (specific), 18-19, 30, 32, 34-35, 40, 43-45, 49-51, 54, 56, 58, 65, 79, 80, 212, 213, 232, 236, 241, 250, 253, 260, 265, 270, 272, 278, 282
Schuncke, Charles, 144
Schwaederlé, J.-J.-S., 282 (and n. 22, p. 352)
Schwarz, Boris, 136-41, 164, 207, 251, 287 n. 32, 313 n. 19, 315 n. 47 and 52, 317 n. 1
Schwenke, Karl, 32
Scudo, P., 154; own statements on individual concerts and series, 5, 53, 57, 129, 154, 226, 249; own statement on music, 157
own statements on the musical scene, 5, 159
Séances Populaires (de Musique de Chambre), 58-60, 82, 96, 101, 124, 156, 160, 257
Searle, Humphrey, 243 (and n. 159, p. 343)
Season, musical, 13-14
Second Empire (1852-1870), 150, 162; music during, 74-82, 92-94, 118-21, 152-60, 162
Second Republic (1848-1852), music during, 72-74, 117-18 (and n. 15, p. 312), 151-54 (and n. 127, p. 323)
Seghers, François-J.B.: as conductor, 37-39, 73, 274-75; *matinées* of, 70-71, 257
Siege of Paris, music during, 15-16
Seligmann, Prosper, 343 n. 158
Servières, Georges, 164, 316 n. 60, 350-51 n. 324
Shanet, Howard, 183
Sieber, Georges-Julien (music publisher, son of Jean-Georges), 23, 144
Sieber, Jean-Georges (music publisher), 23, 107, 229 n. 197
Sighicelli, Vincent, 251, 253
Sivori, Camillo, 73, 154, 249, 254-55, 271, 278; *soirées* with Théodore Ritter, 75, 254-55
Smith, Paul. *See* Monnais, Edouard
Soccanne, Pierre, 164, 221, 319 n. 45, 337 n. 21
Société Académique des Enfants d'Apollon, 15, 65-66, 95, 96, 257-58 (and n. 221, p. 346)
Société Alard-Franchomme, 15, 52-54, 118, 154, 159, 258; secondary references to, 70, 72, 96, 152, 212, 328 n. 216
Société Calco-Philharmonique, 258
Société Classique, 298 n. 189
Société de la Grande Harmonie. *See* Société d'harmonie des premiers prix du Conservatoire
Société de l'Athénée, 76-77, 99, 101, 159, 258-59
Société de l'Athénée Musical (1829-1844), 14-15, 67, 71, 82, 95, 99, 142, 148, 149, 259-60, 314 n. 33
Société de l'Avenir Musical, 80, 260
Société de l'Union Musicale. *See* Union Musicale
Société de Musique Classique, 72, 152, 260-61

Société de Musique de Chambre (?1847-?1872). *See* Société Alard-Franchomme
Société de Musique de Chambre Jacobi-Willaume, 79, 261-62 (and n. 248, p. 347)
Société de Quatuors et Quintetti. *See* Société de Musique de Chambre Jacobi-Willaume
Société de Sainte-Cécile, 74, 262
Société des Amis de l'Enfance, 67
Société des Concerts, 92
Société des Concerts de l'Opéra. *See* Concerts de l'Opéra
Société des Concerts du Conservatoire, 21-37, 67, 233, 262; admission fees of, 24, 36, 38, 47; conservatism of, 21-22, 29, 30, 33-34, 37, 42, 44, 49, 165, 211, 213, 243, 335 n. 1; establishment of, 23-26, 313 n. 19; influence of, 9 (and n. 32, p. 287), 22-23, 67, 70, 80, 208, 231; praise of, 4, 5, 22-23, 37; programming of, 25-28, 30, 33, 34, 43 (*see also* conservatism of; repertory of); promotion of Beethoven at, 9, 28-37, 40, 69, 82, 111, 114, 116, 122-24, 141, 142, 162, 208; quality of performance of, 9, 21-23, 33, 43, 53, 68-70, 142, 159; repertory of, 21-22, 28, 37, 114, 123, 126, 127, 143, 154 (and n. 130, p. 323), 156-58 (and n. 156, p. 325), 161 (and n. 181, p. 327), 175, 233, 316 n. 64 (*see also* conservatism of); social aspects of, 36-37, 99, 100, 145, 147, 149, 328 n. 216, 335 n. 1; subsidization of, 24, 89, 104, 145; success of, 36-37, 46, 100, 142, 143; other references to, 15, 37, 47, 72, 73, 95, 96, 118, 119, 122, 141, 142, 144, 145, 148, 149, 154, 157, 159, 162, 230, 260, 274, 355 n. 1
Société des Derniers Quatuors de Beethoven (or Quatuor Maurin-Chevillard or Maurin *soirées*), 55-56, 82, 154, 212, 262-63; secondary references to, 66, 70, 72, 96, 152, 328 n. 216
Société des Jeunes-Artistes, 38 (and n. 102, p. 294), 42-46, 82, 99, 154, 263; as performers for other series, 67, 89, 245; repertory of, 43-46, 82, 154-55, 213, 315 n. 45 and 46; secondary references to, 73, 75, 117, 119, 152, 212
Société des Musiciens-Exécutants de Paris. *See* Association des Musiciens-Exécutants de Paris
Société des Quatuors de Mendelssohn (or Quatuor Armingaud or Quatuor Armingaud-Jacquard), 56-58, 82, 157, 212, 263; secondary references to, 75, 118, 154, 163, 328 n. 216
Société des Quatuors et Quintetti. *See* Société de Musique de Chambre Jacobi-Willaume
Société des Quatuors Français, 79, 82, 159, 263-64
Société des Quintettes Anciens et Modernes, 75, 264
Société des Quintettes Harmoniques, 79, 96, 157, 264
Société des Symphonistes, 77, 82, 96, 264-65
Société des Trios Anciens et Modernes, 79, 265
Société d'Harmonie, 71, 151, 265-66
Société d'harmonie des premiers prix du Conservatoire, 256
Société du Grand Concert, 157, 266
Société du Gymnase Lyrique, 266-67 (and n. 276, p. 348)
Société Libre des Beaux-Arts, *séances* of, 267 (and n. 277, p. 348)
Société Musicale (I, 1835). *See* Cercle Musical (1834-35)
Société Musicale (II, 1838-39), 70, 82, 148, 267
Société Nationale de Musique, 6-7, 83-84, 160, 161, 195, 206-08
Société Nationale des Beaux-Arts, 261; concert series of, 77, 82, 99, 213, 266-68
Société Philharmonique de la Ville de Paris, 15, 66, 95, 99, 141, 268-69 (and n. 284, pp. 348-49), 321 n. 93
Société Philharmonique de Paris (1850-51). *See* Grande Société Philharmonique de Paris
Société Philharmonique de Paris (I, 1862), 269 (and n. 289, p. 349)
Société Philharmonique de Paris (II, 1866), 78, 156, 269-70
Société Philharmonique du Calvados, 280
Societies, amateur. *See* Amateur performers; Orchestras, amateur
Société Sainte-Cécile (I, 1839), 270 (and n. 297, p. 349), 294 n. 91
Société Sainte-Cécile (1847-48). *See* Société de Sainte-Cécile
Société Sainte-Cécile (II, 1850-55, 1864-?66), 37-42, 153, 270, 275 (and n. 324, pp. 350-51); repertory of, 38-42, 44, 46, 82, 128, 152, 315 n. 44, 334 n. 73; secondary references to, 73, 117, 119, 154, 212, 257, 274
Société Schumann, 79-80, 82, 120, 270-71
Société Symphonique (1852-53), 74, 271 (and n. 302, p. 349)
Société Symphonique de Paris (from 1861), 77, 271
Soirées. See *Salons,* musical
Solar (composer), 264
Sowinski, Wojciech, 62
Spohr, Ludwig [Louis], 97, 122, 139, 181; music of, 175; performance of his music (general), 108-09, 112-13, 117, 121, 128; performance of his music (specific), 30, 50-51, 62, 68, 72, 223, 244, 245, 250, 259, 261, 277, 282
Spontini, Gaspare, 71, 165, 219, 243; performance of his music, 63, 130, 163, 236

Stadtfeld, Alexander, 40
Stainlein, Louis de, M. le comte, 75, 271; concerts of, 75, 271-72
Stamaty, Camille-Marie, concerts of pupils of, 19, 74, 272
State concerts. *See* Concerts, state
Stéphen [probably Etienne-J.-B.-N. Madelaine, *dit* Stéphen de la Madelaine], 143, 348 n. 276
Stoeger, Ernest, 227
Stoepel, François, 4, 87, 148, 166
Stradella, Alessandro, 43, 271
Strakosch, Maurice, 17
Strasbourg, 282 (and n. 22, p. 352); Conservatoire, 282; Hôtel de Ville, 282
Students' concerts. *See* Concerts, pupils'; Conservatoire (Paris); Ecole Beethoven; Institution des Jeunes Aveugles; Société des Jeunes-Artistes
Subscription series, 36, 99, 101
Summer concerts. *See* Concerts, outdoor
Symphony: appreciation of (and lack thereof), 1, 45, 143, 144, 154, 159-60 (and n. 174, p. 326), 322 n. 107; delimitations of, 165, 211, 293 n. 90; "narrative", 160
Szarwady, Wilhelmine (*née* Clauss): concerts with the Müller brothers, 80, 272; other presentations, 278. *See also* Clauss, Wilhelmine

Taeglichsbeck, Thomas, 32
Taffanel, Claude-Paul, 53, 224, 239, 252, 253, 261
Taine, Hippolyte, 88
Tajan-Rogé, D., 25
Tardieu de Malleville, Charlotte (*née* de Malleville), 56, 242, 249; concerts and *séances* of, 72-73, 81, 96, 248-49
Tartini, Giuseppe, 77, 222
Taste, musical, 97-102, 131, 139, 140, 144-47, 155-60, 165-67, 171, 204-05, 209-10, 212-14; changes in, 99, 102, 160, 205, 213-14; concerning the traditional versus the innovative, 131, 144-46, 155, 157-60, 165, 167, 171, 179, 204-05, 209-10, 212-14. *See also* Appreciation of instrumental music
Taylor, Isidore-Justin-Severin, Baron, 71, 219, 243
Telesinski, Joseph, 53, 225, 278
Tellefsen, Thomas, 53, 56
Thalberg, Sigismond, 148, 192
Theaterzeitung [probably the Vienna *Allgemeine Theaterzeitung*], 305 n. 13
Théâtre de la Gaîté, 270
Théâtre du Prince Impérial, 94
Théâtre-Français, 38
Théâtre-Italien (building), 17, 219, 226, 232, 240
Théâtre-Italien (institution), 104, 232, 243; concerts of (*see* Concerts des Italiens); Concert Spirtuel of, 138, 233; orchestra of, 68, 74, 220, 244, 256 (and n. 207, p. 345), 265, 272, 287 n. 5; personnel of, 25, 158, 232, 233
Théâtre Lyrique, 229, 243, 269
Théâtre Montmartre, 39
Thematic transformation, 178, 190-91, 193, 201, 203
Third Republic (1870-1940), 6; music during (*see* Franco-Prusssian War, renaissance after)
Thoinan, E. *See* A.E. Roquet
Thomas, Ambroise, 38, 143, 211, 243, 334 n. 73, 336 n. 6; performance of his music, 67, 161, 231
Tickets: cost of (*see* Concerts, admission fees of); distribution of, 86, 287 n. 4
Tiersot, Julien, 144, 163, 165, 322 n. 107, 333 n. 68
Tilmant *(jeune)*, Alexandre, 83, 261, 322-23 n. 118; compositions with Théophile Tilmant, 273, 311 n. 5; concerts with Théophile Tilmant, 70, 272-73
Tilmant *(aîné)*, Théophile, 83, 322-23 n. 118; compositions with Alexandre Tilmant, 273, 311 n. 5; concerts with Alexandre Tilmant, 70, 272-73; as conductor, 30, 34-36, 66, 71-72, 89, 91, 219, 228, 243, 245, 293 n. 82; as violinist, 153, 224, 261
Tingry, Célestien, 189-90
Tivoli d'Hiver, 66
Tolbecque, Auguste (brother of Jean-Baptiste-Joseph), 59
Tolbecque, Isidore-Joseph (brother of Jean-Baptiste-Joseph), 95(?)
Tolbecque, Jean-Baptiste-Joseph, 4, 69, 91, 95, 148, 282
Toulouse, 48, 281 (and n. 81, p. 352); *société philharmonique* of, 280
Tours, 282
Trémont, M. le baron de Louis-Philippe-Joseph Girod de Vienney, *matinées* of, 70
Trevitt, John, 317 n. 1, 346 n. 218, 350 n. 318
Triébert, Charles-Louis, 64, 242, 249, 264
Trollope, Frances, 87, 90, 91
Trombetta (violist), 53, 61, 64, 222, 237, 241, 252, 259
Trompette, La (concert series), 273-74 (and n. 315 and 318, p. 350)
Trouville, 282
Tuileries, 89, 93
Tulou, Jean-Louis, 142, 174, 227; performance of his music, 30-31, 67, 109, 111-12, 117
Turban, A.-L.-G., 229
Turban, Charles-Paul, 252, 253, 264

Ulrich, Hughes, 171
Union Artistique. *See* Cercle de l'Union Artistique
Union Musicale, (Société de l'), 37, 73-74, 117, 152, 212, 274-75 (and n. 324, pp. 350-51)
Urhan Chrétien, 221, 224, 259, 267, 273; concerts with Franz Liszt, 70, 248

Valentino, H.-J.-A.-J., 68-69, 234, 244. *See also* Concerts Valentino (I, 1837-41)
Valgrand, Clémence. *See* Grandval, Marie-Félice-Clémence de Reiset, Vicomtesse de
Vanden Abeeln (composer), 225
Vander-Gucht (cellist), *séances* with Pierre-Désiré Delcroix and Ménétrier, 236
Van Gelder (cellist), 271, 275
Vansteenkiste, Vincent-Joseph. *See* Dorus, Louis
Varney, P.-J.-A., 246
Vaslin, Olive-Charlier, 221, 249, 259
Vaucorbeil, Auguste-Emmanuel, 34, 79, 263, 265
Vauxhall, 66
Veit, Wenzel Heinrich [originally Václav Jindřich Veit], 60
Verdi, Giuseppe, 324 n. 144
Verlève (brass player), 257
Vernaelde, Albert, 293 n. 81
Véronge de la Nux, G.-M.-F.-Rocheblanche. *See* La Nux, de
Verrimst, Victor-Frédéric, 249
Verroust *(jeune)*, A.-C.-J., 249, 253, 255, 261
Verroust *(aîné)*, L.-S.-X., 62, 249, 255, 261, 276
Versailles, 48, 90
Viard-Louis, Mme. (pianist, wife of Nicolas Louis and, after Louis's death, a merchant named Viard), 245
Viardot, Pauline (*née* García), 64; *soirées* of, 88
Viault, L.-V.-A., 53, 64, 271
Vidal, Jean-Jacques [or Jean-Joseph], 221, 259
Vienna, 151, 152, 275
Vieuxtemps, Henri, 46, 73, 129, 275; concerts with Rosa Escudier-Kastner and Alexandre Batta, 80, 238; performance of his music (general), 108, 113, 118, 121, 128-29; performance of his music (specific), 30, 49, 65, 75, 238, 275; series of, 75, 275-76
Vieuxtemps, Josephine (*née* Eder, wife of Henri), 275
Vignier (composer), 65
Viguier, A. (violist), 55, 263
Viguier, Leonide (*née* Deloigne), 263
Viotti, Giovanni Battista, 31-32, 34, 49-50, 67, 108-09
Vocal music, dominance of, 143-44, 147, 148, 211, 281. *See also* Grand Opera; Opera; *Opéras comiques*
Vogel, Adolphe, 187, 231
Vogt, Gustave, 30-31, 67, 111-12
Volkmann, Robert, 80, 270

Waefelghem, Louis van, 270
Wagner, Richard, 2, 22, 33, 48, 189, 215-16; influence of, 84, 215-16; performance of his music (general), 108, 110, 113, 120, 122, 129-31, 212, 324 n. 144; performance of his music (specific), 31, 34-35, 38-40, 45, 49, 51, 78, 213, 243, 259, 270
Walckiers, Eugène, 62, 65, 174, 242
Wallace, Vincent, 49
Wangermée, Robert, 342 n. 144
Waque (? cellist), 261
Warrack, John, 331 n. 33
Wartel, Thérèsa (*née* Andrien), 249, 261; musical presentations of, 81, 276; *soirées* with Joseph Joachim and Bernhard Cossmann, 73, 247
Weber, Carl Maria von, 144, 155, 165, 323 n. 127; influence of, 181, 202; music of, 157, 165, 181, 194, 202, 204, 209, 210, 212; music of, description of, 181, 316 n. 61; performance of his music (general), 8, 19, 107-20, 122, 129, 130, 159, 181, 283; performance of his music (specific), 18, 27-35, 40-41, 44, 47, 49, 54, 56, 58, 65, 68-69, 74, 90, 222, 223, 225, 229, 234, 236, 237, 244, 248-49, 259, 261-62, 270, 278, 294 n. 112
Weber, William: own statement on concerts of individuals, 85; own statements on audiences, 85, 87, 97-98, 100, 102, 166, 167, 213, 306 n. 41, 310 n. 105 and 108; own statements on individual concert series, 237, 260, 348-49 n. 284, 351 n. 329; own statements on the increasing number of public concerts, 2, 98, 140, 164; own statements on the musical scene, 97-98, 100, 145, 167, 213; own statements on the musical scene before 1828, 136, 139; own statements on outdoor and café concerts, 92, 306 n. 41; 310 n. 108; own statements on *salons,* 87-88; writings of, 97-98
Wekerlin [or Weckerlin], Jean-Baptiste, 37-39
White, [? Joseph], 53, 64, 79, 222, 239, 241, 251, 264, 265, 270
Wieck, Clare (later Clara Schumann), 270
Wieniawski, Joseph [or Józef], 249, 278
Willaume, Jules-Louis, 79, 261
Winter, Peter, 233
Wolff (violist), 241
Wolff, Auguste, 236
Wolff, Edouard, 249
Writings by nineteenth-century musicians and critics, 3-6, 8, 135, 141-62, 164-66

Zimmermann, Emile, 351 n. 329
Zimmermann, P.-J.-G., 62, 88, 276-77, 351 n. 329; *soirées* of, 88, 95, 151, 276-77, 351 n. 329
Zompi, Diomède, 278

A YEAR WITHOUT TIME

BY

CATE ALLEN
&
JEN WHITING

To Kitty —
Strong connections
and calm waters —
these are the things
that make life grand.
Here's to you!
— Jen

ISBN: 1-4140-2060-0 (e-book)
ISBN: 1-4140-2059-7 (Paperback)
ISBN: 1-4140-2058-9 (Dust Jacket)

Library of Congress Control Number: 2003098003

Printed in the United States of America
Bloomington, IN

This book is printed on acid free paper.

1st Books - rev. 07/28/04

Table of Contents

Introduction ix
Ask For What You Want - Jen 1
Ask For What You Want - Cate 11
Leap, Then Look - Jen 21
Leap, Then Look - Cate 24
Laugh At You - Jen 35
Laugh At You - Cate 38
You Don't Have To Please Everyone - Jen 42
You Don't Have To Please Everyone - Cate 46
Welcome Risk Into Your Life - Jen 49
Welcome Risk Into Your Life - Cate 56
Stay Curious - Jen 63
Stay Curious - Cate 68
Paddle Each Bend In The River Gently - Jen 72
Paddle Each Bend In The River Gently - Cate 82
Love More Than You Think You Can - Jen 96
Love More Than You Think You Can - Cate 100
Be What You Always Wanted To Be When You Grew Up - Jen 104
Be What You Always Wanted To Be When You Grew Up - Cate 112
Dreaming Works - Jen 117
Dreaming Works - Cate 125
Follow Your Heart - Jen 131
Follow Your Heart - Cate 140
Don't Let The River Get In The Way Of The River Trip - Cate 145
Don't Let The River Get In The Way Of The River Trip - Jen 148
Afterword - Say Yes 153
Updates from the Web Site 154
About the Authors 175

A Year Without Time

Introduction

Here's what we're up to and why we're doing such a damn fool thing as to make all those mosquitoes happy.

I, starting my 80th year, my spouse, Catherine, a lady of 52 years, my daughter, Jennifer, 30, and her, and our, dear friend, Donna, 36, departed from Kansas City in mid-June. We added Geoff, my grandson, to our group while in Denver. Diva, our opera-loving Brown Labrador, and Gypsy, a Lady Dog Streetwalker, whom we rescued from a life of poverty and degradation on the streets of Moscow (the one in Russia), have accompanied us for moral support, laughs, and love, and maybe a warning or two about rattlesnakes.

Named, oxymoronically, "A Year Without Time ...the expedition," we're traveling without watches or clocks, canoeing the 4,000 miles of the Missouri and Mississippi rivers.

Though we're anticipating much joy on our venture, this is not just a pleasure trip.

For one thing, we'd like to communicate to the geezers of the world that there are adventures they can enjoy regardless of age or sex, that if they're in reasonable health, i.e., if they can walk and breathe, adventure is theirs, if they want it.

Not only that, but people should know that many adventures can be enjoyed right here in the United States, not just in Nepal, or on the Amazon, or in Outer Magnolia. Well, all right, Mongolia.

We also hope to establish that these sorts of quests can be accomplished without the cost of an arm and a leg, literally or financially.

We speak not only for the elderly; younger men and women, burning out from overwork, overscheduling, listening to enhancement tapes to and from the job – these people, too, need to be reminded to back off from whatever grindstone their noses are stuck to, and smell the daisies. Corporations are important, but from the CEO to the loading dock, there's more to life than the corporation.

To see certain parts of America as our forepops and moms, and Lewis and Clark, saw them, to escape Call Waiting, cars, fast food and airport lounges, to escape the clock, itself, these are beckonings that everyone should heed, at least temporarily, before it's time to Buy the Farm.

We aren't writers, in the strict sense, though we've all been published; two of us, Catherine and Donna, have even been paid for it. Nor are we filmmakers or scientists. Catherine is a seminar presenter. How did Lewis and Clark survive without a seminar presenter? Donna worked in the field of information technologies as a trainer, consultant, manager and, most recently, project coordinator at Princeton University. Donna's computer skills will surely come in handy at the end of a canoe paddle. Geoff, an MBA major, will be the financial advisor. I am a retired television news anchor. The adult mayfly, with its 24-hour life span, has greater significance for Mother Earth than news anchors, past or present. Jennifer, computer consultant at Princeton University, is a trained chef, instructor in rock climbing, and our general outdoors personal savior; it is she who will scale us up and down rock walls for spectacular vistas. She will also be our camp cook, preparing meals which our taste buds will recall long after the paddles have been put away and the canoes are upside down on the barn rafters. Our casting office triumphs again!

We used straight thinking, reason, and a little madness to persuade Donna and Jennifer to quit their jobs at Princeton University and to come with us, and it didn't take wild horses to induce Geoff to continue college <u>after</u>

lending his brains (and his muscles) to A Year Without Time.

Using our hand-held Pilot from US Robotics we will provide updates of the folks we meet, the lessons we are learning from the rivers and stars, and any new recipes for sticky-buns we make in our Banks Fry-Bake pans.

We will upload new info every month, and perhaps more frequently, if we can find a phone line.

Bill Allen
from the banks of the Missouri River

Ask For What You Want

Jen

I grabbed the railing as I headed down the narrow stairs in the cottage. The phone rang its third ring and Diva lifted her head to inquire. I pulled on the railing as I jumped to the right of the landing, into the kitchen. A fourth ring and I grabbed it off the hook just before it went to the answering machine. I wondered if it was Mom calling back.

"Hello?" I said.

Diva settled back onto her bed in the living room, her tail taking one ceremonial thump as she assessed that all was under control.

"Jenny, I want to canoe the Missouri River before I die. Want to come?" Bill's voice was a familiar one. I grinned before knowing it.

"Bill," I said, "that's a great idea."

I had dropped the -ny ending on my name years earlier, using the shorter "Jen," somehow thinking it allowed me to escape, at least partially, the taunts of childhood. With Bill, however, it had stuck, and I didn't mind. I was thirteen when we met, he stealing my mother's heart a few years after a quiet divorce. He was canoeing the great Mississippi, and we lived in a small riverside town. The first night he came to dinner was the only night of my life my mother prodded, "Don't you think it's time to go to bed, Jenny?" I awoke to find the car gone, Mom and Bill taking in the Midwest sunrise. They married a year later and my mother had found her mate; Bill is the only person I know who can fit her wanderlust-filled life, a life she had passed on to me.

I shifted my weight onto my other foot, the linoleum cold against my bare feet. "When are you going to do it?" I asked. Having just gotten off the phone with Mom, I wished I could have heard the route they had taken to get to this idea.

"Not me Jenny, us. I think the four of us should do it together, do the whole thing, all the way to the Gulf of Mexico."

He sounded like a little boy, anticipation measuring itself against imagination. I could picture him grinning on the other end of the phone line, his crooked smile giving way to a full-toothed grin. Bill had watched me grow out of girlhood; he had been the adult who found a fit into a girl's life, at the most awkward time of adolescence. Now his seventy-eight years gave way to my twenty-nine, and I wondered if he was serious.

"So what do you think?" he said, "How long do you think it would take?"

I heard Donna move from the smallest bedroom into the bathroom upstairs, her delicate steps making the floorboards creak. "I don't know Bill, how long is it?"

"I'm not sure, let's see, the Mississippi is just over 2000 miles, but the Missouri River starts somewhere in Montana and then meets the Mississip' just above St. Louis. If we went all the way to the Gulf, I think it would be about 4000 miles. Do you think we could do it in a year?"

This is where I began to measure who Bill thought I was against who I was becoming. The past year had found me in a new relationship, I was just completing the first month of a new job – the first job in my life that actually had a salary, not the hourly wages I was earning before – and Donna and I were just getting to know each other's wishes and dreams. She had not mentioned canoeing the Missouri River as one of her dreams, and I was trying to control my wanderlust.

"I think it could be done, Bill, but would Mom do it, too?"

I knew, and Bill knew, that this was a silly question. Cate Allen would do anything, be anything, go anywhere, just because a) she wanted to, b) somebody dared her to, or c) God forbid, someone told her she couldn't. My mother would be in a canoe on the Missouri River for a year just because she knew of no one else who was doing it. That was her way.

"Yes," he said, a smirk in his voice, "I think I could talk her into it."

Now it was down to me, and Donna. My life had been measured with a wanderlust yardstick. As I grew older and moved out of the house I realized that not everyone moved every year, and most families didn't sit down together during Christmas break and wonder where they would be for the next Christmas, asking each other what adventures the coming year would bring. Donna had been reared in three houses, all within thirty miles of each other. She was the yin to my yang, and somehow it was working. The first year we spent together taught me that I could build a career, that maybe the wandering was more costly than I knew, and that indeed, it was with Donna that I wanted to be. There was, however, a glint of doubt in me, that longing to make it over the next hill, just to see what was there. My wanderlust was a part of me that brought me many adventures, and a sense of pride. I was more my mother's daughter than I wanted to admit.

"I don't know, Bill, I just started my job here at Princeton."

After years of hourly wages, this job paid me to think, not just to do. Finally, I had a job and a sense of stability I had not yet been able to hold on to, the slipperiness of stability always foiling my grasp. To be honest, I had scoffed at stability, had bid it folly, for those who couldn't handle the pressure of movement. But now, with Donna, it was stability I longed for. It had taken me years to find her, or more precisely, to find myself, and a river trip seemed threatening to that fragile, new part of my psyche.

"I'll think about it," I said.

A pause landed itself right there in our conversation. Bill was seventy-eight years old. This wasn't a trip I could put off for ten years until my retirement account was a bit fatter and I had racked up a few months of vacation time. Here was the man who had seen me through the transition from a shaky thirteen year-old girl to a young woman who was finding out that life might not hold marriage and kids, but might go down another path, and he had been the first one to tell me that was just fine.

We wished each other goodnight and I dropped the phone back in its cradle. I roused Diva and opened the door to let her out for her last evening pee. The crickets were loud that night, the darkness surrounding the cottage seemed to know the brief struggle going on inside of me. How does one know what the morning's light will bring? And when the lightness comes, will it look the same to us?

Diva trotted back to the front stoop and I reached down to pat her angel-soft brown ears; the ears of a Labrador Retriever are as soft as anything I have ever felt, their softness radiating warmth. We went inside together and I turned off the porch light.

"You coming up?" Donna's voice floated down the narrow stairs.

"Up in a minute," I said.

I sat down on Diva's bed and she nuzzled into my side. Why did a lack of movement signify stagnation for me? And how much movement could my relationship endure? Donna had worked in the same field for the past fourteen years; how could I ask her to quit her job and canoe a river, with people she barely knew? This was ridiculous. Wanderlust was rearing its head again, taking hold of a part of me that I thought I had satisfied. I stroked Diva's brown fur and she sighed her deep end-of-the-day sigh.

I turned down the lights and walked slowly up the stairs, wanderlust and all.

***

"Hi Jenny, JanSport wants to know what gear we want for the trip."

Bill's voice played in my ear as I tried to connect what he was saying to something recognizable. The phone rested on my shoulder as I reached for the spaghetti box on top of the refrigerator.

"Before what trip, Bill?"

It was September, and the warmth of the early autumn night drifted in through the screen door. I could hear Donna returning from the mailbox, her steps crunching the gravel on the driveway.

"Before our river trip – they want to know what gear we need to canoe the Missouri River."

Somehow, the slight crinkle of his lips giving way to a smile made its way across the fields of the Midwest, over the Appalachian Mountains, and into the warm skies above our little cottage in Princeton. Twelve hundred miles of phone wires couldn't conceal his enjoyment.

"Bill, wait, how does JanSport know about our trip?"

And it was there that he had me. I was as good as packed, the mud of the Missouri River already oozing over the soles of my sandals. My possessive pronoun had given me away. He knew it, and I knew it.

What I didn't yet know was that my seventy-eight year old stepfather had written to JanSport, the company that he had grown to love while canoeing the length of the Mississippi River, just after retiring from the desk of a Michigan newsroom twenty years earlier. It was their tent and sleeping bag that he had crawled into every night of his journey. I didn't yet know that he had told them that he was about to canoe the Missouri River, along with his wife, his stepdaughter, and her partner, and would they be interested in sponsoring us, in exchange for a bit of publicity along the way? And he was calling tonight to tell me that they had said yes. They wanted to know what gear we needed for our trip, and if we would kindly send them a list, they'd ship it out pronto.

The phone line was quiet while I breathed in the warm night air. If Bill had written to JanSport, one of the largest gear companies in the world, with a real shipping department, and CEO, and profit margins, and stockholders, and they thought this river trip was a real thing, and something we were actually going to do, and they said “Yes, just tell us what gear you need, and we’ll sponsor you,” well, then…what? Was it a real thing? Would we actually do it?

I moved toward the stove and added a dribble of olive oil to the water boiling for pasta. Donna stepped in and closed the screen door behind her. Diva trotted over and looked up at her longingly for a second dinner. I shook my head “no” as Donna’s raised eyebrows asked me if Diva needed to be fed. Chocolate Labs, at least this Chocolate Lab, are motivated by food.

“Bill…what, exactly, did you tell them?”

I dropped the spaghetti into the boiling water, shuffling the strands through my fingers as one loosely shuffles cards, the better to have each strand flow through the pool of floating olive oil as it enters the water.

“I let them know that we thought the world was moving too fast, and someone, or more specifically, the four of us, wanted to slow it down a bit by taking a year off and canoeing the Missouri River. I told them I thought they would benefit from the stories we would tell to local newspapers and radio stations. And I told them we were bringing the dogs.”

How was it that this man who had lived in an entirely different generation, rather, several generations away from mine, had so closely embraced what was dear to me? He knew that Donna’s Chocolate Lab, Diva, was my new best buddy, next to Donna. I had relayed stories of playing fetch with Diva in a pitch-black backyard, her nose overpowering the darkness, a wriggling chocolate-colored dog diving under a bush until she found the tennis ball covered with her own saliva.

Bill, by understanding the life, and the love, that was embracing me now, had embraced me. And I knew that to be in that embrace, to return the affection of this all-accepting, sweet, deep, gentle man meant understanding him, and his life. If he wanted to do this river trip, and if his desire for this crazy trip included me, then I would return the embrace.

Just as the pasta water boiled over, I realized I wanted to do the river trip.

A breeze caught the sheets as I crawled under them later that evening.

"Bill and Mom are planning to canoe the Missouri River, taking a year off and going from Montana to the Gulf of Mexico."

"MmmHmmm," came Donna's sleepy reply.

"They want us to join them. And Diva, too."

Donna rolled over to face me. She looked directly at me, her brown eyes searching mine. She knew Bill's age; she knew my closeness with my mother and stepfather; she knew my wanderlust tendencies.

"Do you want to do it with them?" she asked.

I paused. Of course I did. Of course I didn't. In my mind I skated across a frozen pond, not knowing where the ice was thin.

I had met Donna in a rock-climbing course in upstate New York, so I knew her sense of adventure was large enough to include a river trip. I wasn't sure about her career including a year of time off, and I couldn't read in her eyes if she knew that this was probably the last time I would be able to answer this question with Bill. If I wanted to spend time with him, significant amounts of time – time to dawdle through our thoughts and conversations, time to build deep trenches of memories, time to know each other as well as we would in this life – then I wanted to do this trip.

How does one measure love? And how does one get past those moments when rational communication fails, and your heart speaks?

"Yes, I want to do the river trip. And I want to do it with you."

It wasn't an ultimatum, simply a statement of fact. Can we speak truth without needing to explain it? With Donna, I could. She put her arm over my back, the warmth of her skin crossing my shoulder blades as delicate calm.

"I know you," was all she said.

And she did. I reached over and clicked off the light, soft darkness settling over us, and the night.

***

Three months slipped past and the river trip stayed in our lives as a book one is reading is always at the bedside. Each night I imagined how it would feel to be on the other side of adventure – to live days full of movement, always on a journey – river towns flowing past as we soaked up the Montana sun. These dreams made their way into my waking life in the form of trips to the local library, stacks of books coming home with me about Lewis and Clark, Montana, camping stove reviews.

Donna seemed to be rolling the idea around in her mind but did not come right out and say she was going to quit her job and take a year off to canoe the Missouri River with my stepfather and mother. Somehow, I couldn't blame her. Our little cottage in central New Jersey welcomed us home each night after the workday ended. The thought, rather the question, of the river trip, was nearly always present.

Then, one crisp fall evening, the Swedish family who lived in the big house on the same property as our little cottage invited us to dinner. They were in the United States for a three-year assignment with a major pharmaceutical company. Lars was a vice president and Elizabeth often watched Diva during the day, bringing her to play with their dog during long, sunny afternoons. As we relaxed after dinner with thick European coffee, Lars asked if we were going to do the river trip. We had shared the story of JanSport and Bill securing the gear, and they were curious about the trip.

I stayed quiet as Donna explained that she didn't know if it was the right time for her to leave her career, put everything on hold, and do this crazy thing. Lars listened and sat back in his chair. He moved his coffee cup slowly across the tablecloth, ripples forming in the cloth as he moved the cup away from him. He leaned forward.

"Donna," he said, "I hire many people. I only get involved with the last cut – I am seeing the best applicants – and every one of them, every one," he slowed his speaking so 'every' had three syllables, "has done something that was crazy. They have hiked the Himalayan mountains, they have taken time off to write a book – they have dreamed, and then made their dreams come true. And each time it happened at what seemed to be the height of their careers."

He stopped for a moment. I looked at Donna and it was as if she and Lars were the only ones in the room. This was a conversation happening between only two people, and neither of them looked away from the other.

"Donna, they made their crazy dreams happen, and that is what I look for. I want to hire someone who has taken risks, someone who has shown that he can be successful making something happen that others are not brave enough to do. These are the best people. These are the people that are successful at whatever they do."

He sat back and sipped his coffee. The room was electric. Donna took in a breath as if she were going to say something, and then stopped. I watched her eyes; they were like gates, guarding her mind from distraction. Later, Donna would describe this conversation as though it were happening in a tunnel that existed only between her and Lars. She said all noise fell away, and it was as if his words had been saved for her, at just that moment.

The next day the river trip question turned into The River Trip. We were doing it.

The first thing we did was to make a list. We tried to think of everything we'd need for a year and then double it. We faxed the list to Bill and Mom and the phone rang three minutes later.

It was Mom. "So... you're... coming with us?"

And so it began. Nightly phone calls to talk about what type of tents we needed, how many frying pans we should bring, and how were we going to pay for all of this. If we really needed all this gear, maybe the tack Bill had taken with JanSport would work with other companies. If I were to make a t-shirt with Bill's life-motto on it, across his chest it would read: Ask for what you want. So we made the list again, this time writing down the name of the company that made the best tents, the company that produced the best cookware, the folks who made the warmest socks – we even listed Diva's dog food and the maker of her favorite kind.

A week of phone calls and faxes later we had defined the river trip well enough to be able to communicate our idea of taking time to slow things down a bit, to throw away our answering machines, our calendars, and even our watches to get to know each other, people who lived along the river, and the land that Lewis and Clark passed through almost 200 years earlier to our prospective sponsors. We each set about writing letters to the CEOs of our list of companies, never asking for money, but rather asking for their particular specialty – tents, socks, sleeping bags – in exchange for publicity through radio shows and newspaper articles along the way. We wrote to twenty companies; nineteen of them became our beloved sponsors. Not only did we outfit ourselves, we even got Diva sponsored with a year's worth of Nutro dog food!

One night Donna came home from work and said, "I've heard of this new thing called a Palm Pilot; we could keep our journals in them."

One stamp, and three weeks later, four Palm Pilots showed up on our doorstep. Ask for what you want. This was becoming our mantra. For a span of about a month, we would receive a letter from a prospective sponsor in our mailbox almost daily. Donna and I would hurry to the cottage, Diva trotting behind. We always opened the sponsor's letter first. I am not certain there is, or has been, anything more exciting than planning this crazy adventure with my lover, my mother and my stepfather. We were watching Bill's vision become reality, and as it did, it became ours as well. We each had a part in the building of this thing called the river trip. It was already becoming a part of us, and we hadn't even put paddle to water.

Ask For What You Want

Cate

Funny how we each remember it differently. I remember having my usual Sunday afternoon call from Jen. She told me Princeton was wonderful and hectic in August, that Angie and Mark were having a baby, that she'd cut her hair, and did I remember that haircut I gave her before the first day of kindergarten. We rambled on, aimlessly as always, and laughed out loud about the year I began a traveling school, pulled her out of fourth grade, and took twelve kids to Baja to study whale migration, lived in snow caves in Yellowstone for a month, studied government in Washington D.C., theatre in New York, and ecology and finance on a little farm in Missouri.

We laughed.

Then she said, "Mom, I miss living with you."

"Jen, take a weekend off, come to Kansas City, and we'll play."

"I was thinking of something longer," she said.

"Tell you what," I said, "I'll take a week off if you will, and we'll travel somewhere."

"Mom, I was thinking of something longer," she said.

"Do you want to canoe a river?"

"What?"

"Do you want to canoe a river? How about the Mississippi?"

We both loved that river. It brought Bill to us.

Twenty years ago, my son, Gig, read a magazine article about a television newscaster who walked into the studio one day, took off his tie, handed it to the floor director, and said, "I quit. I want to see the world I've been reading about for twenty years each evening at six and eleven." Then he hitchhiked around Europe, fell in love in China, taught English in London, and decided to canoe, alone, down the Mississippi River, the river where my three kids and I lived in a tiny river town. Gig wrote to him, told him that if he'd stop in our town his mom would make dinner for him. He stopped, I made him dinner, put my kids to bed early, kissed him on the midnight Grafton ferry ride across the river to Calhoun county and back, and put him back on the river in his canoe the next morning. He called from St. Louis that evening, ten miles downriver, and asked me to join him for dinner. I skipped an evening class, joined him for dinner and put him back in his canoe the next morning. And the next morning. And the next.

Three months later he called to tell me to listen to a radio interview he was doing that afternoon. Jen and I listened. The interviewer asked if he'd had any life-changing adventures along the river. He said, "I think I have. I met a woman upriver and am taking this opportunity to ask her to marry me."

When I asked Jen if I should marry him she said, "Would I get his canoe?"

Now, on this Sunday afternoon, when I said, "How about the Mississippi," she said, "Would I get his canoe?"

"Seriously, Jen," I said, "why don't we take a year off and canoe a river? What about the Missouri?"

"Where does it begin," she asked.

"I don't know, up north somewhere, I guess. Isn't that the river Lewis and Clark explored?"

Jen said, "Ask Bill if he's up for another river in his eightieth year."

"Bill," I yelled into the kitchen, "do you want to canoe the Missouri River?"

"Sure," he yelled back.

"He says sure," I said, "What about Donna?"

"I'll ask her. Love you, Mom. Bye. "

On Wednesday Donna called to report that she'd researched the Missouri River. It began in Three Forks, Montana, and flowed through North Dakota, South Dakota, Nebraska, Iowa, Kansas, and Missouri where it joined the Mississippi River near St. Louis. It would be a 4000-mile canoe trip from Montana to the Gulf of Mexico. We'd need two canoes for the four of us. Taking into account bad weather days, restocking supplies, portages, and cleaning gear, we'd have to canoe twelve miles a day if we were to complete the river in a year. And, since she and Jen had just signed another one-year lease on their house, they couldn't leave for ten months. But, she thought, it would take that long to prepare for such a trip, anyway.

That was just like Donna. She's thorough, rational and thoughtful. From the day Jen told me about Donna, I knew she was a perfect balance for Jen who is impulsive, and a creative and free thinker. Jen and I always think that if we spend four hours in a Saturday class, say, on sailing, or CPR, or chain sawing, that we're experts. We even make t-shirts proclaiming our expertise. Donna, on the other hand, takes year-long courses and then considers herself only a novice. I trust her every decision more than my own.

Donna and I agreed that we'd all think about the river and make a decision when they came to Kansas City for Christmas, four months away. After all, we'd have to quit jobs, jobs we loved, if we were to have this adventure.

Later that fall, in Donna's usual style, she invited a friend, a vice-president at an international corporation, to come to dinner. After dessert, she questioned him about job interviews. She wanted to know how, in an interview, he could be sure an applicant held promise for the company. He told her he looked for someone who has done something unusual, something of his own creating, someone who has accomplished a dream. Any dream. And, certainly, he didn't trust grade point averages.

Donna decided over the kitchen sink that night. While doing the dishes, she told Jen that she felt secure. She thought by quitting her job and doing the river she wasn't destroying her career. Maybe, just maybe, she was ensuring her future.

Everyone came for Christmas. We'd sent messages to all the children, the grandchildren, the nieces and nephews, saying that the only presents we wanted that year was their presence. They all came. Every one. No presents. Sleeping bags everywhere. A two-day game of Whodunit. A candlelit Christmas dinner on the floor, where we announced that they'd better eat up now because the four of us, Jen, Donna, Bill, and I were going to give notice at work next month so we could canoe the Missouri River.

***

It was all set, then. We'd all quit our jobs, the jobs we loved, canoe an unknown river for a year, and then God only knew.

Then reality came crashing in. What equipment would we need? What boats? We had "*E. coli*," Bill's Mad River canoe from the Mississippi trip, but Jen and Donna didn't have a boat. How would we pay for living expenses for four people for a year? What about our two dogs? What would we need in the way of transportation? What was the real purpose of the adventure? Was it just a whim? Is it ok to quit your job for a whim?

Jen was eager to begin to get our gear together, to see what we'd need to buy, and what we could borrow, or repair from our summer camp days. When my kids were old enough to go to summer camp, I volunteered to be a camp counselor. I was only twenty-five when they were old enough to spend summers at camp. For fifteen years we all went off to camp together. Then, one day, Jen was appointed Program Director of the camp, began to boss me around, and I knew I'd retire the next summer. But, we had lots of camping gear. Blanket rolls, climbing rope, crafts supplies, plastic tube tents, dented black pots. None of which we could use on a year-long expedition. We'd need sleeping bags which would take us down to below zero temperatures, and tents which would keep pesky mosquitoes and black flies from our sun-scorched skin.

Jen sent me a fax that listed everything she thought we'd need:
Tents, dry bags, paddles, canoes, cooking equipment, food, dog food, clothing, a stove, life jackets, cameras, sleeping bags, water bottles, Cool Whip containers (on cold, frosty mornings they make great bedside commodes), ground cloths, watches…

"Wait," I said, on a quick return call. "Why watches? Why not spend this whole year without any watches or clocks?"

"A year without time?" she said. "Sounds good. In fact, we could call the whole adventure A Year Without Time …the expedition."

So it was born. We had a purpose to our adventure. We'd spend the whole year without time, simply learning about our inner clocks and how we fit into nature's scheme. We'd eat when we were hungry, sleep when we were sleepy and paddle in between. Twelve miles a day.

Bill offered his $750/month Social Security check to keep us all fed while we were on the river. I could take as much time off my job as I liked, without jeopardizing my future. In the seminar business, schedules are made three months ahead of time. The seminar company offers a schedule of seminars, a different city each day, to the seminar presenter. I was free to accept or decline as many seminars as I wanted. I decided to do a week of seminars every other month. That way, the canoe crew would take a few days off every other month while I flew off to Honolulu or Kennebunkport. They could clean equipment, rest, write, explore, and I'd stay current with business trends and audiences. I'd also be able to keep paying for our Kansas City apartment so we'd all have a place to call home. Just in case.

In one of our phone conversations, which were becoming nightly calls now, I mentioned that Bill had taught me, when we first began to travel together, to ask for what I wanted. Whatever it may be. It had become our mantra. With good reason. Ask for what you want.

I'd seen it work over and over again. Once, during our honeymoon trip, canoeing the Rhein River through Switzerland, Germany, and Austria, Bill and I were celebrating the 4th of July. Mail hadn't reached us for weeks. We'd been away from home for three months, and I was feeling lonely. To cheer me, I tucked a flower behind my ear and we set off to find a place to stay. At an ancient cathedral in Tübingen, standing on cobblestones, I looked up to see a lovely restored home. Four stories, nestled between pale yellow buildings, with shiny black shutters and spunky geraniums in the window boxes.

"That's where I'd like to live." I pouted.

Bill started the search for the owner and found Axel and Gudrun in the garden. "We're looking for a room."

Soon, we were seated on a balcony high above the village, enjoying strawberries as big as lemons, chatting about our families and our journey, and the flower tucked behind my ear.

Axel winked as he spoke, "We want you to be our guests. You could stay in the lavender room on the third floor."

A few mornings later at breakfast, Gudrun asked if we would do them a favor. "We're leaving next week for our holiday in Portugal," she said. "Would you stay here to take care of our house while we're away?"

Would we? A month in this village, getting to know the postman, the baker, the outdoor market where I would go toodling off with a basket under my arm – this all sounded wonderful to us. We had a grand time playing house all summer. Ask for what you want.

What if we asked for the equipment we needed? What if we could actually help suppliers by promoting their products as part of A Year Without Time …the expedition? We'd already begun to get requests from newspapers, magazines, and radio shows for interviews about our plans to follow the Lewis and Clark route (by now we'd learned that we'd actually be doing the reverse of the Lewis and Clark trail). We could talk about our sponsors during interviews.

As if to encourage us, a few evenings later, I was standing at a fancy Chinese take-out counter when a man in cut-offs and a t-shirt, with ratty tennis shoes stepped up and ordered. I'd seen him get out of a truck with a canoe on top. After he ordered, I said, "Have you been canoeing?"

"Yes," he said, "but it was pretty cold."

"Canoe much around here?" I asked.

"Yep." He said.

"What paddles do you use?"

"Wooden for show. Aluminum for getting there." He said.

I laughed.

He said, "Do you canoe?"

Inside, I puffed up, smiled nonchalantly, and said, "Oh, we'll be leaving to canoe the Missouri, come spring." I made it sound as though we did this sort of thing everyday. What fun this was.

My order arrived and while I was writing a check he said, "We should get together. I canoe lots."

Now, I thought, how will I explain this conversation to Bill while I serve up hot Chinese? How will I explain that I'd told our dearest plans at eleven o'clock at night to a straggly-haired, disheveled, muddy guy at a Chinese restaurant?

As I mused, he said, "In fact, I own Kansas City Paddler, a canoe shop down by the river. Come on down someday. If you need anything, say paddles or life jackets, for your expedition, we'd be happy to supply them."

Now inside I took a deep breath. Was this really happening? I hadn't even asked. He had just given us paddles and PFDs between egg rolls and lo mein.

"Oh," he said, "call before you come because I might be in surgery."

"Surgery?" I said.

"I'm a neurosurgeon. Canoes are my play toys."

The next day Jen, Donna, Bill and I made a list of the finest manufacturers of all the things we needed:

> Dry bags, tents, sleeping bags, camping clothes: REI
> Duffels, backpacks: JanSport
> Cooking equipment: Banks Fry-Bake
> Food: Power Bars, Pillsbury, Wild Oats
> Dog food: Nutro
> Warm socks: Wigwam
> Palm Pilots: U.S. Robotics
> Camp chairs: Crazy Creek

Then we drafted a letter to each one and sent it off, hoping to get some equipment crossed off our list. We enclosed a brochure which we'd printed making A Year Without Time …the expedition, a reality. At least in our minds. Then we waited.

That next Thursday I was in a hotel room in New York when Bill called. I was putting the final touches on my seminar for the next day, Organization Skills for Professionals. Bill gave me all the news from Kansas City. The next morning I opened my seminar by saying, "During this seminar, ask for what you want." I went on to explain that if they needed a question answered, ask! If they needed special supplies or equipment back at work, ask! If they needed time off to attend a seminar, ask! Just as we'd asked for a Palm Pilot the week before, and had just received not only one Palm Pilot, but four, one for each member of our soon-to-be expedition. Four Palm Pilots in all. Absolutely free.

We were thrilled. Now we could stop once a week at some riverside town, go to the laundromat, or the gas station, or even a restaurant and post our latest adventures on our website, for our families to read. The Palm Pilots would keep us in touch and all the while we'd feel we were following Lewis and Clark through the wilderness.

Before we knew it, other packages began to arrive. Socks from Wigwam. Thirty-eight pair! A year's supply of dog food from Nutro. And, of course, paddles and PFDs from Kansas City Paddler. We got to know Lynn Lyon, the neurosurgeon/canoer. He taught us the joys of kayaking. In late winter he took us to a Kansas City lake and taught us how to roll out underwater from an over-turned kayak. Jen and Donna bought a kayak to hang from their living room ceiling next to their canoe. Bill said he didn't intend to go down the river upside-down, so we'd stay with his canoe, *E. coli*, named after the garbage and sewage floating down the Mississippi right along with him back in 1980.

We'd sent twenty letters. Nineteen sponsors sent their equipment. Daily packages would arrive with shiny, beautiful gear.

Then one day, we got a reply from REI. They wrote to say that they'd received our request. They'd like to be a sponsor. Only trouble was, if they were going to send anything, they'd like to send a lot. Enclosed was a catalog. Would we please circle everything we might possibly need. In our wildest dreams!

Our small Plaza apartment began to overflow with rubberized, down-filled, color-coded, micro-screened equipment. We sorted it into two piles. One for Jen and Donna. One for us. We'd settle down in the middle of the piles and read canoeing magazines, the three volume set of *The History of the Lewis and Clark Expedition* by Elliott Coues, *How to Shit in the Woods* by Kathleen Meyer, and study river maps from the Corps of Engineers. We'd had a problem getting maps of the Upper Missouri. The Corps only stocked maps from Iowa on down. In our reading we kept seeing references to a place called the Missouri Breaks. What was that, we wondered.

Donna called one night to say that a documentary filmmaker wanted to follow our expedition, taking footage to turn into a documentary.

"Take a look at the website she found." It was a picture of gigantic waterfalls and seething whirlpools. "Read the title," she said.

Morning on the Missouri River.

We hadn't even wondered if the entire Missouri was navigable today. We couldn't tell if there was any whitewater on the river from the maps we had. And why didn't the Corps have Upper Missouri River maps? We'd find out soon enough.

Leap, Then Look

Jen

May 16th came quickly. Donna and I had quit our jobs and gotten out of our lease; furniture was in storage. We put the Talking Heads on loudly as we drove down the on-ramp to I-95 West: *Take Me to the River*. Two hours later we stopped at Donna's sister's house and for the first time felt the mix of emotions that would become standard from people we passed on the river trip. I could see thoughts of "why are you doing this crazy thing, and what about your finances?" mix with a spark of envy, maybe jealousy, and then come back to the crazy part, as we bade our farewells to Donna's sister and family. Two days later we re-conned with Mom and Bill in Kansas City and walked into their gear-laden apartment. Ten thousand dollars worth of donated gear greeted us – so much we could barely fit it all in our cars. Trucks were the right next move, so the cars were traded in. I saw a new side of Donna when she turned to me with a smile at the used car dealer and said, "I've always wanted a truck."

What is it about quitting your job and living out of a tent that lets you see a new side of your lover? I knew this trip would either bring Donna and me together as we wanted to be, or we would split at the first sign of trouble. Everything is more exposed in a tent, and traveling together highlights habits quickly.

It was in Colorado that I realized Donna had not seen the interior of the country. Driving across eastern Colorado, the flatness easily mistaken for Kansas, she was asleep when we got to Denver. I like to think it was the mountains that woke her. She was intrigued, and we ended up spending a week exploring the Colorado Rockies; A Year Without Time time was beginning to take hold. Diva loved the snow in June and Donna loved the starkness of the peaks. I loved watching the two of them relax in a way I'd never seen before; it would take months truly to forget about our work lives.

We had agreed to meet Mom and Bill at the post office in Three Forks, Montana, on June 19th. We wanted to avoid the caravan mentality and be able to explore as we drove north from Denver to Montana. We spent the first night in Sinks Canyon, just outside of Lander, Wyoming. It was Wyoming-cold, and our sleeping bags had frost on them in the morning. But the night was dark and I saw once again the western sky full of stars. Something about this felt like home to me.

Three Forks, Montana has one main street, and the post office was not hard to find. After buying a map at the local drugstore, we scooted out of town to the headwaters of the Missouri River. We had tents to seam-seal and boats to load. As we drove to the Headwaters State Park, the ground was soft, flooded, and marshy. We were excited because we had gotten there early enough in the day to have the pick of tent sites. As it turned out, no one else checked in that day; mosquitoes are a powerful deterrent.

Montana mosquitoes are the kind that like dark clothing, and small children, and old men, and young strapping men, and women, and dogs. We set up our tents as quickly as we could and dived into them. The mosquitoes swarmed outside. Our food and gear lay in a heap by the trucks, and we chuckled at how brave we were turning out to be. We'd been on the river trip all of fifteen minutes and all we could do was run like hell to find the mosquito repellant.

The evening chill scared off most of the mosquitoes and our first dinner (curried chicken and rice) on our camp stove settled us down. As Donna and I crawled into our tent with Diva that night, I wondered if this trip would be too much for us. Could our relationship withstand the tests of traveling, in boats, through the wilderness of the Missouri River and swarms of mosquitoes? Had my wanderlust gotten us in over our heads? Was this really something Donna wanted to do, or was she doing it to make me happy? I heard the night's breeze rattle our tent poles against the nylon ceiling and wondered if I had exposed us to too much, too soon. Diva stirred as she tried to find a comfortable spot. I reached for Donna's hand and squeezed it. Only the night knew how nervous I was.

Leap, Then Look

Cate

We planned a June departure from Kansas City. We would drive to Denver, say goodbye to Bill's daughters and grandchildren, drive to Three Forks, Montana, put our canoes in the river, and, a year later, emerge at the Gulf of Mexico. We thought.

In early May, Jen and Donna packed their household goods into a storage locker, their river gear into their VW, bade farewell to their colleagues and friends, and drove to Kansas City. We all had our teeth cleaned. We packed flour, powdered milk, garam masala, and tampons in plastic baggies. We sorted through equipment, packed and repacked their VW and our Lincoln Continental. We always seemed to have paddles, or bags of clothing, or fresh water bottles left over sitting on the sidewalk. We needed to take everything, it seemed, and there just wasn't room. Late one afternoon I asked my mom to go for a ride with me. We drove down Broadway, where used car lots lined both sides of the street. I pulled into the Ford lot, where I'd spotted a little, used truck. Mom and I took it around the block. "What do you think, Mom?" I said.

"Honey, we've never had a truck in the family. But, if it's what you want…"

An hour later Mom and I drove my new black truck home and honked and honked outside until Bill and Jen and Donna came out. It was perfect. It held all the gear. We all went to sleep that night blessing our lucky stars that we'd realized we couldn't drive a Lincoln Continental to put a canoe into the Missouri River in Montana.

On Saturday at breakfast, Donna said, "I've been researching trucks. Jen and I think we should have a truck, too. That way we could leave one truck where we put in the river, and have another waiting where we think we'll take out. I've been checking blue book values, and have found a truck in southern Missouri which might work for us."

They drove four hours, took a look, drove it to a mechanic, checked it from top to bottom, then drove home to think about it. As I said before, and will say again, Donna does everything right. In the end, they bought the truck. They saved lots of money. Their truck has more power than ours. The trucks look alike, but they definitely got the better deal. The day they brought their truck home, we all allowed as how silly it was to have matching trucks.

Jen and I felt the same way years ago when she was in high school and we were supposed to attend a Mother/Daughter Tea at her school. We would have preferred to stay home and clean, or go to the dentist. At the last minute we bought matching ruffled outfits, and pranced into the Tea, making fun all the while. Only years later did I realize that as silly as I thought the tea party was, to Jen it was more than silly. She'd been feeling things I knew nothing about. She'd been wondering just who she was. Where she was going. And why she loved Aimee.

So, here we stood in Kansas City, packing up trucks, Bill and I, and Jen with maybe not her first love, but certainly her true love, Donna. We not only delighted in the silliness of owning two matching trucks, but all agreed to have signs made for the trucks: "A Year Without Time ...the expedition." The next afternoon we all feigned disgust as we carefully applied the big, white, stick-on letters. Now we were ready for the countdown.

On Monday, Donna went to the bank to start an account to pay her incoming bills automatically. She was nearly out of breath as she dashed into the apartment.

"I did it," she said. "When they asked me my occupation, I said Explorer!"

She was taking this whole adventure seriously. We celebrated that night at the Chinese restaurant where I'd met Lynn Lyon. Our dinner table conversation centered on the radio interview, a talk show, we were to do the next morning.

Early the next morning we lashed canoes on top of trucks, drove to the NPR station and enjoyed talking about our suppliers, our dogs, our proposed riverside meals, and all manner of plans. Then she called.

"I think you are a bunch of parasites."

We were stunned. How had we ever given that impression? Were we, in fact, using people? Using our sponsors? Was this whole idea offensive? Her call put a damper on everything we'd planned. I keep a slip of paper on my desk on which I've written, "true, honest, just, pure, lovely, good report," from a verse I love from Philippians. Each day I try to keep my actions in line with that slip of paper. How had I so blatantly forgotten how others might respond to A Year Without Time ...the expedition?

We had to leave right after the radio show so we could meet a reporter down by the river who was going to do a front page spread in the *Kansas City Star* the next weekend when we were to leave for Montana. We unloaded the canoes from our matching trucks, put in the river near Kansas City's downtown river-side park, and had an hour-long photo shoot and interview. When we returned to the trucks, I found a handwritten note on my windshield. I keep it close, even today.

> "To the Year Without Time Family: Have a wonderful expedition. What a wonderful growth experience for your family, as well as a legacy you are making. Blessings to you all. Best of luck. Rebeccah"

We fell into bed that night tired from our first day on the river, even though it was only a dry run for a reporter. But, everything was all right again. After all, we weren't doing this adventure to please everyone. Or even anyone.

There would be detractors along the way. We knew that. But as long as once in a while a Rebeccah would happen along, everything would be ok.

***

We thought we'd be able to drive to Denver, our first stop, before dark. But it was already getting dark by the time we finished packing and repacking both trucks. Jen and Donna spent the afternoon building a ramp for Diva, Donna's Chocolate Lab, who at twelve, needed help to get up into the back of the truck. We wondered aloud if we should sleep one more night in our apartment and leave in the morning. But we'd waited so long, planned almost a year, and were eager to get on the road.

"Let's head out, stop when we are sleepy and rendezvous at Jane's in Denver."

Jen and Donna and Diva climbed into their truck, Bill and I and Gypsy into ours, and eased onto Highway 70 outside Kansas City.

We'd brought Gypsy home from Russia a few years before. She'd been a Moscow street dog who'd followed us home one day and stayed. When my one-year contract, which I'd extended three times, to manage Abbott Laboratories' Moscow office expired four years later, we arranged for Ivan and Svetlana, our upstairs neighbors, to take Gypsy. After the movers took our last box and we said teary goodbyes to our beloved Russian friends, I handed Gypsy's leash to Ivan. Of all the wonderful friends we found in Russia, the heart surgeon who became our housekeeper, little Luda who surprised us with a glowing pumpkin one October when we were especially homesick, Irina my treasured secretary and confidant, the rocket scientists and teachers and students and taxi drivers and engineers who came to our apartment each Tuesday to speak English, of all those, and so many others, Gypsy was my best friend. She never, ever leaves my side. I imagine that she feels I saved her life by taking her in, and that she owes me for that. She doesn't let anyone come near me unless I say it's ok. She walks at my feet so that I constantly stumble and trip. She has sat at my bedside for days without food or water or walks, when I've been ill. She listens to my secrets. And doesn't tell anyone.

So, as Ivan took her leash and I looked at her beautiful face, I sputtered, "Bill, I can't leave her. Can't we take her with us?"

"It would mean canceling our flight for this afternoon, getting her the proper papers, and taking a train out of Russia. Our visas expire in two days, and you know the bureaucracy we'd face. The hoops we'd have to jump through…"

"I don't care," I cried, "she's my friend."

"She'll be the luckiest Russian I know," Bill said, "to be getting out of Russia. Quick, you flag down a car and get to the vet's office to get her shots and papers before they close. I'll get in the line for train tickets."

In Russia one only has to stand at the curb, wave an arm, and a car, any car, will stop to ask where you're headed. If they're going your way, you hop in. Sometimes there's a bit of negotiating over rubles. It's a grand way to get around the city, especially for a foreigner with hard currency, whom Russians can spot a block away.

"It's because of the way you hold yourself and walk with your head up." Lena had explained, "Oh, and because you don't wear scarves and hats."

So Gyp was going to canoe the Missouri River now, and needed no coaxing to hop in the little black truck just as the setting sun cast a warm glow over Kansas fields. It had been a long day so Gyp and I settled in back for a nap while Bill took the first shift of getting us closer to Denver and Montana and the Missouri. I'd never ridden in the back of a truck. It was bumpy but I managed to scrunch between paddles and tent poles and fall asleep. I was jolted awake by a screech, a crashing sound, and Bill yelling, "No!"

He'd fallen asleep, and run off the road into the median strip which was a deep gully. I was disoriented, sleepy, and had a bump on my head. I couldn't get to the tailgate window, and when I finally did, it was locked. I felt trapped. I lunged to the tiny window which opened into the cab, stuck my head through, and screamed in the darkness, "Are you ok?"

Calmly Bill answered, "Sure."

"What happened?" I screamed.

Calmly Bill answered, "I seem to have fallen asleep and run off the road."

"Good God, Bill!" I screamed.

Calmly Bill answered, "We're all right. Let me just get us back on the highway."

"Tell you what," I said, trying to mimic his calm, "I'll drive. I've had enough sleep."

Calmly he handed me the keys as I pushed and pulled myself through the little window and Bill moved to the passenger side of the cab. Gyp hopped through the window and sat between us. The truck went right up the hill, and we got back on the highway between whizzing trucks.

At the next rest area we pulled in between two eighteen-wheelers, made a pallet in back, and fell asleep with Gyp between us. All night long I coughed exhaust fumes, wondered if our little money was safe under the front seat, had dreams of muggers in Kansas rest area bathrooms, and generally longed for Jane's house where all would be peaceful. Or so we thought.

We arrived at Jane's by lunch the next day. Jane is Bill's middle daughter. Two years my junior. She calls me Mumsy. I sign my letters, Your Wicked Step Mother. I loved her from the moment we met. I'd heard tales of her childhood temper tantrums, and heard that she'd once thrown a whole stack of plates to the floor in protest of something or other, but I found her to be cheery, and loving. Until that day.

Her son, Geoff, was home from college and sat wide-eyed as we told of our plans to canoe the river. He stayed up long into the night talking with Jen and Donna. I felt Jen shake me awake before I could even see her. It was still dark. "Mom, what would you two think if we asked Geoff to join us on the river? He's sort of between semesters in college, doesn't really have any direction, and is enamoured of our plans."

"Jen, this will be the first time all four of us must make a decision together. It's an important one. I don't even know what process we should use to make decisions as a group."

"How 'bout using our hearts?" Jen replied.

"Meet us in the upstairs bathroom in five minutes."

Five minutes later, Jen, Donna, Bill and I sat around the perimeter of the red bathroom and discussed the proposed change in the crew. "It will change the whole complexion of the trip," I said. "But if it's important for Geoff, let's make the change."

Bill said, "He's got a strong pair of arms and could really be helpful."

Jen and Donna winked at each other and told us of staying up all night, talking with Geoff about his dreams, and feeling that we could, maybe, just maybe, help him begin to find those dreams. "Mom," Jen said, "you always insisted that we follow our dreams, and I think it's time we help Geoff learn to do that, too."

"Ok," I said, "what do we do now? Vote?" This group living was new to all of us, and this was our first challenge at making a decision that would affect all of us, intimately, for the whole year. The vote was unanimous.

"Go get Geoff," Bill said.

"Geoff, we want you to join us on the river. Think about it," Bill said.

"Gwamps, I don't have to think about it. I'm ready. What will I need? When do we leave?"

We were all thrilled. It just felt right. It would change everything, but we'd adjust our minds, and move ahead with this new plan. We'd put off our departure from Denver for another few days while we'd help Geoff gather gear, and put his affairs in order, which to a college student really wouldn't take all that long.

"WHAT?" I heard screams from the kitchen. Then a pan slammed on the counter. Geoff had gone to tell the good news to Jane, his mother.

"Dad, you can't just waltz in here and change Geoff's college plans just like that. Cath, you're free to go off and do a river whenever you like, but don't go dragging my son into the scheme! He's not going. He's going back to college in the fall. And that's that!"

Bill said, "Jane, come outside, let's talk."

"NO!"

"Jane," now I was afraid I'd hear dishes dropping to the floor, "come outside. Please."

Again, Bill was calm. If this situation were to be turned from disaster to triumph, it would require Bill's calm approach. A half hour went by. An hour.

"Who wants scrambled? Who wants poached?" Jane called. "Let's eat while Geoff gets his gear together and makes a few calls."

I've never asked Bill what he said to Jane that morning, but I know it must have included something about never ever getting into bed at night wondering what you could have done, what you could have accomplished, if you'd only followed your heart. That was always our coming together point. We'd had choices in life, should we go to Russia, or work in Boston? Should we open our own business or work for someone else? Always we'd make lists on paper napkins, sitting in some deli, or coffee shop, as we discussed our future. We'd write all the pros on the left, the cons on the right, add them up, and then turn to each other and ask what our hearts were telling us. To heck with what seemed the right thing to do. What did our hearts tell us? I think that's one way God speaks to us. By placing a desire in our hearts. Our job, then, is to follow. Sounds simple. In reality, though, it's hard. As it was for Jane that morning. She came around, though, at her father's calm, gentle nudging. We scrambled eggs as Geoff began to pack.

Now we were five. And two dogs. Two canoes and a kayak on top of two trucks. And maps to Three Forks, Montana, where we agreed to meet at noon in three days at the post office. On the way, we stopped at Mary Helen's house in Longmont, Colorado. We'd met her ten years before, and to this day depend on her to keep us abreast of current events. She's like a news hound, always knowing what's going on in politics, in environmental issues, in international affairs, in local communities. She has a special slant on news. She keeps a high ideal, and demands that those around her do the same, so it's always a pleasure to be with her. Besides that, she's a marvelous cook. It was peach season, and we knew her fresh peach ice cream was the best west of the Mississippi. And might be our last ice cream for a year. And we wanted Geoff and Donna to meet her. We had a grand evening together. She'd arranged for a reporter to interview us. After he left, we had fond goodbyes and promised to keep her up-to-date on our location, even using her as a clearinghouse for others to follow our expedition. Then we were off. Oh, one more thing about Mary Helen. She doesn't see. Or hear.

Bill and I decided to spend a couple nights at a hotel, albeit, a rundown, dusty one in Cheyenne, Wyoming, almost a deserted ghost town. The next morning we walked the streets downtown, trying to get a sense of this town. Western cafes, western clothing stores, western gift shops, and a beauty school. A beauty school? We raced through the doors and made appointments for haircuts, facials, manicures, pedicures, wax dips. All afternoon we were buffed, cleaned, clipped, and polished. Just right for the Lewis and Clark trail. I thought of Sacagawea.

The next day we drove through Montana and realized why it's called the Big Sky state. The sky reaches all around you. The land goes right up to it. We arrived in Three Forks just at noon and saw the other truck waiting at the post office, just as planned. Geoff and Donna and Jen had gotten there just a few minutes before. Everything was going just as planned. I'll never be able to write that sentence again.

Jen introduced us to Laura, the filmmaker/documentarian, who immediately began to film our meeting, our beginning of the river. We had lunch in a small café. The locals seemed to be interested in our expedition. They wanted to help in any way they could. One drew maps to the river, another gave us a book on Lewis and Clark, and another gave us two bags of rhubarb from his garden. That night we set up camp on the banks of the dashing Missouri River. We had chicken and rhubarb crisp for dinner. Our pots were shiny. Our tents were sweet-smelling. Our boats were polished. Our hearts were eager. Our night was peaceful. I'll never be able to write those sentences again.

Early the next morning we were awakened by the park ranger. "What are these canoes doing here?" he asked.

"We're going to canoe the river to the Gulf of Mexico," we beamed.

"Not this year, you're not," he said.

"What?"

"The river's running much too fast. The snows were heavy this winter."

"What do you mean?"

"I mean," he said, "The river would eat you up just the way the mosquitoes are doing."

He was right. We were each mosquito-bitten so that our faces were puffed up, and our legs were bloody from where they bit right through our jeans. But what about the river? We were great at adapting our plans, but this, this meant our year was turned completely upside down.

"We're allowed to, right?" I said.

"Sure, but you'd be crazy to put in this river right now. Give it a couple of months to settle down."

A couple of months? A couple of months? What were we supposed to do for a couple of months? Then he was off.

We were dumbfounded. Stunned. And the whole thing was on film. Nobody spoke. I'll never be able to write that sentence again.

Laugh At You

Jen

June in Montana is still spring and the days dawn blustery and cold. Our plans of a mid-June put-in blew away with the winds that chopped the water we so desperately wanted to be on. After prepping our boats at the headwaters and scouting the pace of the river near Three Forks, we decided that a current that swift would surely dump our inexperienced little paddling selves into the river quicker than our egos (and our desire for dry gear) could handle; we moved our put-in to the first lake on the river, Canyon Ferry Lake.

So there we were, a caravan of trucks and boats, heading downriver… on the road. Diehards will say we were chickens, but my experience leading outdoor education courses told me otherwise. "Accurate self-assessment is everything," we said as we stood in the parking lot just below the dam that forms Canyon Ferry Lake, the put-in here a rocky and steep descent. It was getting on toward late afternoon, and our first day on the "river" was not on the river at all, rather, it was spent trying to find a place that would let us get on the river. I found myself thinking that perhaps she didn't want us on her after all. I now know that it wasn't that exactly. No, this day she was teaching us patience, and that maybe we weren't in as much control as we thought we were; she was the one in control. This lesson would take months for me to learn, this yielding to the river, allowing her to dictate our time and motion. We bedded down at a campground on the shores of Canyon Ferry Lake and planned our put-in for the morning.

"Accurate self-assessment is everything," we said the next morning as we stood on the shore and watched the lake throw three-foot rollers toward the sky. We resorted to re-packing the dry bags and putting one more layer of seam-seal on the tents. Months later I would recognize wind as the harshest of the elements we would face. Wind is inescapable. You can't hide from it as you can rain; our wonderful REI tents provided excellent coverage from rain but only magnified the wind's deafening presence. More often it would be wind that would keep us off the river, not rain. These first days were the beginning of the lesson, however, and our frustration with a slow start was beginning to show. The afternoon walk that Donna, Geoff and I took was quiet, save for the howl of the wind. Our inexperience showed through that night as we sat after dinner discussing that tomorrow, indeed, we would put in. No more of this waiting around for us.

But the next two days were windy and wet, and the third morning dawned as the others – windy, windy, windy. The sun was shining and we mistakenly took this as a good sign. We loaded the boats, threw away our watches, and set out. There were waves and cheers. Finally, we were on the river.

Canoeing on a lake with twenty mile per hour crosswinds is not the smartest thing to do. Canoeing on a lake with a thunderstorm rolling in is a stupid thing to do, but we wouldn't recognize that until it was three hours too late. Three boats – two canoes and a kayak – each laden with gear, food, dogs and people, made slow progress along the shores of the windswept lake. After two hours of paddling, shouting through the noise of the wind, and trying to get our paddle strokes synchronized, we pulled into a small sandy beach for a quick re-con. As we got out of the boats, Diva running to investigate the new scenery, we looked back at our campsite from the night before. We could see it plainly. We realized that we had not gone more than a mile.

Donna captured our collective thoughts when she said with a wry smile in her voice, "Well, we've only got 3,999 miles to go."

This first mile will stay with me always. The wind, the sense of self that mistakenly put us on the water in a windstorm that was simply the precursor to the rain that was coming, the sheer joy of having put paddle to water, all of these things stay with me today, and I know, even though I have learned that the river is the one who is in control, that I would repeat this folly just to hear Donna's words and the laughter that followed.

"Only 3,999 miles to go."

We did get rained on, and we didn't melt. The REI tents held up well, the dogs probably slept better than we did, and the next morning came quiet as a lamb. The lake was as smooth as a piece of glass and the miles flew by. I watched as Donna and Geoff drew closer together as paddling partners. I was beginning to better learn the balance points of the kayak, and Mom and Bill seemed to be falling back into their known pattern of paddling *E. coli* together. There was a sweetness in watching them as I listened to the sound of our paddles carrying us across waters that had come out of the Rockies. Mom and Bill had met by a river, and they were returning to one now some twenty years later. There was more than paddling going on.

We had four lakes to cross before getting to free-flowing river, and we paddled on each of them. I can't say that we paddled the length of each of them, but we did paddle on each of them. Some will say that this means we didn't paddle the river as we set out to do. I will say that setting out to paddle the Missouri River and thinking one knows exactly how it is going to turn out is naïve. Of course, we did think we knew how it was going to turn out, but we were learning quickly that we were, simply put, wrong.

Laugh At You

Cate

As I was to learn many times during this adventure, the hardest part was making group decisions. The whirlpools, the freezing cold, the swarms of mosquitoes, even the capsize, wasn't as hard as this new group decision-making, for me. Throughout our lives we make the biggest decisions alone. Now, I had to join a group to decide how to wash the dinner pots, or which side of the river to paddle, and now, what to do about this dubious beginning of A Year Without Time …the expedition.

Two hundred years before, on this very spot, Meriwether Lewis and William Clark had named the three rivers that form the Missouri's headwaters:

> …We were …induced to discontinue the name of Missouri, and gave to the southwest branch the name of Jefferson, in honor of the President of the United States and the projector of the enterprise (the Lewis and Clark expedition). We called the middle branch Madison, after James Madison, Secretary of State. These two, as well as Gallatin river (named for the Secretary of the Treasury), run with great velocity and throw out large bodies of water.

Not much had changed in 200 years! The river was still running "with great velocity." Had we come all this way simply to turn around and go home for a few more months till the river settled down? Could we all have stayed at our jobs longer? Would we have the same passion for the expedition if we went home and came back later? What about our sponsors who'd already begun to advertise our expedition. How much were we each prepared to risk? Our lives? And, how would a group make this decision, which was even bigger than the one we each made, in our own space and time, to do the expedition in the first place? Should we have done more homework?

All these questions were tossed around as we loaded the canoes on top of the trucks, not knowing where we were going with them.

I stood there and thought of our chickens. When Bill and I bought a farm on Beaver Island in the middle of Lake Michigan, my kids gave me five chickens for my birthday. Wonderful, free-range chickens, who produced the biggest, yellowest-yolked eggs I'd ever seen. One day I noticed that one of the chickens didn't look well. I carefully explained to Bill that we'd have to chop off its head and bury it to put it out of its misery. He spent all morning carrying out his assignment while I made a little cross out of twigs to put over the grave. The next day, another chicken had the same look. Bill got out his axe, I made another little cross. At week's end, we had five little crosses on our farm.

On Saturday I went to the local market where a farmer, who knew we didn't know anything about farming, yelled across the market, "Hey, Cate. How ya doin'? How're the chickens doing? Have they started to molt yet?"

MOLT YET? We didn't know chickens lost their feathers each year! We should have done our homework…

"What if we go downriver to where the river runs smoother?" Geoff said. "What about one of the lakes, maybe Canyon Ferry Lake, just twenty miles down? A lake probably runs slower than the river."

When we thought of the entire 4000-mile trip, what was twenty miles?

We had decided that we'd always take a truck, say, 100 miles downriver to be waiting for us when we took out. This time Geoff and Bill drove both trucks to the end of a series of lakes on the Missouri River, and left one truck at Wolf Creek at the end of Holter Lake. They drove the other truck back and joined us at the Canyon Ferry Lake put-in.

By the time they returned it was dark, so we had a quick dinner of sardines, Gatorade, and Oreos. While Laura filmed, we pitched our still-new tents, took the dogs for one last run and snuggled into sleeping bags, dreaming of beginning the river early the next day.

It rained the next day.

And the next.

On the third day, at eight in the morning, we piled into Jenny and Donna's now soggy tent to make a group decision. When we all climbed out fifteen minutes later, the decision was to get our gear together, pack the canoes, and begin A Year Without Time …the expedition. Rain or not. We simply needed to do something. We'd waited long enough. We had cabin fever. And I was beginning to think about the commitment I had to do a week of seminars beginning just two weeks from today. I wanted to do what we came here to do, even if it was just for a few days.

By ten o'clock, we were all packed, the truck was locked and parked where we would pick it up in a couple of weeks. Laura had her tripod set up so she'd get the first paddled strokes of each canoe. We all posed at river's edge to throw our four-dollar watches into the air as we symbolically began A Year Without Time …the expedition. We were all smiles as we zipped our REI fleece jackets up under our chins.

The lake was rough with a few white caps in the middle where the wind was stirring up a bit. We followed one canoe after the other, staying pretty close to shore to avoid the wind and its chill. A few sprays of the Missouri River sloshed over the gunwales and we had to bail water from the bottom of the boats. The wind whipped around us as we each pulled hats lower over our ears. I noticed that my shoes were wet from the light rain. Soon I pulled the bandana from around my neck and tied it over my nose and around in back, bandit style, to protect my cheeks and lips and neck from the wind. It was blowing hard now. I groped for my sunglasses in my jacket pocket between paddle strokes. Although there was no sun, maybe they'd protect my eyes from what was becoming a vicious wind.

Each paddle stroke took us only a few inches, literally. The wind was pushing us back further than the paddles were taking us ahead. Bill and I tried to keep up with Jen and Donna and Geoff, but the fight against the wind was making my arms ache. Now my socks were soaked and my feet were cold and numb. I was in the bow, paddling with all my strength, cursing and crying silently so Bill wouldn't notice. This was not what I had in mind on that day in our cozy Kansas City apartment. This was not what I wanted to do for the next year. I glanced under my arm as I brought the paddle up, and noticed that Bill was shaking. We were cold and wet and tired.

The other boats were just specks in the distance now but we noticed they'd pulled up to shore. Were they waiting for us? Would we always be the slow paddlers? We'd been paddling for three hours and had gone maybe a mile. Another fifteen minutes and we pulled alongside the other boats where Jen and Donna and Geoff were on shore, huddled together to stay warm. Our faces were swollen from windburn, our clothes were sopped, the boats were filling up with water, the dogs were whining.

At river's edge, standing in a circle, shivering, muscles aching, nobody said a word. Was this what the whole expedition would be?

Donna broke the silence. "Well, we only have 3,999 more miles to go."

Our windburned lips parted and we all began to laugh. If this were the way it was to be, as long as we could laugh, it'd be ok.

We pitched the tents, stripped off our wet clothes, crawled into damp sleeping bags, and fell asleep without lunch or dinner.

The next morning was sunny and calm. It was as if we'd passed our test, and were now ready for the reward. We paddled all day, and well into the bright evening, finally on the Missouri River.

You Don't Have To Please Everyone

Jen

The second lake on the Missouri is Hauser Lake. Hauser Lake is probably best known for the marina at the north end that is the launching point for hour-long shuttle boat tours into the Gates of the Mountains, a portion of the Missouri River renowned for its stark cliffs and historical significance. We arrived at the marina in the late afternoon and opted to camp on the spit of land that is nestled between the marina and the point one rounds to enter the Gates of the Mountains. The shore was covered with four-foot high reeds into which we nestled the tents.

By this time we had gotten into a routine of setting up camp in the evening: tents up first, change into dry clothes and socks, place the sleeping bags out to fluff and the sleeping pads to inflate, feed Diva and Gypsy, fire up the little stove and start a pot of water for cocoa (evenings in Montana in June are nippy) and rattle around in the food bins for a dinner plan. Sometime mid-dinner Diva would usually make her way to the door of our tent and wait to be let in, the sinking sun making it too cold for her liking. Donna created what came to be known as the "Diva Burrito," a soft sleeping bag and pad (yes, Diva had her own sleeping bag and pad) all snuggled around her brown body, only her soft ears and snout poking out.

I had read about the Gates of the Mountains, but didn't really believe it: 200-foot high cliffs coming right down to the water's edge. Lewis and Clark had named this passage based on what they saw coming through this section of river. Heading up-river, as they were nearly 200 years earlier, they had seen the Rockies through the narrow passage the cliffs formed, and aptly named this section of river the "Gates of the Mountains." Now, as the sun was setting over Hauser Lake and the marina traffic was calming, I wondered if the spirit and wonder Meriwether Lewis had recorded in his journal would also find us in the Gates of the Mountains. A breeze started up as I zipped the door of the tent. Our tent fly flapped against the interior shell. Donna was already in the sleeping bags and Diva's soft snoring sounded familiar. After a week on the river, the thin nylon tent that separated us from the outer world was slowly becoming home.

Cocoa and oatmeal and packing up the tents warmed us the next morning; an eagerness to get on the water and round the point permeated our movements. Mom was just packing up the last of the pots when she turned to her right and yelled sternly, "Gypsy, No!"

We all stopped moving and turned to watch. "Gypsy, come here!"

Gypsy had her nose in the reeds, just beyond the matted-down patch from Mom and Bill's tent. Gypsy adores my mother, but she is not what one would consider an obedient dog. She stood her ground. "Gypsy, come here!" my mother yelled again, and this time Gypsy slowly trotted to Mom's side.

"What is it, Mom?" I said.

"Listen."

We all fell quiet as a faint rattle came from the spot Gypsy had spied. A rattler was coiled somewhere in those reeds, and Gypsy had found it. The boat packing picked up in pace and we were on the water in record time. Gypsy would prove to be a great finder of wildlife, and would often alert us to animals before anyone else could sense them.

Moving from Hauser Lake into the channel that cuts through the Gates of the Mountains was the first time we felt a current on the river. Geoff was in the kayak this morning, and Donna and I paddled with Diva while Mom and Bill had Gypsy as their mascot. Just as we came into the Gates we noticed a mountain goat on the eastern side of the river, high atop the cliffs.

"Look at that mountain goat!" I said. "Do you think there are many of them here?"

The current carried us past spruce and scrub and further into the canyon. As we approached the first bend in the river I looked back to the eastern cliff. The mountain goat was still there.

"Hey, I think he isn't moving," I said. "Maybe he's sick."

Bill promptly raised his monocular to his eye and, after almost a full minute, chuckled.

"What's so funny, Bill?"

It turns out the mountain goat was plastic, a gimmick used for the shuttle boat tours that launch from the marina. The rattler was real, but the mountain goat a sham. We were batting .500.

Paddling a river is kind of like being on a train – the speed is handled by someone else and the stops are limited by the availability of station platforms. So it was in the Gates of the Mountains. We drifted along, using our paddles only to keep us off fallen trees at the water's edge, and simply drank it all in; even Diva was taking note. The cliffs rose out of the water, giving way to the blue Montana sky after forming a gorge some 200 feet deep. There was a quiet that cut through the excitement, bringing a calm that soothed the frustrations of the past week. This was the beginning of the river for me. I was captivated by the starkness of the cliffs and the quiet that brought me to consider the history of this particular portion of the river. Somehow floating past cliffs that were best inhabited by the native peoples, and that have never been able to be tamed by the white man, brought me a reverence that I hadn't felt since being on a NOLS course in the Wind River Mountains in Wyoming thirteen years earlier. There, standing on the edge of a 2000-foot precipice, newly fallen snow brought a quiet that only nature can produce.

We stopped about midway through the Gates at a landing that is used by the tours, got out and poked around. The dogs investigated the new smells and we each took advantage of stable ground for a long-awaited pee. Five PowerBars later we were back in the boats and heading north. The second half of the Gates of the Mountains brought cliffs that were steeper and rockier. Somehow we couldn't bring ourselves to paddle, the river carrying us along quickly enough, each of us knowing that however much we wanted to stay and soak in the quiet, the current was determining our pace.

The cliffs gave way to rolling green hills, home to what we thought looked like mule deer. I was back in the kayak at this point, and found myself paddling upstream and then down, connecting the canoes with a zigzag trail, as the kayak could cover more ground, so to speak, more quickly. Evening was falling and the search for a campsite was on. The rolling hills were too steep to hold a pitched tent. We pulled the boats alongside the western shore and tied them to boulders covered with lichen. We were in high desert, a dry, green, sandy environment, with (I know this sounds crazy) cactus in Montana. Mom found a purple cactus flower and tied it to *E. coli's* bow.

The only place we could pitch a tent was on top of a hill, so we unloaded just the gear we thought we'd need and started the trek up. The thought of the morning's rattler was with me as I picked my way through the sandy vegetation. A flat rock slab on the top of the hill acted as home for the night and we bunked down. As I slipped into my sleeping bag I realized how the scenery of the day had overloaded my senses and I knew that sleep was not far away. The Gates of the Mountains had taken me from the rush of the world into the calm of the river. This was a different place, a different pace. As I closed my eyes I wondered if I could slow enough to feel only the river's current.

You Don't Have To Please Everyone

Cate

At lunch I called over to Jen's boat, "Jen, I'm making sandwiches, do you want jelly with your peanut butter? Does Donna?"

"Jelly for me, Mom. You'll have to ask Donna what she wants," she replied.

To this day I use that as my guide. The respect Jen and Donna have for each other is stunning, something I've never seen in any other couple. Jen taught me that a closeness, even a marriage, doesn't give one the right to think for another person, to make decisions for another.

The next week was filled with gentle paddling, good campfire meals, laughter, breathtaking views of Montana, and a camera lens in our faces. We tired quickly of having a camera capture our every move.

Laura was nice, but her mission was getting on our nerves. She'd drive her truck and gear several miles ahead, perch her camera on a ledge high above the river and we were supposed to wave as we paddled by. At night she'd film our group meetings, our decision-making, our loving each other, and laughing at each other.

One night, when Laura drove to the closest town to make a phone call, we decided that we wanted this to be a private family expedition, not a filmed one. We were tired of smiling at all the right places, of combing our hair before peeing in the mornings, of being so goddamned nice all the time.

We didn't know how to explain all that to Laura. After lots of discussion we decided that maybe <u>she</u> didn't need to change at all, that maybe we were the ones who needed to change, to forget the camera was even there. We'd try harder.

When she returned from town she called us all together to tell us that she'd made a decision. She said that it wasn't working for her, that she wasn't able to get the story she wanted. Our hearts held our collective breath. Maybe we would offer to help her pack up…

Then she said, "I think I need to be in the boats with you."

Jen's eyes met mine, then dropped to the ground. Our hearts did too. We didn't have a business agreement with Laura. We could have ended it all right there, but we'd promised each other that this expedition was to bring good things to many besides just our family. We truly wanted to share it with as many folks as possible. And here was Laura, trying her best to bring the adventure alive by way of a documentary. Yes, we needed to try harder.

The boat Laura picked was a Russian inflatable dinghy eighty-five year-old Volodya had given me for my birthday one year in Moscow. We would take turns puffing it up whenever he and Klava came to dinner at our one-room apartment. By the time we'd finish blowing it up, he would have finished half a bottle of vodka. Always we'd end up sitting in the dinghy, under the table, singing The Volga Boat Song in the faint morning Moscow light. Now, we'd brought along the dinghy just for fun. Laura said she'd tie it to the back of the last canoe and film from there.

Next morning she did just that. Problem was, Russians are not known for their workmanship. Laura's dinghy sprang a leak, and she and her cameras went down just as we entered the Gates of the Mountains, a spot where steep, towering cliffs line the river for miles, and create a great, echoing canyon. As Laura clambered into our canoe, Gypsy began to whine and didn't stop for the whole year. So now in our canoe were Bill, me, Gypsy,

Laura, all of our gear, and all of Laura's which we could save from gurgling to the bottom of the river.

We couldn't put Laura out. The cliffs come straight to the river's edge, with no take-out possible. She rode with us for the rest of the day. On the second day the cliffs slowly began to give way to forest. Around dinnertime we saw what looked like a tiny village on the river's edge. As we got closer we read a sign, "Indian Creek Restaurant," and paddled right up. The village, it turned out, was only accessible from the river. There were no roads leading to the half-dozen houses. No electricity. No running water. We had the fattest, juiciest hamburgers, and afterwards used the most elaborate outhouse in the West.

That night Laura said that as soon as we came to a take-out, she thought she'd head for home.

"Well, it's not all that interesting, anyway," I said to cheer her. "There really isn't much to film."

But, then, I didn't know what was around the next bend.

Welcome Risk Into Your Life

Jen

Geoff grabbed my bow line as I drifted past. The river was choppy, the surface mimicking what I imagined the bottom of the river looked like: boulders the size of piano benches lined the edge of the river as she moved swiftly through the narrow channel. This pattern had held true for the past week of paddling – the surface of the river appeared to be determined by the edges. When the edge of the channel was a soft, hummocky joinery of water and earth, reeds drooping over themselves, pricking the water as it flowed past, the river itself was soft and mellow. As we dropped out of the mountains and started losing elevation more quickly, the river had eaten through the edge's soil, revealing boulders that would snag… and spit if provoked.

This change in temperament of the river seemed to be telling us to be awake, to stay alert, that she was taking over; now that she was free of those pesky lakes and dams, she was going to have some fun. I had been drifting for some time, the kayak cutting through the water more quickly than either of the canoes. I had learned to point her downstream, or up, and let the current carry me. My double-bladed paddle served as a rudder of sorts, one blade dipping in behind my right hip, steering me into the chop that lapped over the top of my boat.

Just before Geoff grabbed my line, I had spun 180 degrees to face upstream. Paddling alone afforded me time to daydream – thoughts of work dropping away as the sun's shine on my face deepened – but paddling alone was also lonely. I had spun around to watch the canoes coming downriver, to feel the waves in the river bob my boat, and me, backwards.

“Hey there,” Geoff’s voice called.

I was growing to know Geoff over the days. What had grown into a young man in his first nineteen years reminded me of what had grown into a young woman in my first nineteen years; the maleness of brash youth seemed to wash over to my female upbringing and I had thought it natural to be nineteen and wanting strength above all else.

“Hungry?” I said.

“I could go for something to eat, yeah,” came his gentle reply.

“Donna, want some lunch?”

The days without watches were still cordoned by appetites, and we seemed to be eating on the three-square schedule on which we had been reared. Watches or no, our tummies were keeping time just fine.

“Umm-hmmm, how about some PB & J?” she said.

Donna was in the bow of the canoe, which was heading downstream, and she was at this point behind me, as I was facing upstream. I turned around to catch her eye and wink. The first week of the trip had brought rain and wind and miles of paddling, beautiful sunsets and brisk mornings, camp-stove cuisine and sunscreen, but it had not brought much privacy. I winked at her to try to say, ‘I see you. And I know you. And you know me.’ The gesture likely held more significance for me than for her, but it was all the privacy we had at the moment.

“OK – lunch at the next landing. I bet Mom and Bill will be along in a –”

I was in mid-sentence when I saw it. I had been watching Mom and Bill’s silhouette upstream as our two-boat flotilla had been bobbing downstream over the choppy water. As we were pondering lunch, they appeared to have stopped and were getting smaller and farther away from us. The river had just taken a turn around a bend, and I was beginning to lose them in my line of sight, the bow of their canoe getting hidden by the rocks lining the river's edge.

And then, they got shorter.

I was puzzled in my mid-sentence and my mouth stopped forming words. Shorter, in a boat? How does that happen? I tried to form words to explain what I was seeing to Geoff and Donna, but my mind had not caught up. We floated around the bend and I lost sight of them completely.

"I think something is happening with Mom and Bill," I said.

"Are they far behind us?" Geoff asked.

"No, they were right there, it's just that –"

"Jenny, get Bill!"

A shout came from the banks. I looked up and saw my mother running along the railroad tracks on the bank, her paddle in the air.

"Get Bill!" She yelled again and I noticed at this point that she was soaked. I looked upstream and saw her yellow lifejacket bobbing on the tops of the river's choppy waves.

"Geoff – untie us – they've capsized!" Geoff moved quickly to try to disconnect the two boats but couldn't get the lines untied for what seemed like five minutes, but was probably only twenty seconds. I watched as bright red REI dry-bags came floating toward us. Mom had almost reached us and was yelling that they had flipped, that she had been shot toward the shore and that she couldn't see Bill.

I paddled upstream once our flotilla was untied and Geoff and Donna turned their boat around. Around the bend came more gear bags, paddles, food bags, sleeping pads and finally, an upside-down *E. coli*, the red Kevlar canoe

Mom and Bill paddled, with Bill hanging on to the stern. He had done the right thing by staying with the boat; Bill can't swim.

Donna and Geoff reached him first and he grabbed the bow of their boat, smiling to Donna.

"Good to see you," he said.

They headed to shore to deposit him to Mom, and I made my way to *E. coli* as she turned slightly and revealed a soaking Gypsy Dog. I pulled Gypsy into my lap and got to shore just behind Geoff and Donna. The shore here was rocky and reedy and Geoff helped Bill make his way to the railroad tracks as Donna held their boat in the current.

Three soaked beings stood on the tracks, the day grey and cool, and I knew hypothermia was our next concern.

"Get Bill's blue pack – it has his journal in it."

My mother's voice caused my head to turn downstream. I saw the dry bags, backpacks and gear floating toward the next bend. A quick computation told me that if we let the gear go we would lose a lot of time getting re-outfitted. Our trip had gotten off to a shaky start, late and slow, and I didn't want us to delay getting on with our progress. It was at this point that I made what was perhaps the biggest mistake of my backcountry-travel career and yelled to Donna, "I'm going after the gear – see if you can get Bill warm – hypothermia is the biggest danger now."

Donna looked at me with what I have come to understand as a look of wisdom, formed through more years than I have spent on the earth, which is always right.

"Jen, don't go alone – it's crazy to split up," she yelled.

"I can cover more ground in the kayak," I yelled across the wind, the day growing colder. I untied the bags on the kayak and unloaded as much gear as I could.

"Get Bill warm, that's the most important thing right now." And with that, I hopped back in my boat and headed downstream.

As I paddled away I felt heroic, the way young men must feel when responding to testosterone. I was going to save the gear. I was disobeying the rules that I had learned, and later taught, in my time climbing and backpacking: never go out alone, take care of people first, replace the gear second. Perhaps it was the sense that my identity was shifting – that which had defined me at my work just six weeks earlier was gone, and the river trip had yet to set roles for the group.

I had taught Outdoor Leadership courses for three years before being on the river trip, and was always in the role of instructor. I was sensing from the group that the instructor role was not one that existed on this trip, and I was trying to find my spot, my identity. If "Saviour-of-Gear" was up for grabs, I was going after it.

The kayak handled differently without the forty pounds of gear strapped to her deck, and we almost skated across the waves. The first piece of gear I saw bobbing in the water was a water jug. It was behind everything else, as it was mostly full and traveled lower in the water. I pulled up beside it and hauled it onto my lap. Two dry bags were next and I attached them to the deck. I had to drop the gear to make room for more so I made my first stash on the left bank. I headed on downstream and retrieved Bill's blue backpack and another dry bag. Another left-bank stash and I was heading for the lighter items – two paddles and two lifejackets. "Why weren't they wearing them," I thought, as I grabbed them from the rapids. Two sleeping pads later and all that was left was one paddle. It was the nicest paddle Mom and Bill had – a $100 model that Kansas City Paddler had given us – a thing of beauty that lifted itself out of the water with every stroke. Paddling with this paddle was pure heaven. I traversed the river three times before giving up – it had beaten me downstream.

The bends were getting closer together, the channel narrower and the river was starting to form rapids. I had been retrieving gear for what seemed like two hours and knew I had to get off the water if I was going to make it back to camp by nightfall. I looked for that paddle at every bend and seine for the next 1500 miles of paddling. What had made the paddle so luxurious in our hands is also what sped it downriver more quickly than any other piece of gear – its feather-light weight. This truth – the most beautiful quality bringing vulnerability – would be repeated many times in the coming months and years. The river had a premonition that day, the water alerting us. I hadn't expected the lessons to flow so freely and early in the trip.

As I pulled my boat twenty yards inland on the left bank I realized the mistake I had made. I was more than two miles downstream from the group, gear and food; the bank I was on was steep and rocky. I had to retrieve gear that was, at some spots, forty feet down a rocky incline, and I was soaking wet. I had put myself, and therefore, the group, in danger. The Saviour-of-Gear title didn't seem so glamorous as the sun started its decline toward the horizon.

In the coming twilight, I could see a tent pitched on a hill beyond the railroad tracks. Two people were sitting outside of the tent in Crazy Creek camp chairs, the shadows of early evening falling over them. I arrived in camp with the retrieved gear, could tell Mom, yes, I had gotten Bill's blue backpack, and could barely meet Donna's eyes. She had been right, and had, by my exiting the scene, been put in charge of keeping my mother and Bill from getting hypothermic. She didn't mind this task, but had no formal training in it, and felt as if she were in over her head. I learned that night, in the dark of our sloping tent, that my sweetest friend in the entire world had been worried about me, and simply wanted me to be safe. She was right about the gear – it could all have been replaced, yes, even the journal could have been rewritten – and she was right about me.

I learned a new sense of love that night.

After Donna drifted off to sleep and Diva's snore rolled softly through the tent, I realized that my role was to be Donna's partner, her best buddy, and the one person in the world who would not fail her. As I listened to the river's constant flow past our camp I remembered the dim feeling I had experienced months earlier about the cost of wanderlust. I had seen it today, and wondered if I could reconcile my account with my future – if I could absorb the cost and live a new role.

I dreamed that night of being in the river's flow, the boulders glancing me off the shores. As I approached the place my kayak had been stashed, it was not there, as if the reeds had swallowed it up. I saw visions of myself floating the rest of the way downriver, through Montana, the Dakotas, Iowa and Kansas. I was constantly cold and bobbed along feet-first through the rapids and into the high desert.

I found myself at the foot of our incline-pitched tent (the banks didn't have any flat area where the capsize had happened), my knees tucked under me, the nylon of the sleeping bag tight against my skin. I moved my shoulders back up the incline until my head was even with Donna's. Her soft and steady breathing settled me back into the present; the night swallowed me whole.

Welcome Risk Into Your Life

Cate

The rain began again, so we set up camp quickly, emptied the boats and tried to sort gear, all the while sloshing along the muddy bank of a state park. We built a fire under a tarp we rigged in some trees, grilled six of the fourteen trout some fishermen had given us, and tumbled into our tents. I wished we'd had lemons and butter for the trout. And French bread. And pastries. And Hershey bars. And lemon meringue pie.

As we packed up the next morning, and wished Laura all the best, we secretly sighed sighs of relief to be on our own. What kind of documentary would it have been anyway? A whining mother, her eighty year-old husband, a couple of unemployed computer geniuses and a college dropout, letting the river take us where she will.

After the boats were packed the next morning, I asked what had happened to the other eight trout. "We took care of them, Mom." Jenny replied. I saw her exchange glances with Geoff, but thought nothing of it. We shoved off into a calm river, with a warm sun overhead.

As we rounded the first bend in the river we saw Laura high up on a cliff waving goodbye to us and filming our first paddled strokes of the day, and the last strokes she was to film.

That's when it happened. We had just waved our paddles in her direction and saw her take down her tripod and pack up her gear, and head her truck toward Pennsylvania.

"Anyone hungry?" I yelled up river to Jen in her kayak and Donna and Geoff in their canoe. "The river seems calm. Let's float and eat. Put out your anchors."

Their boats slowed, they pulled beside each other, and Bill dropped our anchor. We didn't stop. The anchor wasn't stopping us. Then, all of a sudden, we lurched to an abrupt stop. The anchor must have caught on a rock underwater. *E. coli* trembled slightly. Then she began to rock back and forth. Then she began to roll with the current.

"Bill, pull up the anchor before she rolls over." I called. She was rocking furiously now. Water was pouring into the boat. My water bottle floated away into the river, followed by our spare paddle.

"Bill," I yelled, "Cut the anchor line."

"I just paid twenty dollars for this line," he yelled, "I'm not going to cut it."

"Cut the damn line!" I yelled.

We were both holding on to the gunwales now to keep our balance. Gyp was being tossed from side to side. As I reached for Gyp's collar to steady her, the boat lurched starboard. Gypsy had a look of terror in her eyes as though she'd seen her life pass before her, then she was gone. The river took her.

The next thing I knew I was in the icy water, thrown with such force that in a second my head hit a boulder on the bottom of the river.

I'm a lifeguard. I'm a good swimmer. At that instant, however, with my muscles cramping from the cold, and my head aching, I lost my sense of where I was. It was like being in a blinding snowstorm, not knowing which direction I was going. Which way was up? Where was the shore?

And where was Bill? He wasn't a swimmer. As a Navy recruit, he'd been tossed in a pool at Great Lakes Naval Training Center in 1942 and had been fished out with a pole. Then, in all its wisdom, without as much as one swimming lesson, the Navy put him on a destroyer for three years in the South Pacific.

I put one foot in front of the other till my feet touched bottom. I knew I'd be out of the river if I could just keep going. The temptation to stop, though, was strong. My arms and legs felt like lead. Every fiber of muscle ached. Then I was on rocks along the shoreline. Without thinking, I clambered to the top of the riverbank, and began to run downriver yelling for Bill all the while. I'd lost one shoe and was running on sharp rocks lining a railroad bed. I could see the canoe, which had finally loosed itself from the rock and was floating languidly upside-down.

I couldn't see Bill. As I ran, I saw our gear float by, spreading across the river like a blanket of nylon and rubber and plastic.

I thought of my children's baby pictures I always keep with me.

Years before, while canoeing the Rhein, I'd let Bill out to make camp, but couldn't get the canoe to shore, so took it downriver where there seemed to be a landing. Without Bill and the gear as ballast, the canoe went faster and faster till I was caught in a whirlpool just above a dam and waterfall. I simply couldn't paddle out of the whirlpool, so jumped overboard to safety. The police report in Zurzach, Switzerland told of pulling me out of the river while I cried about losing my children's pictures.

Now, running along the railroad tracks on the banks of the Missouri, dripping wet and shivering, with bleeding feet, I didn't want warm clothes, or dry matches for a fire, or a warm sleeping bag. All I thought about was my children's pictures and Bill. Had he gone down? Had he drowned? Had he frozen to death?

I heard Jen's voice. "Mom, we've got Bill. Grab the bow line." I followed her instructions, not thinking for myself. She'd paddled the kayak upriver to

E. coli, and nudged it to shore, grabbing Bill at the side of the canoe where he'd been clinging since he went overboard.

"Is he ok?" I yelled as I pulled the canoe by the bow line to shore.

"I'm cold," he shouted, "but I'm ok." Then, "Oh, my god… Gyp!" I looked up to see Gyp, a good-sized dog, perched on Bill's head. She'd been trapped under the canoe in an air pocket, whimpering, and climbed to the highest spot, Bill's head, as I pulled the canoe ashore and Jen scooped Gyp into the kayak cockpit.

By now, Donna and Geoff had made their way to where we were collapsed on the rocks on shore. Jen yelled, "Take care of Mom and Bill while I try to retrieve some of their gear." Then she was off across the river trying to save paddles and food and dry bags floating, just as the brochures had promised.

While Bill and I shivered and sputtered, Donna stripped our wet clothes off us, stripped off her own dry ones, and dressed us in her still-warm clothing. Geoff brought their sleeping bags up, stuffed us in them and lay on top of us to get us warm. Donna dashed to their boat to get clothes for herself, and hauled up sopping gear that was beginning to float to shore.

When Geoff left us to help Donna, Bill held me tight and, with dancing blue eyes, whispered, "Isn't this fun?" We both giggled. We'd learned so many times that what seems like misfortune really is The Stuff of Life. The stories we have to tell. The delight of figuring out just what to do. The fun of creating a new plan.

It took maybe two hours to get much of our floating gear from the river, build a fire and begin to talk about what had happened. We each had differing views of the capsize. We each seemed to want to tell our story over and over again. Maybe to put it into perspective. Maybe to confront and chase away the fear of what might have been. Maybe to bless our lucky stars that we were sitting there talking about it. We each decided to pitch in five dollars for Bill's anchor line.

If only we'd had a phone. But, then, whom would we have called. We were all all right. There really wasn't anything anyone could do for us. I thought of the time on Beaver Island when we didn't have a phone. When we moved onto the island, the phone man came around to ask when we wanted him to install a phone. Bill asked how much it would cost. "Seven hundred dollars," he said.

"Forget it," Bill said, "We came here for peace and quiet. We don't want a phone. Not for that amount." When he told me that night, tucked between flannel sheets, we made plans to send letters to our children each week, to write long missives to friends and relatives, and to look forward to the twice-a-week mail delivery from Rosie, the mail lady.

Four years later, as we loaded our belongings onto the ferry for the mainland, our good island friends came to say goodbye. The phone man, a good friend by now, said, "I still don't know why you didn't have a phone all these years, for only seven dollars." Bill's eyes met mine. He'd lost much of his hearing in the war, but this time, his deafness had actually brought us much joy we would have missed if we'd had a phone ringing on our peaceful little farm.

Geoff made biscuits for dinner, as we spread our wet gear out to dry. The hillside looked like a garage sale, with tents and sleeping bags and clothing and kitchen gear spread across bushes and hanging from branches.

Bill propped each page of his soggy journal along the train tracks. It was while we were dipping biscuits into honey that we heard the familiar whistle. Before we could get to the tracks, the train sped by, scattering pages into the air. And the river. And the honey.

Then Gyp encountered her first porcupine. Four of us held her while Donna used pliers to pull quills from her whole head and face.

And none of this day was on film.

We'd lost much of our gear in the capsize but thought if we ate lightly we had enough food and water to last till the next town. As we doubled up in what dry tents and sleeping bags were left, I said I wished for the trout from the night before. Again I saw Jen and Geoff glance at each other.

“What <u>did</u> happen to the trout?” I asked.

“Let’s just say the next people to use the park’s outhouse will not have to worry about stinking it up.” Geoff grinned.

Geoff had established a routine which was to last the whole trip. Each morning he’d get up before anyone else, build a fire, and deliver small pans of hot water to each tent so we could have tea, wash faces, or wipe away dried, caked mosquito blood from our arms and legs and faces.

After morning ablutions, we packed our now damp gear, and shoved off, but by lunchtime were ready to quit paddling for a few hours. Our muscles were still tense. Donna was still testing us every fifteen minutes to see if we had concussions. We still knew our names and where we were. Funny thing though, we couldn’t figure out why on earth we were there.

We found a grassy slope, a backyard to an empty cabin, and took out that afternoon. I busied myself with making a cargo net from ropes and lines and straps and bungies. We’d lost lots of our precious gear, and I wasn’t going to let it happen again. We might go over again, but with my hand-tied cargo net, our gear should stay in the canoe. That cargo net is one of my proudest accomplishments.

Geoff and Bill went scouting and returned with an invitation for us to join a family downriver for breakfast the next morning. That was the easiest group decision we ever made. We pulled the boats up out of the water, pitched tents, crawled in and dreamed of chilled orange juice in real glasses.

We were at the Barrett’s kitchen door by seven. Before 7:30 we’d finished pancakes, eggs, sausage, bacon, muffins, hash browns, toast, and freshly-squeezed orange juice. We were all smiles.

“You are the first canoers we’ve seen in over a year,” Fred told us.

"Be careful," Ruth said.

Then they told us of the man who'd drowned last year just a few yards downriver from their house. "Got caught in a whirlpool. Took him right under."

Fred added, "She's a powerful, raging river. You were lucky two days ago. Don't push your luck. Be careful."

There were hugs and thanks all around. Ruth and Fred were now officially part of A Year Without Time. They'd taken us in. Fed us. As many were to do in the next year.

We shoved off, eager to get back on the river. But, now we had new eyes. We saw whirlpools to the right. Boulders downstream. Maybe we'd never tame her, but we could learn to train ourselves. To respect her. To read her. And, in time, to love her.

Stay Curious

Jen

We'd been on the river for almost a month. Thoughts of work were drifting from the creases of my memory; I found my mind wandering to topics anew for the first time in years. As we were making our way through western Montana, my mind began its own journey. After nearly six weeks of not working, the space "work" had occupied in my mind's patterns was clearing, and wanderings were beginning. I thought of the wind, and what actually caused it to rush past us and push us to the river's edge.

The last time I had asked this question was during a trek over a snowy mountain pass in the Wind River Range in western Wyoming on a three-month outdoor leadership course at the National Outdoor Leadership School. As the temperature fell on a windy hike, I called across the rush to one of the instructors.

"Ed, what makes the wind blow so hard?"

I was seventeen, and it seemed like a reasonable question to me. Ed gave me a look that was gentle, but revealed that he saw me as another of his many students, thrown against the elements with a backpack and a pair of leather boots. His answer contained converging air currents, temperatures that varied with elevation, and the turning of the tides in the distant seas. These same explanations would be given again, after the midpoint of the three-month course, at the head of Dark Canyon in Utah. Utah's Canyonlands were a different section of the course, and Leslie, a tanned, lean instructor was teaching from her ensolite pad, the sandy soil at the head of this 200-foot gash in the earth creeping toward her wool socks as she lectured. A geologist by training, she described the creation of the deserts by the swirling of the tides. I was perched on my own ensolite pad, my elbows pocked by the sand they were resting on. I squinted up at her, the sun poking from behind her shoulder. She spoke for an hour on the evolution of the continents, how landmasses came and went, and how the rising mountains formed the valleys that in turn became deserts...

The wind I remembered in Utah those years earlier had now ceased in Montana, the river's pitch leveling, its pace slowing. My mind had been wandering away from the smooth paddling of my kayak. The day was warm, and the space in my mind's patterns that had been filled with thoughts of computer configurations and e-mail quota just two months before, was now free to be filled with... well, something else.

The river was slowing, bending around the crease in the plains of western Montana that carried the current toward Great Falls. And that current was slowing. I swatted a mosquito and let my mind wander back to the memory of the view into Dark Canyon. My muscles were thirteen years younger as I remembered the sunset that adorned that evening's sky in Utah, watching the ball-of-fire sun drop into the canyon, a brilliant red glow expanding from the horizon, then seeping into the deep blue that becomes black if you watch it closely enough.

This kind of time is only available if your life is centered in the outdoors. This kind of time is a luxury, and one that was allowing my mind to wander from one decade to another. I swatted another mosquito in Montana.

"How you doing?" I called to Donna, her red canoe drifting behind my kayak. I killed a mosquito on my neck with a sharp thwack.

Diva had just perked up her head when I called over to Donna's boat, and I watched Diva go after a mosquito with her mouth, her teeth bared as she snapped her jaws together trying to catch a mosquito that was bothering her. It was at this moment that I realized that during my mind's wanderings, the river had slowed to a crawl, the land had flattened from foothills to fields, and a recent rain had left pools of water along the edge of the fields.

Pools of water get warm in the sun, and warm water breeds all kinds of things, most notably at the moment, mosquitoes. I whacked at one on my arm, and another on my neck. Donna and Geoff were doing their share of chasing mosquitoes, killing most of those on their skin. Donna was attending to Diva, the mosquitoes focusing on her eyelids, ears and jowls, the only places they could get to her blood.

Mom and Bill had paddled ahead and were out of sight. The mosquitoes were growing denser; we knew we needed to find a dry patch of shore to pitch the tents, and find it fast. Rounding the next bend revealed a spit of land, which held Mom and Bill's familiar tent. We paddled fast to get to it. The shore was anything but dry, but looked better than continuing to paddle in the growing swarm of mosquitoes. Mud slipped under our sandals as we jumped from the boats and pulled them out of the water. The three of us, Geoff, Donna and I, looked at each other and then looked to the canoe. We grabbed the first tent we could find and ran to the driest section of land, about ten feet from Mom and Bill's tent.

"Quick, grab a food bag," Donna yelled as she dumped the tent poles from their bag. I ran back to the canoe and grabbed a food bag, headed up to the quickly-assembling tent, then doubled back and grabbed Diva's food bag, too. Geoff and Donna were pitching the tent in double-time, and we threw the food bags into it as the last pole was snapped into place. The three of us, Diva, and two food bags, crammed into the two-person tent and zipped the door shut. We had escaped the swarm of mosquitoes that had found us on the muddy bank of the river, but not entirely.

We smashed mosquito bodies into the clean white nylon ceiling of our REI dome tent as the sun started to set. What had been a pristine white and cream dome tent became the final resting ground for the hundreds of mosquitoes that had followed us into the tent. We smacked and squashed each one. Streaks of mosquito blood turned dark brown as the sun made its way to the horizon.

Outside, a BZZZZZZZZ continued as hundreds more mosquitoes covered the outside of the tent. The noise was constant, and grating. In our hot, humid tent smeared with mosquito guts, our bodies still muddy from the day's paddle, we ate peanut butter by the spoonful for dinner (I had grabbed the food bag that held peanut butter and sardines). Diva ate her dinner from a plastic bag.

"Bill," I called over to their tent, above the mosquito's whine, "on the Mississippi, were the mosquitoes like this?"

"Yes, in Minnesota the pesky little buggers were bigger than these," came his reply.

"And will they go away?"

"Oh, yes, don't worry – they'll be gone by morning." He sounded so sure.

I'm not certain if it was the BZZZing and whining of the thousands of mosquitoes surrounding out tents or the wet from the mud oozing through the bottom of the tent (we had not taken the time to lay down a groundsheet) that kept me awake, but my mind wandered again – this time to dreamland. Hot and humid, my dreams were short. I woke up several times and wasn't certain if I was dreaming the constant whine of mosquitoes or if they were really still there, trying to get to our blood-filled skin through the thin nylon of our tent.

As the sun made its way to the day, I realized I hadn't been dreaming. The whine was still there; along with the source of it – mosquitoes such as I had never seen. A black cloud just outside our zipped-up tent door.

"Bill," I called over the mosquito's whine, "did you mean they would be gone <u>this</u> morning?"

A few more scoops of peanut butter all around, and we made a mad dash for the boats, our nylon tent crammed under a seat and a t-shirt drenched in bug spray on Diva, we paddled like hell to get out of the slow-moving river. And there, before our arms were too tired to keep up the frantic pace (movement, at least, kept the mosquitoes from landing on our skin), was our respite – a house nestled back in the trees, and a three-bay garage. The owner brought us orange soda as we hauled our boats out of the water and made a quick dash for his garage. He helped us get to the road and Mom and Bill hitchhiked back to the trucks. And the trucks took us to showers in Great Falls. Within six hours, we had gone from the incessant whine of mosquitoes, the kind of noise that settles in just below your level of tolerance, and tempers get short, to the clean, crisp feeling you get just after a shower, the mud of days past yielding to the flow of water and suds.

That night, as we drifted to sleep, shamed-laughter filled the campsite, for just twelve hours earlier we had made a list of those we would like to stake to the muddy banks to lure the mosquitoes away from us.

I thought back to the sunset in my Utah memory. I had watched as the horizon changed, the silhouettes of sandstone turning from red to black. As it had happened here, too, in Montana.

Stay Curious

Cate

We paddled leisurely all that day and the next through a light mist. Cans of sardines had survived the capsize, so breakfast, lunch and dinner were sardines on crackers served up on a paddle while we floated toward Craig, Montana.

By the time we reached Craig, the mist had turned into a full-blown storm, with heavy rain pelting down, soaking the gear we'd worked so hard to dry on a hillside just three days earlier.

Craig has one shop and one café/motel. Both of which were closed when we arrived. Fly-fishing season didn't start for another week.

We wandered up the bank, pulling the canoes well out of the river onto mud. Geoff rapped on the door of the café hoping someone was inside, although the door was locked and the lights out. We flipped the canoes upside-down and stashed as much gear as we could underneath. Just then Geoff returned with the good news that the café owner, Karen, would make breakfast for us. Although she didn't have all the things on the menu, she could make pancakes. Blueberry or pecan!

As Karen flipped pancakes on the griddle, we each told of our adventures. She'd come to Montana from Ohio, where she was a college professor. She bought a cabin in the mountains, learned to fly fish, and to tie flies. She opened a tiny shop to sell her flies, built a two-table café next door, and then added a four-room motel, three of which were ours for the next two nights. Thirty-nine dollars each, including hot showers, and sandwiches and fruit she'd leave in the café fridge for late night snacking. We each showered. Twice. As the rain poured outside, we slept lots, used her washer and dryer, wrote, and nearly forgot our canoes in the cold Montana rain just outside our door.

Jen had, years earlier, spent a year in culinary school, and got to talking to Karen one midnight about the café. The next morning, Jen and Donna perched on the end of our bed and asked what we'd think if they ran the café for the season. Karen had offered them jobs. They'd make meals for trout fishermen, and live in one of the motel rooms. Diva was welcome too.

Oh, this dreaming was fun. And, Donna was catching on. I'd always told my children to follow their hearts, to dream lots, to make some of the dreams come true. Not all of them. But without the dreams, there would be nothing to come true.

As our thoughts whirled around, thinking how we'd proceed with A Year Without Time …the expedition, we realized that this is just the sort of thing which can happen without time. Then the reality of a Montana winter set in. If we didn't get through Montana and North and South Dakota before winter, we'd have to stay over and take another year to complete the river. We were paddling leisurely, but knew somewhere in the backs of our minds, that we had to be in Kansas, heading to the Mississippi River and the south in November if we were to survive on the river.

Bill and I so often had found ourselves in this dilemma. Many roads from which to choose. And, all good ones. Dreaming works.

The following morning, as we gathered clean clothes, took one last shower, and stuffed even more pancakes down, Jen and Donna made their decision. Maybe someday they'd come back to Montana. Maybe someday they'd run their own restaurant. But, now, they wanted to get on with canoeing the Missouri River. We thanked Karen for taking us in, piled gear into muddy canoes and set off, still paddling north toward Great Falls where I'd pick up a flight for Honolulu, and my next seminar.

Two days later we picked up the waiting trucks, found a KOA campground, and pitched our now muddy, bloody tents beside shiny, lavender Winnebagos, and all manner of fancy travel trailers. It was the 4th of July weekend, so we'd been lucky just to get a spot for our little tents. That night fireworks kept me awake. Or maybe it was the thought of leaving my crew to go back to the real world.

Bill drove me to the airport. We kissed a long kiss. I urged him to be very careful since I wouldn't be there to pull him out. I reminded him that Gyp would be lonely, so please hug her up now and then. He drove away while I checked my bags, which held my black silk suit, lacy bra, and patent leather high-heels.

I stopped by the restroom on my way to the gate. I found an empty stall, went in, closed the door behind me, put a paper cover on the toilet seat, turned around to undo my belt, and heard a whoosh. The toilet had automatically flushed behind me. I tried again. The paper cover flushed away before I could sit down. I scrambled to sit on the seat before the next flush. I'd been squatting behind bushes for weeks now, and this automated wonder caught me completely unprepared. It was the first of many moments in the real world where I'd wish I were back in the wilderness, which had become my real world.

I traveled in my muddy flannel shirt, jeans, and hiking boots, my hair in pigtails. My contract read, "…and seminar presenters shall wear business attire while traveling to and from seminars." Oh, heck, I thought, who will see me before I get to my hotel where I'll change clothes. It seemed as though everyone saw me. I met colleagues on each flight I took from Montana to Utah to California to Hawaii – seventeen hours after watching Bill drive away in our little black truck. And wishing I were sitting beside him. Well, until the bubble baths and room service.

I incorporated much of what I'd already learned from the river in my seminars. They were the best seminars I'd ever given. I'd always had great customer satisfaction ratings, but now I was getting presents delivered to my hotel room, and was being invited home to meet the participants' families.

What had changed, I wondered? It would all be clear to me when I joined my river crew in Fort Benton, Montana a week later.

Paddle Each Bend In The River Gently

Jen

I stepped into the stream of hot water and closed my eyes. A hot shower in a KOA campground in Great Falls, Montana washed away the grime of the three weeks of paddling we had just finished. My shoulders began to relax under the heat of the water, and soap bubbles ran over my muddy calves.

Donna was in the shower stall next to mine, all hint of romance gone as we sought cleanliness first, and closeness second. It was the July 4th weekend, and the campground was packed. We made our way from the showers past the screaming children at the pool and back to the trucks.

Diva had been waiting under the shade of a small tree, her water bowl next to her. I rummaged through the back of the truck, my clean fingers realizing just how dirty our gear really was, and found her food bag. By this time Diva knew the small blue dry bag with the roll-down cover contained her dog food and treats, and she joined me at the back of the truck as I made her dinner. I put her food bowl down on the ground next to the picnic table in our campsite and watched her eat. This beautiful Chocolate Lab appeared the least affected by the changes of the past several months. She rode in the boat easily, and adapted to each campsite without a thought. The mosquitoes had been annoying to her, but she had endured them without any of the disparaging comments her humans had made. The sweat and stickiness left on her humans' skin at the end of a day were of no concern to her; she reveled in swimming at each stop, pursuing sticks that were floating downstream with us. I would come to recognize that Diva's ease with the river trip was enviable, her apparent nonchalance something to emulate.

As I stood next to her at our KOA campsite, watching her finish her dinner on this 4th of July evening, I admired how her soft ears bounced to the rhythm of her chewing, her tail a rudder in the warm afternoon breeze. My hair was drying as she ate, and I leaned my nose down toward my shoulder, into my clean t-shirt, simply to smell that I was a clean body inside clean clothes.

We paid for two nights at the KOA, knowing we had to deposit Mom at the Great Falls airport for her first journey back into the land of the working the next afternoon. Donna and I slept in the back of our truck that night, Diva wedged at our feet, and fireworks welcomed us back into civilization. I stayed awake for a long time that night. Even though the hot shower had taken away the stickiness on my skin and the grime of camping for three weeks, it had cost me the quiet I had come to know as I drifted off to sleep, the only sound the river running past us on her way to the Gulf.

Mom's departure brought a new "bend in the river" to us. We were to find out how to function without what I can best identify as our matriarch. We entertained ourselves with laundry and ice cream cones and lunches at the Chinese restaurant, but Bill seemed always to be looking to the horizon, checking to see if, by chance, the two weeks till Mom's return had passed.

After a full week of enjoying the "city life" (we had extended our stay at the KOA), mending gear that had already worn, visiting the local thrift shop to find long-sleeved cotton button-down shirts to protect my red-head skin from the sun, and restocking our food bags and cooking fuel, we made our way back to the river.

After arranging the truck drop-offs, we put our boats in the water as the afternoon was coming to a close. Donna, Geoff and Diva were in the canoe, I was in the kayak, and Bill was paddling *E. coli* alone. Well, almost alone. Gypsy was supposed to be in Bill's boat, Mom had sworn us to take care of her beloved dog while she was away. The problem was, however, that Gypsy would not get in the boat. I firmly believe that she had this notion that if she left land, and her beloved Master (my mother) was not with her, that she would never see her Master again. And so, as the sun started its decline toward the horizon, we tried to cajole, and then bribe, and then beg Gypsy to get in *E. coli*. She refused.

Donna and Geoff, having put in before Bill, now paddled back upstream to see what was the problem. I was chasing Gypsy around the parking lot of the put-in, and Bill was in his boat, paddle at the ready. Gypsy was not leaving without her Master, and her Master was in Hawaii giving management seminars.

"Jenny," Bill's voice was strained as he tried to make the best of our current reality, "let's just let her run alongside until she gets tired, then she'll get in the boat." I had her in my arms at this point, and placed her in the bow of *E. coli*.

"Quick, Bill – start paddling!"

As Bill's boat pulled away from shore, Gypsy jumped back to land, turning around to look at Bill as if she had just made a brilliant escape. She was not leaving land, not without her Master.

I looked downstream to survey the river bank. It was level for a good stretch then the bank turned sharply upward, quickly forming a siltstone bluff as the river turned left.

I thought about my mother, working her way back to us through a dozen seminars, each presentation bringing her closer to the river. I knew I would never tell her this story, and it is with this writing that I reveal it to her for the first time. Bill, Donna and Geoff, I have broken our pact of silence, and beg your forgiveness.

"We'll have to get her in the boat before that bluff." I said. And with that, it was decided. If Gypsy wasn't going to paddle with us, she'd have to run along the shore until she would get into the boat.

Bill headed *E. coli* downstream and I slid the kayak into the current. We stayed close to shore, except for the section where an island and a strong current separated us from Gypsy's line of sight. I felt sorry for the little dog from Russia, her blond curly fur getting brambled by the prickers on the river's bank. As we came around the end of the island, I scanned the shore for Gypsy, and she was… gone.

"Donna," I yelled across the current, "do you see Gypsy?"

I watched as Geoff and Donna scanned the bank upriver, Diva even perking her head up to investigate the commotion.

"No, she's not up here," came Donna's reply.

Bill and I were close to each other and I caught his eye. If his wife's little dog didn't make it through the first time she was left in our care, we were in for it, not to mention what it would mean to Gypsy. There would be no explaining how Gyp wouldn't get in the boat; we were doomed.

Bill and I both swung our boats around and headed them back upstream, hoping we would get to the inland side of the island and find her waiting for us. As we paddled furiously to break through the wave at the end of the island, half of the river having flowed on one side of the island and half of the river on the other, I saw a little bobbing head in the water coming around the tip of the island. I strained to make out if it was an opossum or some other animal.

The kayak had broken through the confluence of the currents and the swimming head was approaching me with speed. As it got closer, I realized this was my dog-sister, Gypsy! She had seen us disappear behind the island and jumped in the dashing Missouri River and started swimming to catch up with us! Her front paws scraped against the plastic of the kayak and I grabbed her by her dog-PFD and lifted her into my lap for the second time. As she shook her ears to start them drying, I saw a look in her eyes that made me remember that she had lived the first years of her life on the streets of Moscow, and she and I shared a moment that I remember every time I have seen her since that day; she is a part of our family, and she is going to stay with us.

I paddled over to *E. coli* and Gypsy jumped from my boat into the bow of Bill's boat. She was coming with us, but not entirely happily; her Master was still missing. She whined the rest of the afternoon, just to remind us that someone was missing.

The three boats reconvened and we paddled into the dusk of the Montana evening. The river bends left and right as she makes her way from Great Falls to Fort Benton, the next town on the map. Each of her bends is sided by a siltstone bluff at least 200 feet tall. The siltstone has been eroded by water and wind to reveal faces in the bluffs that watched us as we paddled beneath them. An eerie sense came over me; we were traveling as others have traveled here before. The native peoples, the explorers, the spirits that remained, had all been carried by the current that was now carrying us. We paddled quietly beneath the watching bluffs as the sun hit the horizon, taking with it the heat of the day.

A rocky beach greeted us around the next bend, and we pulled the boats to shore. Gypsy jumped to shore before any of us, she was now the advance scout, and would secure the area for us. Tents went up on the grassy section just beyond the beach, and Geoff found a fire circle.

We made a quick dinner of mashed potatoes and cocoa and then shared the stars and crisp night air with the crackle of a campfire. Diva sat by the door of our tent wanting to be let inside to her bed. As I went back to find another layer, I let her in and tucked her into bed. When we would erect the tent and throw out our sleeping bags to fluff, we would do her bag as well. When she was ready for bed, she would lie down on her unzipped sleeping bag and let us roll the sleeping bag around her and tuck her in, into her Diva Burrito.

I made my way back to the fire just in time to hear Bill, Geoff and Donna talk about the bluffs we had passed that day and how the faces had appeared to be watching us. Indeed, we felt we were not alone.

In the morning, we found that our thoughts from the night before had been true.

I heard Donna unzip the tent door as the chill of the morning tried to make its way into my sleeping bag. As I scooted farther down into my bag, I heard Donna's morning pee start, and then stop.

"Jen, come out here, quick!"

I opened my eyes, looked at Diva, who was looking at me, and threw off my sleeping bag. After fumbling with the door zipper, I made my way outside. Donna was still posed in her pee-position, and we were surrounded by at least forty steer, their eyes following our every move. We knew immediately we were in their breakfast grazing territory, and it was clearly the wrong place to be on this sunny morning. I wasn't at all comfortable with this, and Donna's face told me she wasn't either.

"Geoff, come out here, quick!"

We heard rumbling in Geoff's tent and then he stepped out as well. He peered around and stood, as we were, dead still.

"Bill, come out here, quick!"

Bill's hearing was not what it once was, so Geoff made his way over to Bill's tent. After he opened the door to Bill's tent, Gypsy darted out and started a mad-barking-herding of the steer that were keeping Donna and me stone-frozen, not certain if we should advance or retreat. Gypsy settled it all for us by pulling one of her stark-raving-mad dog impersonations and herding the steer away from our campsite.

The four of us looked at each other, smiled and raised our eyebrows. Perhaps Gypsy wasn't so bad to have along, after all. As we made a pot of oatmeal and packed the boats, Gypsy continued her barking-herding and general craziness, and we appreciated every moment of it.

The morning's sun glinted off the river as the boats pulled into the current. I watched as Donna paddled into a river that was once only a blue line on a map, and was now our home. The sun played with the image in my eyes, bringing the boats into focus as the siltstone rose above them, crystals of light bouncing off the water. The boats bobbed smoothly into the morning sunlight, into this beauty.

That afternoon, the heat of a Montana July swallowed me up as I walked up the cement boat ramp in Fort Benton. We had made the usual 180-degree turn from the downstream current to point the boats upstream and toward the boat ramp on the north side of the river (yes, the Missouri runs west to east through the bulk of Montana; Fort Benton is on the north shore). A swift tug on the canoes set them on the bank, then a tether on the kayak, and the four of us made our way up the boat ramp. An ice cream stand greeted us as we rounded the top of the ramp. I liked Fort Benton immediately.

The heat of the days had gotten into my pores, and the natural state while paddling was a perpetual stickiness. The long-sleeved white dress shirt I had purchased in the Great Falls thrift store was marked with stains from the sweat that pooled under my close-fitting whitewater-style PFD. Whitewater PFDs are significantly evolved from the old orange U-collar life vests worn in the row boats at Girl Scout camp. These chest-snugging PFDs fit like a glove, and although we would not see real whitewater, they were the PFD of choice, becoming almost a part of me as the summer wore on. Part of me, and my ever-present sun-blocking white Brooks Brothers shirt.

I unzipped the right side of my PFD to let some cooler air in as I made my way to the line of townfolk waiting in the ice cream line. As I noticed the stains on my shirt from the days of sweat, I looked back at Donna, Geoff and Bill. I saw, for the first time, a glimmer of how we must have looked to the other people contemplating whether to get chocolate sprinkles – motley, at best.

Our feet were donned in river sandals, the skin between the straps the color of cocoa. Each of us had either baggy shorts or jeans with sweat-stains forming an upside-down moon on our butts. Shirts were soft and sticky, the heat clinging them to our skin, and each of us wore a hat that almost perfectly defined our personalities. Geoff sported a wide-brimmed Australian Outback duster, a leather lanyard draped from brim to chest. Donna tucked her hair up into a dark green, wide-brimmed canvas hat that floated and had a pocket hidden in the seams. I pulled my ponytail through a low-profile JanSport baseball cap. Bill had perched on his head a woven straw hat that had been reshaped after The Capsize; the reshaping hadn't gone so well, and the brim drooped on three sides while the top formed a pitch off to the left.

What had been normal to me for the past several weeks now struck me as chaotic and altogether bizarre. What did we look like to these townfolk? The ice cream line moved forward and the four of us moved with it.

There was something so comforting about standing in that line. I'm not certain if it was knowing that I had re-entered civilization, and the ice cream was cold and cheap, or the anticipation of spending a few days not moving. After wanting the progress of our boats so fiercely in the first few weeks of the trip, I now wanted to base-camp, to have the same ice cream tomorrow afternoon, and to have rested between now and then. Was it a vacation I was seeking? A vacation from the river trip? A vacation from the pressure of not having to be anywhere in particular, on what just might be the most significant trip of my life? Or a vacation from the constant motion and the lack of control one faces when living in nature?

I stepped up to the counter of the ice cream stand and ordered a chocolate shake. Whatever it was I was looking to get away from, it seemed odd that I would need to get away from anything – having started the river trip to "get away from it all."

As I pulled two dollar bills from the plastic bag that carried our cash, the young woman at the register looked at me with a question in her eyes. I could tell she wanted to know why I had bills and coins and receipts in a plastic bag instead of a wallet or purse, and why I was still wearing a PFD, but her youth kept her from forming the words. I handed her the bills in exchange for my shake.

If there was anything I needed to get away from, it certainly was not this chocolate milkshake. It was thick and creamy and rich, and I savored it until it was only a slurping noise in the bottom of my wax-coated paper cup. We sat on a picnic table in the city park adjacent to the ice cream stand, the afternoon heat foiled by the shade of canopy trees. There was no place we needed to be, and we let the afternoon take hold, the time ticking away on clock faces we couldn't see anymore.

After visiting the park office, we learned the camping was free in the town park, the showers were only seventy-five cents in the nearby pool, and that the county fair was happening for the next three nights just outside of town. Whatever it was I was needing to get away from had just turned into what I needed to do: shower, put on clean clothes, and act as if I were a normal person in the normal world, heading to the county fair with my best buddy. And so I learned of my need for normalcy.

"Normalcy" always had a negative connotation in my family. It was what those who couldn't think of anything interesting to do did. It was what everyone else did. And here I was, after months of planning, and then starting, what was perhaps the least normal event of my life, and paddling for two months, yearning to put on clean jeans and a pair of shoes that covered my toes, and go to the county fair. I wanted to blend in. After weeks of doing radio and newspaper interviews, I wanted to go watch the rodeo clowns and buy popcorn and a coke. I wanted to be free of the responsibility of being an adventurer, of moving on each day to see what was around the next bend. I wanted to be stationary, if even for a few days, to stop the flow and become familiar with my surroundings, reaping the benefit of knowing what is around the next street corner.

"Mom comes in two days, how about we camp here for a while and get to know the town?" I said to no one in particular.

Geoff and Bill and Donna were all within earshot and they each glanced my way. The look in their eyes told me they longed for a shower, at least, and that a few days free of paddling was not a bad idea. And so, we stayed.

The town park in Fort Benton became our home for a week, we took showers at the pool almost daily, and we got to know the rangers in the museum as we grilled them for information about what the river was like as she headed through the upcoming Missouri Breaks. We watched every educational video they had, just so we could sit on the tattered orange sofa in the side room of the museum. The biggest treat, however, after the cotton candy at the county fair, was buying rotisserie chickens at the Stop-n-Shop on Main Street and bringing them back to the park for dinner. I'm not certain which I enjoyed more: the taste of the chicken, hot and oily as we picked it from the bone, or the fact that I could wash my hands in the bathroom sink afterward.

The river trip was teaching me my own idiosyncrasies. Nothing is hidden when you have no place to hide.

Fort Benton took us in for a week, folks who lived close to the park brought us blueberry muffins and stayed to talk about what we were doing, the local vet saw Diva *gratis* to help us figure out what the rash on her belly was (Missouri River mites), and we befriended the teenage boy at the Circle-K who sold us burritos after the sun went down. As eager as I had been to stay, once Mom settled back into the group, and a week's time had passed, I became eager to leave. I understood my need for normalcy, but hadn't accepted that it would stay in my heart. The river called to me, especially after my skin had been smooth and clean for six days in a row. We visited the laundromat one last time and packed the boats. Diva was as eager as I to return to the water. Somehow, though, it was all right for her to have fleeting desires, but I was questioning mine.

Paddle Each Bend In The River Gently

Cate

Bill picked me up at the Great Falls airport, and I changed from my black suit to my river clothes as we drove toward Fort Benton. I shoved my hot curlers into my briefcase, and tossed it into the back of the truck, knowing I had only two weeks to wear pigtails before I had to leave for another round of seminars.

I told Bill about my incredible week of seminars. I told him that I felt the crowds got my message more than ever before. And how they took a personal interest in me more than ever before. How I felt successful more than ever before.

Bill said, "Don't you see? Everyone would like to have adventure in his life. They'd like to be doing what we're doing on the river, or living in Spain, or climbing Mount Fuji, or selling their own homemade mustard door to door. They'd like to be following dreams. Whatever that may mean. And by hearing you, it brings them closer to being part of adventure." Then he added, "And maybe, just maybe, after your seminars last week, seeing how an average person can follow her dreams, they'll make changes in their lives. Maybe they'll follow their own hearts… I hope so."

Fort Benton, Montana, where the river crew had paddled while I was away, is a tiny river town with a statue of a Yellow Labrador on the riverbank. Story goes that when the dog's master drowned in the Missouri River, the dog came to the riverbank everyday, not taking his eyes off the river, waiting for his friend to return. Everyday. For years.

Bill and Geoff and Jen and Donna had reached Fort Benton and pitched tents three days earlier to wait for me. They'd already met the laundromat owner, the Visitor Center keeper, the Malt Shop owner, and the local innkeeper, Amy, who'd opened her home as a bed and breakfast instead of going to work in the big city as a nurse. Amy asked our crew what they were doing in Fort Benton, how they'd gotten there, how we were all living on $750 a month, and why didn't we just come on over to her mom's empty house and spend a night in real beds.

Bill drove me straight to the waiting beds. Twin beds. That night Bill wrote:

TWIN BEDS
"You won't be disturbed," they said.
"You'll sleep better," they said.
They said, "You won't be bothered when he turns over,
Or when he's up in the small hours,
And then comes back to bed,
Or when he's restless."

Maybe so.
But I miss you. You're not here anymore.
You might as well be back in the old country
Waiting for me to send you the money to come and join me.
I miss the warmth of you.
I miss the scent of you.
I miss our arms and legs wrapped around each other.
I miss sleeping like spoons.
I miss backs and bottoms touching.
I can no longer hear you sleeping,
Your breath in my ear.
I miss patting you there,
Or rubbing your neck some
As we drift away with Mr. Morpheus.
I miss the gentleness of your breast
When I touch you lovingly.
I miss you.

Wouldn't you like to be disturbed a little?

We slept late, ate cereal with cold milk, something we can't do on the river, then returned to the wonderful city park, where our tents were pitched near the swimming pool. That meant hot showers. Our morning pots of water in our tents had kept our faces clean, and our hands clean, but showers were pure luxury. For seventy-five cents we could be admitted to the public swimming pool, shower in endless hot, steamy water and even wash out underwear and socks to hang up back at our tent site in the park.

We spent a few days in Fort Benton wandering around the town, stocking and packing supplies for the next part of the river, and showering. Since I'd just come from a week in luxury hotels, I waited till the last day to shower before we put in the river. As I stood in the communal cubicle meant for showers before entering the pool, eyes closed, lathered from forehead to feet, I felt someone nearby. I stuck my head under the showerhead so the lather would slip from my eyes, and opened them a little to see. A small, towhead girl was staring at me, looking me up and down. Her eyes were wide open. I smiled. She dropped her jaw. That's when her mother grabbed her arm and yanked her away with a "Humph." That's when I noticed that all the other showerers were clothed. They were taking showers in their swimsuits. I was starkers.

Then I chuckled. We'd been so used to dropping our drawers, draping our fannies over the side of the canoe when we wanted to pee and didn't want to stop paddling, so used to stripping down to our skins to change muddy clothes, so used to each other's bodies, that I'd forgotten that in public places folks frown on nakedness.

After her shower, Donna was eager to show the video footage she had taken of Dung Beetles while I was away. Two hours of Dung Beetle footage. She'd followed one beetle as he scooped and rolled dung into a ball, pushed and pulled it uphill, sat stunned as it rolled back down, and then began the whole procedure over again.

After a long discussion of what each of us thought the Dung Beetles were thinking, we made a huge pot of fried potatoes for dinner. Then came one of my most unhappy days on the river.

It was cold and dark after dinner, and it was my turn to wash the pots, so I hurriedly scrubbed the inside of the blackened, fried potato pot, left it on a stump upside-down to dry, and ran to our tent to snuggle down next to Bill.

After a long while Jen's voice was at our tent door, "Mom, could I talk to you?"

I struggled to get my fleece jacket on before unzipping the tent. "What is it?" I said as my eyes adjusted to the darkness. "Are you ok?"

"It's the pot, Mom. It's still black on the outside. That one belongs to Donna."

I stared incredulously. I wanted to shout "So what?" but realized that Jen was caught in the middle of her mother and her lover. She was cringing from both sides, I was sure. She wanted to please Donna. She wanted to please me. My heart was breaking for her.

"I'm sorry, I'm sorry, I'm sorry," I lied.

I'd decided long ago that I'd always play with and read with and dream with my kids instead of cleaning the house. I was a terrible housekeeper. Now, my hurried cleaning was getting me, and Jen, and Donna into trouble.

Jen and Donna were just finding their way in their new relationship. Jen loved her so. I wanted Donna to like me. No, to love me. And now, already, I was causing trouble between them.

Donna patiently explained that her Grandmother had always said, "If a job is worth doing, it's worth doing well."

"Yes, I agree," I lied again. I didn't. I didn't see why the outside of a pot needed to shine. But Jen's eyes told me just what I needed to do. "I'll do it over now. Just wait till you see it." I said. Then I lied a third time, "I'm so sorry."

It took many bends in the river before Donna and I learned not just to accept each other, or like each other, but to love each other. Just the way we are. She's so wise and so gentle. I love how she loves my daughter. And I love how my daughter loves her. Somewhere along the way we learned that we didn't have to lie to each other if we didn't agree. Somewhere along the way we learned we could be ourselves.

After studying the river, and coordinating it with the next airport for my seminar schedule, we decided to drive the boats north so I'd be able to paddle a couple hundred miles before I had to leave again. Early on our last morning in Fort Benton, the townspeople came to see us off. They brought hot muffins, and juice, and helped us tie the boats to the rooftops, insisting that we return someday.

We drove to Coal Banks where we met Beth Johnson, author of *Yukon Wild*, the adventures of four women who paddled 2,000 miles through America's last frontier. Beth was in Montana with a group of Texans. The campsite was crowded and noisy with a third group – young people with special needs. Each one was partnered with an adult, and together they were canoeing a stretch of the Missouri River. They were camping, paddling, cooking over fires, all the while holding onto crutches, or walkers, or each other.

Beth was the first person really to cheer us on. Others had accepted what we were doing, but Beth understood and encouraged us to spend our lives on some adventure or other. She gave us a copy of her book, which we used as an excuse to stay at camp, reading in our tents, for a few more days. In time, reading aloud would become the reason we'd get off the river earlier and earlier each evening.

That night Donna said, "I think our lives are supposed to be made up of chapters. Work a chapter, play a chapter. Work a chapter, adventure a chapter."

When we finally put in the river and cast off our last line, a billow of dust in the distance caught our attention. We turned the canoes around and let the current take us. We watched as the dust became tiny black specks, then became cars. Four of them. All heading to our campground. We paddled back, against the current, curious what the trouble was. An advance team from the Montana U.S. Senator's office was putting canoes in the river, preparing to take the Senator downriver to see the Eye of the Needle, a breathtaking eleven foot tall natural rock formation in the White Cliffs, high above the riverbank. Lewis and Clark had camped across the river from Eye of the Needle on the 31st of May, 1805.

Now, on Memorial Day, 1997, tourists had a drinking party atop the Eye of the Needle, a huge rock with a hole through which a person could walk. They had taken sledgehammers and crowbars to beat the white sandstone and volcanic rock till it crumbled, and now the landmark was simply two stumps of rock on a beer-can-strewn hilltop. Montanans were outraged, and proposed that public monies be used to restore the rock. Others wanted to leave it exactly as it was, beer cans and all, for others to see, and to weep.

That night, Jen read to us from her journal:

> A beaver is following me. She slaps her tail on the water as I pass the head of an island on the Missouri River Breaks. The morning's sun has just topped the White Cliffs portside and is casting the only relief one can find from the already-too-hot glare.
>
> I ponder the fate of this stretch of river, and what is happening to it. Our passage is causing a breakdown of the systems that have formed the landscape, the scenery that rivals some of the most scenic in the West. I spot heron more frequently than I sip from my water jug. The cliffs that line the river's edge hold delicate formations that the wind caresses. The cottonwood stands provide the only shade, leaves glitter like butterflies in the soft morning breezes.
>
> The sun has rolled another fifteen degrees across the blue. This I calculate by the extremely scientific method of extending my hand to arm's length and assigning each finger fifteen degrees. A flotilla of eight canoes pass the rocky beach on which I am lazing in my Crazy Creek chair. Sixteen people. We exchange the words of travelers. I adjust my hat, noticing the color change of the sweatband as the day matures.

> I think about the impact our group of five is having on the river. We focus on minimizing our impact by going by the guidelines of Leave No Trace, but still we impact this land.
>
> There is no group size limit in the Missouri Breaks, and we have seen groups of thirty-five people camping on the fragile banks. I wonder if the damage that was done to the Eye of the Needle formation is a part of the movement of humanity reaching for meaning, and trying to find it in nature. Are we pushing too many people through what is left of our wild places, without the appropriate change of heart that is needed to preserve the wildness? As a species, are we hell-bent on conquering what is foreign to us? Has this brought us to yet another point in our history: the desecration of beauty?
>
> In the distance I spot the flash of paddles. There are a few cottonwoods across the river – all of them mature and aging. There are no seedlings in the stand of trees shading a campsite. The lack of flooding and the silt that accompanies flooding has stopped the birth of cottonwoods. Larry, a Bureau of Land Management ranger on the river, tells me that in twenty to forty years this stretch will most likely be treeless. Bring an extra sunhat.
>
> I see a familiar hint of red carrying the glint of paddles. If the cottonwoods are gone, will the owls remain? Will the days always be this still?

Stephen Ambrose's book, *Undaunted Courage*, and Ken Burns' film about Lewis and Clark had been blamed for bringing 43,000 tourists to the White Cliffs in just the last year. Only 2,000 had visited the year before. The locals met with the BLM to set in motion a plan to slow down tourism in the area. But, we wondered as we pitched our tents that night, just who should not be allowed to come. Beth Johnson? The young campers in wheelchairs and on crutches? Local fishermen catching dinner? School and church groups getting out of a city for a moment of beauty and peace? Or maybe, the Year Without Time crew?

It didn't make sense. But, then, neither did the Dung Beetles…

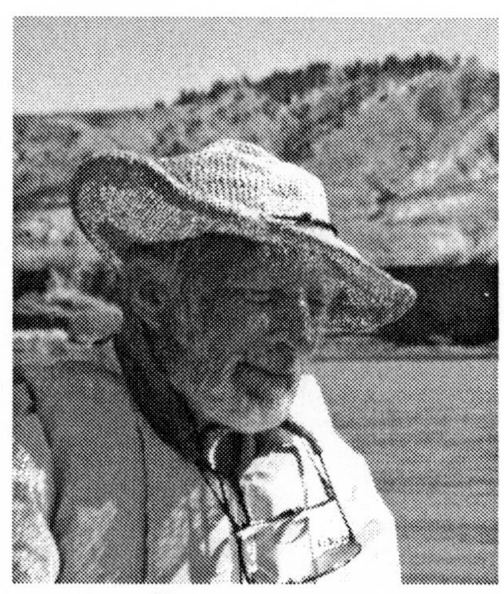

"The reshaping of Bill's hat hadn't gone so well, and the brim drooped on three sides while the top formed a pitch off to the left."

"Donna tucked her hair up into a dark green, wide-brimmed canvas hat that floated and had a pocket hidden in the seams."

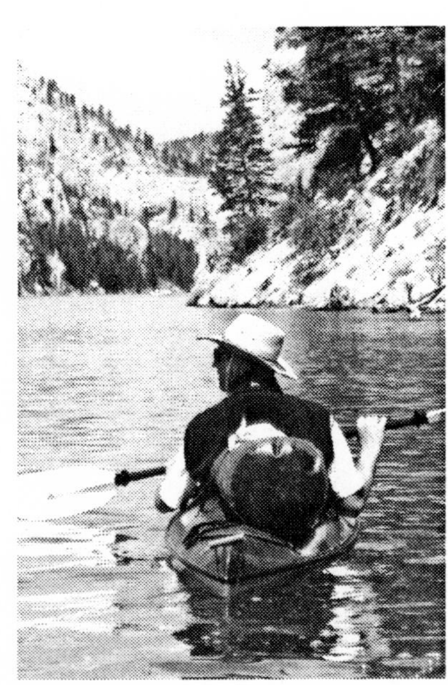

"Geoff sported a wide-brimmed Australian Outback duster, a leather lanyard draped from brim to chest."

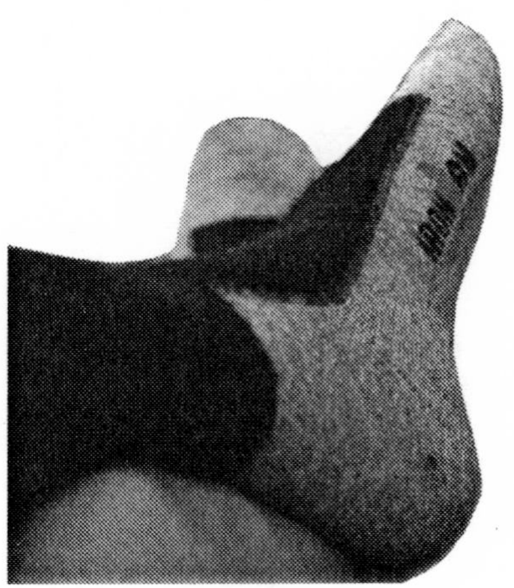

"Socks from Wigwam – 38 pair!"

"Diva, our opera-loving Chocolate Labrador"

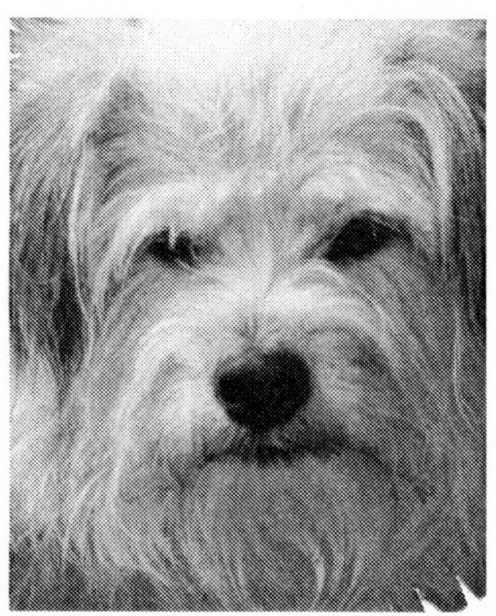

"Gypsy, a Lady Dog Streetwalker"

"Something changed in me that windy morning as a basket formed in my mother's hands."

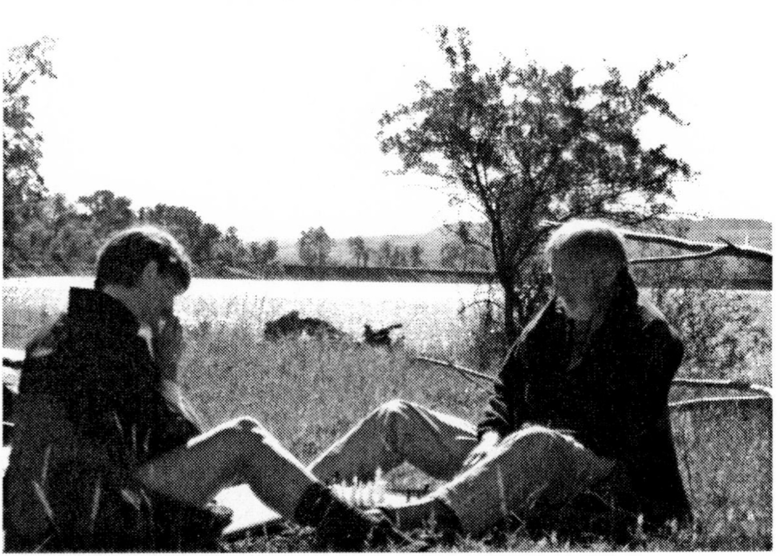

"As long as I live, I'll never forget the day I first won a game."

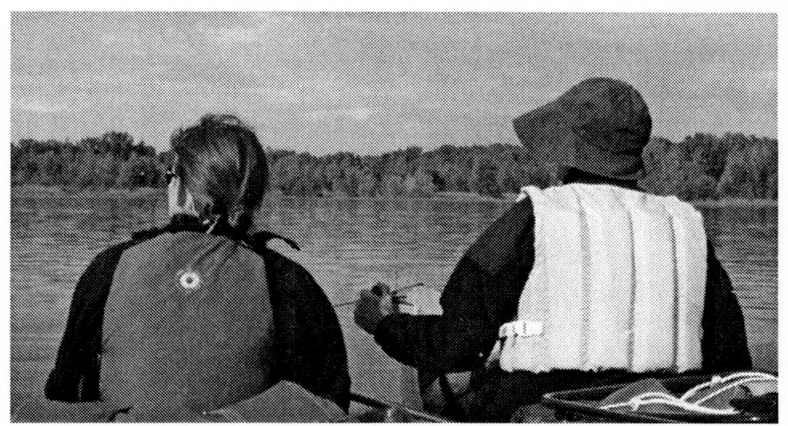

"We held our paddles on the gunwales and let the current take us..."

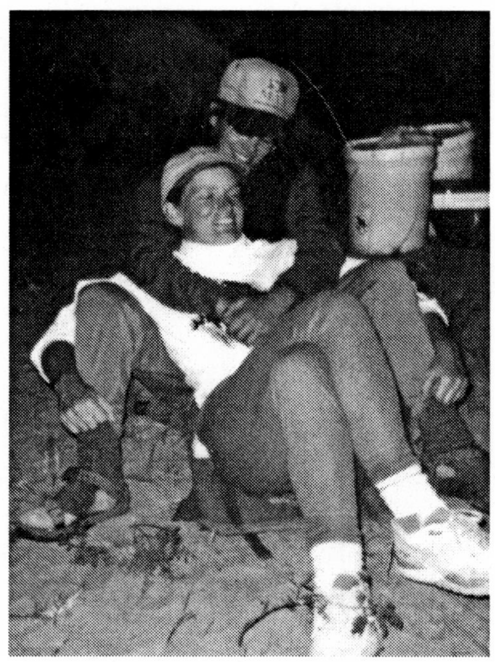

"Donna, I am giving you my daughter."

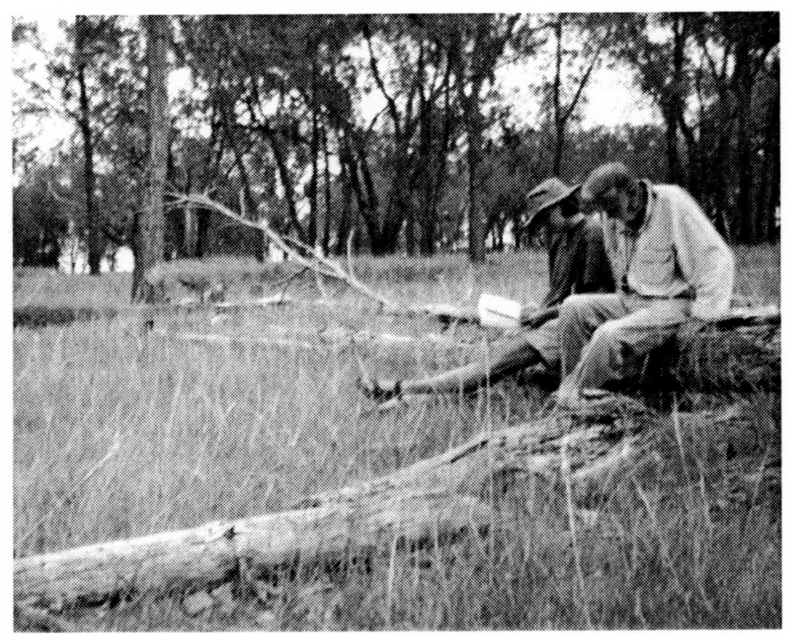

"...reading aloud would become the reason we'd get off the river earlier and earlier each evening."

"It was this damn channel."

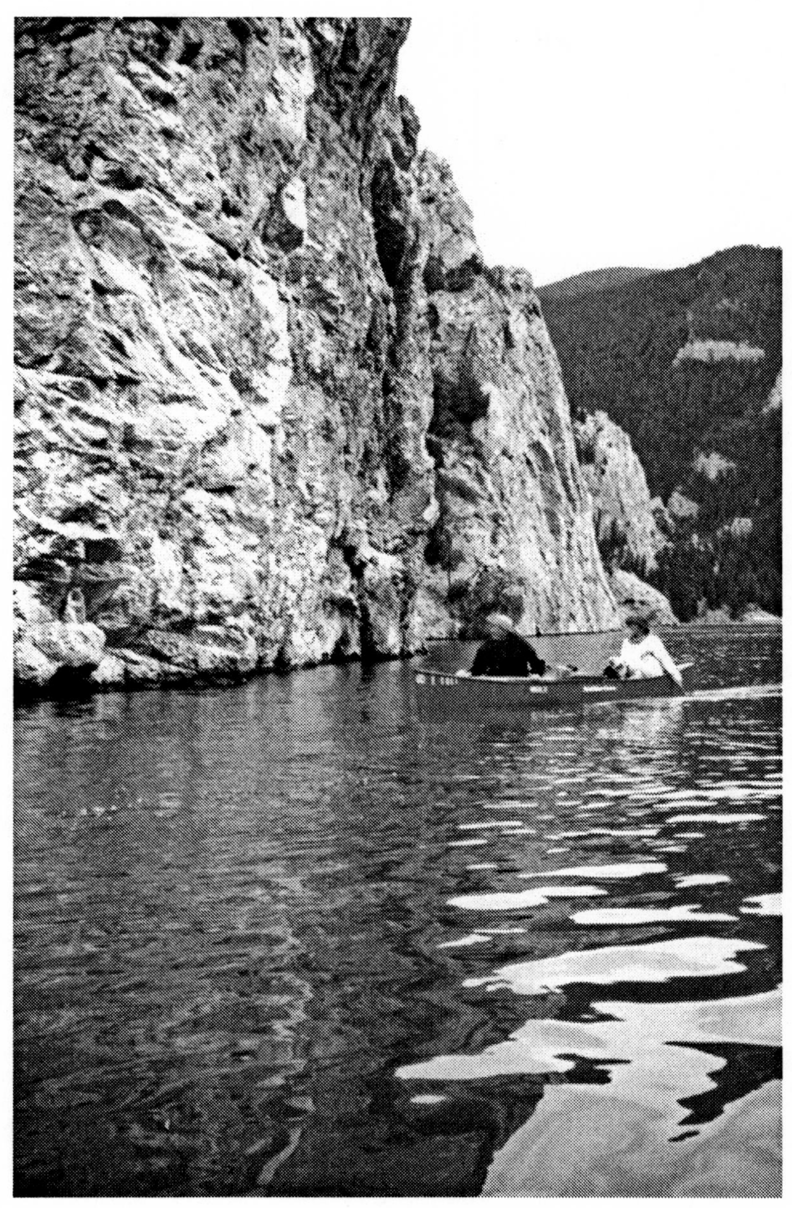

Gates of the Mountains

Love More Than You Think You Can

Jen

The sun was burning the dew off the grass as we carried the boats down the ramp to the river as she flowed past Coal Banks Landing. We came here after fetching Mom from the airport and saying goodbye to our Fort Benton friends, ice cream and all. We quietly put dry bags into their places and cinched tent bags to the thwarts. Water jugs went into the bowels of the kayak, and Diva's treats were placed in a plastic bag underneath the bow seat in her canoe (she had trained us well). We put in under a silence that told me we had done this before, and everyone was focusing on his or her tasks.

Since Mom was with us, Gypsy jumped into *E. coli* as if she did it all the time. Bill and I exchanged glances as he pushed their canoe back from shore. A smirk crossed my lips and he raised his paddle to mock a splash in my direction.

We made our way back into the pulse of the river's current, she seemed to welcome us back, as if we had never left. Was she always there, ready to carry us, to share her movement, her travels, with us? Was it simply our human desires that kept us from flowing freely in her strength? Could we always get on for the ride, steady and full of direction? I was beginning to see that "Yes" was my answer, and I the only impediment.

I felt sweat drop between by breasts, the heat of the morning sun finding my PFD and warming the skin beneath it. My clean white long-sleeved dress shirt seemed to know it was entering another long phase between laundromats, and settled in for the coming stains.

The river is swift just after Coal Banks, entering the region known as the Missouri Breaks. I had read that if Lewis and Clark, the legendary explorers of the Great Northern Passage, were to travel the Missouri River today, they would recognize only 200 miles of it – the 200 miles known as the Missouri Breaks. We were entering the most remote section of the river, with only one outpost of civilization (read: fresh water) between us and the head of Lake Peck on the eastern edge of Montana.

The river carried us through low rolling bluffs, tumbleweed rolling through the high desert we were paddling. We stopped for a late lunch on an island made of smallish rocks, small enough that we could crunch them beneath our feet as we walked across the island. The sun was close enough to the horizon to set up camp for the night. As we sat around the cookstove we wondered aloud if the river would rise enough to cover the island at any point during the night. We realized the rocks the island was made of were the same size as the rocks on the bottom of the river. She ran clear and fast here, and we could see the bottom in spots. We loaded all the unused gear into the boats and pulled them far into the center of the island. As we said goodnight, I wondered if anyone had any clear idea of what we would do if indeed we did wake up to a flood in the middle of the night, but never got around to asking. The first day back on the river after Coal Banks brought me the luxurious feeling of being worn out, and settling in to sleep on the hard bed of rocks beneath the tent was the sweetest sensation.

Morning came quickly, and with it Donna unzipped the tent. She was usually the first one out of our tent, heating water for coffee. Before unearthing the cookstove from the gear stashed in the boats, I heard the familiar sound of her morning pee. It's amazing how intimacy takes on a whole new meaning in the out-of-doors.

Mid-pee she called what was becoming a familiar morning greeting, "Jen, come quick."

I unzipped my sleeping bag and Diva and I poked our heads out of the tent. Donna was frozen in position, looking over her shoulder. A six-foot snake was making its way toward her, dropped drawers and all. It was as if the snake had heard her and was coming to see what she was.

By this time Geoff had made it out of his tent, the memory of the cattle bringing him to action. He grabbed a dry bag full of clothing from one of the boats and started banging it on the ground near Donna.

"Geoff, what are you doing? That will attract it," I said.

"No, I'm telling it we are bigger than it is and that it should go the other way."

Geoff kept banging on the rocky island while Donna pulled up her long johns and slowly turned around. The snake, a thick black ribbon of muscle continued in Donna's direction. Diva backed away as she sensed something was not quite right. And then, as if the snake heard another calling, it turned and headed away from us.

The island was only twenty yards by forty yards, and we weren't certain where the snake had originated, or where it was going. It turned toward the river and we thought it was heading for a hole in the island's rocks. We slowly followed it with our eyes, and Diva stayed nearby. And then, unexpectedly, it slithered into the river. I had seen water moccasins before, and knew that they swam, but I didn't know black snakes also swam. On a diagonal path, the snake made its way across the swift current, hitting the bank almost exactly across from us. It had calculated the angle it needed based on the swiftness of the river. Geometry in motion.

After this second morning-pee event, Donna gained the reputation of being the Attractor of Animals. It would happen many times over; she would go out to pee and come back to get us to show us a group of dung beetles rolling their oversized dung balls uphill to their holes in the wet bank, beaver's peering over their banks, or bear tracks just outside our fire circle. We spent many hours in the Upper Breaks watching Donna's discovered wildlife. There is luxury in ignoring time. By watching the sun instead of the hands of a clock we were starting to move in time with the winds and the warmth of the sun. By spending the better part of an afternoon watching dung beetles, we discovered that they actually push their over-sized dung balls uphill backwards – they use their back legs to roll the dung balls toward their holes in the wet bank by standing on their hands!

Time and learning often don't go hand-in-hand. Real learning was happening as we let ourselves escape the constraints of mornings and afternoons and instead bound our time only by breaking camp, satisfying our hungry tummies, and finding the next campsite. The days were melting into weeks as we made our way toward the high cliffs of the heart of the Missouri Breaks. We still hadn't seen the true Missouri; she was just around the bend.

Love More Than You Think You Can

Cate

We paddled for days, weeks, centuries, I don't know, because we were relaxed and calm and the wilderness along this stretch of the river seemed endless. No towns. No other boats. We stopped one afternoon when we saw something moving in the woods, only to find two small bronze-skinned Indian boys playing on the river's edge. They were shy, so we approached them carefully, quietly, and were soon introduced to their families who were having a summer's eve picnic. As the sun began to set, we washed our muddy sneakers in the river before getting back into the boats. One of the boys, Joseph, tied a string from which a fluffy white feather was suspended around my wrist. We'd become fast friends.

My eyes met Bill's as we settled onto the caned canoe seats and zipped our life jackets up to our chins. He knew what I was thinking. I'd looked in his eyes this way many times before. Once in Germany at a nursery school. Once in Switzerland at a riverside playground. Once in Siberia at a city park. I wanted to stay and get to know these children, and their families, and see their house, and eat their food, and learn new ways of doing things, and new ways of being.

Years ago, on the Rhein River, we'd lost control of our canoe in the swift current and hit a boulder. Hard. Daniel's Swiss family fished us out, took us home, dried and warmed us by the fire, fed us Onion Pie and cups of cocoa, let us work with them at their flower farm for a week, took us to mineral baths, tennis matches, and concerts, to church, and the farmer's market. When we put back in the river they and their friends stood on the bank singing God Bless America, as we paddled toward the Bodensee. And more mishaps.

In Russia, I'd invited the little girls in our apartment block to come play Barbies with me. Before long we had the first ever Moscow Barbie Doll Club, which met all over Moscow at different apartments each Saturday. I learned about tea with strawberry jam, and slimy, pickled mushrooms, and about live chickens on balconies for hard-to-get fresh eggs, and how children with disabilities were hidden in back rooms (well, until we began the Moscow Wheelchair Brigade), and about a mother's delight in seeing her first maxi pad, and all manner of other new ideas. I'd found long ago that being a tourist was not the real stuff of travel. And now, my fluffy white feather bracelet nagged at me to pull ashore and dawdle with this backwoods family.

But, as Jen and Donna had done at the blueberry pancake motel, I knew we had to press on, if only to go to the next airport in time to get me to my next seminar, one week away.

That night as we sat around our campfire, Jen said, "There's something we need to talk about, Mom." Oh, bloody hell, I thought, what have I done now?

"Donna and I have been talking… we want to be sure that all our parents know that if there were a life or death situation, that we each want the other to make decisions for us. If I couldn't make a decision about my health, I'd want Donna to decide for me. She'd be the one to decide whether to pull the plug."

I stood up, walked over the sand to the other side of the fire, took Donna's hand, put Jen's in it, and said, "I'm giving you my daughter. I trust you completely to take care of her."

Plenty of times in the months to come, when Jen walked the shoreline covered in mud, or spilled her pee can in the wee hours, or wanted a chocolate malt from the closest town, I'd remind Donna that I'd given her to her. I was glad, though, that they'd made it clear to all of us, considering stories of legal issues concerning gay couples, that they were, in their own eyes and hearts, each other's.

Geoff announced at that campfire that he wanted to ask his good friend, Sarah, to join us for a week. And what did we all think?

Jeez, I thought, another group decision. This one, however, was easy. Sweet, secure, easy-going Sarah arrived on the next train. With a book. For the next week we all paddled furiously so we could stop early each evening to read *First You Have to Row a Little Boat* by Richard Bode. We loved it! We loved reading aloud to each other. Sometimes we couldn't wait for evening and would read from canoe to canoe as we paddled. My favorite Christmas memories include an entire Christmas Eve and Christmas Day spent reading *Auntie Mame* aloud with my teenaged kids. We all vowed to do more reading aloud for the rest of our lives.

On Saturday afternoon Geoff and Sarah hitchhiked to the nearest town, Wolf Point, so Sarah could catch the train back to Denver. Bill and I went along so we could stock up on groceries. After we waved to Sarah till her train was out of sight, we stopped to shop and were recognized by a woman in the grocery store who'd read an article about A Year Without Time… the expedition, in *Outside* magazine just that morning.

She drove us back to the river where a huge, pink, semi-truck was parked on the shoulder of the road, about a half-mile from the river. And Jen and Donna. There was no driver in the cab. I glanced at Bill as we wrestled the groceries out of the car. His brow was furrowed. He picked up his pace as we made our way through the dark woods toward the river.

As we got closer, I could hear the girl's voices, and a deep-throated rumble of a voice.

"Here they are!" Donna shouted, as she ran to us to help carry the bundles of groceries.

"You've got to come meet Big John. He's staying for dinner."

Our faces must have given us away. Big John, his blue denim shirt wide open, cut-off sleeves, tattoos winding all over his huge torso and hairy arms, said, “I decided to stay with the girls till you returned. You never know what could happen.”

Big John did stay for dinner. Barbecued chicken, roasted potatoes, even fudge cake. We stayed up late into the night talking about John’s wife and children, his little farm, his beloved Pitty Tink, the eighteen-wheeler embossed with gold letters. He explained how his trucking buddies had dared him to buy a ‘titty pink’ truck, and how they honked and waved uproariously when they passed Pitty Tink on the highway. He slept in his luxurious cab that night, joined us for bacon and pancakes the next morning, then was out to the highway. But, not out of our lives. He sends us Christmas cards each year. And we talked about his generosity, his truly kind spirit, for many river miles.

Then it was time to head back to the world of first class airplane seats, pressed sheets and down comforters, hot steamy bubble baths… and room service, and all the while I longed for the sound of my paddle dipping into the Missouri River.

Be What You Always Wanted To Be When You Grew Up

Jen

August had finally found us. After spending two months in Montana, traveling on a river that flows west to east, August took us south into North Dakota. Finally, we were heading toward the sun.

We re-conned just below Garrison Dam, a massive stalwart of land that holds back millions of gallons of water; our campsite would have been flooded had but a trickle made its way through the tonnage of earth that kept the lake contained. The high desert of the Missouri Breaks gave way to the plains of North Dakota. The land rolled away from us, flowing as a duvet covers a bed, softness creeping through from underneath. From our perch on the edge of the river, I could feel the land falling away, as if the river was just skimming the surface, our boats small specks of drifting flotsam on the massiveness that is North Dakota.

Although the river was fed by the release of Garrison Dam, she meandered through scrubby tree-lined banks, poking around bends that were low-lying fingers of sandy soil reaching into the current, fingers that softened as we got closer, welcoming us to shore. Evening brought an orange ball of fire sinking toward the west, a soft glow filling the sky, and our eyes. I was learning about expanse.

Traveling through the lands that make up the American West, one can't help but learn about expanse. Looking at a horizon that goes beyond the normal degree of sight, I was being swallowed up by the expanse of North

Dakota. Everything was big. B-I-G. The kind of big that makes you wonder if you've always been looking at a curved horizon, and just never noticed.

We were paddling under blue and white fluffy clouds that seemed to go on beyond the normal dimensions of sky. I leaned back in the kayak, my legs out of the cockpit, calves resting on the deck of the boat, and closed my eyes. I wondered if, when I opened my eyes, the sky would still be as large as it was when I closed them. I hesitated, not yet wanting to test the limits of a North Dakota sky. I wanted the sky to go on and on, the warmth of the August sun forming a trickle of sweat under my shirt. I wanted the path my mind had been wandering, a sweet spot of probing into the softness of memory, to follow the gentle rocking of the current. I wanted the softness we had come to as a group to continue into some dimension of time I didn't want to identify, as if, by opening my eyes, I would see the boundary, the line of the horizon, and it would place a limit on thought.

The current pulled the blade of my paddle toward the back of the boat and I had the strange sensation of going backwards. I opened my eyes in time to see Mom and Bill's boat tucking neatly into a sandy bank on the eastern shore. The river was wide here, wide and slow, and I sat up in my seat. Pulling my legs into the cockpit, I started paddling back upriver. Donna and Diva were pulling onto the sandy beach just as I was getting within earshot.

"You looked so peaceful." Donna said, as the bow of my kayak poked the sandy shore, heading upstream. The current pulled my stern around, the boat now parallel to the shore, a handy trick I had learned over the last three months.

"The sun is nice," I said, "warm, warm and slow, almost."

I tossed my paddle to shore, put my hands on either side of the cockpit and pressed up and out of the kayak. My sandals hit land and I tested the firmness of the earth. Diva jumped out of the canoe and went searching for a stick on shore, ready to play fetch now that we were home for lunch.

What started as lunch and a quick game of fetch with Diva progressed into an afternoon of exploring. The beach we were on was the beginning of acres of prickly shrubs, vines covering the shrubs and forming fortresses that Diva could explore with her usual curiosity.

Geoff had taken a few weeks off the river to visit his dad. Mom and Bill and Donna and I were getting to know each other as a foursome. Quiet filled our afternoon, as the four of us mimicked the slowness of the river and turned a sunny afternoon into a slow walk through a fortress of vine-bushes.

A chill blew through the air as we were finding our way back to the boats. Our sandy beach came into view and we all seemed to know that we weren't paddling anymore today. We had pulled the boats far up on shore before starting our walk, and now we unloaded tents and gear bags. Donna and I pitched our REI dome tent with the ease of familiarity; we had done this so many times together over the past three months, we communicated through our actions rather than our words. Diva sat next to her blue dry bag of Nutro waiting for her dinner.

Bill was gathering wood for a fire while Mom set up their tent and fluffed their sleeping bags. By the time the four of us rejoined near what Bill was building as a fire circle, the sun was touching the horizon. Potatoes and onions and carrots were placed in foil with a few pats of butter, wrapped tightly and put aside to wait for Bill's fire to turn to coals.

Watching flames start to lick at the wood, a chill settled over us. I caught Mom's eye. We knew summer was fading.

After building up a fire with small sticks so it would quickly turn to coals, we put the foil packs of vegetables on the coals and settled back in our Crazy Creek chairs, fabulous low, legless camp chairs that support your back while you rock away the evening. The sand was cold beneath my feet; I slipped my toes into wool socks. The evening was turning from a dark blue sky to simply a dark sky as I scooched my Crazy Creek closer to Donna. I could smell the potatoes cooking in the butter inside the foil packs. Dinner was just moments away.

As I zipped up the tent after dinner, I heard a few bits of sand hit the nylon wall of the tent. I thought it was just the tent moving as Donna and I settled in, but then I heard more sand hit our tent as I zipped up my sleeping bag. Diva let out a sigh as she fell deeper into sleep in her own bag, and I nestled up close to Donna. As we let the chill of the night settle over our noses, I heard the wind pick up outside, sand being lifted off the beach and drumming lightly on the nylon stretched over our tent poles. The plains were greeting us with a neighborly windstorm.

The next morning's oatmeal came complete with teeth-cleaning grits of sand. As I downed the end of my coffee, sand clung to the inside of my plastic mug. We were truly in a North Dakota storm – a windstorm.

The storm had started slowly as we settled into sleep, but I awoke several times throughout the night to the pitter-patter of sand against the outside of our tent. By morning, the wind had picked up to a good clip, and breakfast was simply a place for the blowing sand to lodge. Paddling was out of the question today, so we stayed in our land-clothes (for me, long pants, a long-sleeved REI fleece pull-over and tennis shoes instead of sandals) and continued the walk we had started the day before.

Mom and Bill, Donna and I, Diva and Gypsy – the six of us – made our way up off the beach into the fields of shrubs that were covered in vines. The wind stayed steady, but grew milder as we found protection among the fortress of bushes. Diva ran ahead and brought back sticks for us to throw for her. Bill and Donna talked about the likelihood of meeting people on this stretch of the river, and how the dam's releases affected the rate and level of the water. Mom and I hung back and talked about the way the river swirled around the edge of the shore, the current leading to places we hadn't yet imagined. Mom picked up a vine, soft and soggy from the moist, sandy earth. She shook the sand from it and curled it back onto itself. I bent down and pulled a long, thin vine from beneath a bush and handed it to her, she wound it around the first one, forming a circle about eighteen inches across.

We changed the subject to her twenty-year-old divorce, and kept walking. As we stepped over a log, Mom made her way toward the riverbank and doused the vine-circle in the water; I pulled a vine off the exposed roots of a tree and handed it to her. And it was in this way that we made our way along the river, walking north, Donna and Bill walking with Diva, Mom and I catching up every once in a while, vines being passed to Mom, her hands winding the vines into a crisscross pattern, then adding ribs. As we turned around to head back to our campsite, my mother's fingers were weaving smaller, pencil-thin vines in between the ribs of what was quickly becoming a basket.

I watched my mother as the basket was forming; I had seen this so many times before. I saw her fingers gently coax a stiff vine between gnarled ribs, slowly pulling the smaller vine through this way and that – slowly so that it wouldn't break, gently telling it where it was needed, how to become a part of the form she was building as we walked away the morning. I thought back to the child I was when I learned my parents were divorcing, and remembered how the divorce had jelled in me, creating a chasm.

"Mom,' I started, "what was it about your marriage that brought you to the divorce?"

She was quiet as we walked, vines trailing to the ground, swishing alongside.

"Jenna," she hesitated, testing what to share, "I needed to be my own woman. I needed to take care of myself, to grow as I wanted to, and to rear you kids just as I wanted."

Gypsy ran between us, sand flying from her pads. She was chasing low-flying birds as they flitted from bush to branch.

Mom continued weaving the smaller vines between the ribs of her basket. As I watched, I noticed how familiar her hands were. I looked down at my own hands and saw the source of the familiarity. The same hands that had grasped my paddle yesterday were now on another body, plying vines from the bank of the Missouri River into a graceful basket; my hands were a likeness of my mother's hands. I stopped in my tracks. Had this always been true? Had she always been this close to me, her hands as mine, my hands nearly identical to hers?

I watched as her fingers again nudged a vine into place, wrapping its wispy end around the thick rim of the now-sure basket. I had thought I was my own woman. I held inside me a notion of being brave and bold in my lifestyle, independent in my living. And here I was, seeing my hands, the connectors between me and everything I touched, on the wrists of my mother. I was quiet as we approached the tents. I was more connected to my mother than I had allowed myself to be. Her desire to be her own woman had passed through her fingertips into me, skin separating all but a few millimeters of likeness. I unzipped the door to the tent and ducked inside. The wind quieted as I closed the door and grabbed for my journal. I opened it and stared at a blank page.

My pen dotted the page as I started to write, and then hesitated. "Even our fingernails are the same," I thought as I looked at my fingers wrapped around the shaft of my pen.

"Yes," I wrote, "I am her daughter."

Something changed in me that windy morning as a basket formed in my mother's hands. It was as if I could feel it in my own hands. As if by being her daughter I could feel her lessons. As if by sharing the same hands, the same wrinkles and fingernails, the same cuticles, I could learn from her lessons, and she from mine. Is that what it means to be a daughter? To be a mother?

I crawled out of the tent and made my way down to the fire circle, now just a dark spot on the sand. Donna and Bill were fishing peanut butter and crackers out of the food bin; Mom was sitting on a log, twisting a flower into the handle of the basket. I filled a water bottle and went to sit next to my mother.

"Nice day, this one." I said.

"Yes." Mom smiled as she placed the basket on the ground and reached for a swig of water from my bottle. "Yes, this is a good day," she said.

The next morning we awoke to what was perhaps the quietest morning we had experienced all summer. A late summer chill hung in the morning air, but the wind that had kept us off the river the day before was entirely absent. We were eager to continue our travels south.

A quick breakfast of oatmeal, a quick stow of our gear, now a habit that came naturally, and we were once again on the river. We were in no hurry, and let the current carry us around the bends that appeared like glass on this windless morning.

Each bend seemed to be spreading the river, the distance between her banks broadening, and the current slowing. We had stopped paddling and were floating in a flotilla, arms holding gunwales and deck straps to keep our boats together. Around a bend we drifted slowly past low trees on the shore, our flotilla pointing downstream.

And it was around this bend that we saw the river in a new way. She was white. Not whitewater, as in rapids, but white on her glassy surface. The calmness of the morning had brought with it an angelic whiteness to the water. It was as if we were witnessing a mirage in the desert, the shimmer of water glancing off the heated sand.

Our boats continued their path downstream with the current, approaching the whiteness. I looked at Donna and she looked at me; we shared a puzzled brow. Even Diva sat up and seemed to see the odd shimmering on the surface of the water. Mom and Bill were transfixed; we were all silent. We held our paddles on the gunwales and let the current take us toward whatever this was, unknowing.

And then, in an instant, the whiteness took flight. One squawk lifted all their wings, and what had looked like a mirage was actually thousands of white pelicans tucked away in this one slow bend of the river. In an instant the roar of their wings, the flapping of their feet against the water as they pushed off to take flight, the massive sound of thousands of wings beating against the air, against their bodies, against our intrusion, came as a deafening noise that lasted for what seemed like several full minutes.

We all sat silent… all except my sweet sister-dog Gypsy, who nearly leapt out of the boat as the birds passed overhead.

And then, just as quickly as the whiteness had launched into a symphony of wings, it was gone. I sat stunned for a minute, having never been so close to such a mass of non-human beings. Every environmental education class I had ever been in, every textbook about the migratory patterns of birds, every professor who had stood at the front of a lecture hall trying to teach me of the grandness of nature had failed in comparison to the liftoff of these thousands of birds that we had disturbed on this slow, quiet morning. My education was complete. I now understood the power of the quiet of nature. The river was teaching me what I couldn't learn on my own.

Yes, I am her daughter.

Be What You Always Wanted To Be When You Grew Up

Cate

"I felt like an apple cut in half," Jen confessed.

Jen and I were walking along the riverbank in North Dakota. The morning was windy, so we'd all decided to stay put, to rest, read, build a blazing campfire and cook up a spicy Chinese lunch.

Jen and I were meandering along the bank, and through pine scrub, half-heartedly looking for kindling. She continued, "When you and Dad called us into your bedroom, I knew what was coming. I knew something horrible had happened. Then when you told us you were going to get a divorce, it was much more horrible than I'd ever imagined."

I had my head down. "I know," I said quietly, "I was so selfish then…"

"Mom, you know I wouldn't have it any other way. You know I love your life with Bill, and Dad is doing just what he wants, so it all turned out fine."

"I don't know if you understand." I said, "It was my idea. I wanted the divorce. I'm the one who insisted."

"I know that," she said.

"I wanted more out of life. I wanted someone to... oh, I don't know, I wanted everything. To feel loved, to feel important, to be what I always wanted to be when I grew up."

"I know," she said.

"And what I really didn't want was to blame someone else for my unhappiness. Or my happiness, for that matter. I wanted to be responsible for myself. And for you. Your beliefs and values."

"I know, Mom, it's ok," Jen said.

"Oh, I don't know," I sighed.

She put her arm around my shoulder and we walked side by side, I stooping down to pick up vines now and then to add to a basket I unthinkingly had begun in my arms. Along the way I tucked pelican feathers into the weaving. We'd been surprised to see huge flocks of pelicans all along the riverbank. In Montana and North Dakota!

Just before lunch we wandered back to the campsite with a lopsided, wet, feather bedecked, vine and tendril basket. Today it hangs from my living room ceiling, one of the treasures of my life.

The Missouri River flows north from its beginnings at Three Forks, Montana, then flows east after Fort Benton. Now, a few miles over the North Dakota border, she finally turns south, just short of Canada. Our sunrises and sunsets changed, the weather changed, the wildlife changed, we were changing.

There were more small towns, grocery stores, laundromats, even casinos. Towns were so close, we could stop to do laundry once a week now, and eat at a restaurant while we waited for our drying, and even watch the World Series as we folded fraying underwear and turtlenecks.

That windy day turned into two, then three windy days. On the third day we decided that since we'd left our chess set in the truck, trying to cut down on the gear we piled high in each canoe, we'd just make a new chess set, and have ourselves a chess tournament. Bill taught me to play chess on our living room floor in Boston many years ago. It was so boring. I feigned interest in the game, wanting to be the first woman who ever played serious chess with Bill. He was a good player, and an even better teacher. He has infinite patience.

Little by little, I learned openings, endgames, and the joys of chess. It became, over many years, a passion for me. Bill and I usually eat brunch each day about 10:30 over a chessboard, craving chess as much as poached eggs.

As long as I live, I'll never forget the day I first won a game. For years Bill would let me win, hoping to keep me interested, hoping I wouldn't wander off to the kitchen to bake a batch of cookies while he contemplated a move. Then, one day, I saw something he hadn't taught me. Something I'd discovered on my own. And with a flourish I checkmated him. He was stunned. Since then I wouldn't wander off if there were a fire or an earthquake, let alone to bake cookies. For me, chess is a sort of Xterra for the mind.

Since then, Bill taught Jenny to play, and helped Donna brush up on her game. On that foggy day we were chess-starved, so we grabbed the small saw we carried in the boat, and headed to the woods, each one with an assignment: sixteen pawns, two queens, four bishops, two kings, four knights, four rooks.

Our pawns were half-inch high disks, slices of inch-in-diameter branches, the bishops had pointy tops, the knights actually had a silhouette of a horse, and the rooks had hatched tops just like real castles. The Kings were fat and each had nubbins of branches on either side which looked like arms, the queens had feathers sticking out of their tops, reminding me of my Scottish friend who described her husband's mistress as a 'fancywoman.' From then on the Queens were called 'fancywomen.'

Now, for a board. With a magic marker we created a chessboard on my sleeping pad, tossed it in a tent, set up the men, and began the tournament. Ever after we prayed for windy days so we could spend the day playing chess.

But, autumn was around the corner, so we paddled whenever possible, with pictures in the backs of our heads of dreaded snow-covered tents, frozen water bottles, and frozen socks warming on our bellies each night.

As the river widened and flattened in the North Dakota plains, it slowed to a lazy creep. We couldn't let the current take us anymore. We had to paddle.

In Washburn, a tiny river town, we instinctively made our way to the only restaurant, ordered chocolate malts, and wandered, sipping, through the town. Jen and I stopped at a garage sale. She held up a toilet seat and said, "Wouldn't this be luxury?" Then, a yellow shower curtain with ruffles along the top. "If only a hot stream of water came with it…" We met up with our crew at the laundromat and headed back to the waiting boats.

As we tucked clean, still-warm clothes into our waterproof duffels and secured them under the wonderful cargo net, Donna said, "I checked my messages when we were at the laundromat. Steven left a message saying they were leaving on their sailing trip." Then she added, "Wouldn't it be nice if we had sails on our canoes?"

I don't know which one of us started running toward town first. But, in less than five minutes Jen and I were at the garage sale, where we bought not only the shower curtain, but shower curtain rings to go with it. And pink bathmats to cushion our canoe seats.

Before we shoved off the Washburn river bank, we tied all the boats together, slid the shower curtain rings over a long paddle handle, attached the shower curtain, tied lines to each free corner, and stood the paddle on end in the bow of *E. coli*, where I was to hold the paddle in place, as the wind took us downriver.

And, that's precisely what happened. We sailed away, making better time than ever before. We traded places about every twenty minutes so the 'paddle holder' could rest.

That night, by flashlight, we rigged a paddle holder from an extra PFD and a water jug. For days we floated while we read, or wrote in journals. We didn't feel the least bit sorry for Lewis, or Clark, or Sacagawea.

Well, until the whirlpools…

Dreaming Works

Jen

The sun crossed the line between morning and afternoon as we rounded a left-handed bend in the river. Cornfields lined both banks while in the distance large factories peeked over the horizon. I knew we were leaving a portion of the river I had grown to love: the long, slow flow of current through mostly uninhabited land. All through Montana and North Dakota we had floated past rock formations and farm fields, Indian reservations and grazing cattle. As we approached the border of South Dakota, I could feel the river changing. She was getting closer to the channelized section, and she seemed to know it.

Large white gas pipes came out from underground on one side of the river, made a sharp bend downward, and crossed under us as we floated past. Billboard-size signs warned of pipelines in the river. She was becoming something to be spanned, something to cross, not simply to follow. It was an unfamiliar feeling.

As we made our way around the left-handed bend, the wind whipped up and our boats drifted apart. As if on cue, we all stopped paddling. Wind caught my paddle and lifted it into the air; I fought to keep it from flying out of my hands. We heard a train go by.

I looked around for the bridge across the river, or the tracks alongside, but saw nothing. Where was the train? The wind continued. Donna started paddling, calling over her shoulder, "We should get to shore, there's a storm coming."

Donna pulled her boat up on a long sandy beach, and Diva jumped out. The other boats came in; paddles were thrown in the bottom while we dragged them farther up onto shore. Donna was heading to a grassy field just off the beach, with Diva close behind her and a tent bag in her hands.

I looked west, back over the river as she flowed past us, and saw black clouds forming funnels in the sky. Donna was yelling something that I couldn't hear – the wind carrying her voice downriver before it got to me. My baggy red nylon shorts and worn sandals came with me as I scooted over the beach to where the tent was being set up. A crack of lightning caught my eye just as I reached Donna.

"We need insulation – the ground is wet, and if this storm brings lightning, we can't be sitting on the ground. We need something to sit on."

This is what she had been yelling to me earlier as I made my way across the beach. I turned around and ran back to the boats while Mom, Bill and Donna started putting the fly on the tent. Sleeping pads, I needed to find the pads. I pulled one off the deck of the kayak, and then grabbed another two from under the bow seat in Donna's boat. Mom and Bill's were inside their gear net; I pulled it back and saw their orange pads underneath two REI dry bags. Armed with five pads, I started to run back to the tent.

I stumbled on the beach and dropped one of the pads. The wind took it just as the rain started. The wind that had forced us off the river was simply a precursor to the rain, and it came just as forcefully. Drops quickly turned to sheets, and sheets quickly turned to torrents as I finally made it to the tent.

Donna unzipped the tent door and I threw the pads in, and then dived in after them. Sleeping pads are a godsend to the weary traveler after a long day. These had a turn-valve on one corner which, when opened, slowly self-inflated or could be inflated quickly with ten or twenty puffs, the air filling a bladder that encases a foam pad. The pad, when inflated, is the camper's version of a pillow-top mattress. The only trouble with these inflatable pads is that in order for them to protect us against lightning traveling through the water in the wet field, we needed to get them inflated. We each unrolled a pad and began to blow.

There are moments in life that should be captured on videotape – this was one of those moments. Four adults and two dogs in a tent on the western bank of the Missouri River, madly blowing into orange sleeping pads while the wind brought rain sheets pelting against our tent, as the lightning crackled wildly.

I finished blowing up one pad and scooched it under Diva. Mom and Bill got on top of their pads, and Mom hugged Gypsy to her, making sure her little feet were not touching the ground. Donna and I shared the last pad. We listened as the thunder and lightning grew closer together in sequence. Bill and Donna debated whether the delay between the thunder and lightning (which they now counted at ten seconds) meant the center of the storm was ten miles away, or closer. I looked at Mom and we both smiled, our partners were applying logic where she and I were applying humor.

"Oh God," my mother yelled over the wind, a chuckle in her voice, "can you picture what my mother would say if she knew we were about to be killed by lightning in a tent along the river? She told me this was crazy."

A clap of thunder punctuated Mom's sentence. Donna started counting. "One-one thousand, two…"

Bill chimed in, "God, if you let me live through this storm, I will not smoke for the rest of my life."

"Three-one thousand, four…" Donna's counting continued.

"Bill, you don't smoke now." Mom punched him softly on the arm.

"Fiv-" and the lightning came.

We all grew quiet. We had experienced windstorms on the river for the past few weeks, but nothing like this. The nylon walls of the tent flapped against the poles, and Diva plastered herself against the orange pad underneath her, her head sandwiched between her paws. Rain continued to come down, the force of it seeping under the floor, making everything wet. The next roar of thunder made us all flinch. Bill and Donna both started counting, but didn't get to two. The lightning cracked and we all held our breath.

We were truly in the heart of the storm. Thunder rolled over us in waves while the lightning prickled the hairs on my skin. I took Donna's hand. I had considered the danger of capsizing a boat or being eaten by bears, but had forgotten to consider that lightning might be the worst danger. I flashed back to my CPR class. Fifteen beats, two breaths.

"Fifteen and two," I said. "Just remember fifteen and two." Donna looked at me knowingly.

And then, just as quickly as the rain had moved in, the storm moved on. Thunder and lightning sequences grew longer. We listened as the rain dimmed to a pitter-patter on the tent. Donna unzipped the tent and stuck her head outside.

Calm greeted us. We emerged from the tent as if emerging from a womb. The field was springy from the water it now held, and Diva and I took a walk downriver. Gypsy scouted for porcupines or snakes and Mom and Donna and Bill made their way back to the boats. The storm that had started by sounding like a train passing in the distance, that had driven us into a tent and highlighted our fear of lightning, and then had left us as babes in the calm that followed, was now making us chuckle.

"No cigarettes for you, Bill." I said, catching his eye.

Mom needed to be at the airport the next morning to fly to her next seminar so we loaded the boats and paddled a calm river to Washburn. The day that had started with the massive flight of birds had ended with a massive storm. In the coming days we would learn from the locals that in the upper Midwest, storms that blow you off whatever you are doing are common. At least our story provided them a bit of entertainment.

I will never look at an orange inflatable sleeping pad again without seeing our bulging cheeks trying to inflate them as lightning bore down on us, our folly mistaken for bravery.

After leaving Washburn, Mom headed back out to the business world, and Donna, Bill and I in two canoes, with a dog in each boat, headed south toward Sioux City, Iowa. We had only a few weeks of paddling left before we hit Sioux City, and the river became channelized for barge traffic. I wanted to savor the remaining free-flowing miles.

The next morning was windy when I awoke, and I was slow to get out of the tent. We decided to put in, even though the wind was coming from the southeast – directly into us as we paddled downriver. We were heading for Clay County Park – just three miles downriver – for breakfast. As a flotilla of two boats we stayed close together. Donna and I were in our canoe with Diva, Bill was in *E. coli* with Gypsy. The bow of his boat was weighted with food bins to help keep it down and out of the wind.

We crossed to the west side of the river and paddled to keep from getting blown into the shore and accompanying snags. Quickly, however, we were deposited by our friend, the river, on the eastern shore – opposite Clay County Park. A concrete boat ramp appeared as we rounded the next bend. Succumbing to the wind, we pulled the boats onto the ramp, tied off the bow lines and came ashore. We spotted an outhouse (heaven) and a trashcan in the empty parking lot.

I unloaded the food bins and retrieved bagels, raspberry jam and cantaloupe. As cantaloupe juice flowed from our elbows, a van pulled into the parking lot. Three men got out, one with binoculars, and started looking toward the river, binoculars picking out an island upstream.

Of the three men, two were middle-aged and one was older. The largest of them – a big bear of a fellow – started to make his way over to us. Gypsy, in her usual fashion, began her wild barking; he stopped and let her sniff him, and, unimpressed, continued making his way toward us. He asked us where we were from, and the usual explanation followed. We had described our trip to so many people along the way – a family making its way down the river, devoid of watches and deadlines and calendars, simply wanting to understand the flow of the river, and each other, better.

We stood in the wind in our baggy shorts and sweat-stained t-shirts, toes poking out from the tips of our sandals. The wind grew colder and I headed back to our canoe for my REI fleece pullover. Jan, the bear-fellow, told us that he and his brother, Jeff, were visiting their hometown of Vermillion, South Dakota (named for the color of the cliffs Lewis and Clark saw here during their journey), back home for their father's eightieth birthday. Bill's ears perk up, his eightieth birthday being but a few months away.

Introductions were made, and we offered bagels and raspberry jam all around. The next three hours were spent talking about Vermillion, Bud's birthday party, their family, our families, their work, dreams, how the river trip came to be, our dreams, and before the sun had reached its high spot, we found ourselves in the company of friends.

Jan and Jeff offered to take us to town for a tour, I declined out of habit, and then reconsidered. Donna and I caught Bill's eye and he nodded a subtle nod.

"No, this is not crazy, this is South Dakota," I caught myself thinking.

It was care we were feeling, complete and innocent care, from these three gentle men we had met by the river.

Donna and I got a local's tour of Vermillion, complete with root beer floats and Chinese food. We brought Chicken Chow Mein and a root beer float back to Bill, and spent the rest of the afternoon in the parking lot on the shore of the river. The wind was still blowing, and we decide to stay put for the night. As Donna and I pitched the tents, Bud, Jeff and Jan interrupted us to invite us to Bud's eightieth birthday party that night. They wanted us to come into town and meet the rest of the family. Somehow, talking the day away, telling of dreams and swapping stories, tucked behind the side of their van to stay out of the wind, we had become part of their family. We put on the cleanest clothes we had, packed the dogs into the tents, one in each, and headed into town.

Clean towels and showers at Bud's house really made us part of the family, and an evening in a restaurant celebrating Bud's birthday was capped off by a sweet round of hugs as they dropped us back at our campsite.

How had this happened? How had we become fast friends, talking about living our dreams and seeking love, in the span of only a few hours? Was it the sense that we were completely exposed as travelers on the river, no escape on a windy day, and no place we needed to be? Or was it simply the offering of care that came from these sweet folks in Vermillion? Did they want to be part of the river trip, as much as we enjoyed sharing it? Could they see their dreams more clearly from taking us into their lives, making us part of their family? And how was it that by becoming part of their family, by being willing to accept the care they were giving, that I got to know my own family better? Does it all work in a cycle?

As the night grew colder and I snuggled down in my sleeping bag, french fries settling in my tummy, I turned to Donna and we talked about what had happened that day. We were both awake from the experience, not able to sleep. Could we have felt this caring had we not been on the river? Did we need to be ready to accept the care, the form of love that was offered that day? Could we have felt this in a city? Or if we were traveling by car?

And did the giving, the offering, have to be done with no thought of getting anything back? We had nothing to offer that day except warm cantaloupe, tales of our trip, and an eagerness to listen to their stories and see their town. Maybe that was why it had worked. All of us, as we moved through the windy day of talking about dreams and ambitions, simply wanted to get to know the other's ambitions and dreams. We had forgotten about ourselves as we were overcome with the care that was being shared.

The crickets sang of a summer that was coming to a close and I felt Donna's hand relax with the coming of sleep. The night's stars were bright and clear through the screen window of the tent. Just before I drifted to sleep the

Vermillion Principle came to me: Give everything you have in yourself to give; allow others to do the same.

Thank you for the gift, and Happy Birthday, Bud.

Dreaming Works

Cate

"Mom, come here. Hurry!" Jen yelled.

I was sorting through muddy clothes, muddy cans of soup, and our muddy beloved REI waterproof duffels. We'd stopped at a park to sort, clean, and organize gear for the next river stretch. I was folding a barely-yellow, tattered shower curtain.

I turned to see Bill on the ground. When I got to him, he was clearly in pain, holding his chest.

"What happened?" I questioned Geoff, Donna, Jen, and Megan, Bill's grand-daughter, Geoff's sister, who had joined us for a week on the river.

Megan's first four days were rainy ones. We stayed in our tents, cooked under tarps, and crowded into one tent to play Bingo with a tiny cardboard set from a dime store. We were gamblers, betting dimes and nickels till we ran out of change, and then betting pot cleaning detail, or sock washing, or an extra potato for dinner.

Geoff squatted next to Bill on the ground, patting his shoulder. "You'll be ok, Gwamps."

"What happened?" I yelled again.

"Well," Geoff said, "he ran out for a pass…"

"What?" I said.

"He was the running back, and I threw him a pass, and…"

"Look, you guys," I said, "Bill's almost eighty. Couldn't you find someone else to be your running back?"

I looked down to see Bill's blue eyes twinkling. Yes, he was nearing eighty, but he was full of life, maybe not Super Bowl material, but nothing would stop him from his mission to get as much as he could out of life. He is the original envelope pusher.

They'd been playing football when Bill slipped, fell, and grabbed his chest. At this point we had a truck, so we put Bill on a pile of soft sleeping bags in the back of the truck, Jen and Donna hunched over him keeping an eye on his color, his pulse, his eyes, then the rest of us piled into the cab, followed directions to the closest hospital, and carried Bill into the emergency room, where they wheeled him off down a long, cold corridor. His nurse said we wouldn't know anything for an hour or two.

We all gathered on the front lawn of the hospital, to talk. "If Bill can't continue," I finally said, pulling at a blade of grass, "what shall we do?" There was silence. I couldn't even picture doing this expedition without Bill. He was the center of the river trip. And of our lives.

Bill has an extraordinary sense of what was and what wasn't important in life. He was teaching us, without knowing it, how to be better at letting the small things of life slide by, while focusing on the largeness, the grandness of life. I've known Bill for twenty-two years and have never seen him angry, upset, blue, or worried. He just doesn't do that. We were all trying to learn from him.

Now, we began to look at a larger picture, and to wonder, and discuss what our next chapters of life would be if we couldn't finish the river. I could easily go back on the road full time to teach business seminars. Geoff still had enough time to enroll in the fall semester at Denver University.

Only yesterday Geoff had told me he'd done lots of thinking during long days of paddling. He knew now what he wanted to do. I was sitting in the water at the river's edge, he was handing me tiny stones while I built a miniature castle. "I want to encourage kids, by using music and art," he said. "Maybe work with an inner-city program, or a home or school of some sort. At least give them an opportunity to find their talents. To follow their dreams. To change their lives."

I kept my eyes on the castle so he wouldn't see my surprise. I didn't know Geoff had lofty goals. I knew he was a great kid, a scholar, had a passion for soccer, was handsome and funny, worked hard during summer breaks, made his own money, and had weathered some hard knocks. But what I didn't know was that his goal was to help kids. In my eyes, at that moment, he was a cactus flower, blooming. And, now, in his eyes, his goal seemed reachable. Had the river done that, I wondered. She's capable of anything, I'd learned.

Jen and Donna had quit good jobs to do the river, but there were always other jobs. "You could always stay in our apartment in Kansas City till you get your own place," I said.

"Mom, we can't live in Kansas City."

"Why not?"

"Mom, when we walk down the street, we hold hands. In the movies we hold hands."

It just didn't make sense. These two lovely, and loving, women had to consider whether they'd be accepted in a Midwest town, or in the world. There was something wrong if they had to worry about their safety because of their loving each other.

I'd often told of the moment Donna just couldn't keep her secret any longer and called her mother and said, "Mom, I have to talk to you about something."

"Sure honey, what is it?"

"No, Mom, I have to come home and sit down and talk with you."

"Ok. Just tell us when to pick you up at the airport."

Donna flew home, and melted into her mother's arms at the gate at the airport. "What is it, honey?" her mom said.

"Not here, Mom, let's go to a restaurant and sit down."

As soon as they were seated, Donna's mom said again, "What is it, Donna?"

Donna took a long breath, "Mom…" Just then a waiter arrived to take their orders. They ordered, and Donna began again. "Mom." She stopped.

"Mom, I'm gay," she blurted.

Donna's mom quickly brushed it aside, "Yes, I know that, honey," then leaning forward, earnestly said, "now, what is it you came to tell me?"

I plucked another piece of grass. "We could continue the river, even without Bill." One glance around the Year Without Time crew told me just what I needed to know. Without Bill, there was no river to continue.

"Katinka, why the sad face?" It was Bill's voice. He was walking down the front steps of the hospital coming toward us. "I've got a couple of broken ribs. No big deal. But, no more football."

The sun had come out, in more ways than one, so we headed back to the river, back to the boats, loaded our gear and paddled four miles before stopping for supper on a muddy bank. That night, in our tent, we zipped our sleeping bags together, and Bill and I held each other long and long. As I drifted into sleep I heard him whisper, "Ain't it fun?"

At breakfast I waited till the oatmeal pot had been shined and put back in the kitchen pack, then I broke the news. "I checked my voice mail yesterday while we were at the hospital," I said lightly. "My stats are better than ever before, and they want to get me into every city they can. Especially the large markets. They've booked me into a whole month of seminars."

Somehow this river trip had improved my business tremendously. I was winning awards, and making bunches of money. Maybe it was confidence, but I never really lacked confidence in the first place. Maybe it was delight at learning. But then I always adored learning anything new. Or maybe it was clean sheets after weeks of a sandy, damp, sleeping bag. Whatever it was, I was considering taking the month of seminars simply because, well, because it felt so good to be so successful.

Seemed like just a few years ago I was a single mother of three, a high school dropout, with no money, no home, no education, never having worked, staying awake nights wondering just how I was going to feed my kids the next day. Little by little I fed them, got a job, went to college, bought a home. In France! And now was at the top of my career. I'd like to write that it was all due to hard work. Fact is, though, that it was all just like a vacation. It was fun. It was a challenge to be overcome. In reality, it was all just a game. A game I happened to win. Not by following the rules, though. But by following my heart.

I knew I had to do that now.

"Whaddya think?" I said. "Should I accept it?"

Donna gave me my answer. "Cate," she said, "Follow your heart. We'll be ok till you return. In fact, maybe we'll use that time to do some traveling of our own. Jen and I have been wanting to spend time in Glacier National Park."

Geoff spoke up, “I’ve been trying to figure out how to tell you that I wanted to go to Denver to pick up my own canoe and van my uncle left me.”

“Wait,” I said, “are you saying we need a vacation from our vacation?” We all laughed. Then Bill said, “I could come with you, Katoushka…”

By the next Friday, we’d all repacked, stashed the canoes, and agreed to meet in one month at a motel near Omaha.

Follow Your Heart

Jen

Rulo, Nebraska is a one stop-sign town. We had pulled our boats up on the Nebraska side of the river, as the entire Iowa side required a permit, and we had already been scolded by one park ranger in Iowa; we camped in Nebraska the whole way down from South Dakota to Kansas. Rulo sported boat ramp access, with the ramp leading to a small park where the camping is free and the folks living in stilt-houses by the river are curious enough to offer a cold beer when the sun goes down.

Rulo had lived through the last flood and now every one was putting his house on stilts in anticipation of the next "Big One." Ron, a tanned, lean-muscled man put down his hammer to watch us haul the boats up the boat ramp; he smiled and then kept working away at the girders he was building to raise his house onto stilts.

Geoff and Donna and I had made it from Omaha in four days, the current strong and our days in the boats long enough to imprint our butts with the moldings of the canoe seats. Diva jumped onto the concrete boat ramp as soon as the gunwales cleared the water; she was happy to be on shore. The days were getting colder, and we knew fall was fully upon us. Rulo was a happy place to take out for the night.

Tents were pitched and the camp stove fired up for our nightly dose of instant bread stuffing and canned corn. Somehow the coming of autumn brought a new diet, and we had been living on canned vegetables and stuffing since leaving South Dakota. Diva sat by the door of our tent, her ritual waiting to go in and snuggle into her Diva Burrito. Donna obliged her the need for warmth and grabbed an extra pile jacket after she had tucked in her beloved, aging Chocolate Lab.

The sun was turning the horizon crimson as Ron sauntered over.

"Where ya' comin' from?" he asked.

"Montana." Geoff replied, as he stood up to shake his hand. Geoff's hat perched on his head in a way it hadn't five months earlier. He approached this stranger in a new way, with more confidence, more intrigue, a bit of pride in his answer, and an eagerness to listen to the story that was bound to come from this soon-to-be friend; a lesson Bill had taught… everyone has a story to tell.

"Just the three of you's? In them two boats, all the way down from Montana?"

"Well, we've been takin' our time about it, so it wasn't that big a deal." Geoff displayed a wonderful bit of self-deprecation to ease this man out of his shell and have him join our trip, if only for an evening.

"Did you get hit by the flood? That why you putting her up on stilts?" Geoff nodded his head toward Ron's house as he queried.

And with that, Ron settled into our trip as surely as our stuffing was settling into our tummies. A tour of his one-room house, all the interior walls torn out because they were too damaged to save after the last flood, a run up the ladder to the web of wood he was weaving onto which his house would be raised by a crane, and his own boat, "mostly for fishing and floating," he said, and we found ourselves on up-turned buckets on his front lawn, sipping cold beer from his cooler in the kitchen.

We watched, almost through his eyes, as the river, which had become so intimate to us, took on a new character. The wind that had buffeted us for the past four days had shown us but an inkling of the force that accompanied the river wherever she went. Ron told of the last flood, how she simply came up the banks, gobbling up everything in sight, last of all, his house, and the houses of all his neighbors. The houses stood, but most everything else floated away. The town itself was covered in eight feet of water, and you could still see the water line on all the buildings.

The mosquitoes joined us as we opened more beer, and the sun sank lower, leaving the night sky a cobalt blue. Ron offered us the use of his "pee bucket," a five-gallon bucket with a toilet seat on top (his house had electricity but no running water). I took him up on his offer, and then followed his direction when I was finished, to empty it into the river, easy as that. I realized the life we had been living, where one of the most intense moments of the day was finding the perfect log on which to balance for the morning constitutional, could have been so much easier if we had simply hauled along a five-gallon bucket and a toilet seat. It would have made for some good front-page photos, too.

Ron had an early day tomorrow, and headed off to bed. We made our way back to the tents to find Diva snoring away in her bed. We checked in on her, Geoff slipped into his tent, and Donna grabbed the camera.

"Let's take a walk," she said.

The evening had grown chilly, but my face was warm from the beer. I slipped my arm through hers and we started a slow walk past the stilt-houses toward what we thought was the town. Three blocks back from the river we spotted a post office with an elevated wooden sidewalk, the door a good six feet above the street. Down from the post office was a feed store and beyond that corn grew five feet tall in rows that butted right up to the side of the store. We could just make out, in the fading light, the depth of the rows. They grew past the light and seemed to go on forever.

But it was across the street that Donna was focused. A neon sign glowed red in the window and Donna crossed the street to capture Rulo on film. The door, again, was elevated off the street, with wooden steps leading up to it. I stepped on the first stair and reached up to jiggle the knob as Donna took a picture. It was locked, but the neon flickered as bright as a Manhattan nightclub: RULO LIBRARY.

Nebraska was good to us – neon, toilet seats and all.

***

Geoff headed off to visit colleges that might be interesting to him come winter, and Donna and I met Bill in St. Joseph, Missouri. We were just above Kansas City, and wanted to get in as much paddling as the weather would allow; we were racing winter.

Bill, Donna and I again settled into our routine of slow mornings packing up the tents and paddling through the afternoons, to take advantage of the heat of the afternoon sun. Diva and Gypsy tolerated each other as they explored close to camp as we secured gear in the boats. Diva came running when Donna said "In the boat," as she knew treats were soon to follow. Gypsy, on the other hand, lingered on shore until Bill was well settled into his stern seat and was just about to swing the bow of *E. coli* into the current, and then she would make a running leap into his boat, sending it rocking. In a way, it was her version of casting-off, but I don't think Bill saw it that way.

We were making headway as the current carried us downriver at a steady six knots. The banks of the channel were high, with reeds flowing over them. The reeds hung down and looked soft in the wind but were thick and dry and cut your skin if you tried to grab them.

That afternoon, we continually looked for a campsite, zigzagging back and forth across the river. Bill and Donna each spying through their monocular to the other shore, looking for a dip in the height of the bank and a potential campsite.

I know you won't believe me when I tell you that not having a campsite, with the sun quickly heading toward the horizon, and the day's warmth going with it, can bring a bit of stress into a group. It was this damn channel. The six-knot current had chewed away the sloping banks we had not known to cherish in Montana and the Dakotas and we were left with having to grab at reeds that cut like deep paper cuts and swing the boats around in the current. We tried this several times and still were drifting downstream.

Donna spied a possible landing and called back to Bill, "How about that one, to your right?"

Bill was about forty yards behind us and knew we were yelling to him, but couldn't hear what Donna was saying. "Follow us," she shouted.

And with that, we started paddling like crazy. We were moving quickly past the point where the speed of the current and our angle of crossing was getting dangerous. I was in the bow and dug into the water with my paddle as if I were shoveling out of quicksand. Donna paddled as hard as she could and we felt the boat start to head to shore. It was then that the constant boils of the channelized river began to worry me.

Boils are, in my best estimation, simply a manifestation of how angry the river is to have been channelized. One could paddle along for a few serene minutes, thinking one was in control, and then she would snarl and spit and throw up a boil to the right of your bow. The force of the boil, some bubbling as large as thirty feet across, would rock the canoe and fully spin the kayak, as the kayak has a deeper draw. Once, I was turned 180 degrees in the kayak by the force of one boil. I learned just to go with it, as fighting it was not only useless, but dangerous.

As Donna paddled in the stern and I was digging away in the bow, our canoe started to turn toward the right bank. As if on cue, a boil came up just off the bow, slightly downstream, as the boil bubbled her rage. The boat swung into it and rocked back toward the upriver side. Again, just as if orchestrated, another boil spat at us from the upriver side of the boat and rocked us back to the other side. Diva bolted upright as she felt her usually stable canoe bed begin to give way and water start to rush in over the gunwales.

Donna and I both yelled something to the other. It simply highlighted the stress of being out of control in the middle of the river, with all of our gear and Diva in the balance. We both instinctively put our paddles across the gunwales and, after we rocked through the water-over-the-gunwale cycle four times, the boat settled down and we were still upright. Diva let us know that she would like to get to dry land and we silently began to paddle again. This was the closest we had come to dumping, and I could feel the chill, not of the approaching winter, but of the realization that we were entirely at the mercy of this river.

Shore came up quickly and I grabbed hold of a branch and the reeds that were our entrance to dry land. The boat swung around as the current carried it downstream, almost smashing the stern into the shore to prove a point. I jumped out and held the boat as Diva, and then Donna, made it to land. The scene was repeated as Bill followed us into the alleged take-out. Finally, we had found a campsite.

It was late that night, after the tents were up and dinner eaten, Bill settled into his tent, his journal ever at the ready, that Donna and I struck out to a ridge separating the river valley from the farm fields in the distance. The sun had disappeared behind the horizon, and the trees on the ridge were silhouetted black as a cast iron pot. I will never forget the feeling of helplessness I had experienced in the boat that day with Donna, more helpless than I have ever felt next to her. What was it about being at the mercy of a river for five months? Had I learned her lessons? Had I taken them in and let them soak into my soul?

I knew the darkened trees of the sunset were bidding me on. I could feel their message, their telling of the days gone by, the slight of the summer's sun spent in the wilderness of Montana, the transition of the Dakotas and now the power of a river forever kept against her will. What had I come here to learn? Was it love, or the boundaries of love? Was it myself, and if I could endure the home of the traveler? I looked to the night sky as she turned from crimson to purple and finally to the rich blue that takes us all to black. Will I remember this feeling, and how it had changed me? When the sun rises tomorrow, will I remain alert, knowing I have been given lessons, gifts, from this river trip, that would not have been given without the endurance of these days, one after the other.

Donna and I made our way back to the tent. Bill's light was out but we whispered "Night, Allen" in voices so soft we knew we wouldn't wake him.

I slipped into our sleeping bag as Diva stretched her legs into my back, reclaiming the space I had tried to stake out. I moved closer to Donna.

***

In the morning, I did remember the lessons. I spent the first of the day's light surveying our tent ceiling as Donna and Diva breathed softly, one on either side of me.

Mosquito blood streaked brown against the faded cream-colored nylon that was once as bright as the REI catalog we'd first seen more than a year ago. My sleeping pad was stained with spilled coffee and the mud that had soaked through during the rainstorm in North Dakota, the six of us huddled on top of the pads to protect us from lightning traveling through the ground. Donna and I had broken down and gotten cotton pillowcases into which we shoved t-shirts and long johns to make pillows in September (not sure why we waited so long), and mine was soft under my neck.

I looked to my left and saw my journal perched on top of my red REI dry bag. The dry bag was half-full and the top flopped over. It had taken me five months to figure out that I could live with very few pieces of clothing for weeks and not mind one bit. Gone were the days of full dry bags. On the other side of Donna, her toilet kit was positioned perfectly to avoid getting squashed by Diva, and her contact lens supplies were waiting for their morning activities. She had learned to live her way in the backcountry, not needing running water or electricity or even clean clothes to be comfortable, or, at least, not un-comfortable.

Comfortable or no, she was more beautiful to me this morning than any other time I had known her. As her lips parted slightly with her breathing, I remembered the evening in the cottage in New Jersey when she placed her hand on my back and said, "I know you." But did she? Did she know what I would be like after three weeks of not showering and the third day in a row of eating warm tuna fish out of a can on soggy saltine crackers? Did she know I would want to vie for my place in the group by rescuing gear after a capsize two weeks into the trip, that it would be me, the one who appeared so prepared for group leadership, that would actually put the group in jeopardy because of pride?

And now, after five months of living with scant privacy, when this was all over, what would our life together look like? Donna rolled over and smiled her morning smile as my mind played out scenarios. I pushed a strand of hair off her forehead and smiled good morning. We were still on the river, at least for now.

The day's paddle held the usual boils and warm PowerBars, mile markers telling us exactly where we were on the Corps of Engineers maps that were detailed down to the last buoy. As the afternoon was approaching, we pulled into a cove on the Missouri side that was littered with driftwood. The bank here, protected in the cove, was almost beach-like and we pulled the boats out easily. Bill immediately set about gathering wood for a fire, although "gathering" is a bit of a stretch. There was so much driftwood on the shore that we had to clear it away to make a spot to pitch the tents. The cove acted almost like a colander for the wood floating downstream; I scanned the shore for the paddle that had eluded me after the capsize.

As Donna and I set up the tents, Bill lighted a fire to bake our dinner of potatoes and onions in foil. After we wrapped the vegetables in the foil and placed them on the quickly-forming coals, Bill continued to add driftwood to the fire. I could hear the vegetables baking and bubbling as Bill added more and more wood to the fire. As we used tongs to pull the foil packs from the flames and let them cool, Bill added more wood to the fire. Bill loves bonfires; we could have cooked a side of beef.

We had dinner that night with a setting sun, gray billowing clouds tempering the sky, a roaring bonfire to beat back the cold, and potatoes and onions cooked in butter and basil. I leaned back in my Crazy Creek chair and savored the onion on my fork. This feeling was beautiful, and I wanted to imprint the moment on my mind. Diva snored lightly in the tent and Donna reached for more potatoes out of the foil packs. There was a calm that I hadn't felt before, as if what we had come for had been achieved, or, more accurately, received. The fire was holding us in its grasp as the flames licked the dry driftwood Bill was feeding it. I watched as he looked out at the river flowing by, and wondered if he was tired. His bones, I am sure, were as cold as Diva's on these nights, and she was already in her sleeping bag.

"What do you think, Bill?" I asked, of nothing in particular.

"This has been a good day, a good trip." He responded as he turned to face me. His crooked smile floated slowly across his face and I remembered the telephone calls and the letters to sponsors and the gear lists I had exchanged with him one year earlier.

What does a daughter do if she doesn't get to know her stepfather on an expedition down the Missouri River?

Follow Your Heart

Cate

Bill came prancing down the aisle with balloons. He stopped at the podium in the front of the ballroom at the Hyatt Regency in Chicago and said, "Isn't she wonderful?"

The crowd roared. And cheered. I blushed, and spurted, "What are you doing? There's a seminar going on here." He had his crooked grin on, and urged the audience to play along. He pledged his love to me, twirled me around, got down on his knees, and presented the balloons.

After a few giggles, and good-hearted chastising, I sent him on his way, and tried to conduct the rest of the seminar. It was the happiest, jolliest, most successful seminar yet. The crowd loved it!

That night, after we turned off the lamp, we tried to figure it all out. Seemed as though businesspeople in an audience in a strange city identified so much more with me, and with my message, when they knew I was a wife, a mother, a canoer who had a playful spouse. The black silk suit, the makeup, the successful businesswoman image wasn't nearly as productive as simply being myself. Now, I practice being me. Just me. And the earth keeps spinning around.

Bill and I had left all our grungy river clothes in the REI dry bags, which after washing with river water, still looked brand new. They're excellent bags. Then we'd driven our truck to the airport in Pierre, South Dakota, checked in at the ticket counter and split up.

Bill and I have different pacing. Different timing. I'd learned that to travel with Bill meant that we'd each have a ticket and meet up at our destination. I like to arrive everywhere early. Bill lollygags. In airports he reads whole chapters of books in the concourse shops on his way to the gate. I find the right gate, then sit there, ticket at the ready, waiting an hour or more, to be sure I'll be on time. Bill stops in the men's room, does whatever men do in a men's room, then washes his hands and face!, combs his hair, perhaps soaks a stamp off an old envelope in the sink, folds several paper towels to take with him, counts his change, washes his hands again, then, and only then, saunters out, only to find someone to report any shortages of soap or towels or toilet paper.

Once, in Siberia, he reported that the men's room was out of towels. The surly attendant said, "Well, wipe your hands on your pants, then," and rolled her eyes. At the breakfast buffet at the same hotel in Irkutsk, Bill told the waitress there was no more juice. "Well, have kefir…" she snarled. After a few more months in Russia, we learned that there really was no Russian word for 'customer.' The idea of satisfying customers was brand new. That all changed in the years we lived there. We arrived in Russia when it was a Communist country. We left after the 1993 revolution, the burning of the Parliament building, the barricades in the streets, the coup, the collapse of the ruble, the privatization of business and property, the growth of the mafia, the idea dawning that one gets paid for the amount of work one does.

We watched our Russian friends learn this lesson, which we, as Americans, had learned when we had our first lemonade stands. For example, I noticed that the people who shoveled the snow on the streets were always bundled up in thick, quilted black jackets. Telograikas, they're called. Nothing fancy. In fact, street cleaners have worn them for over seventy-five years. I was cold from September till May in Russia, but they always seemed to be warm. I thought I'd better get me one of those jackets. I found one at a street sale for forty-five cents. It did keep me warm. One evening I embroidered a few flowers on my jacket and the next day wore it to a meeting at the U.S. Embassy where an American woman saw it and wanted one just like it. I was so busy that I couldn't even offer to find one for her, let alone embroider it, so I asked Ivan, my neighbor, if he'd find one and have his wife, Svetlana, do the embroidery. The next morning, on my doorstep, were two jackets! Beautifully embroidered with Russian designs. Much, much more wonderful than mine. By week's end, we had an order for five more jackets. Within six months we had over 150 Russians working to fill the orders we were receiving from foreigners who loved what we called Moscow Street Sweeper Jackets. Soon the jackets were sold in Japan, England, Greece, France, Germany, and the U.S. Fortune magazine featured the Moscow Street Sweeper Jacket story in an article on doing business in the new Russia. The business was a grand success, but the important part, the life-changing part, was that 150 Russians learned that they could have an idea, work hard, and make it a reality.

Before we knew it would be such a big business, we used our apartment for Russian women to exchange plain jackets to be embroidered for finished ones. They'd come each Saturday morning with the jackets they'd embroidered that week, I'd pay them, and they'd take however many they thought they, and their neighbors, could embroider the next week. One Saturday, Valentina brought a lovely jacket for which I paid her ten rubles. About a half-month's wage in Russia. The next Saturday she brought two jackets and I handed her twenty rubles. She left my apartment – only to return a few minutes later to give me what she thought was an overpayment, ten rubles.

"Valentina," I said, "you worked twice as hard, so you get paid twice as much."

Her eyes got big as saucers and she said incredulously, "You mean I get paid for the amount of work I do?"

Our Russian friends had told us the seventy-year-long Communism joke: they pretend to pay us, we pretend to work. The ruble was never even worth the paper on which it was printed. Their work was cursory. Shoddy. Prideless. Now, Valentina smiled, and asked if she could embroider ten jackets that next week. And could her neighbors do the same. She was catching on. One gets paid for the amount of work one does.

On trips abroad I'd learned to meet Bill in Amsterdam, or Brussels, or Hamburg, so we could each travel at our own pace and be happy to be together, rather than stew and nag and worry. Well, one of us would stew, and nag and worry.

So from Pierre, we flew to Chicago, luxuriated in a candle-lit tub together, ate crab cakes in bed, and enjoyed perhaps the best seminars I'd ever given. Bill flew back to meet up with the crew in St. Joseph, Missouri, while I gave one more week of seminars in Michigan. In October. In a blizzard. In the seminar business, there's no such thing as calling in sick. Or not showing up for a seminar. When a speaker commits to do a seminar, he does it. Rain or shine. Or three feet of snow. The highways were closed by the time I finished my Thursday seminar. I asked the clerk at the front desk of the hotel if he knew anyone who would drive me from Grand Rapids to Traverse City using back roads.

"No, I don't know any fools," he said.

I asked around the coffee shop. I offered a huge bonus to anyone who would drive me up north.

A burly man, stuffed into layers of flannel and quilted denim said, "I'll do it. How are you on snowmobiles?"

Ten hours later he deposited me, and my three boxes and two suitcases, at my Traverse City hotel. I woke up the innkeeper, registered, and asked for a cigarette. I don't smoke.

By Saturday, I was still thawing out at the airport, waiting for the Year Without Time crew to pick me up. We wandered the town, found an Indian restaurant, our collective favorite type of restaurant, and settled ourselves for a long Indian lunch. After paying the bill, we asked when the restaurant opened for dinner.

"In forty-five minutes."

"Do you take reservations?" Bill said.

We walked around the block, telling tales of Glacier National Park, blizzards, and seminars, then headed right back to our table at India Oven.

That was when I told the Year Without Time crew about the phone call from my dad. And everything changed.

Don't Let The River Get In The Way Of The River Trip

Cate

As was my custom, I had called my eighty year-old mom and dad after my Friday seminar, just to check-in before heading back to the river.

"I don't know how much longer I can take care of your mother alone," Dad blurted out.

"What do you mean, Dad?"

"Honey, it's been so long."

Mom had undergone heart surgery ten years before, and now spent her days in her recliner reading every large-print book from the library and watching television, with only an occasional trip to the grocery store where she maneuvered through aisles in an electric cart, sometimes missing pyramids of green bean cans, sometimes not. In spite of Geraldo and Judge Judy, Mom's thinking was sharp. She kept the checkbook, paid the bills, wrote letters, and kept in touch with her five kids each day.

"What do you mean, Dad?" I repeated.

"Honey…" then he stopped.

"What is it, Dad?"

"Honey," he began again, "I'm about to say the hardest thing I've ever said." Then silence.

"Honey… we… Mom and I… need a little help."

Then, what had begun slowly, turned into a torrent of words, of problems they'd been facing. He driving down the wrong side of a highway. She stumbling and falling down and not being able to get up. He trying to prepare meals which had turned into routine, microwaved t.v. dinners.

"Daddy, what can I do?"

"How would you like to live in Arkansas?"

Bill always says that I am a "to-think-is-to-do" person. At that moment I was mentally packing books and dishes for Arkansas and buying hooks for the ceiling to hang a red canoe.

"I'll be there within the month, Daddy. Find us an apartment. Remember they must take dogs. And we need an extra room for an office. Close to the library would be wonderful. Just hold on till I get there. See you in three weeks. Oh, and Daddy… thanks for taking care of Mama all this time."

Now at our Indian restaurant, I ordered Chicken Vindaloo and sat back in the same seat I'd had at lunch just forty-five minutes earlier. "There's something I need to tell you," I began. Then I told the crew about my Dad's plea.

One by one, water glasses were put down, napkins were folded on laps, eight wide eyes were focusing on me and what I'd just said.

Donna was the first to speak. "Remember, Cate, this is A Year Without Time. If the year is up for you, no matter what clocks or calendars say, then we can all adapt and change and work around what you feel you have to do. That's what a year without time is all about. That's what we've all been trying to learn on this river. We can't see around the bends of the river, but we keep paddling and adjust our course as we round each one. Somehow we'll all make it around this bend, I know."

And then Donna reminded me of something I'd said months earlier, "Don't let the river get in the way of the river trip."

I started to cry. At Donna's wisdom. At the thought of leaving the river. And Jenny. At the delight of being able to do any of the river trip at all. At the thought of what we'd all accomplished. And learned. And shared. The thought of the smell of musty tents, and sticky, sandy, nylon sleeping bags, and burned roasted potatoes and onions, and sardine lunches served on paddles, and dogs baying at huge moons outside our zipper door, and gentle laughter coming from downstream canoes, and leathery, peeling sunburned noses, and the sound of a lone paddle dipping into a great river, and Jenny's freckled shoulders, and Montana cottonwood fluff floating with us to the Gulf of Mexico, and river towns, and warm, deflated root beer floats brought to a campsite an hour away, and being with such important people, and I wondered if I could, in this next chapter of my life, apply all the things I'd learned on A Year Without Time.

Don’t Let The River Get In The Way Of The River Trip

Jen

Twenty-four hours later we were in Atchison, Kansas, and Donna was checking the messages on Mom’s voicemail. We had devised this voicemail system as a way for family to get in touch with us in emergencies. Donna found me rummaging in the back of the truck.

“Jen, I have to call my mother, something is wrong.”

“What is it?” I said.

“I’m not sure, she just left a message. I’ll be back in a bit.”

As it turned out, Donna’s mother had just fallen from a ladder while packing their recently-sold house in Utica, New York, and had broken her arm. She needed help, and none of Donna’s siblings could take off work. Donna’s mom and dad had to be out of their house in three weeks.

“Well, let’s go.” I said.

“You mean leave the river just like that?”

“We can always come back to her, she will be here, and your folks need help right now. Let’s go.”

I knew that if we left, winter would keep us from coming back this year. And if we didn't come back this year, I wasn't sure when we would get back to the river, but I knew it was right to go. Maybe not right for our sponsors, or Geoff, or Bill, but I knew it was right for us. It was the river that had taught me that you take the chances that come to you, and let them lead you where they will. These "bends in the river," as my mother calls them, are the stuff we all seek. These paths that we think we are making – but are really at the mercy of the river, and her boils, and her bends – these are the paths that lead us closer to each other. These are the paths that teach us love.

As we pulled out of Kansas City one day later, our gear hastily thrown in the back of the truck and our boats on top, the October sun setting behind us, I put on a melancholy tape and looked at Donna in private for the first time in weeks. Tears fell from my cheeks as she grabbed for my hand with her free hand.

"Oh, Babe," she said, "don't cry."

"No, it's good. If I weren't crying it wouldn't have meant so much, this river trip. If I didn't cry when I left the river, it would mean I hadn't learned anything, anything at all."

Missouri turned into Ohio as night came, and we stopped at a small motel and sneaked Diva into the room. As I crawled into bed (a real bed and real sheets!) with Donna, she took me into her arms and held me for a long time.

"This trip," she said, "this trip will stay with us."

I knew as I lay my head on her shoulder, my tears making her sweatshirt wet, that we wouldn't go back. And I knew then that if ever anything happened to her, that I would return alone, and do the whole thing, top to bottom, in the kayak, and take it all in again. I knew that the banks of that river, those shores, laden with mud and reeds, were the shores where I got to know my partner, my lover. I knew that it was on those shores, vines forming a basket under the direction of my mother's fingers, that I learned about being my mother's daughter. It was there that I got a glimpse of the man Geoff was becoming, and it was there that I saw, full force, the man that Bill had always been.

But it was in the arms of my lover, a low melancholy washing over me, even as I was sure we had made the right decision, that I knew I had seen myself, little by little, change on the banks of that river. I had watched as I grew closer to becoming the woman I had always longed to be. I felt, as one feels hairs on the back of one's neck in an electric storm, a shock of awareness. I had watched Donna become a friend to my mother, a comrade of Bill's. And I had watched Diva, in the lateness of her life, romp on the shores, mud oozing through her pads, a smile on her dog-face that showed her wildness coming to the surface. She was in heaven.

I drifted to sleep that night in a motel room in Ohio as a rainstorm came over the Midwest plains. Donna and I pulled the blanket tighter around us as we missed the closeness of our zipped-together sleeping bags. I missed the feeling of Diva's paws in my back, but knew she was close to us on the floor. This was the first rainstorm in months that hadn't beat against our tent fly. The sky was crying for me.

My tears were done, except for now, as I write this, five years later.

Afterword

Say Yes

The week this manuscript was completed, Bill passed on gently, at home, with Cate lying beside him, whispering sweet stories into his ear.

Even if Cate's seminar business hadn't blossomed, even if Jen and Donna hadn't been asked to return to the staff of Princeton University (and received promotions), even if Geoff hadn't gone on to become the teacher he'd dreamed of being… we know that Bill's teaching us the Lessons of the River — to throw away our watches, to quit our jobs, to say yes, to follow our dreams and our hearts, and to join him for his last adventure — was Bill's legacy to us.

Updates from the Web Site

Donna

During the expedition we maintained a website which was updated when we found phone lines; Donna authored most of the postings. As we would finish writing a section of this book, Donna would add the archived postings from the web site files that corresponded to what we had just written. Undoubtedly we had gotten some detail wrong, dates mixed up, or allowed slight exaggerations. Always, we would chuckle and say, referring to Donna's writings, "And now, the facts." We print them here *exactly* as they appeared on the web during that fabulous Year Without Time.

July 10, 1997

We have been paddling and portaging dams since June 22. We arrived at the Missouri River Headwaters State Park on June 20. Much of the park, including the sign identifying the boat launch area, was under water, and the current ran at about 8 mph. We decided to scout the river downstream and liked the looks of Canyon Ferry Lake as the spot to practice loading the boats, fine tune our weight distribution, and put in. By unanimous decree, the first bit of the river will be run after the fast water has settled.

The trip from Canyon Ferry to Great Falls was mostly lake paddling, sometimes with strong, gusty headwinds and the sounds and sights of motor boats. The river is held back by three dams: Canyon Ferry, Holter, and Hauser. The Missouri is a trout fisher's paradise. Most folks said they were catching rainbow, brown, and land-locked salmon. Below Hauser Dam, the river started to act like a river, running about 5-6 mph. Our arms, shoulders, legs, abdomens rejoiced.

We stopped in at Craig, Montana, a town that we would be happy to rename Jerry-Karen-Chris-ville. That's for Jerry and Karen Lappier and Chris Goodman, owners and operators of the Missouri River Trout Shop and Lodge. Their hospitality is unparalleled: they found us cold and wet outside their door and opened for business a week early to feed us a breakfast from above (you must try the blueberry pancakes) and to provide us a place to take long, hot showers and rest for a couple of days.

We returned to the river, only to watch Bill and Cate demonstrate the anchor trick. Lesson number 1: do not attempt to anchor for lunch on the Missouri in fast moving current. Or if you do, cut the line. From a point further downstream, Jen, Geoff and Donna watched in disbelief as familiar gear bags and a red canoe began moving toward them. There went Cate's yellow lifejacket. There went a Thermarest sleeping pad. And now the situation was plain to see: Bill and Cate had capsized. Bill was holding onto the canoe, buoyed by two of the red REI dry bags that remained attached to the boat. Cate had already swum to shore. Gypsy, briefy trapped under the canoe until Bill freed her, was now trying to climb up and out of the river. Quick action on Jen's part brought Bill and Gypsy to safety. Donna and

Geoff lassoed *E. coli* and paddled her to shore. Cate and Bill needed a day to dry out on the riverbank.

The next day, we were back at it, despite threatening weather conditions. Finally thunder and lightening forced us to shore. Once again, to our delight, we met wonderful people in Fred and Ruth Barrett. We were invited to share lovely conversation over a welcomed breakfast the next morning.

From Dearborn to Cascade, the river kept its 5-6 mph pace. We reached Cascade and stopped in to see Steve Crow. Karen Lappier (from the Missouri Trout Shop and Lodge) had called Steve and made arrangements for him to prepare some of his famous sausage and bacon for us. If you are near Cascade, do stop in and get some of Steve's wonderful meats. (He also ships anywhere. You can write to him at Cascade Meat Processors, 12 N. First St., Cascade, MT).

The river slows to about 1-2 mph right after Cascade. And after another five miles, the current slows further as the terrain drops only five feet across about fifty miles. And the river is once again controlled by five dams around Great Falls. Standing water, warm temperatures, slow current. Mosquito heaven. This was, perhaps, the most difficult paddle. Mosquitoes, millions of them, singing and swarming, relentless.

We are in Great Falls, Montana, resting (a well-deserved one) and catching up with journal writing, web updates, letters and postcards. Since we are in the neighborhood, we'll take a side trip to Glacier National Park. Until the next time.

July 26, 1997

Since the last update... we paddled from just north of Great Falls (after the last of five dams) to a place called Coal Banks Landing. Donna had her first "Mutual of Omaha Wild Kingdom" experience. We were camped out on an island in the middle of the river. We chose the island because it was without many mosquitoes. It was also flat, with rocks and sand and not much vegetation. In the morning, she went behind the tent to empty her bladder. Just before she started, she had a sixth sense feeling to check behind her one more time. When she turned, there was a 5-foot long snake coming in her direction. It was about 4-5 feet away. In an instant, she decided the morning ritual could wait. Donna stepped up and backed away, calling out to the others that we had a visitor and specifically a rather large snake. Geoff quickly picked up a dry bag and began to bang it on the ground to cause vibrations. Snakes feel vibrations and Geoff wanted to send a signal that we were there and to encourage the snake to choose another direction. It worked. The snake headed off the island, into the river (yes, land snakes swim!) and swam upstream for a time. Then it stopped swimming and let the current take it away downstream. It was exciting, to say the least. Geoff, our resident herpatologist, knew it was a non-poisonous bull snake.

After taking a short break at Coal Banks Landing, we put in again and paddled 88 of the 149 miles of the "Wild and Scenic" section of the Missouri. The river is rife with paddlers. The Bureau of Land Management says the folks who wanted to canoe in June waited until the water level dropped. So, July has double the expected number of boats floating. Just now, there are 137 canoes between Eagle Creek and Judith Landing (about 60 miles of river). That probably translates to about 300 people.

The terrain is 'high desert.' It is dry, hot, full of sage brush and cactus, wild flowers, and occasional groves of cottonwood trees along the river. The cottonwood trees are in trouble. Since the river is controlled by dams, the natural cycle of flooding no longer occurs. Cottonwood seeds don't have a chance to be carried over the banks and germinate. Another short and thorny tree that was introduced some time ago is starting to be more prominent along the banks, but it is not as lovely as the cottonwood tree and does not provide much shade. We hope that the Bureau of Land Management figures out a strategy to maintain the cottonwood trees.

The night before we set out from Coal Banks Landing, we realized that Diva's dry bag filled with her Nutro Max Special dog food was missing. It was likely that the group of paddlers camped adjacent to us had mistakenly taken the bag. The group was being led by Wilderness Inquiry, a guide/outfitters organization out of Minneapolis, Minnesota that brings together people — both able-bodied and not — for wilderness experiences. It was impressive to see folks from all walks of life adventuring together. Jen, always ready to take on challenges, set out early the next morning to retrieve the missing bag. We followed about an hour later. We met up with Jen at Eagle Creek. She did track the Wilderness Inquiry group down right there and indeed they had the bag. We all had a good laugh thinking about what the expression on their faces might have been had they opened the bag to discover dog food!

We did some hiking around, looking for the remains of the Eye of the Needle rock formation. The arch-like formation adorns many a postcard. In June, someone or ones destroyed the formation by hammering out the top of the arch. This topic may have gotten some amount of national coverage. There has been a debate here about whether or not to rebuild the formation. Initially there seemed to be a sentiment to restore it. There are also those who say that the Eye of the Needle should be left as it now stands, as a reminder of how people can be destructive. A Montana senator toured the moument and returned believing that the area was too fragile and that it would not be feasible to rebuild the formation.

We met paddler/author/environmental activist Beth Johnson on the river. Beth was one of four women who canoed the Yukon River in 1982. The Yukon River starts in Canada, passes through Alaska and empties into the Bering Sea. It was wonderful meeting Beth along with a great group of paddlers from Texas. They paddled the Wild and Scenic section in 1992 and were at it for the second time. Theirs was a reunion of sorts, said one member of their group. In 1992, they only passed one other party on the river. How times have changed.

Beth graciously presented us with a signed copy of her book, Yukon Wild (Berkshire Travelers Press, 1983). We have been reading her book aloud ever since, and it is thoroughly a treat. Not only is the book extremely well written, it is inspirational, funny, warm, and engaging. We heartily recommend it!

At a site called Slaughter River, we saw a rattlesnake. Of course, this section of the river is prime rattle and other snake habitat. We were camped at one end of the site and a large church group from Canada was camped at the other. The snake swam in to the shore near some of the teenagers and caused quite a stir. Some of the teenagers began throwing rocks and one even came out with a hachet. The snake moved into the brush on the river's bank — most likely to escape the pelting. Geoff and Jen went over to see about the snake. After some discussion with one of the group's leaders, Geoff talked them into leaving the snake alone. It's great to have a super herpatologist in our crew! Until the next time.

August 8, 1997
We have finished paddling the "Wild and Scenic" section of the upper Missouri, all 149 miles of it. From Judith Landing to the James Kipp Rec Area, the river wound its last 66 miles before merging into Fork Peck Lake. Fort Peck Lake is about 8 miles wide and 140 miles long — an inland ocean for a canoe!

Back on terra firma, at Judith Landing, Diva mistook a bull snake for a stick. The snake was sunning itself on the road when Diva came upon it. She sniffed at the tail of the snake and just as it appeared she was ready to reach down and use it to play fetch, Jen hollers, "Diva come!" Diva turned around to head back towards us, the snake coils and perches to strike. By this time, Jen and Donna are hopping up and down, trying to get Diva to hurry up and get her hinny away from the snake. Diva looked at us as if we were nuts, and what's the big deal anyway? We move back away from the snake (we think it was a bull snake, due to the pattern in its back, and the fact that even though we were only 20' from the snake, we heard no rattles), and wish that we had been carrying the camera, and tell Diva that we love her, and not to play with snakes, as they may not like being treated like a stick.

The section of river from Judith Landing to the Kipp Rec Area is called the badlands. It is mile after mile of bluffs, some coming right down to the water. We camped at Cow Island landing the last night of the section, and enjoyed the shade — a rarity on the river as the Cottonwoods became scarcer. About halfway between Judith's Landing and Kipp, evergreen trees started to appear on the land, I suppose from an elevation change.

The next week found us relaxing and re-fueling in Fort Benton as we awaited Cate's return. We are heading to Fort Peck tomorrow, and did not want to drive across the state, only to have to drive back to retrieve Cate from the airport in Great Falls.

If you find yourself in the Fort Benton area, be sure to stop in the BLM office on Front St. and buy a copy of the history digest they have there. It is an amazing retelling of the major events of the area — well written and fascinating. Bill stayed up till 1 a.m. reading it one night at Judith's! Until the next time.

August 22, 1997
Greetings from Wolf Point, Montana. We are here after proceeding from the ramp at Fort Peck to Bridge Park (about six miles past Wolf Point). These sixty miles between put-in and take-out differ significantly from the Wild and Scenic section. Its hills are lower, gentler than the dry, gnarly pillars and cliffs of the White Cliffs. The river here is not heavily paddled. In fact, we saw no other paddlers and only one motorized boat during the week.

We welcomed a guest: Sarah, a friend of Geoff's. She was a delightful addition to our crew, eagerly helping with meal preparation and cleanup. And so this was the week to unpack the Russian raft. We put in just below the Fort Peck spillway. Bill and Cate in *E. coli*, Jen in the kayak, and Donna and Geoff in the Old Town with Sarah in tow in the Russian raft. At first, the river felt like a lake. We could not detect a current and our crossing to the right side was reminiscent of our journey on Canyon Ferry, Holter and Hauser reservoirs almost two months ago. Then the river narrowed and narrowed again.

We had heard that the outflow from the Fort Peck Dam was to be increased from 17,000 cubic feet per second (cfs) to 21,000 cfs beginning in mid-August. The Army Corp of Engineers is decreasing the level of the Fort Peck reservoir by 18 feet before next spring. The vegetation along the banks was covered with water — clearly a sign of high water. So, the increased flow had begun. And lucky for us. There were places in the river where we could touch the bottom with our paddles, just eight inches below.

We used the power of the wind this week. Yes, we sailed. It did not happen at once, but evolved as we coped with tighter boating quarters. Towing the raft was not ideal. On Monday, our first day out, Jen rigged the Russian craft to the kayak. That worked, but paddling side by side meant that each person could paddle only on one side. Still, it was an improvement over towing. The next day, the "Russian Yak" proved riverworthy again. Disaster struck on Wednesday morning. The Russian raft suffered a puncture as we moved her and the kayak into the water. Jen employed her wilderness first aid skills, using items out of the repair and first aid kits, but the leak persisted. That day we paddled two in *E. coli*, three in the Old Town and one in the kayak.

Once on shore, Jen again set out to repair the raft while the others set up camp. This time, her efforts succeeded.

On Thursday morning, the wind came up during breakfast. Cate suggested that we figure out a way to sail. The boats were rigged together, the kayak sandwiched between the canoes and the revived raft roped in behind the kayak. We used a double-ended paddle as a mast and a tent fly as our main sail. It worked beautifully for several hours. In the late afternoon, we began to notice large, gray clouds congregating in the sky and decided that it was time to get off the water.

Once camp was established and dinner was had, Sarah read to us from a wonderful book: *First You Have to Row a Little Boat* by Richard Bode. It's a wonderful, light musing on life and life's lessons. A perfect summer read. It complemented our sailing adventure as well. A steady wind fluttered across our camp; the clouds darkened above our heads. We waited for the rain, but it did not come. Diva began to dig a large, shallow depression in the sandy bank. She dug until the hole was large enough for her. Then she lay down in it. I read somewhere that dogs and other animals can feel weather systems long before we do. This was a message. The sun finished setting and we retired to our tents.

It was a sudden gust of wind that startled each of us in the dark night. Only this gust did not let up. For some amount of time (perhaps 20, perhaps 30 minutes), the wind pressed against the tents, pushing them over, bending tent poles to their limits. The rain and sand came at us horizontally, meeting the nylon shelters with a steady pattering noise. Diva and Gypsy, in their respective tents, lay motionless, while each of us reported stories of grabbing hold of tent material and holding, holding, holding on. When the wind and rain subsided, Cate called out from her tent and asked if we were all right. Jen and I went out to restake and repair any damages. Of the four tents, two sustained broken tent poles. Bill guestimated that the wind was 35-40 miles per hour with stronger gusts. We stayed off the river on Friday as whitecaps dotted the water.

As though the storm were not enough, Gypsy had her share of memorable adventures. On Tuesday, in the middle of the night, she protected our kitchen paraphernalia (food buckets and equipment storage bags) from some kind of wildlife. Wednesday morning, Gypsy sported a new perfume, and we knew it was a skunk. After her bravery, Gypsy was ill for two days. Until the next time.

September 21, 1997
Where are we? Decatur, Nebraska. Forty-one river miles south of Sioux City, Iowa. We have had a month of paddling and portaging and paddling. And two side trips: Glacier National Park (Montana) and the Black Hills (South Dakota). No major misadventures to report and for that we are grateful. And again, we have enjoyed the kindness of wonderful people along the riverside.

Montana residents and even some non-residents told us that it would be a mistake to leave Montana without seeing Glacier National Park. So, Jen and Donna decided to take a side trip to the Park. Afterwards, the group portaged Lake Sakakawea. Sakakawea begins near the Montana-North Dakota border and is held back by Garrison Dam, one of the largest earthen dams in the world. The boats and four of us were paddling again just below Garrison Dam. Donna, Jen, Cate and Bill canoed the stretch of river to Washburn, North Dakota while Geoff headed off on a mission to secure another canoe.

The paddlers faced a persistent headwind on the first day out. We found a place to camp for the night on a sandy beach. Beyond the beach area and raised up on a small bluff was a field of trees, some standing and swaying in the wind, others long ago fallen. The wind continued through the evening and into the night. Although the Milky Way, familiar constellations and even falling stars were sparkling in the sky, you could not help but think the weather was changing.

The next morning the river showed off her whitecaps. We agreed it was best to stay in camp and enjoy what would come to be an arts and crafts day. Donna and Bill wrote in their journals while Cate and Jen created a basket. Someone suggested that we start a chess tournament. Bill searched in his gear bags, but finally announced that he had left the chess set in the truck. Why should that stop us? The fallen tree branches provided the material for the carved and whittled pieces. Using a magic marker, Bill's REI Thermarest sleeping pad was converted into the board.

We were on the water the next day. Despite the gray skies and rainstorms in the distance, the river was calm and inviting. We were treated to the spectacular sight and sound of perhaps a thousand white pelicans and gulls lifting off from the water as our canoes drifted by. A distant storm followed us for most of the day. And finally, about eight miles upstream from Washburn, the storm arrived. Under a thick, gray sky, we pulled off the water and pitched a tent as quickly as possible. We grabbed water, the REI thermarests and some rain gear and ducked into the tent. Lightning — one, two, three, four, five ... nine seconds and then the sound of thunder. The heart of the storm was still in the distance. The next few counts were seven, six, then three. The storm was building in intensity and moving our way. A strong, bright flash of lightning. The crack of thunder was almost simultaneous. We sat on our thermarests, hoping the worst was over. Eventually, the storm passed. When we ventured out we found the water once again calm and inviting.

We portaged Lake Oahee, an enormous lake which starts just before Bismarck, North Dakota and ends in South Dakota. The last dam on the upper Missouri is at Yankton, South Dakota, named Gavins Point Dam. After a side trip to the Black Hills area (home of Mount Rushmore, Crazy Horse Memorial Monument, Wind Cave National Park, and Custer State Park and the Badlands) Bill, Donna and Jen convened at the Yankton, South Dakota U.S. Post Office ready to paddle the only remaining untamed section of the Missouri River. Between Yankton and Ponca State Park (near Ponca, Nebraska), the river is free flowing; there are no dams, and its flow has not been channelized for commercial (barge) traffic. It was another lovely stretch of Old Muddy. Along the way, we were overwhelmed by and thoroughly enjoyed the tremendous hospitality of Bud Murphy and his family in Vermillion, South Dakota. Once again, Happy 80th Birthday, Bud. Then onto Sioux City, Iowa and finally Decatur, Nebraska.

Just after Ponca State Park, the river is channelized. It is tamed. Its banks do not shift and meander. Though its name is the same as the upper reaches of the Missouri, this is a completely different waterway. The banks are protected from erosion by stone filled dikes and timber pilings. (These structures are called revetment in the U.S. Army Corps of Engineers river maps). Barges make use of this river, though we have not encountered any barges to this point. The outflow from the Gavins Point Dam will be increased next week. The net effect: the river below is expected to rise between five and seven inches. The water is already high. Since beginning the channelized waterway, our biggest challenge has been finding a place to pull off and set up camp for the night.

We expect to welcome Geoff back in a day or two. It will be wonderful to be five again. Until the next time.

October 8, 1997

KANSAS CITY, MO - We are staying ahead of the cooler autumn weather and nearing Kansas City. Reaching Kansas City by boat will be a milestone of sorts. It is the place we gathered five months ago to start out on this adventure. In the meantime, here is what we have been up to...

* September 21: We stay at a motel near Decatur, NE thanks to the onset of cold air and rain blowing in from the north.
* September 22: Still raining. Geoff returns with a van and a canoe and his sister, Megan, who joins us for a week of paddling.
* September 23: The weather continues to be cold and rainy. We decide to wait one more day on the promises of the weather forecasters. During a break in the rain, we head out to play a quick game of football. Bill falls while diving for the goal-line.
* September 24: In the morning, Bill mentions that he has some pain in his ribs. We explain to the emergency room staff, "He insisted on playing running back. Yes, he is 79 years old. It was fourth and one on the one yard line. He took the hand-off. Yes, you heard right, 79. He dove for the goal-line." X-rays reveal a fractured rib, but Bill insists paddling will be no problem. We depart from the hospital, ace bandage in hand.
* September 25: We are back on the water and paddle from Decatur to Blair, NE. There we feast on our typical, scrumptious brunch of eggs, potatoes and onions, and toast prepared by Jen. From Blair we paddle on to Tyson Boat Ramp on the Iowa side. Because our daylight was fast running out, we decide to make camp there despite the overgrown weeds and ferocious mosquitoes.
* September 26: From the ramp, we canoe to Wilson Island State Recreation Area, again on the Iowa side.
* September 27: We arrive in Omaha, NE. Folks in Sioux City recommended that we eat at the Indian Oven Restaurant in the Old Market part of town. We find the place just as it is closing for the afternoon. The staff usher us in the door and then turn the Open sign over to read Closed to the crowds strolling along outside the shop. In the now empty restaurant, we dine on naan and chicken masala and aloo goobi and more. "What time do you open for dinner?" we ask.
* September 28: We restock our groceries and cooking fuel and get ready for more paddling.

* September 29: On the water again, we reach a place called Sandpiper Cove and set up camp.

* September 30: A long day on the water. We go thirty-seven miles to a boat ramp near Bartlett, IA. Because the river is channelized, because the water is running so high, and because the banks are often protected with chunks of concrete or wood pilings, it is not as easy as it once was to find a place to pull off for the night. We pass our first barge. The U.S. Army Corps of Engineers Missouri is the name on the push boat, and it looks like big chunks of rock or concrete in the two barges. We stay to the port side (out of the main channel); the barge stays starboard and we do fine handling the big waves.

* October 1: We paddle to Nebraska City, NE. Just ahead of us is a twenty-six year old man paddling from Billings, MT to St. Louis, MO. His plan is to finish his trip in two months — the time of his vacation from work. We don't ever catch him, but we hear about him from people on the riverside. We wish him well. On our way to Nebraska City, we stop at Plattsmouth for the classic brunch.

* October 2: Onto Brownsville, NE. This is a lovely little town on the river. It is home to the Missouri River History Museum, antique shops, and Midge's Brownsville House (restaurant). We pass another barge. This barge is twice as big as the first one we passed. The waves seem come at us from all directions.

* October 3: We start out from Brownsville in a moderate headwind. Destination: Rulo, NE, about thirty-five miles away. Despite our best efforts, the wind picks up to a steady thirty-five mile an hour beat. The waves grow in height. They are at about two to two and a half feet. We are blown off the river toward the port side just past Corning, MO. About ten minutes later, a huge barge rumbles past us.

* October 4: We arrive in Rulo, NE. We are greeted by Ron and Cathy at the boat ramp and we enjoy visiting with them and hearing about their life on the river near Rulo.

* October 5: We move a vehicle ahead to Kansas City and while there, we stop in at Bill's and Cate's apartment for a rest through October 6.

* October 7: Back to Rulo and we prepare to get back on the water. We hear warnings from riverside residents that rain and winds are predicted.

* October 8: Thunderstorms and high winds greet the day. We decide to head back to Kansas City to stay dry and to wait for the storm system to pass.

Until the next time.

January 1, 1998
The Winter News
We hit our south-most point, Atchison, Kansas, near the end of October. The nights were filled with clear skies and bright stars. The moon blessed our campsites, and the barges kept our days exciting. By mid-October our daily mileage had reached nearly 40 miles, a record for our otherwise-meanandering attitudes. Yes, we had thoughts of getting far enough south to beat the winter weather.

Along this stretch of channelized river we met folks in Kansas and Missouri that showed us hospitiality, Midwest style. "Sure, you can leave your boats in my yard while you restock with food." Farmers who cautioned us about the boils and undercurrents of the Missouri, and those who joined us for one of our famous dinners of baked potatoes and onions, shared their evening with us, and even taught us about flat-bottom boats and told stories of the whirlpools that have been known to gobble them up whole.

The days grew shorter, and the shadows colder. Diva spent more and more time in her sleeping bag, and less time looking forward to joining us in the cold canoe. Us humans can don our REI pilejackets and slip into NRS wetsuit booties, but Diva doesn't go in for such antics. We knew our fall paddling was pushing the limits of our comfort and our safety. This is not to say that other folks shouldn't or don't continue in such circumstances — simply that we all choose our own path, following the bends in the river.

It was three days before the first snow fell in and around Kansas City that we officially took our boats out of the water for the winter. Writing beckoned, and the transcribing of our journals. Families beckoned, as well, and we heeded this bend in the river as we had heeded all the others upstream.

If there is anything I (this is Jen writing) had learned in the first 1700 miles of paddling, it was something Cate had said near the headwaters, "Don't let the river get in the way of the river trip." At the time she first said this to me I did not understand one bit of what she was talking about — what do you mean, don't let the river get in the way of the river trip — I came here to paddle the river, and damned if I'm not going to do it! After having quit my job at Princeton and choosing to paddle the river with Mom (Cate's my mom) and Bill and Donna and Geoff, I wanted to paddle and paddle and paddle.

In the beginning I had no idea of what would become so improtrant to me over the course of the trip: meeting the people we did along the way — from those on the banks and in the malt shops and grocery stores along the way to those who joined us on the internet. Nothing could be as important as the connections we were making through paddling the river. It wasn't until Vermillion, South Dakota — nearly 170 days after that first paddle stroke — that I realized what Mom was talking about. Don't let the river get in the way of the river trip. The river trip she was talking about doesn't start in Montana, and doesn't end in the Gulf of Mexico. True, the river flows between those two places, but the river trip is this current we all ride from one connection to the next — and to quote Jan Murphy (who we met in Vermillion, SD), "You have to get out of the house to meet the people who are waiting for you."

And for now the cold winter months find us at our computers, transcribing our journals and doing some repairs on our boats, and dreaming, ever-so-sweetly, of rejoining the current, to meet those waiting for us downstream. We are putting our boats in the water again, where we left off, in Atchison, Kansas, in April. From there we will paddle to St. Louis, MO, and join the Mississippi. It was Donna who said, it the chilly night air of early — October, that as long as we are having so much fun on the Missouri, why do only the lower-half of the Mississippi, as originally planned — why not do the whole thing? Accordingly, we have enlongated our trip to include the entire Mississippi, instead of simply following it from St. Louis to the Gulf. After reaching St. Louis in May, we plan to take our boats to Minnesota, and retrace the paddle strokes that Bill took in 1980, from the headwaters of the Mississippi (in Lake Itasca, Minnesota) to the Gulf of Mexico.

Sorry for the delay in getting this update on-line, and we hope to see everyone who is with us on this journey again, as the river trip continues.

About the Authors

Cate Allen and Jen Whiting, mother and daughter, traveled the Missouri River with husband and partner, by canoe, and together wrote *A Year Without Time*. Each chapter has two voices, two views, published side-by-side.

Cate Allen spent many years in Russia managing Abbott Laboratories' Moscow office, and has lived in Switzerland, Germany, France, England and Scotland. She was a seminar speaker for American Management Association, and now owns her own seminar company, The Throckmorton Group.

Jen Whiting studied writing at Harvard University, attended The National Outdoor Leadership School, taught climbing and outdoor leadership at Cornell University, and now is a manager at Princeton University. She began publishing her writing in newspapers at the age of 15.

Jen Whiting

Cate Allen

Printed in the United States
21659LVS00005B/1-78